READER'S DIGEST BOOK OF FACTS

STAFF FOR THIS EDITION

Editor: Edmund H. Harvey, Jr.
Art Editor: Robert M. Grant
Associate Editor and Copy Editor: Diana Marsh
Picture Editor: Robert J. Woodward
Picture Researcher: Mary Leverty
Research Associates: Megan Newman,
Barbara Guarino
Contributing Copy Editor: Martin Mitchell

READER'S DIGEST GENERAL BOOKS

Editorial Director: John A. Pope, Jr.
Managing Editor: Jane Polley
Art Director: David Trooper
Group Editors: Norman B. Mack, John Speicher,
Susan J. Wernert

READER'S DIGEST BOOK OF FACTS
The credits and acknowledgments that appear
on pages 414–416 are hereby made a part of
this copyright page.

The original British edition of this book was
published by The Reader's Digest Association
Limited, London, in 1985. Consultant Editor:
Magnus Magnusson, Presenter, BBC TV
Mastermind program.

The publishers are grateful for the
assistance of Guinness Books in providing
access to the information contained in their
range of titles.

The lines from a poem by Ogden Nash
on page 335 are reprinted by permission
of Curtis Brown Ltd. Copyright © 1969
by Ogden Nash.

Library of Congress Cataloging in Publication Data
Reader's Digest book of facts.
  Includes index.
  1. Handbooks, vade mecums, etc. I. Reader's
Digest Association. II. Title: Book of facts.
AG105.R32 1987   031'.02 86-29744
ISBN 0-89577-256-6

READER'S DIGEST
and the Pegasus colophon are
registered trademarks of The
Reader's Digest Association, Inc.

Printed in the United States of America

READER'S DIGEST BOOK OF FACTS

THE READER'S DIGEST ASSOCIATION, INC.
Pleasantville, New York   Montreal

CONTENTS

Spooky dancers on strings and rods, page 141

Dr. Jarvik and a special pump, page 206

FACTS ABOUT SCIENCE AND TECHNOLOGY

FACTS ABOUT ANIMALS AND PLANTS

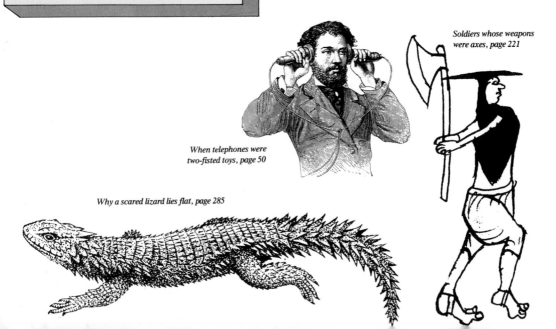

Soldiers whose weapons were axes, page 221

When telephones were two-fisted toys, page 50

Why a scared lizard lies flat, page 285

One side of a great sports rivalry, page 341

Raiders who struck from longboats, page 43

PEOPLE

Prehistoric life

OUT OF THE SOUP

The emergence of life from the the primordial soup of the oceans, some 3.5 billion years ago, cannot be traced completely. Few fossils older than 570 million years exist, and in any case, early forms of life were soft-bodied and therefore left little or no trace. The first life forms were undoubtedly single-celled creatures, perhaps not unlike the primitive amoeba of today. From these single-celled creatures, known as protozoans, evolved the multicelled animals known as metazoans. And from the metazoans developed the chain of species that led to human beings.

THE SURVIVORS

Human beings and the other mammals are descended from reptiles that survived a period of huge climatic and geological change some 225 million years ago. This period, often called the Permo-Triassic Catastrophe, lasted for about 85 million years. During it, two-thirds of all marine animal species, three-quarters of all amphibians, and four-fifths of all reptiles became extinct. With this competition removed, the reptiles that survived evolved in many directions, but two important groups emerged. They are known as thecodonts and therapsids. The thecodonts evolved into the dinosaurs, which dominated the world for 100 million years. The therapsids—a small group of reptiles that may have been hairy, warm-blooded animals—were the forerunners of modern mammals.

After 100 million years of domination, most of the dinosaurs vanished about 65 million years ago. Why they vanished is not clear. Continental upheavals may have played a part by changing the environment, but a possible cause may have been a change in the climate. Cold-blooded reptiles, taking their temperature from the environment, would have been unable to withstand a widespread temperature drop. Warm-blooded mammals—their bodies at a relatively constant temperature and therefore capable of survival in both hot and cold environments—were able to exploit the habitats deserted by the dwindling stocks of reptiles. After millions of years of being subordinate in both numbers and size, probably hiding by day and hunting at night, when the reptiles became torpid, the mammals came out into the open, and the huge population increase that has resulted in their present-day supremacy began.

NEW WORLD

No evidence of man's evolutionary ancestors has so far been found in either North or South America. Fossil and other remains suggest that the first Americans crossed the Bering Strait (which was then dry land) from Asia between 40,000 and 20,000 years ago. These ancestors of the American Indians were already modern men, *Homo sapiens sapiens.*

RETURN FROM THE TREES

When Charles Darwin's evolutionary thesis, *The Origin of Species,* was published in 1859, many people jumped to the conclusion that he was suggesting that man's immediate ancestors were tree-dwelling monkeys. In fact, the first mammals—200 million years ago and long before the apes evolved—lived on the ground. They had developed from reptiles and at first resembled modern, insect-eating animals, such as the hedgehog. It was only later that some of these crea-tures, the forerunners of the primates, took to the trees because trees provided plenty of food and a degree of safety from predators. Man's earliest primate ancestor probably looked something like the modern, squirrellike tree shrew of southern and eastern Asia. Millions of years later some of the descendants of these tiny creatures again came down from the trees. The animals that climbed down evolved into man. Those that stayed behind developed, about 40 million years ago, into the monkey family.

DATING BY VOLCANIC ASH

Although volcanoes destroy life, they have also helped scientists know more about long-vanished living things. Three of the most important fossil sites for man's ancestors—the Olduvai Gorge in Tanzania, Lake Turkana in Kenya, and the lower Omo Valley in Ethiopia—lie in the volcano-studded Great Rift Valley. The well-known carbon 14 method of dating, while quite reliable for fossils less than 40,000 years old, is of little use when testing remains millions of years old. But chemical changes that occur in the mineral components of volcanic ash during the heat and pressure of an eruption set in motion a different kind of atomic clock: the decay of an isotope of potassium into an isotope of argon. By measuring the potassium isotopes' rate of decay, scientists can date layers of volcanic ash, and thus the human remains that lie buried in or near them.

IGNORED BECAUSE OF A HOAX

One of the most important finds in the search for man's ancestors was ignored for years because of the Piltdown Man hoax. The Piltdown skull, "found" in England in 1912, purported to show that human ancestors had large manlike skulls and apelike jaws. So, in 1924, when Raymond Dart, professor of anatomy at Witwatersrand University, found a very different-looking skull at the Tauns Caves in South Africa, his conclusion that it belonged to an early hominid was dismissed. Only when other bones from the same species, *Australopithecus africanus,* were discovered did doubts begin to grow about Piltdown Man, which was exposed as a fake in the 1950s. Today the species Dart discovered is thought to have lived about 5 million years ago, making it one of the earliest stages in the evolution of man.

DRAGON BONE MEDICINE

Nineteenth-century Chinese pharmacists had known for generations that a cave-pocked limestone hill outside the village of Choukoutien (Zhoukoudian), near Peking, was a rich source of fossil bones, which they ground up to make medicine for their patients. What the pharmacists did not know was that some of the bones were those of their own ancestors and about half a million years old. The bones were recognized as human or near-human in 1903, and in the 1920s archeologists began excavating the site. What they found shed new light on human evolution.

In 1927 Davidson Black, a Canadian anatomist, discovered two hominid teeth, and he announced that a new species of primitive man had been discovered: Peking Man. Black's discovery was confirmed in 1929 with the unearthing of part of a skull. Peking Man is now classified as *Homo erectus,* a manlike species that immediately preceded *Homo sapiens* in the evolutionary chain.

LEMURS, THE LIVING LEGACY

The lemur of Madagascar is one of very few of the human species' ancestors that has survived unchanged down the long corridors of evolution. Having developed after the first primates, it is classified as a prosimian, meaning "before monkey," and is one of the ancestors common to both monkeys and men. The prosimians, small insect-eating animals that lived in trees and hunted by night, are known from fossil finds to have flourished from about 60 million to 40 million years ago. They gradually died out in most parts of the world and were replaced by monkeys and apes. They survived in Madagascar because of a geological event that separated the island from Africa at least 30 million years ago and so protected the lemurs from competing species.

NAMED AFTER A CHIMP

A chimpanzee from the London Zoo gave its name to a group of apelike animals that lived 10 to 25 million years ago in Africa. In 1931 the fragmentary remains of a creature thought to be an ancestor of modern chimpanzees were found in Kenya. Arthur Hopwood, of the Natural History Museum in London, suggested that the creature should be given the generic name *Proconsul*—after Consul, one of the chimps then in the London Zoo. Several forms of Proconsul fossils have since been found, including, in 1948, a nearly complete skull of a species now known as *Proconsul africanus*. The Proconsul fossil apes are now often included in the genus *Dryopithecus* (from the Greek *drus*, "tree"). The genus is so called because the fossils are often found with those of oak leaves.

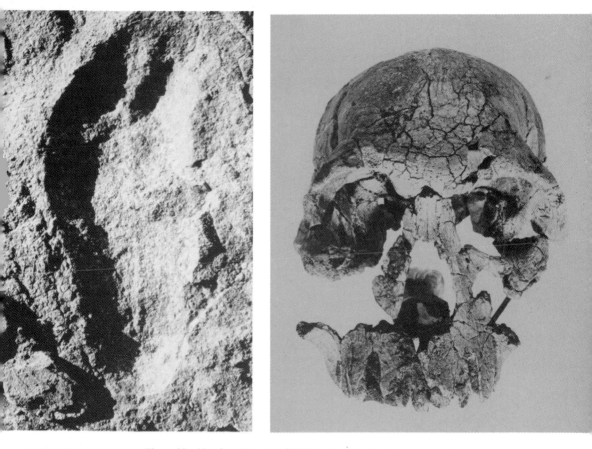

ONE GIANT STEP FOR MANKIND *The world's oldest footprints, one of which is pictured on the left, were made when a group of early manlike creatures walked across a patch of damp volcanic ash near the Olduvai Gorge in Tanzania. The ash later hardened, preserving the prints. Discovered in 1976, they show that man's ancestors were walking upright 3.75 million years ago. By comparison, the world's oldest complete human skull (right), found near Lake Turkana in Kenya, is relatively recent. Known by its museum number as 1470, it is around 2 million years old.*

OUR RELATIVE, THE STARFISH

Humans and other mammals are vertebrates, animals with backbones. And all vertebrates belong to the scientific family called the Chordata, animals with a rodlike structure that supports the body.

The chordates and the echinoderms—creatures such as starfish and sea urchins—diverged into separate evolutionary paths at least 500 million years ago. But scientists believe that both groups descended from a common ancestor, making the starfish one of man's oldest living relatives.

THE LONELY PIONEER

A young 19th-century Dutch anatomist, Eugène Dubois, was the first to establish that early man had lived in Asia as well as Africa. Yet his search for proof was dismissed by orthodox scientists as a waste of time, and his finds went unrecognized until after his death.

Dubois went to the island of Sumatra in 1887 to test the theories of Alfred Russel Wallace, a contemporary of Darwin's, who had argued that the ancestors of man probably lived in Southeast Asia, home of the highly intelligent orangutan. At the time, the attention of the academic world was concentrated on finds in Europe, and nobody was prepared to sponsor Dubois. So he had to support himself and his family by working as a surgeon for the Dutch East India Army.

Dubois found nothing in Sumatra. But in Java, in 1891, he found the skull of a manlike creature. Later he found a thighbone as well. It was only after his death in 1940 that the significance of Dubois's discoveries came to be recognized. As a result of his work, confirmed by other skulls found in the 1930s and 1940s, scientists now know that the Java Man was a specimen of *Homo erectus* ("Upright Man")—a species that is the immediate ancestor of *Homo sapiens* and that lived in Java between about 1.5 million and 500,000 years ago.

THE FIRST FIRE
The human line, the hominids, has known how to use fire for at least 500,000 years and has probably been able to make fire since about 12,000 years ago. Before people learned how to make fire themselves, they must have kept alight fires started by lightning. The folk memory of this practice may account for the religious custom of a "sacred flame" that is never allowed to go out. Peking Man, who lived about 500,000 years ago, seems to have been the first species to make regular use of fire. Charred embers were found with Peking Man's remains in a cave near the Chinese capital in 1929.

THE FIRST TECHNOLOGICAL REVOLUTION
The technological revolution of the mid-20th century is not the first. The first took place during the last Ice Age, between 40,000 and 10,000 years ago. Before that period, man had for hundreds of thousands of years made do with only the most basic of tools: crude knives, spears, and clubs. Then, about 40,000 years ago, an explosion of inventiveness began. More advanced tools—such as the bow and arrow, chisel, adz, and spear thrower, which gave extra leverage for throwing spears—began to appear. The great technological leap forward was created by the successors to Neanderthal Man: our own species, *Homo sapiens sapiens*.

THE FIRST METALWORKERS
Until recently scholars believed almost universally that the development of metalworking techniques began in Mesopotamia in about 3500 to 3000 B.C. and spread to the rest of the world from there. However, in 1974 a discovery in Thailand threw doubt on that theory. American and Thai archeologists working at the village of Ban Chiang Dao in northwest Thailand found graves containing a bronze spearhead, a bronze anklet, and bronze bracelets, and the archeologists believe that the objects date from 3600 B.C.

If the date is correct, the find suggests that the Bronze Age was well established in Thailand at that time, several hundred years before it reached a similar stage in Mesopotamia.

FLOWERS FOR A CAVEMAN'S FUNERAL
A Neanderthal grave found in the 1950s in a large cave near the village of Shanidar in northern Iraq contained the body of a man who had been laid to rest 60,000 years ago with bunches of carefully placed flowers—the first time flowers are known to have been used in a funeral ceremony.

Analysis of the pollen grains, which are now all that remain of the flowers, shows that the cavemen's tributes included cornflowers, hollyhocks, ragwort, grape hyacinths, yarrow, and a species of centaurea known as St. Barnaby's thistle.

RITE OF PASSAGE
The ceremonial practice of burying the dead, rather than just leaving them where they fall, is far more ancient than Neanderthal Man's tradition of paying his respects to the dead with flowers. The first known burial took place in a cave at the Chinese village of Choukoutien (Zhoukoudian), just south of Peking, about 400,000 years ago. Some scholars see the burial as the first evidence of belief in some form of afterlife. At a time when human communities were small and scattered, and when scavenging animals would quickly dispose of an abandoned corpse, hygiene cannot, archeologists believe, have been the reason for burial. So some other factor—perhaps a belief in some sort of immortality, inspired by dreams about the dead person—may explain the start of the custom.

AUSTRALIA'S FIRST COLONISTS
The ancestors of Australia's aborigines braved the open sea to colonize Australia at least 30,000 years ago—thousands of years before anyone else is known to have dared to move out of sight of land. At the time, the last Ice Age had locked up vast quantities of water in the polar ice caps, lowering sea levels around the world by more than 300 feet.

As a result, Europe (including Britain), Asia, Africa, and even the Americas (linked to Asia by a land bridge across the Bering Strait) formed a single vast stretch of dry land across which early human beings could, and did, migrate. But Australia, then uninhabited by man and linked to New Guinea, was separated by at least 40 miles of open sea from the nearest part

---

HOW CARBON 14 DATING WORKS

Early archeologists relied on two major techniques for calculating the age of what they found: the principle of stratigraphy (that the remains of earlier generations are covered over by those of their successors) and the comparison of styles—say, of pottery—to determine whether one style influenced and therefore preceded another. In the 1950s, however, a new technique known as radiocarbon, or carbon 14, dating came into use.

Carbon 14, a radioactive isotope of carbon, is present in tiny quantities in the atmosphere. Living things, such as wood and the bones of living animals, absorb this form of carbon naturally. But when a tree is cut down or an animal dies, the absorption stops and the level of carbon 14 begins to fall.

Rate of decay
Since the level of carbon 14 present in living things is known, and its rate of decay—its half-life—is also known, the age of an object can be worked out by measuring how much carbon 14 is left and comparing it with the original level. Carbon 14 has a half-life of 5,700 years, meaning that half of it is converted to nonradioactive carbon in 5,700 years, and every 5,700 years thereafter half of the remainder is converted. An object with exactly half as much carbon 14 as its living counterpart, therefore, died exactly 5,700 years ago.

For many prehistoric objects—bones, for example, or the charred logs of a cave-dwelling family's campfire—the system is accurate to within a few hundred years. But the margin of error increases with the age of the object, and carbon 14 dating is not reliable for anything more than about 40,000 years old. Older fossils are usually dated by means of a similar method known as potassium-argon dating.

of present-day Indonesia (then linked to Asia). At that distance, given northern Australia's flat terrain, it is unlikely that the coastline of Australia could have been seen by somebody in Indonesia.

Despite the gap, aborigines are known to have crossed over from Indonesia. The earliest known human remains in Australia are of a woman who was cremated and buried between 25,000 and 30,000 years ago. The remains were found in New South Wales—more than 2,000 miles from the northern coast—suggesting that the aborigines had by then already lived on the continent for centuries.

The exact date of the aborigines' first voyage, and the type of boat or raft they used, will probably never be known. The dank tropical coastline on which they are thought to have landed no longer exists. It was drowned by the rising sea at the end of the last Ice Age around 10,000 years ago.

MAMMOTH EATERS

The cave dwellers of Predmosti in Czechoslovakia were mighty hunters who ate mammoths. Their rubbish dumps, which date from 15,000 to 10,000 B.C., have been analyzed by modern archeologists and found to contain the bones of nearly 2,000 mammoths, including stacks of neatly sorted tusks and teeth. Mammoths—cold-climate relatives of the elephant, and now extinct—roamed across much of Europe, Asia, and North America at a time when the Ice Age had buried most of the northern parts of the continents under vast glaciers.

THE AGES OF PREHISTORY

Scholars divide the long span of prehistory into several ages, as a way of describing in shorthand form the dominant features of each set of cultures. However, the dates attached to these ages are only approximate, and since technological developments occurred in different parts of the world at different times, the cutoff dates vary from country to country. The dates shown here are commonly accepted as defining the peak of each period in northwestern Europe.

PALEOLITHIC PERIOD (Old Stone Age)	3,000,000 – 8000 B.C.
MESOLITHIC PERIOD (Middle Stone Age)	18,000 – 2700 B.C.
NEOLITHIC PERIOD (New Stone Age)	2700 – 1900 B.C.
BRONZE AGE	1900 – 500 B.C.
IRON AGE	500 – 51 B.C. (publication of Julius Caesar's *Gallic Wars* in 51 B.C. generally seen as end of prehistory in northwestern Europe)

BULLFIGHT *An enraged bison, above, attacks a human figure in a painting created 15,000 years ago. The painting, one of several vivid animal scenes on the walls of a cave at Lascaux in southwestern France, was discovered by four boys out walking with their dog on September 12, 1940. The dog disappeared down a hole in the ground, and when the boys went to rescue it, they found a large cavern. They returned the next day with ropes and a light, which revealed what is now regarded as some of the world's finest examples of prehistoric art.*

STENCIL ART *Scores of hands wave from cave walls in France and Spain. Many of the 35,000-year-old outlines show mutilations —the result of ritual sacrifice, perhaps, or of frostbite in the bitter Ice Age weather.*

Persia: the first great empire

WORLD RULER
The Persian Empire reached its greatest extent under Darius I, who seized the throne in 522 B.C. It stretched about 2,500 miles from the Indus River in present-day Pakistan to what is now Benghazi in Libya in the west, and from the Arabian Sea in the south to the Caucasus and Macedonia in the north. This, the first "world empire," covered about 2,000,000 square miles, an area about two-thirds as large as the 48 contiguous U.S. states, and had a population of 10,000,000.

THE FIRST SUEZ CANAL
To facilitate trade between Egypt and his ports on the Persian Gulf, Darius I ordered the construction of a canal to link the Mediterranean Sea and the Red Sea. In fact, the value of such a link had long been appreciated by rulers in the region, and there is evidence that a canal was dug and maintained for a time as early as the 20th century B.C. About 1,300 years later, under the Egyptian pharaoh Necho, construction of a new canal was started but abandoned. Darius's workers began completing this canal in about 500 B.C. and, when they finished the job a few years later, they set up five inscribed stelae (stone slabs), of which four survive.

Darius's canal—which ran along a course similar to the modern Suez Canal, from the Nile delta through the Bitter Lakes to a point near the port of Suez—remained in more or less regular use until the 8th century A.D. Then part of it was blocked for military reasons—12 centuries before similar closures of the Suez Canal in 1956 and 1967.

MEN OF MAGIC
The English word *magic* is derived from the Magi, a mysterious Persian priestly clan. A magus was a person wise in religious matters, and the Magi were probably also scribes and keepers of records. The word *magic* may have acquired its modern meaning from a branch of the clan that moved to Babylonia and specialized in telling fortunes and working religious "wonders." It was three of the Persian Magi, "wise men from the east," whose journey to visit the infant Christ is described in St. Matthew's Gospel.

CULT OF WARRIORS
One of the main religions in ancient Persia was the cult of Mithras, who was portrayed as a man slaying a bull. It was a men-only religion, and several of the ceremonies had parallels with those of Christianity, including baptism with water and the sharing of a sacramental meal. Mithraism later spread to the West and, because of its emphasis on manly strength and courage, became popular among Roman soldiers.

GUARDING THE HAREM
The Persian kings kept many wives, and even more concubines, in harems guarded by eunuchs. After Cyrus subdued Babylonia in 539 B.C., the province had to supply already castrated boys each year to learn their trade as eunuchs. Probably none of the kings had more wives and concubines than Xerxes I, who reigned from 486 to 465 B.C. He appears as the amorous King Ahasuerus (the Hebrew version of his name) in the Old Testament book of Esther.

STORMY CROSSING
When the Persian king Xerxes I led an expedition against Greece in 480 B.C., he had some of his Egyptian and Phoenician engineers throw two pontoon bridges across the narrow Hellespont Strait to carry his armies over. But a storm wrecked the bridges, and in a fury Xerxes ordered his men to give the Hellespont 300 lashes and to throw a symbolic pair of shackles into the waves. Some accounts say that he also had the waters branded with hot irons to show his displeasure. The engineers' punishment was not symbolic: they were beheaded. However, their successors kept their heads, because the weather improved and the Persians were able to cross safely. At first the invasion was successful, but after a crushing defeat at Salamis later that year, Xerxes had to withdraw.

LIFESAVING REPLY
Cyrus the Great's son, Cambyses, was a hard-drinking man of violent rages. He was also fond of asking people what they thought of him. It was a question

---

EMPERORS OF PERSIA

The core of the Persian Empire was formed from two kingdoms: the original home of the Persians, known as Fars or Parsa (now in southwest Iran), and Media (northwest Iran). The empire began when Cyrus the Great conquered his Median overlord in the 6th century B.C. Both the Persians and the Medes were Aryans, the word from which Persia gets its modern name, Iran.

Cyrus II, the Great, 559–530 B.C.
Cambyses II, 530–522
Bardiya, 522
Darius I, 522–486
Xerxes I, 486–465
Artaxerxes I, 465–424
Xerxes II, 424
Sogdianus, 424–423
Darius II, 423–404
Artaxerxes II, 404–359
Artaxerxes III, 359–338
Arses, 338–336
Darius III, 336–330

ROYAL CIRCLE *Golden griffins glare from an armlet that may have been worn by Cyrus the Great. Originally encrusted with stones, the armlet was found in a cache thought to have belonged to a wealthy temple in the former Persian province of Bactria, now part of Afghanistan.*

KING'S HEAD *The Persian Empire, toppled by Alexander the Great in 330 B.C., was ruled by the Achaemenian dynasty—named after Achaemenes, a 7th-century ruler of part of Persia. This marble head depicts one of his line, probably either Cyrus the Great, who founded the empire in the 6th century by conquering the neighboring Medes, or Darius I, who won the throne by murdering the previous king, Bardiya. Darius, the first to style himself "king of kings," justified his coup by claiming in public notices that Bardiya had been an impostor—in an early attempt to rewrite history.*

that could cost an undiplomatic vassal his life. But the Greek historian Herodotus, writing in the 5th century B.C., reported that at least one courtier, faced with this dangerous question, found a lifesaving reply. The courtier is said to have told the king: "I do not think you are equal to your father, for you do not yet have a son like the son he left behind him in yourself."

FLAMES OVER THE PALACE

A hall that could hold 10,000 people was a central feature of Persepolis, the enormous palace complex built by Darius I in what is now southwestern Iran. In 1933 archeologists digging among the foundations discovered inscriptions describing the extent of the Persian Empire, as well as an earnest prayer by Darius for his people: "God protect this country from foe, famine, and falsehood." Persepolis—a name later applied also to the city that grew up around the palace—is a corruption of the Greek name for the palace, Perseptolis. The Persians themselves called the palace complex Parsa, after the surrounding province. Darius began building Persepolis in about 520 B.C., and his successors completed it. The wooden-roofed palace remained intact for less than two centuries, however. It was burned to the ground by the invading troops of Alexander the Great in about 330 B.C.

PLEASURE GARDEN

The word *paradise* comes from an old Persian word for a pleasure garden or a deer park. Not only the king had such gardens; many of the provincial governors, known as satraps, had them too.

India: enduring civilization

RAILROAD INTO HISTORY

In the 1850s two British railway builders, the brothers John and William Brunton, stumbled unknowingly on the two most ancient cities in the Indian subcontinent: Harappa and Mohenjo-Daro. Looking for ballast for the line of the East India Railway in what is now Pakistan, they were led by locals to two earth mounds packed with baked-earth bricks.

Unaware of the mounds' importance, the brothers saw them simply as ideal fill to make a solid roadbed for their tracks. Near Harappa, William dug up 164,000 cubic yards of India's priceless heritage to lay 93 miles of railway. It was not until the 1920s that archeologists discovered that the mounds were the remains of a highly developed Indus Valley civilization dating from 2500 B.C.

ENGINEERED FOR PUBLIC HEALTH

The town planners of the Indus civilization built into the city of Mohenjo-Daro the world's first known main-drainage system, and every house was piped into

it. Brick-lined pipes carried sewage from each home into covered channels that ran along the centers of the main streets to disposal points away from the city. The drains took waste from kitchens, bathrooms, and indoor toilets. The main drains even had movable stone slabs that covered inspection points.

FIRST TOWN PLANNERS

The city of Mohenjo-Daro, built about 4,500 years ago, did not just grow up willy-nilly. Its streets were laid out north-south and east-west in the gridiron fashion used today in many U.S. and Canadian cities. Main streets were about 45 feet wide, and side streets about 30 feet. The houses were usually 30 feet by 26 feet, and most were two stories high. They had blank walls facing the streets and opened inward onto courtyards and small alleyways. The walls kept out the heat of the sun and the dust of passing cart traffic.

GODDESS IN CLAY *This terra-cotta figurine, depicting an ancient Indian mother goddess, was found in the ruins of Mohenjo-Daro in the 1920s. It dates from about 2000 B.C.*

FROM DIVERSE ROOTS, A COMPLEX SOCIETY

Between 2000 and 1000 B.C. settlers from central Asia arrived in the Punjab and upper Ganges Valley. They were lighter-skinned than the local Dravidian people, who originated in the south of India, and became known as Aryans, from the Sanskrit word meaning "noble ones." The Aryans brought with them an early form of the Hindu religion, and it was probably at this stage that they devised the rudiments of the caste system to maintain their superiority over the Dravidians. From a fairly flexible set of distinctions, the caste system developed into one of the most complex class systems of any society in the world.

Four main castes were formed. They were the Brahmans, the priestly class; the Kshatriyas, who were warriors and rulers; the Vaisyas, who were originally herdsmen and later merchants and farmers; and the Sudras, who served the other three castes and carried out menial tasks. In Hindu teaching these four classes are said to have been formed from the head (Brahmans), arms (Kshatriyas), trunk (Vaisyas), and feet (Sudras) of the god-creator, Brahma.

Castes within castes

Over centuries, marriage between the four main castes led to the formation of subdivisions, and these were further subdivided by occupations. By the time India became independent in 1947, there were an estimated 2,000 castes within the general framework of the four main classes. The lowest of all was the group known as the Untouchables, or Panchamas. They were confined to occupations that were shunned by the higher castes as unclean, such as clearing excrement or handling the dead.

In each caste there were rules of eating, washing, and religious conduct, and well-defined laws of contact with other castes. Women, for example, could marry into a caste above the one into which they were born, but not below. Today the government of India is committed to abolishing the caste system. The constitution lays down as a principle of law the equality of all Indians, regardless of caste. And Untouchability has been outlawed altogether.

FLOOD RIDDLE

The story of life in the twin cities of the Indus civilization, Harappa and Mohenjo-Daro, is still being pieced together by scholars and archeologists. The cities' economy was based mostly on farming and herding, but trading was also an important activity, and there seems to have been a busy riverside landing place at Harappa. Potters and toolmakers, working in wood and metal, were also part of the cities' commerce.

Nobody knows for certain why the Indus Valley cities suddenly collapsed in about 1500 B.C. Military conquest, economic decline, or an earthquake have all been suggested. Another theory is that the collapse may have been accelerated by a major river flood that inundated the cities and drove the inhabitants away.

MAIDENS IN PERIL

The Lion's Rock at Sigiriya in Sri Lanka, a granite block 600 feet high, was once crowned by a fortified palace built by a Ceylonese king, Kasyapa I, who was killed in A.D. 495. A man-made path spirals up the rock to its 5-acre summit.

A small area of plastered rock is still covered with frescoes depicting 21 voluptuous women, who are known as cloud maidens, because clouds usually obscure their lower parts. Poems to these cold, unyielding beauties were scribbled into the plaster in the 8th through 10th centuries.

During the World War II, vibrations from Allied planes taking off nearby threatened irreversible damage to the maidens. But the frescoes were saved for posterity by a covering of cotton padding held against the rock face by bamboo scaffolding.

THE MOGUL EMPERORS OF INDIA

Indian civilization goes back to 2500 B.C. or even earlier. But although some rulers—particularly the Buddhist emperor Asoka (c. 273–232 B.C.)—came close to dominating the entire subcontinent, it was not until the Middle Ages that all India became a single political unit. The dynasty that established India-wide rule was the Mogul empire—from whose name the English word for a powerful ruler is derived. It was founded by Babur, a Muslim descendant of the central Asian conqueror Tamerlane (1336–1405), and lasted until India became formally a British colony in 1857. India became independent from British rule in 1947 and has been a republic since 1950.

Babur, A.D. 1526–30	Farruk-Siar, 1713–19
Humayun, 1530–56	Mohammed Shah,
Akbar the Great, 1556–	1719–48
1605	Ahmed, 1748–54
Jahangir, 1605–27	Alamgir, 1754–59
Shah Jahan, 1628–58	Shah Alam, 1759–1806
Aurangzeb, 1658–1707	Mohammed Akbar II,
Bahadur Shah I, 1707–12	1806–37
Jahandar Shah, 1712–13	Bahadur Shah II, 1837–57

PILLARS OF WISDOM

Lasting exhortations to the people of India to be kind, benevolent, and peaceful were carved into huge sandstone pillars and set up throughout the country by the emperor Asoka (c. 273–232 B.C.). Asoka was the grandson of Chandragupta (c. 321–298 B.C.) and ruler of the Maurya dynasty, which came to govern much of India from its capital, Pataliputra (now Patna), in the northeast of the country. A bloodthirsty campaign to subjugate the state of Kalinga in about 261 B.C. sickened the victorious Asoka. Full of remorse, he renounced conquest, embraced Buddhism, and spent the rest of his life preaching goodness to his people. His pillars—or rock edicts—ordered tree planting, well digging, kindness to children, and the establishment of hospitals for humans and animals. At the top of each of Asoka's stone pillars was a stone lion holding the wheel of law, a Buddhist symbol of enlightenment. The same symbol is today part of India's national flag.

BATTLE ROYAL *Fights between trained elephants were a popular spectator sport among the Mogul emperors. Here, Jahangir—the father of Shah Jahan, who built the Taj Mahal—watches a fight from horseback. The fights ended when one elephant brought the other to the ground, and usually neither elephant was hurt seriously. But the mahouts, or riders, formally took leave of their families before each fight, because they often did not survive.*

Egypt: land of the pharaohs

HAREM FOR A BOY

No other pharaoh of Egypt can compare with Ramses II for achievement and self-glorification. At the age of 10 he was already a captain in the army and had his own harem. By the time he died in 1225 B.C., he was over 90 years old and had ruled for 66 years, fathered 111 sons and 67 daughters, built the exquisite temples of Abu Simbel, and added to those at Luxor and Karnak. The great Battle of Kadesh in about 1284, in which he claimed to have subdued the Hittites, is celebrated in gigantic relief on one of the walls of the pharaoh's mortuary temples on the Nile's west bank at Thebes.

On an obelisk, which is now in the Place de la Concorde in Paris, Ramses had his glory described in these words: "Ramses, conqueror of all foreign peoples, master of all crown-bearers, Ramses who fought the millions, bids the whole world subdue itself to his power." The massive fallen statue of Ramses at Thebes probably inspired English poet Percy Bysshe Shelley's sonnet of faded glory, "Ozymandias." (Ozymandias is the Greek rendering of one of the pharaoh's names, User-ma'at-re.) The poem ends with these lines:

My name is Ozymandias, king of kings;
Look on my works, ye mighty, and despair!
Nothing beside remains. Round the decay
Of that colossal wreck, boundless and bare,
The lone and level sands stretch far away.

RISE AND FALL OF ANCIENT EGYPT

c. 3100 B.C. Unification of Upper and Lower Egypt by Menes. Invention of hieroglyphic writing.

c. 2650 Imhotep builds the Step Pyramid for the pharaoh Zoser at Sakkare.

c. 2560 Construction of the Giza pyramids and the Sphinx begins.

2181 End of Old Kingdom. Papyrus already in use. Civil wars.

1786 Middle Kingdom collapses in the face of invasions from the east.

1567 New Kingdom established as invaders are repulsed.

c. 1450 Egyptian empire extends from the Sudan to Syria.

c. 1375 Ikhnaton (ruled c. 1375–58), a pharaoh of the 18th dynasty, introduces monotheism, the worship of a single god.

1200–1100 Libyan incursions; decline of the pharaohs' power.

c. 940 Egypt reunited under Libyan kings.

746 Nubian kings conquer Egypt. Assyria makes incursions and becomes steadily more influential.

c. 650 Psamtik I (ruled c. 663–609), a 26th-dynasty pharaoh, breaks with Assyria; Egyptian independence reasserted.

525 Persian Empire absorbs Egypt.

404 Independence restored.

341 Persian rule restored.

332 Alexander the Great conquers Egypt.

305 Ptolemy I (ruled c. 305–285) comes to the throne. Library at Alexandria founded.

285 Ptolemy II (ruled c. 285–246) comes to the throne and makes Alexandria the center of Greek culture. Builds Pharos lighthouse—one of the seven wonders of the ancient world—at Alexandria in about 280.

c. 50 Cleopatra (ruled 51–49 and 48–30) secures the throne with the help of Julius Caesar.

30 Cleopatra commits suicide. Egypt becomes a province of the Roman Empire.

THE SPHINX

The Great Sphinx by the pyramids at Giza, near Cairo, stands 66 feet high, is 240 feet long, and was carved from a knoll left from the quarrying of stone for the Great Pyramid. Only the paws were carved separately and added. It dates from the 26th century B.C., which makes it the oldest known sphinx in Egypt.

Sphinxes were mythological animals, like the unicorns of northern Europe, and they occur in Mesopotamian and Greek mythology as well as in Egyptian tales. Sphinxes were usually male in Egyptian legends and female in Greek ones. Egyptian sphinxes were often constructed with the body of a lion, the tail of a serpent, a human head, and sometimes wings as well. But this design could vary. At Karnak, for example, there is an avenue of sphinxes with the heads of rams. Originally, sphinxes were considered by the Egyptians to be embodiments of the guardian of the Gates of Sunset and were erected to protect tombs from intruders. The features of the Great Sphinx may be those of the pharaoh Khafre, whose tomb is in one of the three nearby pyramids.

BIRTH OF THE MUMMY

The word *mummy,* for the embalmed bodies of Egyptian notables, does not come from Egypt. It is thought to be derived via Arabic from a Persian word, *mummia,* meaning "bitumen," or "tar." Mummies were so named because ancient peoples who came across the age-blackened corpses believed wrongly that the bodies were a source of tar.

THE HEALING ARTS

From the first dynasty onward, medical and surgical knowledge was highly respected in ancient Egypt. The pharaoh Athothis is supposed to have written a book on anatomy around 3000 B.C. Nine medical treatises have survived. One, the oldest surviving book of surgery in the world, contains details of 48 operations, among them trepanning—boring a hole in the skull to relieve pressure on the brain. Other books contain medical advice that is largely based on superstition, but they also list drugs that are still familiar, such as castor oil, wormwood, sodium bicarbonate, and arsenic. Egyptian doctors even used adhesive plasters to protect and promote the healing of wounds.

THREE KINGDOMS OF THE NILE

Egypt before the pharaohs consisted of two countries: Upper Egypt and Lower Egypt. Upper Egypt was the southern part, south of Thebes. Lower Egypt included the Nile delta and the cities of Memphis and Alexandria. The settlement of Egypt seems to have originated in the south, a land of extensive green plains and forests. These turned to desert with a change in climate, and the population gradually moved north up the fertile Nile Valley. Ancient Egyptian history is divided into three main periods, or kingdoms. The time between unification of the country in about 3100 B.C. and the start of the Old Kingdom is known as the Protodynastic Period.

OLD KINGDOM	2686–2181 B.C.
MIDDLE KINGDOM	1991–1786 B.C.
NEW KINGDOM	1567–1085 B.C.

The three kingdoms were separated by periods of foreign domination and civil disorder.

PRESERVING THE DEAD

The first Egyptian mummies date from about 2600 B.C., and the practice survived until Muslim Arabs conquered Egypt in A.D. 641. At its height, around the time of the 21st dynasty of pharaohs (c. 1085–945 B.C.), the most sophisticated techniques of mummification took about 70 days to complete.

The internal organs of the deceased were first removed from the body through a cut about 4 inches long near the left hip. They were cleaned in wine and spices, and the abdominal cavity was flushed out with cedar oil. Parts of the brain were removed by forcing a pointed tool through the soft nasal tissues into the cranial cavity and then scraping out the inside of the skull.

Once cleaned, the body and organs were packed in natron—a natural rock salt that was a mixture of washing soda (sodium carbonate) and baking soda (sodium bicarbonate)—to dry them. Then the organs were individually wrapped and replaced in the body, and the cavity was plugged up with sawdust, linen, tar, or even mud, depending on what was available.

The face and body were restored to a lifelike plumpness by tiny wads of linen inserted under the skin.

Finally, each limb, along with the head and torso, was wrapped separately in layers of resin-smeared linen before the body was handed back to the family for burial. This last stage must have taken considerable time. On some mummies that have been unwrapped by modern scholars, the total length of the bandages has been about 1.5 miles.

ANIMALS' AFTERLIFE *Ancient Egyptians preserved the bodies of sacred animals, such as cats, ibises, and bulls, as well as those of humans. This mummified cat dates from the early 1st century A.D.*

TREASURE OF A TEENAGE KING

Almost 2,000 fabulous objects, including gold figurines and masks and priceless jewelry, were found when British archeologist Howard Carter uncovered the tomb of the pharaoh Tutankhamen in November 1922. It was one of the most stunning archeological finds of all time. Asked what he could see as he peered into the tomb, Carter could only gasp: "Wonderful things. . . ." Yet Tutankhamen, who died in about 1352 B.C. at the age of 18 or 19, was only a minor pharaoh. Far more amazing treasures must have been buried with the more important pharaohs. But their larger and more conspicuous tombs were emptied by grave robbers hundreds of years ago.

SEE-THROUGH CLOTHES *Very fine linen—thought to have been as sheer as modern nylon stockings and probably worn by both men and women—was fashionable for centuries in ancient Egypt. This revealingly dressed statue of Selket, a scorpion goddess, was made of gilded wood for the tomb of Tutankhamen in the 14th century B.C.*

China: behind the Great Wall

TRESPASSERS WILL BE SHOT

China's first emperor, Shih Huang Ti, who died in 210 B.C., wanted to make sure that he would not be disturbed in his final resting place. So he had booby traps positioned around his huge burial mound at Mount Li in northwestern China. According to the historian Ssu-ma Ch'ien (Sima Qian), the emperor ordered hair-trigger crossbows to be loaded and set up in the passages leading to his tomb and in the undergrowth around the mound.

There was much that needed protecting. Ssu-ma Ch'ien also recorded that more than 700,000 men had been conscripted to build the mound and tomb in a project that took 36 years to complete. The imperial treasures buried with the emperor were so valuable that workers who helped to move the riches into the tomb were buried alive to ensure that no details leaked out.

In 1974 a group of astonished peasants sinking a well near Mount Li discovered a number of life-size terra-cotta soldiers. These later proved to be part of a buried army of more than 7,000 clay figures. Since Emperor Shih Huang Ti had been interred, they had maintained their vigil close to the imperial burial mound. Standing in battle formation, complete with life-size models of chariots and horses, the clay men

COMMANDER OF CLAY SOLDIERS *For more than 2,000 years this stern figure—his rank denoted by his uniform and his 6 foot 5 inch height—commanded an underground army. The army, of more than 7,000 life-size clay soldiers, formed a burial guard for Shih Huang Ti, the first emperor of a unified China.*

CHINESE DYNASTIES

Before the 3rd century B.C., China consisted of a number of independent states.

The Chinese empire was founded in 221 B.C. by Shih Huang Ti, who had acquired sufficient strength to defeat his rivals—known as the Warring States—and to establish the first imperial dynasty, Ch'in.

All the imperial dynasties, and the two major pre-imperial ruling houses, are listed here. Gaps in the sequence of dates mark periods when the country was divided between two or more rulers.

China became a republic under the nationalist leader Sun Zhongshan (Sun Yat-sen) in 1912 after the last of the Manchus abdicated. It became a Communist state under Mao Zedong (Mao Tse-t'ung) in 1949, after civil war ended in defeat for the nationalists under Jiang Jieshi (Chiang Kai-shek). The nationalists retreated from the mainland but established an independent state on the island of Formosa (now Taiwan).

Shang, c. 1600–1100 B.C.
Zhou (Chou), c. 1100–256
Ch'in (Qin), 221–206
Han, 206 B.C.–A.D. 220
Wei, Chin, and Northern and Southern, 220–581
Sui, 581–618
Tang, 618–906
Song, 960–1279
Yuan, 1279–1368
Ming, 1368–1644
Manchu (Ching or Qing), 1644–1912

GRIN OF DEATH *A toothy smile leers menacingly from the blade of a Shang dynasty ax, found at the entrance to a large tomb in northeastern China. Inside the tomb, built near the end of the Shang period, were the remains of 48 people. Every one had been decapitated.*

were wearing armor denoting their different ranks, and carrying real weapons. Incredibly, after 2,000 years in the ground, one of the swords was still sharp enough to split a hair.

HOW CHINA GOT ITS NAME

China, the world's oldest surviving civilization, acquired its name in the 3rd century B.C. In 221 Cheng, ruler of the small state of Ch'in, from which the country's modern name comes, annexed the last of six rival kingdoms and took the title of Ch'in Shih Huang Ti, meaning "First August Emperor of Ch'in."

The Anglicized form of Chinese names has changed since the introduction in 1957 of pinyin, a new system for transliterating Chinese characters into Roman letters. In pinyin Cheng became Zheng, Ch'in became Qin, and his title became Qin Shi Huangdi. China itself in pinyin is Zhong Guo.

FIRST HISTORY BOOK

China's oldest comprehensive written history dates from about 90 B.C. Known as the *Shih Chi* (also *Shi Ji* and other variant spellings), which translates as "Historical Memoirs," it was compiled by Ssu-ma Ch'ien (Sima Qian in pinyin), a court scholar and scribe who also gave the Chinese calendar its modern form. The *Shih Chi* represents the history of man according to Chinese records from about 1500 to 90 B.C. The 130-chapter book became the model for a series of 26 standard histories that continued in unbroken succession down to 1912, when Hsüan T'ung (or P'u-i), the last Manchu emperor, abdicated.

EMPEROR WHO PRESCRIBED DEATH

When the young daughter of the Tang dynasty emperor Yizong (who reigned from A.D. 860 to 874) was struck down by fever, 20 leading physicians of China were summoned to the imperial capital, Changan, to minister to her. Each doctor prescribed a remedy, but none was successful, and the princess died. Consumed with grief and frustration, the emperor had the unfortunate experts beheaded.

FROM CHINA TO ROME

Ancient China traded with imperial Rome, but the Chinese and the Romans never met. The only link between the two civilizations was the Silk Road, which ran overland around the northern edge of the Himalayas from China to the eastern Mediterranean coast, with a branch leading south into India. During the 2nd century B.C., camel caravans laden with silk, then a Chinese monopoly, began to move regularly along this arduous 7,000-mile route. The Chinese themselves did not pass their own frontiers, however.

Instead they transferred their bales of merchandise at a point near the Afghanistan border to other traders, often from Persia or central Asia. These merchants in turn sold the silk to Syrians and Greeks near the western end of the route, and from there the silk was shipped to Rome.

BREATH OF LIFE

Ephedrine, a drug derived from the horsetail plant, has been used to treat asthma in the West since the 1920s. But Chinese doctors were using the drug nearly 1,700 years earlier. Its use was being advocated by a doctor called Zhang Zhongjing as early as the 2nd century A.D.

Zhang, who lived from about A.D. 152 to 219, wrote a massive compendium of all the medical knowledge then available in China. In addition, he compiled a detailed list of techniques that doctors could use to diagnose a patient's illness.

TOP MARKS, TOP JOBS

Written examinations were being used to select Chinese civil servants as far back as the 2nd century B.C.—at a time when government jobs elsewhere in the world were largely filled by the relatives or protégés of those in power.

By the time of the Tang dynasty (A.D. 618–906) this principle of selecting public officials on the basis of merit had developed into a system of centralized public examinations open to all. A Jesuit missionary, Matteo Ricci, who arrived in China in 1583, described how the system worked.

Exams lasted several days, he said, and candidates could work nonstop through each day to write their answers. Ricci also reported that the Chinese took enormous trouble to avoid even the possibility of favoritism affecting the examiners' grades. When the exams were over, he said, all the completed papers had to be copied out by another hand in order to conceal the candidates' identity from the examiners.

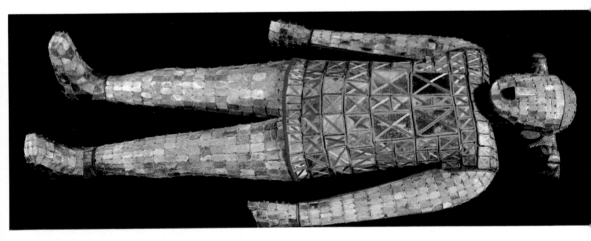

JADE PRINCESS *A burial suit made of 2,160 pieces of jade, tied together with gold wire, was intended to preserve forever the body of the Han princess Dou Wan. The princess was the principal wife of Liu Sheng, son of the fifth Han dynasty emperor Jing Di. She died in about 125 B.C., at a time when jade was believed to be an infallible preservative because of its hardness. The prince, who died in about 113 B.C., had a suit even more elaborate than his wife's; it contained 2,690 polished discs of the highly prized stone. His brother, known as Wu Ti, reigned as the sixth Han emperor (141–87 B.C.). The jade suits were uncovered at Mancheng, about 70 miles southwest of the capital, Beijing (Peking), in 1968.*

19

Mesopotamia: gift of two rivers

BABES IN THE WOOD

The life of a Babylonian princess named Sammu-ramat, the most powerful woman in Mesopotamian history, is also the source of a touching children's tale, "Babes in the Wood." As told by the Greek historian Herodotus, Sammu-ramat, who was born in the 9th century B.C., married Shamshi-Adad V, king of Assyria. When her husband died in 812 B.C., she became regent for her son and helped to establish close political and economic ties between Assyria and the neighboring kingdom of Babylon.

According to a Babylonian myth that grew up later around her life, Sammu-ramat was the child of divine parents, who abandoned her, and she was fed by doves until a shepherd found her and took her in. Modern scholars believe that the myth is the direct ancestor of the European fairy tale about the two infants abandoned in a wood.

FIRST ARCHEOLOGIST

Nabonidus, the last king of Babylonia (556–539 B.C.), was one of the world's first archeologists. Centuries before the modern discipline was invented, he excavated ruined shrines and temples near Babylon and restored the great ziggurat (tower) of Ur. Nabonidus left inscribed cylinders in the foundations for posterity. His daughter, Princess Ennigaldi-Nanna, found southern Mesopotamia a rich source of antiques. She stored them in a temple at Ur, creating the world's first known museum.

ABRAHAM'S HOME *Ur of the Chaldees, as the Bible calls it, was the home of the Old Testament patriarch Abraham. The mosaic at left, on a wooden box thought to have been part of a musical instrument, shows a king of Ur at ease with a drink. The box was made in about 2800–2700 B.C.*

COLLAPSIBLE BOATS

Traders in ancient Sumeria, in southern Mesopotamia, devised a simple but ingenious way to make the best use of river transport. Upstream they built boats of hides stretched over light wooden frames. The boats were loaded with whatever cargo was to be shipped, plus a donkey. The boats then floated downstream with the current to their destination.

Once the cargo was unloaded, the boat was knocked apart, and its wooden parts were sold to the timber-poor cities of the south. The crew then loaded the hides onto the donkey and walked back, having saved themselves all the problems of propelling a boat upriver against the current. At the other end they built a new frame, covered it with the old hides, and were ready to set off again.

A relief carved on the wall of a palace built at Nineveh in the 7th century B.C. for the Assyrian king Sennacherib shows one of these leather boats carrying stone down the river Tigris. Even today, similarly made boats are still used on the Euphrates.

EARLIEST LIBRARIES

Records of commercial transactions, religious practices, political history, popular legends, government accounts, and mathematical and astronomical discoveries are by no means isolated survivals from ancient Mesopotamian civilization. Hundreds of thousands of clay tablets—all covered with the wedge-shaped writing known as cuneiform—have survived to the present day, partly because the Sumerians and Babylonians wrote down a great deal and also because dry, sun-baked clay is almost imperishable.

Several collections of tablets, so numerous that they can only be called libraries, have come to light. Excavations begun in 1933, at a site called Tell Hariri, in eastern Syria, uncovered the archives of the ancient Mesopotamian city of Mari.

The archives contained 23,600 tablets, covering a period of 530 years, between 2285 and 1755 B.C. Another library, compiled for the Assyrian king Assurbanipal in the 7th century B.C., contained specially commissioned Sumerian and Assyrian grammars and dictionaries, which have provided scholars with an invaluable key to these ancient languages.

LAND BETWEEN THE RIVERS

The name *Mesopotamia* comes from Greek words meaning "between the rivers," and the ancient kingdom's prosperity depended on those rivers: the Tigris and the Euphrates. The two rivers irrigated the region, making settled agriculture possible. Farming settlements dating back to about 9000 B.C. grew by about 3500 into independent city-states. Writing, mathematics, astronomy, and complex architecture were developed in Mesopotamia, and the wheel seems to have been first used there.

At times the rulers of individual cities dominated huge territories in the Middle East. The Sumerian city-states, for example, were united under Sargon the Great in the 24th century B.C. to form the first Mesopotamian empire, which set a pattern of dominance that prevailed in the region for the next 2,000 years. Two of the most important cities during this imperial era were Babylon and Ur.

BABYLON

Located 55 miles south of Baghdad on the banks of the Euphrates, Babylon was one of the focal points of southern Mesopotamia and capital of the area that became known as Babylonia. Its first era of magnificence was under Hammurabi in the 18th century B.C. The city's fortunes revived under Nebuchadnezzar II, who built the Tower of Babel and the Hanging Gardens in about 600 B.C.

UR

Built on the Euphrates, Ur was founded between 6000 and 5000 B.C. It came to prominence as a political, commercial, and cultural center in the 26th century B.C., but its political power in southern Mesopotamia was destroyed by the year 2000. Ur remained a trade center until it finally fell into ruin in the 4th century B.C. after the course of the Euphrates changed and river trade bypassed the city.

OLD ALE

Beer may well have been the most popular drink in Mesopotamia. It was being made from malted barley before 6000 B.C., and the Sumerians even had a goddess of intoxicating drink called Ninkasi. Clay tablets found in Babylonia record the words of a hymn to Ninkasi, as well as the words of a drinking song. The tablets also suggest that tippling Mesopotamians enjoyed variety: there is a list of 19 different brews.

MIDDLE EAST OIL

Mesopotamians were exploiting the Middle East's best-known natural asset, oil, thousands of years before the birth of Christ. They probably used natural petroleum, which seeped from the ground in places, as fuel for lamps. They also used the heavier bitumen, or pitch, for bonding brickwork in buildings and for waterproofing boats. The great city of Ur was discovered in the 19th century under mounds, one of which the Arabs called Tall al-Muqayyar, which means "mound of pitch." And the Bible record of the founding of Babylon describes how the builders "used bricks for stone and bitumen for mortar."

THE TOWER OF BABEL

The Book of Genesis tells how the descendants of Noah started to build a tower "with its top in the heavens." Some scholars believe that the foundations of the tower—the Tower of Babel—can still be seen on the site of ancient Babylon in southern Iraq.

The tower was not a straight-sided building like a church tower. It was a ziggurat, a stepped pyramid, about 300 feet high. It was built during the reign of Nebuchadnezzar II, who ruled Babylon between about 605 and 562 B.C. Nebuchadnezzar also built the Hanging Gardens of Babylon, one of the seven wonders of the ancient world. The Babylonians called the tower Etemenanki ("House of the Foundations of Heaven and Earth"). According to the Greek historian Herodotus, it consisted of eight levels, topped by a temple to the city's paramount god, Marduk. Herodotus reported that a room in the temple contained a bed that was used for fertility rites. The room may also have been an astrological observatory.

KING'S PREROGATIVE *Only royalty was allowed to kill lions in Assyria. When Assurbanipal (who ruled from 668 to about 627 B.C.) built a new palace at Nineveh in about 645, he commissioned a series of stone reliefs showing his prowess in the lion hunt to decorate the corridors. Here Assurbanipal spears a charging lion while behind him a wounded lion attacks his spare horse.*

Japan: people of the rising sun

CHARACTER REFERENCE

Japan's oldest book, the *Kojiki* (completed in A.D. 712), describes the nation's history from its mythic origins to about A.D. 600. The book was written to substantiate the imperial family's claim to be descended from the Shinto sun goddess, Amaterasu, the source of Japan's national symbol: the rising sun.

The *Kojiki* marked a turning point in Japanese culture, because it was the first book to use Japanese characters (the script known as *kana*). Before the 8th century Japan made use of Chinese characters.

TEA BREAK

Zen monks in Japan acquired the habit of drinking tea in the 12th century as a "cure" for a variety of ailments and also to keep themselves awake while meditating. Actually the monks imported the custom from China. It later became a stylized ceremony used to teach courtesy and tranquillity.

Guests enter the ceremonial room on their knees through a low door and sip green tea from bowls. The precisely defined protocol extends even to the room in which the ceremony takes place: by tradition, the room is square and only about 9 feet across.

THE SHOGUNS

Few Japanese emperors have wielded personal power. Instead, a military dictatorship (the shogunate) has ruled in the emperor's name for much of Japan's history. The last of the shogun dynasties was the Tokugawa clan, which for more than 200 years kept Japan in seclusion from the world. The dynasty, whose ruling members are listed here, dominated Japan until 1867, when the emperor Meiji reasserted power and abolished the shogunate.

Iyeyasu, 1603–05	Ieshige, 1744–61
Hidetada, 1605–23	Iyeharu, 1761–87
Iyemitsu, 1623–51	Iyenari, 1787–1838
Iyetsuna, 1651–80	Iyeyoshi, 1838–53
Tsunayoshi, 1680–1709	Iyesada, 1853–58
Iyenobu, 1709–13	Iyemochi, 1858–66
Iyetsugu, 1713–16	Hitotsubashi, 1866–67
Yoshimune, 1716–44	

DRESSED FOR COURT *The first Tokugawa chief, Iyeyasu, portrayed in his court clothes, brought internal peace to Japan. He made his base at the port of Edo, later called Tokyo.*

ANCIENT AND MODERN

The 220 sacred wooden buildings at Japan's ancient Shinto shrine at Ise have been pulled down and replaced by identical buildings every 20 years since they were first put up in the 5th century A.D. Only unpainted cypress wood is used, and no nails—just dowels and joints. It is thought that the buildings are rebuilt every two decades to symbolize the coming of a new generation. The last rebuilding was in 1973.

DEATH BEFORE DISHONOR

Hara-kiri, or ritual suicide, was a custom of the feudal samurai warriors—and later, of officers in Japan's imperial army—to avoid dishonor or capture by an enemy. Sometimes hara-kiri was committed to show loyalty to a dead or disgraced lord.

The term *hara-kiri* means, literally, "belly-cutting." The victim first cut open his own stomach with a short sword or dagger and disemboweled himself. Then he was beheaded by a companion. The ceremony, known formally in Japan as *seppuku,* is still occasionally used as an extreme form of protest. The Japanese novelist and playwright Yukio Mishima committed hara-kiri in 1970 in protest against what he saw as the weakness of Japan as a nation.

GUNSLINGERS

Portuguese traders took guns to Japan in 1543, but 100 years later the government banned them. The traditional sword became the sole weapon of the warrior, or samurai. Ordinary citizens were forbidden to carry any weapons at all. Only in 1853, when U.S. warships under Commodore Matthew Perry forced Japan to open its ports to foreign traders, were guns allowed into the country again.

ATISHOO

Paper tissues have been used by the Japanese for more than 300 years. An English traveler in 1637 wrote, "The Japanese blow their noses with a certain soft and tough kind of paper which they carry about them in small pieces, which, having used, they fling away as a filthy thing."

WINDS OF DEATH

World War II suicide pilots who crashed their bomb-laden planes into enemy ships named themselves *kamikaze,* meaning "divine wind." The name had been given first to sudden, providential typhoons that helped to destroy the seaborne invading forces of Kublai Khan, the Mongol emperor, in 1274 and again in 1281. The 1281 storm wrecked the enemy fleet after almost 2 months of fighting, and the stranded invaders were massacred. Not until 1945 did another invading army set foot on Japanese soil.

ROCKS OF AGES

One of the world's oldest stone gardens was laid out at the Zen temple of Ryoanji in Kyoto in 1490. The garden contains just 15 large stones, set apparently at random in a walled area about 70 feet by 30 feet on fine gray-white gravel. The garden is designed to represent nature in the abstract: the stones symbolize islands or mountains; the gravel stands for the sea or trees. The garden contains no plants at all, but the gravel is raked each day.

SAMURAI'S LAST STAND *The 14th-century samurai Kusunoki Masashige killed himself rather than surrender to the enemies of his emperor, and so became a Japanese hero. He committed suicide in 1336 after unsuccessfully defending the capital of the emperor Daigo II against shogun rebels. This print of his last battle was made in 1851.*

BUSHIDO—THE WAY OF THE WARRIOR

The proud warrior class of the samurai (meaning "those who serve") grew from bands of mercenaries hired by feudal landowners in the 11th century to win control of Honshu, Japan's main island. These mercenaries lived by the cult of the sword, worshiping athletic prowess and martial skills. They developed a fierce loyalty to their masters and a fearlessness that made them formidable adversaries. They fought in elaborate armor, wielding their most prized possession, a double-edged saber with which they could cut a man in half.

Later, the spartan principles of Zen Buddhism, with its love of nature, softened their fighting zeal. It became fashionable for samurai to live sparse and frugal lives during the Kamakura era (1192–1333), when the ruling warrior family Minamato moved its seat of power to the eastern city of Kamakura. Confucian thought, with its emphasis on honesty, also influenced the samurai.

Oriental knights
By the 16th century these principles had become codified into Bushido ("the way of the warrior"). First loyalty remained to the samurai lord and to skill with the sword, but the warriors also became an Oriental version of the Christian knights, embracing duty, honor, and nobility of spirit. In 1871 the last 400,000 samurai were pensioned off and became *shizoku,* Japanese gentry. Most were absorbed into the civil service and business management. Five years later it became illegal for anyone but the military to wear a sword.

Nevertheless, the virtues of the samurai were kept as an ideal for the whole nation to follow, with the emperor as the supreme object of loyalty. It was this ethos that in times of crisis turned Japanese nationalism into a potent force.

Greece: democracy's birthplace

RISE AND FALL OF ALEXANDER'S EMPIRE

Alexander the Great created the greatest empire the world had yet seen—and also the shortest-lived. He became king of Macedonia in 336 B.C. at the age of 20 and then subdued the Greek states. Two years later, in 334, he led a large army to conquer Persia. During the next 11 years Alexander conquered an area nearly as large as the United States. His empire extended from Greece and Egypt in the west to beyond the Indus River in the east. When his weary army refused to march farther eastward into India, Alexander retired to Babylon. He died there of a fever in 323 B.C., at 33. The empire he had built in 13 years was broken up as quickly as it had been formed. Within 13 years of his death, the countries Alexander had united were divided again, their territories carved up between his generals.

CONSULTING THE ORACLE

Delphi was the site of Greece's most important oracle, where the advice of the gods was sought. The answer was given by a Pythia, a priestess who went into a trance and shouted wildly. Her cries were "interpreted" by priests, who gave the answers, often very ambiguous, in doggerel verse.

It is said that Croesus, the king of Lydia, in Asia Minor, whose name has become a symbol of wealth, asked the oracle if he should attack the Persian Empire. He was told that if he did he would destroy a great empire. Croesus duly attacked in 546 B.C. and did indeed destroy an empire: his own. Cyrus the Great defeated his army, annexed his kingdom, and took Croesus hostage.

WOMEN WITH RIGHTS *The women of Minoan Crete depicted on this wall-painting from Knossos, which dates from about 1500 B.C., had far greater rights than their contemporaries elsewhere. A Minoan woman's dowry remained wholly at her disposal and could not be used by her husband without her permission. Divorce was a right available to women as well as men, and if the husband was shown to be at fault, the wife could reclaim any property she had given him during the marriage. Women occupied influential roles in Minoan society, partly because Crete was a maritime nation and the men were away for long stretches at sea.*

CITY-STATES OF ANCIENT GREECE

Ancient Greece was not a unified nation. Control of the country was divided between a number of independent city-states, which often formed shifting alliances with each other or fought to expand or preserve their spheres of influence. Below are the major city-states that influenced and sometimes dominated Greek civilization.

ARGOS

Founded in prehistoric times. In Homer's poem, the *Iliad,* it was the kingdom of the sailor-warrior Diomedes. Ascendancy challenged by Sparta in 8th to 7th centuries B.C. Argos later periodically sided with Athens against Sparta.

ATHENS

Founded in prehistoric times. Became the leading city-state in the 5th century B.C., particularly under the statesman Pericles (c. 494–429 B.C.). Defeat by Sparta in 404 led to its political decline.

CORINTH

Founded about 1350 B.C. Important industrial and commercial center in the 7th century. Alternately supported Athens and Sparta. Looted and destroyed by Romans in 146 and rebuilt in 44 B.C.

RHODES

Founded 408 B.C. Became the richest city-state through trade. Sided with Rome against the Syrian king Antiochus the Great, who was defeated at Thermopylae in 191 B.C. Rhodes was later dominated by Rome, and its maritime power declined.

SPARTA

Founded about 1000 B.C. by Dorian Greeks. Defeated Athens in Peloponnesian War (431–404) and became the most powerful city-state. Sparta went into decline after its defeat by Thebes in 371 B.C.

THEBES

Founded in prehistoric times. Helped Sparta defeat Athens in 404 B.C., then drove the Spartans out of central Greece in 371. Briefly became chief city-state, but in 362 was defeated by a Spartan alliance and destroyed by Alexander the Great in 336.

END OF THE MINOANS

The Minoan civilization of Crete, the immediate predecessor of the culture of ancient Greece, came to a sudden and mysterious end in about 1450 B.C. Some scholars believe that the Minoans were destroyed by invaders from the Greek mainland. Other scholars, however, think that the disaster was the result of a volcanic explosion on the nearby island of Santorini (formerly Thera), which sent 300-foot-high walls of water crashing over Crete. The destruction of the Minoans may have given rise to the legend of the drowned island continent of Atlantis.

The center of the Minoan civilization—around the palace of Knossos, which was situated well inland—survived for another 75 years. Then, in about 1375 B.C., Knossos too was destroyed, by fire.

A GIFT OF DEMOCRACY

The Greeks gave democracy to the world. The word itself comes from the Greek words *demos,* meaning "the people," and *kratos,* meaning "rule." Beginning in the 7th century B.C., democracy evolved from the mosaic of independent city-states that then covered Greece.

Not all the city-states were democratic. Sparta, for example, was ruled by landowning aristocrats. But some of the city-states shared more power among more people than had any earlier civilizations. The leading democracy was Athens, which overthrew its aristocracy early in the 6th century and under the reformer Solon (c. 638–559 B.C.) established a constitution giving supreme power to a citizens' assembly known as the ecclesia. The right to vote at the assembly's meetings in the marketplace was by no means universal, however. Only freeborn male citizens—about 40,000 people out of a total population of between 300,000 and 400,000—had the vote. Women, slaves, freed slaves, and immigrants were all excluded.

BORN TO BE SOLDIERS

In the city-state of Sparta the elite male citizens, the Spartiates, were groomed for a life of military service. The Spartan existence began at birth, when babies were inspected by the elders, and weak infants were put on a mountainside to die of exposure. From the time they were 7, boys were trained in the skills of a soldier. They wore no clothes until they reached the age of 12; then they were allowed one mantle a year. They lived in military barracks up to the age of 30 and moved into clubs until they were 60.

The men were encouraged to marry in order to produce strong and healthy children for the state. But they were not allowed to spend the whole night with their wives. They had to slip out after dinner and then return to the barracks to sleep. Spartan girls also received physical training so that they would give birth to sturdy babies.

All the Spartiates' work—including farming and trading—was done by helots, serfs who were owned by the state.

BOUND FOR GLORY *Success in athletic contests was a passport to fame for the ancient Greeks. Competition was almost always between individuals rather than teams, and a champion could become a hero throughout the Greek world. Statues of him would be made and songs composed about his exploits. Success in the Olympic Games—held every 4 years between 776 B.C. and A.D. 393 at Olympia in the western Peloponnesus—was particularly prestigious. Athens welcomed its Olympic champions with banquets. Some athletes were exempted from paying taxes. Theogenes of Thasos, a wrestler who competed in the Olympic Games for 22 years in the 4th century B.C., was so revered that he was declared a descendant of the legendary Heracles (Hercules). The chief events were running, wrestling, boxing, the long jump, throwing the discus, throwing the javelin, and the pankration (a boxing and wrestling contest). Many Games also included horse and chariot races. This picture of a footrace appears on a jar dating from about 350 B.C. Filled with oil from holy olives, the jar was one of the prizes at the Panathenaea, a religious and sporting festival held every year in Athens to celebrate the birth of the goddess Athena. Athletes were traditionally portrayed naked, but many modern scholars believe that was an artistic convention, and Greek athletes may actually have stripped only for boxing and wrestling while remaining clothed for other events.*

The Roman Empire

ETERNAL ROME

At its height in A.D. 117, the mighty Roman Empire was almost as big as Australia, covering an area of around 2.5 million square miles. So confident were Romans of the enduring power of their empire that they spoke of their city as *Roma eterna* ("eternal Rome") and of the Mediterranean as *mare nostrum* ("our sea").

WITH THIS RING

Two modern wedding traditions derive from pagan Roman customs. Brides wore wedding rings on the third finger of their left hand because the Romans believed that a nerve led directly from that finger to the heart. And a bride was carried over the threshold of her new home to avoid the risk that she might stumble in the doorway or enter left foot first. Either happening was thought to bring bad luck from the gods.

HIGH-RANKING HORSE

The mad Roman emperor Caligula, who ruled Rome from A.D. 37 to 41, favored his stallion, Incitatus, above many men who had proved themselves loyal servants of the state. Incitatus was housed in an ivory stall in a marble stable and had a retinue of slaves to care for him. He wore a jeweled collar, and his blankets were woven of imperial purple—a color usually reserved for the highest-ranking Romans.

Caligula is thought to have planned to honor Incitatus further by making him a member of the college of priests and then promoting him to consul, one of the highest offices of state. But when Caligula was assassinated, Incitatus was stripped of his privileges.

WRITING ON THE WALL

The writing and drawing of graffiti is by no means new. It was rife in Roman times. The word *graffiti* itself is derived from the Latin *graphium,* meaning "stylus," a pointed instrument for scratching letters onto tablets. Walls in the coastal town of Pompeii, for instance, preserved by ash from the eruption of Vesuvius in A.D. 79, are still daubed with inscriptions and scribblings of all kinds, from brief election addresses to offers of rewards for the return of stolen property. In addition, there are obscenities, rude drawings, and many complaints from lovers, such as: "What use to have a Venus, if she is made from marble?"

LEATHER BIKINI

The wearing of bikinis goes back at least to Roman times. Girls wearing similar two-piece costumes are portrayed on a Roman mosaic that was found in the ruins of a villa near Piazza Armerina in Sicily. Apparently, the fashion spread as far north as Britain. A leather bikini made by the Romans in the late 1st century A.D. was found in a well in London.

BATHING BEAUTY A painted bikini adorns this statue of Venus from the town of Pompeii. Whether propriety or fashion inspired the painter is not known.

NERO THE FIRE FIGHTER

The story that the emperor Nero (A.D. 54–68) deliberately started the fire that roared through Rome in A.D. 64 is fiction. When the fire broke out, he was at his villa in Actium, 35 miles from the city. Far from celebrating the blaze by playing his favorite instrument, the lyre, Nero raced to the capital to take charge of the fire fighting. His concern was no doubt heightened by the news that his new palace was afire.

The legend appears to have sprung from the resentment that the citizens of Rome felt about Nero's behavior after the fire. He used the destruction as an excuse to begin his most ambitious building project—the so-called Golden House—which he intended as a palace fit for a god. Had it been finished, this monumental building would have covered one-third of the entire city of Rome.

FIGHT TO THE DEATH

Public fights between gladiators were among the most popular spectator sports in ancient Rome. The first of these bloody combats was recorded in 264 B.C. The spectacles continued until they were finally banned by the emperor Honorius (A.D. 395–423) in 404. Most battles were fought to the death, and they were held so often that several hundred gladiators were killed in the arena every year. Some of the fighters were volunteers, but most were prisoners of war, slaves, or condemned criminals.

There were several categories of gladiator. The *retiarius* carried a net to entangle his opponent, and a trident, with which to kill him. The *mirmillo* was armed with a sword, shield, and helmet. The *laqueator* was armed with a noose. All gladiators were trained in their art at special schools.

PAGAN FESTIVALS

Roman festivals were a mixture of public holiday and religious ritual. One of the oldest was a fertility rite called the Lupercalia, which was celebrated every year on February 15.

The celebrations began with the ritual sacrifice of goats and a dog at the Lupercal, a cave on Rome's chief hill, the Palatine, in which Romulus and Remus, the legendary founders of Rome, were reputedly suckled by a she-wolf.

Two youths, naked except for leather girdles, were smeared with the blood from the sacrifices and then ran around the Palatine Hill, carrying thongs cut from the goats' skins. By striking any woman they passed with the thongs, the runners were thought to confer the gift of fertility.

This particular ceremony was known as *februa* ("purification"). It is from this that the name of the second month of the year is derived.

VIRGIN PRIESTESSES

One of the chief rituals in the worship of Vesta, the Roman goddess of the hearth, was keeping a fire burning in her circular temple. This fire was allowed to go out only once a year, on March 1, the Roman New Year's Day.

Tending the fire was the responsibility of six priestesses, the vestal virgins. These were girls of noble birth, who were recruited between the ages of 6 and 10 and remained in the service of the goddess for 30 years. They swore to remain chaste during that time, though at the end of it they could leave their order to marry if they wished.

Discipline could be severe. For even minor offenses a vestal was liable to be flogged, but if she broke her oath of chastity a worse fate lay in store. She would be taken to an underground room beneath a mound near one of the city gates. There, she was given a bed, a lamp, and some food. The entrance to the mound was then closed and covered with earth, and the unfortunate vestal was left, in theory, to starve to death. In some cases, however, condemned vestals were secretly released from their underground tombs, perhaps by their families or lovers.

ROME: ITS EMPERORS AND ITS EXTENT

The Roman Empire was founded in 27 B.C. by Octavian, the grandnephew and adopted son of Julius Caesar (100–44 B.C.), who had become dictator of Rome in 49 B.C. Octavian became known as Augustus Caesar on his accession. The word *caesar* is the origin of the German title *kaiser* and the Russian title *tsar*.

The empire was divided formally into east and west after the death of Theodosius the Great in A.D. 395. The western empire ended less than 100 years later when the German chieftain Odoacer forced the emperor Romulus Augustulus to abdicate in 476. The eastern half survived under mostly Greek rulers as the Byzantine Empire until its capital, Constantinople (now Istanbul), was conquered by the Turks in 1453.

The list shows the dates of all the Roman emperors from the foundation of the empire until its division. Where dates in the sequence overlap, the title of emperor was shared.

Augustus, 27 B.C.–A.D. 14
Tiberius, 14–37
Caligula, 37–41
Claudius, 41–54
Nero, 54–68
Galba, 68–69
Otho, 69
Vitellius, 69
Vespasian, 69–79
Titus, 79–81
Domitian, 81–96
Nerva, 96–98
Trajan, 98–117
Hadrian, 117–38
Antoninus Pius, 138–61
Marcus Aurelius, 161–80
Lucius Verus, 161–69
Commodus, 180–92
Pertinax, 193

FROM SEA TO SEA *The Roman Empire reached its peak of expansion in the reign of Trajan, who died in A.D. 117. At that time it covered approximately 2.5 million square miles and held sway over an estimated 100 million people. The empire stretched from Britain and the North Sea southward along the Atlantic coastline to Africa, then swept eastward on both sides of the Mediterranean Sea into Asia Minor as far as the Persian Gulf, then northward to the Caspian Sea, and back westward across the Black Sea and into eastern and northern Europe. Rome's relentless empire building had begun in the 3rd century B.C. and at Julius Caesar's death in 44 B.C. had absorbed most of the lands bordering the Mediterranean.*

Empire-founder Augustus Caesar was first named Caius Octavius.

Didius Julianus, 193
Septimius Severus, 193–211
Geta, 211–12
Caracalla, 211–17
Macrinus, 217–18
Heliogabalus (Elagabalus), 218–22
Severus Alexander, 222–35
Maximinus, 235–38
Gordianus I Africanus, 238
Gordianus II, 238
Balbinus, 238
Pupienus Maximus, 238
Gordianus III, 238–44
Philip the Arab, 244–49

Decius, 249–51
Hostilianus, 251
Trebonianus Gallus, 251–53
Aemilianus, 253
Valerian, 253–59
Gallienus, 259–68
Claudius II, 268–70
Quintillus, 270
Aurelian, 270–75
Tacitus, 275–76
Florianus, 276
Probus, 276–82
Carus, 282–83
Carinus, 283–85
Numerianus, 283–84
Diocletian, 284–305
Maximian, 286–305; 307–08
Constantius I, 305–06
Galerius, 305–11
Severus, 306–07
Maxentius, 306–12
Maximinus Daia, 308–13
Licinius, 308–24
Constantine I the Great, 306–37

Constantine II, 337–40
Constans, 337–50
Constantius II, 337–61
Julian the Apostate, 361–63
Jovianus, 363–64
Valentinian I, 364–75
Valens, 364–78
Gratian, 375–83
Valentinian II, 375–92
Theodosius I the Great, 379–95

Marcus Aurelius, famous for his Meditations, *was a lenient ruler but saw Christians as enemies of the Roman Empire.*

South America: land of gold

SHORT-LIVED EMPIRE

The Inca empire, which grew to control a 2,500-mile-long stretch of the Andes in South America, survived for less than 100 years. Until the reign of Pachacuti Yupanqui (c. 1440–71) the Incas had spent almost 250 years as a small tribal group centered around their capital, Cuzco, in the Peruvian highlands. Then, after repelling an attack by neighboring Chanca warriors in 1438, Pachacuti and his successors, Tupac Yupanqui (1471–93) and Huayna Capac (1493–1525), launched a series of campaigns that established Inca rule from present-day southern Colombia through Ecuador and Peru to central Chile, spilling over into Bolivia and Argentina.

The culture gets its name from the word *Inca*, a shortened form of *Sapa Inca,* meaning the "unique Inca." The word, which comes from the Quechua term *inka* ("king"), was used as a title by the rulers, who were worshiped as gods. The empire was toppled by a mere 180 Spanish soldiers under Francisco Pizarro. Taking advantage of his men's superior firepower, of epidemics introduced by the Spaniards to which the Indians had no immunity, and of divisions among the Incas themselves after a 7-year civil war, Pizarro conquered the whole of the empire within 6 years of his arrival in 1532.

MUMMIFIED MONARCHS *Inca kings were worshiped even in death. This sketch, from a Spanish chronicle published in about 1610, shows how their mummified bodies were carried out into the main square of the capital, Cuzco, each day. There, the corpses were honored with prayers and the sacrifice of white llamas.*

PIERCING STARE *Funerary masks, placed over the faces of the dead, were a common feature of South American civilizations. This hammered gold mask, painted and decorated with smaller pieces of gold—including two needles jutting menacingly from the eyes—was probably made for a wealthy Chimú nobleman. Found near the Chimú capital of Chan Chan in northwestern Peru, it is thought to date from the early 15th century.*

ROYAL HABIT

Centuries before cocaine became known in the West, the leaves of the coca plant (*Erythroxylon coca*), from which cocaine is derived, were being chewed by the Incas. Originally reserved for the Inca kings and leading nobles, the habit spread to commoners after the Spanish conquest. Chewing the leaves diminishes hunger, increases stamina, and counteracts the effects of exertion at high elevations. Andean Indians today still chew coca leaves.

SKULL SURGERY

In the Inca empire, priests doubled as doctors and surgeons and appear to have been able to carry out some difficult operations. The remains of some Inca skulls, for instance, show that the priests knew how to perform the operation known as trepanning—cutting a hole in the skull. It is uncertain whether the operation was performed to relieve pressure caused by injury or to release evil spirits, but it seems likely that coca was used as an anesthetic.

SAY IT WITH KNOTS

Ignorant of written numbers, the Incas devised an ingenious counting method based on knotted cords called *quipus*. The system, which is still used by Peruvian peasants, made use of single knots, double knots, and slip knots with loops to represent numbers. Different-colored cords identified subjects, such as tax and census information, and even historical records.

Official messages were memorized and delivered by relays of runners, or *chasquis,* who could cover 150 miles in a single day. In this postal service, established by Pachacuti Yupanqui and made possible by the empire's efficient road network, pairs of *chasquis* were stationed in roadside huts about every 2 miles. When a runner approached a hut, he shouted out his message, and a relief *chasqui* took off for the next hut. Complex messages were sent by *quipus*.

FOOD FROM THE HILLS

Besides flooding Spain with looted wealth—nearly 200 tons of gold and 20,000 tons of silver by 1650—the conquistadores introduced several new foods to Europe. These included maize, tomatoes, gourds, manioc (cassava), guavas, and potatoes. The potato had been cultivated by Andean farmers since at least A.D. 200. Its English name is derived from the Taino word for the sweet potato, *batata.*

The potato was so important to the Inca diet that they invented a method of freeze-drying to preserve it. Potatoes were left out to freeze for several nights (they thawed by day). Softened by repeated freezing and thawing, the vegetables were then squeezed by hand to remove most of their moisture and put out in the sun to dry completely. Finally, they reached a stage known as *chuño,* in which they could be kept indefinitely. Andean Indians still use this technique.

THE GOLDEN ROOM

The Inca ruler Atahualpa, backed by thousands of warriors, came face to face with Francisco Pizarro, backed by 180 men and 37 horses, for the first time at Cajamarca in Peru. The encounter was a disaster for the Indians. Pizarro kidnapped Atahualpa, and the demoralized warriors were put to flight by their first experience of firearms and cavalry.

After the kidnapping, Atahualpa offered to ransom himself by giving the Spaniards enough gold to fill his 23- by 16-foot cell as high as he could reach. He was a tall man and standing on tiptoe could reach to 9 feet. Atahualpa also offered to fill a smaller room twice over with silver. The Spaniards accepted, but then changed their minds, realizing that Atahualpa could become the focus of rebellion if he were released. Instead, they tried the king on several trumped-up charges—such as murdering a former Inca king, Huáscar, and plotting against the Spanish forces—and sentenced him to death. He was garrotted in 1533.

CEREMONIAL KNIFE
Gold inlaid with turquoise forms the image of a god sacred to the pre-Inca Chimú civilization of northwestern Peru. Knife handle probably dates from 12th century.

INSTANT GALOSHES

Amazonian Indians invented rubber boots many centuries before they were known in Europe. The Indians dipped their feet and legs in latex, the raw liquid of the rubber tree. It formed a tough extra skin, or boot, that protected against insects and thorns.

MASS MARRIAGES

Marriage by decree was the norm for ordinary people within the Inca empire. Although nobles often had several wives, commoners were limited to one. Furthermore, the state dictated whom and when each commoner could marry. Each year local chiefs assembled all eligible inhabitants (all men over 24, all women over 18), separating them by sex into lines before calling them up to be paired off.

PRINCIPAL PRE-COLUMBIAN CIVILIZATIONS

The arrival of Europeans in the Americas in the late 15th and early 16th centuries brought to an abrupt end a series of cultures that dated back more than 2,000 years. These civilizations are known as pre-Columbian, from the Italian explorer Christopher Columbus (1451–1506).

CHAVÍN
Earliest highly developed Peruvian culture, existing from about 850 to 200 B.C. The Chavíns were a farming society composed of several different regional groups. Their capital was the city of Chavín de Huantar in central Peru.

NAZCA
Mysterious southern Peruvian culture about which little is known. Thought to have been founded about the time of Christ, but its people had disappeared before the Spanish conquest. The major artifacts of Nazca culture are a series of enormous figures and designs drawn with lines of pebbles across the coastal desert of southern Peru, which are best seen from the air. The largest design is of a bird; it is about 900 feet long.

TIAHUANACO
Named after the city of Tiahuanaco, founded in about 800 B.C. near Lake Titicaca in present-day Bolivia. The city was occupied by a series of five different cultures until about A.D. 1200. Then it was largely abandoned, for unknown reasons.

CHIBCHA
Civilization in the Colombian highlands destroyed by Spanish in 16th century. Accomplished goldsmiths, the Chibcha may have inspired the legends of El Dorado.

MOCHICA
Flourished in northern Peru from about 200 B.C. to A.D. 800. Mochica farmers used irrigation systems, built fortifications, and developed distinctive crafts and sculpture.

CHIMÚ
Civilization established on northwest Peruvian coast in about A.D. 1000. Its capital was the city of Chan Chan, which at its peak had a population of 100,000. Expanded into the Andes under Nancen-pinco after 1370. Conquered in about 1470 by Incas.

INCA
Last and largest pre-Columbian civilization in South America. Created vast Andean empire between 1438 and 1532. Destroyed by Spanish conquistadores under Francisco Pizarro in 1530s.

Middle America

NO USE FOR WHEELS

All the pre-Columbian civilizations of Middle America set up brilliantly organized states and trade systems without two developments considered vital in the Old World: they made no use of the wheel and had no draft animals, such as horses or oxen. However, they did have their own form of currency—cacao beans. The absence of practical wheels is all the more remarkable because the principle of the wheel was known in Middle America. Wheeled clay models of animals—possibly toys or religious offerings—have been found in Mexican tombs dating from around the time of Christ. But although several Middle American peoples, in particular the Mayas, built flat, broad roads between their cities, the wheel was never used for transportation or in making pottery.

CLAY TOY *The wheel was not put to work in the Americas until the Spanish conquest. But the principle was known; this clay model was made in Mexico before* A.D. *100.*

STAR STRUCK

Sky-gazing Mayan priests accurately calculated the 365-day solar year more than 1,500 years ago. They broke the year up into 18 months of 20 days each, plus 5 odd days. Superimposed on the Mayan solar year was a sacred 260-day calendar used to indicate days of religious ritual. The Mayas had no clocks or telescopes, but they could predict solar and lunar eclipses and calculated the time Venus took to make a complete circuit of the sky to within 2 hours of the actual figure, 583.92 days.

OLMEC CERAMIC *Naked and hollow "babies" were a favorite subject of Olmec craftsmen, who fashioned them from the whitish clay called kaolin. This one dates from 1200–1000* B.C.

LONELY EMPIRES OF THE INDIANS

Five advanced civilizations flourished in brilliant isolation in Middle America—the term many scholars use to describe the area of Central America stretching from Mexico to the northern edge of Nicaragua—over a period of 3,500 years. Their first contact with Europe in 1519 was decisive and disastrous. In a few decades their societies were swamped by the invader. Not until 300 years later did archeologists and scholars begin to uncover and appreciate the richness of the civilizations so carelessly swept aside.

OLMEC
First of the great ancient Middle American cultures. They dominated the coastal plain along the Gulf of Mexico from about 1200 B.C. to about 400 B.C. Their name comes from a Nahuatl Indian word meaning "inhabitant of rubber country," because of the rubber trees that grew in the region. They began as subsistence farmers but became accomplished pyramid builders, using clay and earth. Their pyramid at La Venta is 100 feet high. The Olmecs were also great sculptors. Giant stone heads, some 10 feet tall, and figurines and animals of jade are Olmec legacies.

MAYA
Most enduring of the Middle American civilizations. The Mayas were a recognizable political group as early as 2000 B.C. in southern Mexico, Guatemala, and parts of Belize. Their golden age lasted from about A.D. 250 to 900. Their hieroglyphic writing is only partly understood. The Mayas were superb astronomers with an advanced knowledge of mathematics and devised an accurate calendar.

TEOTIHUACÁN
City and cultural center of a trade empire that flourished on Mexico's central plateau for about a thousand years after 300 B.C. Archeological evidence suggests that at its peak (A.D. 350–600) Teotihuacán had as many as 125,000 inhabitants, Its grid network of streets covered nearly 8 square miles, more than imperial Rome. The name Teotihuacán means "city of the gods," and its huge Pyramid of the Sun—which soared, in four great terraces, to a height of 212 feet—is Mexico's most imposing pre-Columbian edifice. The city appears to have been destroyed by Toltecs sometime after A.D. 650.

TOLTEC
A warrior culture based at the city of Tollán (now Tula), 56 miles north of Mexico City. The Toltecs forged their civilization from several different ethnic groups. They are believed to have brought about the collapse of Teotihuacán and eventually ruled central Mexico between A.D. 900 and 1200. Between 987 and 1185 the Toltecs also ruled the city of Chichén Itzá in the Yucatán Peninsula.

AZTEC
An originally nomadic civilization of warriors from northern Mexico who settled in the island heart of Lake Texcoco and created Tenochtitlán (now Mexico City) in about A.D. 1200. The Aztecs conquered central Mexico and imposed worship of their gods, Tezcatlipoca and Huitzilopochtli, on the surrounding agricultural villages. They reached their height under Montezuma II (1502–20) but were conquered by the Spanish under Hernán Cortés in 1519–21.

WINNER TAKES ALL—FROM THE FANS

Vigorous ball games played in walled courts were a regular part of Mayan and other Middle American religious festivals. Players were apparently not allowed to use their hands, but bounced the solid rubber ball off padded elbows and hips. Injuries seem to have been common, and sometimes fatal. Losing teams were sometimes sacrificed to the gods.

The Aztecs played a ball game known as *tlachtli*, whose aim was to knock the ball into the opponents' end of the court in much the same way as in modern volleyball. Teams could also win the game outright by knocking the ball through either of two stone rings set on the side walls. Since the rings were often 20 feet off the ground and only just big enough for the ball, goals of this kind were rare. But any player who scored one was allowed to confiscate the clothes and possessions of any spectators he and his friends could catch.

ROCK OF AGES

The Aztecs believed that there had been four previous creations of the world, and that theirs was the fifth and last. They carved this belief into a single stone—the Sun Stone, or Calendar Stone—a huge block 12 feet across. The stone was dug up in 1790 in the Zocalo, the main square of both ancient Tenochtitlán and the modern capital of Mexico, Mexico City.

In the center of the stone is carved the sun god, and on the four panels around it are the four previous creations, their once-bright Aztec colors worn away by time. The stone is now in the city's National Museum of Anthropology.

WELL OF DEATH

Chichén Itzá, last outpost of the Mayan civilization, was built in the heart of the arid Yucatán Peninsula, unlike most of the earlier Mayan cities, which were built in rain forests farther south and east. The city was built around two wells, known as cenotes, which were fed by underwater streams. The city folk drank from one well and used the other as a well of sacrifice. In times of crisis a maiden was hurled at dawn into the 60-foot-deep hole in the limestone rock. If she sur-

vived in the water at the bottom until midday, priests hauled her out to ask what the gods had told her. The Mayas also threw cherished possessions into the hole. Carved jade, gold, copper discs, and human skeletons have all been dredged out of it.

TEMPLES OF BLOOD

Aztecs believed that the sun died every night and needed human blood to give it strength to rise next day. So they sacrificed 15,000 men a year to their fearsome sun god, Huitzilopochtli. Most of the victims were prisoners taken in wars, which were often started solely to round up sacrificial victims.

DEATH ROW DELIGHT

A particularly handsome prisoner was chosen each year by the Aztecs as a sacrifice to their chief god, Tezcatlipoca. Tezcatlipoca was the god of matter—and archrival of the Aztecs' god of wind and spirit, Quetzalcoatl. For 12 months the prisoner was allowed every luxury. He was taught to play the flute, feasted like a king, and was generally doted upon. He spent his last month with four lovely girls. Then he led a procession to the temple of Tezcatlipoca. Four men held him down over the sacrificial altar, and a priest, using a knife of obsidian, a glasslike volcanic stone, cut open his chest and tore out his heart.

RETURN OF THE WIND GOD

Aztec chiefs fell on their knees in awe and hailed the invading Spaniard Hernán Cortés as a god. By an extraordinary coincidence Cortés had unknowingly fulfilled an ancient Aztec prediction. Priests taught that the wind god Quetzalcoatl, who was both fair and bearded, had been forced into exile across the eastern sea, but would one day return. The bearded Cortés, bent only on conquest and plunder in the name of his own country, arrived on the Atlantic coast to begin his invasion of Mexico in 1519—the very year predicted by some priests for the return of Quetzalcoatl.

TERRA-COTTA TRIO *A Mayan woman stares from beneath the arm of a Mayan statuette known as "The Orator." On the right is a model of a Zapotec woman in a poncho. All date from about A.D. 600 to 1000.*

Key dates in world history

The chart that begins on these pages summarizes the most important events in world history since the end of the last Ice Age, some 10,000 years ago. From the earliest farming settlements to the present day, it traces on a global scale man's political, social, commercial, scientific, and cultural development.

POLITICS AND WAR 4000—45 B.C.

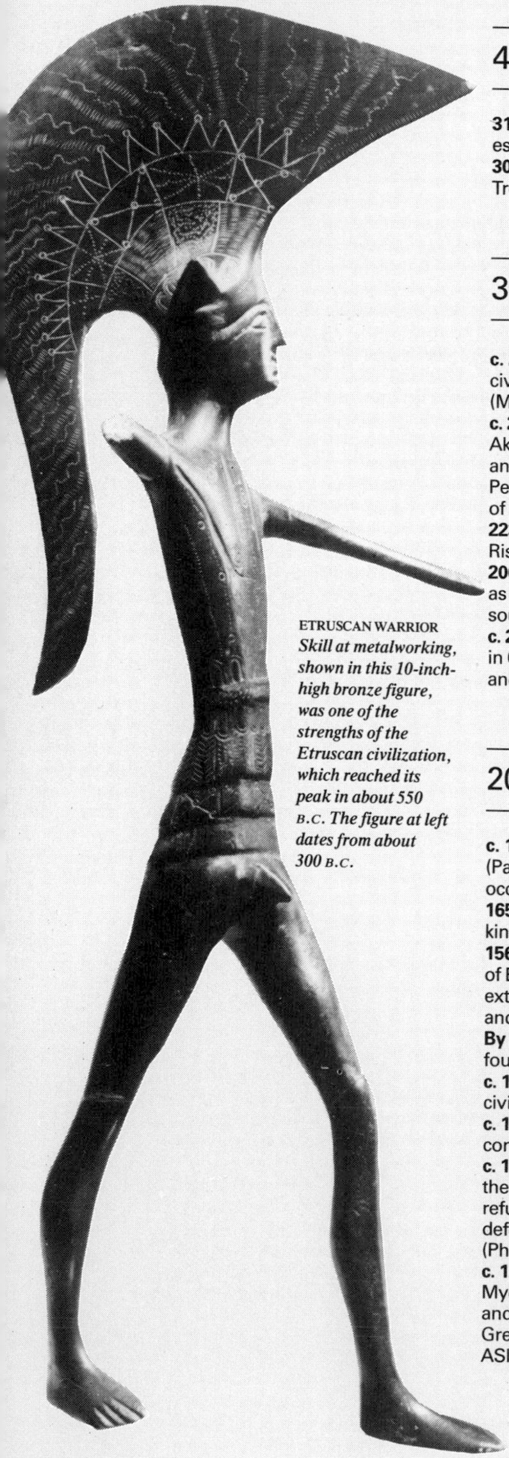

ETRUSCAN WARRIOR
Skill at metalworking, shown in this 10-inch-high bronze figure, was one of the strengths of the Etruscan civilization, which reached its peak in about 550 B.C. The figure at left dates from about 300 B.C.

4000–3000 B.C.

3100 AFRICA Egyptian kingdom established under Pharaoh Menes.
3000 ASIA First city established, at Troy.

3000–2000 B.C.

c. 2500 ASIA Indus Valley civilization begins in India (Mohenjo-Daro, Harappa).
c. 2371–2316 ASIA Sargon I of Akkad conquers Sumerians; creates an empire from Syria to southwest Persia. Establishes Susa as capital of Persia.
2230 ASIA End of Akkadian empire. Rise of Sumerian empire at Ur.
2006 ASIA End of Sumerian empire, as Ur falls to Elamites from southwest Persia.
c. 2000 EUROPE First palaces built, in Crete. Greeks settle in Mycenae and Tiryns.

2000–1000 B.C.

c. 1720 AFRICA Hyksos (Palestinians) invade Egypt and occupy the Nile delta.
1650–1590 EUROPE Minoan kingdom (Crete) at its height.
1567 ASIA/AFRICA New Kingdom of Egypt expels invaders and extends its empire to Nubia and Palestine.
By 1523 ASIA Shang dynasty founded in China.
c. 1500 ASIA Fall of Indus Valley civilization.
c. 1375 EUROPE Mycenaeans conquer Crete; Knossos destroyed.
c. 1250–1150 AFRICA Peoples of the Sea, possibly Mycenaean refugees, attack Egypt; they are defeated (1174), but some (Philistines) settle in Canaan.
c. 1200–1150 EUROPE Fall of Mycenaean civilization in Greece and Crete. Dorians move into Greece.
ASIA Trojan War and fall of Troy.

1100 ASIA Chou (Zhou) dynasty founded in China.
1010–925 ASIA Kingdom of Israel established under David and Solomon. Divided after 925 into Israel and Judah.

1000 B.C.–0

c. 814 AFRICA Phoenicians from Tyre found Carthage in Tunisia. Rise of Nubian kingdom of Kush in the Sudan.
753 EUROPE Foundation of Rome by Romulus and Remus (legendary).
745–727 ASIA Tiglath-pileser III of Assyria conquers Babylon, Syria, and half of Israel.
722–705 ASIA Sargon II of Assyria continues conquests, extending the Assyrian empire from Lebanon to Iran.
689 ASIA Babylon destroyed by Sennacherib of Assyria.
671 AFRICA Assyria briefly conquers Egypt.
c. 650 ASIA Rise of kingdom of the Medes in Persia.
614–612 ASIA Medes, allied with Babylon, overthrow Assyria and destroy its capital, Nineveh.
c. 610 EUROPE Sparta dominates Peloponnesus and adopts rigid constitution (Lycurgan laws).
c. 592 EUROPE Solon establishes constitution in Athens.
587 ASIA Nebuchadnezzar II of Babylon destroys Jerusalem. Many Jews taken captive to Babylon.
559–530 EUROPE/ASIA Cyrus the Great of Persia establishes Persian Empire. Conquers Media (550), Ionian Greek cities, Lydia (547–546), and Babylon (539).
c. 550 EUROPE Etruscans dominate Italy and rule Rome.
546–511 EUROPE Pisistratus and his sons rule Athens as tyrants.
538 ASIA Babylonian captivity of Jews ended by Cyrus the Great.
525 AFRICA Cambyses, king of Persia, conquers Egypt.
509 EUROPE Tyranny in Athens overthrown; democracy begins. Republic established at Rome, with tribunes introduced as representative of the general citizens (*plebs*) about 500.

To clarify what is an enormously complex story, the key events have been divided in three ways. First, they have been grouped under five broad themes. In order, the themes are: politics and war; social and religious history; exploration and trade; science, inventions, and medicine; and the arts.

Second, the events have been divided geographically, by continents, so that it is possible to trace easily the developments in any one part of the world or to make comparisons between different areas.

Third, the events have been grouped into periods—sometimes several thousand years long, sometimes as short as a single decade—so that any particular period can be located and comparisons between different fields of human activity are simplified.

Additional information about many of the events mentioned here can be found elsewhere in the book. For details, see the index.

490 EUROPE First Persian invasion of Greece repelled by Athenians at Marathon.
480–479 EUROPE Xerxes of Persia invades Greece: battles of Thermopylae (Persian victory), Salamis, and Plataea (Greek victories). Persians retreat; Ionia freed.
480 EUROPE Syracuse, in Sicily, repels Carthaginian invasion.
478 EUROPE Athens forms the Delian League, an anti-Persian alliance that becomes nucleus of Athenian empire (460 onward).
461–430 EUROPE Pericles is leading statesman in Athens.
449 EUROPE/ASIA Peace treaty between Persia and Greece.
431–421 EUROPE Peloponnesian War. First stage, primarily between Athens and Sparta, ends in Peace of Nicias.

GIANT-KILLERS *War galleys like this one were part of the Spartan fleet that destroyed the Athenian Navy in 413 B.C. during the Second Peloponnesian War.*

415–404 EUROPE Peloponnesian War, second stage. Athenian expedition against Syracuse, Sicily, fails. Sparta invades and defeats Athens, destroying Athenian Navy and the city's walls. Sparta dominates Greece until 371.

404 AFRICA Egypt regains independence from Persia.
403 EUROPE Democracy restored in Athens.
ASIA Warring States epoch begins in China.
390 EUROPE Rome, head of Latin League, destroyed by Gauls under Brennus.
371 EUROPE Thebes defeats Sparta at Leuctra and becomes dominant Greek city-state.
357 EUROPE Philip II of Macedon begins campaign to rule Greece.
341 ASIA Persia reconquers Egypt.
338 EUROPE Philip of Macedon defeats Greeks at Chaeronea; elected leader for war against Persia. Rome heads federation of central Italy.
336 EUROPE Philip of Macedon murdered, perhaps at the instigation of his wife. Succeeded by Alexander the Great.
334–330 ASIA Alexander invades Persia and defeats King Darius III.
332–331 ASIA/AFRICA Alexander conquers Egypt and Tyre, founds Alexandria.
331–326 ASIA Alexander conquers Bactria (Turkestan, northern Afghanistan) and invades northwest India.
323 ASIA Alexander dies at Babylon. Heirs and generals fight among themselves for 20 years.
321 ASIA Chandragupta founds Maurya dynasty in northern India and expels Greeks.
305 ASIA/AFRICA Alexander's generals divide empire. Ptolemy I (Egypt) and Seleucus I (Syria) found dynasties, with Alexandria and Antioch as capitals. Bactria becomes independent Greek kingdom.
By 280 EUROPE Rome, having defeated Etruscans and Samnites, dominates all Italy except Greek cities in the south.

280–275 EUROPE Pyrrhus, king of Epirus, attacks southern Italy and Sicily but is forced to withdraw despite several victories over Romans. Rome dominates all Italy.
273 ASIA Asoka rules two-thirds of the Indian subcontinent. He becomes a Buddhist (261).
264–241 EUROPE/AFRICA Rome defeats Carthage in First Punic War and acquires Sicily as its first province.
From 221 ASIA Ch'in (Qin) dynasty unites China. Construction of Great Wall is begun.
218–202 EUROPE/AFRICA Second Punic War: Hannibal of Carthage crosses Alps, defeats Romans (notably at Cannae, 216) but is finally defeated by Scipio Africanus in present-day Algeria.
206 ASIA Han dynasty is founded in China.
202 EUROPE/AFRICA Carthage disarmed. Spain becomes a Roman province.
163 ASIA Jews, led by Judas Maccabeus, revolt against Syria and form independent Judaea.
147–146 EUROPE Rome sacks Corinth and rules Greece from Macedonia.
AFRICA Third Punic War: Rome destroys Carthage.
133 EUROPE Reforms of Gracchi brothers (133, 123–121) begin a 100-year challenge to Senate power in Rome.
By 126 ASIA Parthian empire established in Middle East except in Syria and Judaea.
121 EUROPE Rome completes conquest of southern Gaul.
90–88 EUROPE Social War, in which Italians rebel against Rome. Roman citizenship is extended to all peoples of Italy.
By 87 ASIA Chinese empire includes Korea and northern Vietnam.
By 62 ASIA Pompey completes conquest of Syria and Judaea, which become Roman provinces.
58–50 EUROPE Julius Caesar conquers rest of Gaul for Rome and invades Britain and Germany.
49–45 EUROPE First Roman Civil War: Caesar defeats Pompey and Senate and becomes dictator. Assassinated March 15, 44.

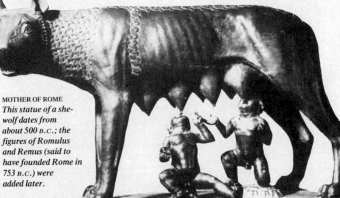

MOTHER OF ROME
This statue of a she-wolf dates from about 500 B.C.; the figures of Romulus and Remus (said to have founded Rome in 753 B.C.) were added later.

POLITICS AND WAR 44 B.C.–A.D. 1529

ASSASSIN
*A Roman
silver coin
showing, on
one side, the
head of
Brutus,
Caesar's
murderer.*

44–31 EUROPE Second Roman Civil War. Mark Antony and Caesar's heir, Octavian, defeat Caesar's assassins (led by Brutus and Cassius) and divide Roman Empire. AFRICA Mark Antony, with help of Cleopatra of Egypt, fights Octavian but is defeated at Battle of Actium (31). Egypt becomes a Roman province.
27 EUROPE Octavian (now Augustus) takes control of Roman Empire and establishes Julio-Claudian dynasty.

A.D. 0–500

41–54 EUROPE/ASIA/AFRICA Emperor Claudius extends Roman Empire to Britain (43), Mauretania (North Africa), Thrace, and Lycia (Asia Minor).
61 EUROPE Boudicca leads revolt in Britain against Rome but fails.
66–70 ASIA Jewish revolt against Rome. Siege of Jerusalem (70). Temple destroyed. Masada, scene of final Jewish resistance, falls (73).
69 EUROPE Year of Four Emperors in Rome; internal conflict ends with Vespasian as first emperor of Flavian dynasty.
69–96 EUROPE Southern Scotland and Rhineland added to Roman Empire. Syria extended eastward.
By 100 AFRICA Rise of Axum kingdom in Ethiopia.
101–06 EUROPE/AFRICA Emperor Trajan adds Dacia (Romania) and Arabia to Roman Empire.
113–17 ASIA Trajan defeats Parthians and annexes their empire.
117–38 EUROPE Emperor Hadrian establishes fixed Roman frontiers. Hadrian's Wall built in Britain (122).
132–35 ASIA Final Jewish revolt suppressed. Judaea becomes Palestine. Jews banned from Jerusalem and dispersed.
161–80 EUROPE Barbarian invasions of Roman Empire begin from the northeast.
220 ASIA Han dynasty ends in China. Country divided into three kingdoms.
224–27 ASIA Artaxerxes I (Ardashir) founds Sassanid dynasty and reestablishes Persian Empire.
306 EUROPE Constantine the Great proclaimed Roman emperor at York, England. He founds Constantinople (now Istanbul) in 330 on the site of Greek Byzantium.
395 EUROPE Roman Empire permanently divided. Rome made capital in west, Constantinople in east (Byzantine Empire).
By 400 ASIA Rise of Japanese empire.
410 EUROPE Alaric leads Visigoths to plunder Rome.
451–53 EUROPE Attila leads Huns into Italy.

455 EUROPE Vandals sack Rome.
476 EUROPE Western Roman empire overthrown by Odoacer, German chief, who becomes first king of Italy.
486–87 EUROPE Franks (German tribe) under Clovis I control all France.
493 EUROPE Theodoric (Ostrogoth) becomes king of Italy.

A.D. 500–1000

507 EUROPE Visigoths invade Spain.
527–65 EUROPE/AFRICA Eastern Roman emperor Justinian reconquers Italy, North Africa, southeastern Spain.
589 ASIA Sui dynasty temporarily reunites China. Great Wall rebuilt.
590–604 EUROPE Pope Gregory I extends secular and spiritual power of the papacy.
622 ASIA Muslims (Arab followers of Muhammad) begin Holy War against nonbelievers in Medina.
632 ASIA Muhammad dies. Caliphate is established.
By 650 ASIA/AFRICA Arabs led by Caliph Omar take Syria, Palestine, Egypt, and destroy Persian Empire.
661–80 ASIA/AFRICA Arabs conquer North Africa and extend empire eastward to Afghanistan and the Indus Valley.
687 EUROPE Venice lagoon settlement elects first doge.
711 EUROPE Arabs invade Spain and southern France.
732 EUROPE Charles Martel (The Hammer), grandfather of Charlemagne, leads Franks to victory over Arabs at the Battle of Poitiers, halting Muslim advance into Europe.

768–814 EUROPE Charlemagne, king of Franks, conquers northern Italy, Germany, northeast Spain.
800 (December 25) EUROPE Coronation of Charlemagne as emperor by Pope Leo III in Rome.
808 onward EUROPE Rise of Bulgarian empire.
810 EUROPE Venice recognized as independent state by both Charlemagne and Byzantines.
878–99 EUROPE Alfred the Great of Wessex defeats Danes and rules southern England.
893–927 EUROPE Height of Bulgarian empire under Simeon I.
By 900 ASIA Khmer Empire established in Cambodia with capital at Angkor.
911 EUROPE Rollo (Hrolf) the Norseman is granted lordship over Normandy in France.
ASIA Byzantium acknowledges power of Kiev Russian state after 50 years of intermittent warfare around Black Sea.
930 EUROPE World's first legislative assembly (the Althing) founded by Norse settlers in Iceland.
962 EUROPE Otto I, the Great, king of the Germans, conquers central Europe and is crowned Holy Roman emperor.
973 EUROPE Edgar of Wessex crowned first king of England at Bath.
987 EUROPE Hugh Capet crowned king of France at Noyon.
992 EUROPE Boleslaus I becomes first king of Poland.

A.D. 1000–1100

1001–22 EUROPE Basil II ("The Bulgar Slayer") restores eastern Roman empire at Constantinople, defeating Bulgars and Armenians.
1001 EUROPE Stephen (later Saint) crowned first king of Hungary with "Holy Crown."
1013–42 EUROPE Danes rule England. (King Knut, or Canute, reigns in Scandinavia and England 1016–35.)
By 1035 EUROPE Rise of Spanish Christian kingdom in Castile under Ferdinand I (1033–65).
1055 ASIA Seljuk Turks take Baghdad. Sultanate established.
1066 EUROPE Normans under William the Conqueror invade England, winning the Battle of Hastings (October 14).
1096–97 EUROPE First Crusade: three armies of Normans and French reach Constantinople, defeat the Turks, on way to free Palestine from Muslims.
1099 ASIA Crusaders take Jerusalem and found a Latin kingdom there under Godfrey of Bouillon.

WARRIOR AND SCHOLAR *This jewel, which may have been a pointer used for reading manuscripts, was owned by Alfred the Great, who drove the Danes out of southern England in 878.*

A.D. 1100–1200

1143 EUROPE Alfonso I becomes first king of Portugal.
1146–48 ASIA Second Crusade, led by King Louis VII of France and Emperor Conrad VII, attacks Damascus but achieves little.
1170 EUROPE State-church power struggle in England between Henry II and Archbishop Thomas Becket ends in Becket's murder at Canterbury.
1175 onward ASIA Muslim rulers established in central India.
1187 ASIA Saladin, sultan of Turkish Syria and Egypt, retakes Jerusalem.
1189 ASIA Third Crusade, led by Emperor Frederick Barbarossa, Philip Augustus of France, and Richard I of England, fails militarily, but truce with Saladin allows Christians access to Jerusalem.

A.D. 1200–1300

1204 EUROPE Venice gains control of the Aegean Sea and the Ionian islands.
ASIA Fourth Crusade is diverted to Constantinople, which is sacked by Crusaders. Latin empire set up while Byzantines flee to Nicaea (now Iznik).
1206–23 ASIA Genghis Khan leads Mongol warriors through China and Persia to defeat the Russians.

KHAN'S CAVALRY
Tough, small ponies, which needed no fodder because they fed on grass, carried the archers who swept through Asia in the army of the Mongol leader Genghis Khan.

1215 EUROPE King John of England sets royal seal on Magna Carta, accepting limits on royal powers demanded by barons.
1218–21 AFRICA Fifth Crusade tries but fails to take Egypt.
1228–29 ASIA Sixth Crusade, led by Emperor Frederick II against pope's wishes, recaptures Holy City. Frederick crowns himself king of Jerusalem.
1235 AFRICA Rise of Mali empire.
1240–1450 ASIA Mongol Khanates of the Golden Horde rule central and southern Russia.
1242 EUROPE Prince Alexander Nevsky defeats Teutonic Knights near Pskov in northern Russia.
1244 ASIA Muslims retake Jerusalem, which remains under Muslim rule until 1917.
1248 ASIA Seventh Crusade, led by Louis IX (St. Louis) of France, fails. Louis captured and ransomed.
1260–94 ASIA Kublai Khan completes Mongol conquest of China and establishes his capital at Peking (Beijing).
1261 EUROPE Greek army from Nicaea (Iznik) reconquers Constantinople and overthrows Latin rule, restoring Byzantine Empire.
By 1262 EUROPE Teutonic Knights complete conquests south of Baltic Sea; bring German influence to Prussia.
1270 AFRICA Eighth Crusade, led by Louis IX and Prince Edward of England, makes expedition to Tunis. Louis dies in Tunis.
1273 EUROPE Rudolf of Hapsburg elected emperor. Dynasty rules Austria until 1918.
1276–84 EUROPE Edward I conquers Wales and unites it with England.
1285–1307 EUROPE Edward I conquers Scotland.
1290–1326 ASIA Osman I founds Ottoman dynasty in Turkey.

A.D. 1300–1400

1307–32 AFRICA Height of Mali empire under Mansa Musa.
1314 EUROPE Robert Bruce reestablishes Scottish independence by defeating English at Bannockburn.
1337 EUROPE Anglo-French Hundred Years War begins as Edward III claims French throne. Edward wins naval battle of Sluis (1340) and land battle of Crécy (1346).
1338–1573 ASIA Ashikaga shoguns dominate Japan, based in Kyoto.
1347–1558 EUROPE Calais, in France, surrenders to English.
1354 EUROPE Ottoman Turks establish foothold in Europe at Gallipoli.
1369–1405 ASIA Tamerlane of Samarkand establishes Mongol empire over all central Asia. It disintegrates after his death.
1389 EUROPE Turkish victory at Kossovo over Serbia and allies gives Ottoman Turks control of Balkan states for 500 years.

A.D. 1400–1500

1415–20 EUROPE Henry V of England defeats French at Agincourt and captures Paris.
1429 EUROPE Joan of Arc leads French to victory at siege of Orléans. Is convicted of sorcery and burned at the stake in Rouen (1431).
1453 EUROPE French defeat of English at Castillon, in Burgundy, effectively ends Hundred Years War.
ASIA Fall of Constantinople to Muhammad II ("The Conqueror") ends Byzantine Empire. Constantinople becomes Ottoman Turks' capital city.
1455–85 EUROPE Civil war in England between dynasties of York and Lancaster, later called the Wars of the Roses. Ends with death of Richard III (of York) at Battle of Bosworth.
1479 EUROPE Spain unified by marriage and joint rule of Fernando (Ferdinand) II, king of Aragon, and Isabella, queen of Castile.
1479–80 EUROPE Turks wrest control of southern Adriatic from the Venetians.
1492–1502 AMERICA Christopher Columbus reaches Bahamas, Cuba, Haiti, Panama, Trinidad, and the mouth of the Orinoco River (in present-day Venezuela).
1492–1529 AFRICA Zenith of the Songhoy empire of the middle Niger region under Askia Mohammed.

POLITICS AND WAR A.D. 1517–1829

A.D. 1500–1600

1517 EUROPE Martin Luther begins German Reformation at Wittenberg.
1519–21 NORTH AMERICA Hernán Cortés and Spanish conquistadores defeat Aztecs and seize Mexico.
1526 EUROPE Turks defeat Hungarians at Mohacs, beginning 150-year Ottoman rule in Hungary. ASIA India: Babur occupies Delhi and sets up Mogul Empire.
1531–35 NORTH AMERICA Francisco Pizarro and Spanish conquistadores defeat Incas and seize Peru.
1546–55 EUROPE Schmalkaldic War in Germany between Holy Roman emperor Charles V and Lutheran princes.
1547 EUROPE Ivan IV ("The Terrible"), on the throne from 1533, crowned first czar of Russia.
1562–98 EUROPE Wars of Religion in France, between Protestant Huguenots and Catholic League; Huguenots massacred on St. Bartholomew's day in Paris (1572).
1571 EUROPE Turkish naval power in Mediterranean destroyed by Christian League under John of Austria at Battle of Lepanto.
1571–1603 AFRICA Idris Alwoma rules Muslim empire from Kanem, north central Africa.
1572 EUROPE Dutch revolt against Spanish rule.
1580 EUROPE Philip II of Spain conquers and absorbs Portugal.
1582–98 ASIA Toyotomi Hideyoshi completes unification of Japan.
1588 EUROPE Spanish Armada defeated by English ships.

A.D. 1600–1700

1603 EUROPE Union of English and Scottish crowns.
1605 (November 5) EUROPE Gunpowder Plot by Catholic extremists, among them Guy Fawkes, fails in attempt to blow up English king and Parliament.
1607 NORTH AMERICA First permanent English settlement in America at Jamestown, Virginia.
1618 EUROPE Thirty Years War begins with Protestant revolt in Bohemian capital of Prague against Emperor Ferdinand II.
1620 NORTH AMERICA Pilgrims in *Mayflower* land and found Plymouth Colony in Massachusetts.
1636–38 ASIA Shogun Iyemitsu forbids Japanese to travel abroad or foreigners to enter Japan. Ban maintained until 1853.
1640 EUROPE Charles I of England forced to summon Long Parliament, which seeks to curb power of English crown and the Church. Disputes lead to Civil War (1642–46).

1643 EUROPE Victory of French general Prince Louis of Condé over Spain at Rocroi marks start of France's military superiority in western Europe.
1644 ASIA Manchu dynasty established in China after period of political anarchy.
EUROPE English Parliamentary leader Oliver Cromwell (1599–1658) beats Royalists at battles of Marston Moor and Naseby (1645).
1648 EUROPE Treaties of Westphalia end Thirty Years War, with gains for France, Sweden, Brandenburg, and Holland. Losers are Spain and the Holy Roman Empire.
1648–53 EUROPE La Fronde, a series of outbreaks of civil unrest in France against Cardinal Mazarin and the growing power of the French throne.
1649 EUROPE Charles I tried for treason in England and beheaded.
1655 NORTH AMERICA Jamaica seized by Britain from Spain.
1660 EUROPE British monarchy restored under Charles II.
1664 NORTH AMERICA British expedition captures New Amsterdam from Dutch and renames it New York.
1667–68 EUROPE War of Devolution. Louis XIV of France gains part of Flanders from Spain.
1668 EUROPE Spain restores Portugal's independence.
1675 EUROPE Frederick William of Brandenburg ("The Great Elector") defeats Sweden at Fehrbellin and lays foundation of Brandenburg-Prussia's military power.
1683 EUROPE Vienna relieved from Turkish siege by army of Polish king, John Sobieski.
1687 EUROPE Venetians bombard Athens. Gunpowder stored by Turks in Parthenon explodes.
1688 EUROPE Britain's Glorious Revolution. Parliament invites Prince William of Orange and his wife, Mary (both Protestants and grandchildren of Charles I), to cross from Holland and succeed the Catholic James II (reigned 1685–88) on the throne (1689). Bifl of Rights (1689) safeguards parliamentary government.
1690 EUROPE William III defeats James II's Catholic rebellion in Ireland at Battle of the Boyne.
1696 EUROPE Peter I ("The Great") becomes sole czar of Russia and captures Azov.

A.D. 1700–1750

1700–21 EUROPE Great Northern War in Baltic. Charles XII of Sweden defeats Russia at Battle of Narva (1700) but loses at Poltava (1709).
1701 EUROPE Brandenburg becomes Kingdom of Prussia.

1701–13 EUROPE War of Spanish Succession: victories of English duke of Marlborough against France at Blenheim (1704), Ramillies (1706), Oudenarde (1708), and Malplaquet (1709). Peace treaties of Utrecht accept Philip V, grandson of French king Louis XIV, as king of Spain, if French and Spanish thrones are never united. French gain land along Rhine; English gain colonies in Canada and West Indies.
1707 EUROPE United Kingdom established by union of English and Scottish parliaments under Queen Anne (1702–14).
1739 ASIA Nadir Shah of Persia sacks Delhi, carries off Peacock Throne.
1740–48 EUROPE War of the Austrian Succession. Britain supports Austria's Maria Theresa against France, Spain, and Prussia.
1745 EUROPE Jacobite rebellion in Scotland in support of Catholic Stuart pretender, Bonnie Prince Charlie. Rebels finally defeated at Battle of Culloden (April 1746).
1748 EUROPE Treaty of Aix-la-Chapelle ends War of Austrian Succession. Austria cedes Silesia to Prussia.
1749–56 EUROPE Diplomatic revolution reverses earlier alliances: France and Austria combine against Britain and Prussia.

A.D. 1750–1800

1754–63 NORTH AMERICA French and Indian War pits British colonies against French colonies, involves Indians on both sides.
1756–63 EUROPE Seven Years War, during which Prussia builds up position in central Europe, and Britain consolidates colonial hold on Canada and India.
1757 ASIA British general Robert Clive wins Battle of Plassey and conquers Bengal in India.
1759 NORTH AMERICA British general James Wolfe defeats French at Quebec.
1768–74 EUROPE Russo-Turkish War. Russia gains Crimea and northern coast of Black Sea.
1772, 1793, 1795 EUROPE Poland partitioned between Russia, Prussia, and Austria.
1773 NORTH AMERICA Boston Tea Party protests British taxation.
1773–75 EUROPE Peasant revolt in Russia led by Cossack Emelian Pugachev is suppressed by Catherine the Great.
1774 NORTH AMERICA Continental Congress at Philadelphia lists American grievances.
1775–83 NORTH AMERICA American Revolution begins. Americans defeat British troops at Saratoga (1777) and decisively at Yorktown (1781).

STAMP ACT
British law requiring payment for tax stamps enraged American colonists in 1765 and inspired this warning.

1776 NORTH AMERICA American Declaration of Independence, July 4.
1783 EUROPE In Treaty of Paris, America's independence recognized by Britain.
1787 NORTH AMERICA U.S. constitution signed. George Washington becomes first president in 1789.
1789–95 EUROPE French Revolution. Bastille falls (1789). Louis XVI beheaded (1793). Radical Jacobins under Maximilien Robespierre institute a reign of terror, in which 35,000 die, mostly on the guillotine (1794). Robespierre is guillotined (July 1794).
1792–97 EUROPE War of the First Coalition against France. French revolutionary armies take over the Netherlands, Switzerland, the Rhineland, and northern Italy.
1794–96 NORTH AMERICA/AFRICA Britain takes over French and Dutch colonies (West and East Indies, southern Africa).
1796–97 EUROPE First Italian campaign of Napoleon Bonaparte; he defeats Austria at Battle of Rivoli.
1796–1802 NORTH AMERICA Slave revolt of Toussaint l'Ouverture in Haiti forces French colonial troops to withdraw from the island.
1798 EUROPE Irish rebellion suppressed.
1798–99 AFRICA Bonaparte occupies Egypt, but French fleet is destroyed by Horatio Nelson at Battle of the Nile.
1798–1802 EUROPE War of the Second Coalition—Austria, Russia, and Turkey. The allies' early successes, against France, are countered by Bonaparte's victory at the Battle of Marengo (1800).
1799 ASIA In India anti-British sultan of Mysore, Tipoo Sahib, killed when British take Seringapatam.
1799–1804 EUROPE Bonaparte becomes ruler of France as first consul (1799); reforms French legal system with new code of law (1804).

A.D. 1800–1850

1800 EUROPE Parliamentary Union of Britain and Ireland. Malta seized by Britain from France.
1803 NORTH AMERICA In Louisiana Purchase, U.S.A. acquires from France 800,000 square miles stretching from the Mississippi River to the Rocky Mountains and from the Canadian border to the Gulf of Mexico. France receives about $15 million for the land.
1804 EUROPE In Vienna, Franz (Francis) I assumes title of emperor of Austria, leading to the abolition of the Holy Roman Empire in 1806. Napoleon is crowned emperor of the French in Paris.
NORTH AMERICA Haiti becomes independent—the second country in the New World after the U.S.A. to do so—under a former slave, Emperor Dessalines.
1805–07 EUROPE War of the Third Coalition—Britain, Austria, and Russia, joined in 1806 by Prussia—against France. British under Horatio Nelson defeat French and Spanish fleets at Battle of Trafalgar, near Gibraltar (1805). Napoleon defeats Russia and Austria at Battle of Austerlitz (1805).
1806 EUROPE Prussia decisively defeated by France at battles of Jena and Auerstadt.
1806–14 EUROPE Napoleon's continental empire attempts to blockade Britain.
1808–14 EUROPE French occupy Spain and Portugal but meet resistance in the Peninsular War.
1809 EUROPE Austria reenters war but is defeated by Napoleon at Wagram.
1809–16 SOUTH AMERICA First South American wars for independence from Spain gain some success in Argentina (1810) and in Paraguay (1811) but fail in Mexico and Venezuela.

1812 EUROPE Napoleon invades Russia, defeating Russians at Battle of Borodino and occupying Moscow. But the city's destruction by fire forces him into disastrous winter retreat to Germany.
1812–15 NORTH AMERICA War of 1812, caused mainly by U.S. resentment of British naval harassment, ended by Treaty of Ghent.
1813 EUROPE War of Liberation in Germany culminates in Napoleon's defeat by Fourth Coalition at Leipzig (October). British duke of Wellington's army wins Battle of Vitoria (June) and crosses Pyrenees to invade France (October).
1814 EUROPE Napoleon abdicates after allies capture Paris and is exiled to Elba. Bourbon dynasty (Louis XVIII) restored in France.
1814–15 EUROPE Congress of Vienna restores old frontiers of France. Russia given mastery over Poland, Austria over northern Italy. Holland and Belgium united. Sweden gains Norway, and 39 states form a confederation dominated by Austria and Prussia. Britain retains colonial gains in West Indies, southern Africa, Ceylon, and Malta.
1815 EUROPE Napoleon returns to Paris and in the Hundred Days seeks to recover his empire. He is defeated at Battle of Waterloo and exiled to St. Helena (dies 1821).
1819–23 ASIA Stamford Raffles develops Singapore for British trade.
1819–25 SOUTH AMERICA Simón Bolívar secures independence from Spain of present-day Colombia, Venezuela, Peru, and Bolivia (named after him).
1821 NORTH AMERICA Mexico declares independence from Spain.
1821–29 EUROPE Greek War of Independence from Turkey. Britain, France, and Russia intervene to sink Turko-Egyptian fleet at Navarino (1827).

BASTILLE DAY *On July 14, 1789, French revolutionaries stormed the hated Bastille prison in Paris.*

POLITICS AND WAR A.D. 1822–1918

1822 SOUTH AMERICA Brazil becomes independent empire under Dom Pedro I, son of the Portuguese king João.
1823 NORTH AMERICA President James Monroe, in message to Congress, asserts that North and South America are no longer open to European colonization; abjures U.S. intervention in Europe.
1830–45 AFRICA France occupies Algiers.

SIGN TO THE VALLEY OF DEATH *In the Charge of the Light Brigade at Balaclava (October 25, 1854), 247 British cavalrymen out of 600 died.*

1848–49 EUROPE Revolutions in France, Italy, and central Europe suppressed after triumphs for Louis Kossuth in Hungary and Giuseppe Garibaldi in Italy.

DRAGON SAILOR
During the Opium War (1839–40) the Chinese saw English sailors as monsters snorting tobacco smoke.

1831 NORTH AMERICA Nat Turner's slave uprising in Virginia is suppressed.
1836 NORTH AMERICA Texas secedes from Mexico.
1838–41 NORTH AMERICA Costa Rica, El Salvador, Guatemala, Honduras, Nicaragua become independent.
1839–40 ASIA Opium War. Britain gains Hong Kong from China.
1840 OCEANIA New Zealand's Maori chiefs accept British rule in return for civic guarantees.
1845–48 NORTH AMERICA Texas joins U.S.A. In war with Mexico, U.S.A. gains New Mexico and California.
1848 EUROPE Karl Marx and Friedrich Engels publish *The Communist Manifesto.*

A.D. 1850–1900

1850–64 ASIA Taiping Rebellion against Manchu rulers in China put down with help of Western and Chinese troops under Charles "Chinese" Gordon (1833–85).
1853 Commodore Matthew Perry sails into Tokyo Bay, the first step in opening Japan to trade with west.
1854–56 EUROPE Crimean War: Britain and France join Turkey against Russia and besiege Sebastopol. At Battle of Balaclava 247 cavalrymen die in Charge of the Light Brigade. Peace congress in Paris, ending the war, limits Russian power in the Black Sea.
1858–61 ASIA France conquers south Vietnam and colonizes Saigon area.
1860–61 EUROPE Unification of Italy completed under Count Camillo di Cavour and Giuseppe Garibaldi.
1860 ASIA British and French troops in China burn Summer Palace in Peking (Beijing).

A TIME TO HEAL *Confederate Gen. Robert E. Lee surrenders to Union Gen. Ulysses S. Grant at Appomattox Courthouse, Virginia, April 9, 1865.*

1861 NORTH AMERICA Confederacy formed by 11 southern states; civil war begins in U.S.A.
1861 EUROPE Russian czar Alexander II emancipates 10 million male serfs and their families.
1863–64 EUROPE Polish rebellion against Russia suppressed.
1863 NORTH AMERICA Union army wins Battle of Gettysburg (Pa.).
1864 EUROPE Prussia and Austria, after war against Denmark, share provinces of Schleswig-Holstein.
1865 NORTH AMERICA U.S. civil war ends in victory for the North. President Abraham Lincoln assassinated.
1865–70 SOUTH AMERICA Paraguayan War: Argentina, Brazil, and Uruguay invade Paraguay.
1866 EUROPE Seven Weeks War: Prussia victorious over Austria and other German states. Prussia's ally, Italy, gains Venice in peace treaty.
1867 EUROPE Otto von Bismarck establishes North German Confederation. Austria grants home rule to Hungary, creating dual monarchy of Austria-Hungary. NORTH AMERICA Mexican emperor Maximilian shot by republicans after withdrawal of French support.
1870–71 EUROPE Franco-Prussian War: France becomes a republic. Italy annexes Rome, which becomes the capital.
1871 EUROPE Wilhelm of Prussia proclaimed German kaiser; Otto von Bismarck is chancellor. NORTH AMERICA Lt. Col. George Custer and troops killed at Little Bighorn, Dakota Territory, by Sioux and Cheyenne Indians under Chief Crazy Horse.
1877 EUROPE Russia attacks Turkey, reaches outskirts of Constantinople.
1879–83 SOUTH AMERICA War of the Pacific: Chile defeats Peru and Bolivia.
1881–98 AFRICA Britain, Germany, France, and Italy vie to carve out colonies in the "scramble for Africa."
1885 AFRICA Congo Free State (later Zaire) set up by Belgian king Leopold II.
1893 OCEANIA New Zealand becomes the first country to give the vote to women.
1895 ASIA Japan gains Formosa (now Taiwan) in war with China.

1896 AFRICA Italian invasion of Ethiopia repelled at Adowa.
1898 AFRICA Britain defeats Sudan at Omdurman. Fashoda Crisis: Britain and France near to war over control of upper Nile.
OCEANIA U.S.A. annexes Hawaii.
NORTH AMERICA/ASIA Spanish-American War ends Spanish rule in Cuba, Philippines, and Puerto Rico.
1899–1902 AFRICA Boer War. Britain defeats Dutch republics of Transvaal and Orange Free State.

A.D. 1900–1950

1900 ASIA Boxer Uprising in China against foreigners is suppressed by international army.
1901 NORTH AMERICA Theodore Roosevelt becomes U.S. president after assassination of William McKinley.
AUSTRALIA Unified Commonwealth of Australia set up.

1904 EUROPE Entente Cordiale: Anglo-French settlement of colonial differences.
1904–05 ASIA Russo-Japanese War gives Japan mastery over Korea and the approaches to Manchuria.
1905 EUROPE Russian liberal revolution forces czar to create a parliament (Duma). Norway given independence from Sweden.
1908–09 EUROPE Austria annexes Bosnia-Herzegovina.
1910 AFRICA Union of South Africa established.
1911–12 ASIA Chinese nationalist revolution overthrows Manchu dynasty. Emperor Hsüan T'ung (P'u-i) abdicates (1912).
EUROPE/AFRICA Italo-Turkish War. Italy gains Libya.
1912 EUROPE First Balkan War. Balkan states—Serbia, Greece, Bulgaria, and Montenegro—defeat Turkey. Albania is created (1913).
1913 EUROPE Second Balkan War. Balkan states fight over spoils of first Balkan War; Russia and Austria-Hungary involved.
1914 EUROPE Sarajevo Crisis: assassination (June 28) of Archduke Franz Ferdinand, heir to Austrian throne, by Bosnian Serb leads rival alliances into World War I. Germany invades Belgium and Russia, defeats Russia at Tannenberg (August). German advance on Paris repulsed at Battle of the Marne (September).
1915 EUROPE/NORTH AMERICA Sinking of passenger liner *Lusitania* by German submarine inflames U.S. public opinion against Germany. U.S.A. Occupies Haiti.
EUROPE Gallipoli: unsuccessful British attempt to defeat Germany's ally, Turkey, by advancing through the Dardanelles.
1915–18 EUROPE Static trench warfare along Western Front from Ypres in Belgium to Franco-Swiss frontier.
1916 EUROPE Easter Rebellion suppressed by British troops in Ireland. Heavy, inconclusive battles in France at Verdun (February–December) and Somme (July–November). British Navy defeats Germans at Battle of Jutland.
1917 EUROPE Russian Revolution. Liberals topple czar (February). Bolsheviks led by Lenin establish Soviet government (October) and seek peace with Germany, Austria-Hungary, and Turkey. U.S.A. declares war on Germany (April). Balfour Declaration promises British support for a Jewish national homeland in Palestine.
1918 EUROPE Military collapse of Germany's allies: Bulgaria (September); Turkey (October); Austria-Hungary (November). Germany signs armistice.

"PAWS OFF!"

HIGH TENSION *The first two decades of the 20th century were torn by war: tensions between Japan and Russia over Korea, noted by Punch in 1901 (above left), ended in war in 1904. In 1917 the U.S.A. entered World War I, and Uncle Sam recruited soldiers to fight in Europe.*

POLITICS AND WAR A.D. 1918–PRESENT

1918–19 EUROPE New republics formed: Germany, Austria, Hungary, Poland, Finland, Czechoslovakia, Lithuania, Latvia, Estonia. Southern Slavs form Yugoslavia, a kingdom dominated by Serbia.

1919 EUROPE Paris Peace Conference. Treaties of Versailles, St.-Germain, and Neuilly signed. Germany loses colonies and European territory; armed forces restricted; made to pay reparations to Allies; blamed for the war. League of Nations established.

1920 EUROPE Hungary becomes a kingdom under Miklós Horthy, but by Treaty of Trianon is limited to one-third of its historic territories.

1921 EUROPE Ireland partitioned. Eire becomes independent (1922). Six Ulster counties remain in United Kingdom.

1922 EUROPE Benito Mussolini ("Il Duce") becomes Italy's Fascist prime minister.
ASIA Turkey proclaimed a republic by Mustafa Kemal (later known as Atatürk).

1924 EUROPE Death of Lenin leads to power struggle in Russia, won by Joseph Stalin.

1925 ASIA Pahlavi dynasty secures throne in Iran and reigns until 1979.

1926 EUROPE General strike in Britain.

1928 WORLDWIDE Kellogg-Briand Pact outlawing war signed by 65 governments, including Britain, Germany, Italy, Russia, Japan, and the U.S.A.

1929 EUROPE Lateran Treaties between Mussolini and papacy create Vatican City state.

1930 EUROPE French troops, occupying Rhineland since 1918, withdraw from Germany.

1931 WORLDWIDE Statute of Westminster defines dominion status with British Commonwealth of Nations. Recognizes Canada, Australia, Newfoundland, South Africa, and New Zealand as "autonomous communities."
EUROPE Spanish monarchy overthrown by republicans.
ASIA Japanese troops occupy Manchuria in China.

1932 EUROPE Antonio Salazar (1889–1970) becomes prime minister and dictator of Portugal.
ASIA Saudi Arabia established as united kingdom by Ibn Saud.

1932–35 SOUTH AMERICA Chaco War between Bolivia and Paraguay after oil is discovered in the desert region. After 100,000 deaths Paraguay gains three-quarters of the disputed territory.

1933 EUROPE Adolf Hitler becomes German chancellor (January 30) and establishes Nazi dictatorship.

1934–35 ASIA Long March across 6,000 miles of China by 100,000 Communists under Mao Tse-tung, to escape besieging army of nationalists under Chiang Kai-shek.

1935–36 AFRICA Abyssinian War: Italy invades and occupies Ethiopia.

1936 EUROPE Rome-Berlin Axis proclaimed (collaboration of Hitler and Mussolini). Germany rearms the Rhineland.

1936–38 EUROPE Stalinist purge of rivals in Soviet Army and Communist party. Hundreds of thousands of Soviet citizens sent to forced labor camps in the Arctic and Siberia.

1936–39 EUROPE Spanish Civil War: Gen. Francisco Franco overthrows republic and becomes dictator with support from Germany and Italy.

1937 ASIA Japan attacks China.

1938 EUROPE Germany annexes Austria. Munich Pact allows Germany to seize Czechoslovak frontier region of Sudetenland.

1939 EUROPE Italy annexes Albania (April). Germany invades Poland (September 1), triggering World War II.

1939–40 EUROPE Russo-Finnish War: Soviet Union pushes back Finnish frontiers.

1940 EUROPE Norway and Denmark occupied by Germany (April). Germany overruns the Netherlands, Belgium, and France (May–June). Latvia, Lithuania, and Estonia occupied and annexed by U.S.S.R. (August). In Battle of Britain, Germany fails to gain air superiority.

1941 EUROPE Germany overruns Yugoslavia and Greece. Germany, Romania, and Finland attack Soviet Union (June 22).
AFRICA British Army liberates Ethiopia from Italians.

OCEANIA Japanese surprise attacks on Pearl Harbor in Hawaii, Malaya, and Hong Kong (December 7). U.S.A. enters World War II.

1942 ASIA Japanese successes in Singapore, Burma, and Philippines checked by U.S. victory at Midway Island (June 4).

1942–43 EUROPE Russians defeat Germans at Stalingrad.
AFRICA British and U.S. troops free North Africa from German and Italian control. Decisive British victory at El Alamein (1942).

1943 EUROPE Italian king dismisses Mussolini (July 25). Allies land in southern Italy (September).

1944 EUROPE Russians relieve Leningrad after 900-day siege (January). Allies enter Rome (June). Allies land in Normandy (D-day, June 6), push across France.
ASIA U.S. troops return to Philippines (October 19).

1945 WORLDWIDE United Nations charter signed in San Francisco.
ASIA U.S.A. takes Okinawa (April). British troops retake Burma (July). U.S.A. drops atom bombs on Hiroshima and Nagasaki, Japan (August). Japan surrenders, ending World War II.
EUROPE Yalta Conference (February). Churchill, Roosevelt, and Stalin meet to discuss postwar settlement of Eastern Europe. Soviet and U.S. troops link up at Torgau in Germany. Hitler shoots himself as Russians enter Berlin (April 30). Germany surrenders (May 7). Communist-dominated governments set up in Poland, Romania, Bulgaria, Hungary, Albania, and Yugoslavia.
NORTH AMERICA Franklin D. Roosevelt dies. Harry S. Truman becomes 33rd U.S. president.

1945–49 ASIA Indonesian war for independence from Dutch rule.

1946 EUROPE Italy becomes a republic (June).
ASIA Philippines given independence by U.S.A. (July).

1946–49 EUROPE Civil war in Greece. Communists defeated.

1946–54 ASIA Pro-Communist Vietminh war against French colonialists.

1947 ASIA India and Pakistan become independent within British Commonwealth.

1947–51 Marshall Plan dispenses more than $12 billion in American aid to Europe.

1948 EUROPE Coup in Czechoslovakia perpetuates Communist control of government. Yugoslavia under Marshal Tito breaks clear of Soviet domination.
ASIA Independence for Burma and Ceylon (Sri Lanka). State of Israel established (May 14); unsuccessfully attacked by six neighboring Arab states.
AFRICA Afrikaner nationalists win South African election and introduce apartheid laws.

PEACE AT LAST *This London* Daily Mirror *cartoon marked Germany's surrender on May 7, 1945. The caption read: "Here you are—don't lose it again."*

1948–49 EUROPE Russian blockade of West Berlin defeated by Anglo-American Berlin airlift.
ASIA Chinese Communists defeat Nationalists and establish Chinese People's Republic, October 1, 1949.
1949 EUROPE/AMERICA Western powers create North Atlantic Treaty Organization (NATO).
EUROPE Federal Republic of Germany established on September 21. German Democratic Republic established on October 7.

A.D. 1950–PRESENT

1950–53 ASIA Korean War: U.N. forces repel North Korean Communists.
1952–54 AFRICA Mau Mau (secret society among Kikuyu tribe) attack Europeans in Kenya.
1954 ASIA France defeated by Vietminh at Dien Bien Phu.
1954–62 AFRICA Algerian War. Nationalist guerrillas win out over French settlers and army leaders.
1955 EUROPE Warsaw Pact created as military alliance of Eastern European states.
1955–60 EUROPE Guerrillas attack British troops in Cyprus, which gains independence in 1960.
NORTH AMERICA Eisenhower administration formulates policy of massive nuclear retaliation as strategic deterrent to U.S.S.R.
1956 EUROPE Hungarian national uprising put down by U.S.S.R.
AFRICA Egyptian president Gamal Nasser nationalizes Suez Canal. Anglo-French-Israeli military action to regain it ends after U.S. and U.N. protests.
1957 AFRICA Ghana becomes independent within British Commonwealth, starting an acceleration of decolonization throughout the world.
1958 EUROPE Fifth Republic set up in France under Gen. Charles de Gaulle.
1959 NORTH AMERICA Fidel Castro seizes power in Cuba.
1960 ASIA Mrs. Sirimavo Bandaranaike, in Ceylon, becomes world's first woman prime minister. Ideological differences split Soviet Union and China.
EUROPE: Khrushchev uses U-2 incident to end detente with U.S.A.
1960–67 AFRICA Belgian grant of independence to Congo (later Zaire) is followed by internal revolts in Katanga and Kasai.
1961 EUROPE Berlin Wall built.
ASIA India seizes Goa, ending Portuguese colonial rule.
AFRICA South Africa leaves British Commonwealth.
1962 NORTH AMERICA U.S. blockade forces U.S.S.R. to remove its missiles from Cuba.

1963 WORLDWIDE Nuclear Test Ban Treaty signed by U.S.A., U.S.S.R., and Britain.
NORTH AMERICA President John F. Kennedy assassinated in Dallas, Tex. (November 22).
1965 AFRICA Southern Rhodesia unilaterally declares independence from Britain.
1965–73 ASIA Vietnam War: U.S. troops support South Vietnam against North Vietnam.
1966–69 ASIA Cultural revolution in China launched by Mao to rekindle revolutionary ideals and wrest party control from rivals.
1967 ASIA Six Day War. In response to armies massed on its borders, Israel attacks Egypt, Syria, and Jordan.
1967–70 AFRICA Nigerian civil war prevents secession of Biafra.
1968 EUROPE Warsaw Pact troops invade Czechoslovakia to crush political reforms.
NORTH AMERICA Martin Luther King, U.S. civil rights leader, assassinated in Memphis, Tenn.
1969 EUROPE British troops first stationed in Northern Ireland.
AFRICA Mu'ammar al-Qaddafi makes Libya a socialist dictatorship.
1970 SOUTH AMERICA Chile elects Communist president, Salvador Allende. Allende killed in right-wing coup (1973).
1971 ASIA Bangladesh becomes independent from Pakistan.
1972 WORLDWIDE First Strategic Arms Limitation Treaty signed by U.S.A. and U.S.S.R.
1973 ASIA Yom Kippur War: Israel fights off surprise attack by Egypt and Syria. U.S. troops withdrawn from Vietnam.

1974 EUROPE Cyprus partitioned into Turkish and Greek regions after Turkish invasion.
1975 WORLDWIDE Helsinki Pact: 35 nations, including the U.S.S.R., agree to respect national frontiers and human rights.
EUROPE Death of Gen. Francisco Franco leads to restoration of democracy in Spain.
ASIA Vietnam unified under Communists. Communists take over Cambodia and Laos. Civil war begins in Lebanon.
1979 ASIA/AFRICA Israel and Egypt sign peace treaty.
ASIA Iranian monarchy toppled; Ayatollah Khomeini establishes fundamentalist Islamic republic. U.S.S.R. invades Afghanistan.
1979–80 AFRICA Rhodesia becomes independent Zimbabwe.
1980 ASIA Iraq-Iran War breaks out over control of Persian Gulf.
1981 NORTH AMERICA Ronald Reagan elected 40th U.S. president. Advocates cuts in domestic budget, tax reform, strong defense.
AFRICA Anwar Sadat, president of Egypt, assassinated.
EUROPE Martial law imposed in Poland to crush Solidarity labor movement.
1982 EUROPE/SOUTH AMERICA Argentina invades Falkland Islands. Ejected by British troops.
1983 AMERICA U.S. troops invade Grenada after left-wing coup.
1985 EUROPE Mikhail Gorbachev becomes Soviet premier.
1986 AFRICA U.S.A. bombs Libya to answer Libyan-backed terrorism. State of emergency declared in face of unprecedented civil unrest in South Africa.

SUMMIT SHAKE *Although tensions persisted, Soviet leader Mikhail Gorbachev and U.S. president Ronald Reagan met cordially in Switzerland in 1985 and Iceland in 1986.*

SOCIAL AND RELIGIOUS HISTORY 8000 B.C.—A.D. 1351

8000–3000 B.C.

8000–7000 ASIA First farming settlements at Jericho in Jordan and Hacilar, Turkey.
7000–6000 ASIA First known urban settlement at Çatal Hüyük, Turkey.
3500–3000 ASIA First Sumerian city-states at Uruk and Ur (now in Iraq).
3000 EUROPE Stone circles built in Hebrides, Scotland.

NEOLITHIC PINUP *This female figure was made in Çatal Hüyük, Turkey, in about 6000 B.C..*

1650–1590

1650–1590 EUROPE Rise of Mycenaean civilization in Greece. ASIA Aryans move into India.
1378–1362 AFRICA Pharaoh Ikhnaton tries to establish monotheism in Egypt.
c. 1300 EUROPE Last stage of Stonehenge built in England.
1100–1000 ASIA/AFRICA Aramaic language (spoken by Christ) becomes common tongue of Middle East.

1000–500 B.C.

c. 950 NORTH AMERICA Olmec civilization flourishing in Mexico.
c. 900 EUROPE First Iron Age cultures begin to appear in continental Europe and Britain.
c. 800 ASIA Hindu caste system developed in India.
c. 550 ASIA Lao-tse founds Taoism in China.
c. 530 ASIA Prince Siddartha Gautama founds Buddhism in India and Nepal.
c. 500 ASIA Teachings of Kong Zi become new religion, Confucianism, in China.
c. 500 EUROPE Celtic cultures develop in mainland Europe, and later in Britain and Ireland.

500 B.C.–0

325–323 EUROPE/ASIA Alexander the Great decrees racial equality within his empire and encourages intermarriage between Greeks, Macedonians, and Persians.
After 221 ASIA Mandarin administrative system of nine ranks of officials, one of the first known efforts to systematize civil service, set up in China.
27 EUROPE/ASIA Roman Empire organized; beginning of imperial civil service.
c. 7 ASIA Jesus Christ (crucified c. A.D. 30) born in Bethlehem.

3000–1000 A.D.

c. 2750 EUROPE Construction of Stonehenge begun in England.
2000 onward EUROPE Indo-Europeans (Aryans) enter Europe. ASIA Canaanites settle in Lebanon at Byblos and in Syria at Ugarit, now Ras Shamra.
c. 1758 ASIA King Hammurabi, ruler of Babylon, codifies and publishes an extensive code of laws.

0–A.D. 500

c. 14 WORLDWIDE Estimated world population is 256 million.
c. 30–60 EUROPE/ASIA Christian communities founded in eastern Mediterranean by disciples of Jesus Christ and linked by the missionary journeys of Paul of Tarsus in Asia Minor, Greece, and Rome.
64 EUROPE Great Fire of Rome. Emperor Nero executes some Christians as scapegoats. Traditional date for killing of St. Peter and St. Paul by Nero.

MARTYR'S HUMILITY *According to legend, St. Peter asked to be crucified upside down because he was not worthy to die in the same way as Christ.*

79 EUROPE Vesuvius erupts, destroying Roman town of Pompeii.
By 100 EUROPE/ASIA Mithraic religion spreads in Roman Empire. Christian gospels written.
166 EUROPE/ASIA Plague in Roman Empire.
250 EUROPE/ASIA General persecution of Christians in Roman Empire, intensified under Emperor Diocletian (284–305). NORTH AMERICA Beginning of golden age of Mayan civilization.

VICTIMS OF VESUVIUS *About 2,000 people died under the ash that buried Pompeii in A.D. 79. These plaster figures were made from holes left by bodies in the ash.*

312 EUROPE Constantine becomes Christian after seeing a flaming cross in the sky before the battle of Milvian Bridge in Italy.
313 EUROPE/ASIA Constantine legalizes Christianity in Roman Empire.
c. 350 WORLDWIDE Estimated world population is 254 million.
360–63 EUROPE/ASIA Emperor Julian (The Apostate) restores paganism briefly.
381 EUROPE/ASIA Emperor Theodosius establishes official Christian Church and bans paganism (391).
c. 400 EUROPE Huns establish empire in central Europe. Saxons settle in Britain.
c. 432 EUROPE St. Patrick goes from France to convert Ireland.
c. 490 EUROPE Last Romano-British stand against Anglo-Saxon invaders at Mount Badon. The Britons' unknown leader is later identified with the legendary King Arthur.
496 EUROPE Clovis I, king of the Franks, becomes Christian.
By 500 ASIA Buddhism spread in China by Indian missionaries.

A.D. 500–1000

528–34 EUROPE *Codex Justinianus* published, reorganizing and restating imperial Roman law.
529 EUROPE Monasticism spreads in western Europe under influence of Italian monk, St. Benedict (c. 480–547), who founds the first Benedictine monastery of Monte Cassino. Irish monasteries become centers of learning.
568 onward EUROPE Lombards settle in northern Italy.
587 ASIA Japanese Emperor Yomei converted to Buddhism.
596–97 EUROPE St. Augustine sent to England, becomes first Archbishop of Canterbury.
c. 600 WORLDWIDE Estimated world population is 237 million.
EUROPE Slavs begin to settle in central Europe.
600–700 AFRICA Earliest settlement of Zimbabwe.
612 ASIA Muhammad begins preaching in Mecca.
622 ASIA Muhammad leaves Mecca for Medina. Islam founded. Islamic calendar is dated from July 16, the start of the lunar year.
645–784 ASIA Japan assumes characteristics of Chinese culture.
651–52 ASIA Definitive text of the Koran, sacred book of Islam, published under Caliph Othman (c. 574–656), Muhammad's son-in-law.
700 onward EUROPE Feudalism begins in western Europe. Personal service to overlord replaces duty to state.

RAIDING FORCES *The dragon-prowed longboats of the Vikings came to be known and feared along the Atlantic coasts of Europe after 780.*

780 onward EUROPE Vikings from Scandinavia start raids on Britain and the Atlantic seaboard of continental Europe.
843 EUROPE Danish Vikings invade France and Germany. Frankish kingdom disintegrates.
862 EUROPE Swedish Vikings enter Russia and found Novgorod, which becomes state of Russia.
863 EUROPE St. Cyril and St. Methodius bring Christianity to South Slavs (modern Yugoslavs and Bulgars); St. Cyril invents a Greek-based script, which becomes the Cyrillic alphabet.
865 EUROPE Danish army invades England and captures York.
867–70 EUROPE/ASIA Orthodox schism: Eastern Church separates from Roman Church.
892 ASIA Baghdad becomes the capital of the Eastern Muslim caliphate.
898 EUROPE Arpad (c. 840–907) leads the Magyar tribe from southern Russia to found Hungary.
c. 980 AFRICA Arab towns founded along east African coast.
988–89 EUROPE Vladimir, prince of Kiev, converted to Christianity. His Russian subjects join the Eastern Orthodox Church.
c. 1000 WORLDWIDE Estimated world population is 280 million.
By 1000 EUROPE Scandinavians converted to Christianity.
ASIA Turks of central Asia converted to Islam.
AFRICA Kingdom of Ghana at zenith of power and culture.

A.D. 1000–1500

1054 AFRICA Muslims enter western Africa.
1086 EUROPE Domesday Book compiled in England.
c. 1100–1450 AFRICA Golden age of Zimbabwe in southern Africa.
1120–30 EUROPE Crusading orders of chivalry founded: Knights Templars (1120); Knights of St. John (1130).
1185 ASIA Rise of feudalism in Japan.

c. 1190 ASIA Teutonic Order of Knights founded at Acre.
c. 1200 EUROPE Italian cities organized as independent communes. Rise of craft guilds in towns of western Europe.
AMERICA Collapse of Mayan civilization in Central America. Rise of Inca civilization in Peru.
1212 EUROPE Children's Crusade: French and German children start out for Palestine. Many die or are sold into slavery before they even reach the Mediterranean Sea, and none, it is thought, ever actually get to the Holy Land. A few children return to their homes. Crusades continue, but with lessening vigor.
By 1223 EUROPE Mendicant preaching orders (Franciscans and Dominicans) established, spread from Italy across western Europe.
1267–73 EUROPE St. Thomas Aquinas writes *Summa Theologica.*
c. 1340 WORLDWIDE Estimated world population is 378 million.

RENT DAY *In the 14th century, peasants began to pay rent in money, one result of new European prosperity that brought decline of feudalism and manorialism.*

1347–51 EUROPE Bubonic plague (Black Death), probably spread by returning Crusaders, sweeps western Europe, killing one person in four.

SOCIAL AND RELIGIOUS HISTORY A.D. 1348–PRESENT

1348–55 AFRICA Egypt devastated by plague.
1376–82 EUROPE Religious reformer John Wyclif (c. 1328–84) and the Lollards in England denounce Church abuses.
1378–1415 EUROPE Great Schism divides Europe as rival popes in Rome and Avignon compete for authority.
1434–68 AFRICA Ethiopian sovereign Zara Yagub institutes social and religious reforms.
c. 1447 ASIA First Dalai Lama recognized as high priest of Buddhism in Tibet.
1470–1570 EUROPE Period of rapid population growth.

DAY OF TRAGEDY *At 9:40 on the morning of All Saints Day in 1755, when most of the population was in church, an earthquake struck Lisbon, killing more than 60,000.*

A.D. 1500–1600

1502–1736 ASIA Shi'ism recognized as official Islamic faith under Safavid dynasty in Persia.
c. 1510–33 ASIA Indian mystic Chaitanya spreads Vaishnava movement (Hindu devotion to the god Vishnu).
1517 EUROPE Martin Luther (1483–1546) begins German Reformation at Wittenberg by posting on a church door 95 theses attacking practices of the Catholic Church (October 31).
1533–34 EUROPE English Reformation led by Archbishop Thomas Cranmer after pope's refusal to annul Henry VIII's marriage to Catherine of Aragon.
1536 EUROPE French theologian John Calvin (1509–64) begins Presbyterian Reformation in Geneva, winning support in France (from Huguenots), Scotland, Holland, and England (from Puritans).
1536–40 EUROPE Dissolution of English monasteries redistributes landed property. Society of Jesus founded by Ignatius of Loyola in Spain (1540).

GENEVA DOODLE *Not all of Calvin's students concentrated on study. This sketch of the Protestant thinker was made at a lecture.*

1545–63 EUROPE Council of Trent reforms Roman Catholic Church.
c. 1550–1600 EUROPE Importation of gold and silver into Spain from Aztec and Inca treasuries in America leads to inflation.
1550–1700 EUROPE/NORTH AMERICA Peak of witchcraft persecution in western Europe; from 1648 in North America.
1598 EUROPE Henry IV signs Edict of Nantes, granting religious freedom to French Protestants (mainly Huguenots).
c. 1600 WORLDWIDE Estimated world population is 498 million.

A.D. 1600–1700

1603–49 EUROPE Movement of serfs restricted in eastern Europe to boost farm output.
1642–60 EUROPE Puritans regulate social mores in Britain.
1665–66 EUROPE Great Plague and fire devastate London.
1685 EUROPE Huguenots flee France after revocation of Edict of Nantes by Louis XIV ends religious freedom for Protestants.

A.D. 1700–1800

1701–25 EUROPE Peter the Great (1672–1725) westernizes Russia, founds St. Petersburg in 1703.
c. 1750 WORLDWIDE Estimated world population is 731 million.
1755 EUROPE Portuguese capital, Lisbon, destroyed by 6-minute earthquake (November 1).
1760 EUROPE Industrial Revolution begins in Britain.
1785–1815 EUROPE English landowners restrict use of common land, pushing more peasants into towns.
1792 EUROPE Denmark bans slave trade.

A.D. 1800–1900

1811–18 EUROPE Recession in Britain leads to destruction of machines by Luddites.
1824 EUROPE Britain legalizes trade unions, the first country to do so.
1833 WORLDWIDE Slavery banned throughout British Empire.
1830–70 EUROPE/NORTH AMERICA The railroad boom: fevered investment in railroads in Britain, France, and U.S.A.
1846–51 EUROPE Famine in Ireland after potato blight devastates crops, spurs emigration.
1849 NORTH AMERICA California Gold Rush begins.
1851 AUSTRALIA Gold Rush in Australia begins after gold is discovered at Ballarat, Victoria.
1861–63 EUROPE Limited-liability laws in Prussia, Britain, and France—limiting shareholders' responsibility for company debts—encourage investment.
1864 WORLDWIDE Geneva Convention sets up International Red Cross.
1865 NORTH AMERICA U.S. constitutional amendment outlaws slavery.
1870 EUROPE Vatican Council recognizes papal infallibility on matters of faith and morals.
1881–82 EUROPE Anti-Jewish laws and violence (pogroms) in Russia. NORTH AMERICA Standard Oil Company founded by John D. Rockefeller. Samuel Gompers founds labor union that becomes AF of L.
1883–89 EUROPE Bismarck pioneers state insurance policy in Germany: workers protected against loss of income from sickness, given accident insurance and pensions.
1886 NORTH AMERICA Coca-Cola introduced at Jacob's Pharmacy in Atlanta, Ga.
1900 WORLDWIDE Estimated world population is 1.67 billion.

GOLD FEVER *One of the 80,000 prospectors who headed for California in 1849.*

A.D. 1900–1950

1909–13 EUROPE Britain, France, U.S.A., and Holland introduce old age and sickness insurance.
1918–28 EUROPE/NORTH AMERICA Rapid social and political emancipation of women in Britain, Germany, U.S.A., and the U.S.S.R.
1918–19 WORLDWIDE Influenza epidemic causes more deaths than World War I.
1920–33 NORTH AMERICA Constitutional prohibition on alcoholic beverages in U.S.A. is exploited by criminals.

1928–33 EUROPE/ASIA First Five Year Plan in U.S.S.R. develops heavy industry and forcibly collectivizes agriculture.
1929–34 NORTH AMERICA World financial depression triggered by Wall Street crash.
1933 NORTH AMERICA U.S.A. abandons gold standard, other Western nations follow.
1935 EUROPE Violent anti-Semitism on rise in Germany.
1938 NORTH AMERICA U.S.A. introduces laws on minimum wages and maximum work hours, and bans child labor.
1941–45 EUROPE Peak of the Holocaust. Systematic extermination of 6 million Jews and others in Nazi-controlled Europe.
1942 EUROPE Beveridge Report in Britain urges social insurance "from the cradle to the grave."
1945 WORLDWIDE International Monetary Fund set up to help nations in financial difficulties.
1946 EUROPE In Fulton, Missouri, speech, Winston Churchill deplores ideological restraint ("Iron Curtain") imposed by Soviet-type governments on the peoples of Eastern Europe.
1947 EUROPE U.S.A. sends $12 billion in aid to speed economic recovery of postwar Europe (Marshall Plan).
1948 EUROPE British National Health Service inaugurated.
1948 NORTH AMERICA Sale of TV sets surges in U.S.A., then in Europe in early 1950s.
1949 EUROPE Comecon established in Moscow to maintain common economic policies in Soviet bloc.
c. 1950 WORLDWIDE Estimated world population is 2.5 billion.

A.D. 1950–PRESENT

1954 NORTH AMERICA In *Brown* v. *Board of Education,* U.S. Supreme Court abolishes racial segregation in public schools.
1956 NORTH AMERICA Dr. Martin Luther King leads boycott against segregated bus lines in Montgomery, Ala.
1957 EUROPE European Economic Community (EEC) of seven (later 12) non-Communist nations formed.
1958–61 ASIA China's Great Leap Forward—a plan for radical agricultural and industrial change.
1959 NORTH AMERICA U.S.A. and Canada open St. Lawrence Seaway.
1960s and 70s WORLDWIDE Women's liberation movement develops after publication of *The Feminine Mystique* by Betty Friedan, and *The Female Eunuch* by Germaine Greer.
1967–74 AFRICA Drought in Sahel region causes mass starvation.
1973 NORTH AMERICA U.S. Supreme Court permits abortion in 1st trimester *(Roe* v. *Wade).*
1978 EUROPE John Paul II becomes first non-Italian pope since 1522.
1984 U.S.A. and Vatican establish diplomatic relations.
1987 WORLDWIDE Estimated world population is 4.9 billion.

VICTORY NEAR *Pressure for woman suffrage grew in the World War I years; the 19th Amendment gave U.S. women the vote in 1920.*

EXPLORATION AND TRADE 7000 B.C.–A.D. 1637

7000–1000 B.C.

7000–6000 EUROPE/ASIA Trade in obsidian from Anatolia to Palestine and Cyprus.
c. 2700 ASIA Egyptian colony set up at Byblos, Lebanon.
c. 2500 EUROPE Trade between Agean Sea ports and Spain.
c. 2400 AFRICA Egyptian trading expeditions explore as far south as Ethiopia.
c. 2371–2316 ASIA Akkadians cross Persian Gulf to trade with Indus peoples.
2065 EUROPE/AFRICA Trade begins in glazed pottery and ivory between Egypt and Crete.
1580 ASIA/AFRICA Canaanites of Byblos and Ugarit trade as middlemen with Egyptians, Hittites, and Mycenaeans.
1100–1000 EUROPE/ASIA/ AFRICA Phoenicians (descendants of Canaanites) settle at Tyre and trade with Britain, Spain, Italy, North Africa. Israel trades with Arabia and Ethiopia.

1000–500 B.C.

884–859 EUROPE Phoenician sailors establish thriving trading post at Cadiz, Spain.

TIMBER TRADE Phoenician sailors load their ship with logs of cedar in a stone relief dating from the 8th century B.C.

750–700 EUROPE Greeks colonize southern Italy and Sicily. Syracuse founded by Corinth (c. 734).
700–500 EUROPE/ASIA Greeks and Phoenicians develop ships with several banks of oars (bireme, trireme, quinquereme).
c. 605 AFRICA Greek trading posts set up in Egypt.
c. 600 EUROPE Phocaeans (Greeks from Asia Minor) colonize southern France, found Marseilles, and trade with Spain.
c. 535 EUROPE Carthage colonizes Sardinia.
ASIA Network of partly paved roads built across Persian Empire, with posting stations.
By 500 EUROPE Carthage controls southern Spain and western Sicily with colonies and trading posts.

500 B.C.–0

c. 480 AFRICA Hanno of Carthage explores West African coast to Sierra Leone.
437 EUROPE Athens colonizes Amphipolis (Thrace), and Athenian leader Pericles (c. 494–429) leads expedition to the Black Sea.
c. 310–306 EUROPE Pytheas of Massilia (Marseilles) reputed to have sailed around Britain and found Thule (Iceland) to the north.
166–69 EUROPE Free port of Delos dominates eastern Mediterranean trade, especially in slaves.
c. 100–66 EUROPE/ASIA/AFRICA Pirates wreck Mediterranean trade.
c. 90 ASIA Silk Road from China opened as far west as Parthia (Iran).

44–31 AFRICA Roman trading posts set up on east African coast.
c. 27 ASIA Sailors utilize monsoon winds to take direct sea route to India from Aden.

0–A.D. 500

1st century EUROPE Rome trades with Germany and Denmark.
c. 61–63 EUROPE/AFRICA Roman expedition to Ethiopia.
c. 66–70 EUROPE Amber route from Danube to Baltic opens.
67 EUROPE Romans, under Nero, begin work on Corinth Canal in Greece but abandon the project.
After 250 EUROPE Decline of Roman trade and travel, except to North Africa.

A.D. 500–1000

606 ASIA First Japanese trade contacts with China.
796 EUROPE Emperor Charlemagne concludes trade treaty with King Offa of Mercia, England. English woven fabric exported.
874 EUROPE Norwegians colonize Iceland.
907 EUROPE Russians trade with Constantinople.
982–86 EUROPE Norseman Eric the Red colonizes Greenland.
c. 1000 NORTH AMERICA Leif Ericson, son of Eric the Red, establishes settlement in Vinland,

on the coast of Newfoundland.
1000 EUROPE Venice dominates Adriatic, and over the next 100 years sets up trading posts throughout eastern Mediterranean.

A.D. 1000–1500

c. 1147 EUROPE Wool trade flourishing between England and Flanders.
c. 1189 EUROPE Cornish tin exported to Rhineland, Flanders, and France.
c. 1228 EUROPE German Gothland Society establishes network of trade routes in northern Europe, linking cities of Lübeck, Cologne, Riga, Hamburg, and Novgorod in Russia.
1252–99 EUROPE Trade war between Venice and Genoa for commercial control of Black Sea and the Levant won by Venice.
1253–55 ASIA Trade mission of William of Rubruck from France to Mongol court at Karakorum opens central Asia to trade.
1255–95 EUROPE/ASIA Venetian trade links with central Asia and China increase.
1271–95 EUROPE/ASIA Venetian traveler Marco Polo crosses central Asia, visits China, India, Sumatra, and Persia.
c. 1337–50 EUROPE Hanseatic League in northern Germany organizes trade from Baltic to Flanders, centered in Lübeck and Bruges.
1418–60 EUROPE/AFRICA Prince Henry the Navigator sponsors Portuguese expeditions to West Africa and opens school of navigation at Sagres.
1488 EUROPE Bartolomeu Dias of Portugal rounds Cape of Good Hope at the southern tip of Africa, opening a new route to India.
1492–1502 SOUTH AMERICA Four Spanish-backed voyages by the Genoese-born explorer Christopher Columbus (1451–1506) reach Bahamas, Cuba, Hispaniola, Trinidad, the mouth of the Orinoco River, and Panama.
1493 WORLDWIDE Papal edict assigns Africa and Brazil to Portugal, rest of South America to Spain.
1497–98 NORTH AMERICA Genoese-born explorer John Cabot (1461–98) makes two English-backed voyages in search of a Northwest Passage to China. Discovers Newfoundland.
1498 (May) ASIA Vasco da Gama (c. 1469–1524) of Portugal reaches west coast of India at Calicut after rounding southern Africa.
1499–1501 SOUTH AMERICA Florentine navigator Amerigo Vespucci (1454–1512) explores coast of South America and gives his name to the continent.

FAITH AND FIREARMS *A preacher (with Bible) accompanies musket-toting Pilgrims to worship at Plymouth Colony, founded by* Mayflower *pioneers in December 1620.*

A.D. 1500–1600

1501 NORTH AMERICA Black slaves brought from Africa to Spain's colony of Santo Domingo in the Caribbean.
1510 ASIA Portugal sets up trading post in India at Goa.
1513 NORTH AMERICA Spanish pioneer Vasco Núñez de Balboa (1475–1519) crosses the isthmus of Panama, becoming the first European to see the eastern rim of the Pacific.
1519–22 WORLDWIDE Ferdinand Magellan, a Portuguese in Spanish service, leads first expedition to circumnavigate the world.
1527–31 NORTH AMERICA Commercial tobacco farming begins in Haiti, the first large-scale farming by Europeans in the New World.
1535 NORTH AMERICA French navigator Jacques Cartier sails up St. Lawrence River, winters at Quebec, and explores site of present-day Montreal.
1542 ASIA First Portuguese reach Japan.
1545 SOUTH AMERICA Spanish find silver deposits at Potosí in modern Bolivia. Convoys of treasure ships begin (1560) carrying bullion to Europe.
1557 ASIA China grants Portugal a treaty to establish Macao as a trading colony.
1562–68 AFRICA/NORTH AMERICA John Hawkins begins English slave trade between West Africa and the Caribbean.

1568 ASIA Nagasaki developed as Portuguese trading center in Japan.
1577–80 WORLDWIDE English seaman Sir Francis Drake (c. 1545–96) sails around the world, landing in California, the Moluccas, and Java.
1584–85 NORTH AMERICA Sir Walter Raleigh (c. 1552–1618) leads English expedition to colonize North American region that he names Virginia, after Elizabeth I, England's "Virgin Queen."
1600 ASIA English East India Company founded.

A.D. 1600–1700

1602 ASIA Dutch East Indies Company set up. Dominates Indonesia by 1641, controls trade with the islands until 1799.
1603 NORTH AMERICA French explorer Samuel de Champlain makes first of 11 voyages to explore Canada as far west as the Great Lakes.
1616–27 AUSTRALIA Dutch vessels explore western coast of Australia.
1618 ASIA Cossack explorers establish trading post in Siberia at Yeniseysk. They reach Okhotsk on the Pacific coast in 1649.
1620 NORTH AMERICA Puritan pioneers aboard the *Mayflower* found Plymouth Colony in present-day Massachusetts.
1637 SOUTH AMERICA Dutch slave trade with Curaçao established from present-day Ghana.

EXPLORATION AND TRADE A.D. 1642–PRESENT

1642 OCEANIA Dutch explorer Abel Tasman (c. 1603–59) discovers Tasmania, sights New Zealand, and discovers Tonga and Fiji.
1652 AFRICA Dutch establish trade settlement at Cape Town and colonize hinterland.
1670 NORTH AMERICA Hudson's Bay Company set up to establish trading stations in Canada.

A.D. 1700–1800

1728 NORTH AMERICA Vitus Bering, a Dane in Russian service, passes through straits between Siberia and Alaska into Arctic Ocean.
1768–71 AUSTRALIA/OCEANIA Capt. James Cook explores coasts of New Zealand and New South Wales.
1772–73 ANTARCTICA Cook discovers Antarctica.
1776 NORTH AMERICA Spanish explorer Juan Bautista de Anza completes exploration of northern California, founds San Francisco.
1784 NORTH AMERICA Russians establish trading post in Alaska.
1788 AUSTRALIA First convict settlement established by Britain at Botany Bay.
1792 EUROPE Denmark becomes the first country to outlaw the slave trade.
1795–1805 AFRICA Scottish explorer Mungo Park leads expeditions along upper Niger River.

MAORI SKILL *The early New Zealanders added carvings even to their weapons.*

A.D. 1800–1850

1803–06 NORTH AMERICA Meriwether Lewis and William Clark lead first expedition across the Rocky Mountains.
1817–18 AUSTRALIA John Oxley begins to explore country's interior.
1819–44 EUROPE Growth of German Free Trade Association (Zollverein) led by Prussia.

1825 NORTH AMERICA Erie Canal completed and era of canal building in U.S.A. begins.
1836 AFRICA Dutch Boers begin Great Trek north of the Orange River to escape British interference.
1840–41 AUSTRALIA British-born pioneer Edward Eyre crosses deserts of southern Australia.
1842 ASIA China opens five Treaty Ports for foreign trade.
1842–46 NORTH AMERICA Three expeditions under John Frémont map whole of American West.
1845–47 NORTH AMERICA Expedition led by British explorer Sir John Franklin discovers Northwest Passage around Canada, but all 129 members perish. Mormons settle in Utah after migration from Illinois.

A.D. 1850–1900

1853–56 AFRICA Scottish missionary David Livingstone (1813–73) crosses Africa and explores Zambezi River.
1854 ASIA U.S. commodore Matthew Perry negotiates treaty with Japan, opening the country to commerce with U.S.A.
1858–60 ASIA Russians develop Far Eastern territories and found Vladivostok; also increase fisheries and trade in Alaska.
1860–61 AUSTRALIA Robert Burke and William Wills cross Australia from south to north, but die on return journey.
1869 NORTH AMERICA U.S. railroads cross continent, link Atlantic and Pacific coasts. AFRICA Suez Canal opened.
1885 NORTH AMERICA Canadian Pacific Railway spans the continent. It is officially opened in 1887.
1891–1917 EUROPE/ASIA Trans-Siberian Railway built.
1893–95 ARCTIC Norwegian explorer Fridtjof Nansen in the *Fram* penetrates the Arctic.
1895–98 AFRICA Jean Marchand leads French expedition from the Congo to the White Nile.

FIRE AND ICE *During his last voyage, in 1778, Captain Cook ventured into the Arctic Ocean. His crew added walrus meat to their diet.*

A.D. 1900–1950

1903–06 NORTH AMERICA Roald Amundsen, Norwegian explorer, navigates Northwest Passage.
1911 ANTARCTICA Amundsen reaches South Pole (December), a month before British expedition led by Capt. Robert Scott.
1914 AMERICAS Panama Canal opened.
1932–39 WORLDWIDE Airlines, air routes proliferate.
1947–48 WORLDWIDE International commerce facilitated by General Agreement on Tariffs and Trade (GATT).

A.D. 1950–PRESENT

1950–60 EUROPE West German postwar recovery termed the "economic miracle."
1953 ASIA Edmund Hillary and Tenzing Norkay scale Mt. Everest.
1955–70 EUROPE/SOUTH AMERICA/AFRICA Common markets in Europe, Latin America, and east Africa establish protected trade zones.
1960 WORLDWIDE Organization of Petroleum Exporting Countries (OPEC) is formed to control world oil prices.
1966 EUROPE Oil discovered in North Sea.
1967 AFRICA Suez Canal closed after Six Day War, encouraging development of supertankers. Canal reopened 1975.
1973 AFRICA/ASIA Following Yom Kippur War, embargo by Arab oil-producing countries causes rise in oil prices.
1973–81 EUROPE Britain, Ireland, and Denmark join European Economic Community. Greece becomes member of EEC in 1981.
1979–82 WORLDWIDE British Transglobe Expedition becomes first team to circumnavigate the earth via the poles.
1986–87 WORLDWIDE Falling oil prices, lessening inflation, cause global trade adjustments.

SCIENCE, INVENTIONS, AND MEDICINE 7000 B.C.–A.D. 1476

7000–2000 B.C.

7000–6000 ASIA Pottery being made in Middle East.
c. 5500 ASIA/AFRICA Copper, gold, and silver worked in Mesopotamia and Egypt.
c. 4000–3500 ASIA/AFRICA Basket making begins. Spindle developed for spinning. Wheel and kiln invented. Mud bricks used.
c. 3500–3000 ASIA Cuneiform writing developed in Sumeria. Plow and cart invented. Bronze is cast.
3100 ASIA/AFRICA Hieroglyphic writing in Egypt. Reed boats used in Egypt and Assyria (now Iraq).
3000 ASIA Cotton cultivated in Indus Valley.
c. 2500 AFRICA Wooden boats used in Egypt. Papyrus writing material and ink made.
2100–2050 EUROPE Linear A writing developed in Crete.
ASIA Glass made in Mesopotamia.

2000–1000 B.C.

1792–1750 ASIA Mathematics and medicine practiced in Babylon.
c. 1740 ASIA Horses (ridden and used for draft) and war chariot introduced from Persia to Mesopotamia (and later Egypt).
1650–1590 EUROPE Linear B writing (syllabic, early form of Greek) developed in Crete.
1372–1354 ASIA Iron weapons used by Hittites. Alphabetic script used at Byblos and Ugarit.
c. 1000 ASIA Industrial use of iron in Egypt and Mesopotamia.

1000–500 B.C.

c. 800 EUROPE Greek alphabet first used.
c. 750 ASIA Babylonian astronomy developed and eclipses predicted. A calendar is established (747).
c. 650 ASIA Coinage invented in Lydia (Asia Minor).
c. 600 EUROPE Etruscans invent the arch. Roman alphabet develops from Greek via Etruscan.
c. 509 EUROPE Pythagoras of Samos establishes community at Croton (southern Italy) for study of mathematics, astronomy, and reincarnation.

SAILOR'S FRIEND *The Pharos lighthouse, built in about 280 B.C., was more than 400 feet high. The light was provided by a wood fire.*

500 B.C.–0

c. 400 EUROPE Hippocrates of Kos, physician and founder of scientific medicine, formulates the Hippocratic oath.
ASIA Crossbow invented in China.
c. 300 AFRICA In Alexandria, Egypt, Euclid teaches mathematics. Spring, screw, pump, lever, cog invented. First use of steam power and water clock.
c. 280 AFRICA Pharos, one of the seven wonders of the ancient world, built at Alexandria.
c. 250 EUROPE Archimedes, Greek mathematician and engineer, formulates law of lever and invents Archimedes' screw for raising water.
c. 133 EUROPE Romans begin to use concrete.
c. 100 EUROPE Hypocaust (underfloor heating) and public baths introduced in Italy.
46 EUROPE Julius Caesar creates the Julian calendar.

0–A.D. 500

Before 21 EUROPE Strabo, Greek writer, produces the *Geographia,* a compendium of historical and geographical knowledge.
By 77 EUROPE Pliny the Elder completes *Historia naturalis,* an encyclopedia of natural science.
c. 100 ASIA Paper invented in China.
By 400 ASIA Decimal system of numbers in use in India; symbol for zero first used.

A.D. 500–1000

By 650 ASIA Persians using windmills—not known in western Europe until about 1100.
786–96 EUROPE Palace school flourishes at Aachen (Charlemagne's capital) under English scholar-monk Alcuin of York (c. 735–804).
c. 813 ASIA Astronomical observatories set up at Baghdad and Damascus.
c. 850 EUROPE University established at Constantinople.
878–99 EUROPE King Alfred the Great establishes schools for English nobles' sons.
c. 868 ASIA First printed book, *The Diamond Sutra,* published in China by means of wood blocks.

A.D. 1000–1500

1040–50 ASIA Printing from movable type invented by Chinese alchemist Pi Sheng.
c. 1164 ASIA Gunpowder in use in China, probably for fireworks.
c. 1250–77 EUROPE Friar Roger Bacon, experimental scientist at Oxford University, England, invents magnifying glass and has knowledge of gunpowder.
1438 EUROPE Johann Gutenberg, German printer, invents a mold for casting individual letters in metal. His first printed books appear in 1450s in Mainz.
1476 EUROPE William Caxton sets up first printing press in England, at Westminster.

SCIENCE, INVENTIONS, AND MEDICINE A.D. 1509–PRESENT

A.D. 1500–1600

1509 EUROPE Earliest known pocket watch made at Nuremberg, Germany.

1527 EUROPE Swiss physician and alchemist Philippus Aureolus Paracelsus (Theophrastus Bombastus von Hohenheim) compiles the earliest manual of surgery, one aspect of his effort to modernize medicine.

1543 EUROPE Polish astronomer Nicholas Copernicus publishes his theory that the earth revolves around the sun.

1550s EUROPE First muskets manufactured in Spain.

1568 EUROPE Flemish geographer Gerhard Kremer, also known as Gerardus Mercator, publishes map of the world, using the projection that now bears his name.

c. 1590 EUROPE Dutch opticians Hans Lipperhy and Zacharias Janssen invent the first true microscope by combining concave and convex lenses.

1592 EUROPE Italian astronomer Galileo Galilei, at Padua, invents the thermometer.

A.D. 1600–1700

1614 EUROPE Scottish theologian John Napier devises logarithms.

1628 EUROPE British physician William Harvey discovers circulation of the blood.

1650 EUROPE Otto von Guericke, mayor of Magdeburg in present-day East Germany, invents the air pump and (1654) demonstrates the vacuum pump.

1659–62 EUROPE Anglo-Irish chemist and physicist Robert Boyle perfects his theories on gases and pneumatics.

1668 EUROPE Isaac Newton, English physicist, invents the reflecting telescope.

1687 EUROPE Newton publishes *Philosophiae naturalis principia mathematica,* a work that includes his laws of motion and theory of gravitation.

1665–1704 EUROPE Newton and German philosopher-mathematician Gottfried von Leibniz independently develop the mathematical system of calculus.

A.D. 1700–1800

1709 EUROPE Abraham Darby first uses coke in a blast furnace to smelt iron at Coalbrookdale, England. His coke-fired furnaces were cheaper and more efficient than ones using charcoal, and they produced iron that could be made in thin castings. This meant iron could compete with brass as an industrial material.

1712 EUROPE First practical steam engine invented by English blacksmith Thomas Newcomen.

1733 EUROPE British engineer John Kay invents flying shuttle to speed cotton weaving.

1735 EUROPE Swedish botanist Carolus Linnaeus publishes *Systema naturae,* which presents his method of classifying plants and animals.

c. 1740 EUROPE Swedish astronomer Anders Celsius invents Centigrade temperature scale.

1752 NORTH AMERICA Scientist Benjamin Franklin installs the first lightning conductor on his home in Philadelphia, Pa.

1757 EUROPE Sextant invented by Capt. James Campbell of British Royal Navy.

1764–69 EUROPE James Hargreaves' spinning jenny and Richard Arkwright's water-driven spinning machine launch first textile factories in northern England.

1769 EUROPE James Watt invents new type of steam engine, with separate condenser and pump.

1774 EUROPE British scientist Joseph Priestley discovers oxygen. Swedish chemist Karl Scheele discovers chlorine.

1781 EUROPE Seventh planet, Uranus, discovered by German-born astronomer William Herschel.

1783 EUROPE First ascents in hot-air balloons, built by Montgolfier brothers, in Paris.

1786 EUROPE Experiments in Italy by Alessandro Volta and Luigi Galvani lead to the first simple electrical battery.

1793 NORTH AMERICA Inventor Eli Whitney devises labor-saving cotton gin, boosting productivity of U.S. cotton industry.

1796 EUROPE English physicist Edward Jenner successfully completes 20 years of experiments in the protective power of vaccination.

1799 EUROPE Metric system is adopted in France.

A.D. 1800–1900

1821–31 EUROPE British scientist Michael Faraday develops electric generator and discovers principle of electromagnetic induction, the basis of electric motors.

1825 EUROPE Steam locomotive is first used on public railroad in England.

1827 EUROPE Law relating current, voltage, and resistance is formulated by German physicist Georg Ohm.

1832–44 NORTH AMERICA Inventor Samuel Morse develops the electric telegraph and sends first message, from Baltimore to Washington (May 1844).

1834 NORTH AMERICA Inventor Cyrus McCormick devises reaping machine, making possible mass harvesting of grain.

1836 NORTH AMERICA Samuel Colt, U.S. inventor, patents the revolver.

1839 NORTH AMERICA Charles Goodyear discovers how to vulcanize rubber.

1846 EUROPE Eighth planet, Neptune, discovered by German astronomer Johann Galle.

1859 EUROPE British naturalist Charles Darwin publishes *The Origin of Species,* setting out his theory of evolution. NORTH AMERICA First commercial oil well dug at Titusville, Pa.

1862 EUROPE First plastic articles—made from "Parkesine," invented by Alexander Parkes—exhibited in London.

1865–66 EUROPE Antiseptic surgery introduced by Joseph Lister in Edinburgh, Scotland. Austrian monk Gregor Mendel publishes findings on heredity.

1867 EUROPE Swedish chemist Alfred Nobel invents dynamite.

1876 NORTH AMERICA Alexander Graham Bell transmits the first telephone message. Four-stroke internal-combustion engine invented by German engineer Nikolaus Otto.

1878–79 EUROPE/NORTH AMERICA Thomas Edison in U.S.A. and Joseph Swan in Britain produce first successful incandescent electric light.

1885 EUROPE French scientist Louis Pasteur develops rabies vaccine.

1887 EUROPE Gottlieb Daimler and Karl Benz produce first successful automobile, in Germany.

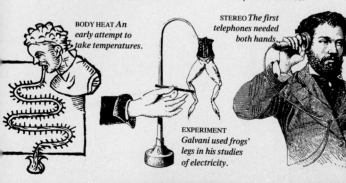

BODY HEAT *An early attempt to take temperatures.*

STEREO *The first telephones needed both hands.*

EXPERIMENT *Galvani used frogs' legs in his studies of electricity.*

CRACKER *A stick of dynamite made in Nobel's factory in 1884.*

SIX-SHOOTER *A Colt revolver from about 1880.*

1889–93 NORTH AMERICA Thomas Edison perfects motion-picture technique through his Kinetoscope.
1892 EUROPE German engineer Rudolf Diesel patents his compression-ignition engine.
1895 EUROPE Radio demonstrated by Italian physicist Guglielmo Marconi.
German physicist Wilhelm Roentgen discovers X-rays.
1896 NORTH AMERICA Research by George Washington Carver, born a slave, shows need for agricultural diversification and conservation in U.S. South.
1898 EUROPE Pierre and Marie Curie discover radium in Paris laboratory.

A.D. 1900–1950

1900 EUROPE Sigmund Freud, Viennese physician, founds science of psychoanalysis; publishes *The Interpretation of Dreams.*
1901 EUROPE/NORTH AMERICA Marconi transmits wireless message across Atlantic Ocean.
1903 NORTH AMERICA Wright brothers make first successful airplane flight at Kitty Hawk, N.C.
1905 EUROPE In Zurich, Switzerland, Albert Einstein formulates his special theory of relativity, revolutionizes basic assumptions of physics.
1906 EUROPE Count Ferdinand von Zeppelin builds first practical rigid airship.
British biochemist Sir Frederick Hopkins identifies nutritional value of "accessory food factors," later renamed vitamins.
1911 EUROPE At Manchester, England, physicist Ernest Rutherford discovers the nucleus of the atom.
1913 EUROPE Danish physicist Niels Bohr explains the structure of the atom.
1915–16 EUROPE First metal aircraft built by Junkers in Germany. Einstein publishes his general theory of relativity in Berlin.
1926 EUROPE Scottish inventor John Logie Baird projects first television images.
NORTH AMERICA U.S. inventor Robert Goddard launches world's first liquid-fueled rocket.
1928 EUROPE Scottish bacteriologist Alexander Fleming discovers antibiotic powers of penicillin.

EARLY SHUTTLE Enterprise *never went into orbit but did pave the way for* Columbia, *first launched on April 12, 1981.*

1930 EUROPE British engineer Frank Whittle patents jet engine.
NORTH AMERICA Ninth planet, Pluto, discovered by U.S. astronomer Clyde Tombaugh at Lowell Observatory, Ariz.
1935–39 EUROPE British physicist Robert Watson-Watt develops radar.
1942 NORTH AMERICA At University of Chicago, first nuclear chain reaction created by Enrico Fermi.
1944 EUROPE German scientist Wernher von Braun produces first long-range rocket (V-2).
1945 NORTH AMERICA Experimental atom bomb exploded in New Mexico (July 16). First truly electronic computer built at University of Pennsylvania.
1948 NORTH AMERICA Transistor—invented by U.S. scientists John Bardeen, Walter Brattain, and William Shockley—signals dawn of electronics revolution.

A.D. 1950–PRESENT

1953 EUROPE James Watson, Francis Crick, and Maurice Wilkins discover the structure of the genetic material DNA.
1954 EUROPE First atomic power station begins generating electricity in Obninsk, U.S.S.R.
NORTH AMERICA First successful organ transplant, of a kidney, carried out at Harvard Medical School, Cambridge, Mass.
1954–59 NORTH AMERICA Dr. Jonas Salk develops first effective polio vaccine, followed by Dr. Albert Sabin's live-virus, orally taken type.
1955 NORTH AMERICA Oral contraceptive developed by U.S. researchers led by Dr. Gregory Pincus.
1957 EUROPE First Soviet test launch of intercontinental ballistic missile. Soviets also orbit *Sputnik,* first artificial earth satellite.
1960 NORTH AMERICA Laser beam developed by U.S. scientists.
1960–63 NORTH AMERICA U.S. geologist Harry Hess develops theory of ocean-floor spreading; leads to theory of plate tectonics.
1961 EUROPE Soviet cosmonaut Yuri Gagarin becomes first man in space aboard *Vostok I.*
1962 EUROPE/NORTH AMERICA First communications satellite, *Telstar,* launched by the U.S.A.
1967 AFRICA First human heart transplant performed in South Africa, by Dr. Christiaan Barnard.
1969 NORTH AMERICA U.S. astronaut Neil Armstrong, in *Apollo 11,* becomes the first man on the moon (July).
1971 EUROPE First space station—U.S.S.R.'s *Salyut*—launched.
NORTH AMERICA First pocket calculators become commercially available in U.S.A. Microprocessor (logic and arithmetic unit of a computer on a single silicon chip) patented by the Intel Corporation. AFRICA Aswan High Dam is completed in Egypt.
1978 EUROPE First test-tube baby born in Oldham, England, following fertilization in a laboratory.
1980 WORLDWIDE U.N. World Health Organization announces the eradication of smallpox.
1981 NORTH AMERICA U.S. space shuttle *Columbia* takes off on maiden flight, 20 years to the day after Gagarin's flight.
WORLDWIDE Virus identified that causes AIDS (*A*cquired *I*mmune-*D*eficiency *S*yndrome); incidence of disease rises sharply in parts of the U.S.A. and Africa.
1982 NORTH AMERICA First implantation of an artificial heart—named for its inventor, Robert Jarvik—in a human being.
1984 ASIA Toxic gas from pesticide plant in Bhopal, India, kills about 2,000 people in world's worst industrial accident to date.
1986 NORTH AMERICA *Challenger* explosion, killing seven astronauts, sets back U.S. space program.
EUROPE Reactor accident at Soviet plant in Chernobyl, the Ukraine, clouds future of nuclear power.

THE ARTS 8000 B.C.–A.D. 1497

DEATH MASK *The face, in beaten gold, of a Mycenaean king. Made about 1500 B.C.*

8000–1000 B.C.

8000–7000 ASIA Painting on plaster and stone. Clay features modeled on human skulls in Jericho.
7000–6000 ASIA Shrines, wall paintings, and figurines being made in the Middle East.
Before 3000 EUROPE First known stone temples built in Malta.
3100 AFRICA Royal tombs of Abydos, Upper Egypt, built.
2800 ASIA Royal cemetery built at Ur, Mesopotamia.
c. 2700 AFRICA Pyramid age in Egypt begins. Pyramids and Sphinx built at Giza (c. 2560).
c. 2600 ASIA "Priam's treasure" of gold and jewelry made in Troy.
c. 2371–2316 ASIA Akkadian statues and bronzes made.
2100 ASIA First ziggurat built at Ur.
1792–1750 ASIA Babylonian palaces and temples built.
1650–1500 EUROPE Cretan palaces built at Knossos and Phaistos.
1567–1330 AFRICA Egypt's New Kingdom culture builds tombs in Valley of the Kings, and temples at Luxor, Karnak, and Abu Simbel. Tutankhamen buried 1352.
c. 1250 EUROPE The Lion Gate and tombs built at Mycenae.
c. 1000 AMERICA Olmec pyramids and pavements built at La Venta, Mexico.

1000–500 B.C.

c. 900 AFRICA Artisans in the Nok culture make pottery heads in central Nigeria.
884–859 ASIA Relief sculptures created at Assyrian palace at Nimrud.
c. 800 EUROPE *Iliad* and *Odyssey*, Greek epic poems said to be composed by Homer.
AFRICA Royal tombs and pyramids built in Nubian kingdom of Kush, in the Sudan.
776 EUROPE First Olympic Games held at Olympia in Greece.
772–705 ASIA Assyrian kings at Nineveh collect libraries of Akkado-Sumerian inscriptions, including the epic poem *Gilgamesh*.
650 EUROPE Archaic Greek sculpture created.
c. 600 EUROPE First civic buildings constructed in Rome.
From 600 ASIA Babylon rebuilt with Hanging Gardens and Tower of Babel ziggurat.
600–500 EUROPE Etruscans begin painting on walls of tombs in northern Italy.
c. 600–400 EUROPE Golden age of Greek poetry and drama.
c. 520 EUROPE Thespis in Athens transforms performance of chorus into primitive drama by introducing solo actor.

500 B.C.–0

490 EUROPE Classic sculpture and temple building begins in Greece.
472 EUROPE Earliest surviving Greek play, *The Persians,* written by Aeschylus (525–456).
458 EUROPE *Oresteia* trilogy, considered the greatest Greek tragedy, written by Aeschylus.
448–438 EUROPE Parthenon in Athens built by Greek architect Ictinus, with sculptures by Phidias.
447 EUROPE Herodotus (c. 484–425) writes first secular history of the ancient world.
c. 425 EUROPE Sophocles writes tragedy of *Oedipus Rex.*
c. 421 EUROPE Socrates (c. 470–399) begins teaching as scientific philosopher in Athens.
c. 385 EUROPE Plato (427–347) founds his Academy in Athens.
335 EUROPE Greek philosopher Aristotle founds his school in Athens, devises laws of logic.
c. 330 EUROPE Greek philosopher Diogenes (c. 412–323) founds philosophy of austerity and self-sufficiency known as Cynicism.
c. 313 EUROPE Zeno of Citium, Greek philosopher, founds philosophy of Stoicism, stressing individual virtue.
c. 300 AFRICA Museum and library founded at Alexandria, on northern coast of Egypt.
From 100 ASIA Buddhist art flourishes in India.
52–51 EUROPE Julius Caesar (c. 100–44) writes *Gallic Wars.*
29 EUROPE Roman poet Vergil (70–19) starts his epic the *Aeneid,* about the founding of Rome.
From 27 EUROPE Golden age of Augustan writers in Roman Empire: poets Vergil, Horace (65–8), and Ovid (43–A.D. 18), and historian Livy (59–A.D. 17). Forum, palaces, and library built on Palatine Hill in Rome.

A.D. 0–500

120–200 ASIA Baalbeck temples built in Lebanon.
From 250 AMERICA Mayan pyramids and temples built in Central America.
From 320 ASIA Classical Indian art begins under Gupta dynasty (c. 320–430)
c. 400 AFRICA St. Augustine of Hippo, in North Africa, writes *Confessions,* a classic of Christian mysticism.
c. 404 ASIA St. Jerome completes translation of the Bible into Latin (Vulgate) in Palestine.

A.D. 500–1200

c. 530 EUROPE Illuminated manuscripts made in northern Europe. Byzantine art—mosaics and painted frescoes—flourishes in Constantinople and Ravenna. Church of St. Sophia built in Constantinople, 532–37.
c. 618 ASIA Art of Tang dynasty in China includes figure painting, lyric poetry.
645–784 ASIA Japanese classical art imitates Chinese style.
731 EUROPE English monk, the Venerable Bede, completes in Latin his *History of English Church and People.*
c. 800 EUROPE *Beowulf,* Anglo-Saxon epic poem, written by an unknown bard.
813–33 ASIA Caliph Mamum sets up a center of learning at Baghdad.
From 887 EUROPE King Alfred of England translates Bede into Anglo-Saxon and encourages start of the *Anglo-Saxon Chronicle.*
c. 900 AMERICA Mayan city of Chichén Itźa rebuilt under Toltecs.
c. 912 EUROPE Cordoba, Spain, becomes Moorish cultural center under Caliph Abdurrahman III and his successors.
By 1000 EUROPE Latin love lyrics produced in France and Germany. ASIA Tales of *The Thousand and One Nights* compiled in Arabia.
c. 1000–1200 EUROPE Romanesque architecture flourishes in Italy and France.
1049–1109 EUROPE Hugh of Semur rebuilds the abbey of Cluny, France—landmark in the flowering of ecclesiastical architecture in England and France.
1063–73 EUROPE St. Mark's Basilica built in the Byzantine style in Venice.
By 1100 EUROPE University of Bologna founded in Italy.
c. 1100 AFRICA Timbuktu founded as center of culture in western Africa.
From 1100 EUROPE Medieval *Chansons de geste* ("songs of deeds") written down.
1144 EUROPE Choir of Benedictine Abbey of St. Denis built outside Paris; the first example of Gothic architecture.
From 1150 ASIA Averroes (1126–98), Spanish-born Arab philosopher and physician (known in Arabic as Ibn Rushd), influences Jewish and Christian thought through his commentaries on Aristotle.
1150–1200 EUROPE Oxford University founded in England.
c. 1170 EUROPE Poets of courtly love, such as Chrétien de Troyes (c. 1150–83), write in French. Vernacular literature begins to

ROTTEN TEETH *The mason who carved this figure in Wells Cathedral, England, in the 12th century must have known what agony a toothache could be.*

emerge in Europe. University of Paris founded.
c. 1180 EUROPE Giraldus Cambrensis (c. 1146–1223) describes history and topography of Ireland and Wales.
1194–1260 EUROPE Chartres Cathedral, France, extensively rebuilt in Gothic style.

A.D. 1200–1300

1209 EUROPE Cambridge University founded in England.
c. 1237–80 EUROPE Allegorical poem *Le Roman de la Rose* written in France.
1267–73 EUROPE St. Thomas Aquinas (1225–74), Italian philosopher, writes his *Summa Theologica,* attempting to reconcile Aristotle and Christianity.
c. 1280–1450 ASIA Classical drama flourishes in China.
From 1300 ASIA Japanese Noh theater established.

A.D. 1300–1400

1305–08 EUROPE Italian artist Giotto paints fresco "The Lives of the Virgin and Christ" in Padua, signaling a turn toward naturalism and beginning of the Renaissance.
1307 EUROPE Italian poet Dante begins *The Divine Comedy,* medieval vision of God's unchanging universe.
1348–53 EUROPE Giovanni Boccaccio's *Decameron* published, concerned with secular themes.
c. 1360 EUROPE Italian poet Petrarch publishes *Canzoniere,* perfects sonnet form. ASIA Ming blue-and-white porcelain first made in China.
1385 EUROPE Heidelberg University founded by Elector Rupert I in Germany.
1360–1402 EUROPE Moorish artisans build Alcazar ("castle") in Seville, Spain.
1362–63 EUROPE William Langland writes visionary religious poem *Piers Plowman.*
1387–1400 EUROPE Geoffrey Chaucer writes *The Canterbury Tales* about life and people of 14th-century England.

A.D. 1400–1500

1401–52 EUROPE Italian sculptor Lorenzo Ghiberti works on bronze doors for baptistry in Florence.
1420–36 EUROPE Italian architect Filippo Brunelleschi (1377–1446) builds dome of Florence Cathedral—marks main flowering of the Renaissance.
c. 1420 EUROPE Brunelleschi develops system of perspective.
c. 1420–50 EUROPE Guild mystery plays performed in England.
From 1430 EUROPE Flemish artist Jan van Eyck perfects oil-painting technique in Flanders.
1430–35 EUROPE In Italy, Donatello creates "David," the first monumental nude sculpture since the Roman Empire.
1446–1515 EUROPE King's College Chapel, Cambridge, built in English perpendicular (Gothic) style.
1480–85 EUROPE Sandro Botticelli (c. 1445–1510) paints "The Birth of Venus" in Florence.
1485 EUROPE *Morte d'Arthur,* tales of King Arthur, written by Englishman Sir Thomas Malory.
From 1495 EUROPE Aldine Press in Venice prints the Greek classics, spreading rebirth of Greek learning.
1497 EUROPE Leonardo da Vinci (1452–1519) paints "Last Supper" in Milan.

LINES BY LEONARDO *One of da Vinci's sketches for the portrait of St. James in the "Last Supper."*

THE ARTS 1501–1867

A.D. 1500–1600

1501 EUROPE First printed music published in Venice by Ottaviano dei Petrucci.

1501–04 EUROPE Michelangelo, sculptor, painter, and architect, makes statue "David" in Florence.

1502 EUROPE Leonardo da Vinci paints the "Mona Lisa" in Florence.

1505 EUROPE New St. Peter's begun in Rome by architect Donato Bramante; completed 1655.

c. 1507 EUROPE In Venice, Giorgione (1475–1510) paints "The Tempest," one of the earliest Western landscapes.

From 1508 EUROPE Raphael (1483–1520), painter and architect, decorates the papal apartments in the Vatican with frescoes.

1508–12 EUROPE Michelangelo paints frescoes in the Sistine Chapel in Rome.

1509 EUROPE Erasmus (1466–1535), Dutch humanist philosopher, writes *Praise of Folly*, exposing worldliness of medieval Church.

From 1510 EUROPE Venetian Renaissance at its peak. Major painters include Titian (1487–1576), Veronese (1528–88), and Tintoretto (1518–94).

1516 EUROPE English lawyer Sir Thomas More (1478–1535) publishes his fantasy *Utopia*.

FLORID GRANDEUR
Bernini's statue of an angel was carved in 1669, at the height of Italian baroque.

1532 EUROPE *The Prince,* by Italian political theorist Niccolò Machiavelli (1469–1527), published.

1534 EUROPE French comic writer François Rabelais publishes the ribald and satirical romances *Gargantua.* in Lyons.

1550 EUROPE Italian painter and writer Giorgio Vasari (1511–74) publishes *Lives of the Most Excellent Painters, Sculptors and Architects.*

1552 EUROPE Architect Andrea Palladio begins building the Villa Rotonda in Vicenza, Italy.

1572 EUROPE Luis de Camões (1524–80) writes epic poem *The Lusiads* in Portugal.

1580 EUROPE French writer Michel de Montaigne (1533–92) invents new literary form, publishes his *Essais.*

c. 1590–92 EUROPE William Shakespeare writes his first plays: *Henry VI* parts 1, 2, and 3 and *Richard III.*

1590–96 EUROPE English poet Edmund Spenser (1552–99) writes *The Faerie Queene.*

1597–1625 EUROPE English statesman and philosopher Francis Bacon (1561–1626) composes his *Essays,* the first examples of the essay form in English.

1600 EUROPE New musical form, the oratorio, emerges as sacred equivalent of opera.

A.D. 1600–1700

1605 EUROPE Spanish author Miguel de Cervantes writes tragicomic burlesque *Don Quixote.*

1607 EUROPE In *Orfeo,* Italian composer Claudio Monteverdi develops opera as an art form.

c. 1613 EUROPE Lope de Vega (1562–1635), first major Spanish dramatist and poet, publishes *The Sheepfold,* the best known of the estimated 1,500 to 2,000 plays he wrote.

From 1630 EUROPE Baroque art flourishes in Rome.

1636 NORTH AMERICA Harvard, first university in North America, founded in Cambridge, Massachusetts Colony.

1637 EUROPE French dramatist Pierre Corneille (1606–84) writes *Le Cid.* French philosopher René Descartes (1596–1650) publishes his *Discours de la Méthode,* an essay setting out the basis of his scientific philosophy. First public opera house, Teatro di San Cassiano, opens in Venice.

1640–60 EUROPE French painter Claude Lorrain perfects his influential style of poetic classical landscapes.

1642 EUROPE Rembrandt van Rijn paints "The Night Watch" in Amsterdam.

1651 EUROPE Thomas Hobbes publishes *Leviathan,* mechanistic view of human life, in England.

1660–80 EUROPE Great age of French drama led by Molière (1622–73). Chapel and palace built at Versailles by Jules Hardouin-Mansart (1646–1708). The gardens are created by André Lenôtre.

1667 EUROPE English poet John Milton publishes religious epic *Paradise Lost.*

1669 EUROPE *Thoughts on Religion* by Blaise Pascal (1623–62) is published in France.

1675 EUROPE Sir Christopher Wren (1632–1723) begins new St. Paul's Cathedral in London. Rationalist philosopher Benedict Spinoza (1632–77) publishes *Ethics* in Holland.

1678–84 EUROPE English author John Bunyan (1628–88) writes *The Pilgrim's Progress,* a precursor of the modern novel.

1680 EUROPE Comédie Française, French national theater, established in Paris.

1690 EUROPE English empiricist philosopher John Locke (1632–1704) publishes *An Essay Concerning Human Understanding.*

A.D. 1700–1800

1710 EUROPE Irish philosopher Bishop George Berkeley (1685–1753) publishes *The Principles of Human Knowledge* in Dublin.

1714 EUROPE German philosopher Gottfried Leibniz (1646–1716) publishes *Monadologie.*

1719 EUROPE Daniel Defoe publishes *Robinson Crusoe,* considered first true English novel.

1721 EUROPE Johann Sebastian Bach completes the *Brandenburg Concertos* in Cöthen, Germany.

1726 EUROPE Jonathan Swift (1667–1745), Irish satirical writer and poet, publishes *Gulliver's Travels.*

1728 EUROPE First performance of *The Beggar's Opera,* by John Gay, is given in London.

1729 EUROPE Bach composes *St. Matthew Passion.*

1734–37 EUROPE Scottish philosopher David Hume (1711–76) writes *Treatise of Human Nature.*

1735 EUROPE "A Rake's Progress" painted by English artist William Hogarth (1697–1764).

1742 EUROPE *Messiah,* by German-born composer George Frideric Handel, given first performance in Dublin.

1747 EUROPE English critic-essayist Samuel Johnson (1709–84) starts compiling the first useful English dictionary.

1749 EUROPE Henry Fielding (1707–54) publishes his picaresque novel *Tom Jones* in London.

1751–66 EUROPE *L'Encyclopédie* written in France, with contributions by Diderot (1713–84), Voltaire (1694–1778), Rousseau (1712–78), and Montesquieu (1689–1755).
1754 EUROPE English furniture maker Thomas Chippendale (1718–79) publishes his book on furniture design, *Gentleman and Cabinet Maker's Director.*
1759 EUROPE Voltaire's satirical novel *Candide* published in France.
From 1761 EUROPE Austrian composer Franz Joseph Haydn (1732–1809) perfects the classical form of the symphony.
1762 EUROPE Swiss-born philosopher Jean-Jacques Rousseau publishes *On the Social Contract* and *Émile.*
1774 EUROPE Johann Goethe, leading figure of the romantic *Sturm und Drang* ("Storm and Stress") literary movement in Germany, publishes *The Sufferings of Young Werther.*
1781 EUROPE German philosopher Immanuel Kant (1724–1804) publishes the *Critique of Pure Reason.*
1786 EUROPE Wolfgang Amadeus Mozart composes *The Marriage of Figaro,* his first major opera.
1791 EUROPE Scottish writer James Boswell publishes landmark biography, *The Life of Johnson.*
1798 EUROPE English poet Samuel Taylor Coleridge publishes romantic collection, *Lyrical Ballads,* with William Wordsworth; includes his *The Rime of the Ancient Mariner* and Wordsworth's *Tintern Abbey.*

A.D. 1800–1850

1803 EUROPE Beethoven composes his Third Symphony, the *Eroica,* a transition from classical to romantic music.
1807 EUROPE German philosopher Georg Hegel (1770–1831) publishes the *Phenomenology of Mind.*
1808 EUROPE Goethe publishes the first part of *Faust.* (Second part is published in 1832.)
1811 EUROPE *Sense and Sensibility,* by Jane Austen (1775–1817), is published in London, followed by *Pride and Prejudice* and several more novels that secure a lasting reputation for Austen.
1815–23 EUROPE English architect John Nash (1752–1835) reconstructs the Brighton Pavilion in Regency style.
1816 EUROPE Italian composer Gioacchino Rossini writes his opera *The Barber of Seville.*
1817 EUROPE John Keats (1795–1821) publishes his first volume of poetry in London.
1818 EUROPE Mary Shelley (1797–1851) publishes her Gothic horror romance *Frankenstein.*

1818–30 ASIA Japanese painter and print designer Katsushika Hokusai (1760–1849) produces his best work.
1820 EUROPE French poet Alphonse de Lamartine (1790–1869) publishes lyrical poetry in *Méditations Poétiques.*
In England, painter John Constable paints "The Haywain."
1823 EUROPE Beethoven's Ninth (and last) Symphony, the *Choral,* composed.
1828 NORTH AMERICA Noah Webster publishes his *American Dictionary of the English Language.*
1830 EUROPE In France, Hector Berlioz composes the *Symphonie Fantastique.* Stendhal publishes his novel *Le Rouge et le Noir* ("The Red and the Black").
1831 EUROPE Victor Hugo (1802–85) leads the French Romantic movement in literature with his drama *Hernani.*
1833 EUROPE Russian poet Alexander Pushkin (1799–1837) begins his novel in epic verse, *Eugene Onegin.*
1835 EUROPE French novelist Honoré de Balzac publishes *Le Père*

ALICE AND THE RED QUEEN *Sir John Tenniel illustrated the first edition of Lewis Carroll's* Through the Looking Glass, *published in 1872.*

Goriot. Hans Christian Andersen publishes his first book of fairy tales, *Eventyr,* in Denmark.
1836–37 EUROPE English novelist Charles Dickens (1812–70) writes *The Pickwick Papers.*
1843 EUROPE Soren Kierkegaard (1813–55), Danish philosopher, publishes *Either/Or,* the foundation of existentialism.
1847 EUROPE *Jane Eyre,* novel by Charlotte Brontë, and *Wuthering Heights,* by her sister Emily, published in London.
1848 EUROPE Pre-Raphaelite brotherhood of painters founded in London by John Everett Millais (1829–1910) and Dante Gabriel Rossetti (1828–82).
1850 NORTH AMERICA U.S. author Nathaniel Hawthorne (1804–64) publishes his novel of moral conflict, *The Scarlet Letter.*

A.D. 1850–1900

1851 EUROPE Great Exhibition held in London's Crystal Palace, designed by English architect Sir Joseph Paxton (1801–1901).
1851–53 EUROPE In Italy, Giuseppe Verdi writes dramatic operas *Rigoletto, Il Trovatore,* and *La Traviata.*
1854 EUROPE Hungarian composer Franz Liszt (1811–86) invents the symphonic poem with *Les Préludes.*
NORTH AMERICA Henry Thoreau (1817–62) writes antimaterialist narrative *Walden.*
1856 EUROPE French novelist Gustave Flaubert (1821–80) writes *Madame Bovary.*
1857 EUROPE Charles Baudelaire publishes *Les Fleurs du Mal,* considered the first modern poetry.
1861–64 NORTH AMERICA Mathew Brady's photographs record U.S. Civil War.
1862 EUROPE Russian novelist and playwright Ivan Turgenev (1818–83) publishes *Fathers and Sons,* introduces concept of nihilism.

1863 EUROPE French painter Édouard Manet (1832–83) exhibits "Déjeuner sur l'Herbe," causing a scandal.
English philosopher John Stuart Mill (1806–73) publishes *Utilitarianism.*
1865 EUROPE English writer Lewis Carroll (1832–98) publishes *Alice's Adventures in Wonderland.*
1866 EUROPE Russian author Feodor Dostoevski (1821–81) publishes *Crime and Punishment.*
1867 EUROPE Karl Marx (1818–83) publishes Volume 1 of *Das Kapital.* Volumes 2 and 3 are published posthumously (1885 and 1894).

THE ARTS 1868–PRESENT

1868–72 EUROPE Modest Mussorgsky composes his opera *Boris Godunov* (first performed in 1874).

1869 EUROPE Russian writer Leo Tolstoy (1828–1910) finishes his epic novel *War and Peace*.

1870 EUROPE French novelist Jules Verne pioneers modern science fiction with *Twenty Thousand Leagues Under the Sea.*

1874 EUROPE First exhibition of Impressionist painting in Paris.

1875 EUROPE Georges Bizet opera *Carmen* is performed in Paris.

1876 EUROPE *The Ring,* cycle of four operas by Richard Wagner, first performed at Bayreuth, Germany.

1878 EUROPE Russian composer Peter Ilyich Tchaikovsky (1840–93) composes his opera *Eugene Onegin.*

"The Age of Bronze," first major sculpture by Auguste Rodin, is exhibited in Paris.

1879 EUROPE Norwegian dramatist Henrik Ibsen (1828–1906) publishes *A Doll's House.*

1881 NORTH AMERICA U.S. author Henry James (1843–1916) writes *The Portrait of a Lady.*

1884–86 EUROPE French artist Georges Seurat (1859–91) paints "Sunday Afternoon on the Island of La Grande Jatte." Develops technique known as pointillism.

1885 NORTH AMERICA Mark Twain writes influential novel *Huckleberry Finn.*

William Jenney, a member of the Chicago School of architects, led by Louis Sullivan (1856–1924), completes the first skyscraper, the Home Insurance Building, in Chicago.

1885–87 EUROPE Paul Cézanne produces a series of paintings of Mont St. Victoire.

1886 EUROPE German philosopher Friedrich Nietzsche (1844–1900) publishes *Beyond Good and Evil.*

1887 EUROPE French author Émile Zola (1840–1902) writes *La Terre* ("The Earth").

1891 EUROPE English novelist Thomas Hardy (1840–1928) publishes *Tess of the d'Urbervilles.*

1893 EUROPE Norwegian artist Edvard Munch paints "The Cry."

1895 EUROPE In England, H.G. Wells publishes science-fiction novel *The Time Machine.* Oscar Wilde publishes classic comedy *The Importance of Being Earnest.* NORTH AMERICA Stephen Crane writes *The Red Badge of Courage,* searing account of U.S. Civil War.

1896 EUROPE Giacomo Puccini composes the opera *La Bohéme* in Milan.

1898–1904 EUROPE Moscow Art Theater under Konstantin Stanislavsky (1865–1938) presents plays by Chekhov. Stanislavsky's theories on acting lead to "method" acting in the U.S.A.

JAZZMAKER *Master musician, master showman, Louis "Satchmo" Armstrong (1900–71) helped transform the music of New Orleans funeral marches into an all-American institution.*

1899 EUROPE Jean Sibelius (1865–1957) composes tone poem *Finlandia.* Russian dramatist Anton Chekhov writes *Uncle Vanya.* English composer Edward Elgar writes the *Enigma Variations.*

A.D. 1900–1950

1900 EUROPE Polish-born novelist Joseph Conrad writes *Lord Jim* in English.

1902 EUROPE *Voyage to the Moon* by French filmmaker Georges Méliès (1861–1938) is made.

1903 EUROPE *The Way of All Flesh,* by English novelist Samuel Butler, is published posthumously. NORTH AMERICA First narrative film, *The Great Train Robbery,* produced in the U.S.A.

1904 EUROPE Scottish dramatist and novelist James Barrie (1860–1937) publishes Peter Pan.

1905 EUROPE *Salomé,* erotic opera by German composer Richard Strauss, is produced in Dresden. Fauvist painting develops in France.

1906–21 EUROPE English novelist and dramatist John Galsworthy writes *The Forsyte Saga.*

1907 EUROPE "Les Demoiselles d'Avignon," by Spanish artist Pablo Picasso, begins the Cubist movement in painting.

1909 EUROPE Russian impresario Sergei Diaghilev brings the Ballets Russes to Paris, with Vaslav Nijinsky as the leading dancer.

1910–13 EUROPE British philosophers Bertrand Russell (1872–1970) and A.N. Whitehead (1861–1947) publish *Principia Mathematica.*

1913 EUROPE Russian musician Igor Stravinsky (1882–1971) composes *Rite of Spring* for Diaghilev's Ballets Russes. English novelist D.H. Lawrence publishes *Sons and Lovers.* French novelist Marcel Proust (1871–1922) starts his 8-part work, *À la recherche du temps perdu* ("Remembrance of Things Past"). Last volume published 1927. George Bernard Shaw publishes his play *Pygmalion* in London. NORTH AMERICA Armory Show in New York City introduces modern European art to U.S.A.

1914 NORTH AMERICA D.W. Griffith (1875–1948) directs long epic film *Birth of a Nation.*

1915 EUROPE Czech novelist Franz Kafka (1883–1924) completes *The Trial* (published 1925). Radical Dadaist movement, rejecting all previously accepted artistic standards, founded in Zurich, Switzerland, by poet Tristan Tzara. Surrealism develops from it.

1918 EUROPE British essayist Lytton Strachey (1880–1932) publishes *Eminent Victorians,* enlivens traditional biographical style.

1919 EUROPE German designer Walter Gropius (1883–1969) founds Bauhaus, school for functional architecture and design, in Weimar.

1921 EUROPE Italian dramatist Luigi Pirandello (1867–1936) publishes *Six Characters in Search of an Author.* Austrian philosopher Ludwig Wittgenstein (1889–1951) publishes *Tractatus Logico-Philosophicus.*

1922 EUROPE American-born poet T.S. Eliot (1888–1965) publishes *The Waste Land.* Irish novelist James Joyce's *Ulysses* is published, but is banned in Britain and the U.S.A. until the 1930s for obscenity. NORTH AMERICA Jazz trumpeter Louis Armstrong (1900–71) joins King Oliver's band in Chicago.

1923 EUROPE Austrian composer Arnold Schoenberg (1874–1951) writes *Five Piano Pieces* using a new musical language, serialism.

1924 EUROPE German novelist Thomas Mann (1875–1955) publishes *The Magic Mountain.* Surrealist movement founded in Paris, led by painters Salvador Dali (1904–) and Max Ernst (1891–1976). English novelist E.M. Forster publishes *A Passage to India.*

1925 EUROPE Soviet film director Sergei Eisenstein (1898–1948) makes *The Battleship Potemkin.* NORTH AMERICA Comedian Charles Chaplin (1889–1977) directs and stars in the film *The Gold Rush.*
1926 EUROPE German director Fritz Lang (1890–1976) makes futuristic film *Metropolis.*
1927 NORTH AMERICA First commercially successful talking picture, *The Jazz Singer,* released.
1928 EUROPE German composer Kurt Weill (1900–50) writes the caustic *Threepenny Opera* in Berlin. NORTH AMERICA Film animator Walt Disney (1901–66) makes the first cartoon talkie, *Steamboat Willie,* in which Mickey Mouse makes his debut.
1929 EUROPE Russian-born choreographer George Balanchine (1904–83) creates the ballet *Le Fils Prodigue* ("The Prodigal Son"). NORTH AMERICA William Faulkner (1897–1962) publishes *The Sound and the Fury.* Ernest Hemingway (1898–196l) publishes *A Farewell to Arms.*
From 1930 NORTH AMERICA Dance bands spread jazz, in the form of swing, to large U.S. cities.
1935 EUROPE British publisher Allen Lane founds Penguin paperback books, revolutionizes public's reading habits.
1936 EUROPE British philosopher A.J. Ayer publishes *Language, Truth and Logic,* first account of logical positivism in England.
1936–39 NORTH AMERICA Frank Lloyd Wright builds Taliesin West in Arizona, founds influential school of architecture.
1937 EUROPE Pablo Picasso paints *Guernica,* in an anguished reaction to the destruction of undefended Basque town by German bombers during the Spanish Civil War. NORTH AMERICA Andrew Wyeth has first one-man show of paintings, gains immediate acclaim.
1938–39 EUROPE German Marxist dramatist Bertolt Brecht (1898–1956) writes *Mother Courage.*
1940 NORTH AMERICA U.S. playwright Eugene O'Neill writes *Long Day's Journey Into Night* (produced 1956).
1941 NORTH AMERICA U.S. film director Orson Welles (1915–85) makes *Citizen Kane.*
After 1945 NORTH AMERICA Abstract Expressionist movement in painting, also called the New York school and action painting, develops in U.S.A.
1947 NORTH AMERICA In U.S.A., Tennessee Williams (1914–83) produces *A Streetcar Named Desire.* U.S. dramatist Arthur Miller (1915–) writes *Death of a Salesman.*
1949 EUROPE George Orwell publishes prophetic novel *Nineteen Eighty-Four.*

A.D. 1950—PRESENT

From 1950 WORLDWIDE Steel and concrete used in building.
1951 NORTH AMERICA U.S. author J.D. Salinger (1919–) publishes *The Catcher in the Rye.*
1953–60 EUROPE Theater of the Absurd movement founded by Romanian-born Eugene Ionesco and Irish-born Samuel Beckett.
1954 EUROPE Radio play *Under Milk Wood,* by Welsh poet Dylan Thomas (1914–53), first broadcast. English novelist William Golding (1911–) writes *Lord of the Flies.* ASIA Japanese film director Akira Kurosawa (1910–) produces *Seven Samurai.*
1955 EUROPE Italian film director Michelangelo Antonioni (1912–) makes *L'Avventura.* NORTH AMERICA "Rock Around the Clock," by Bill Haley and the Comets, boosts popularity of rock and roll music in U.S.A.
1956 EUROPE Playwright John Osborne has *Look Back in Anger* produced. NORTH AMERICA Elvis Presley (1935–77) dominates rock music after release of "Heartbreak Hotel." "Beat" poet Allen Ginsberg (1926–) publishes "Howl," an attack on American social values.
After 1956 EUROPE/NORTH AMERICA Pop Art gains respect.
1957 EUROPE Russian writer Boris Pasternak (1890–1960) publishes *Doctor Zhivago.* Alain Robbe-Grillet (1922–), founder of French "anti-novel," publishes *Jealousy.* NORTH AMERICA *West Side Story,*

by Leonard Bernstein, is landmark in U.S. musical theater.
1958 SOUTH AMERICA Construction of Brasilia, as capital of Brazil, begun by architects Oscar Niemeyer and Lucio Costa.
1959 EUROPE Emergence of *nouvelle vague* ("new wave") in French cinema—includes *Breathless,* directed by Jean-Luc Godard (1930–).
1960 EUROPE Beatles pop group forms in England (break up 1970).
1962 EUROPE Russian poet Yevgeny Yevtushenko (1933–) publishes his poem "Babi Yar," an attack on Soviet anti-Semitism. NORTH AMERICA U.S. playwright Edward Albee (1928–) produces *Who's Afraid of Virginia Woolf?*
1967 SOUTH AMERICA Colombian writer Gabriel Garcia Márquez (Nobel Prize winner 1982) publishes *One Hundred Years of Solitude.*
1968 NORTH AMERICA U.S. film director Stanley Kubrick (1928–) makes *2001: A Space Odyssey.*
1969 EUROPE Art historian Kenneth Clark (1903–83) makes 13-part series on the arts, *Civilisation,* for British television.
1973 EUROPE Russian novelist Alexander Solzhenitsyn publishes *The Gulag Archipelago,* depicting Soviet labor camps.
1972–77 EUROPE Pompidou Center in Paris designed by Renzo Piano and Richard Rogers.
1976 AUSTRALIA Film director Peter Weir's *Picnic at Hanging Rock* wins international recognition for Australian film industry.
1980s Urban architecture influenced by Postmodernists, rebelling against boxy Modernist buildings.

BEATLEMANIA BEGINS TV *variety-show emcee Ed Sullivan (center) introduced the Beatles, a rock group little known outside Britain, to U.S. audiences in 1964.*

Kings and queens

SLOW COACH TO DEATH

Marie Antoinette and Louis XVI might well have avoided the guillotine during the French Revolution if the queen had not changed their original escape plan. In 1791, instead of allowing the king to leave Paris separately in a fast coach, as was first agreed, she insisted that the royal family travel together. A larger and therefore slower coach had to be used. Because of the delay, the family missed their rendezvous with an armed escort of loyalists, and it was pitch-dark and difficult to find fresh horses by the time they reached the village of Varennes, only 37 miles from the French border and safety.

As a result, a young man named Drouet, who had recognized them, was able to catch up with them and have their escape route blocked by pro-Revolution troops. Drouet had spotted the family when they changed horses at his stables in the village of Sainte-Menehould earlier in the day. The royal family were captured and sent back to Paris under guard. Louis XVI was guillotined in January 1793, followed 9 months later by Marie Antoinette.

PROCREATION

Augustus the Strong, the elector of Saxony who was elected king of Poland in 1697, is believed to have fathered more than 300 children. Nevertheless, when he died there was no difficulty about choosing the king's successor: only one of his sons was legitimate.

SOLDIER-KING

King Karl Gustaf of Sweden is the direct descendant of an unrenowned French lawyer who had a practice in the small town of Pau, in southern France, during the 18th century. The lawyer's son, Jean Bernadotte, joined the French Army as a common soldier and rose through the ranks to become a marshal under Napoleon. In 1810 he was elected crown prince of Sweden—after the Swedes had sent a delegation to Paris to consult Napoleon, then the master of continental Europe—because the existing Swedish royal line was on the point of dying out. Jean Bernadotte had earlier impressed the Swedes when he led troops in northern Germany and Denmark. With Napoleon's blessing, Jean Bernadotte became in 1818 King Karl XIV Johan, and founded Sweden's present ruling house.

LOST AND FOUND

After Charles I of England met his death on the scaffold in January 1649, his body was interred without ceremony in the vaults of St. George's Chapel at Windsor Castle, where it was to lie undisturbed for nearly 200 years.

This had not been the government's or the royal family's intention, however. At the restoration of the monarchy in 1660, Charles II was voted £70,000 by Parliament to pay for his father's reburial beneath a magnificent monument in Westminster Abbey. Then, to general consternation, it was announced that the body had mysteriously vanished; but such was the nation's sympathy toward the bereaved king that no one dreamed of asking him to return the money.

There the matter rested until 1813, when workmen in St. George's Chapel accidentally broke into the tomb of Henry VIII. There, next to the coffins of Henry and Jane Seymour, was that of Charles I. The royal physician, Sir Henry Halford, was summoned

and positively identified the remains as those of the beheaded Charles I. The lid of the tomb was then closed and the king left to rest. But it seems that Sir Henry had a most unprofessional bent toward souvenir hunting.

He removed the severed vertebra from the king's neck, had it set in gold, and for the next half century he and his descendants used it as a saltcellar—until Queen Victoria heard about it and ordered that the bone be returned to the royal coffin.

THE EMPEROR WHO COULDN'T WRITE

Though Charlemagne (c. 742–814), the founder of the Holy Roman Empire, was a great patron of learning, he never learned to write properly. The king kept writing materials under his pillow so that he could practice penmanship in his spare time. But, perhaps because he tried to learn late in life, his efforts were of little avail. The few surviving examples of Charlemagne's handwriting show a childishly unformed scrawl.

PRETENDER'S PORTRAIT

In London's National Portrait Gallery hangs a painting believed to be of James Scott, duke of Monmouth and supposed son of Charles II. He was beheaded in 1685 for trying to seize the throne by force of arms, his claim being that Charles had married his mother, Lucy Walter, while in exile in Holland. If this claim was true, then Monmouth and not James II—Charles's younger brother—was the rightful king of England.

In 1685, when Charles II died, Monmouth attempted to seize the throne; but his uprising was a disaster. His pitiful army of farmboys was annihilated, and the duke himself was captured after being found hiding in a ditch. Since he had declared himself king, he could not hope for mercy.

There was no trial. A special law had already been passed against Monmouth that in effect sentenced him to death without judicial proceedings. The execution was carried out 2 days after he was brought back to London. It is said that just as his corpse was being taken for burial, it was remembered that no portrait of Monmouth existed, a state of affairs that could not be permitted for a member of the royal family, however misguided. The head was therefore hastily stitched back into place, the body propped in a chair, and the portrait was painted.

THE BAVARIAN STUART

A descendant of the Stuart kings of Britain was a general who commanded German armies on the western front in World War I. After the direct Stuart line failed with the death of Bonnie Prince Charlie in 1788 and his brother, Henry, in 1807, the mantle of possible successors passed to the descendants of Princess Henrietta, the sister of Charles II and James II. A series of dynastic marriages brought the Stuart claim to Mary Theresa of Este, who married King Louis III of Bavaria in 1868. The German general was their son, Crown Prince Rupprecht (Rupert) of Bavaria.

POISONPROOF

King Mithridates VI of Pontus in Asia Minor made himself so immune to poison that he was unable to poison himself when he wanted to. The king spent his life taking small doses of poison in order to build up a resistance to it, because he was frightened of being assassinated. Mithridates was so successful that when he tried to commit suicide in 63 B.C., to avoid imminent capture by the Romans, the poison he took had no effect. In the end a slave killed him with a sword.

SAME FAMILY, NEW NAME

The present British royal family's surname was chosen by one of the staff. Originally the family's name was Saxe-Coburg and Gotha. But in 1917, during World War I, it was changed because of its German connotations. The name Windsor was suggested by Lord Stamfordham, George V's private secretary.

UNFAITHFUL DEFENDER

Britain's Protestant kings and queens—who are forbidden by law from becoming Roman Catholics or even marrying them—still bear a title given to them by the Catholic Church. The title is Defender of the Faith, meaning the Catholic faith. It appears on British coins as the abbreviation F.D. or Fid. Def. (for the Latin phrase *Fidei Defensor*). Pope Leo X gave the title to Henry VIII in 1521, rewarding him for writing

a treatise against Martin Luther, just 13 years before the king—angered by Rome's opposition to his divorce from Catherine of Aragon—broke with the papacy and made himself head of the new Church of England. Although the pope granted the honorary title only for Henry's lifetime, British sovereigns hung on to it even after 1701, when the Act of Settlement made it illegal for a monarch to adopt the Catholic faith, and after 1772, when the Royal Marriages Act made it illegal for a monarch to marry a Catholic. They have kept it ever since.

ARTIFICIAL SNOW

An Arab king once had a Spanish hillside planted entirely with almond trees—to instruct and delight his favorite wife. The king, Almotamid, ruled the region around Seville in the middle of the 11th century A.D., when Spain was largely a Moorish colony. His wife, a Christian slave named Itimad, did not know what snow looked like, and the king decided he must try to show her. In spring the falling petals of the almond trees turned the slopes white, the closest approximation to snow available in southern Spain's climate.

QUEEN MOTHER *Queen Victoria (1819–1901) and Prince Albert (1819–61), who were married in 1840, play with their three eldest children in this popular print made in 1843. The couple went on to have four sons and five daughters in all, most of whom married into other royal houses. As a result of these dynastic links, almost all the crowned heads of Europe in the 20th century have been descendants of the English queen. They include Wilhelm II, the kaiser of Germany during World War I; Alexandra, the wife of Nicholas II, the last Russian czar; the present monarchs of Spain, Norway, Denmark, and Sweden; the former royal families of Greece, Romania, and Yugoslavia; and both Elizabeth II of Britain and her husband Prince Philip, along with all their children and grandchildren. On Victoria's death in 1901, her eldest son became King Edward VII.*

THE QUEEN AND PRINCE ALBERT AT HOME.

HARSH JUSTICE

Frederick the Great of Prussia was so badly treated at home that he tried to run away to France at the age of 18. But his father, Friedrich Wilhelm I, caught him and threw him into prison. During the prince's imprisonment in 1730, Lieutenant Katte, a friend who had helped him in his attempt to escape, was executed before Frederick's eyes. He fainted at the sight. Frederick was kept under arrest for 15 months before being grudgingly set free. As king, though, he far outshone his harsh father. He stayed on the throne for 46 years—nearly twice as long as his father—and doubled his country's territory.

GOOD KING MACBETH

The real King Macbeth of Scotland was very different from the tragic hero of Shakespeare's play. Far from being an ambitious usurper, as Shakespeare describes him, Macbeth had a claim to the Scottish throne that was at least as good as that of his rival, Duncan. Furthermore, Duncan was killed in open battle in 1040 and not murdered by Macbeth, as Shakespeare's play claims. In fact, Duncan was a young, ineffectual king—not Shakespeare's venerable and gracious sovereign. And after Macbeth seized the throne by force, he went on to reign in Scotland for 17 prosperous years, from 1040 to 1057.

EUROPE'S KINGS AND QUEENS/Britain/France/Austria

These lists give the dates of the major royal houses of Europe. Some dates overlap, usually because two or more monarchs ruled different parts of what is now one country. Sometimes a monarch ruled more than one country, with a different title in each. The 16th-century Holy Roman emperor Charles V, for example, known in Germany as Karl V, was also king of Spain as Carlos I. On other occasions, countries were without a monarch for a time because of civil wars or periods of republicanism.

ENGLAND AND GREAT BRITAIN

Saxons and Danes
Egbert, 827–39
Ethelwulf, 839–58
Ethelbald, 858–60
Ethelbert, 860–66
Ethelred I, 866–71
Alfred the Great, 871–99
Edward the Elder, 899–925
Athelstan, 925–40
Edmund, 940–46
Edred, 946–55
Edwy, 955–59
Edgar, 959–75
Edward the Martyr, 975–78
Ethelred II, 978–1016
Edmund Ironside, 1016
Canute (Knut) the Dane, 1016–35
Harold I, 1035–40
Hardicanute, 1040–42
Edward the Confessor, 1042–66
Harold II, 1066

Normans
William I, 1066–87
William II, 1087–1100
Henry I, 1100–35
Stephen, 1135–54

Plantagenet
Henry II, 1154–89
Richard I, 1189–99
John, 1199–1216
Henry III, 1216–72
Edward I, 1272–1307
Edward II, 1307–27
Edward III, 1327–77
Richard II, 1377–99

Lancaster
Henry IV, 1399–1413
Henry V, 1413–22
Henry VI, 1422–61, 1470–71

York
Edward IV, 1461–70, 1471–83
Edward V, 1483
Richard III, 1483–85

Tudor
Henry VII, 1485–1509
Henry VIII, 1509–47
Edward VI, 1547–53
Jane Grey (9 days), 1553
Mary I, 1553–58
Elizabeth I, 1558–1603

Stuart
James I, 1603–25
Charles I, 1625–49

Commonwealth
Council of State, 1649–53
Oliver Cromwell (Protector), 1653–58
Richard Cromwell (Protector), 1658–59

Stuart Restoration
Charles II, 1660–65
James II, 1685–68

Orange
William III, 1689–1702
and Mary II, 1689–94

Stuart
Anne, 1702–14

Hanover
George I, 1714–27
George II, 1727–60
George III, 1760–1820
George IV, 1820–30
William IV, 1830–37
Victoria, 1837–1901

BORN TO BE KING *Two poles and a drape become a makeshift tent for the future George III, sketched at play in his nursery in the 1740s.*

Saxe-Coburg-Gotha
Edward VII, 1901–10

Windsor
George V, 1910–36
Edward VIII (325 days), 1936
George VI, 1936–52
Elizabeth II, 1952–

VIRGIN QUEEN *Framed by a starched lace ruff, Elizabeth I—known as the Virgin Queen because she never married—stares impassively from a portrait by the English miniaturist Nicholas Hilliard. Only four British monarchs have reigned for longer than the 45 years Elizabeth spent on the throne: Henry III (56 years), Edward III (50), George III (60), and Victoria (64).*

ZULU KINGS' SENIOR WARRIORS

The Zulu army that defeated the British at the Battle of Isandhlwana in 1879 included a regiment of men in their sixties. They were the oldest troops in a culture that built itself into a nation of warriors under the Zulu king Chaka (who died in 1828) and later his nephew Cetewayo (c. 1826–84). The youngest troops were about 13 years old.

The regiments were divided according to age, and each regiment lived in a separate village, where the soldiers worked the land in peacetime. The warrior culture did not last long. Six months after the Battle of Isandhlwana the Zulus, whose major weapons were spears, were defeated by British guns at Ulundi, in Natal, now a province of South Africa and the site of government-designated "Zulu lands."

SONS OF THE DESERT

Abdul-Aziz, who in 1932 became the first king of what is now Saudi Arabia, had at least 79 children. Also known as Ibn Saud, the king used his numerous marriages to form alliances with powerful families in Arabia. At his death in 1953 there were 34 sons surviving, plus about the same number of daughters, and today the Saudi royal family has at least 8,000 princes and princesses. King Fahd, who came to the throne in 1982, is one of Abdul-Aziz's sons.

FRANCE

Carolingian dynasty
Pépin the Short, 751–68
Charlemagne, 768–814
Carloman, 768–71
Louis I, the Pious, 814–40

ROME'S SUCCESSOR
Charlemagne, the Christian king of the Franks, was crowned emperor of the West on Christmas Day A.D. 800.

END OF A MONARCHY *An executioner ~lds out the head of Louis XVI, guillotined in 1793 during the French Revolution. ~his body still lies beside the blade. Louis's wife, Marie Antoinette, followed him to the guillotine later the same year.*

West Francia
Charles II the Bald, 843–77
Louis II, 877–79
Louis III, 879–82
Carloman, 879–84
Karl III, Holy Roman emperor, 884–87
Eudes, 888–98
Charles III, the Simple, 893–923
Robert I, 922–23
Raoul, 923–36
Louis IV, 936–54
Lothair, 954–86
Louis V, 986–87

Capetian kings
Hugh Capet, 987–96
Robert II, 996–1031
Henri I, 1031–60
Philippe I, 1060–1108
Louis VI, 1108–37
Louis VII, 1137–80
Philippe II (Auguste), 1180–1223
Louis VIII, 1223–26
Louis IX (St. Louis), 1226–70
Philippe III, 1270–85
Philippe IV, 1285–1314
Louis X, 1314–16
Jean I, 1316
Philippe V, 1316–22
Charles IV, 1322–28

House of Valois
Philippe VI, 1328–50
Jean II, 1350–64
Charles V, 1364–80
Charles VI, 1380–1422
Charles VII, 1422–61
Louis XI, 1461–83
Charles VIII, 1483–98
Louis XII, 1498–1515
François I, 1515–47
Henri II, 1547–59
François II, 1559–60
Charles IX, 1560–74
Henri III, 1574–89

Bourbon dynasty
Henri IV, 1589–1610
Louis XIII, 1610–43
Louis XIV, the Sun King, 1643–1715
Louis XV, 1715–74
Louis XVI, 1774–92

First Republic, 1792–1804

House of Bonaparte
Napoleon I, emperor, 1804–14
Hundred Days, 1815

Bourbon Restoration
Louis XVIII, 1814–24
Charles X, 1824–30

House of Bourbon-Orléans
Louis Philippe, 1830–48

Second Republic, 1848–52

House of Bonaparte
Napoleon III, 1852–70

HUNTING PARTY *One of the last Hapsburg rulers of Austria, Franz Josef I, poses for the camera with his son Rudolf.*

AUSTRIA

Hapsburg dynasty
Friedrich III, 1453–93
Maximilian I, 1493–1519
Carlos I (of Spain), 1519–21
Ferdinand I, 1521–64
Maximilian II, 1564–76
Rudolf II, 1576–1611
Mathias, 1611–19
Ferdinand II, 1619–37
Ferdinand III, 1637–57
Leopold I, 1657–1705
Joseph I, 1705–11
Karl II, 1711–40
Maria Theresa, 1740–80
Joseph II, 1765–90
Leopold II, 1790–92
Franz I, 1792–1835 (also held title of Franz II of Holy Roman Empire until 1806)
Ferdinand I, 1835–48
Franz Josef I, 1848–1916
Karl I, 1916–18

RISING TIDE

King Canute, the Dane who ruled England from 1016 to 1035, got his feet wet to prove that only God could control the tide. He set his throne on the beach and commanded the tide not to rise in order to show his courtiers how limited—and not how great—his powers were. He allowed the tide to come in over his feet and the waves to lap around his legs. Then he leaped up, saying that nobody was worthy of the name king "save Him whose nod heaven and earth and sea obey under laws eternal." Afterward, Canute never wore his crown again. As a mark of respect he placed it instead on a crucifix, above Christ's head.

THE KING WITH TWO WIVES AT ONCE

When Britain's future king, George IV, married Caroline of Brunswick in 1795, he was already married—and had been for 10 years. In 1784 George had fallen in love with Maria Fitzherbert, a Catholic widow. He married her in secret in 1785. The marriage was valid in the eyes of the Catholic Church but not under English law, which bans British monarchs or heirs to the throne from marrying Roman Catholics.

George and Caroline parted after a year when their daughter, Princess Charlotte, was born, and George went back to Mrs. Fitzherbert. Caroline spent most of her time in Italy after the separation, and outraged

EUROPE'S KINGS AND QUEENS/Holy Roman Empire/Prussia/

HOLY ROMAN EMPIRE

Carolingian dynasty
Charlemagne, 800–14
Louis (Ludwig I) the Pious, 814–40
Lothair I, 840–55
Ludwig II, the German, 850–75
Karl II, the Bald, 875–77
Karl III, the Fat, 877–87
Arnulf, 887–98
Ludwig III, the Child, 899–911

Franconian house
Konrad I, 911–18

Saxon house
Heinrich I, the Fowler, 919–36
Otto I, the Great, 936–73
Otto II, 973–83
Otto III, 983–1002
Heinrich II, the Saint, 1002–24

Franconian (Salian) house
Konrad II, 1024–39
Heinrich III, 1039–56
Heinrich IV, 1056–1105
Heinrich V, 1105–25

Saxony-Supplinburg house
Lothair II, 1125–37

Hohenstaufen house
Konrad III, 1138–52
Friedrich I Barbarossa, 1152–90
Heinrich VI, 1190–97
Philipp of Swabia, 1198–1208

Saxon house
Otto IV of Brunswick, 1198–1215

Hohenstaufen house
Friedrich II, 1215–50
Konrad IV, 1250–54

Great Interregnum, 1254–73

Rulers of various houses
Rudolf I of Hapsburg, 1273–91
Adolf of Nassau, 1292–98
Albrecht I of Austria, 1298–1308
Heinrich VII of Luxembourg, 1308–13
Ludwig IV of Bavaria, 1314–47
Karl IV of Luxembourg, 1347–78
Wenzel of Bohemia, 1378–1400
Rupprecht of Palatinate, 1400–10
Sigismund of Luxembourg, 1410–37

Hapsburg dynasty
Albrecht II, 1438–39
Friedrich III, 1440–93
Maximilian I, 1493–1519
Karl (Charles) V, 1519–56
Ferdinand I, 1558–64
Maximilian II, 1564–76
Rudolf II, 1576–1612
Matthias, 1612–19
Ferdinand II, 1619–37
Ferdinand III, 1637–57

KAISER AT THE HELM
Wilhelm II steers the ship of state in a print popular in Germany before World War I.

Leopold I, 1658–1705
Josef I, 1705–11
Karl VI, 1711–40
Karl VII, 1742–45
Franz I, 1745–65
Josef II, 1765–90
Leopold II, 1790–92
Franz II, 1792–1806

PRUSSIA

Hohenzollern dynasty
Friedrich I, 1701–13
Friedrich Wilhelm I, 1713–40
Friedrich II (Frederick the Great), 1740–85
Friedrich Wilhelm II, 1786–97

Friedrich Wilhelm III, 1797–1840
Friedrich Wilhelm IV, 1840–61
Wilhelm I, 1861–71 (ruled as kaiser of Germany, 1871–88)
Friedrich III (kaiser), 1888
Wilhelm II (kaiser), 1888–1918

SPAIN

Houses of Aragon and Castile
Fernando (Ferdinand) II of Aragon and Isabella I of Castile, 1479–1504
Fernando II and Joanna the Mad, 1504–06
Fernando II, 1506–16

Spanish Hapsburgs
Carlos I (as Holy Roman emperor Charles V), 1516–56
Felipe (Philip) II, 1556–98
Felipe III, 1598–1621
Felipe IV, 1621–65
Carlos II, 1665–1700

Spanish Bourbons
Felipe V, 1700–46
Fernando VI, 1746–59
Carlos III, 1759–88
Carlos IV, 1788–1808
Fernando VII, 1808

House of Bonaparte
Joseph, 1808–13

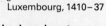

DEFENDER OF THE FAITH *Felipe (Philip) V of Spain slays the dragon of heresy in an 18th-century painting of himself and his family. Beside him is the figure of Blind Faith. In the center is El Escorial, the combined palace and monastery built near Madrid for his great-great-great-grandfather, Philip II.*

George by her intimacy with her chamberlain, Bartolomo Bergami. So when she returned to England to claim her rights as queen after George's father died in 1820, George would have none of it.

He ordered her not to attend his coronation in Westminster Abbey in 1821, and when she turned up anyway, he had her forcibly prevented from entering. The humiliated queen fell ill and died a month after the coronation.

KNAVE OF HEARTS *Bartolomo Bergami pays extravagant court to George IV's wife, Caroline, while slipping a secret note to her lady-in-waiting. The affair, caricatured in this 19th-century print, outraged the king.*

Spain/Greece/Italy/Russia/Sweden

1st Bourbon Restoration
Fernando VII, 1813–33
Isabel II, 1833–68

House of Savoy
Amadeo, 1870–73

1st Spanish Republic, 1873–74

2nd Bourbon Restoration
Alfonso XII, 1874–85
Maria Cristina, 1885–86
Alfonso XIII, 1886–1931

2nd Spanish Republic, 1931–39

Fascist dictatorship, Gen. Francisco Franco, 1939–75

3rd Bourbon Restoration
Juan Carlos, 1975–

GREECE

House of Wittelsbach
Otto, 1832–62

House of Oldenberg
George I, 1863–1913
Constantine I, 1913–17
Alexander I, 1917–20
Constantine I, 1920–22
George II, 1922–24

1st Greek Republic 1924–35

George II, 1935–47
Paul I, 1947–64
Constantine II, 1964–74

ITALY

House of Savoy
Vittorio Emanuele II, 1861–78
Umberto I, 1878–1900
Vittorio Emanuele III, 1900–46
Umberto II, 1946

RUSSIA

Grand Princes of Vladimir
Vsevolod III, 1176–1212
Yuri II, 1212–16
Konstantin, 1216–19
Yuri II, 1219–38
Yaroslav II, 1238–46
Andrei II, 1246–52

Princes of Novgorod and Grand Princes of Vladimir
Alexander Nevsky, 1238–63
Yaroslav III, 1263–72
Vasili, 1272–76
Dmitri, 1276–94
Andrei III, 1294–1304
Mikhail II, 1304–19
Yuri III, 1319–24
Dmitri II, 1324–27
Alexander II, 1327–28

Grand Princes of Moscow
Ivan I, 1328–41
Simeon, 1341–53
Ivan II, 1353–59
Dmitri Donskoi, 1359–89
Vasili I, 1389–1425
Vasili II, 1425–62
Ivan III, the Great, 1462–1505
Vasili III, 1505–33

Czars of Russia
Ivan IV, the Terrible, 1533–84
Fedor I, 1584–98
Irina, 1598
Boris Godunov, 1598–1605
Fedor III, 1676–82
Dmitri I, 1605–06
Vasili IV, 1606–10

Romanov dynasty
Mikhail, 1613–45
Alexis, 1645–76
Fedor III, 1676–82
Ivan V and Peter I, the Great, 1682–96
Peter I, the Great, 1696–1725
Catherine I, 1725–27
Peter II, 1727–30
Anna, 1730–40

Ivan VI, 1740–41
Elizabeth, 1741–62
Peter III, 1762
Catherine II, the Great, 1762–96
Pavel (Paul), 1796–1801
Alexander I, 1801–25
Nicholas I, 1825–55
Alexander II, 1855–81
Alexander III, 1881–94
Nicholas II, 1894–1917

SWEDEN

House of Vasa
Gustaf I, 1523–60
Eric XIV, 1560–68
Johan III, 1568–92
Sigismund, 1592–99
Karl IX, 1599–1611
Gustaf II Adolf, 1611–32
Christina, 1632–54

House of Zweibrücken
Karl X Gustaf, 1654–60
Karl XI, 1660–97

Karl XII, 1697–1718
Ulrika Eleonora, 1718–20

House of Hesse
Fredrik I, 1720–51

House of Holstein-Gottorp
Adolf Fredrik, 1751–71
Gustaf III, 1771–92
Gustaf IV Adolf, 1792–1809
Karl XIII, 1809–18

House of Bernadotte
Karl XIV Johan, 1818–44
Oskar I, 1844–59
Karl XV, 1859–72
Oskar II, 1872–1907
Gustaf V, 1907–50
Gustaf VI Adolf, 1950–73
Karl XVI Gustaf, 1973–

LAST OF THE CZARS *Nicholas II and his wife, Alexandra, glitter with gems in a 1903 print. In July 1918 they and their children were reportedly shot dead by Bolsheviks in a grimy cellar.*

ASCENT OF WASHINGTON *George Washington, the first U.S. president, is carried to heaven by angels in a painting created soon after his death in December 1799. The painting, on glass, was made in China for the U.S. market, and illustrates the almost reverential adoration accorded Washington by the people of his own country and in many nations around the world.*

U.S. presidents

WHO CAN BE PRESIDENT?

The U.S. Constitution stipulates that, to be eligible for the presidency, a candidate must be "a natural-born citizen," must have lived in the United States for a minimum of 14 years, and must be at least 35 years old. The requirement to be native-born was waived at first, because before the Revolution all Americans were British subjects. Candidates had merely to be U.S. citizens at the time the Constitution was adopted in 1788; Martin Van Buren, the eighth president, was the first not to have been born a British subject. But there are no other legal qualifications for the post, so theoretically there is nothing in U.S. law to prevent a lunatic, a bankrupt, or a convicted criminal from becoming president.

TRACK TO THE WHITE HOUSE

Most presidents have been Protestants. All have been white, and so far no woman has held the post. Until John F. Kennedy was elected in 1960, no Roman Catholic had been president. Although Alfred E. Smith, a Catholic, was nominated as the Democratic presidential candidate in 1928, he lost the election to a Quaker, Herbert Hoover. And, although U.S. women have had the vote since 1920, as of 1987 no woman had won either the Democratic or Republican nomination to run for president, although Geraldine Ferraro was the Democrats' candidate for vice president in 1984. She and presidential candidate Walter Mondale, a white male Protestant, lost badly to Ronald Reagan and George Bush, both white male Protestants.

YOUNG AND OLD

John F. Kennedy was the youngest man to be elected president, at 43. But he was not the youngest president. Theodore Roosevelt was only 42 when he moved up from the vice presidency after the assassination of William McKinley in 1901. The oldest man to become president was Ronald Reagan, who was 69 when he first took office.

FAMILY TIES

John Quincy Adams, the sixth president, was the son of John Adams, the second president. And Benjamin Harrison, who took office in 1889, was the grandson of William Henry Harrison, who was president in 1841. The two Roosevelts who have been presidents— Theodore and Franklin—were related only as distant cousins.

TWO-EDGED COMPLIMENT

Known for his sharp wit and sense of history, President John F. Kennedy displayed both at a White House dinner honoring Nobel Prize winners in 1962— and in the bargain paid graceful tribute to the third U.S. president. "I think this is the most extraordinary collection of talent, of human knowledge, that has ever been gathered together at the White House," he told his distinguished dinner guests, "with the possible exception of when Thomas Jefferson dined alone."

RESIGNED TO THE PRESIDENCY

Gerald Ford, president from 1974 to 1977, is the only person to hold the office who was never elected either president or vice president. He became vice president under Richard Nixon in 1973 after the elected vice president, Spiro Agnew, resigned after being accused of taking bribes prior to assuming the vice presidency. Ford took over as president 8 months later when Nixon resigned over the Watergate scandal.

I CANNOT TELL A LIE

The story of young George Washington nobly confessing to chopping down his father's cherry tree was almost certainly an invention. The fable seems to have been created by an American clergyman and notorious romanticizer, Mason Locke Weems, who wrote a biography of the first president with the avowed intention of extolling his virtues. The story was first published in the book's fifth edition, issued in 1806, seven years after Washington's death.

KILLED IN OFFICE

Four of America's 39 presidents have died at the hands of assassins. Abraham Lincoln was shot in a Washington theater in 1865 by John Wilkes Booth, an actor who had supported the defeated South during the Civil War. James Garfield was shot only 4 months after his inauguration, in 1881, by Charles Guiteau, a disappointed office-seeker. William McKinley was shot by an anarchist, Leon Czolgosz, in 1901. John F. Kennedy was shot in 1963 by Lee Harvey Oswald, a deranged drifter.

LAST WALTZ *This image-boosting melody, entitled "Log Cabin March," was written for William Henry Harrison's presidential campaign in 1840 and may have helped him win. In fact, however, Harrison was brought up in a palatial home in Virginia, and the closest he came to the shack shown here was a sturdy five-room cabin that he lived in briefly around the end of the 18th century. Ironically, Harrison's campaign music turned out to be his swan song. Conscious of his image as a rugged soldier, he insisted at his presidential inauguration on standing hatless and coatless in a freezing wind. He caught a chill and died exactly a month later, on April 4, 1841—making his term of office the shortest of any president's.*

LINCOLN'S FIRST CHOICE

Robert E. Lee, who became commander-in-chief of the Confederate forces toward the end of the Civil War, was originally offered command of the Union Army of the North. He turned down the offer, made by President Abraham Lincoln via Francis Blair, on April 18, 1861—the day after Lee's home state of Virginia seceded from the Union at the start of the war. Although he opposed secession, Lee could not bring himself to fight against his own state.

Two days later he resigned from the Union Army, and on April 23 he took command of Virginia's military and naval forces.

BARGAIN BUY

When President Thomas Jefferson began negotiations to buy Louisiana from France (which had itself only just acquired the territory from Spain), what he had in mind was to buy an area around the mouth of the Mississippi River for no more than $10 million. But in the end the French, preoccupied with the threat of war in Europe, were so eager to sell that in 1803 Jefferson was able, for a mere $15 million, to buy almost all the land between the Mississippi and the Rocky Mountains. The territory covered more than 800,000 square miles, doubling at a stroke the area of the United States.

PRESIDENTS OF THE UNITED STATES/Washington—Pierce

MAJOR EVENTS AND ACHIEVEMENTS

GEORGE WASHINGTON
1st President/1789–97
Born 1732 at Wakefield, Virginia; died 1799. Chosen as president after leading Continental Army of the infant United States to victory against the British in the American Revolution (1775–83). Established a stable government, based on a strong currency. Against fierce opposition, kept U.S.A. neutral when the Anglo-French war broke out in 1793 following the French Revolution. Failed in his struggle against the rise of partisan politics.

JOHN ADAMS
2nd President/1797–1801
(Federalist)
Born 1735 at Quincy, Massachusetts; died 1826. Despite attacks by French privateers on American shipping, resisted pressure from his own party for all-out war. Clamor against the Alien and Sedition Acts (1798), under which critics of the government could be jailed, led to collapse of his Federalist party.

THOMAS JEFFERSON
3rd President/1801–09
(Democratic-Republican)
Born 1743 at Shadwell, Virginia; died 1826. Doubled area of United States by purchasing Louisiana Territory from France (1803) for $15 million. Sponsored Lewis and Clark Expedition (1804–05) that blazed a pioneer trail across America to the Pacific Northwest. His Jeffersonian

Democracy emphasized freedom of choice for the individual and was to have far-reaching effects on American political thinking.

JAMES MADISON
4th President/1809–17
(Democratic-Republican)
Born 1751 at Port Conway, Virginia; died 1836. Led United States into War of 1812 against Britain, which began as a protest against British blockade of American ships trading with France. Was forced to flee Washington, D.C., when British troops captured and set fire to the city in 1814. War was ended, with no gains for either side, by Treaty of Ghent (December 1814). Two weeks later Gen. Andrew Jackson (later to become president)—unaware that a peace treaty had been signed—defeated a British army at the Battle of New Orleans (January 1815).

JAMES MONROE
5th President/1817–25
(Democratic-Republican)
Born 1758 in Westmoreland County, Virginia; died 1831. Presided over the acquisition of Florida from Spain for $5 million in 1819. Expounded the Monroe Doctrine

(1823), the principle that Europe should not intervene in the affairs of independent countries in the New World. North-South quarrel over the extension of slavery was ended temporarily by the Missouri Compromise (1820–21), under the terms of which Missouri was admitted to the Union as a slave state, but slavery would be prohibited in future states.

JOHN QUINCY ADAMS
6th President/1825–29
(Nonpartisan)
Born 1767 at Quincy, Massachusetts; died 1848. Alienated politicians by advocating a professional civil service free of patronage and, with neither wide popular support nor the backing of a political party, could achieve little. Later, as a congressman (1831–48), he was an effective campaigner against proslavery measures.

ANDREW JACKSON
7th President/1829–37
(Democratic)
Born 1768 at Waxhaw Settlement, South Carolina; died 1845. Strengthened the role of the presidency with the help of a

ON TO VICTORY *On Christmas night 1776, George Washington led his troops across the ice-strewn Delaware River into New Jersey. The next day he surprised and defeated a British force at Trenton—one of the first major American victories of the Revolution.*

INVISIBLE NAME

The *S* in Harry S Truman does not stand for a name. Truman was christened Harry S because both his grandfathers had names beginning with the letter— Anderson Shippe Truman and Solomon Young—and each grandfather would have been offended if young Truman had been given the other's name, or so the future president's parents feared.

DEATH IN THE FAMILY

Abraham Lincoln was not the first member of his family to die violently. Years before the president was born, his grandfather, also named Abraham, was shot dead by an Indian at his Kentucky farm. The raider was about to carry off Thomas Lincoln, the future father of the president, when he was shot in his turn by Thomas's elder brother, Mordecai.

WHITE ON GRAY

The White House, the president's official home, was originally gray, the color of the pale Virginia sandstone used to build it. During the War of 1812, British troops captured Washington, D.C., in August 1814— forcing President James Madison and his wife, Dolley, to flee—and put the mansion to the torch. When it was rebuilt after the war, the outside walls were painted white to hide the smoke stains.

---

kitchen cabinet of close advisers, and extended the practice of rewarding party supporters with government posts. The practice came to be known as the spoils system.

MARTIN VAN BUREN
8th President/1837 – 41 (Democratic)
Born 1782 at Kinderhook, New York; died 1862. Lost popular support by opposing use of federal money to alleviate distress during financial panic of 1837, caused by the collapse of the western land boom and general distrust of paper currency. Resisted extension of slavery and opposed annexation of Texas, because he felt it would provoke war with Mexico.

WILLIAM HENRY HARRISON
9th President/1841 (Whig)
Born 1773 in Charles City County, Virginia; died 1841. As governor of the Indiana Territory (1800– 12), led troops to victory at the Battle of Tippecanoe (1811) against the Shawnee Indians and settled the territory's claims to 4,680 square miles of Indian land. Died of pneumonia a month after inauguration, the first president to die in office.

JOHN TYLER
10th President/1841 – 45 (Whig)
Born 1790 in Charles City County, Virginia; died 1862. Earned the enmity of his party by vetoing Whig bills to reestablish the national bank (dismantled by President Andrew Jackson in favor of state banks). His secretary of state, Daniel Webster, settled a serious dispute over the Canadian boundary of Maine by negotiating the Webster-Ashburton Treaty with Britain. Successfully supported the annexation of Texas as a new state.

JAMES KNOX POLK
11th President/1845 – 49 (Democratic)
Born 1795 in Mecklenburg County, North Carolina; died 1849. Believed that the United States had a "manifest destiny" to expand across the continent. The phrase was coined by newspaper editor John O'Sullivan in 1845 to justify the annexation of Texas and the occupation of Oregon. Tried to buy California and New Mexico from Mexico, and the Mexican War followed (1846– 48) when his offer was rejected. Under the Treaty of Guadalupe Hidalgo, ending the war, Mexico got $15 million in return for land that became the states of California, Nevada, and Utah and parts of Wyoming, New Mexico, Arizona, and Colorado. By the Oregon Treaty of 1846, Polk set the 49th parallel as U.S. – Canadian border.

ZACHARY TAYLOR
12th President/1849 – 50 (Whig)
Born 1784 in Orange County, Virginia; died 1850. Although a slave owner and conservative, Taylor became a supporter of the antislavery views of the Whigs and championed in 1850 the admission to statehood of California, an antislavery state. Died of cholera on July 9, 1850.

MILLARD FILLMORE
13th President/1850 – 53 (Whig)
Born 1800 at Locke, New York; died 1874. Sought to preserve the Union by conciliating the South over slavery but succeeded only in alienating both sides. Approved the dispatch of Commodore Matthew Perry to open Japanese ports to U.S. trade.

FRANKLIN PIERCE
14th President/1853 – 57 (Democratic)
Born 1804 at Hillsboro, New Hampshire; died 1869. Backed the $10 million Gadsden Purchase (1854) of the southern parts of Arizona and New Mexico from Mexico. Tried to conciliate the South over slavery, but guerrilla warfare broke out between proslavery and antislavery factions in Kansas in 1855– 56, heightening national tensions.

RAISING THE FLAG *A 19th-century etching records the announcement in 1845 of Texas's admission to the Union as the 28th state, just 9 years after the siege of the Alamo.*

KENTUCKY CONTEMPORARIES

Abraham Lincoln and Jefferson Davis, rival leaders during the Civil War, were both born in Kentucky. Their homes were a mere 100 miles apart. The men were also close in age—less than 9 months separated their dates of birth. Davis was born on June 3, 1808, and Lincoln on February 12, 1809.

THE 20-YEAR CYCLE OF FATE

Seven of the eight presidents who have died in office—either through illness or assassination—were elected at precisely 20-year intervals. The seven were William Harrison (elected 1840), Abraham Lincoln (1860),

James Garfield (1880), William McKinley (elected to a second term in 1900), Warren Harding (1920), Franklin Roosevelt (elected to a third term in 1940), and John Kennedy (1960).

The eighth was Zachary Taylor, who was elected in 1848 and died in office in 1850.

UNBEATABLE

Franklin Roosevelt, who won four presidential elections and spent 12 years in the White House—longer than any other president—is unlikely to have his record beaten. Since 1951 a constitutional amendment has barred presidential candidates from being elected to more than two 4-year terms.

PRESIDENTS OF THE UNITED STATES/Buchanan–Taft

JAMES BUCHANAN
15th President/1857–61
(Democratic)

Born 1791 at Cove Gap, Pennsylvania; died 1868. Proposed maintaining a "sacred balance" between North and South in an attempt to defuse the slavery crisis. Disapproved of slavery, yet recommended admission of Kansas as a slave state. Deplored talk of secession, yet balked at strengthening federal forces in the South. In the last months of his administration South Carolina and six other states—Mississippi, Florida, Alabama, Georgia, Louisiana, and Texas—seceded to form the Confederate States of America, with Jefferson Davis as president.

ABRAHAM LINCOLN
16th President/1861–65
(Republican)

Born 1809 in Hardin County, Kentucky; died 1865. Four more states—Virginia, Arkansas, North Carolina, and Tennessee—joined the Confederacy within 10 weeks after Lincoln's inauguration on

March 4, 1861. The Civil War began with a Confederate attack on federal troops at Fort Sumter, Charleston, South Carolina, on April 12, 1861. Lincoln called for 75,000 militia to fight the rebels and ordered a blockade of southern ports. Lincoln issued the Emancipation Proclamation in 1862, proclaiming freedom for slaves in Confederate-controlled states, but fighting was indecisive until the Union Army defeated a Confederate force led by Gen. Robert E. Lee at the Battle of Gettysburg (July 1–3, 1863) in Pennsylvania. Lee surrendered to the Union commander, Ulysses S. Grant, at Appomattox in Virginia on April 9, 1865, ending the Civil War. Lincoln was assassinated in a Washington theater 5 days later.

ANDREW JOHNSON
17th President/1865–69
(Democratic)

Born 1808 at Raleigh, North Carolina; died 1875. Angered Republicans—who had formed an alliance with prowar Democrats during the Civil War—by his conciliatory policies toward the

defeated South. Johnson's dismissal of Secretary of War Edwin Stanton in defiance of the Tenure of Office Act (1867) led to his impeachment; but the Senate failed by one vote to reach the two-thirds majority needed to convict him. Purchase of Alaska from Russia for $7.2 million was negotiated in 1867.

ULYSSES SIMPSON GRANT
18th President/1869–77
(Republican)

Born 1822 at Point Pleasant, Ohio; died 1885. Harsh postwar Reconstruction policy, with federal troops occupying the South, gave economic supremacy to northern bankers and industrialists. Speculators and politicians went south to exploit the defeated southerners, often carrying only a single bag made of a carpetlike material. They became known by the contemptuous term "carpetbaggers." First transcontinental railroad completed (1869). Constitution amended to give male blacks, including former male slaves—but not women of any

HIGH COMMAND *President Lincoln with high-ranking officers at Antietam, Maryland, the site of a bloody Union victory in 1862.*

TEDDY AND THE BEAR

Children's teddy bears get their name from President Theodore "Teddy" Roosevelt, who always disliked his nickname. On a hunting trip in Mississippi in 1902, Roosevelt refused to shoot a bear cub. The *Washington Post* publicized the incident in a cartoon, and an enterprising Boston shopkeeper, Morris Michtom, cashed in on the publicity by making toy bears and christening them "Teddy's bears."

HUNTER WHO WOULDN'T SHOOT *This* Washington Post *cartoon led to the invention of teddy bears, cuddly toys named after President "Teddy" Roosevelt.*

color—the vote (1870). Gen. George Custer and his troops killed by Sioux Indians at Battle of Little Bighorn in Montana (1876).

RUTHERFORD BIRCHARD HAYES
19th President/1877–81 (Republican)
Born 1822 at Delaware, Ohio; died 1893. Withdrew last federal troops from the South (1877), ending Reconstruction. Banned sale of firearms to Indians in an attempt to halt Indian wars in the West.

JAMES ABRAM GARFIELD
20th President/1881 (Republican)
Born 1831 at Orange, Cuyahoga County, Ohio; died 1881. Shot on July 2, 1881, by Charles Guiteau, just under 4 months after his inauguration on March 4. Died on September 19.

CHESTER ALAN ARTHUR
21st President/1881–85 (Republican)
Born 1829 at Fairfield, Vermont; died 1886. Supported the Civil Service Reform Act (1883), which was designed to limit the spoils system, under which political supporters got government posts.

GROVER CLEVELAND
22nd and 24th President 1885–89, 1893–97 (Democratic)
Born 1837 at Caldwell, New Jersey; died 1908. Established an Interstate Commerce Commission to bring national railways, and later interstate trade, under federal control. In September 1886 the Apache Indian war in the Southwest ended with the capture of the Apache chief Geronimo. The only president to serve two separate terms—Cleveland lost the 1888 election but won the presidency again in 1892. Economic slump in 1893 led to the collapse of more than 15,000 businesses.

BENJAMIN HARRISON
23rd President/1889–93 (Republican)
Born 1833 at North Bend, Ohio; died 1901. Supported Sherman Antitrust Act of 1890, which outlawed industrial monopolies and led to a series of "trust-busting" court cases. On December 29, 1890, federal troops massacred 200 Sioux Indians at Wounded Knee, South Dakota, ending the last Indian war in the West.

ALL ABOARD *A gaudy poster announces the opening of the first transcontinental U.S. railroad on May 10, 1869. Boosted by such promotions, the railroad rapidly became the main route to the Pacific Coast, replacing the slower wagon trains and sea voyages, and opened the West to a flood of new settlers.*

WILLIAM McKINLEY
25th President/1897–1901 (Republican)
Born 1843 at Niles, Ohio; died 1901. Declared war on Spain in April 1898 after influential U.S. newspapers blamed Spain for an explosion that sank the U.S. battleship *Maine* in Havana, Cuba, harbor. Spanish repression of 1895 Cuban rebellion had earlier led to large U.S. property losses on the island. After U.S. victory 4 months later, Cuba was placed under U.S. military rule. Spain ceded Puerto Rico, and the island of Guam, and sold the Philippines to the United States for $20 million. McKinley also annexed Hawaii and, through the Gold Standard Act of 1900, established gold as the backing for U.S. currency. McKinley was shot by an anarchist on September 6, 1901, and died 8 days later.

THEODORE ROOSEVELT
26th President/1901–09 (Republican)
Born 1858 at New York City; died 1919. Strengthened government controls over big business by attacking monopolies through the courts. In foreign affairs his slogan was "Speak softly and carry a big stick." After Colombia refused the United States permission to build a canal across Panama (then a Colombian province), Roosevelt backed a Panamanian rebellion, then in 1904 bought the Canal Zone for $10 million from the new regime. For his initiative in arranging negotiations to end the Russo-Japanese War, Roosevelt became in 1906 the first American to win the Nobel Peace Prize.

WILLIAM HOWARD TAFT
27th President/1909–13 (Republican)
Born 1857 at Cincinnati, Ohio; died 1930. Endorsed a constitutional amendment in 1913 authorizing a federal income tax. Admitted Arizona and New Mexico to the Union, bringing the number of states to 48.

PRESIDENTS OF THE UNITED STATES Wilson–Reagan

WOODROW WILSON
**28th President/1913–21
(Democratic)**
Born 1856 at Staunton, Virginia; died 1924. Centralized U.S. banking system through the Federal Reserve Act (1913), supported laws limiting the use of child labor and restricting hours of work, and backed a constitutional amendment giving women the vote. Sought to maintain U.S. neutrality in World War I, but after Germany refused to end submarine attacks on transatlantic shipping, declared war on April 6, 1917. Approved the purchase of Virgin Islands from Denmark for $25 million (1917). Unsuccessfully opposed Prohibition, which took effect in 1920.

WARREN GAMALIEL HARDING
**29th President/1921–23
(Republican)**
Born 1865 at Blooming Grove, Ohio; died 1923. Postwar recession led to high unemployment. Immigration was restricted by a quota system for the first time. After Harding's death on August 2, 1923, Senate investigations revealed widespread government corruption. The most damaging scandal involved the leasing of naval oil reserve lands, including an area in Wyoming called the Teapot Dome, to a private oil company. The secretary of the interior, Albert Fall—who had been appointed by Harding—was later jailed for accepting bribes totaling $350,000 to approve the leases.

CALVIN COOLIDGE
**30th President/1923–29
(Republican)**
Born 1872 at Plymouth, Vermont; died 1933. Aggressively pro-business, Coolidge encouraged tax cuts and government thrift. Was unable, though, to control the speakeasies that flourished in the cities in defiance of Prohibition or to stop the gang wars over their control. In 1929 American Samoa became a U.S. territory.

HERBERT CLARK HOOVER
**31st President/1929–33
(Republican)**
Born 1874 at West Branch, Iowa; died 1964. Great Depression triggered by stock market crash on October 24, 1929. By early 1930s more than 37,000 businesses had shut down and 12 million people were out of work. Hoover set up government-funded banks to funnel loans to businessmen and farmers in an effort to revive the economy, but the measures were ineffective.

FRANKLIN DELANO ROOSEVELT
**32nd President/1933–45
(Democratic)**
Born 1882 at Hyde Park, New York; died 1945. Launched a series of emergency measures, the New Deal, to revive the economy by massive government spending and to reorganize agriculture and industry under government controls. Led United States into World War II after Japanese surprise attack on Pearl Harbor, Hawaii (December 7, 1941). Backed formation of United Nations to ensure lasting peace after the war, but died of a cerebral hemorrhage on April 12, 1945, less than a month before Germany surrendered to the Allies.

HARRY S TRUMAN
**33rd President/1945–53
(Democratic)**
Born 1884 at Lamar, Missouri; died 1972. Authorized dropping atom bombs on Hiroshima and Nagasaki. Led effort to contain Communism during the Cold War, which was triggered by Soviet imposition of Communist regimes in nations of Eastern Europe after World War II. Set up the Marshall Plan to help postwar recovery in Europe and founded the North Atlantic Treaty Organization (NATO) as an anti-Communist military alliance. Sent troops to Korea. Administration marked by anti-Communist zeal of Sen. Joseph McCarthy, who alleged Communist infiltration of U.S. government.

DWIGHT DAVID EISENHOWER
**34th President/1953–61
(Republican)**
Born 1890 at Denison, Texas; died 1969. Was Allied commander-in-chief from 1943 to end of World War II, and his tremendous popularity as a war hero served him well when he entered politics. Settled the Korean War with an armistice signed in July 1953. Sponsored formation of the Southeast Asian Treaty Organization (1954) and sent military advisers to South Vietnam (1955). Senator McCarthy's power subdued by Senate censure (December 1954). Efforts to ease Cold War tensions with Moscow collapsed in May 1960 when a U.S. U-2 spy plane was shot down over the Soviet Union. A year later

THE SINKING OF THE LUSITANIA *Nearly 1,200 people, including 128 U.S. citizens, died when the British liner* Lusitania *was sunk by a German submarine on May 7, 1915. Anger over the attack helped fuel support for the U.S.A.'s entry into World War I two years later.*

Eisenhower broke diplomatic relations with Cuba, which had become a Communist under Fidel Castro. Alaska and Hawaii admitted to Union (1959).

JOHN FITZGERALD KENNEDY
35th President/1961 – 63
(Democratic)

Born 1917 at Brookline, Massachusetts; died 1963. Approved unsuccessful Bay of Pigs invasion of Cuba (April 1961). Provided armed helicopters and crews to fight Communists in South Vietnam, expanding U.S. involvement. In October 1962 ordered air and naval blockade of Cuba, forcing Soviet Union to withdraw nuclear missiles based on the island. Later set up the first hot line and teletype link between the White House and the Kremlin, and in October 1963 signed a nuclear test ban treaty with Britain and the Soviet Union. Was assassinated November 22, 1963.

LYNDON BAINES JOHNSON
36th President/1963 – 69
(Democratic)

Born 1908 at Stonewall, Texas; died 1973. Pushed through much of Kennedy's New Frontier program of laws designed to ease poverty and extend civil rights for blacks. Later, in his own social reform program, the Great Society, he cut taxes, enforced black voting rights, and set up the Medicare plan giving medical insurance to people over 65. Committed U.S. troops to ground combat in South Vietnam (1965) and approved the bombing of North Vietnam. Black civil rights leader Martin Luther King was shot dead in Tennessee (April 1968), sparking race riots in more than 100 cities. Sen. Robert Kennedy, brother of President Kennedy, was assassinated in Los Angeles (June 1968).

RICHARD MILHOUS NIXON
37th President/1969 – 74
(Republican)

Born 1913 at Yorba Linda, California. Improved relations with Communist powers. Supported China's admission to United Nations (1971). First president to visit China and the Soviet Union while in office (1972). Pioneered SALT treaties on arms limitations with U.S.S.R. (1972). Ended direct U.S. participation in Vietnam War (1973), the longest war in the nation's history. Forced to resign by domestic Watergate scandal (1974) following attempts to cover up crimes committed by aides during his 1972 reelection campaign.

GERALD RUDOLPH FORD
38th President/1974 – 77
(Republican)

Born 1913 at Omaha, Nebraska. Granted a pardon to President Nixon a month after taking office "for all offenses" committed during Nixon's administration. Inflation, largely caused by Arab oil price increases, triggered a recession that put 8.5 million people out of work in 1975. Signed the Helsinki Accords (1975) with the U.S.S.R., recognizing European border changes imposed by the Soviet Union after World War II in return for a guarantee of human rights in nations of Eastern Europe.

JAMES EARL CARTER
39th President/1977 – 81
(Democratic)

Born 1924 at Plains, Georgia. Pardoned Vietnam War draft evaders (1977). Negotiated treaty with Panama (1978), agreeing to give up U.S. control of the Canal Zone by 1999. Lost popularity because of high inflation and unemployment and because of his inability to rescue more than 50 Americans captured by Iranian militants at U.S. embassy in Tehran on November 4, 1979, and held hostage until January 20, 1981, the day Carter left office.

RONALD WILSON REAGAN
40th President/1981 –
(Republican)

Born 1911 at Tampico, Illinois. Cut taxes and government spending, reducing inflation from 13 percent in 1981 to near zero in the mid-1980s, and called for tax reforms. Oversaw a major economic recovery beginning in late 1982, but annual budget deficits topping $100 billion, the highest in U.S. history, and unprecedented balance-of-trade deficits posed new economic challenges. Early anti-Soviet talk gave way in second term to efforts at negotiation on arms control and other issues of mutual concern, while U.S. military defense was strengthened.

HEADLINES
Eisenhower's 1952 election victory, as seen by a newspaper in Abilene, Kansas, where he spent his youth. The 1963 assassination of President Kennedy. The 1974 resignation of President Nixon.

World leaders and losers

THE PRIME MINISTER WHO WASN'T

Robert Walpole, Britain's first prime minister, formally held the post only of first lord of the treasury. He became George I's chief minister because the German-born king had little knowledge of or interest in British affairs, and since he spoke no English he could not follow cabinet discussions. Since Walpole spoke no German, the two men were able to communicate with each other only in Latin.

Before Walpole's appointment British monarchs had themselves been the "prime" ministers, choosing and directing the government as they saw fit. But since Walpole's time the influence of the monarchy has gradually waned, and since the reign of Queen Victoria the prime minister has generally been the leader of the largest party in the House of Commons.

YOU . . . PRIME MINISTER!

The title of Britain's top political office was originally a term of abuse. It was used to describe the chief minister of a despotic monarch, and carried overtones that the politician was merely a lackey of the crown. Robert Walpole, George Grenville, and Lord North all denied hotly that they were prime ministers.

The title was given official recognition only in 1937, when the Salaries of the Ministers of the Crown Act made provisions for paying "the First Lord of the Treasury and Prime Minister"—the two offices that have, since the late 18th century, usually been held by the prime minister. Despite the recognition, the brass plate outside the front door of the prime minister's Downing Street residence in London still bears only the title of first lord of the treasury.

TURNING POINT

The Austrian archduke Franz Ferdinand might well have escaped assassination in Sarajevo in 1914—and World War I might not have broken out then—if his chauffeur had been told of a change of plan. At the beginning of the archduke's visit to the capital of Bosnia, then under Austrian rule, a bomb was thrown at the car, but it fell into the road and injured the occupants of the car behind. Panicked by the failure, six other would-be assassins, who were all members of the bomb thrower's group, left their posts along the route.

Later, after an official reception in the city hall, the archduke announced that he wanted to go to the hospital to see the injured men, rather than make a scheduled visit to a museum. Nobody told the chauffeurs, though, so the leading car turned to follow the route originally planned, and Franz Ferdinand's driver followed.

Realizing the mistake, the governor of Bosnia, who was riding with the archduke, told the chauffeur to turn the car around. The driver stopped—precisely opposite the spot where one of the remaining conspirators, Gavrilo Princip was standing on the pavement. With his target only a few yards away in an almost motionless car, Princip could hardly miss. He shot both the archduke and his wife, and was about to shoot himself when he was seized by bystanders. Because Princip was just 19, he escaped the death penalty, but he died 4 years later of tuberculosis in an Austrian prison. A member of a secret Serbian nationalist society, Princip is to this day regarded as a hero by many Serbians.

POLITICAL PUT-DOWNS, BRITISH STYLE

Politicians, who take special care not to offend voters, often seem to reserve their venom for use against fellow politicians. These are some of the memorable put-downs that have been aimed at British prime ministers—mostly by other prime ministers.

● "It is fitting that we should have buried the Unknown Prime Minister by the side of the Unknown Soldier." (Herbert Asquith on Bonar Law)

● "A sophisticated rhetorician, inebriated with the exuberance of his own verbosity." (Benjamin Disraeli on William Gladstone)

● "An arch-mediocrity, presiding over a cabinet of mediocrities." (Benjamin Disraeli on Lord Liverpool)

● "He is a self-made man, and worships his creator." (Member of Parliament John Bright on Disraeli)

● "His smile was like the silver plate on a coffin." (Member of Parliament Daniel O'Connell on Robert Peel)

● "He saw foreign policy through the wrong end of a municipal drainpipe." (Lloyd George on Neville Chamberlain)

● "He couldn't see a belt without hitting below it." (Margot Asquith on Lloyd George)

● "A sheep in sheep's clothing." (Attributed to Winston Churchill on Clement Attlee)

● "Churchill on top of the wave has in him the stuff of which tyrants are made." (Newspaper publisher Lord Beaverbrook on Churchill)

● "If Harold Wilson ever went to school without any boots, it was because he was too big for them." (Harold Macmillan on Wilson)

HIEDLER, HUTTLER, HITLER

Adolf Hitler, Nazi fuehrer of Germany from 1933 to 1945, was never known as Adolf Schicklgruber, despite the popular belief that he was.

Hitler's father, Alois, was the illegitimate son of a servant girl called Maria Schicklgruber. Five years after the birth of Alois, she married one Johann Georg Hiedler, but Hiedler took no steps to legitimize the boy, who used his mother's name until he was nearly 40. Then his stepfather's brother, Johann Huttler, persuaded the local priest to amend the parish register to show that Hiedler acknowledged paternity of Alois, though Huttler himself may well have been the father. From then on Alois called himself Hitler. He was 52 when Adolf was born in 1889 and died when the boy was 14.

The variations in the spelling of the family name seem to have resulted simply from the illiteracy that was then common in rural communities. The amendment took place 12 years before Adolf's birth. The name Schicklgruber was forgotten until Hitler's political opponents tried to discredit him by publicizing his father's illegitimacy.

WHAT KILLED NAPOLEON?

By the time Napoleon died on the island of St. Helena in 1821 at the age of 52, he was a very sick man. But the nature of the illness that killed him remains a mystery. Some doctors have argued that he died of cancer, others that he was poisoned by a servant. Still others have argued that Napoleon's death was hastened accidentally by toxic vapors from wallpaper dyed with arsenic in his house on St. Helena.

In 1982, however, a U.S. endocrinologist, Dr. Robert Greenblatt, came up with a new diagnosis: that far from being a sick *man,* the former emperor of France was becoming a sick *woman.* Dr. Greenblatt, who specializes in the study of hormones, says that Napoleon was suffering from a glandular disease known as Zollinger-Ellison syndrome. This explains, he says, why one of the doctors who examined the emperor's body after his death observed: "His type of plumpness was not masculine; he had beautiful arms, rounded breasts, white soft skin [and] no hair."

The disease, which was not understood at the time, left another clue, according to Dr. Greenblatt. Napoleon was an ardent lover during his marriage to his first wife, Josephine. But he himself admitted that he had little interest in lovemaking after he married his second wife, Marie Louise, in 1810.

DUKE OF LONDON

Winston Churchill turned his back on an offer of the highest rank in England's peerage for the sake of his son. When Churchill retired from the premiership in April 1955, he was offered a dukedom (rather than the usual earldom) in recognition of his unique wartime services. He toyed with the idea of becoming duke of London, but decided to decline the offer, mainly at the request of his son Randolph, who hoped to make a career in the House of Commons. At that time Randolph would not have been able to disclaim the peerage when his father died, and so would have been forced to serve in the House of Lords, which has prestige but no longer a great deal of power in the British political system.

NICKNAME THAT STUCK

The name *Tory,* now used for members of the Conservative Party in Britain, was once an insult. It comes from the Irish word *toiridhe,* meaning "pursuer." It was used to describe Irish robbers who preyed on travelers. From about 1680 it was applied sneeringly to the supporters of royal power, because they were thought to be chasing royal favors—and thus to politicians who supported traditional policies. In the United States the term *Tory* was used to describe people who supported the British during the Revolutionary War.

THE ALIEN RAJAHS

For over a century Sarawak, on the island of Borneo, was ruled as a virtually independent state by a family of English rajahs. The founder of the dynasty was James Brooke, an ex-employee of the East India Company. While sailing along the Borneo coast, Brooke helped the sultan of Brunei to suppress a revolt and, as a reward, the grateful sultan made him rajah of Sarawak in 1841.

The country prospered under Brooke's rule and that of his successor, his nephew, Sir Charles Brooke. Though Sir Charles placed Sarawak under British protection in 1888, the country retained its independence until the Japanese invaded it during World War II. After the defeat of Japan, the third and last of the white rajahs, Sir Charles Vyner Brooke, relinquished Sarawak to Britain. In 1963 Sarawak became a part of the newly independent state of Malaysia.

TAMERLANE THE TERRIBLE

The 14th-century Mongol warlord Tamerlane (1336–1405), who built an empire stretching from China to Turkey, had an insatiable appetite for death. In 1387, after a rebellious mob in Isfahan (in present-day Iran) had massacred 3,000 of his occupying troops, Tamerlane ordered his commanders to collect a sickening ransom. By the time the army moved on, 70,000 heads were heaped in grisly pyramids outside the city.

The city of Sivas in Turkey fell victim to a lethal trick. Tamerlane is said to have promised the city

HICCUPS OF FATE Napoleon (1769–1821) tried to poison himself once, in April 1814, after his enemies had achieved a military advantage in Europe. But the vial he used was 2 years old and had lost its potency. It merely gave him a violent attack of hiccups, which made him vomit and saved his life. Without the hiccups the Battle of Waterloo (June 18, 1815) would probably never have taken place.

ARSENIC AND OLD PAPER Napoleon spent the last 6 years of his life in exile, at Longwood House (above) on the South Atlantic island of St. Helena. The house's drawing room was decorated with wallpaper patterned with green-and-brown rosettes (detail, left). An English chemist tested a scrap of the paper in 1982 and found that the green shades (the lighter parts of the rosette) had been dyed with a commonly used pigment containing arsenic.

73

elders that not a drop of the defenders' blood would be shed if the city surrendered. He kept his promise to the letter: 4,000 Armenian soldiers who had led the city's resistance were buried alive; Christians were strangled or tossed in a moat to drown; and children were herded into a field to be trampled to death by Tamerlane's Mongol cavalry.

Despite his savagery, Tamerlane encouraged the arts and sciences, as well as construction of public works. He died not on the battlefield but in bed, possibly from the effects of a wild drinking party.

MING DYNASTY

Australia has had its own Ming dynasty. Prime Minister Sir Robert Menzies, who served two terms (1939–41 and 1949–66) covering a total of 21 years, longer than any other Australian prime minister, became known as Ming the Merciless—after one of the villains in the Flash Gordon comic strips and films—and his term at the official residence in Canberra was nicknamed the Ming dynasty.

DEATH AT POINT-BLANK RANGE

Only one British prime minister has been assassinated: Spencer Perceval, who was shot at point-blank range in the lobby of the House of Commons on May 11, 1812. The assassin was John Bellingham, a bankrupt merchant who believed that the government owed him compensation because the British ambassador had refused to intervene when he was arrested and imprisoned while trading in Russia. Bellingham was tried, convicted, and hanged within a week.

PICKLED HERO

The British admiral Horatio, Lord Nelson (1758–1805), who joined the navy at the age of 12 and was made a captain at 20, made his last sea voyage in a barrel. Mortally wounded in his hour of triumph at the Battle of Trafalgar in 1805, Nelson died aboard his flagship, *Victory*. His body was brought back to England for burial pickled in brandy to prevent it from decomposing on the long journey home.

HEADS OF GOVERNMENT/Australia–China

PRIME MINISTERS OF AUSTRALIA

1901 Edmund Barton
1903 Alfred Deakin
1904 John Christian Watson
1904 George Houston Reid
1905 Alfred Deakin
1908 Andrew Fisher
1909 Alfred Deakin
1910 Andrew Fisher
1913 Joseph Cook
1914 Andrew Fisher
1915 William Morris Hughes
1923 Stanley Melbourne Bruce
1929 James Henry Scullin
1932 Joseph Aloysius Lyons
1939 Earle Christmas Page
1939 Robert Gordon Menzies
1941 Arthur William Fadden
1941 John Joseph Curtin
1945 Francis Michael Forde
1945 Joseph Benedict Chifley

"SUPERMAC" *Harold Macmillan's term as British prime minister (1957–63) was marked by his success in improving U.S.-British relations, which had been strained by Britain's move to take over the Suez Canal in 1956. He also oversaw the transition to independence of 11 former British colonies.*

1949 Robert Gordon Menzies
1966 Harold Edward Holt
1967 John McEwen
1968 John Grey Gorton
1971 William McMahon
1972 Edward Gough Whitlam
1975 John Malcolm Fraser
1983 Robert James Lee Hawke

PRIME MINISTERS OF BRITAIN

1721 Robert Walpole
1742 Earl of Wilmington
1743 Henry Pelham
1754 Duke of Newcastle
1756 Duke of Devonshire
1757 Duke of Newcastle
1762 Earl of Bute
1763 George Grenville
1765 Marquess of Rockingham
1766 Earl of Chatham
1768 Duke of Grafton
1770 Lord North
1782 Marquess of Rockingham
1782 Earl of Shelburne
1783 Duke of Portland
1783 William Pitt

BOSTON MASSACRE *Five men were killed when British troops fired on a rioting crowd in Boston on March 5, 1770, fueling American resentment against British rule. Lord North later came to be blamed for the loss of the colonies despite his opposition to Britain's tough policies.*

1801 Henry Addington
1804 William Pitt
1806 Lord Grenville
1807 Duke of Portland
1809 Spencer Perceval
1812 Lord Liverpool
1827 George Canning
1827 Viscount Goderich
1828 Duke of Wellington
1830 Earl Grey
1834 Viscount Melbourne
1834 Robert Peel
1835 Viscount Melbourne
1841 Robert Peel
1846 Lord John Russell
1852 Earl of Derby
1852 Earl of Aberdeen
1855 Viscount Palmerston
1858 Earl of Derby
1859 Viscount Palmerston
1865 Lord John Russell
1866 Earl of Derby
1868 Benjamin Disraeli
1868 William Ewart Gladstone
1874 Benjamin Disraeli
1880 William Ewart Gladstone
1885 Marquess of Salisbury
1886 William Ewart Gladstone
1886 Marquess of Salisbury
1892 William Ewart Gladstone
1894 Earl of Rosebery
1895 Marquess of Salisbury
1902 Arthur Balfour
1905 Henry Campbell-Bannerman
1908 Herbert Henry Asquith
1916 David Lloyd George
1922 Andrew Bonar Law
1923 Stanley Baldwin
1924 James Ramsay MacDonald
1924 Stanley Baldwin
1929 James Ramsay MacDonald
1935 Stanley Baldwin
1937 Arthur Neville Chamberlain
1940 Winston Churchill
1945 Clement Attlee
1951 Winston Churchill
1955 Anthony Eden
1957 Harold Macmillan
1963 Alec Douglas-Home
1964 Harold Wilson

SAVED BY DEFEAT

William Lyon Mackenzie King, who was Canada's prime minister three times, was a fervent believer in the supernatural. In 1930 his fortune-teller predicted that if King called an election that year he would emerge from it stronger than ever. King called the election—and lost to Richard B. Bennett. But the fortune-teller turned out to be right. By losing the election, King avoided being blamed for the worst of the Depression. In 1935 he led his Liberal Party back to power, and remained prime minister for 13 years.

KNIGHT FLIGHTS

Canada's first prime minister, Sir John A. Macdonald, was a shrewd politician and an enthusiastic drinker. In a political career that spanned 47 years he fired off a hail of barbed aphorisms.

The teetotaling Liberal Party leader, George Brown, once criticized Macdonald in parliament for drunkenness. The prime minister was unflustered.

The honorable members, he retorted, "would rather have John A. drunk than George Brown sober."

BENNETT BUGGIES

During the early 1930s, when 1.5 million Canadians were out of work and the western plains were a dustbowl, many farmers hitched horses to their cars because they could not afford to license or buy gasoline for them. The strange vehicles came to be called "Bennett buggies" after Richard B. Bennett, who was prime minister during the worst years of the Depression. An abandoned farm was similarly dubbed a "Bennett barnyard," and hoboes brewed "Bennett coffee" with scavenged wheat or barley.

MAO ON THE MARCH

Mao Tse-tung (1893–1976), or Mao Zedong in the officially approved Pinyin spelling, ruled China from 1949 until his death. He rose to power largely through his leadership of the Long March during the 1930s, in which some 100,000 Chinese Communists, some with

1970 Edward Heath
1976 James Callaghan
1979 Margaret Thatcher

PRIME MINISTERS OF CANADA

1867 John A. Macdonald
1873 Alexander Mackenzie
1878 John A. Macdonald
1891 John J. C. Abbott
1892 John S. D. Thompson
1894 Mackenzie Bowell
1896 Charles Tupper
1896 Wilfrid Laurier
1911 Robert L. Borden
1920 Arthur Meighen
1921 W. L. Mackenzie King
1926 Arthur Meighen
1926 W. L. Mackenzie King
1930 Richard B. Bennett
1935 W. L. Mackenzie King
1948 Louis S. St. Laurent
1957 John G. Diefenbaker
1963 Lester B. Pearson
1968 Pierre E. Trudeau
1979 Joe Clark

COMBATIVE *Margaret Thatcher, Britain's first woman prime minister, battled inflation in the early 1980s, then won popularity by standing up to Argentina in the 1983 Falkland Islands war.*

1980 Pierre E. Trudeau
1984 John N. Turner
1984 Brian Mulroney

CHINA

Republic
1912 Sun Yat-sen
  (Sun Zhongshan)
1912 Gen. Yüan Shih-kai
  (Yüan Shikai)
1916 Li Yüan-hung (Li Yüanhong)
1917–28 China divided into
  Northern and
  Southern regimes
1928 Chiang Kai-shek
  (Jiang Jieshi)

Communist
1949 Mao Tse-tung
  (Mao Zedong)
1976 Hua Kuo-feng
  (Hua Guofeng)
1978 Ye Chien-ying (Ye Jianying)
1981 Deng Xiaoping

FIVE IN ONE *Five British prime ministers appear in this detail from "Statesmen of World War I," a canvas painted by Sir James Guthrie in the 1920s and now in the National Portrait Gallery, London. Perhaps prophetically, the artist made the central and most brightly lit figure Sir Winston Churchill, who was a cabinet minister for part of World War I but did not become the head of government until 1940, at a time when Britain's prospects in World War II were far from bright.*

Balfour

Bonar Law

Asquith

Lloyd George

Churchill

wives and families, marched and fought the staggering distance of 6,000 miles from the southeastern part of China to the northern province of Shenshi to escape the Nationalist forces of Chiang Kai-shek.

The march began in October 1934 and ended in October 1935. As many as 80,000 died—including Mao's two small children and his younger brother.

SERGEANT-MAJOR GANDHI

Mohandas K. ("Mahatma") Gandhi (1869–1948), advocate of nonviolence and leader of India's struggle for independence from Britain, served twice with British forces and was awarded a British decoration.

On the outbreak of the Boer War in South Africa in 1899, Gandhi was living in Natal, an adjacent British colony. For a mixture of motives, but primarily because he believed that civil rights for Indians would come about only when they assumed responsibilities, Gandhi raised an Indian ambulance corps of more than 1,000 men. At the end of the war, he and 37 others received the war medal.

FUNERAL FOR A LEG

A Mexican president once held a funeral for his own leg. Antonio de Santa Anna was the general who in 1836 led Mexican troops to victory over Texan rebels at the siege of the Alamo. American frontiersmen James Bowie—after whom the Bowie knife was named—and Davy Crockett died in the siege. Santa Anna's leg was amputated below the knee after he was wounded during a battle with French troops in December 1838. The general kept the leg at his hacienda near Veracruz for 4 years, during which he rose to become the virtual dictator of Mexico and the center of an adoring political cult.

On September 26, 1842, Santa Anna's supporters paraded his leg through Mexico City to the music of bands, then laid it to rest in a shrine known as the Pantheon of St. Paula. Two years later, the leg was stolen during the riots that accompanied Santa Anna's fall from power. Santa Anna died in 1876 at the age of 62. The fate of his leg remains unknown.

HEADS OF GOVERNMENT/France–Italy

PRESIDENTS OF FRANCE

1906 Clément Armand Fallières
1913 Raymond Poincaré
1920 Paul Deschanel
1920 Alexandre Millerand
1924 Gaston Doumergue
1931 Paul Doumer
1932 Albert Lebrun
1940–44 France occupied
1944–47 Provisional government
1947 Vincent Auriol
1954 René Coty
1959 Gen. Charles de Gaulle
1969 Alain Poher (interim)
1969 Georges Pompidou
1974 Alain Poher (interim)
1974 Valéry Giscard d'Estaing
1981 François Mitterand

CHANCELLORS OF GERMANY

Empire
1900 Bernhardt, Prince von Bülow

1909 Theobald von
      Bethmann-Hollweg
1917 Dr. Georg Michaelis
1917 Count Georg von Herling
1918 Prince Maximilian of Baden
1918 Friedrich Ebert

Republic
1919 Philipp Scheidemann
1919 Gustav Adolf Bauer
1920 Hermann Müller
1920 Konstantin Fehrenbach
1921 Karl Joseph Wirth
1922 Wilhelm Carl Josef Cuno
1923 Dr. Gustav Stresemann
1923 Wilhelm Marx
1925 Dr. Hans Luther
1926 Wilhelm Marx
1928 Hermann Müller
1930 Dr. Heinrich Brüning
1932 Franz von Papen
1932 Gen. Kurt von Schleicher
1933 Adolf Hitler
1945 Adm. Karl Dönitz

Federal Republic (West Germany)
1949 Konrad Adenauer
1963 Prof. Ludwig Erhard
1966 Dr. Kurt Georg Kiesinger
1969 Dr. Willy Brandt
1974 Walter Scheel
1974 Helmut Schmidt
1982 Helmut Kohl

PRIME MINISTERS OF INDIA

1947 Jawaharlal Nehru
1964 Lal Bahadur Shastri
1966 Indira Gandhi
1977 Morarji Desai
1979 Charan Singh
1980 Indira Gandhi
1984 Rajiv Gandhi

PRIME MINISTERS OF IRELAND

1922 Arthur Griffith
1922 Michael Collins
1922 William Thomas Cosgrave

Michael Collins of Ireland

Charles de Gaulle of France

Emperor Hirohito of Japan

DETAINED WITHOUT TRIAL

John Vorster, who as South African prime minister in the 1960s and 1970s backed the detention without trial of political dissidents, was himself imprisoned without trial for 2 years during World War II. He was arrested in 1942 under wartime regulations because of his activities as a leader of the anti-British, right-wing organization known as Ossewa-Brandwag (literally, "ox-wagon sentinel"). Vorster was kept in police detention for 3 months, then sent to an internment camp, where he passed his time lecturing in law and studying German, genetics, and sociology. He was released in 1944.

FROM BALLROOM TO BEEHIVE

For 10 years members of the New Zealand parliament debated measures and passed laws in the elegant surroundings of a ballroom. Their previous home, Parliament House in Wellington, burned down in 1907. Lord Plunket, the governor (the title changed to governor-general in 1917), moved out of his nearby residence, Government House, so that parliament could use the building. Debates were held in the ballroom there.

When the new Parliament House was finally ready in 1917, the governor's house was not handed back. It continued to be used as offices for another 52 years until it was torn down in 1969 to make room for a high-rise block of government offices nicknamed the Beehive (after a New Zealand national symbol). The Beehive was opened by Queen Elizabeth II in 1977, although it was unfinished. The prime minister, Sir Robert Muldoon, moved in with his cabinet in 1979.

NUMBER 10

The official residence of British prime ministers— Number 10 Downing Street—was built in about 1680 by Sir George Downing, a diplomat, spy, and turncoat whom the diarist Samuel Pepys called "a perfidious rogue." Downing supported Oliver Cromwell after the English Civil War (1642–49). But after the resto-

1932 Eamon de Valera	
1948 John Costello	
1951 Eamon de Valera	
1954 John Costello	
1957 Eamon de Valera	
1959 Sean Lemass	
1966 Jack Lynch	
1973 Liam Cosgrave	
1977 Jack Lynch	
1979 Charles Haughey	
1981 Dr. Garret FitzGerald	
1982 Charles Haughey	
1982 Dr. Garret FitzGerald	

PRIME MINISTERS OF ISRAEL

1948 David Ben-Gurion
1953 Moshe Sharrett
1955 David Ben-Gurion
1963 Levi Eshkol
1969 Golda Meir
1974 Yitzhak Rabin
1977 Shimon Peres (acting)
1977 Menachem Begin
1983 Yitzhak Shamir
1984 Shimon Peres
1986 Yitzhak Shamir

PRIME MINISTERS OF ITALY

Kingdom
1919 Francesco Nitti
1920 Giovanni Giolitti
1921 Ivanoe Bonomi
1922 Luigi Facta
1922 Benito Mussolini
1943 Marshal Pietro Badoglio
1944 Ivanoe Bonomi
1945 Ferruccio Parri
1945 Alcide de Gasperi

Republic
1946 Alcide de Gasperi
1953 Giuseppe Pella
1954 Amintore Fanfani
1954 Mario Scelba
1955 Antonio Segni
1957 Adone Zoli
1958 Amintore Fanfani
1959 Antonio Segni
1960 Fernando Tambroni
1963 Amintore Fanfani
1963 Giovanni Leone
1963 Aldo Moro

REBEL AND RULER *Gen. Francisco Franco, shown here in 1944, led the Nationalist forces that overthrew Spain's democratic republic in the Spanish Civil War (1936–39). Then he ruled Spain until his death in 1975.*

FASCIST FRIENDS *Italy's Benito Mussolini (second from left, front row) stands next to his ally and fellow dictator, Adolf Hitler, as they review troops in 1940. Mussolini, or Il Duce, as he liked to be called, entered World War II when Hitler's conquest of Europe seemed unstoppable. Five years later both men were dead.*

ration of the monarchy in 1660, Downing entered Charles II's service and betrayed some of his former associates, who were excuted. In 1738 George II offered Number 10 to Robert Walpole, Britain's first prime minister, as a present. Walpole declined it as a personal gift, but accepted it as an official residence for the holder of the premiership. Not all prime ministers have lived there, and not all its occupants have liked it. Herbert Asquith's wife, Margot, found it "an inconvenient house with three poor staircases." And Winston Churchill called it "shaky and lightly built."

PEACE OFFERING FROM A WARRIOR

The Cullinan diamond, pieces of which are now the largest stones in the British crown jewels, was given to Edward VII by a man who fought against Britain throughout the Boer War (1899–1902). The man was Gen. Louis Botha, who became South Africa's first prime minister in 1910. He was premier of the Transvaal when he persuaded his government to buy the 3,025-carat stone in 1907 and offered it to the king "as

an expression of . . . loyalty and affection." The diamond—which was found in January 1905 when a mine manager's walking stick accidentally knocked it out of a tunnel wall—was named after Sir Thomas Cullinan, who had discovered the mine, near Pretoria, in 1902. The gem was later cut into 9 large stones and 96 smaller ones, all flawless. The largest, the 530-carat Star of Africa, was set in the British royal scepter. Another, the 317-carat Cullinan II, is now the most valuable stone in the imperial crown. The two stones, which are kept in the Tower of London, are the world's largest cut diamonds.

IF AT FIRST . . .

The band of aristocrats who plotted the murder of Grigori Rasputin (c. 1871–1916) in St. Petersburg (now Leningrad) took on more than they bargained for when it came to carrying out their scheme.

According to Prince Yussupov, the leader of the conspirators, the dissolute Siberian monk and mystic, who virtually ruled Russia through his dominance of

HEADS OF GOVERNMENT/Japan–U.S.S.R.

1968 Giovanni Leone	1948 Shigeru Yoshida	1837 Gen. Anastasio Bustamante
1970 Mariano Rumor	1955 Ichiro Hatoyama	1841 Gen. A. López de Santa Anna
1970 Emilio Colombo	1956 Tanzan Ishibashi	1844 José Joaquín Herrera
1972 Giulio Andreotti	1957 Nobusuke Kishi	1846 Mariano Paredes
1973 Mariano Rumor	1960 Hayato Ikeda	1846 Gen. A. López de Santa Anna
1974 Aldo Moro	1964 Eisaku Sato	1848 José Joaquín Herrera
1976 Giulio Andreotti	1972 Kakeui Tanaka	1851 Mariano Arista
1979 Francesco Cossiga	1974 Takeo Miki	1853 Gen. A. López de Santa Anna
1980 Arnaldo Forlani	1976 Takeo Fukuda	1855 Juan Alvarez
1981 Giovanni Spadolini	1980 Zenko Susuki	1855 Ignacio Comonfort
1982 Amintore Fanfani	1982 Yashuhiro Nakasone	1858 Benito Juárez
1982 Giovanni Spadolini		1864 Austrian archduke Maximilian (emperor)
1982 Amintore Fanfani	**PRESIDENTS, EMPERORS, AND RULING GENERALS OF MEXICO**	1872 Sebastián Lerdo de Tejada
1983 Bettino Craxi		1876 Gen. Porfirio Díaz
	1821 Agustín de Iturbide (emperor)	1880 Manuel González
PRIME MINISTERS OF JAPAN	1824 Gen. Guadalupe Victoria	1884 Gen. Porfirio Díaz
	1828 Vicente Guerrero	1911 Francisco Madero
1945 Prince Naruhiko Higashikuni	1829 Gen. Anastasio Bustamante	1913 Gen. Victoriano Huerta
1945 Baron Kijuro Shidehara	1833 Gen. A. López de Santa Anna	1914 Venustiano Carranza
1946 Tetsu Katayama		1920 Álvaro Obregón
1946 Shigeru Yoshida		1924 Plutarco Elías Callas
1947 Tetsu Katayama		1929 Emilio Portes Gil
1947 Hitoshi Ashida		1929 Pascual Órtiz Rubio
		1932 Abelardo Rodríguez
		1934 Lázaro Cárdenas
		1940 Gen. Manuel Ávila Camacho
		1946 Miguel Alemán Valdéz
		1952 Adolfo Ruiz Corines

FAMILY TIES *Indira Gandhi (below), India's prime minister 1966–1977 and from 1980 until her assassination in 1984, was the daughter of Jawaharlal Nehru (right), India's first prime minister, 1947–64; and her son succeeded her.*

CHINESE HEAD
Deng Xiaoping, who turned 82 in 1986, emerged as China's tough, pragmatic boss after bitter infighting following the death of Mao in 1976.

Czar Nicholas II and his wife, was lured to a cellar in the prince's house late in the winter of 1916 by the promise of an evening of debauchery. There, he was first offered cakes and wine containing potassium cyanide. Rasputin may not have eaten a cake—he is reported to have disliked sweets—but to Yussupov's dismay, even the wine Rasputin drank had no apparent ill effects. Drawing a revolver, the prince shot Rasputin near the heart. Rasputin fell, but when Yussupov approached the apparently lifeless corpse, the monk attacked him and then crawled up the cellar stairs on his hands and knees in an attempt to reach the safety of the street. Another of the conspirators shot him in the shoulders and head while Yussupov beat his body with a rubber club. Convinced that they must have at last killed the monk, the conspirators bound and weighted Rasputin's body and threw it in the Neva River.

Even then Rasputin was apparently not yet dead. After the recovery of his corpse from the river, a postmortem examination revealed water in his lungs, indicating that he was still breathing at the time he was thrown in. In addition, there were deep marks on his wrists, suggesting that, having regained consciousness through the shock of the freezing water, he had struggled to break his bonds.

THE RED PRIEST

The mother of Joseph Stalin, dictator of the Soviet Union from 1927 until his death, intended her son to become a priest, not a revolutionary. In 1894, when the young Stalin was 14, he was awarded a scholarship to study at the theological academy in Tiflis, the capital city of his native province of Georgia. In 1899, however, Joseph left the academy.

According to his own account, Stalin was expelled for preaching Marxism, but according to his mother, he left for reasons of health. At the time, Stalin was known by his original name of Joseph Vissarionovich Dzhugashvili. Only later, after he became a revolutionary, did he adopt the name by which he is known to history: Stalin, or "man of steel."

1958 Adolfo López Mateos
1964 Gustavo Díaz Ordaz
1970 Luís Echeverría Álvarez
1976 José López Portillo
1982 Miguel de la Madrid Hurtado

PRIME MINISTERS OF NEW ZEALAND

1893 Richard John Seddon
1906 William Hall-Jones
1906 Joseph George Ward
1912 Thomas Mackenzie
1912 William Ferguson Massey
1925 Francis H. D. Bell
1925 Joseph Gordon Coates
1928 Joseph George Ward
1930 George William Forbes
1935 Michael Joseph Savage
1940 Peter Fraser
1949 Sidney George Holland
1957 Keith Holyoake
1957 Walter Nash
1960 Keith Holyoake
1972 John Ross Marshall
1972 Norman Eric Kirk
1974 Wallace Edward Rowling
1975 Robert Muldoon
1984 David Lange

PRIME MINISTERS OF SOUTH AFRICA

1910 Louis Botha
1919 Jan Christiaan Smuts
1924 James B. M. Hertzog
1939 Jan Christiaan Smuts
1948 Daniel François Malan
1954 Johannes Gerhardus Strijdom
1958 Hendrik Frensch Verwoerd
1966 Balthazar Johannes (John) Vorster
1978 Pieter Willem Botha

SPAIN

Prime Ministers
1923 Gen. Miguel Primo de Rivera
1930 Gen. Damaso Berenguer
1931 Adm. Juan Batista Aznar
1931 Niceto Alcala Zamora
1931 Manuel Azaña
1933 Alejandro Lerroux
1933 Diego Martínez Barrio
1933 Alejandro Lerroux
1934 Ricardo Samper
1934 Alejandro Lerroux
1935 Joaquin Chapaprieta
1935 Manuel Portela Valladares
1936 Manuel Azaña
1936 Augusto Barcia
1936 Santiago Casares Quiroga
1936 Diego Martinez Barrio
1936 José Giral

1936–39 Spanish Civil War
1939–73 Gen. Francisco
        Franco
1973 Adm. Luis Carrero Blanco
1973 Carlos Arias Novarro
1976 Adolfo Suárez González
1981 Leopoldo Calvo Sotelo
1982 Felipe González Márquez

U.S.S.R.

Provisional government
1917 Prince Georgy
        Yevgenyevich Lvov
1917 Alexander Fedorovich
        Kerensky

Soviet Socialist Republic
1917 Yakov Sverdlov
1919 Mikhail Kalinin

Union of Soviet Socialist Republics
1922 Vladimir Ilyich Lenin
1924 Grigori Zinoviev,
        Lev Kamenev, and
        Joseph Stalin
1927 Joseph Stalin
1953 Georgi Malenkov
1955 Marshal Nikolai Bulganin
1958 Nikita Khrushchev
1964 Alexei Kosygin and
        Leonid Brezhnev
1982 Yuri Andropov
1984 Konstantin Chernenko
1985 Mikhail S. Gorbachev

RED GIANTS *Vladimir Lenin (left), a leader of the 1917 Communist Revolution and then Soviet dictator until his death in 1924, meets with the man who succeeded him, Joseph Stalin, at Lenin's villa in central Russia in 1923. Stalin's one-man rule lasted from 1927 until his death in 1953.*

Laws and lawyers

THE FIRST LAWS

Rules and laws—and the conventions or customs from which they are descended—have been a part of human life ever since our ancestors first began to live in large and settled groups. But our knowledge is vague of laws that were in effect before the invention of writing in about 3500 B.C. The earliest known legal text was written by Ur-Nammu, a king of the Mesopotamian city of Ur, in about 2100 B.C. It dealt largely with compensation for bodily injuries, and with the penalties for witchcraft and runaway slaves.

LAWS OF BABYLON

One of the most detailed ancient legal codes was drawn up in about 1758 B.C. by Hammurabi, a king of Babylonia. The entire code, consisting of 282 paragraphs, was carved into a great stone pillar, which was set up in a temple to the Babylonian god Marduk so that it could be read by every citizen.

The pillar, lost for centuries after the fall of Babylon in the 16th century B.C., was rediscovered by a French archeologist in 1901 amid the ruins of the Persian city of Susa. Hammurabi's words were still legible. The pillar is now in the Louvre museum in Paris.

The laws laid down by Hammurabi were more extensive than any that had gone before. They covered crime, divorce and marriage, the rights of slave owners and slaves, the settlement of debts, inheritance and property contracts; there were even regulations about taxes and the prices of goods.

Punishments under the code were often harsh. Not only murderers but also thieves and false accusers faced the death penalty. And a child who hit his father could expect to lose the hand that struck the blow.

Nevertheless, Hammurabi's laws represented an advance on earlier tribal customs, because the penalty could not be worse than the crime—no more than an eye could be forfeit for an eye.

The code outlawed private blood feuds and banned the tradition by which a man could kidnap and keep the woman he wanted for his bride. In addition, the new laws took account of the circumstances of the offender as well as of the offense. So a lower-ranking citizen who lost a civil case would be fined less than an aristocrat in the same position—though he would also be awarded less if he won.

NAPOLEON'S LAW

The laws of much of continental Europe (particularly France), of Quebec in Canada, and of much of Latin America—along with the civil laws of Louisiana—owe their modern form largely to the work of a man who never even studied law. Napoleon Bonaparte, the Corsican soldier who became emperor of France after the French Revolution, established in 1800 five commissions to refine and organize the disparate legal systems of France. The result, enacted in 1804, was the Code Napoléon.

Some of its original 2,281 articles were drafted by Napoleon himself, and all were affected by his thinking, even though he was completely self-taught in legal matters. The code was a triumphant attempt to create a legal system that treated all citizens as equals, without regard to their rank or previous privileges. It was also so clearly written that it could be read and understood by ordinary people at a time when only Latin

scholars could make sense of the earlier laws handed down since Roman times. The code was adopted intact in most of the areas of Europe that Napoleon dominated and spread from there across the Atlantic, taking root particularly in French-speaking American communities. Many of its principles are still in force today.

BIRTH OF THE JURY

Juries first came into being in Norman Britain because of the Church. In medieval Europe, trials were usually decided by ordeals—in which it was believed God intervened, revealing the wrongdoer and upholding the righteous. In the ordeal by water, for instance, a priest admonished the water not to accept a liar. The person whose oath was being tested was then thrown in. If he floated, his oath was deemed to have been perjured. If he was telling the truth, he might drown but his innocence was clear.

In 1215, however, the Catholic Church decided that trial by ordeal was superstition, and priests were forbidden to take part. As a result, a new method of trial was needed, and the jury system emerged.

At first the jury was made up of local people who could be expected to know the defendant. A jury was convened only to "say the truth" on the basis of its knowledge of local affairs. The word *verdict* reflects this early function; the Latin word from which it is derived, *veredictum,* means "truly said." It was not until centuries later that the jury assumed its modern role of deciding facts on the sole basis of what it heard in court. Today the jury system has spread to numerous other countries. Every year more than 100,000 jury trials are held in U.S. courts—90 percent of the world total.

GOOD MEN AND TRUE

G. K. Chesterton (1874–1936), the English author who created the detective stories featuring a Roman Catholic priest named Father Brown, was also a powerful champion of the virtues of traditional common sense. After serving as a juror himself, Chesterton wrote an essay in which he summed up the value of the jury system in this way:

"Our civilization has decided, and very justly decided, that determining the guilt or innocence of men is a thing too important to be trusted to trained men. . . . When it wants a library catalogued, or the solar system discovered, or any trifle of that kind, it uses its specialists. But when it wishes anything done which is really serious, it collects 12 of the ordinary men standing round. The same thing was done, if I remember right, by the Founder of Christianity."

SUNDAY BLUES

The so-called blue laws in the United States might better be called Sunday laws, because their intent has been to restrict or forbid business, trade, paid work, or other commercial activities on Sunday, the Sabbath of the major Christian sects. In the mid-1980s blue laws had been repealed or simply ignored in many parts of the nation but continued to be observed in certain religious communities.

Secular arguments against blue laws are that they violate the constitutional guarantee of separation of church and state and favor one religion, Christianity. A secular argument supporting them is that everybody needs a day of rest each week. Proscribing work on Sundays goes back at least to 4th-century Rome under Constantine the Great, and the practice was strictly supported in the religion-oriented American colonies. The term *blue law* is said to have arisen from a list of Sabbath rules printed on blue paper for residents of New Haven, Connecticut, in 1781.

A CRY FOR JUSTICE

Residents of the Channel Islands still have a legal right to call for help from a nobleman who died more than 1,000 years ago: Rollo, the first duke of Normandy, who died in 932. Householders can invoke the right by falling on their knees in the presence of witnesses and shouting "*Haro, haro, haro, à l'aide, mon prince; on me fait tort*" ("Haro, haro, haro, help, my lord; I am being wronged") and then reciting the Lords's Prayer in French. The Clameur de Haro, as the law is known, was used as recently as April 1950 on the Isle of Guernsey to stop the local water board from digging up the road outside the home of a local citizen.

Once the cry has been made, the work in dispute must be stopped for 12 months so that the issue can be settled in court. If work is not stopped, the offender can be imprisoned for 24 hours in a castle dungeon— as can a citizen who raises the cry wrongfully.

"LET THE BODY BE BROUGHT . . ."

In the United States, Britain, and many other English-speaking countries, the law of habeas corpus guarantees that nobody can be held in prison without trial.

Habeas corpus became law because of a wild party held in 1621 at the London home of a notoriously rowdy lady, Alice Robinson. When a constable appeared and asked her and her guests to quiet down, Mrs. Robinson allegedly swore at him so violently that he arrested her, and a local justice of the peace committed her to jail.

When she was finally brought to trial, Mrs. Robinson's story of her treatment in prison caused an outcry. She had been put on a punishment diet of black bread and water, forced to sleep on the bare earth, stripped, and given 50 lashes. Such treatment was barbaric even by the harsh standards of the time; what made it worse was that Mrs. Robinson was pregnant.

Public anger was so great that she was acquitted, the constable who had arrested her without a warrant was himself sent to prison, and the justice of the peace was severely reprimanded. And the case, along with other similar cases, led to the passing of the Habeas Corpus Act in Britain in 1679. The law is still on the British statute books, and a version of it is used in the United States, where the law was regarded as such an important guarantee of liberty that Article 1 of the Constitution declares that habeas corpus shall not be suspended except in cases of "rebellion or invasion."

Habeas corpus is part of a Latin phrase—*Habeas corpus ad subjiciendum*—that means "Let the body be brought before the judge." In effect, a writ of habeas corpus is an order in the name of the people (or, in Britain, of the sovereign) to produce an imprisoned person in court at once.

WIG AND PEN *A bewigged and pompous judge props up two dozing colleagues in a satirical engraving by the English artist William Hogarth (1697–1764). Judges and lawyers in Britain have been wearing wigs for at least 300 years. Originally, the wigs were made of human hair; today they are made of horsehair or nylon. Barristers also wear gowns in court. Junior barristers wear gowns made of alpaca wool; senior barristers, known formally as queen's counsel, are more commonly called "silks," because their gowns are made of silk. The gown of every barrister has a small pouch sewn into the left shoulder—a reminder of the time when barristers were not allowed to solicit fees and instead solicitors would quietly slip golden guineas into the pouch. Another legacy from the past is Britain's Privy Council, which was set up after the Norman Conquest in A.D. 1066 to advise the monarch. Today the council's judicial committee acts, on petition, as a final court of appeal for nine independent nations, all former British colonies: Australia, the Bahamas, Fiji, Jamaica, Kiribati, New Zealand, Singapore, Trinidad and Tobago, and Tuvalu. It also hears certain kinds of appeals from the United Kingdom.*

MORALITY REPEALED

Ratified in January 1919, the 18th Amendment to the U.S. Constitution prohibited "the manufacture, sale, or transportation of intoxicating liquors" within the United States. A little less than 15 years later, the 21st Amendment repealed Prohibition. Viewed as a triumph of morality by its backers, Prohibition forced a double standard on many tippling politicians, among them the next U.S. president, Warren G. Harding. As a senator in 1919, he had spearheaded passage in the Senate of some tough laws to enforce the 18th Amendment. Two years later Harding brought many of his drinking buddies with him as advisers into the White House.

ONLY A TRICKLE *The impossible task of stopping the flow of liquor during Prohibition fell to a few federal agents, such as these.*

WAYWARD WILLS

● When Margaret Montgomery of Chicago died in 1959, she left her five cats and a $15,000 trust fund for their care to a former employee, William Fields. The will stipulated that Fields was to use the trust income solely for the cats' care and feeding, including such delicacies as pot roast. If, however, he outlived all the cats, Fields would inherit the trust principal. Nine years after the last cat, Fat Nose, died at 20, and Fields, 79, was $15,000 richer.

● Probably the largest single group of pets to be named specifically in a will were the 150 or so dogs given $4.3 million by Eleanor Ritchey, an oil company heiress who died in 1968. The dogs were mostly strays she had collected at her 180-acre ranch in Deerfield Beach, Florida. When the last dog, Musketeer, died in June 1984, the entire estate—by then grown to nearly $12 million—went under the will to the Auburn University School of Veterinary Medicine to support research on dog diseases.

● Charles Vance Millar, a Canadian lawyer and financier who died a bachelor in 1926, bequeathed the bulk of his fortune to whichever Toronto woman gave birth to the largest number of children in the 10 years after his death. Four women eventually tied in the "stork derby" that followed the publication of his will. Each had 9 children, and they shared between them $750,000. A fifth woman who had 10 children was ruled out because 5 were illegitimate.

● One of the world's shortest wills was left by an Englishman named Dickens. Contested in 1906 but upheld by the courts, it read simply: "All for mother."

● A 19th-century London tavernkeeper left his property to his wife—on the condition that every year, on the anniversary of his death, she would walk barefoot to the local market, hold up a lighted candle, and confess aloud how she had nagged him. The theme of the confession was that if her tongue had been shorter, her husband's days would have been longer. If she failed to keep the appointment, she was to receive no more than £20 a year, just enough to live on. Whether the wife decided to take the bigger bequest or spare herself humiliation is not known.

THE MAN THEY COULDN'T HANG

It is no mere legend that if a condemned man survived three attempts to hang him, his sentence was automatically commuted to life imprisonment. In 1885 John Lee, a 19-year-old footman, was found guilty of murdering his spinster employer. Condemned to death, Lee then survived three attempts by a hangman, John Perry, to execute him at Exeter Gaol in Devon, England.

The wooden gallows had warped in the rain, and three times the trapdoor refused to open when Lee was placed on it—although it worked perfectly when he was moved down to the ground. So Lee was sentenced to life imprisonment and spent 22 years in jail. Released in 1907, he emigrated to the United States, married there, and died of natural causes in 1933 at the age of 67.

SILENT WITNESS

A slander case in Thailand was once settled by a witness who said nothing at all. According to the memoirs of Justice Gerald Sparrow, a 20th-century British barrister who served as a judge in Bangkok, the case involved two rival Chinese merchants, Pu Lin and Swee Ho. Pu Lin had stated sneeringly at a party that Swee Ho's new wife, Li Bua, was merely a decoration to show how rich her husband was. Swee Ho, he said, could no longer "please the ladies."

Swee Ho sued for slander, claiming Li Bua was his wife in every sense—and he won his case, along with substantial damages, without a word of evidence being taken. Swee Ho's lawyer simply put the blushing bride in the witness box. She had decorative, gold-painted fingernails, to be sure, but she was also quite obviously pregnant.

STIFF SENTENCES

One of the most bizarre methods of execution was inflicted in ancient Rome on people found guilty of murdering their fathers. Their punishment was to be put in a sack with a rooster, a viper, and a dog, then drowned along with the three animals. In ancient Greece the custom of allowing a condemned man to end his own life by poison was extended only to full citizens. The philosopher Socrates died in this way. Condemned slaves were beaten to death instead.

In medieval Europe some methods of execution were deliberately drawn out to inflict maximum suffering. Some felons were tied to a heavy wheel and rolled around the streets until they were crushed to death. Others were strangled, very slowly. One of the most terrible punishments was hanging, drawing, and quartering. The victim was hanged, cut down, and disemboweled while still alive—then finally beheaded and the body cut into four pieces. It remained a legal method of execution in Britain until 1814.

The first country to abolish capital punishment was Austria in 1787. Russia abolished it for every crime except treason on the orders of Czar Nicholas I in 1826, but it was reintroduced after the Communist Revolution in 1917.

KILLER TORTOISE

In July 1981 a tortoise was sentenced to death for murder. Tribal elders in Kyuasini, a village in Kenya, formally condemned the tortoise because they suspected it of causing the death of six people, apparently through magic. However, because none of the villagers was prepared to risk the tortoise's wrath by carrying out the execution, it was chained to a tree instead. The tortoise was later freed after the government promised an official inquiry into the deaths.

INTERNATIONAL COURTS

Since the creation of the United Nations in 1945 and the European Economic Community in 1958, four major international courts have been set up.

INTERNATIONAL COURT OF JUSTICE
Often known as the World Court. Composed of 15 judges, all of different nationalities and all elected by the U.N. General Assembly and the Security Council. Sits in The Hague in the Netherlands. Deals with cases involving disputes between nations and the interpretation of international treaties.

EUROPEAN COURT OF JUSTICE
Composed of 10 judges, all of different nationalities and appointed by the 10 member governments of the European Economic Community (EEC). Sits in Luxembourg. Interprets EEC law at the request of national courts and deals with cases brought by states or individuals against EEC institutions, or by EEC institutions against member states; but cannot impose fines or prison sentences.

EUROPEAN COURT OF HUMAN RIGHTS
Composed of 21 judges (one for each of the 21 nations in the Council of Europe) appointed by the council's parliamentary assembly. Sits in Strasbourg, France; hears cases involving alleged breaches of the 1950 European Convention for the Protection of Human Rights and Fundamental Freedoms.

INTER-AMERICAN COURT OF HUMAN RIGHTS
Composed of seven judges elected by the General Assembly of the Organization of American States. Sits in San José, Costa Rica. Hears cases involving the interpretation of the 1969 American Convention on Human Rights.

HOW LAWS ARE MADE

UNITED STATES
The U.S. Congress, the lawmaking arm of the federal government, consists of two houses: the House of Representatives and the Senate. Any congressman in either house, or the president, may initiate new legislation.

The proposed legislation, or bill, is first introduced in the House of Representatives, then referred to one of the standing committees, which organizes hearings on it and may approve, amend, or shelve the draft. If the committee passes the bill, it is considered by the House of Representatives as a whole. If passed there, it goes to the Senate for a similar sequence of committee hearings and general debate.

In cases of disagreement, the House of Representatives and the Senate confer together. Once passed by the Senate as a whole, the bill has to be examined by two more standing committees—the Committee on House Administration and the Senate Committee on Rules and Administration—and is then signed by the speaker of the House and by the president of the Senate. Finally, it must be signed by the president, who has the right to veto it. If the president vetoes a bill, it can still become law—but only if it is passed by a two-thirds majority in both houses of Congress.

BRITAIN
New legislation in Britain usually starts in the House of Commons and then goes on to the House of Lords. In each house a bill is considered in three stages, called readings. The first reading is purely formal, to introduce the bill. The second reading is usually the occasion for debate. After the second reading the bill is examined in detail by a committee.

The bill is then returned to one of the houses for the report stage, when it can be amended. If passed after its third reading, it goes to the other house. Amendments made to a bill by the House of Lords must be considered by the Commons. If the House of Commons does not agree, the bill is altered and sent back to the Lords. In the event of persistent disagreement between the two houses, Commons prevails.

Finally, the bill goes to the reigning monarch for the royal assent. Nowadays the royal assent is merely a formality. In theory the queen could still refuse her consent, but the last monarch to use this power was Queen Anne, who vetoed the unpopular Scottish Militia Bill in 1707.

SOVIET UNION
New legislation is initiated by the Presidium of the Communist Party's Central Committee. It is then considered by either the Presidium of the Supreme Soviet or the Presidium of the Council of Ministers. Once approved by either body, the legislation has the force of law, though it may also be formally approved by the Supreme Soviet.

ORDER! ORDER! *The speaker, or chairman, bangs his gavel while congressmen chat, shout, or read newspapers, in this mocking English view of the U.S. House of Representatives in 1861.*

Great explorers

THE LONG SHORTCUT

To the end of his life the Italian explorer Christopher Columbus clung to his belief that by sailing westward he had found, not a new continent, but merely a short sea route to Asia. Like many other geographers, Columbus underestimated the size of the earth and overestimated the east-west extent of Asia. A globe made at the time of Columbus's first voyage in 1492 showed the distance from the Azores westward to Japan as no greater than the length of the Mediterranean. Thus, when Columbus reached the Bahamas, he thought he had arrived at the Indies (the collective name then used for India, Southeast Asia, and Indonesia), which is why the Caribbean islands are called the West Indies. During Columbus's second voyage, in 1494, the crew had to swear that Cuba's coast, along which they sailed, was "the mainland at the beginning of Cathay." The penalties for breaking the oath depended on rank: offenders paid a fine, had their tongue cut out, or received 100 lashes.

QUARREL THAT ENDED IN TRAGEDY

A disagreement about the source of the Nile River may have cost the life of the Victorian explorer John Hanning Speke. He died on the day he was to debate the question with his fellow explorer and archrival, Sir Richard Burton. Burton and Speke had twice gone to East Africa together. On the second expedition, when Burton became too ill to travel, Speke went off on his own in July 1858 and found the lake he named Victoria. This he believed, correctly, to be a main source of the Nile, but Burton disagreed. The controversy rumbled on until 1864, when Speke agreed to the public debate. He is known not to have been looking forward to it, because he was less articulate than Burton. On the afternoon prior to the confrontation, Speke went bird hunting—and was later found dead from shotgun wounds. Whether it was an accident or suicide is uncertain.

THE FAITHFUL FOLLOWERS

Ten Africans gave their lives to get the body of the Scottish missionary and explorer David Livingstone back to Britain after his death in 1873. When he died at the village of Chitambo in what is now Zambia, the 60 Africans of his party determined to take the body to the coast near Zanzibar so that it could be returned home for burial. They removed and buried the heart and other internal organs, embalmed the body with raw salt, and dried it in the sun. The grueling journey, which covered 1,000 miles, took from May 1873 to February 1874, and 10 men died during it. But the survivors' only reward was their normal wages, paid by the British consul in Zanzibar, and a commemora-

DR. LIVINGSTONE, I PRESUME *The Anglo-American explorer and journalist Henry Stanley (left) steps forward to utter his famous greeting to the Scottish missionary David Livingstone after finding him at a village beside Lake Tanganyika on November 10, 1871. This engraving, drawn with Stanley's guidance, was published in 1872.*

tive medal struck by the Royal Geographical Society, which probably very few of them received. Only the two Africans who led the journey—Chuma and Susi—gained real benefit, because they were brought to Britain to help fill gaps in Livingstone's journals. The fame they gained in Europe made them sought-after guides when they returned to Africa.

THE SHIP THAT CHANGED ITS NAME
The *Golden Hind,* the flagship in which the English explorer Sir Francis Drake sailed around the world in 1577–80, started the voyage with a different name. Originally called the *Pelican,* the flagship was suddenly renamed after Drake suppressed a threatened mutiny and had the ringleader, Thomas Doughty, beheaded. The execution created a political problem for Drake, because Doughty had been secretary to Sir Christopher Hatton, a major shareholder in the expedition and a man who stood high in Queen Elizabeth's favor. Drake solved the problem by an astute gesture of flattery. The crest on Hatton's coat of arms was "a hind statant or," which means "a standing golden female deer without antlers." And by the time Drake's ships entered the Strait of Magellan a few days after Doughty's execution, the *Pelican* had become the *Golden Hind* in Hatton's honor.

SAVED BY ABORIGINES
John King, the first European to cross the Australian continent and survive, did so only because of the generosity of aborigines. King was a member of the Burke and Wills expedition that set out from Melbourne in 1860. After the expedition established a supply camp at Cooper's Creek in South Australia, four men went on northward and reached the tidal marshes at the edge of the Gulf of Carpentaria. They were Robert Burke, William Wills, King, and Charles Gray. But supplies ran out on the return journey, and Gray died of starvation before the party reached Cooper's Creek.

The three exhausted survivors were horrified to discover at the camp a message saying that the support party had given up waiting and gone back south that same morning. Even though the support party had left a cache of supplies, the three men were so weak and ill that they could not get far without help. Aborigines had helped the explorers on their outward trip by giving them fish. However, Burke, crazed by hunger, lost his head when they approached again and ordered

King to fire over their heads to drive them away. Burke and Wills later died of starvation. But King used his rifle to shoot birds for aborigines and so win their help. A relief party found him, emaciated but alive, 6 months later.

DOGS VERSUS PONIES
The British explorer Capt. Robert Scott made a fatal decision during the preparations for his journey to the South Pole. He chose ponies as his principal hauling animals, although he did use a few dogs. The Manchurian ponies were specially purchased in Siberia by one of the team members. Scott insisted on the ponies being white, because he believed they were hardier than brown ponies. But since few Manchurian ponies are white, the dealers were able to demand and get inflated prices for them.

Preliminary trips across the Antarctic ice painfully exposed the vulnerability of the ponies, but Scott refused to alter his plans. As a dog lover, he also refused to kill and eat dogs. On the drive to the pole, the ponies were killed one by one to provide meat for both men and dogs. And after the dogs were taken back to the base camp, sledges pulled by men in harness became the only way of shifting equipment and stores. The Norwegian explorer Roald Amundsen, meanwhile, relying on his experienced dog teams, reached the pole in December 1911, 34 days ahead of the British expedition. Scott and his four companions all died on the return journey.

LAST WORDS Capt. Robert Scott and the last of his companions died of cold and hunger in Antarctica just 11 miles from a supply base and safety. This is the last page of Scott's diary, discovered later beside his frozen body.

PRISON DIARY
Marco Polo's account of his years of travel in Asia, *The Description of the World,* or *The Travels of Marco Polo,* was written when he was a prisoner of war. After his return from his travels he served in the Venetian forces fighting Genoa. He was captured in 1298 and imprisoned in a Genoese jail. There he and another prisoner, Rusticiano of Pisa, an experienced writer, collaborated on the book. It was widely read and was given the nickname *Il Milione* ("The Million"), perhaps because of the innumerable tall stories it was thought to contain.

DOUBLE FIRST
A few days before Robert Peary announced he had reached the North Pole in 1909, another American, Dr. Frederick Cook, claimed he had done so a year earlier, and many believed Cook and doubted Peary. Peary's critics doubted that Peary could have made the journey as quickly as he claimed. Peary insisted that he had covered 800 miles at an average speed of 34 miles a day, and that at times he had traveled at least 46 miles in a day—figures that British explorer Wally Herbert, who led the first crossing of the Arctic ice cap in 1968–69, has described as incredible. Some critics also pointed out that the only non-Eskimo

witness of Peary's dash to the Pole was his servant. In addition, Peary's book on the expedition contained many discrepancies because it was ghostwritten, and Peary undermined his own credibility by refusing to admit that he had been helped with the writing, even in the face of much evidence the contrary.

Later, however, Frederick Cook's account was questioned. His claim to have climbed Mount McKinley was shown to be false, and later imprisonment for a financial fraud did not improve his reputation.

Nevertheless, the case for or against Peary or Cook is not settled, and probably never will be. The reason: the North Pole is merely a point on a constantly shifting ice pack. So nothing remains there to substantiate either man's claim.

WESTWARD HO
Huge Chinese fleets were traveling westward into the Indian Ocean on diplomatic and trading missions more than 60 years before the Portuguese explorer Vasco da Gama became the first European sailor to round Africa in 1498. Chinese records show that between 1405 and 1433 Cheng Ho, a navigator, made seven voyages into the South China Sea and on to the coasts of India and East Africa. On his fifth expedition Cheng took a fleet of 63 ships and 27,000 men, including 180 doctors, as far as the Persian Gulf. His largest vessels, well over 1,500 tons, were more than 600 feet long.

FIRST EXPLORERS BY AIR
In 1897 three Swedish explorers set off from Spitsbergen, an island in the Arctic Ocean, to fly a balloon to the North Pole. They were never seen again. The explorers had hoped to control the balloon's course by keeping low and dragging trail ropes along the ground, which would reduce their speed to less than that of the wind. Sails could then be used to steer. But soon after the balloon was launched it almost came down in the sea, and some of the trail ropes and a quantity of sand ballast were lost. Relieved of weight, the balloon disappeared into the clouds. The full story emerged only in 1930 when some of the expedition's remains were found by sealers. What seems to have happened is that the balloon became so coated with ice that it was forced down well short of the North Pole.

The marooned explorers spent nearly 2 months struggling to get back over the moving ice, but they finally died on White Island—only a few miles from the spot where they had taken off.

ERIC THE SALESMAN
The frigid island of Greenland was given its name as a sales ploy. The island, most of which lies under a permanent ice cap, was discovered by the Norseman Eric the Red, who sailed from Iceland in A.D. 982. He said that he chose the name to make the island sound more attractive to potential settlers. The strategy worked. In 986 about 25 small shiploads of emigrants followed Eric from Iceland to Greenland and founded a Norse colony that lasted for 500 years.

MUTINY ON THE *DISCOVERY*
Mutiny cost the British explorer Henry Hudson his life. He and his young son (thought to have been about 12 years old), along with seven other men, were set adrift in an open boat in the Canadian bay that now bears his name. In November 1610, while Hudson was seeking a northwest passage to the Orient, his ship *Discovery* became trapped in the ice in James Bay, a southern arm of Hudson Bay. Food ran short, and Hudson was accused of distributing it unfairly.

When the ice began to break up, the crew mutinied, and Hudson and the others were put over the side in June 1611.

None of the occupants of the boat was ever seen again. Of the 13 mutineers, four were killed in a fight with Eskimos, one died of scurvy, and eight managed to get back to England. Despite the mutiny, the sailors appear to have escaped punishment, probably because their experience made them too valuable to future exploration. Only four of the mutineers were finally brought to trial—5 years later—and, though most of the trial records have been lost, it is thought that they were able to save themselves from the gallows by throwing the blame onto the five dead men.

GOLDEN AGE OF DISCOVER'

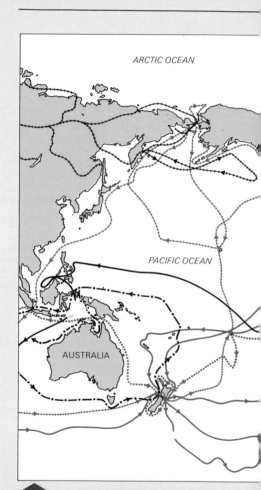

World exploration 1492–1780
Europeans were not the first to explore unfamiliar parts of the world—Polynesians sailed across the Pacific and aborigines colonized Australia centuries earlier. But Europeans were the first to draw together knowledge of the globe as a whole. The map shows the routes of the major explorers. The dates of their voyages are given in the key below.

·············	*Christopher Columbus 1492–93*
-------	*Vasco da Gama 1497–99*
————	*Ferdinand Magellan 1519–22*
– – – –	*Willem Barentz 1594–97*
·············	*Jacques Cartier 1534–36*
–·–·–·	*Abel Tasman 1642–44*
·············	*Robert La Salle 1679–82*
+++++++	*Vitus Bering 1728–30, 1741*
·············	*James Cook 1st journey 1768–71*
————	*James Cook 2nd journey 1772–75*
++++++	*James Cook 3rd journey 1776–80*

BARGAIN EXPEDITION

For much of its way, the Lewis and Clark expedition of 1804–06 was led by a woman, Sacagawea, a Shoshone Indian. With her husband, a French Canadian trapper named Toussaint Charbonneau, she guided the party westward from her home in what is now central North Dakota. In November 1805, having traveled up the Missouri River and down the Columbia River, the expedition reached the Pacific Ocean. A bronze statue in Helena, Montana, commemorates Sacagawea's contribution to the westward expansion of the United States.

The famous trip was one of the biggest bargains in U.S. history. President Thomas Jefferson was eager to know more about the commercial potential of the vast lands west of the Mississippi—even though not all belonged to the United States—and selected two friends in their thirties, Meriwether Lewis (1774–1809) and William Clark (1770–1838), to mount the expedition, which set out from its camp near St. Louis, Missouri, in May 1804. The year before, Jefferson had asked Congress to approve funds for the expedition. The lawmakers fretted that France, Spain, England, and other Euopean nations, which claimed pieces of the western lands, would object to the venture. But Congress ultimately agreed to Jefferson's request: $2,500 to finance the whole trip.

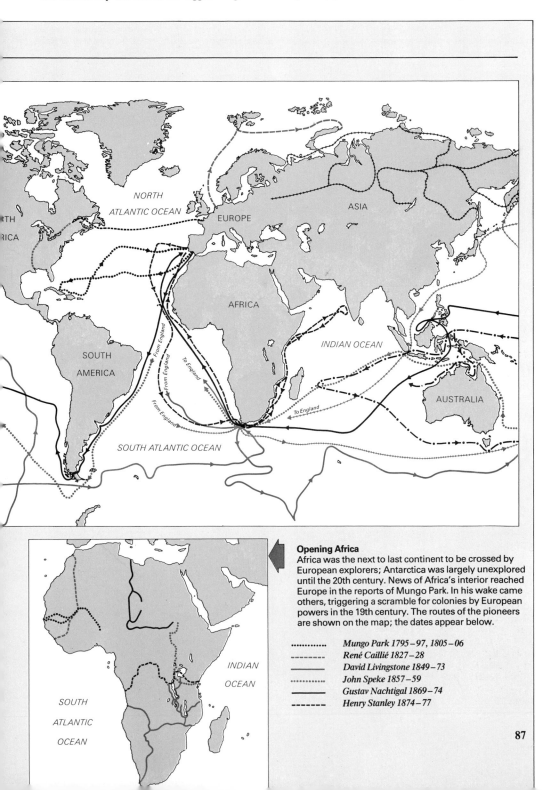

Opening Africa

Africa was the next to last continent to be crossed by European explorers; Antarctica was largely unexplored until the 20th century. News of Africa's interior reached Europe in the reports of Mungo Park. In his wake came others, triggering a scramble for colonies by European powers in the 19th century. The routes of the pioneers are shown on the map; the dates appear below.

....	*Mungo Park 1795–97, 1805–06*
- - - - - -	*René Caillié 1827–28*
————	*David Livingstone 1849–73*
••••••••••	*John Speke 1857–59*
▬▬▬▬	*Gustav Nachtigal 1869–74*
– – – –	*Henry Stanley 1874–77*

The rich and their money

THE HISTORY OF CASH

Without money, people must exchange tangible goods for any they receive. This system, known as barter, was the earliest form of trade. It still has its uses today. A certain amount of barter is sometimes written into East-West trade agreements because Soviet-bloc countries are often short of the "hard" currencies that the West recognizes as being of value. Nevertheless, barter is extremely limiting. Some goods perish easily and are difficult to transport. And if a woman requires, say, eggs, and has only sacks of corn, then she has to find a person with eggs who wants corn. In addition, large objects are often not divisible. A cart seller, faced with a buyer's offer of 12 sacks of corn, may not need so much grain. But he has nothing to give but a whole cart.

Because of these difficulties, divisible or widely available items, such as beads or salt, have often become means of exchange—that is, money.

By around 2000 B.C. metal, which was attractive and durable, had become a means of exchange in the Middle East. By the 7th century B.C. bronze was being cast in China into miniature knives or spades, each assigned a fixed value.

The forerunners of modern coins first appeared in Lydia, in what is now eastern Turkey, between 690 and 650 B.C. They were crudely cast slugs of electrum, a natural alloy of gold and silver found locally. Their value depended on their weight.

Paper money
The use of paper money is believed to have started in China between the 7th and 9th centuries A.D., to overcome shortages of coins. In Europe in medieval times, letters of credit—amounting to personal banknotes—were exchanged between tradespeople who knew and trusted each other. Later, a practice grew in which goldsmiths gave receipts for gold left in their charge, and these receipts were exchanged as money. During the 18th and 19th centuries, first private bankers, then central banks, took over this role. They issued notes, each of which was a "promise to pay"—words that still appear on many banknotes. Until the 1930s—when many countries, including the United States, went off a strict gold standard—the holders of banknotes were usually entitled, in theory, to demand from the issuing bank that the notes be redeemed in gold. Since then, however, notes have resumed the status of primitive beads—a means of exchange that has value only because the paper is trusted.

Both checks and credit cards are essentially "promises to pay," backed by the person signing the check or guaranteed, within limits, by a bank or credit card company. More recently still, in much of the developed world, electronic accounting has begun to replace notes and coins altogether. The transaction takes place only on a computer screen—without a trace of metal or paper.

CROESUS'S GOLD *The fabulously wealthy King Croesus of Lydia, in present-day Turkey, issued the first coins with fixed values. This 0.3-ounce gold coin, bearing the imprint of a lion and a bull, was issued by Croesus in about 550 B.C. It was worth 10 silver coins.*

CASH FLOW
Many of the great personal fortunes of the past 100 years have flowed from holes in the ground: oil wells. Once the steam engine had been adapted to drive a drill, and a method of cleaning, or "refining," oil had been developed in the mid-19th century, the way was open for oil products to become an indispensable fuel for modern industry. For those who foresaw this and had the chance to invest in the new oil business, there were vast riches to be gained.

It was oil that gave American tycoon John D. Rockefeller the opportunity to acquire probably the biggest personal fortune of modern times. At present-day values, it would be worth more than $50 billion. Rockefeller (1839–1937) began his business life at 16 as a bookkeeper. By the age of 19 he had saved enough to help start a small company, and he then entered the oil business, backing Samuel Andrews, the inventor of an oil-refining process. In 1870 Rockefeller helped found the Standard Oil Company, which swallowed smaller firms and by 1879 controlled 90 percent of U.S. oil refineries, making Rockefeller master of 75 percent of the world's oil production. His huge conglomerate survived until 1911. Then the U.S. Supreme Court ordered it to be broken up because of its overwhelming commercial power.

Arab oil sheiks are now often thought to be the wealthiest people in the world, but they are usually rulers of states rather than gatherers of purely personal riches. Sheik Zayed bin Sultan al Nahayan of the United Arab Emirates was said at the peak of oil prices in the early 1980s to be entitled to over $10 billion a year—more than $20 million a day—from oil royalties that were not made over officially to the state. He is not thought to draw anything approaching that amount, however, and so the remainder of the money is kept by the emirates.

HALF A BILLION IN A DAY
The eccentric American recluse Howard Hughes (1905–76) once made half a billion dollars in one day. He received a single banker's draft for $546,549,171 in 1966 in return for his 75 percent holding in Trans World Airlines (TWA).

WEALTH OF THE STARS
Great fortunes can be made by the stars of pop music, films, and sports. Paul McCartney is said to have earned more than $57 million since 1979, mostly from royalties for songs written and recorded while he was with the Beatles. The actor Marlon Brando is said to

HIGH FLIER *In the 1930s Howard Hughes was on top of the world as a business tycoon, moviemaker, and dashing daredevil who built and flew planes that set many world records. But he died a recluse, tormented by phobias and paranoia.*

WHY MONEY IS VALUED

Money by itself is not wealth. It is a means by which people can exchange goods that do have value. Money is a piece of trust that is passed from hand to hand, and it can easily be stored without perishing. It has value as long as the trust lasts.

To be trusted, it seems that money must be in limited supply. If there is too much, people trust it less. They then want more and more of it in return for goods. It can become practically worthless, as in times of chronic inflation. If there is too little money, people cannot expand their activities because they cannot find the credit in the form of loans to keep themselves going while they develop new ventures. This can lead to economic depression, or recession, which means not enough investment, not enough money in people's pockets to cause demand for goods, and not enough jobs.

Lines and quotas
The problem of achieving the delicate balance between too little and too much money has bedeviled 20th-century governments all over the world. Some Communist countries have tried to find a way around the problem by fixing prices artificially and planning their economies, allocating quotas of goods to state factories. But shortages and lines, reminiscent of wartime rationing, often result.

have collected a fee of $3.7 million, plus $15 million in profit percentages, for a mere 12 days' work in the 1978 film *Superman*—a rate of more than $1,500,000 a day.

By those standards, athletes are not so well paid, although Czech-born U.S. tennis star Martina Navratilova earned $2,173,556 in 1984, placing herself among the highest-earning sports celebrities.

EXECUTIVE PRIVILEGE
Naming the top-paid corporate executive is often a difficult matter because of the many kinds of compensation awarded to executives. Some payments may be deferred, for example, or relate to the exercise of stock options. For 1985 *Business Week* gave Victor Posner, chairman of the DWG Corporation, a U.S. conglomerate, the top spot with his total compensation for the year of $12,739,000; but *Forbes* magazine named Lee Iacocca, chairman of the Chrysler Corporation, who earned $11,499,000.

These figures were barely out when another contender appeared. In a registration statement for the Securities and Exchange Commission, a document that U.S. law requires be made public, Aaron Spelling reported that in 1985 he earned $15,700,000 as the president of his own television production company. The Hollywood producer of such shows as *Dynasty, Hotel,* and *Love Boat* began his career as an actor in

1953, but lack of steady work made him turn to writing and producing. By the mid-1980s he had become one of the most successful independent producers in the history of commercial TV.

RICH AND POOR
The Persian Gulf oil states, among them the United Arab Emirates and Kuwait, are the world's richest nations in terms of the average income per person. The richest of all in the early 1980s was the United Arab Emirates, with an income of almost $25,000 a year for every man, woman, and child. The poorest was Bhutan—a Himalayan nation whose citizens have an average income of less than $100 a year.

BIG SPENDER
On inheriting more than $1 million in cash and oil wells, one of the fastest fortune-losers in modern times deserted his wife, moved into a smart New York hotel, and began offering champagne and oysters to all comers. In one year of riotous living in 1864, John Washington Steel, known as Coal-Oil Johnny, ran through his entire inheritance. Then, sober and bankrupt, he went back to his wife, moved west to Nebraska, and found a job as a railway depot supervisor. Steel died—solvent again, but not rich—in 1920.

NOT WORTH THE PAPER
● In Germany after World War I the government printed money frantically as the mark's value plunged. Wheelbarrow loads of paper notes were needed to buy bread and ordinary household goods. In 1921 the German rate of exchange was 81 marks to one U.S. dollar. By September 1923 a U.S. dollar was worth 100 million German marks.

● The world's worst inflation occurred in Hungary in 1946. Hungary, like many other countries, had gone off the gold standard in 1931. By June 1946 one 1931 gold pengö was worth 130 million million million paper pengös, and prices in Budapest were being raised as often as 10 times a day. The pengö was later replaced as a unit of currency by the present forint, and by 1980, inflation was down to a modest 4 percent a year.

THE FIRST INCOME TAX
Taxes have been collected since ancient times. The earliest—recorded in Mesopotamia and Egypt—were taxes on imported goods (the equivalent of customs duties) and on houses and land. Income tax, however, is a relatively recent invention. It was first introduced in Britain in 1799 by British prime minister William Pitt—with a top rate of just 10 percent—to help pay for the Napoleonic Wars. Progressive income tax—increasing in proportion as earnings rise—was developed in Prussia in 1853 and has been used in Britain since 1907, in the United States since 1913, and in France since 1917.

PRACTICAL CASH *Central African "coins" included the* din kouga, *a spearhead (left), and the* swenga, *a spade (below).*

WIVES FOR RODS *Among the Palaboroas of South Africa, one of these copper rods (below) would buy two cows, but a wife was worth five rods.*

SHELLING OUT *Shells have been widely used as currency in Africa and the Pacific islands. These shell-like seed husks, strung on a cord, were used by the Olemba people of southern Africa.*

MONEY BELT *Seashell beads from Indian wampum belts were used as money by 17th-century American settlers. Five purple beads equaled one English penny.*

Languages 1: the beginnings

HOW WRITING DEVELOPED

Pictures are the basis of the earliest known examples of writing. The symbols used were simplified pictures of objects or people, such as the sun or a king. But other symbols were needed to express more abstract ideas, such as "love" or "happy," and since concepts could not be drawn directly, early writers borrowed and adapted from symbols already in use, often adding new distinguishing marks. The early deciphered scripts—among them the cuneiform script of Mesopotamia, and early Chinese and Egyptian hieroglyphics—all developed symbols for abstract concepts in this way. The word *cuneiform* is from the Latin *cuneus,* meaning "wedge," and cuneiform script is so called because of its wedge-shaped outlines, made by scribing on wet clay with reeds. *Hieroglyphics* comes from Greek words meaning "sacred writings" (or "carvings").

These pictorial scripts later gave way to writing in which the symbols came to stand for words themselves, rather than the things the words represented; the pictorial element disappeared or became marginal. Symbols that represent entire words are called logograms; they include the modern English symbols &, =, +, and % as well as all the numerals.

Symbols for syllables

Later, symbols were used to stand for the sound of a word or its various syllables. Called syllabaries, they developed alongside or as an alternative to logograms in many cultures. The first syllabaries appeared in the Middle East in about 2000 B.C. Chinese characters—derived from a form of picture writing first devised in about 1500 B.C.—still combine symbols for words with symbols for syllables. They are often called logo-syllabic for this reason. However, Japanese script, which developed from Chinese in about A.D. 800, is wholly syllabic. Known as *kana,* it is still in use in Japan.

The last major step in the development of writing was from the syllabary to the alphabet. Syllabaries were an advance over picture writing and logograms in that they broke down a language into simpler units and vastly reduced the number of symbols in use. Alphabets took this process of simplification further, breaking down the language into individual sounds. Alphabets seem to have been invented only in the West, beginning with the early consonantal alphabets of the eastern Mediterranean in about 1700 B.C., and followed by Greek, which added separate symbols for vowels to those for consonants.

MESSAGE IN STONE *Primitive languages used pictures—sometimes stylized—to convey ideas. This Central American carving, or glyph, is the symbol for grass.*

THE FIRST SPEAKERS

Using plaster casts of ancient human remains, anthropologists have tried to estimate when the human skull and vocal tract became suitable for speech. Even Neanderthals, who lived between about 100,000 and 40,000 years ago, probably could not produce the range of sounds found in known languages. Our species, *Homo sapiens sapiens,* first appeared about 35,000 years ago; and this has led some anthropologists to conclude that speech developed sometime between then and about 20,000 years ago. Unfortunately these conclusions tell nothing about the origins of language. Between the first *H. sapiens sapiens* and the earliest reconstructed spoken languages is a gap of at least 20,000 years.

Most European languages, and many of southwest Asian and Indian tongues, belong to a single family: the Indo-European. This is the largest group of spoken languages—more than 80 in all. No written evidence of the parent language has been found, but scholars have reconstructed parts of it by comparing common elements in related languages, and have called the parent tongue Proto-Indo-European. Opinions differ on where Proto-Indo-European was first spoken. Some scholars believe that it was the language of farming peoples in an area of northeastern Europe around 4000 B.C. Others assert that it was spoken by nomadic tribes who ranged across southeastern Europe and southern parts of Russia.

WHERE WRITING BEGAN

The earliest known examples of writing are forms of picture writing found on clay tablets in parts of the Middle East and southeastern Europe. The pictures—such as a foot, representing the idea of walking—were drawn on clay while it was soft. The tablets were then baked in the sun. Many have been found in what is now Iraq and Iran. The earliest tablets date from around 3500 B.C. and usually record land sales, business deals, and tax accounts. Linguistic symbols from this period have been found on clay tablets in Romania as well.

In addition, archeologists have found even older tokens in the Zagros Mountains of Iran. The tokens are marked with symbols that seem to represent numbers and specific objects, such as animals and garments. The tokens date from about 8500 B.C.—some 5,000 years before the accepted date for the invention of writing. But scholars are divided as to whether the symbols were a form of artistic decoration or whether they qualify as the beginnings of a written language.

CHILDREN WHO INVENTED A LANGUAGE

In the 1880s thousands of immigrants from Europe and Asia came to Hawaii to work in the islands' new sugar industry. The result was linguistic chaos. The immigrants—mostly Chinese, Japanese, Korean, Spanish, and Portuguese—could understand neither the largely English-speaking owners of the sugar plantations nor the native Hawaiians.

At first a crude pidgin English emerged while each group struggled to make sense to the others. But by about 1910—in other words, within a single generation—a remarkably sophisticated language had developed. Now known as Hawaiian Creole,

NEW LETTERS FOR OLD

All the alphabets in use around the world today can be traced to a North Semitic alphabet that emerged in about 1700 B.C. at the eastern end of the Mediterranean. From this alphabet developed Hebrew, Arabic, and Phoenician. The Phoenician alphabet was adopted and adapted by the Greeks, who introduced it into Europe in modified form around 1000 B.C. The Greeks standardized the direction of the written lines to read from left to right and added some symbols for vowels. The Greek alphabet gave rise to both the Roman alphabet, now used for all modern Western European languages (including English), and the Cyrillic alphabet. Cyrillic—devised by two Greek missionaries, St. Cyril and St. Methodius, in the 9th century A.D. and named after St. Cyril—is now used in Eastern Europe and the Soviet Union. The North Semitic alphabet also gave rise to the Aramaic alphabet, which spread eastward to develop into Asian alphabets, such as Hindi.

Phoenician	Old Hebrew	Early Greek	Early Latin	Cyrillic (Russian)	Arabic	Hindi (Devanagari)	Roman (English)
ⲕ	⳨	Δ	⋀	⋀	∣	ⴺ	A

TAKE A LETTER *The same letter can appear very different in different alphabets. Yet all the forms can be traced back to a common ancestor. The word* alphabet *itself comes from the first two Greek letters:* alpha *and* beta.

BABIES WHO SUFFERED FOR SCIENCE

More than 2,500 years ago two babies were kept in isolation for at least 2 years in an effort to track down the world's first language. The cruel experiment was the work of an Egyptian pharaoh, Psamtik I, who ruled from about 663 to 609 B.C. He believed that without anyone they could mimic, children would instinctively talk the world's "original language." So he ordered two newborn babies of poor parents to be put into solitary confinement.

A shepherd was given the job of looking after the babies, and Psamtik insisted that nobody should speak in their presence. When after 2 years the shepherd reported that the children had begun to repeat a sound like *bekos*—the Phrygian word for bread—Psamtik concluded that Phrygian was the oldest language. But he overlooked the fact that *bekos* sounds like the bleating of sheep, something the children had often heard. So the experiment proved nothing.

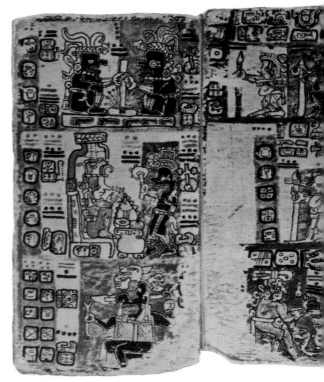

the language included ready-made words from all the original languages in the islands' mix, but its grammar bore little resemblance to any of them.

Hawaiian Creole's astonishingly rapid evolution was studied in detail by Derek Bickerton, a professor of linguistics at the University of Hawaii. In his book *Roots of Language,* Professor Bickerton concluded that Hawaiian Creole had been invented entirely by children at play. Only the children could have done it, he argues, because there was no time for their parents to have learned the new language and passed it on. Indeed, he points out, the parents did not understand Hawaiian Creole when it first appeared; they had to learn it from their offspring.

THE MYSTERY OF THE RUNES

The runic alphabet is one of the oldest in northern Europe, with most early examples dating from about the 3rd century A.D. Long associated with magic and witchcraft, runes have been found in some 4,000 inscriptions and a few manuscripts, mainly in Britain, Scandinavia, and Iceland. Nobody knows for certain where the alphabet came from. Some scholars believe that it was derived from the Etruscan alphabet, which was used in southern Europe after about 800 B.C., and brought north by the Goths after their invasions of the Roman Empire.

WOLF CHILDREN

Children left in the wild or otherwise deprived of human contact do not learn how to speak spontaneously, linguistic experts believe. There are now more than 50 recorded cases of "wolf children"—mostly in India—who have been found living among animals. All were mentally retarded and unable to speak.

A report on a similar case in the United States was published in 1977. It concerned a girl called Genie, who was locked up in her home for 14 years—and who later made very limited progress in speaking.

LEFT, RIGHT, RIGHT, LEFT *The first scripts known to have been written in regular lines are two Minoan scripts from Crete dating from about 2000 B.C. Known as Linear A and Linear B, they are thought to have been written in lines arranged like the furrows in a plowed field, so that the words ran alternately from left to right and right to left. The Western habit of writing consistently from left to right down the page became established only around 1000 B.C. Elsewhere other patterns dominated. The Mayas of Central America, for example, wrote numbers in columns read from bottom to top. In the detail pictured above from a Mayan manuscript, the numbers appear as groups of dots and dashes between pictorial symbols; in each group, each dot stands for 1, and each dash for 5. Semitic languages, such as Arabic and Hebrew, are still written from right to left. In traditional Chinese, words are arranged in vertical columns rather than in horizontal lines. The columns are read from top to bottom and right to left.*

Languages 2: the way we talk

BABY'S FIRST WORDS

Babies begin to recognize elements of speech sounds very shortly after birth, and they imitate the patterns of speech before they begin to form intelligible words. At the age of 1 month they begin to distinguish between certain features of the spoken language that will later represent vowels and consonants. In English, for example, the presence or absence of the vocal cord vibration that distinguishes *pin* and *bin*, *to* and *do*, is picked up at this early age.

At about 4 months babies can gauge the mood of an adult from his tone of voice. And at 6 months the sounds infants make begin to mimic the rhythm and intonation of adult speech. Soon afterward it is possible to tell English, French, and Chinese children apart simply on the basis of tape recordings of their unintelligible babblings.

PLAY LANGUAGES

Children all over the world devise their own secret play languages, mostly just for fun. But some scholars argue that these play languages introduce changes into the languages of adults and should be taken seriously. Two British researchers, Iona and Peter Opie, even suggested in a book published in 1959 that, in every generation, some developments in language are due to innovations first created by children at play. Records of these children's languages go back only to the 19th century, when experts began to consider their significance. But play languages probably have a far longer history. Three used in Britain are back slang, pig Latin, and eggy-peggy speech.

Back slang takes its name from saying words backward, as in "Tup taht koob yawa" (for "Put that book away"). The colloquial British word *yob*, for example, is back slang for "boy." A commoner version of back slang takes the final sound and moves it to the front of the word, adding an occasional consonant for ease of pronunciation, as in "Teput tetha keboo yawa." In pig Latin the first sounds are placed at the end of the word and "ay" or "e" added, as in "Utpay atthay ookbay wayay." Eggy-peggy, or aygo-paygo, speech inserts an extra syllable, as in "Pegut thegat begook egaway."

RHYMING SLANG

Rhyming slang, the traditional language of Cockney Londoners, can be traced back to the 17th century, though it did not become widely known until the 19th century. It probably began as a kind of thieves' jargon in the East End of London, though rhymes of this kind are also known in other parts of the world and have been found among criminals and certain other groups, such as gypsy clans, whose desire to preserve secrecy is strong.

More than 1,000 examples of English rhyming slang have been recorded, though not all are still in use. Among them are *Hampstead Heath* (teeth), *Barnet Fair* (hair), *bottle and glass* (class), *bird-lime* (time in prison), *saucepan lid* (kid, meaning "child" or "to fool"), *china plate* (mate), *Scapa Flow* (go), *jam jar* (car), *tit for tat* (hat), *lean and lurch* (church), *Cain and Abel* (table), *frog and toad* (road), *apples and pears* (stairs), *plates of meat* (feet), *whistle and flute* (suit), *half-inch* (pinch, in the sense of steal), *butcher's hook* (look), and *loaf of bread* (head—whence comes "use

WHO SPEAKS WHAT

There are almost 5 billion people in the world, and all told they speak some 9,000 languages and dialects. The 12 most widespread languages are the mother tongues of about 2.5 billion people.

The largest number, a billion, speak Chinese, but since spoken Chinese has several mutually unintelligible dialects, it is perhaps misleading to call it one language. The Mandarin dialect, however, is spoken by more than 500 million Chinese and will probably become even more widespread now that it is taught in schools throughout China.

English is the next most widely spoken language. It is the mother tongue of 350 million people and is used by another 1.2 billion people—in all, about one-third of the world's population. Below it in the world league table are Hindi (145 million); Russian (130 million); Spanish (125 million); German (120 million); Japanese (116 million); and Arabic and Bengali, each with 100 million speakers.

GRIMM'S LAW

Grimm's law is one of several linguistic laws that explain the different forms taken by words in languages with a common origin. It takes its name from the pioneering German scholar Jacob Grimm (1785–1863). He showed, for example, that many *p* sounds in Latin and Greek had become *f* sounds in English and German. Thus the Latin word *pater* had become *father* in English and *Vater* (pronounced fah-ter) in German. And the Latin word *pisces* became *fish* in English and *Fisch* in German. Grimm—who with his brother Wilhelm was the author of *Grimm's Fairy Tales*—charted the transformation of whole groups of vowels and consonants in several Indo-European languages. He was also the first to prove that such changes take a regular form and are not, as had been thought, random processes affecting only certain words.

your loaf"). In most cases only the first, nonrhyming half of each phrase is used—*Barnet*, say, or *bottle*—and to a stranger the conversation is incomprehensible.

English rhyming slang has sometimes been exported. Australians still call a bar, or pub, a *rubbedy*, from the expression "rub-a-dub-dub."

TYPING MADE DIFFICULT

The Japanese, whose mechanical genius has put them in the forefront of the industrial world, have had trouble producing a practical typewriter that can handle their own language. The reason is that even everyday Japanese requires more than 2,000 characters—far more than would fit on a conventional keyboard.

Written Japanese is a blend of three writing systems: *kanji*, which is borrowed Chinese ideograms (characters that symbolize the idea of a word rather than its sound), and two systems of *kana*, which are phonograms (characters that represent spoken sounds). Large dictionaries can contain more than 10,000 *kanji* symbols, but after World War II the government revised the language, creating a simplified vocabulary of about 1,800 *kanji* symbols for everyday use. The two *kana* systems, *hiragana* and *katakana,* date from the 9th century, and each contains 112 symbols.

A Western typewriter can cope with an entire language, including numbers and punctuation, with fewer than 50 keys. In comparison, a Japanese typewriter is a cumbersome machine with a limited vocabulary. It consists of a single key and 2,000 symbols held in a matrix. The typist moves the matrix each time to get the appropriate *kanji* or *kana* character opposite the key. A second set of 2,000 symbols is available for more complex subjects. If one of these additional symbols is required, the character is selected and placed in an empty space in the matrix. Because of this laborious procedure, a typewriter is seldom used for Japanese business correspondence.

HOW MANY WORDS
Precise estimates of the number of words in any language are almost impossible. Living languages are always changing. The Merriam-Webster *Third New International Dictionary*—one of the largest English dictionaries—has a vocabulary of over 450,000 words. But even this massive number is thought by linguistic scholars to represent barely half the total vocabulary of the English language. There are hundreds of dialects in English, each with many words for which no dictionary entries exist, and new words are constantly appearing in such fields as literature and science. Even highly educated people are likely to know less than 10 percent of the words in the total vocabulary. And they are likely to make regular use in speech or writing of less than 10 percent of that fraction—usually fewer than 10,000 words in all.

DIVIDED BY A COMMON LANGUAGE
Dialects in China can be mutually unintelligible—as different from one another as French, Italian, and Spanish. But they share the same written language, which is understood by literate Chinese in all parts of the world, whatever dialect they speak. As a result, a Cantonese-speaking businessman in Hong Kong could not discuss a project by phone with a Mandarin-speaking businessman from Beijing (Peking), but he could do so by letter. And Chinese films often have Chinese subtitles to help Chinese audiences understand what is being said. Chinese dialects fall into six main groups: Mandarin (in the north), Wu, Min, Kan, Hsiang, and Cantonese (in the south). The Mandarin dialect of the Beijing area is now taught in schools all over China as the standard language, although it will be some time before everyone speaks it.

TAKE A LETTER, JULIUS
The Roman general Julius Caesar knew how to write shorthand. He used a system invented by a scholar named Marcus Tullius Tiro in 63 B.C. Tiro devised the system to record the speeches of the orator Cicero. Tiro's system, the first known complete shorthand, remained in use for 1,000 years.

Several new shorthand systems were devised in the

TOWER OF CONFUSION *According to the Bible, the world's huge variety of languages began at the Tower of Babel, shown here in a painting by the Flemish artist Pieter Bruegel the Younger (1564–1638). Some 9,000 languages and dialects are now in use, and new ones are still being discovered in remote areas. Another 1,000 languages, such as ancient Egyptian, are known but no longer used.*

17th century, but modern shorthand is a product of the 19th and early 20th centuries. Pitman's shorthand, still widely used in Britain and Europe, was devised by Sir Isaac Pitman in 1837, and the commonest American system, Gregg's shorthand, was created in 1888 by J. R. Gregg. Both systems use straight lines, curves, dots, and dashes, though Pitman's also uses different thicknesses of stroke, to distinguish between phonetically similar letters. The symbol for *p*, for instance—an oblique line—is a lighter version of the symbol for *b*. Several other systems, among them Speedwriting, invented in the 1920s by an American named Emma Dearborn, consist of abbreviations of the Roman alphabet. The Pitman system holds the world records for shorthand of 300 words per minute for 5 minutes and 350 words per minute for 2 minutes. Both records were set by an American, Nathan Behrin, in New York in 1922.

Among the names for shorthand are brachygraphy (small writing), stenography (little or narrow writing), and tachygraphy (rapid writing).

STRINE

Just as American English has developed its own accents and vocabulary, so Australian English has diverged from the way it is spoken in Britain. Australians have developed a vivid set of verbal images: words and phrases often known collectively as Strine, from a comic exaggeration of the Australian pronunciation of the word *Australian*. Among the phrases are colorful descriptions of people: "lower than a snake's belly," "so mean he wouldn't shout in a shark attack," "as busy as a one-armed bill-poster in a high wind," and "mad as a cut snake."

There are at least 5,000 words or expressions that are Australian by birth. Some, such as *kangaroo*, *boomerang*, and *bush telegraph*, are well known outside Australia. Others, less well known, include *lolly* for "sweet" and *station* for "ranch." There is also a lively collection of Australian slang words, such as *sheila* for "girl," *crook* for "ill" or "angry," *drongo* for "fool," *ocker* for "an uncultured person," and *wowser* for "killjoy."

UPSIDE-DOWN DOWN UNDER

Boys undergoing initiation rites among the Warlpiri tribe of Australian aborigines learn to speak a special upside-down language. Called *Tjiliwirri*—meaning "funny" or "clown"—it expresses every idea as its opposite. Instead of saying, for example, "You are tall," a boy speaking *Tjiliwirri* would say "I am short." And instead of saying "Give me water," he would say "I won't give you water."

IN-LAW LANGUAGE

Among Australian aborigines many tribes have a special language for speaking to in-laws. In Djirbal, for example, spoken in parts of northeast Queensland, the basic language is known as Guwal, but when a man wants to talk to his mother-in-law, he speaks a special language called Dyalnguy. In Guugu-Yimidhirr, spoken farther north, the men use a special language with their brothers-in-law and

WORDS FROM ABROAD

English belongs to the Germanic branch of the Indo-European family of languages. It began about 1,300 years ago as Anglo-Saxon, the language of the Angles, Saxons, and Jutes, who invaded Britain from the Continent at that time. But dozens of other languages from all over the world have also contributed to its rich vocabulary as a result of invasion, trade, and scholarship.

These are some of the languages that English has drawn on, and some of the words they have given it:

Anglo-Saxon Answer, folk, freedom, go, kill, life, love, night, old, thing, what, when, where, who, year.

Norse Anger, awe, clumsy, crooked, enthrall, fog, husband, law, ransack, root, skill, snare, they, wrong.

Norman French Baron, beauty, Bible, court, crown, dress, feast, joy, justice, liberty, market, marriage, navy, parliament, peace, people, pleasure, power, prayer, reign, soldier, treasure, verdict, war.

Modern French Ballet, café, camouflage, elite, espionage, garage, menu, police, regime, soup.

German Noodle, nix, snorkel, spiel.

Latin Accommodate, bacillus, circus, exit, focus, invention, manufacture, penicillin, persecute, refrigerator, status, tradition, vacuum.

Greek Agnostic, alphabet, character, clinic, cycle, electron, epidemic, idea, irony, museum, neurology, parallel, polystyrene, rhythm, telegraph, theory.

Italian Arcade, concerto, sonnet, replica, vendetta.

Dutch Brandy, decoy, landscape, schooner.

Spanish Bravado, cafeteria, lasso, rodeo, tornado.

Caribbean languages Barbecue, canoe, hammock, hurricane, maize, mosquito, tobacco.

Aztec Chili, chocolate, coyote, tomato.

Chinese Ketchup, kowtow, tea, typhoon.

Japanese Judo, karate, kimono, tsunami.

Malay Amok, bamboo, caddy (box), sago.

Turkish Caviar, coffee, kiosk, tulip.

Arabic Alcohol, algebra, amber, assassin, cipher, crimson, cotton, ghoul, mattress, sofa, zero.

Indian languages Bangle, bungalow, chintz, jungle, khaki, pepper, pajamas, teak, thug, veranda.

Persian Azure, candy, caravan, checkmate, divan, lemon, magic, taffeta, talcum.

African languages Banana, banjo, chimpanzee, cola, mumbo jumbo, raffia, tote (to carry), voodoo, yam, zombie.

fathers-in-law. Some tribes address all their in-laws in this way. Aboriginal words for family members are also quite different from those used in Western languages. In some tribes the word for "father" is also used for the father's brothers and cousins, or a wife may call not only her husband but also her husband's brothers "husband."

Crossed wrists means odds-on

TALKING HANDS *British bookmakers use a special sign language called tic-tac to keep in touch with fluctuating betting odds among their rivals around the racecourse.*

Patting the shoulder means 33-1

Hands on the head means 9-4

THUS SPAKE THE TRADER

Pidgin languages are simplified linguistic forms invented by people with mutually unintelligible tongues as a bridge of communication. Well over 100 pidgins are in use today; all are versions of Portuguese, Spanish, French, Dutch, Italian, or English. Spoken mostly in colonies or former colonies, where there might be hundreds of local dialects, pidgins began as trading languages. The word *pidgin* is thought by some scholars to derive from a pidgin rendering of the English word *business,* in which the first syllable has been stretched into two and the final "ess" sound has been lost. Pidgins have served traders, sailors, and local merchants for more than 500 years. In some countries, such as Papua New Guinea, pidgins have become an official national language—and road signs, newspapers, and even parliamentary debates make use of pidgin.

More than 60 varieties of pidgin English still flourish, and some are very widely spoken. Tok Pisin (meaning "talk pidgin"), the pidgin of Papua New Guinea, is spoken by at least 1 million people; and 2 million people speak Cameroon Pidgin.

WORDS BELONG HAMLET

Numerous works of literature have been translated into pidgin languages. Translated into the pidgin English of the Solomon Islanders, Shakespeare's most famous speech appears in these words:

Which way this time? Me killem die finish body
    b'long me
Or me no do 'im? Me no savvy.
Might 'e better 'long you-me catchem this fella
    string for throw 'im this fella arrow,
Altogether b'long number one bad fella, name
    b'long him fortune? Me no savvy.
Might 'e better 'long you-me. For fightem 'long
    altogether where him 'e makem you-me sorry
    too much,
Bimeby him fall down die finish? Me no savvy.

In English the same lines—from the prince's soliloquy on suicide in *Hamlet* (Act 3, Scene 2)—are:

To be, or not to be: that is the question;
Whether 'tis nobler in the mind to suffer
The slings and arrows of outrageous fortune,
Or to take arms against a sea of troubles,
And by opposing end them?

THE SOUNDS OF LANGUAGE

The number of different sounds varies enormously from language to language. Spoken English has about 20 vowel sounds, but some languages have far more or far fewer. The languages of Southeast Asia have the largest numbers of vowel sounds. Bru, a Vietnamese language, has 41 vowel sounds; and Sedang, also spoken in Vietnam, has 55. However, many languages—including some from the Caucasus mountains of southern Russia, such as Abhaz and Adygh—have only one type of vowel, usually a kind of open *a,* as in the English word *are.*

Spoken consonants, too, show a wide range. English accents usually have 24; but many of the languages spoken in the Caucasus have more than 70, and one—Ubykh—has 80. By contrast, several languages make do with fewer than 10 consonants—among them Mohawk, an American Indian language, which has only 7.

THE LONG AND SHORT OF ALPHABETS

Alphabets (in which each symbol stands for a single sound or small group of sounds) are a far more economical method of representing a language than syllabaries or pictographic scripts, in which the symbols stand for complete syllables or words. Even so, some alphabets are longer than others. The world's longest is Cambodian. It has 74 letters, nearly three times as many as English. The shortest alphabet is Rotokas, from the Solomon Islands, which has only 11 letters.

CLICKS OF THE TONGUE

The disapproving clicking noise often written as "tut-tut" in English is used as a consonant in several African languages. Some southern African languages have as many as 15 different click consonants, including the sound made with the sides of the tongue to urge on a horse. Zulu, the most widespread language with clicks, has 3 million speakers, but Bushman, Hottentot, and Xhosa contain clicks too.

Other sounds quite foreign to Indo-European languages also serve as consonants in other tongues. One such consonant, resembling the glug-glug sound that imitates a bath emptying, is used in West African languages.

WHISTLE FOR IT

The Mazateco Indians of Mexico can hold a complete conversation just by whistling. Mazateco whistled speech, which is used only by the men of the tribe, is based on the tones and rhythms of the spoken language. By varying the speed, pitch, and intensity of the whistles, the men can deal with a wide range of subjects. For example, a trader can strike a bargain with a customer, spelling out in whistles exact details of quantity and price, without either man speaking a word. A similar language of whistles, called *silbo,* is used on the Canary Island of Gomera. The sounds carry so well across the valleys that a speaker can be understood up to 5 miles away.

ODD MAN OUT

Basque is unique among the languages of Europe. It is spoken by probably a million people in the French and Spanish Pyrenees but bears no relationship to any other European language.

Baffled by Basque's linguistic independence, scholars have developed a number of theories to explain it. Some experts see it as the last example of the language spoken in southwestern Europe before the Roman invasion. Some see a relationship between Basque and an extinct Iberian language found on inscriptions along the Mediterranean coasts. Others link it with the languages of North Africa or with those of the Caucasus region in southern Russia. No theory, however, has yet won universal support.

Right hand on the nose means 2-1

Clenched fists shaken means 50-1

Arms raised in a circle means 11-10

Number one, or the first horse on the race card

Wit and wisdom

A DWARFISH WHOLE
Epigrams were originally inscriptions; the word comes from the Greek *epi,* meaning "upon," and *graphein,* "to write." Ancient Greek inscriptions tended to be short because they were usually carved in stone, a laborious process.

These Greek roots are preserved in two English words: *epigraph,* used for a short and serious observation, as on a monument; and *epigram,* meaning a short, witty expression of a point of view. The English poet Samuel Taylor Coleridge (1772–1834) defined the epigram with another epigram:

What is an Epigram? A dwarfish whole,
Its body brevity, and wit its soul.

VERSE OR PROSE?
Classic epigrams were always meant to be in verse, but prose has long been an acceptable alternative. The poet Alexander Pope (1688–1744) was entirely at ease in epigrammatic verse, as:

Words are like leaves: and where they most abound,
Much fruit of sense beneath is rarely found.

In prose, however, Pope could express similar sentiments in an equally scathing manner. "It is with narrow-souled people as with narrow-necked bottles," he wrote. "The less they have in them, the more noise they make in pouring out."

WIT AND WISECRACKING
The American critic Dorothy Parker (1893–1967), who observed that "wit has truth in it; wisecracking is simply calisthenics with words," was expert at both sorts of humor.

She once demolished a performance by the actress Katharine Hepburn with the jibe: "She ran the whole gamut of emotions from A to B." But she also wrote the thoughtfully humorous lines:

Four be the things I am wiser to know:
Idleness, sorrow, a friend, and a foe.
Four be the things I'd been better without:
Love, curiosity, freckles, and doubt.

DOCTOR'S DIAGNOSIS
Britain's Dr. Samuel Johnson (1709–84), creator of the first modern dictionary, was once asked by a novice writer to give his opinion on a piece the young man had written. "Sir," Johnson supposedly responded, "this piece is both original and good. Unfortunately the parts that are original are not good, and the parts that are good are not original."

REQUEST STOP
George Bernard Shaw was at one time more celebrated as a music critic than as a playwright. One night, it is said, he was eating in a restaurant where the orchestra was inferior, to say the least, and the bandleader asked him what he would like the musicians to play next. "Dominoes," said Shaw.

HIGH SOCIETY
The essence of the retort (from the Latin *re,* meaning "back," and *torquere,* meaning "to turn or twist") is to use the first speaker's words to deflate him or her. Few people can have been so effectively put down as was the actress Jean Harlow, who, having recently emerged as a Hollywood sex goddess, met the immensely patrician

Margot, Lady Asquith, wife of the British prime minister Herbert Asquith.

Harlow insisted on addressing Lady Asquith by her first name, which might have been a sufficient social offense, but made it worse by pronouncing the *t* on the end of Margot. Lady Asquith, tiring of this ignorant impertinence, set Jean Harlow straight: "My dear, the *t* is silent—as in Harlow."

ANIMAL CRACKS
Mark Twain (1835–1910), American wit and prolific author, took a dim view of most of his fellowmen and was blunt about it. On human gullibility, for instance, he declared: "One of the most striking differences between a cat and a lie is that a cat has only nine lives." And on the human capacity for gratitude he said: "If you pick up a starving dog and make him prosperous, he will not bite you. This is the principal difference between a dog and a man."

THE QUIET AMERICAN
Calvin Coolidge, the Vermonter who was the 30th U.S. president, had a reputation for saying as little as possible. One story about him involves a friend who had missed a sermon on sin that Coolidge had sat through. The friend asked Coolidge what the preacher had said about sin, and Coolidge replied, "He said he was against it." Where taciturnity stopped and wit began was always hard to gauge in Coolidge stories. At a public dinner a woman told him that she had bet some friends that she could make him speak at least three words to her in the course of the evening. All he said to her was, "You lose."

Dorothy Parker, as so often, had the last word. It is reported that when she was told Coolidge was dead, she merely asked, "How can they tell?"

SHOWDOWN AT THE DOOR
Clare Boothe Luce, the American writer and diplomat, liked to upstage people. But according to one story the tables were turned when she stood aside and gestured Dorothy Parker to precede her through a door, saying, "Age before beauty." Parker swept on, commenting, "Pearls before swine."

CHINESE REVENGE
A British member of parliament was squashed in the early 1930s by a Chinese delegate to the League of Nations, C.T. Wang, at a banquet in Nanking. The two men found themselves sitting close to one another, and the MP, not knowing what to say, opened with "Likee soupee?" Mr. Wang did not dignify this remark with a reply, and at the end of the dinner made an address to the gathering in impeccable, erudite, elegant English. He then turned to the MP and asked politely, "Likee speechee?"

BULLDOG HUMOR
Winston Churchill's scathing gruffness would have been simple rudeness in many another man, but some Churchill remarks are so witty that the insults they contain are almost pardonable. Nancy Astor, for example, the society hostess and member of Parliament, was particularly irritated at Churchill one day and is supposed to have said, "Winston, if I were married to you, I'd put poison in your coffee." To which Churchill retorted, "Nancy, if you were my wife, I'd drink

it." Then there is the story involving Bessie Braddock, a formidable and outspoken political opponent of Churchill's. "Winston, you're drunk," she told him one day, and must have regretted it immediately, for he replied, "Bessie, you're ugly. And tomorrow morning I shall be sober."

Churchill crossed swords with the playwright George Bernard Shaw as well. The story goes that Shaw sent Churchill two tickets for the first night of one of his plays with a note saying, "Bring a friend—if you have one." Churchill returned the tickets, saying he could not attend but would be grateful for tickets for the second night, "if there is one."

PRISON HARVEST

Horatio Bottomley, a British journalist and member of Parliament jailed for fraud in 1922, kept his sense of humor even in prison. A prison visitor, noticing him stitching mailbags, said, "Ah, Bottomley, sewing?"

"No, sir," said Bottomley. "Reaping."

FAMOUS LAST WORDS

The last words of a dying person are sometimes a matter for argument among scholars. Incoherence, the chance presence or absence of witnesses, and family sentiment can all interfere with an accurate record. The sayings quoted here are widely accepted by historians.

Ludwig van Beethoven, German composer who suffered progressive impairment of his hearing for the last 29 years of his life; died in 1827: "I shall hear in heaven."

Leonardo da Vinci, Italian artist and inventor; died in 1519: "I have offended God and mankind because my work did not reach the quality it should have."

Douglas Fairbanks, Sr., American movie star; died in 1939: "I've never felt better."

Henry Fox, Lord Holland, British politician; died in 1774: "If Mr. Selwyn [a rival politician] calls again, show him up. If I am alive I shall be delighted to see him, and if I am dead he would like to see me."

Ned Kelly, Australian outlaw and gang leader, who was hanged in 1880: "Such is life."

Hugh Latimer, Protestant reformer and bishop of Worcester in England, burned at the stake in 1555 with the bishop of Rochester, Nicholas Ridley, on the orders of the Catholic queen Mary: "Be of good comfort, Master Ridley, and play the man. We shall this day light such a candle, by God's grace, in England, as I trust shall never be put out."

Niccolò Machiavelli, Florentine diplomat and political philosopher; died in 1527: "I desire to go to hell and not to heaven. In the former place I shall enjoy the company of popes, kings, and princes, while in the latter are only beggars, monks, and apostles."

Karl Marx, German philosopher who died in 1883, to his housekeeper after she asked if he had a last message for the world: "Go on, get out! Last words are for fools who haven't said enough."

William Somerset Maugham, British author; died in 1965: "Dying is a very dull, dreary affair. And my advice to you is to have nothing whatever to do with it."

Sir Thomas More, English Catholic statesman who was beheaded in 1535 on the orders of Henry VIII: "Assist me up [onto the scaffold] and in my coming down I will shift for myself."

Sir Isaac Newton, British scientist; died in 1727: "I do not know what I may appear to the world; but to myself I seem to have been only like a boy playing on the seashore, and diverting myself in now and then finding a smoother pebble or prettier shell than ordinary, whilst the great ocean of truth lay all undiscovered before me."

Lawrence Oates, British explorer; walked to his death in 1912 in an attempt to aid his starving companions during Scott's polar expedition: "I am just going outside and I may be some time."

Cecil Rhodes, South African tycoon and statesman; died in 1902: "So little done—so much to do."

Gen. John Sedgwick, Union commander in the Civil War, shot at the Battle of Spotsylvania Courthouse, Virginia, in 1864 while looking over a parapet at the enemy lines: "They couldn't hit an elephant at this dist—"

DEATH IN VICTORY *The British admiral Horatio Nelson died at the battle of Trafalgar in 1805. His last words were not "Kiss me, Hardy," as is often supposed, but, "Now I am satisfied. Thank God, I have done my duty."*

THE ALWAYS-OPEN MOUTH

Talk is the lifeblood of politics—or, as the American politician Adlai Stevenson put it: "A politician is a statesman who approaches every question with an open mouth." In fact, some of the wittiest epigrams come from politicians. Adlai Stevenson himself came up with: "Man does not live by words alone, despite the fact that sometimes he has to eat them."

A biblical turn of phrase was also favored by Jeremy Thorpe, then leader of the British Liberal Party, when he summed up British prime minister Harold Macmillan's dismissal of several close colleagues in a 1962 Cabinet reshuffle: "Greater love hath no man than this, than to lay down his friends for his life."

THE ANGELIC ELECTION

Sir Robert Menzies, twice prime minister of Australia, was making a campaign speech. A heckler, so the story goes, shouted, "I wouldn't vote for you if you were the Archangel Gabriel." Menzies shouted back, "If I were the Archangel Gabriel, madam, you would scarcely be in my constituency."

THE EPIGRAMS OF OSCAR

The Irish playwright Oscar Wilde (1854–1900) is perhaps the most quoted of wits because of his brilliant epigrams. On the generation gap, for example, he wrote: "Children begin by loving their parents; after a time they judge them; sometimes they forgive them." On a novel: "The good ended happily, and the bad unhappily. That is what Fiction means." On experience: "Experience is the name everyone gives to their mistakes."

On gossip: "There is only one thing in the world worse than being talked about, and that is not being talked about." On hunting: "The English country gentleman galloping after a fox—the unspeakable in full pursuit of the uneatable."

And on the cynic: "A man who knows the price of everything and the value of nothing."

Another famous wit, Dorothy Parker (below), paid this charming verse tribute to Wilde: "If, with the literate, I am/Impelled to try an epigram,/I never seek to take the credit;/We all assume that Oscar said it."

WITH A STILETTO *"To those she did not like . . . she was a stiletto made of sugar,"* wrote the American literary critic John Mason Brown of Dorothy Parker, pictured at left in 1937. Though sometimes portrayed as the soul of malice, Parker championed many humanitarian causes, often crossing swords with another forceful woman of her day, Clare Boothe Luce. Told that Mrs. Luce was kind to inferiors, Parker asked, "Where does she find them?"

CARVED IN STONE

Epitaphs—brief inscriptions usually carved on tombs or gravestones—are often memorable and even humorous. These are some striking examples.

Sir Christopher Wren, the architect of St. Paul's Cathedral in London, has his epitaph carved in Latin over the interior of the Cathedral's north door: *Si monumentum requiris circumspice* (If his monument you seek, look around).

At Reading, in Berkshire, England:
> *Here lies the body of William Gordon.*
> *He'd a mouth almighty and teeth accordin';*
> *Stranger, tread lightly on this sod*
> *For if he gapes you're gone, by God.*

In Tombstone, Arizona, on the grave of a Wells Fargo agent:
> *Here lies*
> *Lester Moore*
> *four slugs*
> *from a .44*
> *no less*
> *no more.*

On a tombstone in Edinburgh, Scotland:
> *Erected to the memory of*
> *John MacFarlane, Drowned in the Water of Leith*
> *By a few affectionate friends.*

On a grave in Nantucket, Massachusetts:
> *Under the sod, under the trees*
> *Lies the body of Jonathan Pease.*
> *He is not here*
> *But only his pod:*
> *He has shelled out his peas*
> *And gone to God.*

On a Staffordshire tombstone in England:
> *Here lies father and mother and sister and I.*
> *We all died within the space of one short year:*
> *They all be buried at Wimble, except I,*
> *And I be buried here.*

On a grave in Lillington churchyard, near Leamington Spa, Warwickshire, England:
> *Poorly lived,*
> *And poorly died,*
> *Poorly buried,*
> *And no one cried.*

On a grave in Stoke-on-Trent, England:
> *All who come my grave to see*
> *Avoid damp beds and think of me.*

On a tombstone in Devon, England:
> *Here lie I by the chancel door,*
> *They put me here because I was poor.*
> *The further in, the more you pay,*
> *But here lie I as snug as they.*

From a Cornish tombstone dated 1869

World religions

STRANGLED AT THE STAKE

One of the world's most familiar Bible translations was made and printed by the English religious scholar and reformer William Tyndale in the early 16th century. His versions of the Old and New Testaments were largely taken over by the Authorized Version, also known as the King James Bible, which was first published in 1611 and is still in use today. Tyndale wrote in ordinary, everyday English—language, he said, that every plowboy would be able to understand. But his efforts outraged the orthodox churchmen of his day. They felt that Tyndale was usurping the church's role as guardian and sole interpreter of the Scriptures. Only scholars could read the Latin and Greek translations then in existence, and almost all scholars were priests. To escape persecution, Tyndale fled to Germany in 1524. The following year his New Testament translation was published in Cologne, and copies of it were smuggled into England—much to the annoyance of Henry VIII, who accused Tyndale, a Protestant, of spreading sedition.

Tyndale later moved to Holland, where he published English versions of parts of the Old Testament and revised versions of the New Testament. But in 1535 he was arrested by the authorities in Antwerp and accused of heresy. He was taken to the state prison for the Low Countries at Vilvorde and brought to trial the following year. After being found "guilty" he was strangled at the stake and his body burned. To the end, his greatest regret was that his work had been banned in his homeland. And his last words were "Lord, open the king of England's eyes!"

HOW THE GREAT RELIGIONS BEGAN

BUDDHISM
Founded about 2,500 years ago by Prince Siddhartha Gautama, who lived from about 563 to 483 B.C. in northeast India. He was known as Buddha, a Sanskrit title meaning "Enlightened One." The chief Buddhist writings are contained in a number of sacred books called the Pali Canon (Pali being the Indian language in which they are written) and in a vast collection of Sanskrit, Tibetan, and Chinese sacred texts. There are now some 256 million believers, mainly in Southeast Asia and the Far East.

CHRISTIANITY
Founded about 2,000 years ago by Jesus Christ, who lived from about 7 B.C. to A.D. 30. Its writings are contained in the Bible. There are now about 1.2 billion believers in the world—including some 806 million Roman Catholics, 343 million Protestants, and 74 million members of the Eastern Orthodox Church.

CONFUCIANISM
Founded about 2,500 years ago by the philosopher K'ung Fu-tzu ("The Master Kung"), known by the Latin name Confucius, who lived from about 551 to 479 B.C. His teachings are contained in what is now called the Analects, from the Greek word *analekta,* meaning "a collection of facts and sayings." There are now about 175 million believers, mainly in China and Taiwan.

HINDUISM
Hinduism is the European name for the *Sanatana Dharma,* "the Eternal Law." The earliest Hindu text, the Rig Veda, dates from before 1000 B.C. But the best-known texts are the Upanishads, Brahmanas, and Puranas, collectively called the Veda, or "Knowledge." The most popular text is the Bhagavad Gita. There are now about 500 million believers in India and in Indian communities throughout the world.

ISLAM
Founded about 1,400 years ago by the prophet Muhammad, who lived from about A.D. 570 to 632. Its holy scripture is the Koran, written by Arab scholars in about A.D. 651. Tradition has it that Muhammad himself was unable to read or write. There are now more than 1 billion believers throughout the world.

JUDAISM
Founded about 4,000 years ago by the Hebrew chieftain Abraham, who taught his people to worship one God: Jehovah, or Yahweh. The chief writings are contained in the Torah—which reveals the will of God as stated in the first five books of the Old Testament, the Pentateuch—and the Talmud, which contains the Jewish religious and civil laws. There are now about 17 million Jews in the world, of whom some 7 million live in the United States, almost 4 million in Israel, and about 7 million in Europe and the U.S.S.R.

SHINTO
Dates from antiquity as a Japanese folk religion. It has no holy book, and its ethical principles are derived from Confucianism and Buddhism. From the early 6th century A.D. the emperor of Japan was regarded as the religion's god, but the idea of divinity was officially renounced in 1946 by Emperor Hirohito, who instead became a constitutional monarch. As a way of life, Shinto is followed by a majority of the Japanese people.

SIKHISM
Founded in India in about A.D. 1500 by Guru Nanak, who lived from 1469 to 1539 and was the first of the ten gurus, or teachers, of the Sikhs. The main writings are contained in the Adi Granth, a Punjabi phrase meaning "The Original (or First) Book," compiled by the fifth guru, Arjun, in 1604. There are now about 14 million believers throughout the world.

TAOISM
Founded in prehistoric times and described about 2,600 years ago by the philosopher Lao-tze (Lao Zi), who lived in about 600 B.C. He believed in a life of contemplation and passivity. Tao is the Chinese word for "path" or "way," and refers to the path of contentment and withdrawal that Lao-tze declared should be chosen above the path of self-seeking and worldly ambition. Lao-tze's beliefs are contained in the Tao Te Ching ("The Classic of the Way and Its Virtue"). There are now more than 20 million believers throughout the world.

ZOROASTRIANISM
Founded more than 2,500 years ago in Persia by the prophet Zoroaster, or Zarathustra. His philosophical and moral teachings—concerning the endless war between the forces of good and evil—are preserved in the Zend Avesta, especially in *Gathas,* or "hymns," written in Old Iranian, a sister language of Sanskrit. Zoroastrianism was once the faith of the Persian empire, but today it is the smallest major religion in the world, with some 250,000 believers, mainly in northwest India and Iran.

MARTYRS OF THE PAPACY

When Pope John Paul II—the first non-Italian pope since the Dutch-born Adrian VI (reigned 1522–23)—was shot and wounded by a Turkish gunman in Rome in 1981, the Christian world was outraged. But Pope John was by no means the first pope to be a target of violence. Of the 266 churchmen who have so far held office as head of the Roman Catholic Church, 33 have died by violence.

The earliest martyr was St. Peter, regarded by Catholics as the first pope, who is believed to have been crucified upside down in about A.D. 64 during the reign of the Roman emperor Nero.

The first pope to be assassinated (rather than executed on a government's orders) was John VIII, who was killed in December 882.

Despite the pomp that often surrounds the Vatican, the pope—the word comes from the Greek *pappas*, meaning "father"—has long had a formal reminder of humility. Since the reign of Gregory I (590–604) every pope has called himself the Servant of the Servants of God.

ROOTS OF RELIGION

Judaism is the oldest of the world's three Western religions. Both Christianity and Islam have evolved from it. Christianity takes from Judaism the idea of one all-powerful Creator and God, and the concept of how He has revealed himself in human history. Churches followed synagogues as centers of prayer and worship. The Eucharist—the sharing of a consecrated meal—incense, and psalm singing all have their basis in Jewish ceremonies. The names of Abraham and Moses, familiar in the Christian Bible, appear often in the sacred book of Islam, the Koran, as Ibrahim and Musa. Muslims, too, accept that Jesus was a prophet of God, though not that he was the Son of God. And Islam's weekly Sabbath and its regular fasting parallel Jewish beliefs.

PATRON SAINTS OF WORKING PEOPLE

Since the beginnings of Christianity certain saints have come to be adopted as the patrons of specific groups of people, and the process has continued into the 20th century. This list shows the names of some of the saints associated with particular occupations.

Accountants: St. Matthew
Actors: St. Genesius
Advertisers: St. Bernardino of Siena
Altar boys: St. John Berchmans
Anesthetists: St. René Goupil
Archers: St. Sebastian
Architects: St. Thomas the Apostle, St. Barbara
Artists: St. Luke, St. Catherine of Bologna
Astronomers: St. Dominic
Athletes: St. Sebastian
Aviators: Our Lady of Loreto, St. Teresa of Lisieux, St. Joseph of Cupertino
Bakers: St. Elizabeth of Hungary, St. Nicholas
Bankers: St. Matthew
Barbers: St. Cosmas and St. Damian, St. Louis
Blacksmiths: St. Dunstan
Bookkeepers: St. Matthew
Booksellers: St. John of God
Brewers: St. Augustine of Hippo, St. Luke
Bricklayers: St. Stephen
Builders: St. Vincent Ferrer
Butchers: St. Anthony, Abbot, St. Luke
Cabinetmakers: St. Anne
Carpenters: St. Joseph
Comedians: St. Vitus
Cooks: St. Lawrence, St. Martha
Dairy workers: St. Brigid
Dentists: St. Apollonia
Doctors: St. Pantaleon, St. Cosmas and St. Damian, St. Luke, St. Raphael
Editors: St. John Bosco
Engineers: St. Ferdinand III
Farmers: St. George, St. Isidore the Farmer
Firemen: St. Florian
Fishermen: St. Andrew

Florists: St. Dorothy, St. Teresa of Lisieux
Gardeners: St. Dorothy, St. Adelard, St. Tryphon, St. Fiacre, St. Phocas
Glassmakers: St. Luke
Gravediggers: St. Anthony, Abbot
Grocers: St. Michael
Housewives: St. Anne
Hunters: St. Hubert, St. Eustachius
Innkeepers: St. Amand
Jewelers: St. Eligius, St. Dunstan
Journalists: St. Francis de Sales
Jurists: St. Catherine of Alexandria, St. John of Capistrano
Laborers: St. Isidore, St. James, St. John Bosco
Lawyers: St. Ivo, St. Genesius, St. Thomas More
Librarians: St. Jerome
Maids: St. Zita
Merchants: St. Francis of Assisi, St. Nicholas
Messengers: St. Gabriel
Metalworkers: St. Eligius
Miners: St. Barbara
Mountaineers: St. Bernard of Menthon
Musicians: St. Gregory the Great, St. Cecilia, St. Dunstan
Nurses: St. Camillus de Lellis, St. John of God, St. Agatha, St. Raphael

Orators: St. John Chrysostom
Painters: St. Luke
Paratroopers: St. Michael
Pawnbrokers: St. Nicholas
Pharmacists: St. Cosmas and St. Damian, St. James the Greater
Philosophers: St. Justin
Plasterers: St. Bartholomew
Poets: St. David, St. Cecilia
Policemen: St. Michael
Postal workers: St. Gabriel
Priests: St. Jean-Baptiste Vianney
Printers: St. John of God, St. Augustine of Hippo, St. Genesius
Public relations: St. Bernardino of Siena
Radio workers: St. Gabriel
Sailors: St. Cuthbert, St. Brendan, St. Eulalia, St. Christopher, St. Peter Gonzales, St. Erasmus
Scholars: St. Brigid
Scientists: St. Albert the Great
Sculptors: St. Claude
Secretaries: St. Genesius
Servants: St. Martha, St. Zita
Shoemakers: St. Crispin, St. Crispinian
Singers: St. Gregory, St. Cecilia
Skaters: St. Lidwina
Skiers: St. Bernard
Social workers: St. Louise de Marillac
Soldiers: St. Hadrian, St. George, St. Ignatius, St. Sebastian, St. Joan of Arc, St. Martin of Tours
Students: St. Thomas Aquinas, St. Catherine of Alexandria
Tailors: St. Homobonus
Tax collectors: St. Matthew
Taxi drivers: St. Fiacre
Teachers: St. Gregory the Great, St. Catherine of Alexandria, St. John Baptist de la Salle
Theologians: St. John the Evangelist, St. Augustine, St. Alphonsus Liguori
Travelers: St. Anthony of Padua, St. Christopher, St. Nicholas of Myra, St. Raphael
TV workers: St. Gabriel
Undertakers: St. Dismas, St. Joseph of Arimathea
Writers: St. John the Evangelist, St. Francis de Sales

Gospel author St. John the Evangelist, patron of writers and theologians.

THE FACE OF CHRIST *Because the early Church disapproved of idols, there is no contemporary record of Christ's physical appearance. The earliest representations, showing him as a beardless youth, date only from the 3rd century. And the traditional vision of a bearded Christ, as in this 12th-century English carving, began only in the 4th century. Christ's life and teachings, however, were set down very quickly in the New Testament, all of which was written within about 70 years of his death in* A.D. *30. The earliest document was St. Paul's letter to the Romans, written in about* A.D. *58. Then, in succession, came St. Mark's Gospel, St. Matthew's (written for Jewish readers), and St. Luke's (written for Gentiles). The last, St. John's, was written in about* A.D. *100.*

WILL OF GOD

Devout Jews obey no fewer than 613 commandments, including the ten of the Christian faith. The commandments are derived from the Pentateuch—the first five books of the Old Testament—which is for Jews the most important religious text. Together, the commandments provide a moral framework for life. Among the rules are several restrictions on food. Like Islam, Judaism prohibits the eating of pork because the pig, a scavenger, is held to be unclean. But in addition a *kosher*, or "clean," kitchen in an orthodox Jewish home should contain no shellfish; nor should a Jew prepare meat and dairy products in the kitchen at the same time, or serve them at the same meal.

THE TONGUE OF THE PROPHET

Arabs today still use the language of the prophet Muhammad, more than 1,300 years after his death. Modern written Arabic—and the spoken language of educated Arabs—is not significantly different from classical Arabic, the language on which the Koran is based; and the Koran was written soon after Muhammad died. Modern colloquial Arabic, however, has diverged from the written language. It appears in numerous dialects, which are as different from one another as German is from English. So although Muhammad would be able to converse today with educated Arabs, he would probably need an interpreter to talk with unschooled Arabs.

101

THE MONKS WHO NEVER SPOKE
Until the 1960s Trappist monks spent their lives in perpetual silence. But the Second Vatican Council of 1962–65 relaxed this rule. Now the monks are allowed to talk during the day. They are still not allowed to talk in the cloisters, however, nor at night except in emergencies.

In some monasteries Trappists still sleep in common dormitories on straw mattresses—sometimes homemade—and rise at 3:15 A.M. They are allowed to eat meat only after an illness but may eat eggs anytime. They have fish twice a week.

The Trappists' proper name is the Cistercians of the Strict Observance. Until 1892 they were based at La Trappe, the abbey from which they get their common name, near Soligny-la-Trappe in northwest France. Today there are about 4,000 Trappist monks in more than 60 monasteries scattered throughout the world. They can be recognized by their habit: white with a black scapular.

ADAM, MAN
Adam, the first man, is mentioned by name 30 times in the Authorized Version of the Bible. Part of the reason is that the word in Hebrew is not a name; it simply means "man." Eve's name, by contrast, appears only four times.

PILGRIMAGE TO MECCA
Every Muslim is supposed to make the pilgrimage to Muhammad's birthplace, the holy city of Mecca in Saudi Arabia, at least once in his lifetime. A Muslim who completes the pilgrimage—known as the hajj—gains the right to add the title hajji to the end of his name. For many Muslims the hajj means a journey of thousands of miles and the spending of their life savings.

Once they reach the outskirts of Mecca, the pilgrims change into a two-piece white robe. In addition, the women are veiled from head to toe so that all appear alike and equal in the presence of God. The sacred Black Stone of the Kaaba shrine must be touched or kissed. The Black Stone, which is set in the wall of the shrine, is thought to be a meteorite dating from prehistoric times. In fact, Mecca was a place of worship centuries before Muhammad was born. Muslims believe that the shrine was built by Abraham and Ishmael in biblical times as a place to worship.

HOLY MAP *Islamic tradition forbids Muslims to portray living creatures. Instead, their art has to take other themes, such as texts from the Koran, or, as in this 17th-century tile, a plan of the Great Mosque in Mecca.*

THE HOLY FAST
The Muslim month of Ramadan—the holy month in which the Koran was revealed to Muhammad—is a time of fasting and atonement. During this period no Muslim may drink, eat, or smoke between sunrise and sunset. Only the sick and those traveling abroad are exempt. But even they must perform or complete their fast at a later date.

The start of Ramadan, the ninth month of the Muslim calendar, varies each year because Muslim months are set by the moon. The self-denial during Ramadan resembles the 40 days of Lent, which mark Christ's fasting in the wilderness, and the Jewish Day of Atonement, Yom Kippur.

THE SIGNIFICANCE OF 7
The number 7 appears to have a special significance in religions throughout the world. But it is particularly important in religions of Semitic origin—Judaism, Christianity, and Islam—which reckon time in periods of 7 days.

The seven deadly sins in the Christian tradition were first compiled by Pope Gregory I around the year 600. They are pride, covetousness, lust, anger, gluttony, envy, and sloth. Gregory also compiled a list of the seven virtues: faith, hope, charity, justice, prudence, temperance, and fortitude.

The number's religious significance seems to stem from pre-Christian times, when it was regarded as a sacred or mystical number. In the 6th century B.C., for instance, the followers of the Greek philosopher Pythagoras believed 3 and 4 to be lucky numbers—and thought that by adding them together the two numbers became even more lucky.

"FROM THE CHAIR"
Although in the understanding of the Roman Catholic Church the doctrine of papal infallibility, like all other doctrines, was implicitly contained in revelation from the beginning of the church, it was not *formally* declared a dogma until the 19th century. As defined by the First Vatican Council, in 1870, it holds that when the pope, "exercising his authority as teacher of all the faithful," propounds a matter of faith or morals, he is divinely protected from error. Such teaching is said to be *ex cathedra*—literally, "from the chair"—symbolizing the pope's authority as the chief bishop.

In modern times the popes have twice *formally* defined dogmas, both dealing with the dignity of the Blessed Virgin Mary. In 1854 Pope Pius IX proclaimed the dogma of the Immaculate Conception (that Mary was, from the first moment of her existence, free from original sin). And in 1950 Pius XII proclaimed that at the end of her life Mary was taken to heaven body and soul (the Assumption). In both cases, solemn definition had been requested by great numbers of the faithful.

CENTURIES OF PERSECUTION
The Nazis were by no means the first people to persecute Jews. Jews were expelled from England in 1290 by Edward I and not allowed back until Oliver Cromwell ended the ban in 1650. Jewish communities in southern Italy were almost wiped out between 1290 and 1293. Jews were expelled from France in 1306 by Philip IV. And they were falsely accused, among other things, of poisoning wells and causing the Black Death that killed some 75 million people in Europe and Asia between 1347 and 1351.

In medieval Spain, where Jews were squeezed between the twin zeals of Christianity and Islam, attacks on their communities reached a peak in 1391, and thousands were driven abroad. A century later, in 1492, Spain forced another exodus by giving Jews the choice of being converted to Christianity or deported. Martin Luther, the 16th-century founder of the Protestant Reformation, initially showed tolerance toward Jews, but he later denounced them in violent outbursts. And in the following century Jews were attacked in Germany, Poland, and the Ukraine.

In most instances, Jews were unpopular because of their moneylending activities—despite the fact that these activities were largely forced on them by Christian laws that forbade Christians from charging interest on loans and Jews from owning land.

THE SIGN OF THE FISH
Born-again Christians today often display a sketch of a fish to show their faith. This is not just because the Bible calls the Apostles fishers of men. It is because letters of the Greek word for fish, *ichthus,* match up with the Greek words *Iesous Christos Theou Uios Soter* (Jesus Christ, Son of God, Savior). From the 2nd century A.D. on, the fish appears as a symbol of Christ and the newly baptized.

THE FORTUNES OF SAINTHOOD
St. George, who has been the patron saint of England since the Middle Ages, was in 1969 dropped from the list of those saints whose feasts must be observed universally throughout the Roman Catholic Church. However, his name was retained in the liturgical calendar, and his feast may be observed locally. Another well-known saint whose feast need no longer be observed universally is St. Nicholas, bishop of Myra, who is perhaps better known to generations of children in various countries as Santa Claus.

Some 30 other saints were removed from the liturgical calendar because modern scholarship has been "unable to find any accurate historical basis for their veneration." Among these are St. Barbara, who was known as the patron saint of artillerymen, miners, and architects, and St. Catherine of Alexandria, for whom the Catherine wheel (a type of spinning firework) is named.

Still other saints, though dropped from the universal calendar, may be commemorated locally if popular devotion or historical association (e.g., with the town where the saint lived) warrants it.

THE BIBLE SAID IT FIRST
Some of the English language's most familiar sayings and words come from the Bible, especially from the Old Testament. For instance, the word *scapegoat* was coined by the 16th-century English scholar William Tyndale in his translation of the Old Testament. It comes from Leviticus 16 and refers to a goat that was ritually laden with the sins of the community. Other familiar sayings derived from the Old Testament include: Can the Ethiopian change his skin, or *the leopard his spots*? (Jeremiah 13:23). *Pride goeth* before destruc-

tion, and an haughty spirit *before a fall* (Proverbs 16:18). Come not near to me; for I am *holier than thou* (Isaiah 65:5). And after the earthquake a fire; but the Lord was not in the fire: and after the fire *a still small voice* (I Kings 19:12). He kept him as *the apple of his eye* (Deuteronomy 32:10). And Moses sent them to *spy out the land* of Canaan (Numbers 13:17).

SWEEPING AWAY THE INSECTS
The religious sect of Jainism, which has more than 200 million members in India, developed in the 6th century B.C. when its disciples broke away from conventional Hinduism. Jains believe that the worst act a person can commit is to take any form of life. Therefore they are not allowed to be butchers or soldiers. The eating of meat and fish is forbidden, and deeply devout Jains do not eat eggs.

Jain priests also gently sweep the paths before them so that they do not step on and kill any insects. The 20th-century Indian leader Mohandas Gandhi,

PREACHING POSTURE *A stone statue carved in Pakistan in the 2nd century B.C. shows Buddha in a traditional preaching posture, fingers interlaced and legs crossed in the lotus position. The spot in the middle of his forehead symbolizes the third eye of enlightenment. Unlike the adherents of most major religions, Buddhists do not believe in an all-powerful God, nor do they accept the existence of an individual soul.*

103

who was a Hindu, came from an area on the west coast of India steeped in Jainism. He adopted the Jain principle of *ahimsa* (nonviolence) and gave it political as well as social significance.

Strict Jains take the principle of nonviolence to such extremes that they will risk their own lives rather than harm anything. In the mid-1970s many

Jain householders in Mangalore on India's west coast refused to let government health workers spray their homes with DDT as protection against mosquitoes. They chose to risk catching malaria and other insect-borne diseases rather than to give approval to the death of the insects.

PEACE TO ALL *Devout Jains, like the 15th-century monk Kalaka shown here, abhor violence in any form and will avoid harming even insects.*

HOW HINDUS GOT THEIR NAME
The name Hindu comes originally from the Sanskrit word *sindhu,* meaning "river." From this, Persian settlers—migrating about 1500 B.C. into the main river valley of what is now Pakistan—derived their own word, *Hind.* In time the land beyond the river became known as Hind (from which India gets its name), and the people who lived there were called Hindus. The same word was the source of the modern name for the river along which the Persians settled. It became known as the Indus.

DARK AS A CLOUD
The modern religious sect of Hari Krishna—whose shaven-headed disciples can be seen on city streets throughout the world—takes its name from the Hindu god Krishna. *Krishna* means "dark as a cloud," and the deity is always depicted with blue or black skin. Hari is another name for the god Vishnu, whose eighth incarnation on earth was as Krishna.

Tradition has it that Krishna was raised by foster parents near Agra in northern India. He grew up to be an amorous, fun-loving young man, and he is supposed on one occasion to have stolen the clothes of some milkmaids as they bathed naked in a river. He became renowned for his romantic adventures and is usually depicted playing a flute and surrounded by adoring and beautiful maidens.

His weak spot was his heel, and he was fatally wounded in the back of the foot by a hunter who mistook him for a deer. This parallel with the fate of the Greek hero Achilles is probably the result of Greek influence after Alexander the Great invaded India in 326 B.C.

MEN OF THE LION
One of the world's youngest religions is Sikhism, which stems from the beginning of the 16th century. It aims to unite Muslim and Hindu thinking and teaches that the one reality is God, although he may be known by various names. The Sikhs later clashed with the Mogul emperors, who ruled much of India from the early 16th to the mid-18th centuries and who persecuted those who were not Muslims like themselves. In 1699 the Sikh leader Govind Singh organized a fighting group in which the men took the name of Singh, meaning "lion."

Since then every orthodox male Sikh has taken the same name, and has followed five symbolic rules of appearance, which help to establish Sikh identity. These rules are known as the Five K's because each has a key word beginning with that letter in Punjabi. The rules are to keep one's hair (*kesh*) uncut (hence the Sikh turban to keep it tidy, though the turban itself is not required by the five rules); to keep a comb (*kangha*) in the hair; to wear shorts (*kaccha*) under one's trousers; to wear a steel bangle (*kara*); and to carry a short dagger (*kirpan*).

The uncut but tidy hair, together with the comb, symbolizes the Sikh's liking for moderation and compromise. The shorts and steel bangle represent moral restraint and chastity. And the dagger— today, usually a tiny and purely ornamental blade attached to the comb—stands for readiness to take up arms in defense of the faith.

SONG OF THE LORD
Hinduism's most important sacred text is the *Bhagavad Gita,* or "Song of the Lord"—a poem of about 700 verses. It is just one section of the *Mahabharata* (Great Epic of the Bharata Dynasty), a work of 100,000 Sanskrit couplets, one of the longest poems ever written. It was composed between 200 B.C. and A.D. 200.

TOWERS OF SILENCE
Hindus and Buddhists traditionally burn the bodies of their dead on funeral pyres, whereas Muslims bury their dead. For Eastern followers of the ancient Persian religion of Zoroastrianism, however, neither method is permissible because both fire and earth are regarded as holy and not to be polluted by such "unclean" acts. So Zoroastrians place their corpses on platforms known as Towers of Silence. The circular towers are built on high ground, and the bodies are exposed to the air, allowing them to be quickly devoured by vultures.

BENEATH THE BO TREE
Buddha ("Enlightened One") was the title given to Siddhartha Gautama, the founder of Buddhism. He was a Hindu of noble birth who grew up in the foothills of the Himalayas on what is now the India–Nepal border. According to legend, he led a life of luxury as a young man. But in about 530 B.C., when he was married and had a baby son, he left his family and wandered for 6 years in search of spiritual enlightenment.

He found it after meditating for more than 40 days under a bo tree (pipal, a type of fig tree) beside a tributary of the Ganges. From then on Gautama devoted his time to teaching his new religion, which emphasized right living and meditation. Buddhism spread quickly in Asia, and many forms of the religion are practiced throughout the world today. Some Buddhists believe that there were other Buddhas before Gautama, that they also achieved enlightenment, and that another Buddha will come one day.

CONFUCIUS'S GOLDEN RULE
Confucius, the Chinese philosopher and social reformer who lived between about 551 and 479 B.C., was the first person to advocate what has come in ethics to be called the Golden Rule: "Do to others as you would be done by." This was the key to the

philosophy named after him, which was a moral and ethical code as well as a religion. His real name was K'ung Fu-tzu ("The Master Kung"), and its Latin form was bestowed by Jesuit missionaries centuries after his death. Confucius worked as a minor civil servant and teacher, and he stressed the virtues of truthfulness, loyalty, learning, and moderation in eating and drinking. He believed in the modest, regular life, urging his followers not to be extremists. He considered war to be one of the greatest evils and called for people to negotiate and compromise rather than fight.

About a week before he died, Confucius told a disciple of a prophetic dream he had had. He had learned, he said, that "the great mountain must crumble; the strong beam must break; the wise man must wither away like a plant." If by "wise man" he meant himself, he would be interested in what happened to his reputation for wisdom nearly 2,500 years later.

In the 20th century a movement to establish Confucianism as a state religion failed. As a defender of traditional values, Confucius has been regarded as a conservative, and his teachings were officially discouraged when the Communists came to power in 1949. Indeed, the dictator of Red China, Mao Tsetung (Mao Zedong), stated that from the age of eight he had hated Confucius.

YIN AND YANG

Disciples of Taoism—a Chinese mystical religion that advocates a life of passivity—believe that each individual's personality is a mixture of two opposite sets of qualities: Yin and Yang. Yin is feminine, mother, soft, wet, dark; Yang is masculine, father, strong, dry, light. The contrasts of Yin and Yang, and their coming together as one, are thought to be responsible for all that happens in the world.

The principle of Yin and Yang is depicted by a circle divided into halves—one dark, the other light—and each half is shaped like a raindrop with a long tail. The symbol decorates many Chinese buildings, banners, crockery, and ornaments.

THE GODS OF A HINDU

In every devout Hindu home there is a shrine with images of one or more of the thousands of gods worshiped. The two major gods are Shiva and Vishnu. Most of the great Hindu temples belong either to the Shaiva cult, which worships Shiva, or to the Vaishnava cult, which worships Vishnu.

Shiva is a god of violence whose frenzied dancing—sometimes shown as taking place within a circle of fire on the body of a dwarf demon—symbolizes the eternal cycle of creation and destruction. He is portrayed with a blue throat caused by swallowing a deadly scum, which arose from the oceans when they were churned by rival deities in an attempt to destroy mankind.

Shiva's consort—just one of whose forms is the fierce goddess Kali—is worshiped as a leading divinity by most orthodox Hindus.

Vishnu, the preserver, is a kindly god who protects those who worship him, restores health, and banishes bad luck. He is said to come to earth periodically as an *avatar*—an incarnation in various forms—to help mankind in times of crisis. His consort is Lakshmi, the goddess of good fortune. Another major god is Brahma, the creator, whose consort Sarasvati is the patroness of arts and learning.

Limbs of power

Among other gods who are widely worshiped are two of Shiva's sons: Ganesh and Karttikeya. Ganesh, the elephant god, is the bringer of good fortune. Karttikeya, a god of war, is usually depicted with 6 heads and 12 arms, a sign of his power. Other popular gods include Sitala, to whom mothers traditionally pray to protect their children from disease; Rama, the personification of reason, virtue, and chivalry; Hanuman, the monkey god, who is revered as a guardian spirit; and Krishna, the eighth incarnation of Vishnu, who is depicted with blue or black skin and who is honored for his skills as a warrior and lover.

WAY OF LIFE *The contemplative Chinese philosophy of Taoism—whose founding figure, Lao-tze (Lao Zi), is shown here with disciples—holds that one can overcome all difficulties by following the natural path of life, in much the same way that water finds its own course. Lao-tze is believed to have written Taoism's central book, the* Tao Te Ching (The Classic of the Way and Its Virtue) *in the 6th century* B.C.

Philosophers and philosophy

WHO SAID WHAT

Aristotle (384–322 B.C.) "Man is by nature a political animal."

Jeremy Bentham (1748–1832) "The greatest happiness of the greatest number is the foundation of morals and legislation."

Cicero (106–43 B.C.) "The good of the people is the chief law."

René Descartes (1596–1650) "Cogito, ergo sum." (Latin for "I think, therefore I am.")

Friedrich Engels (1820–95) "The state is not 'abolished,' it withers away."

Georg Hegel (1770–1831) "What experience and history teach is this—that people and governments have never learned anything from history, or acted on principles deduced from it."

Thomas Hobbes (1588–1679) "The life of man [in a state of nature] is solitary, poor, nasty, brutish, and short."

Immanuel Kant (1724–1804) "Happiness is not an ideal of reason but of imagination."

John Locke (1632–1704) "No man's knowledge here can go beyond his experience."

Karl Marx (1818–83) "A specter is haunting Europe—the specter of Communism."
  "The proletarians have nothing to lose [in this revolution] but their chains. They have a world to win. Workers of the world, unite!"
  "Religion is the opium of the people."
  "The class struggle necessarily leads to the dictatorship of the proletariat."

John Stuart Mill (1806–73) "Liberty consists in doing what one desires."

Friedrich Nietzsche (1844–1900) "I teach you the Superman. Man is something to be surpassed."

Blaise Pascal (1623–62) "Man is but a reed, the weakest in nature, but he is a thinking reed."

Jean Jacques Rousseau (1712–78) "Man was born free, and everywhere he is in chains."

Bertrand Russell (1872–1970) "It is undesirable to believe a proposition when there is no ground whatever for supposing it true."

Seneca (about 4 B.C.–A.D. 65) "Even while they teach, men learn."

Socrates (about 470–399 B.C.) "The life which is unexamined is not worth living."

Henry David Thoreau (1817–62) "It takes two to speak the truth—one to speak, and another to hear."

Voltaire (1694–1778) "If God did not exist, it would be necessary to invent Him."
  "I disapprove of what you say, but I will defend to the death your right to say it."

NOTHING ON PAPER

Although the Athenian thinker Socrates (about 470–399 B.C.) is regarded as the father of Western philosophy, he seems never to have written down his ideas. Our only knowledge of him comes from the writings of his Greek contemporaries: Aristophanes, Xenophon, and particularly his pupil Plato.

Socrates is the main character in Plato's *Dialogues*. Most scholars believe, however, that in the book Plato was giving his own views, not those of Socrates, who was being used only as a mouthpiece.

Condemned to death for impiety and corrupting the youth of Athens, Socrates continued to discuss philosophy with his friends and pupils in jail. He refused their offers to help him escape, and expressed his lifelong commitment to democratic rule by drinking the executioners' hemlock.

THINKER WITHOUT CREDENTIALS

David Hume (1711–76), the Scottish thinker now recognized as one of the founders of empiricism—the doctrine that experience, not reason or God, is the supreme touchstone of truth—was never able to teach philosophy. He lacked the proper academic credentials. Unable to secure the chair of philosophy at either Edinburgh or Glasgow university, Hume worked as a general's secretary on a military expedition to Brittany and on a diplomatic mission to Turin, and as keeper of the Advocates Library in Edinburgh.

His major works, such as *A Treatise of Human*

Nature and *An Inquiry Concerning Human Understanding,* were largely ignored in his lifetime, but later influenced such thinkers as the Englishman Jeremy Bentham (see next page) and the German Immanuel Kant (1724–1804).

LASTING LEGACY

One of the major influences on Western philosophy has been the Greek philosopher Aristotle (384–322 B.C.). Personal tutor to Alexander the Great and later his protegé, Aristotle established a philosophical school, called the Lyceum, outside Athens in 335 B.C. This wide-ranging research center bequeathed to the world numerous academic disciplines, including logic, ethics, physics, rhetoric, metaphysics, economics, and psychology.

TYCOON'S SON WHO TURNED GARDENER

Despite a wealthy background, the Austrian philosopher Ludwig Wittgenstein (1889–1951) preferred to live a simple existence. The son of a steel tycoon, Wittgenstein gave away the fortune he inherited and

divided his time between an active academic life and jobs as a schoolmaster, gardener, and hospital porter. His book *Tractatus Logico-Philosophicus,* published in 1921, took as its basic axiom that "all philosophy is a critique of language," and attempted to construct a language system as precise and logical as mathematics. Although Wittgenstein became a teacher of philosophy at Cambridge University from 1929 to 1947, he never abandoned his taste for the simple life. He wore open-necked shirts—at a time when most teachers and students wore ties—and furnished his college rooms with nothing more luxurious than deck chairs.

SEEING IS BELIEVING

The Irish philosopher Bishop George Berkeley (1685–1753) offered a startling theory to prove the existence of God. Stating that no material objects existed unless they were perceived by the senses, Berkeley claimed that objects continued to exist when they were not being observed by human senses only because they were being continuously observed by God. Berkeley's beliefs were lampooned two centuries later in a pair of limericks by the English theologian Ronald Knox (1888–1957):

> *There was a young man who said: "God*
> *Must think it exceedingly odd*
> *If he finds that this tree*
> *Continues to be*
> *When there's no one about in the Quad."*

To which the reply was:

> *Dear Sir, Your astonishment's odd.*
> *I am always about in the Quad;*
> *And that's why the tree*
> *Will continue to be,*
> *Since observed by Yours faithfully, GOD.*

Despite the criticism, Berkeley's reputation as a major theological thinker was largely unchallenged. The university city of Berkeley, California, is named after him.

DESTITUTE ECONOMIST

Karl Marx (1818–83), whose ideas revolutionized the way workers and nations looked at money, was almost hopeless at acquiring it himself. Shortly after arriving in London as a political exile from Europe in 1849, Marx and his family were evicted from their rooms in Chelsea for nonpayment of rent, losing most of their possessions in the process.

The Marx family rented rooms in Soho from 1851 to 1856, a desperate period during which two of their children died. Although Marx worked as a correspondent for the *New York Tribune,* he could

A DOG'S LIFE *A Roman sculpture of the 1st century A.D. records the meeting of Alexander the Great with the Greek philosopher Diogenes (about 412–323 B.C.). Diogenes—who lived for a time in an earthenware tub (not, as is often claimed, in a barrel) on the grounds of an Athenian temple—is said to have been asked if there was anything he wanted. He replied, "Yes, get out of my sunlight!" Impressed by such directness, the conqueror is said to have remarked, "Were I not Alexander, I would wish to be Diogenes." The philosopher dressed like a beggar and lived so austerely that he was nicknamed The Dog. As a result his disciples came to be known sneeringly as Cynics, from the Greek kunikos, meaning "doglike." Cynics accepted the insult proudly, saying they were watchdogs of morality. Diogenes asked to be buried like a dog: thrown into a ditch and covered with rubbish. Instead, he was given a splendid funeral at Corinth, and in memory of his nickname his tomb was topped with a carving of a dog.*

not earn enough to feed his family. They were saved from starvation only by the generosity of Marx's friend Friedrich Engels, who gave Marx part of his income.

After inheriting about $700 from his wife's mother in 1856, Marx moved his family to a house in Kentish Town, North London, where he wrote the basic material for *Das Kapital,* the first volume of which was published in 1867.

DEATH WISH
Jeremy Bentham (1748–1832), the English utilitarian philosopher, had very decided views on what should happen to bodies after death. He even wrote a book on the subject: *Auto-Icon, or the Uses of the Dead to the Living,* in which he suggested that "if all bodies were embalmed, every man might be his own statue."

Bentham, who had been a founder of University College, London, bequeathed his body to the college so that his remains could be used for medical research. That was done, but the college authorities went a step further. Bentham's skeleton was reconstructed, given a wax head, dressed in a suit of Bentham's best clothes, and placed in a glass case. Thus for many years the deceased Bentham presided over meetings of the college committee—and was always described in the minutes as "present, but not voting."

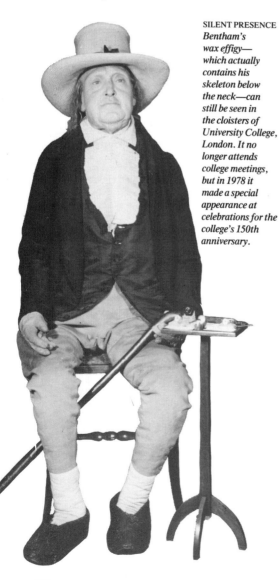

SILENT PRESENCE
Bentham's wax effigy— which actually contains his skeleton below the neck—can still be seen in the cloisters of University College, London. It no longer attends college meetings, but in 1978 it made a special appearance at celebrations for the college's 150th anniversary.

HOTHOUSE EDUCATION
The 19th century's most influential English liberal thinker, John Stuart Mill (1806–73), never went to school. Instead, he was given a highly intensive education at home by his father, James—an economist, historian, and disciple of Jeremy Bentham, whose utilitarian ideas John Stuart Mill later embraced.

Mill started learning Greek at the age of 3; Latin, algebra, and geometry when he was 8; and logic at the age of 12. By the time he was 14, Mill had digested most of the Greek and Roman classics in their original languages. Although Mill's hothouse education helped him to become one of Britain's leading scholars, it seems to have exacted a heavy psychological price as well: Mill suffered a nervous breakdown when he was 20 years old.

ALL THINGS IN MODERATION
The Athenian philosopher Epicurus (341–270 B.C.)—from whose name is derived the word *epicure,* meaning a high-living gourmet—was actually an advocate of moderation. Epicurus felt that pleasure was preferable to pain, but warned that overgratification of physical desire led to greater pain than pleasure. Temperance, courage, and justice, he said, were the qualities that promoted an enjoyable life.

His philosophy, known as hedonism, acquired its modern sense of wallowing in idle pleasure when a distorted form of it was adopted by wealthy pleasure seekers in France in the 17th and 18th centuries and used to justify their self-indulgent lifestyles.

PIONEER DOCTOR
The Greek physician and philosopher Hippocrates (about 460–370 B.C.)—often regarded by scholars as the father of modern medicine, and the man after whom the doctors' Hippocratic Oath is named— knew less about the workings of the human body than most 20th-century schoolchildren. He believed that veins carried air, not blood, and claimed that illness was caused by vapors secreted by undigested food from unsuitable diets. The vapors seeped into the body, he thought, producing disease. Hippocrates' modern reputation stems from his then radical but now widely accepted view that medical treatment had to take account of the patient's body as a whole, not just the affected part. The same illness, he asserted, might require different treatments depending on the patient's age, condition, and way of life.

DEMOLISHED BY FACT AND FICTION
The satiric tale *Candide,* by the French writer Voltaire (1694–1778), helped to demolish the philosophy of a German thinker, Baron von Leibniz.

Leibniz (1646–1716) developed his complicated theories in an attempt to reconcile the existence of God with the presence of evil. He concluded in his *Théodicée,* published in 1710, that since the universe had been created by God, it was "the best of all possible worlds," and that all was for the best in it.

But Leibniz's system foundered on the twin rocks of *Candide* and the Lisbon earthquake of 1755, in which about 60,000 people were killed. *Candide,* published in 1759, scathingly caricatured the disciples of Leibniz in the ludicrously optimistic character of Dr. Pangloss. At the time, Leibniz's conclusions were already targets of attack and ridicule because of the quake that had struck the Portuguese capital on November 1, 1755. Most scholars found it difficult to reconcile Leibniz's devout views with the scale of the disaster—and the fact that many of the victims died in the rubble of the churches in which they had been celebrating All Saints' Day.

VICTORIAN BEST-SELLER

Charles Darwin's argument for evolution, known as *The Origin of Species*, was a best-seller. Despite its length and technical nature—its full title was *On the Origin of Species by Means of Natural Selection, or the Preservation of Favored Races in the Struggle for Life*—it sold out on publication day in 1859 and by 1872 had run through six more editions.

DOWN FROM THE FAMILY TREE *A terrified flunky announces the arrival of a gorilla in a 19th-century* Punch *cartoon lampooning Darwin's theories.*

MAJOR SCHOOLS OF THOUGHT

ARISTOTELIANISM
A philosophy originated by the Greek thinker Aristotle (384–322 B.C.), who held that virtue was a middle way between extremes. The founder of logical reasoning, he classified everything in a "ladder of nature," with inanimate matter at the bottom and man at the top.

CYNICISM
Originated by the Greek philosopher Diogenes (c. 412–323 B.C.), who urged a simple, self-sufficient life as the way to happiness. His scorn for conventional values gave rise to the present meaning of cynicism.

DIALECTIC
Effort to reach truth by proceeding from an assertion, or thesis, to a denial, or antithesis, and reconciling the two by a synthesis, which becomes a new thesis; devised by Georg Hegel (1770–1831) and later used by Karl Marx (1818–83).

EMPIRICISM
Seventeenth-century British theory that all knowledge is derived from sensory experience, by observation and experimentation. Proponents included Francis Bacon (1561–1626), John Locke (1632–1704), and David Hume (1711–76).

EPICUREANISM
Philosophy originated by the Athenian thinker Epicurus (341–270 B.C.), who argued that pleasure was good and that pain was evil. But he also stressed the importance of virtue and moderation in all things.

EXISTENTIALISM
Doctrine stressing the freedom of human beings to make choices—and bear the consequences—in a world that has no absolute values outside human experience; advanced by Sören Kierkegaard (1813–55), Martin Heidegger (1889–1976), Jean Paul Sartre (1905–80), and Albert Camus (1913–60).

HUMANISM
Renaissance philosophy, revived in the 20th century, that champions human dignity and worth.

IDEALISM
Doctrine that matter is an illusion and that the only reality is that which exists mentally. Proponents included the German philosopher Georg Hegel (1770–1831) and the Irish philosopher Bishop George Berkeley (1685–1753).

LOGICAL POSITIVISM
School of 20th-century thinking that tried to base knowledge on sense-experience—that is, observations—governed by scientific principles. Also called the Vienna Circle, after its city of origin. Strongly influenced by Austrian-born Ludwig Wittgenstein (1889–1951), it was promoted in the work of Englishman A.J. Ayer (1910–   ) and others.

MARXISM
Nineteenth-century philosophy, sometimes called dialectical materialism, that interprets history as a struggle between opposing economic forces. According to Karl Marx (1818–83) and Friedrich Engels (1820–95), the ultimate result of this struggle is the emergence of a classless society: Communism.

PLATONISM
Philosophical systems deriving from Plato's belief that unchanging Ideas (models) are absolutes of which earthly things are copies. Plato (c. 427–347 B.C.) was perhaps the most seminal of philosophers.

PRAGMATISM
Nineteenth-century American philosophy that the meaning or value of an idea lies in its practical consequence: what its leading proponent Charles Peirce (1839–1914) called "its bearing upon the conduct of life." Other proponents were William James (1842–1910) and John Dewey (1859–1952).

RATIONALISM
Seventeenth-century European philosophy that reason is the only true source of knowledge. The opposite of empiricism. Main proponents included the Dutch thinker Baruch Spinoza (1632–77) and the German philosopher Baron von Leibniz (1646–1716).

SCHOLASTICISM
Western Christian philosophy of the Middle Ages reconciles faith and reason, and holds that knowledge comes via the senses. Chief proponent was Thomas Aquinas (1225–74). Leaders of Neoscholastic revival in 20th century include Jacques Maritain (1882–1973) and Mortimer Adler (1902–   ).

SKEPTICISM
Greek doctrine that everything is open to doubt. Later adopted by the French philosopher René Descartes (1596–1650), who, as a starting point, doubted everything except the workings of his own mind.

STOICISM
Philosophy that virtue—not glory or possessions—is the only worthy aim in life. Proponents included the Greek thinker Zeno (c. 334–262 B.C.) and the Roman statesman Seneca (c. 4 B.C.–A.D. 65).

TRANSCENDENTALISM
Nineteenth-century doctrine that philosophy must extend beyond the limits of experience. Proponents included the Americans Henry David Thoreau (1817–62) and Ralph Waldo Emerson (1803–82).

UTILITARIANISM
Belief that good consists in creating the greatest happiness for the greatest number of people. Main proponents included Jeremy Bentham (1748–1832), James Mill (1773–1836), John Stuart Mill (1806–73), and Henry Sidgwick (1838–1900).

Spies and spying

OPENING THE MAILS

Alexander the Great (356–323 B.C.), the Macedonian who conquered much of Asia in his twenties, is credited with inventing a spying technique that is still widely used today. During his campaigns in the Middle East and Asia between 334 and 326 B.C., Alexander encouraged his officers to write frequent letters home. He then intercepted the mail to discover and eliminate men whose loyalty was questionable.

PRIESTLY SPY RING

One of the earliest known spying coups occurred in 539 B.C. when the Persian leader Cyrus the Great (ruled 559 to 530 B.C.) secretly recruited a force of dissident Babylonian priests to help him defeat Belshazzar, the ruler of Babylon. Although the exact nature of the priests' help is unknown, Babylonian documents show that Cyrus's soldiers were able to enter Babylon without having to fight their way in.

TUDOR SPYMASTER

Sir Francis Drake, the English naval commander, is said to have amused himself by lawn bowling as the Spanish Armada approached the British Isles in 1588. He could afford to be unconcerned: he already knew the enemy's invasion plans. They had been discovered by an English secret service organization created by Sir Francis Walsingham, one of Queen Elizabeth I's leading advisers. Walsingham recruited agents in England and sent them into "deep cover" in enemy territory. One spy, Anthony Standen, styled himself as a courtier named Pompeo Pellegrini and penetrated the entourage of the Marquis de Santa Cruz, Grand Admiral of the Spanish fleet. By intercepting letters between Santa Cruz and Philip II of Spain, Standen was able to warn his English employer of the preparations for the Armada in 1587—months before it sailed, to ultimate defeat.

FROM RUSSIA WITH DEATH

SMERSH, the Soviet spy organization made familiar by James Bond's creator, Ian Fleming, is a real KGB department. Named after its motto, *Smert Shpionen* ("death to spies"), SMERSH has the job of eliminating enemies of the Soviet Union who live abroad. Its most important victim was Leon Trotsky, the former Bolshevik leader in the 1917 Revolution, who was murdered in Mexico in 1940.

CRACKING THE ENIGMA

Fifteen thousand people kept the secret of one of Britain's most important intelligence advantages during World War II. The 15,000 were employed by the British Secret Intelligence Service, MI-6, at Bletchley Park, a country estate, monitoring and decoding Germany's secret communications. At the heart of their achievement was the German Enigma code machine and . . . a simple weather report.

Each morning at dawn a German double agent, with the help of the British Security Service, MI-5, prepared a routine weather report. The report was transmitted to German spy chiefs in Hamburg, then coded on the Enigma and sent on to Berlin.

The codes used on the Enigma were regarded by the Germans as unbreakable, and as an extra safeguard they were altered each day. In fact, all the precautions were useless. By monitoring the coded signal to Berlin and comparing it with the original weather report, the Bletchley code breakers were able to work out the Enigma code for the day within a few hours of dawn. The rest of the day's messages could then be deciphered almost as soon as they were transmitted.

FATEFUL BUS STOP

Between 1945 and 1972 Britain's security services captured only one Soviet spy without American help—and even that was by accident. In April 1952 an MI-5 surveillance expert was on his way home for lunch when, as he got off a bus in Kingston, London, he spotted a Soviet diplomat talking to a young man. The unknown man was trailed and found to be a 24-year-old radio operator named William Marshall, who worked for Britain's diplomatic wireless service, handling secret radio transmissions to and from British embassies around the world. Three months later Marshall was caught red-handed selling secrets to the Soviet diplomat and was jailed for 5 years.

SAVAGE PENALTY

Jail is one of the lesser risks a spy runs. In the late 1950s Lt. Col. Yuri Popov, an officer in Russia's military intelligence service, the GRU, was discovered to be a double agent working for the West. His reported penalty—supposedly leaked by the Soviets as a warning to Western intelligence agencies—was savage. He was tossed alive into a furnace in front of his GRU colleagues in 1959.

OUTFOXING A SPY SATELLITE

During the battle for the Falklands in 1982, Britain's Royal Air Force claimed that pinpoint bombing of Port Stanley's only runway had effectively closed the airport to Argentina's air force. This view was supported by high-resolution photographs taken by U.S. satellites, which showed what appeared to be several deep bomb craters. After the fighting ended, however, it was discovered that a handful of Argentine soldiers, equipped only with buckets and shovels, had fooled the most advanced military equipment simply by constructing, under cover of darkness, convincing-looking crater walls of loose earth. The bogus craters were left in view during the day for the satellites to photograph, then cleared away after dark. By this simple and cheap expedient the Argentine forces were able to fly in supplies and reinforcements every night, right up to the time of their final surrender.

A SPY NAMED CICERO

A British ambassador's early-morning bath led to one of the most notorious espionage episodes of World War II. For it was while Sir Hughe Knatchbull-Hugessen—His Majesty's ambassador in Ankara, the capital of neutral Turkey—was soaking in his tub that his Turkish valet, Elyesa Bazna, made a wax impression of the key to the top-secret documents box that stood on the desk in Sir Hughe's study. It was October 1943, a time when Turkey was debating whether to join in the fight against Hitler, and by the end of the month Bazna had copied 52 documents, which he sold to Nazi officials in Ankara.

The Germans gave Bazna the code name Cicero, after a Roman statesman (106–43 B.C.) noted for

INTELLIGENCE AGENCIES AROUND THE WORLD

CIA (United States) Founded in 1947 by President Harry Truman. Known to staff as The Company. Headquarters at Langley, Virginia, just outside Washington. Estimated to employ 25,000 staff, mostly analysts openly engaged in reviewing data collected from around the world. Covert work is by a smaller nucleus in the Plans Division, which runs CIA sections—called stations—in U.S. embassies. CIA stands for Central Intelligence Agency.

MI-6 (Britain) Founded in 1909 and known to staff as The Firm. Also called the British Secret Intelligence Service. Based in Westminster Bridge Road, London, and responsible for gathering intelligence outside Britain. MI stands for military intelligence.

MI-5 (Britain) Also founded in 1909 and originally called the Special Intelligence Bureau. Known to staff as The Office. Based at Curzon Street in London and responsible for internal security and counterintelligence in Britain.

KGB (Soviet Union) Known as The Center. The Committee for State Security (KGB) was founded in 1953, the latest in a line of Russian intelligence organizations stretching back to the 16th century. Based in Moscow with headquarters at Dzerzhinsky Square. Employs an estimated 200,000 staff, including 70,000 censors, and is thought to have recruited more than 750,000 non-Russian agents abroad. Eighty percent of Soviet embassy staff around the world are thought to be KGB agents. Responsible for internal security and, with its military counterpart, the GRU, for overseas espionage.

SDECE (France) The Service de Documentation Extérieure et Contre-Espionage was created in 1958. Headquarters in eastern Paris at Boulevard Mortier. The building is known to staff as *La Piscine* ("the swimming pool") because of a nearby public pool. Responsible for gathering overseas intelligence. Estimated to employ 4,000 people.

MOSSAD (Israel) Founded in 1950. Based in Tel Aviv, its headquarters is moved to new premises at irregular but frequent intervals for security reasons. Estimated to employ about 1,200 people, it is responsible for overseas espionage. The name Mossad comes from Hebrew words meaning Institution for Intelligence and Special Assignments.

HOW THE CIA BEGAN

America's Central Intelligence Agency can trace its existence to the British. Before World War II the United States had no centralized intelligence organization. However, in 1940, at the urging of the British, President Franklin Roosevelt authorized the creation of the Office of Strategic Services (OSS) to coordinate the nation's spying activities. The OSS was officially disbanded after the war, but many of its personnel remained in government service and provided the nucleus for the CIA when it was established by President Harry Truman in 1947.

MATA HARI: THE SPY WHO WASN'T

Mata Hari, who was executed by firing squad in France in October 1917, is probably the most famous spy of all time. She is renowned for her beauty, her numerous military lovers, her provocative Oriental dancing, and, above all, her espionage. Yet in fact she was not Oriental, or even a spy. Mata Hari was the stage name adopted by a plump, middle-aged Dutch divorcée named Mrs. Margaretha MacLeod, who had left her alcoholic Scottish husband in the Netherlands East Indies (now Indonesia) and opted to become a dancer in Europe.

The evidence of her alleged espionage on behalf of the German kaiser is based merely on her being mistaken for a known German agent, Clara Benedix, by the British in November 1916. In that month Mrs. MacLeod was arrested in Falmouth, Cornwall, on board the SS *Hollandia* while she was on her way to Holland. The police released her when they realized the mistake. Later she was arrested in France and charged with having been in contact with German intelligence officers in Madrid. At her trial in Paris her lurid life-style was used to damning effect. It was only in 1963, when the secret files relating to her case were released, that the legend was reassessed.

his eloquence. Bazna continued his work as a spy until April 1944, by which time Turkey had decided not to enter the war. From his spying he amassed over $1,000,000, which he hid under the floorboards of his British embassy bedroom. He then quit Sir Hughe and dropped out of sight, taking his fortune with him. At the end of World War II, Bazna resurfaced in Istanbul with the idea of building a luxury hotel for tourists. It was then that he discovered that he too had been betrayed. The money the Germans had given him turned out to be worthless forgeries. The man whose plot had revealed so many British secrets had become the victim of a nasty little German plot.

OF MOLES AND MEN

The word *mole* for a long-term agent who burrows into a rival intelligence agency was devised by an author. British thriller writer and former MI-6 officer John Le Carré (real name David Cornwell) coined the term in 1974 in his spy novel *Tinker, Tailor, Soldier, Spy.*

INNOCENT VICTIM *Most historians now think that, far from being a spy, Mata Hari (photographed here at the height of her dancing career) was simply an innocent scapegoat—shot because the French government wanted to cover up its military ineptitude by fabricating an all-powerful ring of German agents.*

Fashion—the pursuit of beauty

LOOKING LIKE A MILLION
The costliest dress ever made was priced at $1.5 million, a high-waisted and embroidered white muslin evening gown decorated with 516 diamonds. An armored car took it from the makers, Schiaparelli, to a fashion show at the Ritz hotel in Paris in 1977. Shoes extravagant enough to match it could not be found, so the model wore it barefoot. The dress was eventually bought for an Arab princess whose identity has not been revealed; and according to the makers, she still has it.

FEATHER-FOOTED
Feather-light shoes created by New York designer Yanturni in the 1920s took up to 3 years to make, and he refused even to start on a pair without a $1,000 deposit. He made plaster casts of clients' feet and molded the shoes around the contours.

Yanturni made 300 pairs for the Spanish-American hostess Rita D'Acosta Lydig. Some were made with 12th-century velvet, some of lace appliqué, others of brocade or gold and silver foil. Mrs. Lydig collected violins so that Yanturni could use the fine wood to make his shoe trees. Designer Cecil Beaton once claimed that a Yanturni shoe, complete with its tree, weighed no more than an ostrich feather.

THE TROUSER REVOLUTION
Only at the start of the 19th century did fashion-conscious men begin to prefer trousers over knee-breeches or knickers. Czar Alexander I of Russia regarded trousers as subversive, probably because they were worn by extremists of the French Revolution. In 1807 Alexander ordered his troops to stop all carriages, and if any man inside was wearing trousers, they were instantly cut off at the knee.

FRAGRANT THOUGHT
French actress Leslie Caron, as a small girl, had the idea of boiling her underclothes in a tub of expensive perfume to give them lasting fragrance. It seems to have worked—and Leslie had no need to worry about the economic impracticality of her idea. The tubful of scent cost her nothing. Her family owned the perfume house of Caron.

COSMETICS THROUGH THE AGES

7500 B.C. Egyptian shepherds and hunters in the Nile valley used oil crushed from castor beans to protect their skin from the sun.

3500 Women in Egypt and Mesopotamia used henna dyes to color their feet and hands. Eye shadow called kohl—made from lead ore, antimony, and malachite—was believed to drive away danger.

1370 Queen Nefertiti of Egypt painted her fingernails and toenails ruby red—a color forbidden to all but royalty.

750 Greek women dyed their hair black and whitened their skins with lead powder.

150 Romans applied gold-colored saffron pigments around their eyes and used wood ash to blacken their eyelids.

50 Cleopatra, queen of Egypt, rouged her cheeks with red ocher; she also painted her upper eyelids blue-black and lower lids green.

A.D. 10 Ovid, the Roman poet, wrote the first book on cosmetics. He recommended a face pack of barley-bean flour, eggs, and mashed narcissus bulbs as the key to smoother skin.

65 The Roman emperor Nero and his wife, Poppaea, applied lead and chalk to whiten their faces, rouged their cheeks, and used kohl to darken the edges of their eyelids.

200 The Greek physician Galen mixed water, beeswax, and olive oil into a cream. On the face the water evaporated, cooling the skin. Modern cold cream is virtually the same mixture.

1580 Queen Elizabeth dyed her hair red, plucked her eyebrows, and whitened her face. She was the first English queen to see herself in a clear glass mirror. She banned mirrors from court as she aged.

1660 In Restoration England women painted their faces and decorated them with black patches shaped as stars, crescents, and suns. The fashion evolved from a trick used by the Duchess of Newcastle to cover her blemishes.

1700 Powder rooms became fashionable in Europe and America because men and women powdered their hair, wigs, and faces. In bed, women put oiled cloths on their foreheads and wore gloves to prevent wrinkles.

1840 Heavy makeup began to go out of fashion in Britain and America. The Victorian ideal was peaches-and-cream skin.

1886 David McConnell went knocking on doors in the United States to sell sets of Shakespeare . . . and launched the cosmetics industry. His gimmick was a free bottle of perfume, but McConnell found that customers wanted the perfume more than the bard. He began making cosmetics and shrewdly used housewives as a sales force. Thus began the California Perfume Company, which grew into a cosmetics giant and became Avon, in remembrance of Shakespeare's hometown river.

1916 Liquid nail polish and mass-produced bright red lipstick were big nits in the United States.

1920 Hollywood set new ideals of appearance for both men and women, based on the celluloid images created by studio makeup teams. For women, arched eyebrows, cupid-bow lips, and bright colors were the rage.

PALE AND INTERESTING Suntans are a 20th-century notion of beauty. This 19th-century advertisement extols the virtues of a skin-whitening cream that "never fails to remove Freckles [and] Sunburn."

COVER GIRL

A Dutch model named Wilhelmina still holds the world record for appearances on the covers of the world's top fashion magazines: 250 covers between 1960 and 1967, when she retired. That is nearly twice the combined total amassed by the runners-up, British models Jean Shrimpton and Twiggy. Despite the exposure, Wilhelmina's name remained almost unknown to the general public.

SILENT MODEL

The first women models, a century ago, were hardly seen, never heard, and chosen purely as clothes-horses. They had no status and were typically plain looking so that they would not steal the show from the creations they were modeling.

In 1920, Paul Poiret, a Parisian couturier, took his models on tour, all dressed alike in semimilitary uniforms with belts, buckles, epaulets, and peaked caps. Lunching at the Carlton Hotel in London with fashion writer Alison Settle, Poiret was startled when she turned to address a silent model beside her. "No, mademoiselle, do not speak to the girls," he warned Miss Settle. "They are not there."

THE BARE-LEGGED LOOK

Victorian women considered even the merest glimpse of female leg indecent—much more so if the leg was unclad. Right up to the mid-20th century, no fashion-conscious woman would go stockingless, despite severe wartime shortages of materials used to make stockings. In Britain, when supplies of cotton and rayon stockings ran out in World War II, many women used specially prepared leg makeup, which preserved some decorum in the midst of war.

The first real attempt to abandon stockings was made during World War I by actress Gaby Deslys, mistress of King Manuel of Portugal. She shocked women and amused men by declaring that she would not wear stockings again until Germany surrendered to the Allies. In the 1920s Hollywood femme fatale Pola Negri went bare-legged, and actress Joan Crawford rejected stockings as evening wear in 1926.

In 1934, after much debate, the British fashion weekly *Sketch* concluded that "going bare-legged is inartistic and tends to spoil the softness of the skin." But in 1942 the wartime British government came close to official disapproval of stockings, declaring that if women did not stop wearing them in summer, there would be none by winter.

As late as the 1960s, matrons in Melbourne, Australia, disapproved when model Jean Shrimpton appeared as guest of honor at Flemington racecourse hatless, gloveless—and stockingless. Then, in 1983, the Princess of Wales attended a Government House party in Canberra with her legs covered only by a golden Australian suntan. The bare-legged look had finally won the royal seal of approval, at least as far as Princess Di was concerned.

À LA MODE *A 19th-century engraving shows the extravagant costumes worn at Versailles, the court of France's Sun King, Louis XIV (1643–1715). The fashions set there were eagerly imitated all over Europe. The coat became part of everyday wear, having developed from the military dress sometimes worn by the king. Louis promoted French fashions— sometimes by force. When his troops occupied Strasbourg (then an independent city) in 1681, its citizens were ordered to adopt French styles within 4 months.*

MUSTACHE BAN

Faded photographs of mustachioed Victorian males show only one side of 19th-century society's love-hate relationship with the hairy upper lip. A wealthy Englishman named Henry Budd died in 1862 leaving one London estate, Pepper Park, to his son Edward and another estate, Twickenham Park, to his second son, William—on condition that they did not wear mustaches. Seven years later a British upholsterer left the sum of £10 to each employee "if no mustaches." In 1904 some London clothiers stopped employing assistants who wore mustaches (or parted their hair in the middle). The Bank of England, however, scrupulously avoided interfering with employees' private lives. Mustaches were forbidden only "during working hours"!

MEET MR. BEETON

Mrs. Isabella Beeton's encyclopedic *Book of Household Management* instructed generations of proper English matrons. But her unsung husband, Samuel Orchard Beeton, also had a powerful influence on women. He invented the fashion magazine.

In 1852, four years before he married, 21-year-old Samuel published *The Englishwoman's Domestic Magazine*. With each issue, he gave away a paper dress pattern, starting in Volume I with "A Lady's Jacket and Vest." There were then no retail stores selling ready-to-wear fashions. Mr. Beeton's patterns and the do-it-yourself instructions in his magazine gave fashion to British housewives for just the price of material—and, of course, the magazine itself. It was not long before the idea caught on in America.

FALSE EYELASHES

False eyelashes were invented by the American film director D. W. Griffith while he was making his 1916 epic, *Intolerance*. Griffith wanted actress Seena Owen to have lashes that brushed her cheeks, to make her eyes shine larger than life.

A wigmaker wove human hair through fine gauze, which was then gummed to Owen's eyelids. *Intolerance* was critically acclaimed but flopped financially, leaving Griffith with huge debts that he might have been able to settle easily—had he only thought to patent the eyelashes.

WASP WAIST

For about 100 years women laced themselves into ever-tighter corsets in pursuit of the 19th-century ideal of the hourglass figure, which featured a very slender, or wasp, waist. Wasp waists as tiny as 16 inches, 15 inches, and even 13 inches were claimed.

Photographs of the French dancer Polaire suggest that her claim to a 17-inch waist was genuine, but anything less may be anatomically impossible. An English museum curator, Doris Langley Moore, measured the waists of 200 Victorian and Edwardian dresses in Bath's Museum of Costume; all were

HATS AROUND THE WORLD

Derby

The hat called a derby in the United States is named after the British Lord Derby—but the British call it something else. English landowner William Coke ordered the first such hat to protect his head from low branches while he was shooting on his Norfolk estate. On December 17, 1849, he tested the new design in the shop of the London hatters, Lock's, by stamping on it twice. It was undamaged, and Coke bought it for 12 shillings. The hat became known as the bowler after Thomas Bowler, who made it to Lock's order; however, Lock's still calls it a coke, after the man who first ordered it. The bowler was adopted by British office workers and was their standard wear until its use declined in the 1950s.

Fez

A tasseled red felt hat, shaped like a flat-topped cone, the fez became a symbol of Middle Eastern Muslims. In Turkey it was banned by Mustafa Kemal, otherwise known as Ataturk, father of the Turkish revolution, who swept aside the ruling sultans in 1922 and westernized the nation.

Trilby

Actors playing Bohemian characters in the 1894 stage production of George du Maurier's novel *Trilby* wore soft felt hats with wide brims and a dented crown. This style of hat became known as the trilby, after the name of the novel's heroine, Trilby O'Ferral, a singer swept to fame under the hypnotic influence of a magician named Svengali.

Topper

Mobs of curious Londoners crowded around James Heatherington when he first wore his tall, shiny "topper" hat in the city in 1797. Women fainted in the crush, one boy had an arm broken, and Mr. Heatherington was arrested. He was fined £50, an enormous sum then, for disturbing the peace. But his top hat later became obligatory headgear for racegoers at Ascot, at society weddings, and for ambassadors presenting their credentials to the British monarch at the Court of St. James's.

more ample, suggesting that the extravagant claims were wishful thinking.

For a modern comparison, the actress Twiggy, who was a legend of slenderness during her 1960s modeling career, had a 22-inch waist.

POKE BONNET

Nothing evokes a more appealing image of demure 19th-century femininity than the poke bonnet. Yet it was originally meant to conceal the face rather than add allure to it. It was devised by an aristocrat named Baroness Oldenburg in 1818 to hide her unfortunate looks. The bonnet's side flaps curled around and all but covered her face.

Intrigued by the new style, pretty women of the day began decorating the bonnet with ribbons and flowers and turning back its sides to give coy and provocative glimpses of their faces.

A straw version common in the 1880s was adapted by Quaker women and by the English-

PUTTING ON THE AGONY
A 19th-century cartoon hints at the discomfort involved in achieving a minuscule waistline.

woman Catherine Booth for her new battalions of Salvation Army women—not because of its simple charm, but because the stiffened straw offered protection against stones and missiles hurled at the courageous pioneers.

FASHIONABLE BEGINNINGS

Tweed Two simple mistakes gave this fabric its lasting name. A Scots weaver offered London merchant James Locke some twilled (diagonally ribbed) cloth in 1832. But in his letter, the Scotsman, whose penmanship may have been careless besides, spelled *twilled* in its Scottish form, "tweeled." Locke misread "tweeled" as "tweed," and the name stuck.

Worsted Also known as wusted, worsett, wirsed, and wossat, this woolen fabric is made from twisted yarn and originated in the English village of Worstead, Norfolk. No one knows exactly when it was first made, but by the 14th century worsted was frequently mentioned in home inventories, wills, and lawsuits as a material for garments or household use. The cloth is now manufactured in places far from Norfolk, including the United States and Australia.

Tawdry The term *tawdry,* meaning cheap and gaudy, once meant something very different. Tawdry is an abbreviation of St. Audrey, whose name was given to St. Audrey's lace, a silk ribbon worn around the neck in the Middle Ages. The saint died in A.D. 679 of a throat tumor, which she blamed on the vanity of wearing pretty necklaces. Merchants at medieval fairs offered cheap, bright substitutes to country girls who could not afford real silk, and they called it "tawdry."

Poplin Originally a corded fabric in which a silk warp was mixed with a worsted weft, poplin was first made in France in the mid-17th century at Avignon—a *papalino,* or papal city—and that is the origin of its name. The silk has long since gone, and poplin is now generally a mixture of worsted and cotton.

Mae West The name was given to an automatically inflatable life jacket issued to British Royal Air Force crews in World War II. When inflated, it rose in two great curves on the wearer's chest, suggesting the shape of the U.S. comedienne.

Jeans The hard-wearing work trousers, thought to have been invented by a sailmaker named Levi Strauss in San Francisco in 1850, get their name from gene (or jene) fustian, a heavy twilled cotton cloth first made in Genoa, Italy. Denim comes from the French phrase *serge de Nîmes* (serge of Nîmes).

Tuxedo Man-about-town Griswold Lorillard shocked his fellow members at the Tuxedo Park Country Club, Tuxedo Park, New York, when he appeared at the 1886 Autumn Ball wearing a short black coat with shiny satin lapels instead of the conventional white tie and tailcoat. Lorillard explained that his "dinner jacket" was a more formal version of the British smoking jacket; and the club's name came to be used for the style Lorillard had launched there.

Blocked by a stile

Getting dressed

At the ball

Romantic leanings

CUPID AND THE CRINOLINE *A series of cartoons published in 1835—one making an atrocious pun on the words "stile" (for turnstile) and "style"—pokes fun at the hazards of the crinoline. This fashion for billowing skirts, formed by vast quantities of material draped over wicker or steel frames hung from the waist, emerged in France in the mid-19th century. By the late 1850s crinolines had become so enormous that two ladies could not enter a room at the same time, or sit on the same sofa—and presented male suitors with an almost impassable barrier. At the height of the fashion a single dress could use up 1,100 yards of lace and gauzy tulle. Yet despite this extravagant design, white crinolines were often worn only once and then discarded, because their freshness was thought to have been lost. Underneath the whole elaborate structure, ladies wore ankle-length lacy pantaloons to protect their legs from indecent exposure in high winds.*

Mythology and legends

ATLAS In Greek legend Atlas was a Titan, an early Greek god. After the Titans were defeated by the classical gods of Olympus under Zeus, Atlas was condemned to carry the heavens on his shoulders. Later, when he refused hospitality to the Greek hero Perseus, Perseus turned him to stone by showing him the head of the Gorgon Medusa. His body became the Atlas Mountains of northwest Africa. Bound collections of medieval maps often featured the image of Atlas as the frontispiece, which gave rise to the modern use of his name.

CASSANDRA The name Cassandra is often applied to anyone who predicts a future of gloom and doom. But the original Cassandra was gloomy not because of any bleak prophecy but because nobody would believe her, no matter what she forecast or however accurate she proved to be. The daughter of Priam, king of Troy, she was given the gift of prophecy by Apollo on condition that she would accept him as her lover. When Cassandra withheld her side of the bargain, Apollo was unable to retract his gift; but he got even by ordaining that her predictions would always be ignored.

HALCYONE The phrase *halcyon days,* which describes any period of peace and tranquillity, comes from the Greek legend of Halcyone, the daughter of Aeolus, god of the winds. When her husband, Ceyx, was drowned, Halcyone threw herself into the sea in despair. But the gods intervened and changed the couple into kingfishers, or halcyons. Zeus also forbade the winds to blow for a week on either side of the winter solstice (onset of winter, about December 22), giving the kingfishers calm "halcyon days" for brooding their eggs.

The English word for cleanliness, **hygiene,** *comes from the name of a Greek goddess. She was Hygieia, goddess of health and the daughter of Asclepius (Roman Aesculapius), the god of healing.*

HERMES Son and messenger of the supreme Greek god, Zeus, Hermes (the Roman Mercury) in his winged cap and sandals was among the busiest of the gods. When not carrying tidings or leading the dead to Hades, he was god of roads, fraud and cunning, commerce—and luck. The serpent-entwined

SNAKES ALIVE *The Gorgon Medusa, depicted here on a clay tablet dating from the 7th century* B.C., *was one of three sisters made hideous by the gods for their misdeeds. Her face, surrounded by a mass of writhing serpents instead of hair, was so awful that, according to Greek mythology, anyone who looked upon it turned instantly to stone. Medusa was finally killed and beheaded by the legendary Greek hero Perseus. He avoided looking at her directly during the battle by using his polished shield as a mirror. Medusa's blood gave birth to the winged horse Pegasus, her son by the Greek sea god Poseidon.*

staff of Hermes is still the emblem of the medical profession. The staff is known as the caduceus. To the ancient Greeks a snake's ability to slough its skin was a symbol of renewal and fresh vigor, and hence of the healing power of medicine.

HERACLES Greatest and strongest of the Greek demigods, Heracles (known to the Romans as Hercules) was the son of Zeus by a mortal woman and was hated by Zeus's wife, Hera. He began his life of heroic violence by strangling two serpents while still in his crib. In manhood, driven mad by Hera, he murdered his wife and children and, as penance, spent 12 years in the service of his rival Eurystheus. Hoping to destroy Heracles, Eurystheus set him 12 supposedly impossible tasks, but the hero completed them all.

The 12 labors of Heracles were (1) strangling a lion that terrorized the valley of Nemea; (2) striking off the many heads of the poisonous water snake Hydra of Lerna; (3 and 4) delivering alive to Eurystheus the terrifying Erymanthian boar and the Arcadian stag sacred to Artemis; (5) killing the man-eating birds of Lake Stymphalis; (6) cleaning in one day (by diverting two rivers) the stables of Augeas, king of Elis, which contained 3,000 oxen and had not been cleaned for 30 years; (7) capturing and bearing on his shoulders to Mycenae the white Cretan bull, sire of the Minotaur; (8) capturing the man-eating mares of Diomedes (a Thracian king and son of the war god Ares) and feeding them with the flesh of Diomedes; (9) fetching for Eurystheus's daughter the girdle of the Amazon queen, Hippolyte; (10) killing the three-bodied monster Geryon, along with his giant herdsman Eurytion and the two-headed dog Orthrus, in order to capture Geryon's oxen; (11) freeing Prometheus and temporarily bearing the weight of the world for Atlas, who went to fetch for him the golden apples of the Hesperides; and (12) descending to the underworld to bring the three-headed dog Cerberus to its master, Hades.

His servitude ended, Heracles took part in the voyage of Jason and the Argonauts to find the Golden Fleece. He was reconciled with Hera only after his death when, in recognition of his exploits, he was made a god.

The endless chatter of Echo, a mountain nymph, foiled the jealous goddess Hera's attempts to catch her husband, Zeus, making love to other women. The enraged Hera punished Echo by leaving her only able to repeat the last words spoken to her. Echo's unrequited love for Narcissus, who loved only his own image, made her fade away until only her voice was left.

TANTALUS Eternal tantalizing torment was the lot of Tantalus, mythical Greek king of Phrygia. He cut up his son Pelops and presented the flesh to the gods at a banquet to test their all-powerful knowledge. The gods duly detected the outrage, restored Pelops to life, and condemned Tantalus to an eternity of suffering in Tartarus, the lower depths of the underworld reserved for those who defied the gods. Racked by endless hunger and thirst, Tantalus was forced to stand up to his neck in water surrounded by luscious

THE GODS OF GREECE AND ROME

As well as absorbing Greece into the Roman Empire in the 2nd century B.C., the Romans adapted many of the Greek myths, linking the legends and deities of Greece with their own gallery of gods.

GREEK	ROMAN	
Aphrodite	Venus	Goddess of love and beauty
Apollo, Phoebus	Apollo, Phoebus	Greek god of sun, god of music, poetry, and prophecy
Ares	Mars	God of war
Artemis	Diana	Virgin huntress, goddess of the moon
Asclepius	Aesculapius	God of medicine
Athena (Pallas)	Minerva	Goddess of wisdom and art
Cronus	Saturn	Father of the supreme god, Zeus, or Jupiter
Demeter	Ceres	Goddess of the harvest
Dionysus	Bacchus	God of wine and fertility
Eros	Cupid	God of love
Hades, Pluto	Dis	God of the underworld
Hephaestus	Vulcan	God of fire and metalworking
Hera	Juno	Queen of heaven, wife of Zeus/Jupiter, goddess of women and marriage
Hermes	Mercury	Messenger of the gods, god of roads, cunning, commerce, wealth, and luck
Hestia	Vesta	Goddess of the hearth
Hymen	Hymen	God of marriage
Irene	Pax	Goddess of peace
Pan	Faunus	God of flocks and shepherds
Persephone	Proserpina	Goddess of corn and the spring, goddess of the dead
Poseidon	Neptune	God of the sea
Zeus	Jupiter, Jove	Supreme ruler of gods and men, king of heaven, and overseer of justice and destiny

fruit trees. But every time he stooped to drink, the water level dropped, and every time he stretched up for a fruit, the trees drew away—keeping both water and fruit perpetually just out of his reach.

HYACINTHUS The hyacinth flower is said to have sprung from the blood of Hyacinthus, a golden youth loved by both the sun god, Apollo, and Zephyrus. Because the youth preferred Apollo, Zephyrus, the god of the west wind, had him killed by a quoit flung by Apollo. Marks on the petals, the Greeks thought, resembled the letters *a* (alpha) and *i* (iota), standing for Hyacinthus's dying cry, "*Ai, ai*" ("Alas, alas").

PANDORA In Greek myth Pandora was the first woman. Zeus created her and sent her on a mission of vengeance against the rebellious Titans and their allies, men. She was given a box to take with her, with orders not to open it. Because she was curious, Pandora disobeyed, opened the box, and released all the evils of the world. Only Hope was left. Pandora's box is thus a symbol for any action whose consequences are dangerously unpredictable.

PSYCHE Psychology, the science of the mind, gets its name from Psyche, a beautiful girl in Greek mythology who was desired by Eros, the god of love. He forbade her to look at him because he was a god, and when she disobeyed by lighting a lamp in the dark, he abandoned her. Eventually she was reunited with Eros and joined the immortals. She was revered as the personification of the human soul.

TITANS Before Mount Olympus became the home of the gods, the ancient Greeks believed the Titans had ruled over a golden age on earth. The 12 Titans

GODS THE EGYPTIANS WORSHIPED

Ancient Egyptians bound together the folktales and legends of several civilizations that had lived in the Nile Valley before Egypt was unified in about 3100 B.C. From these ancient tales, the Egyptians wove a complex network of myths around their chief god, Ra, or Re.

Originally, ancient Egyptians believed, the earth arose as a hill from the featureless ocean Nun. Darkness was dispersed by the sun god Ra, who alit as a phoenix on the hill. His offspring were Shu, the god of air, and Tefnut, goddess of water. Shu and Tefnut in turn had twins—the earth god Geb and the sky goddess Nut—who remained locked in incestuous embrace until Shu parted them to create heaven and earth.

Each day Nut, who was depicted as a cow, gave birth to the sun anew. Each dawn the sun rose as Khepri, a giant scarab beetle, and crossed the sky as Ra in a ship crewed by other gods. Each night it sank below the horizon as an old man, then crossed the underworld to begin the cycle again.

Other major Egyptian gods and goddesses included:

AMON
Supreme god of Thebes, later identified with Ra.

ANUBIS
Jackal-headed god of embalming, son of Nephthys and Osiris. He supervised the weighing of souls at judgment.

HATHOR
Goddess of joy and beauty in all their expressions, daughter of Ra. As the Eye of Ra, she was the enemy of rebellious mortals. She was later identified with other goddesses of love, including Aphrodite.

HORUS
Originally a falcon-headed god of the sky and son of Nut. He was later regarded as the son of Isis and Osiris, and grew up to defeat his evil uncle Set.

ISIS
Fertility goddess, daughter of Nut and sister and wife of Osiris. She was founder of marriage and teacher with Osiris of agriculture, spinning, and weaving.

NEPHTHYS
Funerary goddess and sister of Isis, she befriended dead mortals at judgment.

OSIRIS
Corn god, son of Nut and Geb. He married his sister Isis while still in the womb, became king on earth, and abolished cannibalism. Murdered by his brother Set, he was restored to life by Isis and became supreme judge of the dead and ruler of the underworld. He was usually shown as a mummified pharaoh.

PTAH
High god of Memphis, said by his devotees to be creator of all other gods. Magician and patron of arts and crafts. Later Ptah became a judge of the dead and was represented as a mummy.

SET
Son of Nut and Geb, and brother of Osiris. In early myths he was Ra's chief defender; later he became the personification of evil, murdering Osiris and persecuting Horus. Also regarded as lord of Upper Egypt. His eventual destruction by Horus, lord of Lower Egypt, symbolized the unification of the country. Usually depicted with red hair, Set personified the desert and its sterility.

THOTH
Magician and inventor of speech and hieroglyphics, Thoth became chief aide of Osiris and teacher of the arts of civilization. He was represented as an ibis or a dog-headed baboon.

GODDESS WHO WADED IN BLOOD Hathor was Egypt's goddess of beauty, fertility, love, and marriage. In one tale about her from early mythology she was ordered by her father, Ra, to destroy the human race and was depicted wading in blood. However, Hathor was tricked into drinking a mixture of beer and red ocher resembling blood, became drunk, and thus failed to complete the slaughter.

To kill a cat in ancient Egypt brought immediate death. To the Egyptians cats were sacred to Bast, the cat-headed goddess of pleasure, and cat funerals were so numerous that the animals' cemeteries are still used by modern Egyptians as a source of rich fertilizer.

were the offspring of Uranus, god of the heavens, and Gaea, the goddess of earth. Cronus, the youngest of the 12, became their leader when he overthrew his father. Cronus, the god of time, was later overthrown in his turn by his son, Zeus.

> *The planet Jupiter is named for Rome's supreme god, Jupiter. His name and that of his Greek counterpart, Zeus, come from an ancient Indo-European word for the sky—suggesting that concepts of Zeus and Jupiter had a common origin in primitive beliefs involving a weather god.*

NARCISSUS Narcissists—people who are obsessed with their looks—are named after Narcissus, a handsome youth in Greek mythology. Narcissus refused all offers of love, including that of the nymph Echo. He was punished by Aphrodite, the goddess of love, for his indifference by being made to fall in love with his own reflection in a forest pool. Unable to possess the image, he pined away and was changed into the flower that bears his name. The modern psychological term *narcissism,* meaning immoderate love of oneself, was coined by the Austrian psychiatrist and pioneer of psychoanalysis, Sigmund Freud (1856–1939).

THESEUS The mythical Greek hero Theseus, who killed the bull-headed Minotaur, escaped from the monster's labyrinth on Crete afterward with the help of a ball of thread that he had let out behind him as he entered the underground maze. When the legend was told in medieval England—where the word for a ball of thread was *clew*—a guide to the solution of any problem became known as a clew, or clue.

WEIGHED AGAINST A FEATHER *An Egyptian papyrus dating from about 1300 B.C. shows Anubis, the jackal-headed god of embalming (bottom, center), weighing a heart—symbolizing the conscience of a dead person—against a feather, the symbol of truth. The heart is that of a senior administrator called Ani, shown on the left in white robes with his wife. Above, a jury of gods sits in judgment. To the right of Anubis stands Thoth, scribe of the gods, recording the results; and behind Thoth crouches the monster Amemit, waiting to devour Ani's soul if it is found wanting.*

LUCKY BEETLE Dung beetles, or scarabs, were venerated by ancient Egyptians as lucky. The insect was revered because its habit of rolling a ball of dung to its nest seemed to symbolize the sun god, Ra, rolling the ball of the sun across the heavens. Crocodiles, too, were sacred, and the Nile crocodile god, Sebek, was worshiped at his own city, appropriately named Crocodilopolis.

MUMMY AND THE ARMY OF RATS Egyptian mythology came to depict Ptah, who had been high god of a cult that flourished at Memphis (south of modern Cairo), as a mummy who judged the dead. Ptah was said to have won a war for the Egyptians against the Assyrians by raising an army of rats that chewed through the enemy's bowstrings and shield thongs, in effect disarming the Assyrians.

Mythology and legends

HORSE SENSE In Norse legend Odin's eight-legged steed, Sleipnir, was born soon after the gods built Asgard as their home. A giant turned up and offered to build a great wall around the stronghold before summer came again—with no help other than that of his stallion, Svadilfari. If he completed the work by the first day of summer, the giant would be given the fertility goddess, Freya, and the sun and the moon. Otherwise he would get nothing.

With the help of his horse, the giant made swift progress, and to the alarm of the gods the wall was rapidly completed. With 3 days left, only the gates remained to be fitted. But Loki, the god of mischief, turned himself into a mare and lured the stallion away from his work. The giant failed to fulfill his contract and was slain by Thor, the god of thunder. Several months later, however, Loki gave birth to a gray colt with eight legs: Sleipnir.

ONE-EYED KING *Odin, the supreme Norse god—shown here on his eight-legged steed Sleipnir—is said to have sacrificed an eye in return for wisdom.*

The Vikings believed that the northern lights, which blaze from time to time in the skies of the far north, were caused by the flashing armor and spears of Odin's handmaidens, the Valkyries, as they rode out to collect warriors slain in battle and take them to Odin's palace, Valhalla.

MEAD OF INSPIRATION One legend about the Vikings' supreme god, Odin, tells how he brought poetic inspiration to mortals by stealing a magic potion of mead made from the blood of the wisest of all creatures in Norse myth, the giant Kvasir. A giant called Suttung hid the mead in three casks inside a mountain under the care of his daughter, Gunnlöd.

Odin crawled into the mountain in the shape of a snake and spent three nights with Gunnlöd. Swayed by his ardor, she allowed him three drinks of the mead. Odin emptied all three casks, then changed into an eagle and flew off toward Asgard, the home of the gods, hotly pursued by Suttung.

The gods had placed a line of vats on the walls of Asgard, and Odin managed to regurgitate the precious mead into these vessels before Suttung could catch him. Some splashed from the vats and fell outside the walls of Asgard; and this spilled brew inspired mortal versifiers and writers of doggerel.

BEWARE THE MISTLETOE Many ancient religions held the mistletoe to be a sacred plant. The Druids believed that a sprig of mistletoe, fastened above a doorway, would ward off evil and enhance the hospitality and fertility of the household. Hence the Christmas custom of kissing under the mistletoe.

But to Norsemen the mistletoe was a baleful plant because it brought death to Baldur, the shining god of youth. Odin, his father, who knew the future, sought to prevent Baldur's fate. Odin and other gods made almost every conceivable object promise not to harm Baldur. But they did not bother to get a pledge from the mistletoe, thinking it too feeble.

Since Baldur was apparently impervious to injury, he entertained the other gods by letting them try to hurt him. One day, when the gods were at this sport, Loki, the god of mischief, noticed that Baldur's blind brother, Hödur, was taking no part in the game. So Loki cut a branch of mistletoe in the shape of a javelin, gave it to Hödur, and made the blind brother throw it toward Baldur. The mistletoe pierced Baldur to the heart, killing him.

Baldur's death was the signal for the Battle of Ragnarök—the Norse equivalent of Armageddon—to begin. The gods were overwhelmed by the giants and monsters of evil. The whole universe was consumed in a holocaust of destruction. But after Ragnarök, Baldur rose from the grave to a new and revitalized world of mortals with one god: Baldur. This was a poetic foreshadowing of the conversion to Christianity, which pushed the cruel warrior Viking gods out of the mainstream of belief.

BIRTH OF THE NORSE GODS

The main sources for Norse mythology are two medieval books, both called Edda: the Poetic Edda and the Prose Edda. The meaning of the word *Edda* is not known. The Poetic Edda, a collection of heroic and mythological poems, was written down in Iceland in the 1270s. The poets and the collector are anonymous.

The Prose Edda was written around 1220 by the Icelandic scholar and historian Snorri Sturluson, as a handbook for aspiring poets. According to the Edda, the universe emerged out of a Great Void. The first living being to emerge was a giant called Ymir, ancestor of the evil race of Frost Giants. From the blocks of salty ice around Ymir's head, a primeval cow licked into shape another being called Búri, the ancestor of the gods. Búri married a giantess who was born in Ymir's left armpit, and their descendants were the first three gods: Odin and his two brothers.

How the first man was made
Together the three offspring set upon Ymir and slew him, fashioning the world from his carcass. The first men and women were whittled out of two pieces of driftwood by Odin and his brothers and were given a home in Midgard (sometimes written as Midgarth), a name meaning the Middle Enclave. In the heart of Midgard the gods built their own fortified home, Asgard, on a high crag connected to earth by the shining rainbow-bridge of Bifrost.

Belief in the Norse gods continues to the present day. In Iceland there is a small cult of the Norse gods called Ásatrú ("belief in the gods"). Its members conduct marriages and funerals according to ancient Norse rites, and the ceremonies are recognized as legal by the state.

CRUSADERS' SAINT *A Spanish picture painted in about A.D. 1400 shows St. George, patron saint of England, killing a dragon. The story is said by some to be a medieval adaptation of the Greek legend about the hero Perseus rescuing Andromeda from a monster. St. George was a Christian martyred for his faith at Lydda in Palestine in about 300. He was a little-known figure until he was adopted as a soldier-saint by medieval Crusaders. At the height of his cult in the late Middle Ages, he was adopted as patron of Venice, Genoa, Portugal, and Catalonia as well as England. In 1969 he was dropped from the list of saints whose feasts must be observed universally. But his name remains in the Roman Catholic liturgical calendar, and his feast may be observed locally.*

MAN WHO MET A ZOMBIE Belief in zombies, the "living dead" of the black magic religion known as voodoo, may be based on fact. In 1983 a Canadian scientist from Harvard University, Wade Davis, reported that he had actually met one. The zombie was a Haitian known as Louis Ozias, who said that he had been certified dead at a U.S.-run hospital on the Caribbean island, buried, then dug up and made to work as a slave on a remote sugar plantation for 2 years. He had escaped only after his master died.

Davis believes that Ozias and other zombies are victims not of magic but of powerful natural drugs

Mythology and legends

known to voodoo initiates. Davis identifies three such types of drugs. One type, tetrodotoxin, is derived from puffer fish and can induce paralysis and other symptoms that are part of the zombie legend. Curiously, puffer fish are eaten as a delicacy in Japan, where they are known as *fugu*. The prized *fugu* stew is supposed to be prepared only by cooks specially trained to remove the puffer toxin; but slipups happen, and puffer poisoning, while rare statistically, is a medical fact of life in Japan. There are cases in Japanese medical annals of victims being pronounced dead and then reviving. In one case reported in 1880, a gambler poisoned after eating *fugu* recovered in a mortuary 7 days after being declared dead. According to Davis, tetrodotoxin is an exceptionally potent anesthetic, 160,000 times stronger than cocaine.

The second group of drugs is derived from a New World toad, *Bufo marinus,* and is known to boost physical strength—matching voodoo legends that say that a new zombie must be tied and beaten to subdue him. The third group, from *Datura* plants, has hallucinogenic properties—capable of inducing the dazed, trancelike state associated with zombies.

CATHERINE'S WHEEL   The Vatican removed St. Catherine of Alexandria from the liturgical calendar in 1969 because it found no proof of her existence. Legend says that she was a virgin of noble birth, martyred at Alexandria in the 4th century A.D. for protesting to the Roman emperor Maxentius about his persecution of Christians. The legend further relates that Catherine was tortured on a spiked wheel, which broke when she was bound to it, and the pieces flew in all directions, injuring bystanders.

The episode gave rise to her emblem, the Catherine wheel, which is also a rotating firework. Eventually she was beheaded, and milk is said to have flowed from her severed head. According to the legend, angels transported her body to Mount Sinai, and it was there that her cult began in the 9th century. The legend appealed to medieval artists, and her cult flourished among the Crusaders.

SEA SPIRITS
As in this ceremonial mask, sea creatures were prominent in the legends of the Northwest Coast Indians—Chinooks, Kwakiutls, Tlingits, and others—who prospered before 1900 on the Pacific Coast from Alaska south to present-day northern California. Blessed by a cornucopia of ocean resources, including the mighty salmon runs, these people spent only a few months getting a year's food. In ceremonies they asked sea spirits never to desert them.

EASTER AND THE BUNNY   Children's stories in many countries tell how Easter eggs are brought not by a chicken but by hares and rabbits. These long-eared hopping mammals have represented fertility in many cultures because they breed so quickly. In traditional Christian art the hare represents lust, and paintings sometimes show a hare at the Virgin Mary's feet to signify her triumph over temptations of the flesh. Yet as a symbol of life reawakening in the spring—often portrayed as the innocent and cuddly Easter bunny—the rabbit coexists in many places with the solemn Christian rites of Easter.

DISAPPEARING TRICK   The legend of the vanishing hitchhiker is told as a true story in many parts of the world. According to the legend a young girl is given a lift and mysteriously disappears during the journey. The baffled driver calls at the address she gave him, only to discover from her parents that she died some years ago at the very spot where he picked her up. He goes to look at her nearby grave and finds the sweater that he had lent her during the car journey draped over the tombstone. This modern ghost story dates from the turn of the 20th century. With variations, it is told in Britain, Ireland, China, Turkey, Europe, and the United States. In Hawaii a rickshaw replaces the car.

One of the most persistent modern legends concerns the New York blackout of November 9, 1965. A power failure put out the lights all over the city; and 9 months later, so the story goes, up leaped the city birthrate. In fact, nothing of the sort happened. Any rise in the birthrate would have shown up between July 27 and August 14, 1966. But demographers have found that the number of births in New York City for that period was slightly below the average—13.9 percent of all births for the year, against a 5-year average of 14 percent for the same period in 1960–65.

THE REAL FATHER CHRISTMAS   The original Santa Claus lived nowhere near the North Pole. If he existed at all, he lived in the Near East. Santa Claus is a corruption of the Dutch name Sinte Klaas, for St. Nicholas, who seems to have been a 4th-century bishop of Myra in Turkey. St. Nicholas was the patron of children and unwed girls. Tradition says that he saved three daughters of a noble but impoverished family from a life of prostitution by giving each daughter a bag of gold as a dowry. As the legend developed in the Netherlands, the three bags of gold became a bulging sack of presents that Santa Claus handed out to children on December 6, St. Nicholas's feast day. Dutch settlers took this custom to North America, where it fused with northern European legends about a winter spirit who gave gifts to good children and punished the bad.

WITCHES' SABBATH   Walpurgis Night, when German witches traditionally ride to meet their master, the Devil, is named after an English abbess who was a formidable opponent of witchcraft. St. Walpurgis, or Walburga, was the niece of St. Boniface, who helped to introduce Christianity to the Germans. She founded several religious houses in Germany during the 8th century A.D. and became known as a protectress against witchcraft. Her name is linked with the witches' sabbath on April 30 only because her feast day falls on May 1. The night of April 30 was simply the eve of Walpurgis Day.

In Roman times May was associated with the spirits of the dead, and it was believed that the month, and particularly May Day, was a time for practicing witchcraft. In general, witches were thought to be particularly active at turning points of the year—for instance, when cattle were taken to summer pasture early in May. On Walpurgis Night villagers in Germany used to light fires to drive any passing witches away from their homes and their cattle.

SACRIFICIAL FIRE Grief-stricken Indian widows used to sacrifice themselves on their husbands' funeral pyres to commemorate an episode in Hindu mythology. The episode concerned Sati—meaning "chaste wife"—who was a wife of Shiva, one of the principal Hindu deities, and daughter of a sage named Daksha. When her husband and father quarreled, she killed herself in sorrow by walking into a fire. Suttee, the custom named after Sati of burning a Hindu woman on her husband's funeral pyre, dates from the 4th century B.C., and by the 6th century A.D. it was obligatory for devout Hindus. The widows, or satis, who immolated themselves in this way were promised 35 million years in Svarga, the Hindu paradise. The satis also became female saints and were believed to possess miraculous healing powers. The practice of suttee was outlawed in British India by the governor-general, Lord William Bentinck, in 1829.

> *Ethiopians, who contend that they are God's chosen people, have a legend to back their belief. According to the legend, God molded the first men from clay. He put the first batch in the oven to bake but left them too long. They came out burned and black, so He threw them away to the southern part of Africa. He took the second batch out too soon, and they were pasty white, so He threw them away to the north, where they became Arabs and Europeans. The third batch came out just right, and He put them in Ethiopia. Other peoples, such as the Eskimos, have similar creation legends expressing ethnic pride.*

THE ALLIGATORS OF NEW YORK Some American children still believe that the sewers of New York City are infested with giant drug-crazed alligators. The 20th-century legend maintains that vacationers returning from Florida brought baby alligators home as souvenirs. When the animals grew larger, their owners panicked and flushed them down the toilet. In the sewers the alligators flourished on a diet of rats and sewage, grew to enormous size, and bred prolifically. Without natural light the giant reptiles turned white and went blind. They supplemented their diet by devouring illicit drugs supposedly flushed into the sewers during police raids. The origin of these wild tales is unknown, although a February 1935 *New York Times* story actually describes the capture of a 7-foot-long alligator in a city sewer. The story reports that the alligator was killed by its rescuers after it turned on them, threatening their lives.

ANNIVERSARY GIFTS

Particular wedding anniversaries have come to be associated in the Western world with particular types of gifts. The gift may vary in different countries. This list is one of the most common.

1st	Paper	25th	Silver
2nd	Cotton	30th	Pearl
3rd	Leather	35th	Coral
4th	Fruit, flowers, linen	40th	Ruby
5th	Wood	45th	Sapphire
6th	Sugar, iron	50th	Gold
7th	Wool, copper	55th	Emerald
8th	Bronze	60th	Diamond
9th	Pottery	70th	Platinum
10th	Tin		
11th	Steel		
12th	Silk, linen		
13th	Lace		
14th	Ivory		
15th	Crystal		
20th	China		

BIRTHSTONES AND FLOWERS

The origins of birthstones and of the flowers associated with each month of the year go back at least to the Middle Ages, when astrologers and magicians taught complicated systems of "correspondences" involving such things as jewels, plants, planets, and the signs of the zodiac. The combinations vary in different parts of the world. This list is widely used in North America and Britain.

January
Garnet
Carnation or snowdrop

July
Ruby
Larkspur or water lily

February
Amethyst
Violet or primrose

August
Peridot or sardonyx
Gladiolus or poppy

March
Aquamarine or bloodstone
Jonquil or violet

September
Sapphire
Morning glory or aster

April
Diamond
Daisy or sweet pea

October
Opal or tourmaline
Calendula or cosmos

May
Emerald
Hawthorn or lily of the valley

November
Topaz
Chrysanthemum

June
Pearl, alexandrite, or moonstone
Rose or honeysuckle

December
Turquoise or zircon
Narcissus, holly, or poinsettia

123

Customs and festivals

FEASTING WITH THE DEAD

Macabre graveside picnics take place in Mexico on the Day of the Dead, when, according to Indian folklore, the dead return to life. Marigolds, tequila—a potent alcoholic drink—and food are first offered to the dead by families, who then proceed to consume the food and drink right in the cemeteries. Typical of the picnic fare are chocolate hearses and coffins; sugar skulls, skeletons, and funeral wreaths; and fancy breads patterned with skulls and crossbones. The occasion is widely celebrated as a national holiday on November 2, All Souls' Day in the Roman Catholic liturgical calendar, when prayers are offered for souls in purgatory.

SWEET HEAD
Mexicans eat skulls made of sugar in cemetery picnics on the Day of the Dead.

THE MONARCH'S MONEY

Every Maundy Thursday—the day before Good Friday—the British monarch distributes money to the poor in Westminster Abbey, London. The recipients, one man and one woman for every year the sovereign has lived, each get a purse containing specially minted silver pennies, two-pennies, three-pennies, and four-pennies. Selected from a different area each year, the recipients are recognized for having given long and exceptional service to church or community. The custom commemorates Christ washing the Apostles' feet.

Until William III and Mary II took the throne in 1689, the monarch personally washed the feet of a group of poor people; but thereafter money was given instead. The money, known as maundy money, is legal tender in Britain but is worth much more than its face value.

EASTER SOAKING

Hungarian men splash their girlfriends with water until the splashers are rewarded with colored easter eggs on Water Drench Monday, as Easter Monday is sometimes called in Hungary. In big cities the old-fashioned water-drenching ritual has been replaced by a ceremony in which a few drops of perfume or eau de cologne are sprinkled over women by their boyfriends. The ceremony is meant to bring a good harvest and ensure good health.

HOLY SMOKE

Every year Chinese families burn one of their own gods. This fiery ritual takes place before the Chinese New Year (held between late January and early February) as part of the Festival of the Kitchen God, Tsao Chun. Wishing to court Tsao Chun's favor so that he will speak well of them to the other gods, families offer cakes and sweets to his picture, smear his mouth with syrup, and dip him into wine to make him tipsy and amiable. Afterward they burn his picture in the belief that the god will ascend to heaven in the smoke. Tsao Chun is believed to return to the household on New Year's Day, when a new picture of him is hung on the kitchen wall.

HORSE RACING, ITALIAN STYLE

Twice a summer, jockeys dressed in medieval costume honor the Virgin Mary by racing bareback around the main square of Siena, Italy. Jockeys ride for individual city wards after having their mounts blessed in church, and the winner gets a silk banner depicting the Virgin. The contest—known as the Palio—was started by the Papal States in the 13th century and is held every July 2 and August 16. Each jockey is given a whip before the start, and under the rules he is allowed to use it not only on his own mount but on other horses as well—and on their riders.

MOON'S BIRTHDAY

In China there is no man in the moon. Instead, there is a toad in the moon, as well as moon rabbits and a goddess, all of which appear as decorations on moon cakes, baked to celebrate the moon's birthday on the 15th day of the 8th moon (September). These cakes—which are traditionally circular to symbolize the full moon—are exchanged between friends, while children receive toy pagodas made from clay. The birthday marks the end of the harvest, when debts are meant to be settled.

SPRING BEANS

Japanese families shout "Good luck in! Evil spirits out!" and throw beans in their homes every February 3, one bean for every year in each bean thrower's life. The origin of the custom is unknown, but in many cultures beans are thought to have magical properties—perhaps because they resemble human kidneys and testicles, symbols of renewal and fertility. The festival, known as Setsubun ("Bean-Throwing Night"), celebrates the end of winter and the onset of spring. It is also observed in shrines and temples.

FLYING THE CARP

Giant kites depicting red and black carp are flown every May 5 by Japanese families in honor of their young sons. This ancient festival, known as Tango-No-Sekku, meaning "Boys' Festival," is intended to encourage the development of manly qualities in

small boys. Carp were chosen as symbols of strength and virility because the fish battle their way up fast-flowing rivers to mate and breed.

LIVING DOLL
Dolls are honored in Japan as a way of encouraging the development of feminine qualities in young girls. During the Festival of Hina Matsuri ("Girls' Festival") dolls are arranged in a special alcove, known as the tokonoma, in family living rooms. The dolls often represent a medieval emperor, empress, and retinue of courtiers. As with family guests, the dolls are offered fruits and vegetables on miniature dishes by young girls dressed in the finest kimonos. The ceremony takes place every March 5.

QUEENS OF THE LIGHT
A December custom in Sweden is for girls to place little electric candles in their hair to honor St. Lucia, the patron saint of light. Long white dresses, scarlet sashes, and evergreen garlands complete their costumes. Communities throughout Sweden elect their own St. Lucias, or Queens of the Light. Candles are burned in homes, shops, and offices during the day. And saffron buns, shaped like cats for luck, are specially baked for the occasion.

MOVABLE FEAST
Thanksgiving Day in the United States can be as early as November 22 or as late as November 28. Only since 1941 has the holiday been on the fourth Thursday in November. Before then, starting with Lincoln, U.S. Presidents proclaimed the last Thursday in November as Thanksgiving—but Franklin Roosevelt in 1939 moved the day back a week to give more shopping time between Thanksgiving and Christmas. At this point Congress enacted the "fourth Thursday" compromise. The first American Thanksgiving, celebrated in 1621 by the Pilgrims of Plymouth Colony, actually occurred in October.

Canada has its own Thanksgiving holiday, observed on the second Monday in October.

CHIVALROUS INDIANS
Hindu men of India pledge their lives and loyalty to their women in return for a bracelet made of cotton, silk, a colored material, or gold thread. The Hindu custom originated in ancient times when a Rajput princess is believed to have sought help by sending part of her silk bracelet to a Muslim emperor in Delhi. After aiding her the emperor kept her bracelet as a token of loyalty between them. The deed is celebrated in the Rakhi Festival, which takes place in the Indian month of Sravana in July and August.

TRAMPLED . . . A FEAT OF FLOWERS
Every Easter, Andean farmers and villagers transform the small market town of Tarma, northeast of the Peruvian capital, Lima. In a double ceremony—first on Good Friday and again on Easter Sunday—every square inch of the town center's streets is covered with thousands upon thousands of glowing

CHARIOT OF THE GOD *Borne on a monstrous wagon, a statue of the Hindu god Krishna is pulled through Delhi in this 1822 painting of Rathayatra, a Hindu festival. Held each year, the ceremony is also known as the Juggernaut Festival, after one of Krishna's titles—Jagannath, meaning "Lord of the World"—and the name has passed into English to describe a huge machine that crushes all in its path. Variations of the ceremony take place throughout India in June and July, but the largest is held in the city of Puri. There, the wagon is pulled by hundreds of devotees, and fanatics are said to have hurled themselves to death under its 16 massive wooden wheels. After each procession the wagon is broken up and the pieces sold to pilgrims. A new wagon is built for the next year.*

flower petals arranged in exquisite designs. Preparations start the day before Good Friday, when village women pluck the petals from flowers harvested locally and separate them by color into sacks. As dusk falls, designers from each village crouch in the street, making chalk sketches on the dusty tarmac. They draw outlines of llamas, bulls, Andean pipers, geometric patterns reminiscent of Persian carpets, and even whimsical cartoons of such familiar Western characters as Donald Duck.

The villagers then spend all night filling in the designs with petals, so that by dawn the streets are a continuous series of flower carpets, each about 30 feet long and displaying in petals the name of the group or village that created it.

Soon after dawn on Good Friday the doors of the Catholic church swing open, and a towering statue of the Virgin Mary is carried out on a litter. A priest walks ahead, blessing each village as he reaches and crosses its carpet. Behind him the statue sways upon the shoulders of some 30 men. And as the procession passes, the designs—many of which were still being frantically completed only minutes before—are trampled into a litter of scuffed and bruised plant matter. The floral designs have vanished; yet the next day, Easter Saturday, the villagers repeat the entire procedure, often with new designs.

THE RACE THAT IS FIXED

Since the 12th century the people of Gubbio in central Italy have staged a rigged race to commemorate St. Ubaldo, who is believed to have saved the town from invasion then. Every May statues of St. Ubaldo, St. George, and St. Anthony are paraded through the town atop 30-foot poles during the Festival of Candles. Then townspeople carry the statues in a race up the nearby 2,690-foot Monte Ingino to the Church of St. Ubaldo. However, because the track is too narrow to allow passing, the race always ends in the order it began. The statues reach the church as they have since the race's origin—first St. Ubaldo, then St. George, and finally St. Anthony.

BLESSING THE ANIMALS

Animals attend church services on St. Anthony's Day in Mexico. The popular saint, regarded as a healer of men and animals, is asked to protect pets, which are decorated with flowers and ribbons for the occasion. In rural areas, peasants bring bags of insects and worms to be blessed in church, too, in the hope that this will prevent these creatures from damaging crops. The saint, whose feast day is January 17, lived in Egypt between A.D. 251 and 356 and founded the first Christian monastery there.

GREEN POWER

Christians in parts of Central Europe believe that green plants and green food acquire special healing powers on Green Thursday, the name given locally to Maundy Thursday, the Thursday before Easter. The belief may have developed because excommunicated sinners, wearing sprigs of green as a sign of joy, were readmitted to the early Christian church on this day.

THE LIVING GODDESS

Hindus in Nepal worship a living goddess—a young girl. Known as Kumari Devi, a title meaning "Living Goddess," she is chosen from the Buddhist goldsmith's caste when she is 3 years old and must be without any physical blemish. She assumes divinity after proving her bravery by remaining alone for a while in a darkened room filled with skeletons and gruesome objects. Thereafter she spends much of her time reciting prayers to Hindu gods until puberty, when she ceases to be divine and is replaced by a new goddess. During her term of office Kumari Devi is supported by the state and lives with her family and friends in a temple in Katmandu's Durbar Square. She is allowed out once a year. Worshipers, including the King of Nepal, visit her temple and place their heads between her knees for luck. The period of divinity can affect a girl's marriage prospects, however. Nepalese men, possibly daunted by the thought of marrying a goddess, often avoid the erstwhile divinities. In addition, Nepalese folklore predicts an early death for husbands of former goddesses.

RITE OF SPRING

Children in parts of Czechoslovakia burn a straw effigy before Easter to mark the passing of winter. The effigy is of a figure of death called Smrt and is decorated with colored rags and strands of eggshells. The straw figure is carried into the fields and either burned or thrown into a river. After Smrt's destruction the children carry flower garlands home to symbolize the arrival of spring.

CHEAP RENT

A small tricolor flag is used to pay the rent on one of the properties of the British monarch. Every June 18, on Waterloo Day, the current duke of Wellington formally presents the queen with the flag at a dinner held in the Waterloo Chamber at Windsor Castle. The flag is the rent due for the Strathfield Saye estate, granted to the first duke after his victory over Napoleon at the Battle of Waterloo in 1815. The rent has never gone up.

GIFTS FROM THE GODS

When modern technology meets primitive society, confusion can result. The so-called cargo cults, for example, sprang up among many isolated New Guinea and Melanesian tribes after initial contact with European culture. Some of these tribal cults came to believe that airplanes were messengers from the gods or from the spirits of their dead ancestors. And tribesmen prayed to their gods for gifts such as radios, canned foods, and refrigerators. Sometimes they even destroyed or abandoned everything they owned and built storehouses to hold the gifts and gadgets they hoped soon to receive.

LOOK, NO HANDS

In Greek and Bulgarian families belonging to the Eastern Orthodox Christian Church, children help their parents prepare for Lent by trying to eat food dangled on strings from the ceiling, without using their hands. The food is typically cheese lumps and other dairy products, which—proscribed for Lent by the church—might otherwise spoil and go to waste. The festival is called Cheese Week. In Russia, Eastern Orthodox Christians have Butter Week, using up butter and eggs in rye-flour pancakes known as *blini*.

GORGING BEFORE FASTING

A 1,000-egg omelet is eaten on the Friday before Lent at Ponti in Italy. This is one of many such customs associated in Christian countries with Lent, a period of fasting and abstinence commemorating Christ's 40 days in the wilderness. In most Christian churches the Lenten period actually runs 46 calendar days, with Sundays being excluded as fast days.

Lent begins on Ash Wednesday. Ever since the church forbade meat and dairy products during Lent, devout Christians have made a practice of using up these foods beforehand. Eggs and butter are often eaten on Shrove Tuesday, popularly called Pancake Day in Britain, and on Mardi Gras, meaning "Fat Tuesday," in France. In Germany the ritual is called Fastnacht (eve of the fast). In many Catholic countries, pre-Lenten feasting came to be called a carnival, a word derived from the Latin *carnem levare,* meaning "to remove the meat."

Some places have expanded the carnival into a boisterous festival—marked by parades, dancing, fireworks, masquerades, and feasting—that may last a fortnight. The most spectacular carnivals are at Rio de Janeiro in Brazil and at New Orleans.

SPRING CLEANING
Every March 1, Greeks smash jugs against their front doors, crying "Away with fleas and mice!" and children bang pots and pans and shout "Away February. Welcome March!" According to superstition, only if the ritual is observed on this specific day will homes be rid of fleas and mice for the remainder of the year. Spring cleaning traditionally occurs in many countries at about the same time.

HOPE YOU LIKE IT
Swedish men sometimes give themselves as presents to their girlfriends at Christmas. Concealed in huge gift-wrapped boxes, they have themselves delivered to their girlfriends' homes. Alternatively, presents known as *julklapp* are sometimes elaborately disguised so that they seem much bigger than they really are. This is done by placing a small present in progressively larger boxes, each covered with paper and tightly tied with string—rather like Chinese boxes.

EIGHT-DAY WONDER
One of the most famous Jewish emblems is the seven-stemmed candelabrum (*menorah* in Hebrew), which commemorates the seven lamps of Solomon's Temple. But once a year Jews use a larger, nine-stemmed menorah to commemorate a victory. In 164 B.C. the Jewish leader Judas Maccabeus defeated the Syrian king Antiochus Epiphanes and occupied Jerusalem. When the Jews entered the temple, they discovered that there was only enough oil left to keep the lamps lit for one day. Miraculously, however, the oil lasted for 8 days, until more oil was found. The episode is celebrated in the 8-day Festival of Lights, called *Hanukkah* in Hebrew, which begins in December. On the first evening of the festival a single branch of the menorah is lit. Each subsequent evening another branch is lit, until by the end of the festival all the branches are alight. The ninth branch of the menorah is a pilot light and is kept burning throughout the festival. Special pancakes, called latkes, are eaten, and children play with a top bearing four Hebrew letters standing for the words "a great miracle happened here." The festival starts on the eve of the 25th day of the Hebrew month of Kislev.

LAMP OF FAITH *Aaron, the elder brother of Moses and first high priest of the Jews, fills the seven-branched lamp known to Jews as the menorah in this detail from a late 13th-century Hebrew manuscript.*

JUNE WEDDINGS
The popularity of June weddings goes back to the ancient Romans, who believed that Juno, the goddess of marriage, would bring prosperity and happiness to all who wed in her month. The custom also has practical advantages, at least in agrarian societies. Marriage in June meant that the bride was likely to bear her first child in early spring, allowing her time to recover and resume her full duties before the fall harvest. As an old Scottish proverb put it: "He's a fool that marries at Yule; for when the corn's to shear, the bairn's to bear."

SECRET BRIDES
Brides have traditionally gone to great trouble to conceal their identity from evil spirits. In ancient Sparta brides disguised themselves as men and cut their hair short to confuse malevolent spirits. The bridal veil may also have first been adopted to hide the bride from evil spirits who might cast a spell on the bride and groom and ruin their marriage. Even bridesmaids may have originated as a way of protecting the bride; for it was hoped that if she surrounded herself with girls of her own age in similar dress, the spirits would be confused and only the groom would recognize her.

HOW TO TREAT THE ELEPHANT GOD
Hindus celebrate the birthday of their elephant god, Ganesh, by parading his statue through the streets and then dunking it in a river or lake. Ganesh is depicted as a fat red man with a pot belly, four arms, and an elephant head with a single tusk. He is usually shown riding on a rat. Regarded as the remover of obstacles, he is particularly popular with merchants, who often invoke his favor at the start of a new business enterprise. Many banks display his image outside their premises, and if they go bankrupt, they turn his face to the wall.

CALENDAR OF FESTIVALS

Many festivals around the world are based on the lunar calendar, so that—like Easter—they fall on different dates each year. In this list specific dates are given only for festivals that always fall on the same day. The entries also identify places or groups associated with each event.

JANUARY

January – February
Kitchen God Festival
China
January – February
Yuan Tan (Chinese New Year)
China
January 1
New Year's Day
Gregorian Calendar
January 1
First Footing
Scotland and Northern England
January 6
Epiphany
Christian
January 6 – 7
Christmas Eve and Christmas Day
Eastern Orthodox
(Julian Calendar)

FEBRUARY

February – March: week before Lent
Butter and Cheese Week
Eastern Orthodox
February – March: day before Ash Wednesday
Shrove Tuesday
Christian
February – March
Carnival
Catholic countries
February – March
Ash Wednesday (1st day of Lent)
Christian
February – March
Purim (Feast of Lots)
Jewish
February – March
Holi (Festival of Fire)
Hindu
February – April
Lent
Christian
February 2
Candlemas Day
Christian
February 3
Setsubun
(Bean-Throwing Night)
Japan
February 14
St. Valentine's Day
Christian

MARCH

March – April
Pesach (Passover)
Jewish
March – May
Easter
Christian
March 3
Hina Matsuri
(Girls' Festival)
Japan
March 17
St. Patrick's Day
Ireland
United States
March 21
Noruz (New Year's Day)
Iran
March 25
Feast of the Annunciation
Christian

APRIL

April – May
Baisakhi (New Year Festival)
Hindu
April – May
Wesak
Southeast Asia
Buddhist

MAY

May – June
Pentecost (Feast of Weeks)
Jewish
May – June: 50 days after Easter
Pentecost/
Whitsunday
Christian
May – June: Sunday after Pentecost
Trinity Sunday
Christian
May – June: Thursday after Trinity Sunday
Corpus Christi
Roman Catholic

GOING A-MAYING *An English sketch published in 1826 shows May Day revelers in Norfolk celebrating the start of summer.*

May 1
May Day
Worldwide
May 5
Tango-No-Sekku
(Boys' Festival)
Japan

JUNE

June – July
Juggernaut festivals
India

JULY

July 2 (and August 16)
Palio
Italy
July 4
Independence Day
United States
July 14
Bastille Day
France

AUGUST

August – September
Birthday of Krishna
Hindu
August 15
The Assumption of the Virgin Mary
Roman Catholic

SEPTEMBER

September
Chinese Moon Festival
China
September – October
Rosh Hashanah
(New Year)
Jewish
September – October
Yom Kippur
(Day of Atonement)
Jewish

September – October
Sukkoth (Harvest Festival)
Jewish

OCTOBER

October – November
Devali (Harvest Festival)
Hindu
October: 2nd Monday
Thanksgiving, Canada
October 31
Halloween
N. Europe, United States

NOVEMBER

November – December: Sunday nearest to St. Andrew's Day
First Sunday
of Advent
Christian
November 2
Day of the Dead, Mexico
November 5
Guy Fawkes Day
England
November 11
Remembrance Day
Canada
November: 2nd Sunday
Remembrance Sunday
Britain
November: 4th Thursday
Thanksgiving, United States
November 30
St. Andrew's Day, Scotland

DECEMBER

December
Hanukkah (Festival of Lights), Jewish
December
Winter Solstice Feast
China
December 13
St. Lucia's Day, Sweden
December 16 – 24
Posadas (Nativity)
Mexico
December 24
Christmas Eve
Christian
December 25
Christmas Day
Christian
December 26
Boxing Day, Britain
December 31
New Year's Eve
Gregorian calendar

ANY MONTH

Ramadan, ninth month of the Muslim year. It can fall in any month because the Muslim calendar, which is lunar, does not keep in step with the seasons.

PLACES

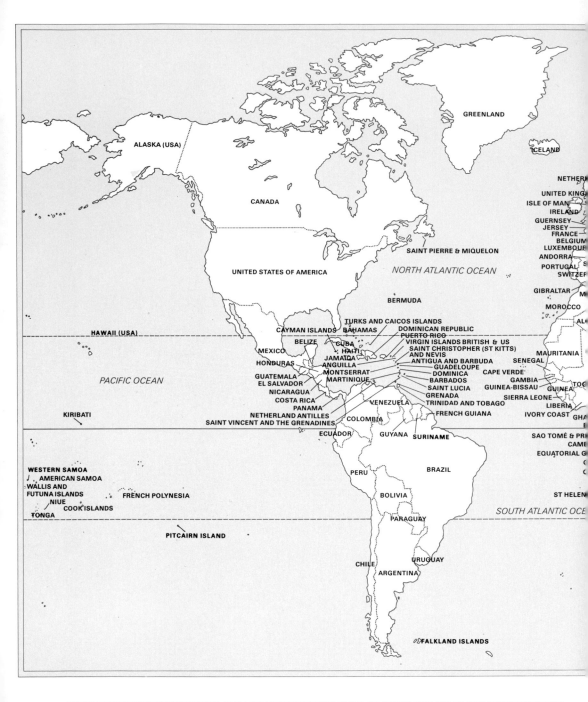

Nations of the world

COUNTRY WHERE NO ONE IS BORN

The world's smallest independent state is the Vatican City, with a population of about 1,000—and a zero birthrate. Its area is 0.17 square mile. The country with the largest area is the U.S.S.R. It covers 8,649,538 square miles.

The country with the largest population is the People's Republic of China, estimated to have in 1986 nearly 1,054,000,000 inhabitants—almost one in four of the world's people.

SHRINKING FROM INDEPENDENCE

Two wars and one near-war have cost Bolivia more than half the territory to which it laid claim when it became independent in 1825. In the 1879–83 War of the Pacific, Chile annexed Bolivia's Pacific seacoast, along with the port of Antofagasta and the mineral-rich Atacama Desert. In 1903, when war with neighboring Brazil was narrowly avoided, Bolivia was forced to cede the rubber-producing Acre territory to Brazil. Finally, after the 1932–35 Chaco War with

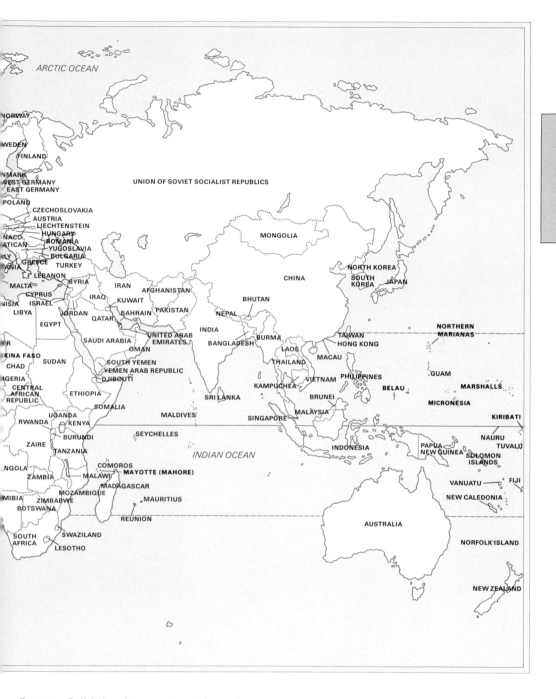

Paraguay, Bolivia lost three-quarters of the southern Chaco region that it claimed. It also abandoned hope of an outlet of its own to the Atlantic along the Paraguay River, at a point where the river is navigable for large vessels. Despite having no coastline, Bolivia still has a navy of some 4,000 men. They are confined to the waters of Lake Titicaca, high in the Andes, and to stretches of some rivers on the fringes of the Amazon Basin.

THE NEED FOR AN HEIR
If Monaco's ruling house of Grimaldi should ever be without an heir (male or female), the country will cease to be a sovereign state. Under a 1918 treaty between France and Monaco, the principality would become a self-governing French protectorate.

VENICE, SOUTH AMERICAN STYLE
While sailing along the Caribbean coast of South America in 1499, the Spanish explorer Alonso de Ojedo saw Indian houses built on stilts over the water. The area recalled Venice, and he named it Little Venice, which in Spanish is Venezuela.

COASTLINE OF ISLANDS
Indonesia consists entirely of islands—somewhere between 13,000 and 14,000 of them, though the number has never been precisely determined. As a result, Indonesia has the world's second longest coastline at 22,888 miles but is only the 15th largest nation. The nation with the longest coastline is Canada, which has five times the land area of Indonesia.

THE FRENCH FOR FALKLANDS

Islas Malvinas, the Argentine name for the Falkland Islands, is not of Spanish but of French origin. Many of the sailors who went there early in the 18th century to fish and hunt seals were from St. Malo in Brittany, so the French called the islands Îles Malouines, after the townsfolk. In Spanish this became Islas Malvinas. "Falklands" probably came from an English sailor, Capt. John Strong, who in 1690 named the sound between the two main islands (now known as East Falkland and West Falkland) Falkland Sound after Viscount Falkland, then the British Navy treasurer.

CHANGING HANDS

In the 17th and 18th centuries the West Indian island of Tobago changed hands 31 times as one country after another sought to use it as a Caribbean naval base. The keenest rivals were the British, Spanish, French, and Dutch—but they were challenged by

NATIONS A–Z / Afghanistan–Bhutan

This list contains basic data about all the independent nations of the world, and about major dependent territories. Population figures are 1986 estimates. Details of national capitals are on pages 154–61; flags are on pages 162–65.

AFGHANISTAN

Area 249,995 square miles.
Population 15,000,000.
Climate Harsh winters, hot summers; average temperature in Kabul ranges from 18°–36°F in January to 61°–91°F in July.
Government Communist state; under Soviet occupation.
Language Pushtu, Dari (Persian).
Religion Muslim.
Currency Afghani (Af) = 100 puls.

ALBANIA

Area 11,100 square miles.
Population 3,111,000.
Climate Mediterranean; average temperature in Tirana ranges from 36°–54°F in January to 63°–88°F in July.
Government Communist state.
Language Albanian.
Religion Largely Muslim; also Greek Orthodox and Roman Catholic. Officially atheist.
Currency Lek (Lk) = 100 quintars.
National anthem *The flag that united us in the struggle.*

ALGERIA

Area 919,590 square miles.
Population 22,611,000.
Climate Mediterranean on the coast, hot and dry in the south. Average temperature in Algiers ranges from 48°–59°F in January to 72°–84°F in August.
Government One-party socialist republic.
Language 80% Arabic; also Berber and French.
Religion Muslim.
Currency Algerian dinar (AD) = 100 centimes.
National anthem *A Vow to God.*

ANDORRA

Area 179 square miles.
Population 42,000.
Climate Winters are snowy, summers cool and usually sunny and dry. Average temperature in

Les Escaldes ranges from 20°–43°F in January to 54°–79°F in July.
Government Principality.
Language Catalan; also Spanish and French.
Religion Mainly Roman Catholic.
Currency French franc and Spanish peseta.
National anthem *The great Charlemagne, my father.*

ANGOLA

Area 481,351 square miles.
Population 8,256,000.
Climate Tropical; average temperature in Luanda ranges from 64°F to 86°F.
Government Communist state.
Language Portuguese, African languages.
Religion Mainly tribal.
Currency Kwanza (Kw) = 100 lwei.

ANGUILLA

Area 35 square miles.
Population 6,500.
Climate Subtropical; average temperature ranges from 75°F to 81°F.
Government U.K. dependency with internal self-government.
Language English.
Religion Christian.
Currency East Caribbean dollar (EC$) = 100 cents.
National anthem *God Save the Queen.*

ANTIGUA AND BARBUDA

Area 170 square miles.
Population 82,000.
Climate Tropical; average temperature ranges from 72°F to 86°F.
Government Parliamentary state.
Language English.
Religion Christian.
Currency East Caribbean dollar (EC$) = 100 cents.

ARGENTINA

Area 1,077,639 square miles.
Population 31,065,000.
Climate Subtropical in the north to subantarctic in the south. Average temperature in Buenos Aires ranges from 23°–57°F in June to 63°–84°F in January.
Government Federal republic.
Language Spanish.
Religion Mainly Roman Catholic.
Currency Austral (Arg$) = 100 centavos.
National anthem *Hear, O mortals! the sacred cry.*

AUSTRALIA

Area 2,967,892 square miles.
Population 15,924,000.
Climate Generally hot and dry. Average temperature in Canberra ranges from 34°–52°F in July to 55°–82°F in January.
Government Federal parliamentary state.
Language English, aboriginal languages.
Religion 36% Church of England, 33% Catholic, 29% other Christian.
Currency Australian dollar (A$) = 100 cents.
National anthem *Advance, Australia fair.*
National emblem Wattle (Australian acacia).

AUSTRIA

Area 32,368 square miles.
Population 7,499,000.
Climate Temperate. Average temperature in Vienna ranges from 25°–34°F in January to 59°–77°F in July.
Government Democratic federal republic.
Language 99% German; also Slovene, Croat, Hungarian, Czech.
Religion 88% Roman Catholic, 6% Protestant.
Currency Schilling (Sch) = 100 groschen.
National anthem *Land of mountains, land of streams.*

AFGHANISTAN *Traditional Afghan musical instruments, resembling the sitars of neighboring Pakistan and India.*

settlers even from such minor powers as Latvia (now part of the Soviet Union). Tobago was eventually ceded to Britain in 1814 and was joined with Trinidad in 1899 as a British Crown Colony. The two islands became an independent nation in 1962.

LAKE LAKE LAND

When Nyasaland adopted the name Malawi on its independence in 1964, it partially removed from the map of Africa a reminder of a misunderstanding that had arisen 105 years earlier. Nyasaland was originally named after Lake Nyasa, a name bestowed by the Scottish explorer David Livingstone. Livingstone reached the lake in 1859 and asked local people what it was called. He was told *nyasa,* and he therefore called the water Lake Nyasa. However, *nyasa* was not the name, simply a word meaning "mass of waters." So Lake Nyasa meant, in effect, "Lake Lake."

In 1964 Malawi's new government renamed the lake Lake Malawi, a name derived from Maravi, a

---

BAHAMAS

Area 5,380 square miles.
Population 237,000.
Climate Mild and subtropical; average temperature in Nassau ranges from 64°–77°F in February to 75°–90°F in August.
Government Parliamentary state.
Language English.
Religion Mainly Anglican, Roman Catholic, Methodist, and Baptist.
Currency Bahamian dollar (Ba$) = 100 cents.
National anthem *March on, Bahamaland.*

BAHRAIN

Area 230 square miles.
Population 447,000.
Climate Very dry; very hot summers with high humidity. Average temperature ranges from 57°–68°F in January to 84°–100°F in August.
Government Monarchy.
Language Arabic, Persian, English.
Religion Muslim.
Currency Bahrain dinar (BD) = 1,000 fils.

BANGLADESH

Area 55,598 square miles.
Population 104,663,000.
Climate Tropical; monsoons from June to September. Dry season between January and March. Average temperature in Chittagong ranges from 55°–79°F in January to 77°–88°F in June.
Government Martial law.
Language 85% Bengali, English.
Religion 85% Muslim, 14% Hindu.

Currency Taka (Tk) = 100 poisha.
National anthem *My Bengal of gold, I love you.*
National emblem Water lily.

BARBADOS

Area 166 square miles.
Population 264,000.
Climate Subtropical; average temperature in Bridgetown ranges from 70°–82°F in February to 73°–88°F in June to September.
Government Parliamentary state.
Language English.
Religion Mainly Anglican.
Currency Barbados dollar (Bds$) = 100 cents.
National anthem *In plenty and in time of need.*
National emblem Head of a trident.

BELAU (also spelled Palau or Pelew)

Area 190 square miles.
Population 14,000.
Climate Tropical; mean temperature at Koror, the capital, is 82°F; frequent typhoons.
Government Self-governing republic in final stage of transition from U.S. Trust Territory of the Pacific Islands; compact of free association with the U.S. provides aid and defense for Belau.
Language English, Malayo-Polynesian (Palauan).
Religion Christian.
Currency U.S. dollar ($) = 100 cents.

BELGIUM

Area 11,783 square miles.
Population 9,892,000.
Climate Temperate; average temperature in Brussels ranges from 30°–39°F in January to 54°–73°F in July.
Government Parliamentary monarchy.
Language Netherlandic (Flemish) and French.
Religion 90% Roman Catholic.
Currency Belgian franc (BFr) = 100 centimes.
National anthem *The Brabançonne.*
National emblem Lion.

BELIZE (formerly British Honduras)

Area 8,867 square miles.
Population 165,000.
Climate Subtropical; average temperature in Belize City ranges from 66°–81°F in January to 75°–88°F in August.
Government Parliamentary state.
Language English and Spanish; also Creole and local languages.
Religion Christian.
Currency Belizean dollar (Bz$) = 100 cents.
National anthem *Land of the free.*

BENIN (formerly Dahomey)

Area 43,483 square miles.
Population 4,135,000.
Climate Tropical; average temperature in Cotonou ranges from 73°F to 82°F.
Government One-party socialist republic.
Languages French, tribal.
Religion 65% tribal; also Christian and Muslim.
Currency African Financial Community franc (CFAFr) = 100 centimes.

BERMUDA

Area 21 square miles.
Population 72,000.
Climate Subtropical; average temperature ranges from 46°F to 70°F.
Government U.K. dependency with internal self-government.
Language English.
Religion Christian.
Currency Bermuda dollar (Bda$) = 100 cents.
National anthem *God Save the Queen.*

BHUTAN

Area 18,000 square miles.
Population 1,450,000.
Climate Temperate; average temperature in Thimphu ranges from 39°F in January to 63°F in July.
Government Constitutional monarchy.
Language Dzongkha (Tibetan/Burmese), Nepali, English.
Religion 75% Mahayana Buddhist, 25% Hindu.
Currency Ngultrum (N) = 100 chetrum.

BELGIUM *A detail from a Flemish lace veil showing the Virgin Mary. The veil was made in the 17th or 18th century.*

133

kingdom said to have ruled from the Zambezi river to the eastern port of Mombasa in the 16th and 17th centuries. But other countries bordering the lake still call it Lake Nyasa.

THE INTERNATIONAL ANTHEM

Scholars differ on exactly who wrote the tune of *God Save the Queen* (or King), but they agree that it was written before 1745 by a British composer. Despite its British origin, the tune has been used as a national anthem by many countries besides Britain. Germany's national anthem between 1870 and 1922, *Heil Dir im Siegerkranz* ("Hail to thee in victor's garlands"), was sung to the same tune. So was the Swiss song *Rufst du, mein Vaterland* ("Do you call, my Fatherland"), which did duty as a national anthem until 1961, when Switzerland officially adopted a new anthem.

In the United States, immediately after the Declaration of Independence in 1776, the old British anthem was often used with new words—such as

NATIONS A–Z / Bolivia–Colombia

BOLIVIA

Area 424,062 square miles.
Population 6,527,000.
Climate Tropical; cooler at altitude. Temperature in La Paz varies little from the annual average of 50°F. Very dry.
Government Republic.
Language Spanish; also local languages.
Religion Roman Catholic.
Currency Bolivian peso (B$) = 100 centavos.
National anthem *Bolivians, propitious fate has crowned our hopes.*

BOPHUTHATSWANA

Area 17,010 square miles.
Population 1,650,000.
Climate Subtropical, hot summers.
Government Republic; declared independent by South Africa in 1977 but not recognized as sovereign by other nations.
Language Setswana, English, Afrikaans.
Religion Tribal, Christian.
Currency South African Rand (R) = 100 cents.

BOTSWANA (formerly Bechuanaland)

Area 224,605 square miles.
Population 1,118,000.
Climate Subtropical and dry; average temperature in Francistown ranges from 41°–72°F in June to 64°–91°F in December/January.
Government Parliamentary multiparty democracy.
Language Setswana, English.
Religion Christian, tribal.
Currency Pula (P) = 100 thebe.

BRAZIL

Area 3,286,470 square miles.
Population 138,820,000.
Climate Mainly tropical and subtropical. Average temperature at Rio de Janeiro ranges from 63°–75°F in July to 73°–84°F in February.
Government Federal republic.
Language Portuguese.
Religion Roman Catholic.
Currency Cruzado (Cr) = 100 centavos.
National anthem *From peaceful Ipiranga's banks.*

BRUNEI

Area 2,226 square miles.
Population 235,000.
Climate Tropical; generally very humid and wet. Average temperature ranges from 75°F to 86°F.
Government Monarchy.
Language Mostly Malay, English, Chinese.
Religion Muslim, Confucianist, Buddhist, Taoist.
Currency Brunei dollar (Br$) = 100 sen (cents).

BULGARIA

Area 42,823 square miles.
Population 9,239,000.
Climate Varied in the mountains and the north, Mediterranean in the south-facing valleys. Average temperature in Sofia ranges from 25°–36°F in January to 61°–81°F in July.
Government Communist state.
Language Bulgarian.
Religion Mainly atheist; Bulgarian Orthodox, Muslim.
Currency Lev (Lv) = 100 stótinki.
National anthem *Dear Bulgaria, land of heroes.*

BURKINA FASO (formerly Upper Volta)

Area 105,870 square miles.
Population 7,083,000.
Climate Tropical, very dry, especially in the north. Average temperature in Ouagadougou ranges from 61°–91°F in January to 79°–102°F in April.
Government Military junta.
Language French, also local languages.
Religion 50% tribal.
Currency African Financial Community franc (CFAFr) = 100 centimes.
National anthem *Proud Volta of my ancestors.*

BURMA

Area 261,217 square miles.
Population 40,069,000.
Climate Tropical; monsoons from May to September. Average temperature in Rangoon ranges between 64°–90°F in January and 75°–97°F in April.
Government One-party socialist republic.
Language Burmese; also tribal.
Religion Mainly Buddhist.
Currency Kyat (Kt) = 100 pyas.
National anthem *We shall love evermore Burma.*

BURUNDI

Area 10,747 square miles.
Population 4,759,000.
Climate Tropical; average temperature in Bujumbura is 75°F.
Government One-party republic.
Language French, Kirundi.
Religion Roman Catholic, tribal, also Muslim.
Currency Burundi franc (BuFr) = 100 centimes.

CAMEROON

Area 183,569 square miles.
Population 9,826,000.
Climate Tropical; average temperature in Yaoundé ranges from 64°F to 84°F.
Government One-party republic.
Language French, English, tribal.
Religion Tribal, Roman Catholic, Muslim.
Currency African Financial Community franc (CFAFr) = 100 centimes.
National anthem *O Cameroon, cradle of our ancestors.*

CANADA

Area 3,851,787 square miles.
Population 25,899,000.
Climate Arctic, temperate, and marine; average temperature in Ottawa ranges from 5°–21°F in January to 59°–79°F in July.
Government Federal parliamentary state.

134

BOTSWANA *A 20th-century basket, painted with a traditional tribal design.*

"God save George Washington" and "God save the Thirteen States." Another version, which began "My country, 'tis of thee," was written in 1831 and shared the honors with *The Star-Spangled Banner* as the U.S. national song until 1931, when Congress officially chose the second song as the American anthem.

Other nations to use the tune of *God Save the Queen* for their anthems were Denmark, Sweden, Russia, and several German states. One independent country that still does so is Liechtenstein.

THE KINGDOM THAT VANISHED

In 1771 the kingdom of Poland was larger in area than any other European country except Russia and had a bigger population than any other European country except France. But within 25 years it had vanished from the map. In 1772 Russia, Prussia, and Austria between them annexed about one-fifth of Poland. Twenty years later Russia took over half of what remained, and all three powers shared in a final

Language English and French.
Religion Mainly Christian.
Currency Canadian dollar (C$) = 100 cents.
National anthem *O Canada!*
National emblem Maple leaf.

CAPE VERDE

Area 1,557 square miles.
Population 326,000.
Climate Tropical maritime; average temperature at Praia ranges from 66°–77°F in March to 75°–84°F in October.
Government One-party state.
Language Portuguese, Crioulo (blend of West African and Portuguese words).
Religion Roman Catholic.
Currency Cape Verde escudo (CVEsc) = 100 centavos.

CAYMAN ISLANDS

Area 100 square miles.
Population 19,000.
Climate Subtropical; average temperature in George Town ranges from 64°–75°F in January/February to 75°–86°F in July/August.
Government U.K. dependency.
Language English.
Religion Mainly Protestant.
Currency Cayman Islands dollar (CI$) = 100 cents.
National anthem *Beloved isle Cayman.*

CENTRAL AFRICAN REPUBLIC

Area 240,534 square miles.
Population 2,626,000.
Climate Tropical; average temperature in Bangui ranges from 70°–84°F in July/August to 70°–93°F in February.
Government Military rule.
Language Sango, French.
Religion Mainly tribal; also Christian, Muslim.

Currency African Financial Community franc (CFAFr) = 100 centimes.

CHAD

Area 496,000 square miles.
Population 5,129,000.
Climate Tropical; average temperature in N'Djaména ranges from 57°–91°F in December to 73°–108°F in April.
Government Rule by decree.
Language French, Arabic, tribal.
Religion 52% Muslim, 43% tribal.
Currency African Financial Community franc (CFAFr) = 100 centimes.

CHILE

Area 292,258 square miles.
Population 12,237,000.
Climate Varies from desert in the north to cold and rainy in the south. Average temperature in Santiago ranges from 37°–57°F to 54°–84°F in January.
Government Military rule.
Language Spanish.
Religion Mainly Roman Catholic.
Currency Chilean peso (Ch$).
National anthem *Pure, Chile, is your blue sky.*
National emblems Condor and Chilean guemal (small South American deer).

CHINA

Area 3,705,387 square miles.
Population 1,054,000,000.
Climate Temperate and humid in the southeast and central south, dry in the north and northeast. Average temperature in Beijing ranges from

34°–46°F in January to 72°–88°F in July/August.
Government One-party Communist state.
Language Chinese (including dialects), Tibetan, Korean.
Religion Confucian, Buddhist, Taoist, Muslim, and others.
Currency Yuan (Y) = 100 fen.
National anthem *March on, brave people of our nation!*

CISKEI

Area 3,025 square miles.
Population 700,000.
Government One-party state; declared independent by South Africa in 1981 but not recognized as sovereign by other nations.
Language Xhosa.
Religion Christian, tribal.
Currency South African Rand (R) = 100 cents.

COLOMBIA

Area 439,735 square miles.
Population 29,304,000.
Climate Tropical; temperate on the plateaus. Average temperature in Bogotá ranges from 50°–64°F in July to 48°–68°F in February.
Government Republic.
Language Spanish.
Religion Roman Catholic.
Currency Colombian peso (Col$) = 100 centavos.
National anthem *Oh unfading glory!*

CONGO *A Bembe tribal mask, representing an old woman.*

CHINA *Sandalwood struts scent this delicate fan.*

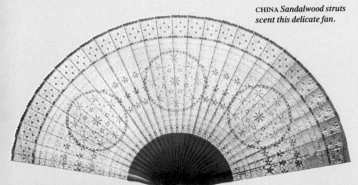

carve-up in 1795. It was not until 1918, in the aftermath of World War I, that an independent Poland reemerged under the powerful Joseph Pilsudski.

FIVE STATES IN ONE
The number of states in the United States could increase at any time from 50 to 54. The reason is that Texas could still exercise an option granted when it became, in 1845, part of the Union. Congress decreed that the new state could divide itself into as many as

five states whenever it chose. So far, though, the Lone Star State has remained intact—the second largest U.S. state after Alaska.

KNOWN BY ITS NUMBERS
Yugoslavia is one country with two alphabets, three religions, four principal languages, five main nationalities, and six republics. The alphabets are the Roman (used in English) and the Cyrillic (used in Russian). The religions are Roman Catholicism,

NATIONS A–Z / Comoros–French Polynesia

COMOROS
Area 838 square miles.
Population 468,000.
Climate Tropical; average temperature in Moroni ranges from 66°–81°F in August to 75°–88°F in March.
Government One-party republic.
Language Swahili, Arabic, French.
Religion Muslim.
Currency Comoros franc (CFr) = 100 centimes.

CONGO
Area 132,000 square miles.
Population 1,784,000.
Climate Tropical; average temperature in Brazzaville ranges from 63°–82°F in July to 72°–91°F in April.
Government Military rule.
Language French, tribal.
Religion 50% tribal, 48% Christian.
Currency African Financial Community franc (CFAFr) = 100 centimes.

COOK ISLANDS
Area 90 square miles.
Population 20,000.
Climate Tropical; average temperature in Rarotonga ranges from 64°–77°F in July to 73°–84°F in January.
Government Self-governing state in free association with New Zealand.
Language English, Polynesian.
Currency New Zealand dollar and Cook Islands dollar (CI$) = 100 cents.

COSTA RICA
Area 19,600 square miles.
Population 2,667,000.
Climate Tropical; temperate on plateaus. Average temperature in San José ranges from 57°–75°F in December/January to 63°–81°F in May.
Government Republic.
Language Spanish.
Religion Roman Catholic.
Currency Costa Rican colón (CR¢) = 100 céntimos.
National anthem *Noble motherland, your beautiful flag.*

CUBA
Area 42,827 square miles.
Population 10,086,000.
Climate Subtropical; average annual temperature ranges from

66°F to 95°F.
Government Communist one-party state.
Language Spanish.
Religion Roman Catholic.
Currency Cuban peso (Cub$) = 100 centavos.
National anthem *The Hymn of Bayamo.*

CYPRUS
Area 3,572 square miles.
Population 675,000.
Climate Mediterranean; average temperature in Nicosia ranges from 41°–59°F in January to 70°–99°F in July.
Government Republic. Since the 1974 invasion by Turkey the island has been effectively divided into north (Turkish sector) and south (Greek sector).
Language Greek, Turkish, English.
Religion Greek Orthodox (80%), Muslim.
Currency Cyprus pound (C£) = 100 cents.
National anthem *Hymn to Liberty.*

CZECHOSLOVAKIA
Area 49,370 square miles.
Population 15,700,000.
Climate Continental; warm summers and cold winters. Average temperature in Prague ranges from 25°–34°F in January to 57°–73°F in July.
Government Communist state.
Language Czech and Slovak.
Religion Mainly Roman Catholic.
Currency Koruna, or crown (Krcs) = 100 haleru.
National anthem *Where is my home?*

DENMARK
Area 16,633 square miles.
Population 5,148,000.
Climate Maritime; average temperature in Copenhagen ranges from 27°–36°F in February to 57°–72°F in July.
Government Constitutional monarchy.
Language Danish.
Religion Lutheran.
Currency Danish krone (DKr) = 100 öre.
National anthem *King Christian stood by the lofty mast.*
Royal anthem *There is a lovely land.*

DJIBOUTI
Area 8,600 square miles.
Population 300,000.
Climate Very hot and dry; average temperature in Djibouti City ranges from 73°–84°F in January to 88°–106°F in July.
Government One-party republic.
Language French, Arabic.
Religion Muslim.
Currency Djibouti franc (DjFr) = 100 centimes.

DOMINICA
Area 290 square miles.
Population 74,000.
Climate Subtropical; average temperature ranges from 68°–84°F December to March to 73°–90°F February to May.
Government Republic.
Language French patois, English.
Religion Christian.
Currency East Caribbean dollar (EC$) = 100 cents.
National anthem *Isle of beauty, isle of splendor.*
National emblem Sisserou parrot.

DOMINICAN REPUBLIC
Area 18,703 square miles.
Population 6,385,000.
Climate Subtropical and maritime tropical; average temperature in Santo Domingo ranges from 66°–84°F in January to 73°–88°F in August.
Government Republic.
Language Spanish.
Religion Roman Catholic.
Currency Dominican Republic peso (DR$) = 100 centavos.
National anthem *People of Quisqueya, we bravely raise our voices in song.*

ECUADOR
Area 109,483 square miles.
Population 9,661,000.
Climate Tropical; cooler at high altitudes. Average temperature in Quito ranges from 46°F to 70°F.
Government Republic.
Language Spanish, local languages.
Religion Roman Catholic.
Currency Sucre (Su) = 100 centavos.
National anthem *Long live the country.*

EGYPT
Area 387,000 square miles.

Eastern Orthodox Christian, and Islam. The four languages are Serb, Croat, Slovene, and Macedonian—although the first two are often grouped together as Serbo-Croat. The five nationalities are Serbs, Croats, Slovenes, Macedonians, and Montenegrins. The republics are Serbia, Croatia, Bosnia-Herzegovina, Slovenia, Macedonia, and Montenegro. And Yugoslavia has a common border with seven other countries: Italy, Austria, Hungary, Romania, Bulgaria, Greece, and Albania.

NEAR NEIGHBORS

Although the United States and the Soviet Union are divided by a wide gulf politically, they are, at their closest point, only 2.5 miles apart. This is the distance between two islands in the Bering Strait: Big Diomede, which is Russian, and Little Diomede, which is American. However, the two islands are also a whole day apart—because the international date line runs between them.

Population 48,000,000.
Climate Hot and dry; average temperature in Cairo ranges from 46°–64°F in January to 70°–97°F in July.
Government Republic.
Language Arabic.
Religion Mainly Muslim.
Currency Egyptian pound (E£) = 100 piastres = 1,000 millièmes.
National anthem *My homeland.*

EL SALVADOR

Area 8,124 square miles.
Population 5,285,000.
Climate Subtropical, cool in the highlands; average temperature in San Salvador ranges from 61°F to 91°F.
Government Republic.
Language Spanish.
Religion Roman Catholic.
Currency El Salvador colón (ES¢) = 100 centavos.
National anthem *Let us proudly salute our motherland.*

EQUATORIAL GUINEA

Area 10,830 square miles.
Population 290,000.
Climate Tropical; average temperature in Malabo ranges from 70°F to 90°F.
Government Military rule.
Language Spanish, also African languages.
Religion Roman Catholic.
Currency Ekwele (E) = 100 céntimos.

ETHIOPIA

Area 472,393 square miles.
Population 33,465,000.
Climate Temperate on plateau; hot in lowlands. Average temperature in Addis Ababa ranges from 41°F to 77°F.
Government Marxist military rule.
Language Amharic.
Religion Ethiopian Orthodox (Coptic), Muslim.
Currency Birr (Br) = 100 cents.
National anthem *Ethiopia, Ethiopia.*

FALKLAND ISLANDS

Area 6,300 square miles, including Sandwich Island group and South Georgia.
Population 2,000.
Climate Generally cool and windy; average temperature in Port Stanley ranges from 30°–39°F in July to 43°–55°F in January.
Government U.K. dependent territory.
Language English.
Religion Christian.
Currency Falkland Islands pound (FI£) = 100 new pence.

FIJI

Area 7,078 square miles.
Population 697,000.
Climate Tropical; average

DENMARK *This piece of Copenhagen porcelain, showing a couple with their two dogs, was made in about 1870.*

temperatures range from 68°F in August to 86°F in March.
Government Parliamentary state.
Language English, Fiji, Hindi.
Religion Christian, Hindu.
Currency Fiji dollar (F$) = 100 cents.
National anthem *God bless Fiji.*

FINLAND

Area 130,119 square miles.
Population 4,900,000.
Climate Temperate, with cold winters. Average temperature in Helsinki ranges from 16°–25°F in February to 54°–72°F in July.
Government Republic.
Language Finnish and Swedish.
Religion Lutheran.
Currency Markka (FMk) = 100 penni.
National anthem *Our Land.*

FRANCE

Area 211,207 square miles.
Population 54,780,000.
Climate Temperate, with dry, hot summers on the Mediterranean coast. Average temperature in Paris ranges from 34°–43°F in January to 57°–77°F in July.
Government Republic.
Language French.
Religion Roman Catholic.
Currency Franc (Fr) = 100 centimes.
National anthem *The Marseillaise.*

FRENCH GUIANA

Area 35,000 square miles.
Population 73,000.
Climate Hot and humid; average temperature in Cayenne ranges from 73°F to 91°F.
Government French overseas department.
Language French.
Religion Roman Catholic.
Currency French franc (Fr) = 100 centimes.

FRENCH POLYNESIA

Area 1,500 square miles.
Population 150,000.
Climate Tropical; average temperature in Papeete ranges from 68°F to 90°F.
Government French overseas territory.
Language French, Polynesian.
Religion Christian.
Currency French Pacific Community franc (CFPFr) = 100 centimes.

137

NATIONS A–Z / Gabon–Israel

GABON

Area 103,347 square miles.
Population 1,100,000.
Climate Tropical; average temperature in Libreville ranges from 68°F to 90°F.
Government One-party state.
Language French; also African languages.
Religion Christian, tribal.
Currency African Financial Community franc (CFAFr) = 100 centimes.
National anthem *United in concord.*

GAMBIA

Area 4,361 square miles.
Population 733,000.
Climate Tropical; average temperature is 61°F from November to April and 100°F from May to September.
Government Republic.
Language English, African languages.
Religion 80% Muslim, tribal, Christian.
Currency Dalasi (Di) = 100 butut.

GERMANY, EAST (GERMAN DEMOCRATIC REPUBLIC)

Area 41,827 square miles.
Population 16,548,000.
Climate Temperate; average temperature in Potsdam ranges from 34°F in January to 64°F in July.
Government Communist state.
Language German.
Religion Mainly Protestant.
Currency Mark (DDR mark, or "Ostmark") = 100 pfennig.
National anthem *Arisen from the ruins.*

GERMANY, WEST (GERMAN FEDERAL REPUBLIC)

Area 95,976 square miles.
Population 60,970,000.
Climate Temperate; average temperature in Frankfurt ranges from 30°–37°F in January to 57°–77°F in July.
Government Federal republic.
Language German.
Religion 49% Protestant, 45% Roman Catholic.
Currency Deutsche mark (DM) = 100 pfennig.
National anthem *Unity and right and freedom.*
National emblem Eagle.

GHANA

Area 92,100 square miles.
Population 13,890,000.
Climate Tropical; average temperature in Accra ranges from 72°F to 88°F.
Government Military-civilian junta.
Language English, tribal.
Religion Tribal, Christian, Muslim.
Currency Cedi (¢) = 100 pesewas.
National anthem *God bless our homeland Ghana.*

GIBRALTAR

Area 2.2 square miles.
Population 35,000.
Climate Temperate; average temperature ranges from 46°–61°F in February to 68°–84°F in August.
Government U.K. dependency.
Language English; also Spanish.
Religion 77% Roman Catholic.
Currency Gibraltar pound (Gib£) = 100 new pence = £1 sterling.
National emblem Castle and key.

GREECE

Area 50,944 square miles.
Population 10,080,000.
Climate Mediterranean; average temperature in Athens ranges from 46°–61°F in February to 73°–91°F in July.
Government Republic.
Language Greek.
Religion Greek Orthodox.
Currency Drachma (Dr) = 100 lepta.
National anthem *Hymn to Freedom.*

GREENLAND

Area 840,000 square miles.
Population 54,000.
Climate Very cold; average temperature in Godthaab ranges from 10°–19°F in January to 37°–52°F in July.
Government Self-governing province of Denmark.
Language Danish; also Inuit.
Religion Mainly Lutheran.
Currency Danish krone (DKr) = 100 Øre.

GRENADA

Area 133 square miles.
Population 116,000.
Climate Subtropical; average temperature in St. George's ranges between 73°F and 88°F.
Government Parliamentary state.
Language English.
Religion Christian.
Currency East Caribbean dollar (EC$) = 100 cents.

GUADELOUPE

Area 687 square miles.
Population 330,000.
Climate Subtropical; average temperature in Point-à-Pitre ranges from 63°–75°F in February to 70°–82°F in August/September.
Government Overseas French department.
Language French.
Religion Mainly Roman Catholic.
Currency French franc (Fr) = 100 centimes.
National anthem *The Marseillaise.*

GUAM

Area 212 square miles.
Population 111,000.
Climate Tropical; year-round average temperatures in Sumay range from 73°F to 88°F.
Government U.S. "unincorporated" territory, self-governing.
Language English, Chamorro.
Religion 96% Roman Catholic.
Currency US dollar ($) = 100 cents.
National song *Stand, ye Guamians.*

GUATEMALA

Area 42,042 square miles.
Population 6,975,000.
Climate Subtropical, temperate in highlands. Average temperature in Guatemala City ranges from 54°–73°F in January to 61°–84°F in May.
Government Republic.
Language Spanish; also local languages.
Religion Roman Catholic.
Currency Quetzal (Q) = 100 centavos.
National anthem *Guatemala, blessed land.*

GUINEA

Area 94,925 square miles.
Population 5,890,000.
Climate Tropical; average temperature in Conakry ranges from 72°F to 90°F.
Government Military rule.
Language French, local languages.
Religion Muslim, tribal.
Currency Syli (Sy) = 100 cauris.

GUINEA-BISSAU
(formerly Portuguese Guinea)

Area 13,948 square miles.
Population 873,000.
Climate Tropical; average temperature in Bolama ranges from 66°F to 90°F.
Government One-party republic.
Language Portuguese; also Creole.
Religion Muslim, tribal, Christian.
Currency Guinea-Bissau peso (GBP) = 100 centavos.

GUYANA
(formerly British Guiana)

Area 82,999 square miles.
Population 845,000.
Climate Tropical; average temperature in Georgetown ranges between 73°F and 88°F.
Government Republic.
Language English; also Creole, Hindi, Urdu, and local languages.
Religion Christian, Hindu, Muslim.
Currency Guyanese dollar (G$) = 100 cents.
National anthem *Dear land of Guyana.*

HAITI

Area 10,714 square miles.
Population 5,033,000.
Climate Tropical; average temperature in Port-au-Prince from 68°F to 93°F.
Government Republic.
Language French, Creole.
Religion Roman Catholic, voodoo.
Currency Gourde (Gde) = 100 centimes.

HONDURAS

Area 43,277 square miles.
Population 4,525,000.
Climate Tropical; average temperature in Tegucigalpa ranges from 43°–77°F in December/January to 52°–88°F in July/August. Wet season May to October.
Government Republic.
Language Spanish; also English.
Religion Roman Catholic.
Currency Lempira (La) = 100 centavos.
National anthem *Your standard serves.*

HONG KONG

Area 411 square miles.
Population 5,660,000.
Climate Subtropical; monsoons from May to September. Average temperature ranges from 61°F in February to 84°F in July/August.
Government U.K. dependency.
Language English and Chinese.
Religion Mainly Buddhist and Taoist.
Currency Hong Kong dollar (HK$) = 100 cents.
National flower Bauhinia (orchid tree).

HUNGARY

Area 35,919 square miles.
Population 10,745,000.
Climate Continental; average temperature in Budapest ranges from 25°–34°F in January to 61°–82°F in July.
Government One-party Communist state.
Language Magyar (Hungarian).
Religion 65% Roman Catholic, 25% Protestant.
Currency Forint (F) = 100 fillér.
National anthem *God bless the Hungarians.*

ICELAND

Area 39,800 square miles.
Population 245,000.
Climate Temperate; warmed by the Gulf Stream. Average temperature in Reykjavik ranges from 28°–36°F in January to 48°–57°F in July.
Government Republic.
Language Icelandic.
Religion Lutheran.
Currency Icelandic new króna (1Kr) = 100 aurar (singular: eyrir).
National anthem *Iceland's thousand years.*

INDIA

Area 1,269,084 square miles.
Population 778,435,000.
Climate Tropical; monsoons from June to September. Average temperature in New Delhi ranges from 45°–70°F in January to 79°–106°F in May.
Government Parliamentary republic, union of states.
Language Hindi and English; also other languages and dialects.
Religion Mostly Hindu; also Muslim, Christian, Sikh, Buddhist, Jain, and others.
Currency Indian rupee (IR) = 100 paise.
National anthem *Thou Art the Ruler of Minds.*

INDONESIA

Area 735,354 square miles.
Population 168,100,000.
Climate Equatorial; average year-round temperature in Jakarta ranges from 73°F to 91°F.
Government Republic under strong presidential rule.
Language Bahasa Indonesia; also other languages and dialects.
Religion 91% Muslim; also Roman Catholic, Protestant, and Hindu.
Currency Rupiah (Rp) = 100 sen.
National anthem *Indonesia the Great.*

IRAN

Area 636,000 square miles.
Population 46,466,000.
Climate Harsh winters, hot summers; average temperature in Tehran ranges from 27°–45°F in January to 72°–99°F in July.
Government Islamic dictatorship.
Language Farsi (Persian).
Religion Muslim.
Currency Rial (RI) = 100 dinars.

IRAQ

Area 167,924 square miles.
Population 16,175,000.
Climate Very hot summers, cool winters; average temperature in Baghdad ranges from 39°–61°F in January to 75°–122°F in July/August.
Government Socialist one-party state.
Language Arabic; also Kurdish, Turkish, and Assyrian.
Religion Muslim.
Currency Iraqi dinar (ID) = 20 dirhams = 1000 fils.
National anthem *Land of Two Rivers.*

IRELAND, REPUBLIC OF

Area 27,136 square miles.
Population 3,632,000.
Climate Temperate; warmed by the Gulf Stream. Average temperature ranges from 39°–45°F in January/February to 57°–61°F in July/August.
Government Parliamentary republic.
Language English and Irish.
Religion Roman Catholic.
Currency Irish punt (pound) (I£) = 100 pighne (new pence).
National anthem *The Soldier's Song.*
National emblem Harp.

ISRAEL

Area 10,715 square miles.
Population 4,318,000.
Climate Subtropical; average temperature in Jerusalem ranges from 41°–55°F in January to 64°–88°F in August.
Government Republic.
Language Hebrew and Arabic.
Religion Jewish.
Currency Shekel (Sk).

IRAN *A Persian plate made in the 9th or 10th century.*

ITALY *Gleaming with gold leaf, this 16th-century glass goblet, which stands about 5 inches high, was probably made in Venice.*

NATIONS A–Z / Italy–Malta

National anthem *The Hope*.
National emblem Menorah.

ITALY

Area 116,303 square miles.
Population 56,562,000.
Climate Mediterranean; average temperature in Rome ranges from 39°–52°F in January to 68°–86°F in July.
Government Republic.
Language Italian.
Religion Roman Catholic.
Currency Lira (L) = 100 centesimi.
National anthem *Brothers of Italy*.

IVORY COAST

Area 124,503 square miles.
Population 9,775,000.
Climate Tropical; average temperature in Abidjan ranges from 72°F to 90°F.
Government One-party republic.
Language French, tribal.
Religion 64% tribal, 24% Muslim, 12% Christian.
Currency African Financial Community franc (CFAFr) = 100 centimes.
National anthem *The Abidjanaise*.
National emblem Elephant.

JAMAICA

Area 4,244 square miles.
Population 2,437,000.
Climate Tropical at sea level, temperate in mountain areas; average year-round temperature in Kingston ranges from 66°F to 90°F.
Government Parliamentary state.
Language English.
Religion Roman Catholic, Protestant.
Currency Jamaican dollar (J$) = 100 cents.

JAPAN

Area 143,750 square miles.
Population 120,931,000.
Climate Monsoon climate modified by the influence of the sea. Average temperature in Tokyo ranges from 28°–46°F in January to 72°–86°F in August.
Government Parliamentary monarchy.
Language Japanese.
Religion The majority adhere to both Shintoism and Buddhism.
Currency Yen (Y) = 100 sen.
National anthem *The Reign of Our Emperor*.

JERSEY

Area 45 square miles.
Population 76,100.
Climate Temperate.
Government U.K. dependency with internal self-government.
Language English, French.
Religion Christian.
Currency U.K. pound and Jersey pound (J£) = 100 new pence.

JORDAN

Area 37,740 square miles.
Population 3,630,000.
Climate Hot and dry in summer, cool in winter; average temperature in Amman ranges from 39°–54°F in January to 64°–90°F in August.
Government Constitutional monarchy.
Language Arabic.
Religion Muslim.
Currency Jordan dinar (JD) = 1,000 fils.
National anthem *Long Live the King*.

KAMPUCHEA (Cambodia)

Area 69,900 square miles.
Population 6,365,000.
Climate Tropical; monsoons from April to October. Average annual temperature in Phnom Penh is 81°F.
Government One-party Communist state.
Language Khmer.
Religion Buddhist.
Currency Riel (KRL) = 100 sen.

KENYA

Area 224,960 square miles.
Population 21,415,000.
Climate Tropical; temperate inland. Average temperature in Nairobi ranges from 52°F to 79°F.
Government One-party republic.
Language Swahili and English; also other African languages.
Religion 50% Christian, 35% tribal, Muslim.
Currency Kenya shilling (KSh) = 100 cents.
National anthem *O God of all creation*.

KIRIBATI (formerly the Gilbert, Phoenix, and Line islands)

Area 318 square miles.
Population 63,000.
Climate Tropical; average temperature on Tarawa ranges from 77°F to 90°F.
Government Republic.
Language English, Gilbertese.
Religion Christian.
Currency Australian dollar (A$) = 100 cents.
National anthem *Stand Up, Kiribati*.

KOREA, NORTH

Area 46,540 square miles.
Population 20,544,000.
Climate Harsh winters, warm summers; average temperature in Wonsan ranges from 18°–30°F in January to 68°–81°F in August.
Government One-party Communist state.
Language Korean.
Religion Buddhist, Confucian, Shamanist, Chundo kyo.
Currency North Korean won (NKW) = 100 jun.
National anthem *The Song of General Kim Il Sung*.

KOREA, SOUTH

Area 38,025 square miles.
Population 40,450,000.
Climate Harsh winters, hot summers; average temperature in Seoul ranges from 16°–32°F in January to 72°–88°F in August.
Government Republic under strong authoritarian rule.
Language Korean.
Religion Buddhist, Christian, Confucianist, Chundo Kyo (Ch'ŏndogyo).
Currency South Korean won (SKW) = 100 chon (jun).
National anthem *May God bless Korea*.

KUWAIT

Area 6,880 square miles.
Population 1,888,000.
Climate Hot and dry; average temperature in Kuwait City ranges from 46°–64°F in winter to 84°–113°F in summer.
Government Parliamentary emirate.
Language Arabic, Persian, English.
Religion Muslim.
Currency Kuwaiti dinar (KD) = 1,000 fils.

LAOS

Area 91,400 square miles.
Population 3,895,000.
Climate Tropical; monsoons May to October. Average temperature in Vientiane ranges from 57°–82°F in January to 73°–93°F in April.
Government Communist one-party state.
Language Lao.
Religion Mainly Buddhist.
Currency Kip (Kp) = 100 att.
National anthem *For all time the Lao people have glorified their fatherland*.

LEBANON

Area 4,036 square miles.
Population 2,663,000.
Climate Subtropical; cool in highlands. Average temperature in Beirut ranges from 52°–63°F in January to 73°–90°F in August.
Government Republic.
Language Arabic.
Religion 50% Christian, 50% Muslim.
Currency Lebanese pound (L£) = 100 piasters.
National anthem *We are all for the motherland*.
National emblem Cedar tree.

LESOTHO (formerly Basutoland)

Area 11,720 square miles.
Population 1,556,000.
Climate Average temperature in Maseru ranges from 27°–63°F in July to 59°–91°F in January.
Government Authoritarian monarchy.
Language Sesotho, English.

Religion 70% Christian.
Currency Loti (Lo) = 100 lisente.

LIBERIA

Area 43,000 square miles.
Population 2,261,000.
Climate Tropical; average temperature in Monrovia ranges from 72°F to 88°F.
Government Authoritarian rule.
Language English, tribal.
Religion Tribal, Christian, Muslim.
Currency Liberian (L$) and U.S. dollars = 100 cents.
National anthem *All hail, Liberia, hail.*

LIBYA

Area 679,358 square miles.
Population 3,835,000.
Climate Hot and dry, especially in the south; average temperature in Tripoli ranges from 46°–61°F in January to 72°–86°F in August.
Government Socialist military dictatorship.
Language Arabic.
Religion Muslim.
Currency Libyan dinar (LD) = 1,000 dirhams.

LIECHTENSTEIN

Area 62 square miles.
Population 28,000.
Climate Temperate.
Government Constitutional monarchy.
Language German.
Religion 82% Roman Catholic, 7% Protestant.
Currency Swiss franc, or franken (SFr) = 100 centimes, or rappen.
National anthem *Above the young Rhine river Liechtenstein is perched.*

LUXEMBOURG

Area 998 square miles.
Population 368,000.
Climate Temperate; average temperature in Luxembourg City ranges from 14°–48°F in January to 45°–88°F in July.
Government Parliamentary monarchy.
Language Luxembourgish (a spoken language but not a written one); French and German as well.
Religion Roman Catholic.
Currency Luxembourg franc (LFr) = 100 centimes.
National anthem *Our Motherland.*
National emblem Lion with crown.

MACAU (Macao)

Area 6 square miles.
Population 300,000.
Climate Subtropical.
Government Territory under Portuguese administration.
Language Chinese and Portuguese.
Religion Buddhist and Roman Catholic.
Currency Pataca (Pat) = 100 avos.

MADAGASCAR

Area 226,658 square miles.
Population 10,285,000.
Climate Tropical; average temperature in Antananarivo, the capital, ranges from 48°–68°F in July to 61°–81°F in December.
Government Socialist republic.
Language Malagasy and French; also local dialects.
Religion 51% tribal, 38% Christian, 5% Muslim.
Currency Madagascar franc (MgFr) = 100 centimes.

MALAWI (formerly Nyasaland)

Area 45,747 square miles.
Population 7,230,000.
Climate Tropical; cooler in the highlands. Average temperatures are 45°–73°F from November to April and 63°–84°F from May to October.
Government One-party republic.
Language Chichewa, English.
Religion Christian, tribal.
Currency Malawi kwacha (MK) = 100 tambala.

MALAYSIA

Area 127,580 square miles.
Population 15,880,000.
Climate Tropical; average temperature in Kuala Lumpur ranges from 72°F to 91°F. Monsoon season is October to February in east, May to September in west.
Government Parliamentary monarchy.
Language Malay; also Chinese, English, and others.
Religion 50% Muslim, 26% Buddhist.
Currency Ringgit or dollar (Ma$) =

100 sen or cents.
National anthem *My country.*

MALDIVES

Area 115 square miles.
Population 183,000.
Climate Tropical; average temperature ranges from 77°F to 84°F; monsoons from June to August.
Government Republic ruled by decree.
Language Divehi, English.
Religion Mainly Muslim.
Currency Maldivian rufiyaa (MvRf) = 100 laris.

MALI

Area 479,000 square miles.
Population 8,190,000.
Climate Hot and dry; average temperature at Bamako ranges from 61°–91°F in January to 75°–102°F in April.
Government One-party republic.
Language French, local languages.
Religion 65% Muslim, 30% tribal.
Currency Mali franc (MFr) = 100 centimes.

MALTA

Area 122 square miles.
Population 360,000.
Climate Mediterranean; average temperature in Valletta ranges from 50°–57°F in January and 73°–84°F in August.
Government Republic.
Language Maltese, English.

MALAYSIA *Shadow puppets, manipulated by thin rods, are usually made of cowhide.*

NATIONS A–Z / Isle of Man–Norfolk Island

Religion Roman Catholic.
Currency Maltese lira (LM) = 100 cents = 1,000 mils.
National anthem *Guard her, O Lord.*

MAN, ISLE OF

Area 227 square miles.
Population 67,900.
Climate Temperate.
Government U.K. dependency with internal self-government.
Language English; also Manx.
Religion Mainly Church of England.
Currency U.K. pound and Isle of Man pound (IoM£) = 100 new pence.

MARSHALLS

Area 70 square miles.
Population 36,000.
Climate Tropical.
Government Self-governing parliamentary republic in final stage of transition from U.S. Trust Territory of the Pacific Islands; compact of free association with U.S.A. provides aid and defense for Marshalls.
Language English and Malayo-Polynesian languages.
Religion Christian.

MARTINIQUE

Area 425 square miles.
Population 330,000.
Climate Subtropical; average temperature at Fort-de-France ranges from 70°F to 88°F.
Government French overseas department.

Language French, Creole.
Religion Roman Catholic.
Currency French franc (Fr) = 100 centimes.

MAURITANIA

Area 398,000 square miles.
Population 1,687,000.
Climate Hot and dry; average temperature in Nouakchott ranges from 55°–82°F in December to 75°–93°F in September.
Government Military rule.
Language Arabic, French.
Religion Muslim.
Currency Ouguiya (U) = 5 khoums.

MAURITIUS

Area 790 square miles.
Population 1,065,000.
Climate Subtropical; June to October average temperatures range from 45°F to 77°F; November to April, 75°–88°F.
Government Parliamentary state.
Language English, French, Creole.
Religion Hindu, Roman Catholic, Muslim.
Currency Mauritius rupee (MR) = 100 cents.

MAYOTTE (Mahore)

Area 144 square miles.
Population 57,000.
Climate Tropical.
Government French dependency, status in dispute; also claimed by Comoros.
Language French; local dialects.
Religion Mainly Christian; also Muslim.
Currency French franc (Fr) = 100 centimes.
National anthem *The Marseillaise.*

MEXICO

Area 764,015 square miles.
Population 81,100,000.
Climate From tropical to temperate, depending on altitude. Average temperature in Mexico City ranges from 43°–66°F in January to 54°–79°F in May.
Government Federal republic.
Language Spanish; also local languages.
Religion Roman Catholic.
Currency Mexican peso (Mex$) = 100 centavos.
National anthem *Mexicans, at the call of battle.*

MICRONESIA

Area 271 square miles.
Population 85,000.
Climate Tropical.
Government Four-state federal republic in final stage of transition from U.S. Trust Territory of the Pacific Islands; compact of free association with U.S.A. provides aid and defense for Micronesia.
Language English; also Malayo-

Polynesian languages.
Religion Christian.

MONACO

Area 0.7 square mile.
Population 29,000.
Climate Mediterranean; average temperature in Monaco ranges from 46°–54°F in January to 72°–79°F in August.
Government Principality.
Language French.
Religion Roman Catholic.
Currency French franc = 100 centimes. Monégasque franc (MnFr) also in circulation = 100 centimes.
National anthem *The March of Monaco.*

MONGOLIA

Area 604,000 square miles.
Population 1,952,000.
Climate Dry and cold; average temperature in Ulan Bator ranges from −26°F to −2°F in January to 52°–72°F in July.
Government Communist state.
Language Mongolian.
Religion Buddhist.
Currency Tugric or Tögrög (Tug) = 100 möngö.
National emblem The Soyombo (ideogram for freedom and independence).

MONTSERRAT

Area 39 square miles.
Population 14,000.
Climate Tropical but windy; average temperature ranges from 73°F to 86°F.
Government U.K. dependency.
Language English.
Religion Christian.
Currency East Caribbean dollar (EC$) = 100 cents.
National anthem *God save the Queen.*

MOROCCO

Area 275,000 square miles, of which approx. 100,000 square miles, known as the Western Sahara, is claimed by Saharan nationalists (the Polisario Front) as an independent nation called the Sahara Arab Democratic Republic.
Population 22,893,000.
Climate Warm; average temperature in Rabat ranges from 46°–63°F in January to 64°–82°F in August.
Government Monarchy.
Language Arabic; also Spanish, French.
Religion Muslim.
Currency Dirham (DH) = 100 francs.
National anthem *Hymne Cheri Lien.*

MOZAMBIQUE

Area 309,494 square miles.
Population 14,470,000.

MOROCCO
Tall brass water jars and coffeepots, resembling Russian samovars, are common in Morocco.

Climate Tropical; average temperature in Maputo, the capital, ranges from 55°–75°F in July to 72°–88°F in February.
Government One-party Communist state.
Language Portuguese; African languages and dialects.
Religion 70% tribal; also Muslim and Christian.
Currency Metical (MT) = 100 centavos.
National anthem *Long live the Frelimo party, guide of the Mozambican people.*

NAMIBIA (formerly South West Africa)

Area 318,259 square miles.
Population 1,190,000.
Climate Very dry; average temperature in Windhoek ranges between 43°–68°F in July and 63°–84°F in January.
Government Independence disputed by South Africa, which retains administrative control.
Language Afrikaans, German, English; also African languages.
Religion 50% Christian.
Currency South African rand (R) = 100 cents.

NAURU

Area 8 square miles.
Population 8,000.
Climate Tropical; average temperature ranges from 73°F to 90°F; monsoons from November to February.
Government Parliamentary republic.
Language Nauruan, English.
Religion Christian.
Currency Australian dollar (A$) = 100 cents.

NEPAL

Area 54,362 square miles.
Population 17,200,000.
Climate Temperate except in the Himalayas; average temperature in Katmandu ranges from 36°–73°F in January to 68°–84°F in July.
Government Constitutional monarchy.
Language Nepali; also other local languages.
Religion 90% Hindu; also Buddhist.
Currency Nepalese rupee (NRe) = 100 paise (pice).
National anthem *May glory crown you, courageous sovereign.*

NETHERLANDS

Area 15,892 square miles.
Population 14,568,000.
Climate Temperate, maritime; average temperature ranges from 30°–39°F in January to 55°–72°F in July.
Government Parliamentary monarchy.
Language Netherlandic (Dutch).

Religion Roman Catholic, Dutch Reformed.
Currency Guilder or florin (Gld, Fl) = 100 cents.
National anthem *Wilhelmus.*
National emblem Lion.

NETHERLANDS ANTILLES

Area 384 square miles.
Population 272,000.
Climate Tropical; average temperature in Willemstad, Curacao, ranges from 73°F to 90°F.
Government Netherlands territory; Aruba promised independence in 1996.
Language Dutch; also Papiamento, English, and Spanish.
Religion Christian (80% Roman Catholic).
Currency Netherlands Antillian guilder or florin (NAGld, NAFI) = 100 cents.
National anthems *Wilhelmus. Bonairiano Hymn.*

NEW CALEDONIA

Area 7,358 square miles.
Population 149,000.
Climate Subtropical; average temperature all year round in Nouméa ranges from 61°F to 86°F.
Government French overseas territory.
Language French; also many languages and dialects.
Religion 65% Roman Catholic.
Currency French Pacific Community franc (CFPFr) = 100 centimes.
National anthem *The Marseillaise.*

NEW ZEALAND

Area 103,787 square miles.
Population 3,315,000.
Climate Temperate; average temperature in Wellington ranges from 43°–54°F in July to 55°–70°F in January.
Government Parliamentary state.
Language English.
Religion Mainly Protestant.
Currency New Zealand dollar (NZ$) = 100 cents.
National anthems *God Defend New Zealand. God Save the Queen.*
National emblems Southern cross, fern, kiwi.

NICARAGUA

Area 50,194 square miles.
Population 3,145,000.
Climate Tropical; average temperature throughout the year in Managua ranges from 68°F to 93°F.
Government Marxist socialist state.

Language Spanish.
Religion Roman Catholic.
Currency Córdoba (C$) = 100 centavos.
National anthem *Hail to you, Nicaragua.*

NIGER

Area 489,000 square miles.
Population 6,700,000.
Climate Hot and dry; average temperature in Niamey ranges from 57°–93°F in January to 81°–106°F in May.
Government Military rule.
Language French and local languages, especially Hausa.
Religion Mainly Muslim.
Currency African Financial Community franc (CFAFr) = 100 centimes.

NIGERIA

Area 356,669 square miles.
Population 94,280,000.
Climate Tropical; average temperature ranges from 73°F to 90°F.
Government Military rule.
Language English, Hausa, Ibo, Yoruba.
Religion Muslim, Christian.
Currency Naira (₦) = 100 kobo.
National anthem *Arise, O compatriots.*

NIUE

Area 100 square miles.
Population 4,000.
Climate Subtropical; average temperature in Niue ranges from 66°F to 88°F.
Government Self-governing state in free association with New Zealand.
Language Niue (Samoan) dialect.
Religion Mainly Ekalesia Niue.
Currency New Zealand dollar (NZ$) = 100 cents.
National anthem *Our Lord in heaven.*
National emblem War club and javelin.

NORFOLK ISLAND

Area 14 square miles.
Population 2,000.
Climate Subtropical; average temperature ranges from 55°F to 77°F.
Government Australian external territory.
Language English and "Norfolk" (Old English/Tahitian).
Currency Australian dollar (A$) = 100 cents.

NETHERLANDS *Carved wooden clogs are now more often sold as ornaments than as footwear.*

NATIONS A–Z / Northern Marianas–Seychelles

NORTHERN MARIANAS

Area 184 square miles.
Population 18,200.
Climate Tropical; temperatures on Saipan, the largest island, range between 79°F and 82°F.
Government Part of the U.S. Trust Territory of the Pacific Islands, the Northern Marianas is in the final stage of becoming a U.S. commonwealth with internal self-government.
Language Chamorro, English.
Religion Mainly Roman Catholic.
Currency U.S. dollar ($) = 100 cents.

NORWAY

Area 125,182 square miles.
Population 4,162,000.
Climate Temperate; cold in the north. Average temperature in Oslo ranges from 19°–28°F in January to 55°–72°F in July.
Government Parliamentary monarchy.
Language Norwegian.
Religion Lutheran.
Currency Norwegian krone (NKr) = 100 öre.
National anthem *Yes, we love this country.*
National emblem Lion.

OMAN

Area 82,030 square miles.
Population 1,250,000.
Climate Hot and dry; average temperature in Muscat is 61°–90°F in winter and rises to 120°F in summer.
Government Absolute monarchy (sultanate).
Language Arabic, English.
Religion Muslim.
Currency Omani rial (OR) = 1,000 baizas.
National anthem *May God keep his majesty the sultan.*

PAKISTAN

Area 310,403 square miles.
Population 103,000,000.
Climate Subtropical; monsoon from June to October; average temperature in Karachi ranges from 55°–77°F in January to 82°–93°F in June.
Government Martial law.
Language Urdu; also English and Punjabi.
Religion Muslim (97%).
Currency Pakistan rupee (PRe) = 100 paisa.
National anthem *Blessed be the sacred land.*
National emblem Jasmine.

PANAMA

Area 29,761 square miles.
Population 2,225,000.
Climate Tropical; average temperatures range from 72°F to 90°F.
Government Republic.
Language Spanish.
Religion Roman Catholic.
Currency Balboa (B/) = 100 centésimos.
National anthem *Himno Istmeño.*

PAPUA NEW GUINEA

Area 178,260 square miles.
Population 3,500,000.
Climate Tropical; average temperature in Port Moresby ranges from 73°F to 90°F.
Government Parliamentary state.
Language English, Tok Pisin (Pidgin English), and more than 700 languages and dialects.
Religion Christian.
Currency Kina (K) = 100 toea.
National emblem Bird of paradise.

PARAGUAY

Area 157,047 square miles.
Population 3,770,000.
Climate Subtropical; average temperature in Asunción ranges from 54°–72°F in July to 72°–95°F in January.
Government Authoritarian rule.
Language Spanish and Guaraní.
Religion Roman Catholic.
Currency Guaraní (₲) = 100 centimos.
National anthem *Once the lands of America.*

PERU

Area 496,225 square miles.
Population 20,208,000.
Climate Temperate, cooler at high altitudes; average temperature in Lima ranges from 55°–66°F in August to 66°–82°F in February.
Government Republic.
Language Spanish and Quechua.
Religion Roman Catholic.
Currency Sol (S/ or $) = 100 centavos.
National anthem *We are free, we will always be free.*

PHILIPPINES

Area 116,000 square miles.
Population 57,450,000.
Climate Tropical; average temperature all year round in Manila ranges from 70°F to 93°F.
Government Republic.
Language Pilipino (Tagalog); also English, Spanish, and local dialects.
Religion 85% Roman Catholic.
Currency Philippine peso (PP) = 100 sentimos (or centavos).
National anthem *Beloved country.*

PITCAIRN ISLAND

Area 2 square miles.
Population 70.
Climate Subtropical.
Government U.K. dependency.
Language English and English-Tahitian dialect.
Religion Christian.
Currency New Zealand dollar (NZ$) = 100 cents.

POLAND

Area 120,727 square miles.
Population 37,890,000.
Climate Temperate; average temperature in Warsaw ranges from 23°–32°F in January to 59°–75°F in July.
Government Communist state.
Language Polish.
Religion Roman Catholic.
Currency Zloty (Zl) = 100 groszy.
National anthem *Poland has not yet perished.*
National emblem Eagle.

PORTUGAL

Area 35,553 square miles.
Population 10,122,000.
Climate Hot, dry summers, warm, moist winters; average temperature in Lisbon ranges from 46°–57°F in January to 63°–82°F in August.
Government Republic.
Language Portuguese.
Religion Roman Catholic.
Currency Escudo (Esc) = 100 centavos.
National anthem *The Portuguese.*

PUERTO RICO

Area 3,435 square miles.
Population 3,190,000.
Climate Subtropical; average temperature throughout the year in San Juan ranges from 70°F to 84°F.
Government U.S. commonwealth with internal self-government.
Language Spanish, English.
Religion Roman Catholic.
Currency U.S. dollar ($) = 100 cents.

QATAR

Area 4,416 square miles.
Population 296,000.
Climate Hot, mild in winter. Summer temperature rises to 104°F.
Government Independent emirate.
Language Arabic, English.
Religion Muslim.
Currency Qatar riyal (QR) = 100 dirhams.

REUNION

Area 969 square miles.
Population 516,000.
Climate Subtropical, warm and humid; average temperature in Hell-Bourg ranges from 46°–66°F in August to 59°–75°F in February.
Government French overseas department.
Language French.
Religion Roman Catholic.
Currency French franc (Fr) = 100 centimes.

ROMANIA

Area 91,700 square miles.
Population 23,185,000.
Climate Continental; average temperature in Bucharest ranges from 28°F in winter to 70°F in summer.

Government Communist state.
Language Romanian.
Religion Mainly Romanian Orthodox.
Currency Leu (plural: lei) = 100 bani.
National anthem *Three colors.*

RWANDA

Area 10,169 square miles.
Population 6,300,000.
Climate Tropical; average annual temperature in Kigali, the capital, is 66°F.
Government One-party authoritarian rule.
Language Kinyarwanda, French.
Religion Tribal, Roman Catholic, Muslim.
Currency Rwanda franc (RwFr) = 100 centimes.

ST. CHRISTOPHER (ST. KITTS) AND NEVIS

Area 101 square miles.
Population 44,000.
Climate Subtropical; average temperature in Basseterre (St. Kitts) ranges from 72°F to 86°F.
Government Parliamentary state.
Language English.
Religion Christian.
Currency East Caribbean dollar (EC$) = 100 cents.

ST. HELENA and dependencies

Area St. Helena, 47 square miles; Ascension, 34 square miles; Tristan da Cunha, 40 square miles.
Population St. Helena, 5,220; Ascension, 1,020; Tristan da Cunha, 325.
Climate St. Helena: mild with little variation. Ascension: tropical but dry. Tristan da Cunha: temperate and oceanic with rapid weather changes.
Government U.K. dependency. Governor on St. Helena; Ascension and Tristan da Cunha have administrators.
Language English.
Religion Christian.
Currency U.K. pound (£) = 100 new pence.

ST. LUCIA

Area 238 square miles.
Population 123,000.
Climate Subtropical; average temperature 79°F. Dry season January to April.

PORTUGAL *A traditional port boat on the River Douro. The boat is steered from the high platform.*

Government Parliamentary state.
Language English, French patois.
Religion Mainly Roman Catholic.
Currency East Caribbean dollar (EC$) = 100 cents.
National anthem *Sons and daughters of St. Lucia.*

ST. PIERRE AND MIQUELON

Area 93 square miles.
Population 6,100.
Climate Temperate with cold winters and cool summers; average temperature in St. Pierre ranges from 18°–30°F in February to 50°–63°F in August.
Government French overseas department.
Language French.
Religion Roman Catholic.
Currency French franc (Fr) = 100 centimes.
National anthem *The Marseillaise.*

ST. VINCENT AND THE GRENADINES

Area 150 square miles.
Population 147,000.
Climate Subtropical; average temperature ranges from 64°F to 90°F. Dry season January to May.
Government Parliamentary state.
Language English.
Religion Christian.
Currency East Caribbean dollar (EC$) = 100 cents.

SAMOA, AMERICAN

Area 76 square miles.
Population 34,000.
Climate Tropical.

Government Unincorporated U.S. territory.
Language Samoan, English.
Religion Christian.
Currency U.S. dollar ($) = 100 cents.
National song *Amerika Samoa.*

SAN MARINO

Area 24 square miles.
Population 23,600.
Climate Mediterranean.
Government Republic.
Language Italian.
Religion Roman Catholic.
Currency San Marino lira (SML) circulates at par with Italian and Vatican lira.
National emblem Feathers.

SÃO TOMÉ AND PRÍNCIPE

Area 372 square miles.
Population 96,000.
Climate Warm and humid; average temperature in the capital city of São Tomé ranges from 70°F to 88°F.
Government One-party socialist state.
Language Portuguese and local languages.
Religion Roman Catholic.
Currency Dobra (Db) = 100 céntimos.

SAUDI ARABIA

Area 830,000 square miles.
Population 11,667,000.
Climate Hot and dry; average temperature in Riyadh, the capital, ranges from 46°–70°F in January to 79°–108°F in July.
Government Monarchy.
Language Arabic.
Religion Muslim.
Currency Saudi rial (SAR) = 20 qursh = 100 halala.
National anthem *Long live our beloved king.*

SENEGAL

Area 75,750 square miles.
Population 6,900,000.
Climate Tropical; average temperature in Dakar, the capital, ranges from 64°–79°F in January to 75°–90°F in September and October.
Government Socialist republic.
Language French; also native languages.
Religion Mainly Muslim.
Currency African Financial Community franc (CFAFr) = 100 centimes.
National anthem *Hope.*
National emblem Baobab tree.

SEYCHELLES

Area 171 square miles.
Population 66,000.

NATIONS A–Z / Sierra Leone–Turkey

Climate Tropical; temperature ranges from 75°F to 85°F on the coast.
Government One-party socialist state.
Language Creole, English, French.
Religion 90% Roman Catholic, 8% Anglican.
Currency Seychelles rupee (SR) = 100 cents.

SIERRA LEONE

Area 27,700 square miles.
Population 4,013,000.
Climate Tropical; average temperature in Freetown, the capital, ranges from 73°F to 88°F.
Government One-party republic.
Language English and local languages.
Religion Muslim and Christian.
Currency Leone (Le) = 100 cents.
National anthem *High we exalt thee, realm of the free.*
National emblem Lion.

SINGAPORE

Area 239 square miles.
Population 2,600,000.
Climate Equatorial; average daily temperature is 81°F.
Government Parliamentary state.
Language Chinese, Malay, English, Tamil.
Religion Buddhism, Islam, Hinduism, Chistianity, others.
Currency Singapore dollar (S$) = 100 cents.
National anthem *Let Singapore Flourish.*

SOLOMON ISLANDS

Area 11,500 square miles.
Population 284,000.

SYRIA *This inlaid chair is typical of the furniture still made in Damascus.*

Climate Equatorial; average temperature in Honiara, the capital, is 81°F.
Government Parliamentary democracy.
Language Pidgin English, English, more than 50 tribal dialects.
Religion Mainly Christian.
Currency Solomon Islands dollar (SI$) = 100 cents.
National anthem *God save our Solomon Islands.*

SOMALIA

Area 246,200 square miles.
Population 6,800,000.
Climate Hot and dry; average temperature in Mogadishu, the capital, ranges from 73°F to 90°F.
Government One-party socialist republic.
Language Somali, Arabic, English, Italian.
Religion Muslim.
Currency Somali shilling (SoSh) = 100 cents.

SOUTH AFRICA

Area 471,442 square miles (if the areas of the tribal homelands of Bophuthatswana, Ciskei, Transkei, and Venda are included).
Population 33,185,000 (including the tribal homelands).
Climate Temperate; average temperature in Cape Town ranges from 48°–63°F in July to 61°–81°F in February.
Government Minority-controlled republic.
Language Afrikaans, English, and African languages.
Religion Christian, tribal, Hindu, Muslim.
Currency Rand (R) = 100 cents.
National anthem *The Call of South Africa.*

SPAIN

Area 194,897 square miles.
Population 39,320,000.
Climate Mediterranean in the southern and eastern coastlands, temperate elsewhere. Average temperature in Madrid, the capital, ranges from 34°–46°F in January to 63°–88°F in July.
Government Parliamentary monarchy.
Language Spanish (Castilian), Catalan, Galician, Basque.
Religion Roman Catholic.
Currency Peseta (Pa) = 100 céntimos.
National anthem *Marcha Real.*
National flower Carnation.

SRI LANKA

Area 25,430 square miles.
Population 16,660,000.
Climate Tropical; average temperature ranges from 79°F to 82°F in the low country and from 57°F to 75°F in the high country.
Government Parliamentary

democracy, with president.
Language Sinhala, Tamil, English.
Religion Buddhist (67%), Hindu, Christian, Islam.
Currency Sri Lanka rupee (SLR) = 100 cents.
National anthem *Sri Lanka Motherland.*
National emblem Lion.

SUDAN

Area 967,500 square miles.
Population 22,177,000.
Climate Tropical; average temperature in Khartoum, the capital, ranges from 59°–90°F in January to 79°–106°F in June.
Government Military dictatorship.
Language Arabic; also local languages, especially Nubian.
Religion Muslim (70%), tribal (25%), Christianity.
Currency Sudanese pound (S£) = 100 piastres = 1,000 millièmes.
National anthem *We are the soldiers of God.*

SURINAME

Area 63,037 square miles.
Population 386,000.
Climate Tropical; average temperature in Paramaribo, the capital, ranges from 73°F to 91°F.
Government Socialist military junta.
Language Netherlandic (Dutch), English, Spanish, Hindi, Javanese, Chinese, and local languages and dialects.
Religion Hindu, Muslim, Christian.
Currency Suriname guilder or florin (SGld, SFl) = 100 cents.

SWAZILAND

Area 6,705 square miles.
Population 668,000.
Climate Subtropical; average temperature in Mbabane, the capital, ranges from 43°–66°F in June to 59°–77°F in January/February.
Government Monarchy.
Language English, Swazi, Zulu.
Religion 60% Christian, tribal.
Currency Lilangeni (plural emalangeni; Li or Ei) = 100 cents.
National anthem *Creator of benevolence.*
National emblem Lion and elephant.

SWEDEN

Area 173,732 square miles.
Population 8,340,000.
Climate Short, warm summers and long, cold winters. Average temperature in Stockholm ranges from 23°–30°F in February to 57°–72°F in July.
Government Parliamentary monarchy.
Language Swedish.
Religion Lutheran.
Currency Swedish krona (SKr) = 100 öre.

National anthem *Thou ancient, thou freeborn.*

SWITZERLAND

Area 15,941 square miles.
Population 6,596,000.
Climate Warm summers, cold winters; average temperature in Zurich ranges from 27°–36°F in January to 55°–75°F in July.
Government Federal republic.
Language German, French, Italian, Romansch.
Religion 48% Roman Catholic, 44% Protestant.
Currency Swiss franc, or franken (SFr) = 100 centimes or rappen.
National anthem *Swiss Psalm.*

SYRIA

Area 71,500 square miles.
Population 10,894,000.
Climate Mediterranean on the coast, very hot and dry inland. Average temperature in Damascus ranges from 32°–54°F in January to 68°–113°F in August.
Government Socialist republic.
Language Arabic, Armenian, Kurdish, French, English.
Religion Muslim.
Currency Syrian pound (£S) = 100 piasters.
National anthem *Defenders of the realm, we salute you.*
National emblem Eagle.

TAIWAN

Area 13,895 square miles.
Population 19,800,000
Climate Subtropical; average temperature in Taipei ranges from 54°–64°F in February to 75°–91°F in July.
Government One-party republic.
Language Chinese, English, Japanese.
Religion Confucian, Buddhist, Taoist, Christian.
Currency New Taiwan dollar (NT$) = 100 cents.
National anthem *San min chu I.*

TANZANIA (formerly Tanganyika and Zanzibar)

Area 364,900 square miles.
Population 23,122,000.
Climate Tropical; average temperature in Dar es Salaam ranges from 66°F to 88°F.
Government One-party socialist republic.
Language Swahili, English.
Religion Muslim, Christian, tribal.
Currency Tanzanian shilling (TSh) = 100 cents.

THAILAND

Area 198,457 square miles.
Population 53,754,000.
Climate Tropical; monsoons from May to October. Average temperature in Bangkok ranges from 68°F to 95°F.
Government Parliamentary monarchy.
Language Thai.
Religion Buddhist (95%), tribal.
Currency Baht (Bt) = 100 satangs.

TOGO

Area 21,925 square miles.
Population 3,100,000.
Climate Tropical; average temperature in Lomé, the capital, is 81°F.
Government One-party dictatorship.
Language French, local languages.
Religion Tribal, Christian, Muslim.
Currency African Financial Community franc (CFAFr) = 100 centimes.

TONGA

Area 270 square miles.
Population 110,800.
Climate Subtropical; average annual temperature in Nuku'alofa is 75°F.
Government Constitutional monarchy.
Language Tongan, English.
Religion Christian.
Currency Tongan pa'anga (T$) = 100 seniti.
National anthem *O Almighty God above.*

TRANSKEI

Area 16,070 square miles.
Population 3,010,000.
Climate Mild, especially on the seacost; summers are warm to hot, winters dry and cool with an occasional frost.
Government Parliamentary

republic; declared independent by South Africa in 1976 but not recognized as sovereign by other nations.
Language Xhosa, English, Afrikaans, Sesotho.
Religion Methodist, tribal.
Currency South African Rand (R) = 100 cents.

TRINIDAD AND TOBAGO

Area 1,981 square miles.
Population 1,225,000.
Climate Tropical; average temperature ranges from 72°F to 88°F.
Government Parliamentary republic.
Language English, Spanish.
Religion Roman Catholic, Anglican, Hindu, Muslim.
Currency Trinidad and Tobago dollar (TT$) = 100 cents.
National anthem *Forged from the love of liberty.*
National emblem Hummingbird.

TUNISIA

Area 63,170 square miles.
Population 7,400,000.
Climate Temperate on the coast, very dry inland. Average temperature in Tunis, the capital, ranges from 43°–57°F in January to 70°–91°F in August.
Government Republic.
Language Arabic, French.
Religion Muslim.
Currency Tunisian dinar (TD) = 1,000 millimes.

TURKEY

Area 301,382 square miles.
Population 52,387,000.
Climate Mediterranean on the coast, continental inland. Average temperature in Ankara ranges from 25°–39°F in January to 59°–88°F in August.
Government Republic with powerful presidency.

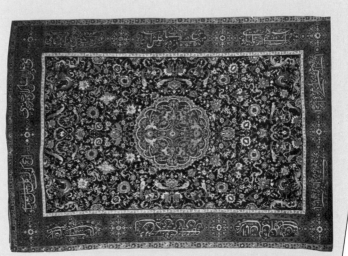

TURKEY *Islamic quotations surround the intricate central design of a 19th-century Turkish carpet.*

NATIONS A–Z / Turks and Caicos Islands–Zimbabwe

Language Turkish, Kurdish, Arabic.
Religion Muslim.
Currency Turkish lira (TL) = 100
kurus or piasters.
National anthem *March of
Independence.*
National emblem Crescent and star.

TURKS AND CAICOS ISLANDS

Area 166 square miles.
Population 8,300.
Climate Equable; average
temperature ranges from a low of
61°F in midwinter to a high of 90°F
in midsummer.
Government U.K. dependency.
Language English.
Religion Christian.
Currency U.S. dollar ($) = 100 cents.
National anthem *God Save the
Queen.*

TUVALU (formerly Ellice Islands)
Area 10 square miles.
Population 8,000.
Climate Tropical; average
temperature 86°F.
Government Parliamentary state.
Language Tuvaluan, English.
Religion Christian, Baha'i.
Currency Australian dollar (A$) =
100 cents. Tuvaluan coins.

UGANDA

Area 91,133 square miles.
Population 15,560,000.
Climate Tropical; temperature
ranges from 59°F to 79°F. Cooler in
mountain areas.
Government Military rule.
Language English, Luganda,
Swahili, Lwo, Ateso.
Religion Christian, tribal, Muslim.
Currency Ugandan shilling (USh) =
100 cents.

UNION OF SOVIET SOCIALIST
REPUBLICS

Area 8,649,538 square miles.
Population 281,057,000.
Climate Spans many climate zones;
arctic in the north. Average
temperature in Moscow ranges
from 3°–16°F in January to 55°–
73°F in July.
Government Communist one-party
state.
Language Russian, Ukrainian,
Belorussian, and others.
Religion Officially atheist, but

Christian, Muslim, Jewish religions
observed.
Currency Ruble (Rub) = 100
kopecks.
National anthem *Unbreakable
union of freeborn republics.*
National emblem Hammer and
sickle.

UNITED ARAB EMIRATES

Area 32,278 square miles.
Population 1,400,000.
Climate Average temperature in
Sharja ranges from 54°–73°F in
January to 82°–100°F in August,
with peak temperatures of over
120°F.
Government Federation of
monarchies.
Language Arabic, Persian, English.
Religion Muslim.
Currency UAE dirham (UAEDh) =
10 dinar = 1,000 fils.

UNITED KINGDOM OF GREAT
BRITAIN AND NORTHERN IRELAND

Area 94,515 square miles.
Population 56,050,000.
Climate Temperate; average
temperature in London ranges from
36°–43°F in January to 55°–72°F
in July.
Government Parliamentary
monarchy.
Language English.
Religion Christian.
Currency Pound (£) = 100 new
pence.
National anthem *God Save the
Queen.*

UNITED STATES OF AMERICA

Area 3,618,770 square miles.
Population 240,000,000.
Climate Temperate, subtropical in
the south. Mainly hot summers,
cold winters in the north. Average
temperature in Washington, D.C.,
ranges from 27°–43°F in January to
68°–88°F in July.
Government Republic; federation of
50 states.
Language English, with a sizable

*U.S.A. An Algonquin Indian chief is
thought to have given this deerskin
cloak to a settler in Virginia
in about 1608.*

*U.S.S.R. This north
Russian walrus-bone
comb dates from the
17th century.*

minority whose language is
Spanish.
Religion Protestant (66%), Roman
Catholic (26%), Jewish (3%).
Currency Dollar ($) = 100 cents.
National anthem *The Star-
Spangled Banner.*
National emblem Bald eagle.

URUGUAY

Area 68,037 square miles.
Population 3,028,000.
Climate Temperate; average
temperature in Montevideo, the
capital, ranges between 63°–82°F in
January and 43°–57°F in July.
Government Multiparty republic.
Language Spanish.
Religion Roman Catholic.
Currency Uruguayan new peso
(UrugN$) = 100 centésimos.
National anthem *People of the East,
the country or the grave.*

VANUATU (formerly New Hebrides)

Area 5,700 square miles.
Population 137,000.
Climate Tropical; average
temperature throughout the year in
Vila, the capital, on the island of
Efate ranges from 66°F to 88°F.
Government Parliamentary
republic.
Language Bislama (pidgin), English,
French, and other Melanesian
languages and dialects.
Religion Christian, tribal.
Currency Vatu (VT) = 100
centimes.

VATICAN CITY

Area 0.17 square mile.
Population 1,000.
Climate Mediterranean.
Government Ecclesiastical state,
seat of the pope of the Roman
Catholic Church.
Language Italian, Latin.
Religion Roman Catholic.
Currency Vatican City lira (VL) at par
with the Italian lira, also in use.

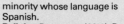

VENDA

Area 2,150 square miles.
Population 417,400.
Climate Subtropical; rainfall plentiful.
Government Republic; declared independent by South Africa in 1979 but not recognized as sovereign by other nations.
Language Venda, English, Afrikaans.
Religion Christian, tribal.
Currency South African Rand (R) = 100 cents.

VENEZUELA

Area 352,145 square miles.
Population 19,617,000.
Climate Tropical; average temperature ranges from 77°– 82°F at sea level to 59°– 64°F in the mountains.
Government Republic.
Language Spanish.
Religion Roman Catholic.
Currency Bolívar (B) = 100 céntimos.
National anthem *Glory to the brave nation.*

VIETNAM

Area 127,242 square miles.
Population 60,826,000.
Climate Tropical; temperatures vary with seasons in the north but hardly at all in the south. Average temperature in Hanoi ranges from 63°F in January to 84°F in June.
Government Communist state.
Language Vietnamese.
Religion Buddhist (70%), Roman Catholic (10%).
Currency Dong (D) = 10 hao = 100 xu.
National anthem *Soldiers of Vietnam, we march forward.*

VIRGIN ISLANDS, BRITISH

Area 59 square miles.
Population 12,600.
Climate Subtropical; average temperature ranges from 63°– 82°F in winter to 79°– 88°F in summer.
Government U.K. dependency.
Language English.
Religion Christian.
Currency U.S. dollar ($) = 100 cents.

VIRGIN ISLANDS, U.S.

Area 133 square miles.
Population 104,000.
Climate Same as British Virgin Islands.
Government Unincorporated U.S. territory.
Language English.
Religion Mainly Christian.

Currency U.S. dollar ($) = 100 cents.
National song *Virgin Islands march.*

WESTERN SAMOA

Area 1,100 square miles.
Population 168,300.
Climate Tropical; average temperature in Apia, the capital, ranges from 73°F to 86°F.
Government Parliamentary democracy.
Language Samoan, English.
Religion Christian.
Currency Western Samoan tala (WS$) = 100 sene.
National anthem *The Banner of Freedom.*

YEMEN (NORTH) ARAB REPUBLIC

Area 75,290 square miles.
Population 6,600,000.
Climate Warm and humid on the coast, cooler in the mountainous interior.
Government Republic under military rule.
Language Arabic.
Religion Muslim.
Currency Yemeni riyal (YR) = 100 fils.
National anthem *Under the shadow of the flag of the revolution we declared our republic.*

YEMEN (SOUTH), PEOPLE'S DEMOCRATIC REPUBLIC OF

Area 128,560 square miles.
Population 2,330,000.
Climate Hot and dry; average temperature in Khormaksar ranges from 72°F to 99°F.
Government Communist (only Arab Marxist nation).
Language Arabic, English.
Religion Muslim.
Currency Yemeni dinar (YD) = 1,000 fils.

YUGOSLAVIA

Area 98,766 square miles.
Population 23,392,000.
Climate Mediterranean on coast, temperate inland. Average temperature in Belgrade ranges from 27°– 37°F in January to 63°– 82°F in July.
Government Communist state.
Language Serbo-Croatian, Slovene, Macedonian, Hungarian, Albanian.
Religion Eastern (Serbian) Orthodox (41%), Roman Catholic (32%), Muslim (12%).
Currency Yugoslavian dinar

(YuD) = 100 para.
National anthem *Fellow Slavs.*

ZAIRE

Area 905,365 square miles.
Population 33,972,000.
Climate Tropical; average temperature in Kinshasa ranges from 64°F to 90°F.
Government One-party rule.
Language French, tribal dialects.
Religion Christian, tribal.
Currency Zaïre (Z) = 100 makuta = 10,000 sengi.

ZAMBIA (formerly Northern Rhodesia)

Area 290,586 square miles.
Population 6,987,000.
Climate Tropical, cool on the plateaus. Average temperature in Lusaka ranges from 48°– 73°F in July to 64°– 88°F in October.
Government One-party republic.
Language English, local languages.
Religion Tribal (70%), Christian.
Currency Kwacha (K) = 100 ngwee.
National anthem *Stand and sing of Zambia, proud and free.*

ZIMBABWE (formerly Southern Rhodesia)

Area 150,804 square miles.
Population 9,064,000.
Climate Subtropical; average temperature in Harare ranges from 45°– 70°F in June/July to 61°– 81°F in November.
Government Parliamentary state.
Language English, Shona, Ndebele.
Religion Tribal, Christian.
Currency Zimbabwe dollar (Z$) = 100 cents.
National anthem *God bless Africa.*
National emblem Zimbabwe bird.

ZAIRE *This carved and polished wooden head is in fact a cup. It stands 8 inches high and was made by a craftsman of the Kuba tribe, which lives near the Kasai River, east of the nation's capital, Kinshasa.*

International organizations

SAVED FROM EXTINCTION

Since its foundation in 1961 the World Wildlife Fund has helped to stop or at least delay the extinction of some 30 animal species—including tigers, polar bears, and African elephants. The fund, which works closely with an international team of scientists, raises money to provide sanctuaries for threatened species. But there are still about 1,000 different kinds of animals—among them the Japanese crested ibis, the California condor, the American alligator, the blue whale, and the Javan tiger—in danger of dying out. Some 25,000 plant species are also threatened with extinction.

With headquarters in Gland, Switzerland, and branches in almost 30 countries, the fund has raised more than $50 million to finance more than 6,000 lifesaving projects in 135 countries.

PAVING THE WAY FOR PEACE

Amnesty International—the worldwide organization for the defense of human rights—is one of the few institutions to have won a Nobel Peace Prize. Most prizewinners have been individual people. The only institutions to have won more than once are the United Nations Office of the High Commissioner for Refugees, in 1954 and 1981, and the Red Cross, in 1917, 1944, and 1963. Amnesty's prize was awarded in 1977 for the organization's help in paving the way "for freedom, for justice, and thereby also for peace in the world."

Amnesty International was founded in 1961 by a British lawyer, Peter Benenson, and is financially independent and without any political ties or affiliations. The organization, which handles 5,000 to 6,000 individual cases a year, campaigns for the release of all prisoners of conscience, provided they have not used or advocated violence; fair and prompt trials for all political prisoners; and the abolition of torture and capital punishment. It estimates that around the world there may be as many as 500,000 prisoners of conscience, and many others who have been summarily executed by governments.

THE $8.5 MILLION GIFT

The United Nations—most of whose members are poor Third World countries—meets on a site donated by one of the world's richest men. The gift came from the multimillionaire philanthropist and industrialist John D. Rockefeller, Jr., son of the founder of the giant U.S. oil company, Standard Oil. Rockefeller bought the 18-acre tract of land beside New York's East River for $8.5 million in 1946. He then gave it to the U.N. as a site for its headquarters building, which was opened in 1952. The land is now officially international territory, and a team of guides shows about a million visitors around the headquarters each year.

THE MAN WHO STARTED THE RED CROSS

In the summer of 1859 a young Swiss businessman named Jean Henri Dunant, traveling through northern Italy, became an eyewitness at the Battle of Solferino during the Risorgimento. He was so appalled by the bloodshed and slaughter—altogether some 30,000 soldiers were killed or wounded as France tried to free Italy from Austrian domination—that he stayed on to organize local relief work.

The following year Dunant, who became a full-time philanthropist, published a booklet, *A Memory of Solferino*, in which he called for the formation of

INTERNATIONAL ALLIANCES

Arab League
Founded March 22, 1945. Headquarters in Tunis, Tunisia. Promotes cooperation among Arab nations.

Association of Southeast Asian Nations (ASEAN)
Founded August 9, 1967. Headquarters in Jakarta, Indonesia. Promotes economic growth in the region.

Commonwealth, The
Founded April 27, 1949. Also known as The (British) Commonwealth of Nations. Secretariat in London, England. Includes countries and dependencies formerly in British Empire that maintain friendly ties with Britain.

Colombo Plan
Founded July 1, 1951. Headquarters in Colombo, Sri Lanka. Aids economic development of southern Asia.

Council for Mutual Economic Assistance (COMECON)
Founded January 25, 1949. Headquarters in Moscow, U.S.S.R. Economic organization of Communist-bloc nations. Promotes trade and economic growth.

Council of Europe
Founded August 3, 1949. Headquarters in Strasbourg, France. Promotes social and economic progress among members. But, unlike the EEC, it does not concern itself with international commerce.

European Economic Community (EEC, or Common Market)
Founded January 1, 1958. Headquarters in Brussels, Belgium. Promotes economic unity among member states—most of the nations of Western Europe—and has trade agreements throughout the world.

European Free Trade Association (EFTA)
Founded May 3, 1960. Headquarters in Geneva, Switzerland. Promotes free trade among members, none of which is a member of the EEC.

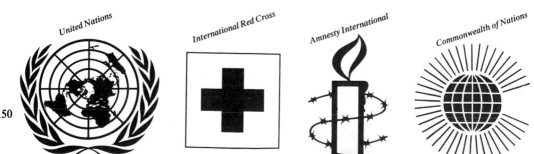

United Nations   International Red Cross   Amnesty International   Commonwealth of Nations

permanent relief societies for those wounded in war. Four years later, in 1864, Dunant formed the International Red Cross in his hometown of Geneva, and in 1901 he was a cowinner of the first Nobel Peace Prize.

Today the Red Cross has about 200 million members in 131 countries, and its work has expanded to help relieve the suffering caused not only by war but also by political upheavals and natural disasters.

The international symbol of the Red Cross—a red cross on a white background—reverses the colors of the Swiss flag, in honor of the society's birthplace. In most Islamic countries, however, the organization displays a red crescent instead of the cross. And in the Soviet Union, the Red Cross uses the cross and crescent combined.

WHEN INTERPOL WORKED FOR THE NAZIS
Adolf Hitler was so impressed by the efficiency of the International Criminal Police Organization (Interpol) that he made it part of the Gestapo, the Nazi secret police. This followed the German occupation of Austria in 1938, when Interpol had its headquarters in Vienna. The organization's records were taken to Berlin, where Gestapo officials used the files to keep track of wanted criminals—and in some cases, to capture them and persuade them to work for the Nazi cause.

Interpol was founded in 1923 at a special criminal police congress held in Vienna and attended by delegates from some 20 countries. In 1946, after the end of World War II, the organization was reconstituted and a new headquarters was set up in Paris. Interpol now has more than 125 member countries, but only one Communist member: Yugoslavia.

POWER OF THE VETO
The Security Council of the United Nations has five permanent members, all nuclear powers: Britain, the United States, France, China, and the Soviet Union. Each has the power to block any motion put before the council, even if all the other members support it. The council can also veto any proposal for membership to the U.N. Only when a new nation has been accepted by the council can its membership be approved by a vote of the General Assembly. Furthermore, the Security Council is the executive arm of the U.N. This means that the U.N. cannot order any action to be taken—though it can make recommendations to governments—unless it wins the support or acquiescence of the five nuclear powers. A no vote by any one of them is enough to overrule the wishes of the other 158 member nations.

All U.N. proceedings are recorded in the organization's six official languages: English, French, Russian, Chinese, Spanish, and Arabic. And the U.N. employs about 620 translators and interpreters to keep pace with its output of words.

THREE VOTES IN ONE
The Soviet Union can always rely on three votes in the United Nations General Assembly because two Soviet republics have seats normally given only to fully independent sovereign states.

At the Dumbarton Oaks Conference in Washington, D.C., in 1944—which led to the establishment of the United Nations—the Soviet Union demanded separate representation for all of its republics. At the time there were 16 of them, each with its own ministries of defense and foreign affairs. But at the Yalta Conference held in the Crimea in the following year, the Russians backed down. The main agenda of the conference—which was attended by the Soviet dictator Joseph Stalin, U.S. President Franklin D. Roosevelt, and British prime minister Winston Churchill—was the unconditional surrender of Germany. But the Allied leaders also agreed on a compromise over Soviet representation: U.N. seats would be given to the Ukrainian and Byelorussian Soviet socialist republics as well as to the Soviet Union as a whole.

North Atlantic Treaty Organization (NATO)
Established September 17, 1949. Headquarters in Brussels, Belgium. Guarantees mutual defense among members, all of which are Western-bloc nations.

Organization for Economic Cooperation and Development (OECD)
Founded September 30, 1961. Headquarters in Paris, France. Promotes economic cooperation among members. Members are all Western-bloc nations with the exception of Yugoslavia.

Organization of African Unity (OAU)
Founded May 25, 1963. Headquarters in Addis Ababa, Ethiopia. Promotes unity and development among more than 40 African member states.

Organization of American States (OAS)
Founded December 31, 1951. Headquarters in Washington, D.C. Promotes cooperation and defense among its members, nearly 30 nations in the Americas.

Organization of Petroleum Exporting Countries (OPEC)
Founded November 14, 1960. Headquarters in Vienna, Austria. Aims to control production and pricing of crude oil.

United Nations (U.N.)
Founded October 24, 1945. Headquarters in New York. In 1986 had 159 members. Some fully independent nations are not members, including North and South Korea, Switzerland, Taiwan, and Vatican City. Includes International Monetary Fund (IMF) and World Health Organization (WHO). Promotes international cooperation, peace, and security.

Warsaw Pact
Founded June 5, 1955. Headquarters in Moscow, U.S.S.R. Military alliance, the Communist counterpart of NATO.

Arab League   World Wildlife Fund   European Economic Community   Interpol

Great cities

YOU MEAN KRUNG THEP?

Krung Thep has been the correct name for the capital of Thailand for more than 130 years, but foreigners persist in calling it Bangkok. The city has changed its name four times since its foundation in 1767, a few years after the destruction of Ayutthaya, the old capital of the the Thai kingdom.

The first site was at Thonburi, just down the Chao Phraya River from Ayutthaya. But in 1782 King Rama I began building a new capital on the opposite bank at Bangkok, then a small village. In 1787, two years after completion, the city was named Rattanakosin. Finally, during the reign of Rama III (1824–1851), the name was altered to Krungthep Maha Nakorn, Amarn Rattanakosindra, Mahindrayudhya, Mahadilokpop Noparatana Rajdhani Mahasathan, Amorn Piman Avatarn Satit, Sakkatultiya Vishnukarn Prasit. Or Krung Thep for short.

The full name translates as "The city of gods, the great city, the residence of the Emerald Buddha, the impregnable city (of Ayutthaya) of God Indra, the grand capital of the world endowed with nine precious gems, the happy city, abounding in an enormous Royal Palace that resembles the heavenly abode where reigns the reincarnated god, a city given by Indra and built by Vishnukarn."

INSIDE THE HUNDRED GATES

Some of the most conservative of the Orthodox Jews who live in the Mea Shearim ("Hundred Gates") quarter of Jerusalem do not recognize the state of Israel, because it is secular rather than religious. They refuse to pay taxes or send their children to state schools, and the women refuse to do military service.

Mea Shearim was founded in 1875 outside the Old City by Orthodox Jews from eastern and central Europe. The district has a variety of synagogues, theological institutions, and religious schools. Strict rules govern modesty of dress, and only Yiddish is spoken. Hebrew, the language of prayer, is deemed too sacred for ordinary speech.

ABOUT-FACE

It was toward Jerusalem, not Mecca, that the founder of Islam, Muhammad, and his followers first turned to pray. Because Muhammad revered the Old Testament and claimed to be the successor of Abraham and Moses, it was natural for him to face the holy city of Jerusalem. But Jews formed an important group in Mecca, where Muhammad was born, and they rejected his claim that Abraham was a Muslim and that he, Muhammad, was the prophet foretold by Moses.

Finally he broke with them and began to pray facing Mecca, believing—as do all Muslims—that the Kaaba, Mecca's sacred shrine, was built by Abraham.

SILENT—THE BIGGEST CANNON

A portrait of the Russian czar Fedor Ivanovich (1557–98), son of Ivan the Terrible, decorates the largest-caliber cannon ever made. The 45-ton gun stands in the Kremlin, the complex of old palaces, cathedrals, and churches that dominates Moscow and now serves as the seat of Soviet communist power. The cannon's bronze barrel is 10 feet 5 inches long, with a bore of 36 inches. It has never been fired.

SILENT—THE BIGGEST BELL

The Kremlin also boasts the heaviest bell in the world. It weighs more than 200 tons and stands 19 feet 3

NEW YORK, NEW YORK Famous the world over for the frenetic pace and dazzle that go with being a financial, entertainment, and communications capital, the "Big Apple" owes its preeminence in large part to a splendid physical location. Its magnificent harbor is fed by the Hudson River (left in photo), flowing from the north, and by the East River (right), crossed by the historic Brooklyn Bridge. Shown here is the southern tip of Manhattan (one of five New York City boroughs), site of Wall Street and the financial district. Farther north, at top of picture, can be glimpsed the Empire State Building, eclipsed in 1971 as the city's tallest building by the twin-tower World Trade Center (left mid-distance).

inches high. Known as the Czar Kolokol, the bell was cast in 1735 but cracked 2 years later in a fire. The bell remains on a platform at the foot of the 263-foot-tall bell tower for which it was originally intended. It has never been rung. The original Kremlin—the word means "walled town" or "fortress"—was built of wood early in the 10th century. Its walls were rebuilt in red brick during the 15th century. Since then new buildings have been added to the Kremlin and old ones repaired and altered.

CAPITAL CHOICE

Four cities were bitter rivals for the honor of becoming Canada's capital: Quebec, Montreal, Kingston, and Toronto. Each made clear that any three of them would stoutly oppose the choice of the fourth; so in 1858 Queen Victoria was asked to arbitrate. She chose none of the four and named Ottawa.

Toronto was more than 100 years old; Quebec, Montreal, and Kingston were founded in the 17th century. Ottawa, which was barely three decades old, had been a city for only 4 years.

FASHIONS BY MICHELANGELO

The Vatican City's Swiss Guard still wears a uniform designed by the Italian artist Michelangelo early in the 16th century. The guard was formed in 1506 under Pope Julius II. As part of the Vatican's contract with the Swiss Confederacy, no other country could recruit in Switzerland or employ Swiss mercenaries without papal permission.

The original force, 6,000 strong, was raised to defend the church and its worldly possessions. Now there are just 100 men, who form the papal guard within the Vatican City.

COOK'S COTTAGE—MAYBE

Captain Cook's Cottage, which can now be seen in the Fitzroy Gardens in Melbourne, Australia, was originally built in Yorkshire, England. The English explorer Capt. James Cook landed at Botany Bay, Australia, in 1770. But the cottage got to Melbourne only in 1934, when it was shipped there from England.

The cottage was built in Yorkshire by Cook's father in 1755. But by then the son was 27 and had been at

sea for about 10 years; so it is unlikely that he ever actually lived in the cottage, although he may have slept in it when visiting his parents.

SINKING CITY
Mexico City is built on top of an underground reservoir. As wells draw out more and more water for the city's expanding population of more than 15 million people, the entire city is slowly sinking at the rate of 6 to 8 inches per year.

CIRCUS COLLAR
Piccadilly Circus in London gets its name from ornamental collars called piccadills, which used to be made in the area by a 17th-century tailor named Robert

Baker. Baker built himself a grand house, Piccadilly Hall, with the fortune he made, and the name came to include the whole neighborhood.

NAMED AFTER A GAME
The grandest street in London's West End, Pall Mall, is built on the site of a long green where Charles I played paille maille, a then fashionable game that was the forerunner of croquet. Paille maille seems to have arrived in England from France in the second quarter of the 17th century. After Charles II was restored to the throne in 1660, he replaced the old pall-mall green with a new one running parallel to it, and the new green later became the site of the Mall, which links Buckingham Palace and Trafalgar Square.

CAPITAL CITIES OF THE WORLD / Afghanistan—Comoros

The capitals of nations—and of many dependent lands—are listed here, together with the dates of their founding and the origin of their names, if known, and other facts.

AFGHANISTAN, Kabul
Founded on Kabul River more than 3,000 years ago. Made capital in 1776. The name is the Persian for "warehouse."

ALBANIA, Tirana (Tiranë)
Founded early 17th century by the Turkish general Suleiman Pasha. Thought to be named in honor of a Turkish victory at Tehran. Made capital in 1920.

ALGERIA, Algiers (Alger)
Founded by Berber dynasty in 10th century on site of ancient city of Icosium. Name comes from the Arabic *Al-Jazair,* meaning "the island."

ANDORRA, Andorra la Vella
Founded probably during the reign of the 8th-century emperor Charlemagne. The name may be related to the Basque word *andurrial,* meaning "heath."

ANGOLA, Luanda
Seaport, founded in 1575 by Portuguese traders. Made colonial capital in 1627 and capital of Angola in 1975.

ANGUILLA, The Valley
Island supposedly named by Christopher Columbus in 1493 from Spanish *anguila,* meaning "eel," because of island's long, thin shape.

ANTIGUA AND BARBUDA, St. John's
Island of Antigua named by Christopher Columbus in 1493 after a church in Seville, Spain, called Santa María la Antigua ("St. Mary the Ancient").

ARGENTINA, Buenos Aires
Founded in 1536 by Spanish settlers, with the full name of Ciudad de la Santísima Trinidad y Puerto de Nuestra Señora la Virgen María de los Buenos Aires ("City of

ANCESTRAL HALL *Brussels' soaring city hall, built between 1402 and 1480, still dominates the main square of the Belgian capital. The spire is 315 feet tall.*

the Most Holy Trinity and Port of Our Lady the Virgin Mary of Good Winds"). The name was chosen because the city was founded on Trinity Sunday and because the Virgin Mary was a patron saint of sailors (who needed favorable winds for their ships). By the 19th century the name had been shortened to the last two words.

AUSTRALIA, Canberra
Chosen in 1909 to replace Melbourne as the capital, but construction delayed by World War I. Became official seat of national government in 1927. Name comes from an aboriginal word, *canberry,* meaning "meeting place." Canberra itself covers about 12 square miles of the Australian Capital Territory, which covers 939 square miles.

AUSTRIA, Vienna (Wien)
Founded by Celts as a fortified settlement on the Danube River during the 1st millennium B.C.

BAHAMAS, Nassau
Founded on the site of a pirate haven as Charlestown, in honor of King Charles II. Renamed Nassau in the 1690s when William III, of the Dutch House of Orange-Nassau, succeeded to the British throne.

BAHRAIN, Manama (Al Manamah)
The island kingdom gets its name from the Arabic word *bahr,* meaning "sea."

BANGLADESH, Dacca (Dhaka)
Founded 1st millennium A.D. Named after Durga, goddess of fertility and wife of the Hindu deity Shiva.

BARBADOS, Bridgetown
Founded in 1628 by British settlers. Originally named Indian Bridge.

BELAU (PALAU), Koror
Nation includes 350 Pacific islands. Over half of 14,000 population lives in Koror.

BELGIUM, Brussels (Brussel or Bruxelles)
Developed A.D. 580 on marshy island in River Senne. Its name comes from the Flemish *brock,* "marsh," and *sali,* "building."

BELIZE, Belmopan
Capital city originally Belize, on the Caribbean coast, named for the Belize River. Because of hurricane damage in 1961, the capital was moved inland to Belmopan on the Mopan River in 1970.

BENIN, Porto Novo
Founded in 15th or 16th century by Portuguese slave traders. Its name is Portuguese for "new port."

BHUTAN, Thimphu
Himalayan kingdom named after the Sanskrit words *Bhyot* ("Tibet") and *anta* ("end"), because it lies on the frontier of Tibet.

BOLIVIA, La Paz
Founded in 1548 by Spanish conquistadores. Originally called Pueblo Nuevo de Nuestra Señora de la Paz, meaning "New Town of Our Lady of Peace."

THE 530-MILE BOOKSHELF

The world's largest library, in Washington, D.C., rose from the ashes of its predecessor. When British troops set fire to the American capital in 1814, they burned almost every book in the government's library. But a former president, Thomas Jefferson, then donated 6,487 of his own books to start the present Library of Congress.

The huge library now contains more than 20 million books, 10 million prints and photographs, and 4 million atlases and maps. They are housed in three buildings, with 64 acres of floor space and 530 miles of shelving. The library is still growing and is running out of space.

VOLCANO PROTECTION

People tend to carry umbrellas even in fine weather in the Japanese seaport of Kagoshima, on the island of Kyushu. They use the umbrellas for protection against showers of fine ash that descend on the city, blown over from the nearby volcano of Sakurajima. The volcano itself was a small island until 1914, when a tremendous eruption spewed forth enough lava and ash to form a land bridge to Kyushu.

PILES OF STRENGTH

Exactly 13,659 piles were driven into firm clay to form the foundations of the Dutch capital, Amsterdam. The city's name means "dam on the Amstel." The

---

BOTSWANA, Gaborone
Capital since 1966. Country named after the Tswana group of Bantu tribes.

BRAZIL, Brasília
Laid out in 1957. Became capital in 1960. The names of the capital and country come from *brasilium,* the Latin name of a red dyewood imported to Rome from the Orient. A similar wood was found in Brazil by European settlers, and the country became known as *terra de brasil,* meaning "land of red dyewood."

BRUNEI, Bandar Seri Begawan
The name of the country comes from the Malay word *berunai,* meaning "plant."

BULGARIA, Sofia (Sofija)
Founded by Romans in 2nd century A.D. on site of a Thracian settlement. It was named *Sofia*—the Greek word for "wisdom"—in the 14th century, possibly after the 6th-century church of St. Sofia in the city. Became capital in 1879.

BURKINA FASO, Ouagadougou
Seat of the Mossi Dynasty from the 15th century until 1896, when France established a protectorate in the region.

BURMA, Rangoon
Developed as a port by 18th-century Burmese ruler King Alaungpaya. Became capital in 1755. Name may be derived from the Burmese word *yangun,* meaning "peaceful." Name may also be linked with Dagon, the god whose golden-spired Shwe Dagon pagoda dominates the city.

BURUNDI, Bujumbura
Formerly Usumbura, country's chief port and capital, renamed upon independence in 1960s.

CAMEROON, Yaoundé
Founded in 1888. Country named from Portuguese *camarão,* meaning "shrimp," because Portuguese explorers found plentiful supplies along the coast.

CANADA, Ottawa
Grew up in 1820s around riverside headquarters of British Royal Engineers. Became capital in mid-19th century. It gets its name from an Algonquian Indian word *adawe,* probably meaning "to trade."

CAPE VERDE, Praia
Islands named *Cabo Verde* ("green cape") by the Portuguese.

CAYMAN ISLANDS, George Town
Islands colonized by British in 1670; named after the Spanish word for alligator, *caimán.*

CENTRAL AFRICAN REPUBLIC, Bangui
Named after Ubangi River, on whose banks it lies.

CHAD, N'Djaména
Town founded in 1900 by French as Fort-Lamy. Renamed in 1973, 13 years after independence of Chad.

CHILE, Santiago
Founded in 1541 by Spanish conquistadores. The city is named after the Spanish name for St. James, *San Iago.*

CHINA, Beijing (Peking)
Founded about 3,000 years ago on the site of a former Chinese capital, Ch'i. Its name comes from the Chinese words *bei* and *kin,* meaning "northern capital."

COLOMBIA, Bogotá
Chibcha Indian center conquered by Jiménez de Quesada in 1538 and renamed *Santa Fé de Bogotá* to honor Santafé in Spain and the Indian chief Bacatá.

COMOROS, Moroni
Capital near Kartala volcano. Islands once associated with moon worship. Their name derives from the Arabic *Jebel-el-Komr,* "moon mountains."

HAVANA UNDER SPAIN *Crosses pierce the skyline of Havana, Cuba, in an 18th-century sketch made when the island was still a colony of Catholic Spain. Taken from Spain by the United States in 1898, Cuba became independent in 1902 and since 1959 has been a Communist state under Fidel Castro.*

Amstel River was dammed in 1240, and the city was first mentioned in a charter in 1275. The canals of Amsterdam were built to drain and reclaim low-lying land—unlike those of Venice, which were built to facilitate travel around the city. The modern city of Amsterdam consists of some 90 islands.

BRIDGE OF NO RETURN

The Bridge of Sighs, most famous of the 400 bridges in Venice, Italy, connects the Doge's Palace to the old state prisons and a place of execution. It was built in 1600 and is believed to have got its name from the sighs of the condemned.

The designer was Antonio da Ponte, who also designed the city's Rialto Bridge.

MAO'S WESTERN BASE

China's Communist Party was founded in the nation's most westernized city, Shanghai. The founders, including Mao Zedong (Mao Tse-t'ung), met there in 1921 in a house that is now preserved as a national shrine. Foreign companies, which moved into the city after an international settlement was established in 1863, were ousted after the communist takeover in 1949. But Shanghai, with about 11 million inhabitants, is still China's main industrial center and largest city.

MURDER STATS

The U.S. city with the highest murder rate is Detroit, with 45.3 homicides per 100,000 people, according to

CAPITAL CITIES OF THE WORLD/Congo—Haiti

CONGO, Brazzaville
Founded about 1880 by French explorer Pierre Savorgnan de Brazza, after whom it is named.

COOK ISLANDS, Avarua
Islands named in honor of Capt. James Cook, who discovered some of them in 1773–74.

COSTA RICA, San José
Founded 1736 by Spanish settlers. Name comes from the Spanish for St. Joseph. Made capital in 1823.

CUBA, Havana (Habana)
Founded 1519 by Spanish explorer Diego Velásquez. Originally called San Cristóbal de la Habana in honor of Christopher Columbus. Cristóbal is the Spanish equivalent of Christopher.

CYPRUS, Nicosia
Founded before 7th century B.C. Name may be derived from a Greek word for the white poplar tree.

CZECHOSLOVAKIA, Prague (Praha)
Began as settlement in 9th century A.D. There are many possible sources of the name, including the Czech *praziti,* meaning "a place where wood has been burned," and *praha,* meaning "threshold."

DENMARK, Copenhagen (Kobenhavn)
Founded 12th century. Named from Danish *kiopman,* meaning "merchant" (from Old Norse *kaupmanna,* meaning "of the merchants"), and *havn,* "harbor."

DJIBOUTI, Djibouti
Constructed as a port by the French in 1888. Made capital of French Somaliland in 1892.

DOMINICA, Roseau
Island named by Columbus, who discovered it on Sunday (in Latin *dominica*), November 3, 1493.

DOMINICAN REPUBLIC, Santo Domingo
Founded on a Sunday in 1496 by Christopher Columbus's brother, Bartolomew. Named Santo Domingo ("Holy Sunday") in 1697.

ECUADOR, Quito
Named by Spanish conquistadores in 1534 after a local Indian tribe. Until Ecuador was formed in 1830 the entire region was called Quito.

EGYPT, Cairo (Al-Qāhira)
Founded in A.D. 969 by the Fatimites, members of a Muslim dynasty. Originally named al-Kahira ("The Triumphant One"). This refers to the planet Mars (*Kahir*), which was in the ascendant when the foundation stones of Cairo were laid.

EL SALVADOR, San Salvador
Founded 1524 by Spanish settlers. City's name is Spanish for "Holy Savior," possibly because the city was founded on August 6, the Feast of Transfiguration.

EQUATORIAL GUINEA, Malabo
Country's name probably comes from the Berber word *aguinau,* meaning "black-skinned people."

ETHIOPIA, Addis Ababa (Addis Abeba)
Site chosen in 1887 by Emperor Menelek II. Name comes from the Amharic *addis,* meaning "new," and *abeba,* meaning "flower."

FALKLAND ISLANDS, Port Stanley
Founded 1833. Named in 1842 after Lord Stanley, then Britain's colonial secretary.

FIJI, Suva
Shipping center became colonial capital 1882, national capital 1970.

FINLAND, Helsinki
Founded 1550 by Swedes. Originally named by them *Helsingfors* from the name of the tribe *Helsingi* and the Swedish word *fors,* meaning "waterfall." Helsinki is the Finnish version of the Swedish name.

FRANCE, Paris
Founded about 5th century B.C. by the Parisii, a Gallic tribe after whom it is named. Established as French capital in A.D. 987 by Hughes Capet.

FRENCH GUIANA, Cayenne
Founded by the French in 1643 on Cayenne Island, where Cayenne pepper grows.

GABON, Libreville
Founded 1848 as a home for liberated slaves. The French name means "free town."

GAMBIA, Banjul
According to tradition, the city's name arose when Portuguese settlers, who discovered the country in the 15th century, asked what the place was called. The question was thought to be "What are you doing?" and the natives replied *"Bangjulo"* ("Making rope mats").

GERMANY, EAST, East Berlin
Two 13th-century villages on the Spree River, Kollin and Berlin, were united under the name Berlin. East Berlin made capital in 1949.

GERMANY, WEST, Bonn
Founded as a Roman garrison in the 1st century A.D. Made capital in 1949.

CANNON OVER CAIRO *The Egyptian capital sprawls below the Citadel, the fortress built by the 12th-century ruler Saladin. On the horizon are the pyramids of Giza.*

latest available statistics compiled by the Federal Bureau of Investigation. Detroit was followed by Miami (42.4), New Orleans (37.1), Houston (26.2), Chicago (24.6), Los Angeles (24.1), New York (20.2), and Las Vegas (15.3). The homicide rate for the United States as a whole was 7.3 per 100,000.

DOOMED SHIP

One of Sweden's most popular tourist attractions is a ship that sank within hours of leaving dockside on her maiden voyage. The *Wasa* set sail in August 1628, despite being known to be dangerously unstable. While she was still in the shelter of Stockholm harbor, a squall caught her and she tipped over and sank. The ship was the newest addition to the royal fleet and one of the largest. Her overall length was about 200 feet, and she carried a total of 64 bronze guns. A Swedish admiral, Klas Fleming, had earlier conducted a stability test during which 30 men ran together from one side of the ship to the other. The test had to be stopped after only three such drills because the *Wasa* was in danger of capsizing, but for some reason the admiral took no action.

The most successful early salvage attempt was made in the 1660s by Albrecht von Treileben, who used an early type of diving bell and managed to bring up most of the guns. However, not until 1961 was the entire hull raised to the surface—333 years after it went down. The restored ship is now in the Wasa Museum in Stockholm.

GHANA, Accra
Grew in 19th century around three 17th-century English and Dutch forts. Name probably comes from *Akan ukran*, meaning "black ant," an epithet given to Nigerian tribes that settled in the region in the 16th century.

GIBRALTAR, Gibraltar
Name comes from the Arabic Jebel-al-Tarik, meaning "mountain of Tarik." Named after an Arab general, Tarik ibn Zaid, who captured Gibraltar in A.D. 711.

GREECE, Athens (Athínai)
Possibly named after the goddess Athena, protector of Greek cities. But the name may come from an ancient word meaning "hill," from the language of the Pelasgians, who inhabited the area before 3000 B.C.

GREENLAND, Godthaab
Founded 1721. Name of the capital comes from Scandinavian words for "good hope." The city is known to Greenlanders also as Nuuk.

GRENADA, St. George's
Island named Concepción by Columbus in 1498 but seems to have been called Granada by Spanish sailors because it reminded them of Granada in Spain; spelling later changed to Grenada under French and British.

GUADELOUPE, Basse-Terre
Island discovered in 1493 by Columbus, who named it Santa María de Guadelupe after a monastery on the Guadelupe River in Spain.

GUAM, Agana
Present name of island derived from the original name San Juan ("St. John"), distorted in local dialects to San Guam. Island first sighted by Portuguese explorer Ferdinand Magellan on St. John's Day in 1521.

GUATEMALA, Guatemala City
Founded 1527 as Santiago de los Caballeros by Spanish conquistador Pedro de Alvarado. After floods in 1541 the capital was moved to Antigua, but in 1776 the city was rebuilt on the present site with its modern name. It became the capital in 1779.

GUINEA, Conakry
The name Guinea may have derived from a Berber phrase meaning "land of the black men."

GUINEA-BISSAU, Bissau
Established in 17th century as slave-trading center. Capital transferred from Bolama in 1941.

GUYANA, Georgetown
Founded by the British in 1781. Occupied by the Dutch 1784–1812 and named Stabroek ("standing pool"), but renamed in honor of George III (1738–1820) when annexed by Great Britain in 1812.

HAITI, Port-au-Prince
Named after the *Prince*, a French or possibly English ship that took shelter there. Made capital of Haiti in 1749.

LIGHTWEIGHT *Paris's Eiffel Tower, built in 1887–89 and named after its designer, Gustave Eiffel, is 984 feet high and weighs about 8,000 tons. It is so light for its size that a scale model 1 foot tall would weigh only 0.25 ounce.*

CAPITAL CITIES OF THE WORLD / Honduras—Pitcairn Island

HONDURAS, Tegucigalpa
The name Honduras probably comes from the Río Hondo (Spanish for "deep river"), which forms the border with Belize. Founded in 1578 as a gold and silver mining center in the mountains, Tegucigalpa became the permanent capital of the country in 1880.

HONG KONG, Victoria
Name of the territory, ceded to Britain by China in 1842, comes from the Chinese *hiang kiang,* meaning "favorable water" or "good harbor." The capital was named after the British queen.

HUNGARY, Budapest
Name dates from 1873, when Buda and Pest—two villages founded in the 13th century—were united.

ICELAND, Reykjavík
First settled in 874. Name comes from the Old Norse *reykr* ("smoke"), which refers to the steam from local hot springs, and *vik* ("inlet"). Became national capital in 1918.

INDIA, New Delhi
Founded 1912 to replace Calcutta as capital of British India. Adjacent to "Old" Delhi, which dates from the 15th century B.C. Delhi was the name of an ancient capital in Hindu legends.

INDONESIA, Jakarta
Founded 1619 by Dutch and became headquarters of the Dutch East India Company. Made capital 1949. Name may come from the Sanskrit *Jaya-kerta,* meaning "place of victory," or from the Persian word *kert,* meaning "place."

IRAN, Tehran
Constructed in 12th century A.D. and made national capital in 1788. Name may mean "plain."

IRAQ, Baghdad
Built by the Islamic caliph Mansur in the 8th century A.D. on the site of an earlier settlement. Name is probably Persian for "God's gift."

IRELAND, Dublin
Founded 9th century A.D. by Norsemen. Named from the Gaelic *dubh linn,* meaning "black pool."

ISRAEL, Jerusalem
In existence by 15th century B.C. Name may come from Old Hebrew words *ieru* and *shalom,* meaning "city of peace."

ITALY, Rome (Roma)
In legend, founded in 753 B.C. by Romulus, after whom it was named. But the name may come from Ruma, the ancient name for the Tiber River.

IVORY COAST, Yamoussoukro
Country a trading center for elephant tusks since 15th century.

JAMAICA, Kingston
City founded 1692 by British and named in honor of King William III.

JAPAN, Tokyo
Founded in 12th century as Yedo. Became imperial capital in 1868 and given present name, which means "eastern capital."

JORDAN, Amman
Capital of the biblical Ammonites. Named after the ancient Egyptian god Amon.

KAMPUCHEA, Phnom Penh
Founded in the 14th century. City's name comes from Khmer words meaning "mountain of abundance."

KENYA, Nairobi
Founded 1899 as headquarters of Mombasa–Uganda railroad. Name comes from the Swahili word for "swamp."

KIRIBATI, Tarawa
The national government center is on Bairiki, an islet of the Tarawa atoll, which was also the site of the capital of the Gilbert Islands before they achieved independence as Kiribati in 1979.

KOREA, NORTH, Pyongyang
Site of a Chinese colony in 2nd century B.C. In Korean, *p'hyon* means "plain."

KOREA, SOUTH, Seoul (Sŏul)
Name comes from the Korean word *sieur,* meaning "capital." Made capital August 15, 1948.

KUWAIT, Kuwait
Arabic name is *Al-Kuwayt,* meaning "the enclosed." This may refer to a Portuguese fort built there in the 16th century. National capital since 1961.

LAOS, Vientiane
Country named after the Lao people. Ancient city of Vientiane made national capital in 1899.

LEBANON, Beirut (Bayrūt)
Site of an ancient Phoenician settlement. Name comes from the Greek word *berytos,* meaning "well" or "spring."

LESOTHO, Maseru
City founded 1869 by Moshesh, a Basuto chief.

LIBERIA, Monrovia
Liberia founded 1822 by the National Colonization Society for freed slaves. Monrovia named after James Monroe (1758–1831), then U.S. president.

LIBYA, Tripoli
Name comes from the Greek word *tripolis,* meaning "three towns." Name refers to the ancient cities of Oea, Sabratha, and Leptis.

LIECHTENSTEIN, Vaduz
The principality came into possession of the Liechtenstein family in 1719.

LUXEMBOURG, Luxembourg
Name comes from Old Saxon words *lytel* and *burh,* meaning "little town." The duchy was named after the town.

MADAGASCAR, Antananarivo
Name of world's fourth largest island derives from Malagasy, the major language. Capital grew from 17th-century village into major trading center.

MALAWI, Lilongwe
Became capital, replacing Zomba, in 1975.

MALAYSIA, Kuala Lumpur
Founded 1857 as a tin-mining camp. *Lumpur* is Malay for "estuary mud."

MALDIVES, Malé
Name of islands may come from Sanskrit words *malai,* meaning "mountain," and *dwipa,* "island."

MALI, Bamako
Country's name, first used by Africans in 11th to 15th centuries, may come from the Mandingo word *mali,* meaning "hippopotamus."

MALTA, Valletta
Founded 1565 by Jean de la Valette, grand master of the Knights of Malta. Made capital in 1570.

MARSHALLS, Majuro
Majuro is one of 34 atolls of this tiny island nation named for Capt. John Marshall.

MARTINIQUE, Fort-de-France
Island discovered by Columbus on St. Martin's Day, June 15, 1502, and named for that saint.

MAURITANIA, Nouakchott
Name of country comes from the Greek word *mauros,* meaning "black."

MAURITIUS, Port Louis
Founded in 1736 by the French and probably named in honor of the French king Louis XV.

MEXICO, Mexico City (Ciudad de México)
Founded by Spanish on an island in a lake, the site of the 14th-century Aztec capital Tenochtitlán. Named, like the country, after an earlier name for the city, *Metz-xih-co,* meaning "in the center (literally navel) of the waters of the moon."

MICRONESIA, FEDERATED STATES OF, Kolonia
Islands' name comes from the Greek *mikros* ("small") and *nesos* ("island").

MONACO, Monaco
Probably founded by the Phoenicians. Name comes from Greek word *monoikos,* meaning "hermit" or "monk." The rock on which it stands bore a temple to the god Hercules the Hermit in the 7th to 6th centuries B.C.

MONGOLIA, Ulan Bator (Ulaanbaatar)
City founded in 17th century. Originally named Urga but renamed in 1924 in honor of Sukhe Baator (1893–1923), who founded the modern republic of Mongolia.

MONTSERRAT, Plymouth
Island discovered by Christopher Columbus in 1493. He named it after a revered monastery and shrine in Spain, Santa María de Montserrat.

MOROCCO, Rabat
Founded 1306 on the site of a camp established in 12th century. Name may come from an Arabic word meaning "place of faith" or "small town."

MOZAMBIQUE, Maputo
City's name changed from Lourenço Marques in 1976.

NAMIBIA, Windhoek
Name comes from Dutch words meaning "windy cape." There are prevailing southeast winds.

NAURU, Yaren
Island formerly called Pleasant Island. Discovered in 1798 by British whaling captain John Fearn.

NEPAL, Katmandu (Kathmandu)
Founded A.D. 723. Name may mean "border place," or the city may be named after the ancient temple of Kastamandap, whose name means "wooden temple."

NETHERLANDS, Amsterdam
Started as 13th-century fishing village. Named for dam built c. 1240 at mouth of Amstel River.

NETHERLANDS ANTILLES Willemstad
Founded 1634; became a center for oil refining after 1918.

NEW ZEALAND, Wellington
Founded 1840, the city is named after the Duke of Wellington (1769–1852), the victor at the Battle of Waterloo in 1815.

NICARAGUA, Managua
Made capital in 1857. Country discovered by Spanish explorer Gil González de Ávila, who named it after the region's Indian chief.

NIGER, Niamey
Made capital 1926. Country, like Nigeria, is named after the Niger River that flows through it, from the Tuareg word *n'eghirren,* meaning "flowing water."

NIGERIA, Abuja
Planned city to replace Lagos as the federal capital in the 1980s.

NORWAY, Oslo
Founded in about 1050 by King Harold III at the head of Oslo Fjord. First became Norwegian capital in 1299. Its name may come from Old Norse word *ōss,* meaning "river's mouth." Known as Christiania, 1624–1925.

OMAN, Muscat (Masqat)
The sultanate was founded before 6th century B.C., when it was taken over by Persians.

PAKISTAN, Islamabad
Built in the early 1960s, it became the capital in 1967, replacing Karachi. Name means "city of Islam."

PANAMA, Panama City
Original city, founded in 1519, was destroyed by the Welsh pirate Henry Morgan in 1671; later rebuilt on a new site about 7 miles to the west.

PAPUA NEW GUINEA, Port Moresby
Harbor where city now stands discovered in 1873 by British explorer John Moresby (1830–1922) and named for his father.

PARAGUAY, Asunción
Spanish explorers built a fort here on the Feast of the Assumption (August 15), 1537, and named it Nuestra Señora de la Asunción ("Our Lady of the Assumption").

PERU, Lima
Founded 1535 by Spanish explorer Francisco Pizarro. He named it Ciudad de los Reyes ("City of the Kings"), but its present name is a derivation of Rimac, the river on whose banks the city stands.

PHILIPPINES, Manila
Founded 1571. Name probably comes from Tagalog, the principal language in the Philippines. It translates as "place where there is indigo," from *may,* meaning "to be," and *nila,* meaning "indigo."

PITCAIRN ISLAND, Adamstown
Island discovered in 1767 by the British explorer Philip Carteret. He named it after the midshipman who sighted it.

JERUSALEM *A detail from a 12th-century map shows Calvary (just below and to the left of the central crossroads) and Bethlehem (bottom right beyond the walls).*

CAPITAL CITIES OF THE WORLD/Poland—Zimbabwe

POLAND, Warsaw (Warszawa)
Site first settled 11th century. City founded about 1300. Name said to be derived from Czech founding family called Warsew, but may come from the Polish word *var*, meaning "castle." A castle was built in the area in the 9th century.

PORTUGAL, Lisbon (Lisboa)
The original settlement on the site was colonized by Phoenicians and Carthaginians. The city's modern name is probably Phoenician; it may come from the word *ippo*, meaning "fortress," or from *alisubbo*, meaning "bay of happiness."

PUERTO RICO, San Juan
City founded 1521 by Spanish explorer Juan Ponce de Léon as Puerto Rico. Later named after St. John.

QATAR, Doha
Arabic name, *ad-Dawhah*, comes from a Persian Gulf Arabic word meaning "bay."

RÉUNION, Saint-Denis
Island discovered by the Portuguese in 1513. Given its present name in 1793, during the French Revolution, to celebrate the union of the revolutionaries from Marseilles with the National Guard on August 10, 1792.

ROMANIA, Bucharest (Bucureşti)
City is said to have been founded in 15th century by shepherd named Bucur.

RWANDA, Kigali
Name of country comes from that of the inhabitants.

ST. CHRISTOPHER (ST. KITTS) AND NEVIS, Basseterre
Founded 1643. Island discovered by Christopher Columbus in 1493 and probably named by him after his patron saint. "Kit" is an English familiar nickname for Christopher. Capital's French name means "lowlands."

ST. LUCIA, Castries
Island discovered by Columbus on the feast day (December 13) of St. Lucy in 1502 and named after her.

ST. PIERRE AND MIQUELON St. Pierre
Islands first named Eleven Thousand Virgins because they were discovered by the Portuguese explorer José Alvarez Faguendez in 1520 on the feast day of St. Ursula and the 11,000 virgin martyrs, October 21. Renamed by 1536.

ST. VINCENT AND THE GRENADINES, Kingstown
Island probably named by Columbus, who is thought to have discovered it on January 22 (St. Vincent's Day), 1498.

SAN MARINO, San Marino
Tiny republic said to have been founded in the 4th century A.D. by St. Marinus of Dalmatia, a stonecutter.

SÃO TOMÉ AND PRÍNCIPE, São Tomé
Islands discovered by the Portuguese in 1470–71. *São Tomé* is Portuguese for St. Thomas.

SAUDI ARABIA, Riyadh
Became the center of Sheik Ibn Saud's conquest of Arabia, 1902–25, and capital of Saudi Arabia in 1932.

SENEGAL, Dakar
Built in 1857 on volcanic rocks. Name probably comes from Wolof word meaning "waterless."

SEYCHELLES, Victoria
Named after Queen Victoria by British, who acquired Seychelles from France in the 1814 Treaty of Paris.

SIERRA LEONE, Freetown
Founded 1787 by British as settlement for freed slaves, and named for that reason.

SINGAPORE, Singapore
Important Malay city in 13th century. Name from Sanskrit words *singa* ("lion") and *pura* ("town").

SOLOMON ISLANDS, Honiara
Islands named by Spanish explorer Alvaro de Mendaña, who thought they were the biblical land of Ophir from which gold was brought to King Solomon (1 Kings 9:28), because of the gold ornaments worn by the islanders.

SOMALIA, Mogadishu (Mogadiscio)
City founded by Arab settlers in 9th century A.D. and became trading center. Made capital of Italian Somaliland in 1905 and national capital upon independence in 1960.

SOUTH AFRICA, Pretoria
City founded 1855 and named after Andries Pretorius (1799–1853), a Boer leader. Made national capital in 1881.

SPAIN, Madrid
Moorish fortress captured by Alfonso VI of Spain in 1083. Made capital in 1561. Name may be an adaptation of the Arabic name *Medshrid*, which comes from *materia*, meaning "timber," abundant in the area.

SRI LANKA, Colombo
Founded 8th century A.D. by Arab traders. City's name probably comes from old Sinhalese word for port, *kolamba*.

SUDAN, Khartoum
Founded 1823 as an Egyptian army camp. Name comes from the Arabic *Ras-al-hartum* ("end of the elephant's trunk"), referring to the city's position on a trunk-shaped piece of land at the confluence of the Blue Nile and the White Nile.

SURINAME, Paramaribo
Founded by French in 1540 on site of ancient Indian village. Name comes from Indian words *para*, meaning "water" or "sea," and *maribo* ("inhabitants").

SWAZILAND, Mbabane
Country named after the first Bantu settlers, the Swazis. Swazi was a chief whose name meant "the rod."

SWEDEN, Stockholm
By tradition, founded by a Swedish baron, Birger Jarl, in about 1255, but the settlement probably existed before then. Name may come from Swedish words *stäk*, meaning "bay" (or *stock*, meaning "pole"), and *holm*, meaning "island."

SWITZERLAND, Bern
Founded 1191 by Zähringen family. Made capital 1848. According to one legend, a count, unable to think of a name for the city he had founded, met a bear out hunting and so decided on Bear Town. (*Bär* is German for "bear.")

SYRIA, Damascus (Dimashq)
City's name dates back at least 3,000 years and may mean "place of industry."

TAIWAN, Taipei
City founded 1708 by immigrants from China. Taiwan ("terraced shore") describes island's coast.

TANZANIA, Dodoma
Country's name formed by combining elements of the names Tanganyika and Zanzibar when the two countries were united in 1964. Dodoma became the official capital in 1983, replacing Dar es Salaam.

THAILAND, Bangkok (Krung Thep)
Became capital 1782. The name Bangkok probably comes from the Bengali word *bangaung*, meaning "forest village" or "olive groves."

TOGO, Lomé
Togo means "behind the sea."

TONGA, Nuku'alofa
Native name for islands is Tonga or Tongatabu, meaning "holy."

TRINIDAD AND TOBAGO Port of Spain
Tobago discovered by Christopher Columbus in 1498. Its Indian name was Tapuago. Trinidad named by Columbus in 1498, after Trinity Sunday or for three island peaks.

TUNISIA, Tunis
City known in pre-Phoenician times. Country named after city, which became capital of Aqlabite dynasty in the 13th century A.D.

TURKEY, Ankara
Became capital of modern Turkey in 1923. Name may come from Indo-European root *ank,* meaning "hook" (in the sense of anchor).

TUVALU, Fongafale
One of world's smallest nations, Tuvalu consists of nine islands. Funafuti, site of the capital, discovered in 1819.

UGANDA, Kampala
Capital's name may come from a Bantu word meaning "antelope" or "basket."

UNION OF SOVIET SOCIALIST REPUBLICS, Moscow (Moskva)
Named after the Moskva River, on whose banks it stands. Earliest historical records date to 12th century A.D. Made national capital in 1918.

UNITED ARAB EMIRATES Abu Dhabi
State was formed in 1971–72 by the union of seven emirates. Formerly known as the Trucial States.

UNITED KINGDOM, London
Founded 1st century B.C. by Romans. Its Roman name, *Londinium,* may derive from the name of a tribe.

UNITED STATES OF AMERICA Washington
Laid out 1791. Named after George Washington, first U.S. president, who selected the site.

URUGUAY, Montevideo
Area explored by Ferdinand Magellan in 1520. Montevideo settled in 1726 by Spanish. Name means "I see the mountain."

MOSCOW BOATMEN *The Kremlin palace towers above the Moskva River in a woodcut of the Russian capital carved in the 1830s.*

VANUATU, Vila
Islands, formerly New Hebrides, discovered in 1606 by Portuguese explorer Pedro de Queiros.

VATICAN CITY, Vatican City
Papal residence since 5th century A.D. City named after *Mons Vaticanus,* the Roman hill on which it stands, and the hill's name may come from the Latin *Vaticinia,* meaning a "place of divination," perhaps because it was the site of a pre-Christian shrine.

VENEZUELA, Caracas
Founded by Spanish explorers in 1567. Named after the Caracas, a local Indian tribe. Its original name was *Santiago de Caracas,* "St. James of the Caracas."

VIETNAM, Hanoi
City founded about A.D. 43 by the Chinese. Name is from Chinese for "inside (the loop) of a river."

VIRGIN ISLANDS (British) Road Town
Islands discovered by Christopher Columbus in 1493 and said to have been named after the feast day of St. Ursula and the virgin martyrs (October 21), the day when Columbus first sighted them.

VIRGIN ISLANDS (U.S.) Charlotte Amalie
Capital named for the princess consort of King Christian V of Denmark (1646–1699). Islands bought from Denmark in 1917 for $25 million.

WALLIS AND FUTUNA ISLANDS Mata-Utu
Futuna islands discovered by Dutch in 1616. Wallis islands—the site of

the capital—occupied in 1842 by France, which established a protectorate in 1887.

WESTERN SAMOA, Apia
Island of Samoa named after the *Moa,* an extinct family of large, flightless birds, by the New Zealand Maoris or the Samoans.

YEMEN (NORTH) ARAB REPUBLIC Sana
Believed to have been founded about 1st century A.D. Yemen derived from Arabic word for oath.

YEMEN (SOUTH), PEOPLE'S DEMOCRATIC REPUBLIC OF Aden ('Adan)
Port at Aden active as a trading center since biblical times.

YUGOSLAVIA, Belgrade (Beograd)
Capital grew up around a 4th century B.C. Celtic fort. Belgrade means "white fortress."

ZAIRE, Kinshasa
Transportation hub on Congo River was formerly Leopoldville, named for Leopold II of Belgium. Became capital of Belgian colony of Congo in 1920s and of independent state in 1960. Renamed in 1966.

ZAMBIA, Lusaka
City became capital of Northern Rhodesia in 1935 and of Zambia on independence in 1964. Country named after Zambezi River, which rises in the northwest of the republic.

ZIMBABWE, Harare
City founded in 1890 with the name of Fort Salisbury (later Salisbury), after the British prime minister Lord Salisbury. Name changed to Harare in 1982.

Flags of the world

OLD GLORY, REVISED

The United States' "Stars and Stripes" flag was introduced in 1777, and it has been changed 26 times as new states have joined the Union—sometimes singly and sometimes in groups. The flag that in 1814 inspired lawyer Francis Scott Key to compose the words of *The Star-Spangled Banner* (now the U.S. national anthem) had 15 stripes and 15 stars, because at that time a stripe as well as a star was added for each new state. But since 1818 only the number of stars has been increased—to the present total of 50—and the number of stripes has reverted to 13, one for each of the original states.

BATTLE STAINED

The simple red-and-white Austrian flag is derived from the original arms of Austria. According to legend, these were granted to the crusader Leopold V, duke of Babenberg, at the Battle of Ptolemais in 1191

NATIONAL FLAGS/Afghanistan—Iran

Flags have been flown as rallying signs or as distinguishing marks for at least 3,000 years. The Chinese emperor Zhou, who founded the Zhou (Chou) dynasty in about 1100 B.C., used to have a white flag carried before him on horseback to announce his presence. In the West, objects raised on staffs were used to identify particular groups, but the first proper flags were Roman. Known as *vexilla,* these emblem-bearing cloths were carried by Roman soldiers to distinguish one legion from another.

Flags have become powerful patriotic symbols, the focus of nationalistic sentiments; and each new independent state designs for itself a unique flag as an expression of national pride. Often, too, flags carry symbols of historical events.

The national flags of Australia, New Zealand, Fiji, South Africa, and Tuvalu, for instance, all contain the Union Jack. And in Africa almost a quarter of the countries use the colors red, green, and yellow, known as the Pan-African colors, in their flags.

The colors are those of Ethiopia, the continent's oldest independent country. The first modern African state to adopt them was Ghana, when it gained its independence from British rule in 1957.

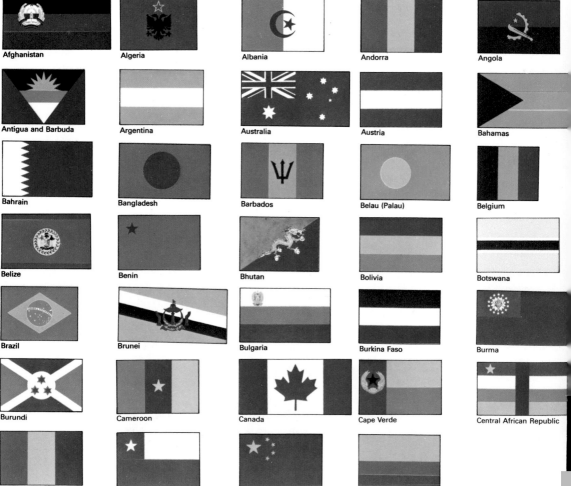

Afghanistan · Algeria · Albania · Andorra · Angola
Antigua and Barbuda · Argentina · Australia · Austria · Bahamas
Bahrain · Bangladesh · Barbados · Belau (Palau) · Belgium
Belize · Benin · Bhutan · Bolivia · Botswana
Brazil · Brunei · Bulgaria · Burkina Faso · Burma
Burundi · Cameroon · Canada · Cape Verde · Central African Republic
Chad · Chile · China · Colombia

by the Holy Roman emperor Henry VI. The battle, between the Crusaders and the Muslim Saracens, resulted in the recapture of the strategic Holy Land town of Acre from the Saracen leader Saladin. Leopold is said to have raised his blood-stained white tunic to rally his troops—and the tunic became the inspiration for the flag. However, the Austrian arms almost surely come from the old Poigen-Hohenburg-Wildberg family of Lower Austria.

TRIPLE ALLIANCE

The British flag—the Union Flag, known popularly as the Union Jack—records two major constitutional changes. The first Union Flag—combining the red-on-white English cross of St. George with the white-on-blue Scottish cross of St. Andrew—was introduced in 1606 after England and Scotland were united under James VI of Scotland (who also became James I of England). The modern flag appeared when Ireland was joined to the United Kingdom in 1800. The new flag included the diagonal red-on-white Cross of St. Patrick. This cross probably came from the arms of the powerful and largely pro-English Fitzgerald (or Geraldine) family, and it was used to complete the slightly asymmetrical modern design.

TWO IN ONE

The national flag of Paraguay is not the same on both sides. One side features red, white, and blue stripes, with the national arms on the white stripe. The other side has the same stripes—but the white stripe carries the treasury seal.

Comoros

Congo

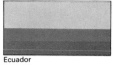
Costa Rica

Cuba

Cyprus

Czechoslovakia

Denmark

Djibouti

Dominica

Dominican Republic

Ecuador

Egypt

El Salvador

Equatial Guinea

Ethiopia

Fiji

Finland

France

Gabon

Gambia

East Germany (GDR)

West Germany (GFR)

Ghana

Greece

Grenada

Guatemala

Guinea

Guinea-Bissau

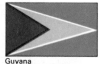
Guyana

Haiti

Honduras

Hungary

Iceland

India

Indonesia

Iran

NATIONAL FLAGS/Iraq—Zimbabwe

Iraq

Ireland

Israel

Italy

Ivory Coast

Jamaica

Japan

Jordan

Kampuchea (Cambodia)

Kenya

Kiribati

North Korea

South Korea

Kuwait

Laos

Lebanon

Lesotho

Liberia

Libya

Liechtenstein

Luxembourg

Madagascar

Malawi

Malaysia

Maldives

Mali

Malta

Marshalls

Mauritania

Mauritius

Mexico

Micronesia

Monaco

Mongolia

Morocco

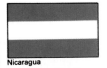
Mozambique

Nauru

Nepal

Netherlands

New Zealand

Nicaragua

Niger

Nigeria

Norway

Oman

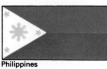
Pakistan

Panama

Papua New Guinea

Paraguay

Peru

Philippines

Poland

Portugal

Qatar

Romania

Rwanda

St. Christopher and Nevis

St. Lucia

St. Vincent and the Grenadines

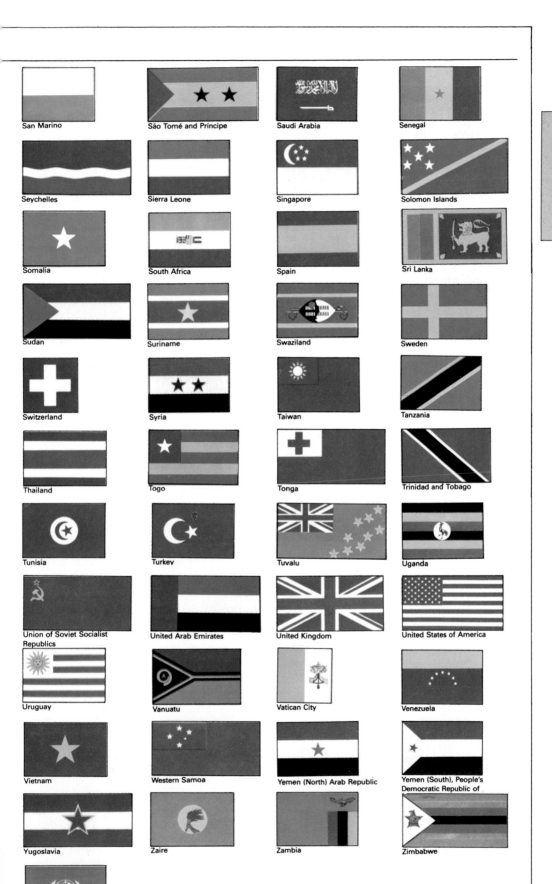

San Marino

São Tomé and Príncipe

Saudi Arabia

Senegal

Seychelles

Sierra Leone

Singapore

Solomon Islands

Somalia

South Africa

Spain

Sri Lanka

Sudan

Suriname

Swaziland

Sweden

Switzerland

Syria

Taiwan

Tanzania

Thailand

Togo

Tonga

Trinidad and Tobago

Tunisia

Turkey

Tuvalu

Uganda

Union of Soviet Socialist Republics

United Arab Emirates

United Kingdom

United States of America

Uruguay

Vanuatu

Vatican City

Venezuela

Vietnam

Western Samoa

Yemen (North) Arab Republic

Yemen (South), People's Democratic Republic of

Yugoslavia

Zaire

Zambia

Zimbabwe

United Nations Organization

FACTS ABOUT PLACES

165

Scenic treasures

PRINCIPAL MOUNTAINS OF THE WORLD

Inaccessibility, changing depths of ice on the peaks of high mountains, and instrument errors caused by the gravitational pull of the mountains themselves all combine to make accurate height measurements difficult. However, these figures are widely accepted.

Name and location	Height in feet (meters)
Everest, Nepal–Tibet	29,028 (8,848)
K2 (Godwin Austen), Pakistan	28,250 (8,611)
Kangchenjunga, Nepal–Sikkim	28,215 (8,600)
Lhotse, Nepal–Tibet	27,890 (8,501)
Makalu, Nepal–Tibet	27,805 (8,475)
Dhaulagiri, Nepal	26,810 (8,172)
Mansalu, Nepal	26,760 (8,156)
Cho Oyu, Nepal–Tibet	26,750 (8,153)
Nanga Parbat, Pakistan	26,800 (8,126)
Annapurna, Nepal	26,504 (8,078)
Gasherbrum, Pakistan	26,470 (8,068)
Broad Kashmir	26,400 (8,047)
Gosainthan (Xixabangma Feng), Tibet	26,291 (8,013)
Nanda Devi, India	25,645 (7,817)
Rakaposhi, Pakistan	25,550 (7,787)
Kamet, India–Tibet	25,447 (7,756)
Namcha Barwa, Tibet	25,447 (7,756)
Gurla Mandhata, Tibet	25,355 (7,728)
Muztagh, Tibet	25,338 (7,723)
Kongur Shan, China	25,325 (7,719)
Tirich Mir, Pakistan	25,230 (7,690)
Minya Konka (Gongga Shan), China	24,790 (7,556)
Muztag Ata, China	24,757 (7,546)
Skyang Kangri, Pakistan	24,750 (7,544)
Kommunisma, U.S.S.R.	24,590 (7,495)
Jongsang Peak, Nepal	24,472 (7,459)
Pobedy, U.S.S.R.–China	24,407 (7,439)
Chomo Lhari, Bhutan–Tibet	23,993 (7,313)
Lenina, U.S.S.R.	23,406 (7,134)
Aconcagua, Argentina	22,834 (6,960)
Ojos del Salado, Argentina–Chile	22,572 (6,880)
Bonete, Argentina	22,541 (6,870)
Tupungato, Argentina–Chile	22,310 (6,800)
McKinley, Alaska (highest point in North America):	20,320 (6,194)

MOUNTAIN HIGH *An early watercolor of Everest, painted soon after an 1852 British survey put its height at 29,002 feet. Its official height has since been recalculated as 29,028 feet.*

THE GIANT "TREE STUMP"

The Devils Tower erupts like a monstrous tree stump above the Belle Fourche River in the Black Hills northwest of Sundance, Wyoming. This flat-topped freak mountain is 869 feet high, and its summit is 279 feet across. Geologists estimate that its history began about 50 million years ago, when a mass of molten rock thrust up through sedimentary rocks laid down on the bed of an ancient inland sea millions of years before. The molten rock cracked as it cooled, forming a mass of innumerable columns. Over succeeding millennia, the softer sedimentary rocks were eroded away by the weather and the Belle Fourche River, leaving the spectacular formation we see today.

RIDDLE OF THE CANYON

Scientists have yet to unlock the secrets of the Grand Canyon (pictured at right), through which the Colorado River runs. The canyon is more than 217 miles long, some 4 to 13 miles wide, and up to 5,300 feet deep. More than 2.6 trillion cubic yards of rock were swept away in its making, but nobody has yet worked out where this vast quantity of debris went.

Until recently most scientists believed that the canyon took shape during the world's last major period of mountain formation. They thought that the river established its course, and then maintained it by eroding its bed at the same rate as the land rose during subsequent earth movements. However, these movements ended more than 50 million years ago, and no older river deposits have been found downstream from the canyon.

In fact, there is evidence that, while the river above the canyon was established in its present course 30 to 40 million years ago, the river's course below the canyon was formed less than 9 million years ago. Before then, the river must have followed another route to the sea, one that has yet to be found.

Curiously, the river now barely reaches the sea, mainly because so much water is taken out of it by a series of dams and canals that provide irrigation and drinking water for the dry Southwest. Most of the year, by the time the Colorado reaches the Gulf of California, it is a mere trickle, no deeper than a wading pool and only about 10 feet wide. At times it dries out completely before reaching the sea.

PREHISTORIC PINES

Trees more than 4,000 years old, some of the most ancient living things on earth, were discovered in the White Mountains of eastern California during the 1960s. The oldest is a bristlecone pine dating back 4,600 years. By studying the tree rings of such pines and matching their pattern against the rings of even older dead trees, scientists have been able to produce a reliable chronological sequence going back more than 6,000 years. This method has led to revision of dates arrived at earlier by the carbon-14 method of radioactive dating.

FOREST OF STONE

Thousands of conifer trees were turned to stone to form the Petrified Forest in Arizona. Some 175 million years ago the desert plateau where the petrified trees are now found was part of a swampy flood plain. The trees, some of them as tall as 200 feet, were

A SPECTACLE AND MORE *The Grand Canyon, seen here at sunset from Hopi Point on the South Rim, has been carved out of the Arizona desert by the Colorado River and its tributaries, which flow as far as a mile below the canyon's rims. "The canyon is at least two things besides spectacle," observed U.S. author Joseph Wood Krutch (1893–1970). "It is a biological unit and the most revealing page of earth's history anywhere open."*

somehow borne to the site—probably by an ancient river or flood—from an area about 100 miles to the west. In time a layer of volcanic ash, rich in silicon compounds, covered the dead trees. Then rain and groundwater began to pull silicon oxides (silica) from the ash, making a silica solution that slowly replaced the cell walls in the dead trees. Each former woody cell was in effect rebuilt into a stony cell made of silica. As a result, each solid stone trunk assumed the precise shape and grain of the original wood. As more millions of years passed, earth movements lifted the fossilized trunks and the softer rock layers around them. Then erosion did its work, gradually stripping away the softer layers and leaving the more resistant trunks high and dry. In the future the dead forest can be expected gradually to "grow" as erosion eats into still lower rock layers.

HIGH WATER
The first steamship to cross Lake Titicaca—the highest navigable lake in the world, 12,500 feet up in the Andes—was carried up to the lake in pieces. The *Yavari,* weighing 180 tons, was built in Scotland in 1862 and taken in pieces around Cape Horn to Chile. After being transported by rail into Peru, the ship's parts were loaded onto mules for the arduous climb to Puno, by the lakeside.

The *Yavari* was reassembled by Peruvian Indians working under a Scottish engineer, and went into service in 1874 as a ferry, crossing the lake from Puno in Peru to the Bolivian shore near La Paz, 50 miles away. Still afloat, she is used as a warehouse by the Peruvian Navy. The main passenger ferry is now the *Ollanta,* which was built in Hull, England, in 1931, then dismantled and reassembled at the lake.

Titicaca is the largest lake in South America. It covers an area of 3,200 square miles, stretches 110 miles at its longest point, and has a maximum depth of 903 feet. Although Lake Maracaibo in Venezuela is larger than Titicaca, it is not strictly a lake but a landlocked bay of the Caribbean Sea.

THE DEAD SEA LIVES
Fish cannot live in the supersalty waters of the Dead Sea, but some salt-tolerant microorganisms thrive there. One of these is *Halobacterium halobium.* It contains a purple pigment that, like the chlorophyll of green plants, enables living cells to photosynthesize—to absorb the energy of sunlight and use it to convert water and carbon dioxide to energy-giving carbohydrates, such as glucose. Another salt-tolerant microorganism found in the Dead Sea is the alga *Dunaliella,* from which petroleum can be made.

Thus the sea is not dead—and neither is it a sea. It is a salt lake occupying a northern extension of the Great Rift Valley on the Israel–Jordan border. Its shore, 1,302 feet below the mean sea level of the eastern Mediterranean, is the lowest place on the earth's land surface. Summer temperatures along its shores frequently exceed 104° F. The Dead Sea is the world's saltiest body of water, some seven to eight times more salty than seawater. Nearly 30 percent of the water is dissolved salt and other minerals, such as potash and bromides, which are extracted for the chemical and fertilizer industries. The extraction plant is at the village of Sodom, in the region of the biblical Sodom, near which Lot's wife is said to have been turned into a pillar of salt.

MEN OF STONE
Dome-shaped Stone Mountain, 12 miles northeast of Atlanta, Georgia, is the largest mass of exposed granite in North America. It is some 1.5 miles across and rises more than 800 feet above the surrounding plain. Like Mount Rushmore in South Dakota, Stone Mountain has been embellished with giant figures. In the case of Stone Mountain, they are mounted figures, each about 90 feet high, of three Civil War heroes of the Old South: Jefferson Davis (president of the Confederacy); Gen. Robert E. Lee (commander in chief); and Gen. Thomas "Stonewall" Jackson, the revered officer killed in action in 1863. On Mount Rushmore are carved the faces of four American presidents: George Washington, Thomas Jefferson, Abraham Lincoln, and Theodore Roosevelt.

THE TRUTH ABOUT TAMERLANE
The bones of the dreaded Mongol conqueror Tamerlane (1336–1405) rest in a magnificent mausoleum in Samarkand, in the Soviet republic of Uzbekistan. His tomb, topped by an enormous slab of jade, was opened in 1941 by Russian archeologists, who were able to confirm the truth behind his name: Tamerlane is a corruption of Timur-i-Lenk, meaning "Timur the Lame." The skeleton revealed that Tamerlane had tuberculosis in his right thigh and shin, and that both his right knee joint and right arm were immobilized.

Modern Samarkand was built after the Russian Revolution of 1917, but the city was already old when Alexander the Great destroyed it in 329 B.C. The Arabs took it in A.D. 712 and made it a cultural center, but it was destroyed again by the Mongol emperor Genghis Khan in 1220.

The city flourished anew under Tamerlane. Later it was ruled by the Chinese and the emirs of Bukhara before falling to the Russians in 1868.

SUNSET SPECTACLE *Ayers Rock at sunset glows like a burning coal. Australian Aborigines, who call the rock Uluru, revere it as sacred. One blood-streaked cave was used until earlier this century for initiation rites: Pitjandjara Aborigines opened veins in their arms there as a sign of approaching manhood. The rock was given its European name in 1873 by the explorer William Gosse. He named it after Sir Henry Ayers, premier of South Australia.*

SACRED HEART

Ayers Rock, close to the geographical center of Australia, is a sacred place to the country's Aborigines. The native Pitjandjara people believe that each of its features represents an important person or event in their history, and some of the rock's caves contain Aborigine paintings of epic journeys made by distant ancestors. One pothole, they believe, is the spot where a spear fell during a battle between rival clans of Aborigines; and one cave entrance is seen as the mouth of a woman weeping for her lost son. In another cave the Pitjandjara tribe carried out manhood and fertility rites.

The rock, 1,143 feet tall and 5.5 miles around, sits alone on a desert plain, the remnant of a vast sandstone formation that once covered the entire region. It changes color dramatically at sunset, glowing deep red just before the sun drops below the horizon, a spectacle that draws more than 50,000 visitors a year.

Ayers Rock is not the world's largest monolith. It is surpassed by Mount Augustus in Western Australia, which is about twice as big.

BRIGHT BLUE

The Blue Grotto of the island of Capri in the Bay of Naples, Italy, has been a popular tourist attraction for more than 150 years. But it became popular only as a result of some quick-thinking sales promotion. In 1826 a landslide suddenly blocked the Grotta Oscura ("Hidden Grotto"), then a favorite attraction, so a local hotelkeeper had the bright idea of offering the Grotta Azzura ("Blue Grotto") as a substitute. The Blue Grotto can be reached only by boat and must be seen on a calm, sunny day. As sunlight enters the grotto from a small opening half below the sea, it is refracted and bathes the cave in a brilliant blue light.

OUT OF SPACE

Despite its enormous size, Meteor Crater—also known as Barringer Crater and Coon Butte—drew no particular public attention until it was "discovered" by Daniel Moreau Barringer, a mining engineer and

PRINCIPAL OCEANS AND SEAS OF THE WORLD

Name	Area in square miles (square kilometers)	Greatest depth in feet (meters)
Pacific	64,186,000 (166,241,000)	35,810 (10,915)
Atlantic	33,420,000 (86,558,000)	28,232 (8,605)
Indian	28,350,000 (73,427,000)	23,376 (7,125)
Arctic	5,105,000 (13,221,950)	17,881 (5,450)
South China	1,148,500 (2,974,615)	18,090 (5,514)
Caribbean	971,400 (2,515,926)	25,197 (7,680)
Mediterranean	969,100 (2,509,970)	16,896 (5,150)
Bering	873,000 (2,261,070)	16,800 (5,121)
Gulf of Mexico	582,100 (1,507,640)	14,360 (4,377)
Sea of Okhotsk	537,500 (1,392,125)	11,400 (3,475)
Sea of Japan	391,100 (1,012,690)	13,123 (4,000)
Hudson Bay	281,900 (730,120)	850 (259)
East China	256,600 (664,590)	9,841 (3,000)
Andaman	218,100 (564,880)	14,600 (4,450)
Black	196,100 (507,900)	7,360 (2,243)
Red	174,900 (452,990)	7,370 (2,246)
North	164,900 (427,090)	2,170 (661)
Baltic	160,000 (414,400)	1,440 (439)

ISLAND IN THE STORM *Angry South Atlantic waves heave and froth around St. Helena, the island where Napoleon died.*

geologist, in 1891. Located about 20 miles west of Winslow, Arizona, the nearly circular crater is 4,150 feet across and about 575 feet deep. Its rim stands 130 to 155 feet above the surrounding land. Most people thought it was an extinct volcano, but Barringer was convinced that it had been caused by the crash of a huge meteorite.

Later studies proved him correct. Barringer Crater is now recognized as the world's largest known meteor crater. The hole is thought to have been blasted out by an iron-nickel meteorite weighing about 2 million tons that fell to earth about 25,000 years ago.

FARMERS IN 6700 B.C.

Fourteen different crops were being grown 8,600 years ago by some of the world's earliest farmers: the inhabitants of a settlement at Çatal Hüyük in what is now southern Turkey. Wheat, barley, peas, lentils, and vetch were among the plants they cultivated.

Scientists have discovered that the farmers, who also kept sheep and goats, lived in timber-framed houses with mud-brick walls that were plastered and decorated with red paint. The ancient farmers built shrines and buried their dead under their sleeping

PRINCIPAL RIVERS OF THE WORLD

Name and location	Approximate length in miles (kilometers)
Nile, Africa	4,160 (6,695)
Amazon, South America	4,000 (6,437)
Chang Jiang (Yangtze), China	3,964 (6,379)
Mississippi-Missouri, U.S.A.	3,740 (6,019)
Ob-Irtysh, U.S.S.R.	3,362 (5,410)
Huang (Yellow), China	2,903 (4,672)
Zaire (Congo), Africa	2,900 (4,667)
Amur, Asia	2,744 (4,416)
Lena, U.S.S.R.	2,734 (4,400)
Mackenzie-Peace, Canada	2,635 (4,240)
Mekong, Asia	2,600 (4,184)
Niger, Africa	2,590 (4,168)
Yenisey, U.S.S.R.	2,543 (4,092)
Paraná, South America	2,485 (3,999)
Murray-Darling, Australia	2,310 (3,717)
Volga, U.S.S.R.	2,194 (3,531)
Purus, South America	2,100 (3,379)
Madeira, South America	2,013 (3,239)
São Francisco, South America	1,988 (3,199)
Yukon, U.S.A. – Canada	1,979 (3,185)
Rio Grande, U.S.A. – Mexico	1,885 (3,033)
Brahmaputra, Asia	1,800 (2,897)
Indus, Asia	1,800 (2,897)
Danube, Europe	1,776 (2,858)
Orinoco, South America	1,600 (2,575)
Salween, Burma – China	1,500 (2,414)
St. Lawrence, Canada – U.S.A.	800 (1,287)

DEEP AND WIDE *The Orinoco about 370 miles inland.*

platforms. The site was occupied beginning about 6700 B.C. *Hüyük* is the Turkish equivalent of the Arabic *tel*, meaning "an ancient mound." And though the site is no longer inhabited, much of the town's original layout has been excavated by archeologists. It is known, for instance, that the residents moved around their city over the rooftops because there were no streets. Each house was built up against its neighbors, so that the whole city was like a series of huge honeycombs, with clusters of homes separated by irregular courtyards. There were no front doors. The only way into each mud-brick home was by a ladder through a hole in the roof, which also served as a chimney. One advantage of this arrangement, similar to that of the Indian pueblos of the southwestern United States, was that it formed a formidable defensive citadel.

The farmers of Çatal Hüyük were among the world's first potters. Clay pots have been found there dating from before 5000 B.C. The pots were not thrown on a wheel, for potter's wheels were not invented until about 3500 B.C. Instead they were molded by hand. Some scientists believe that the first pots may have been created by accident. They speculate that soft clay was pushed into woven baskets to make them waterproof and that accidental burning of these baskets left hard shells of baked clay.

200,000-YEAR-OLD ESCALATOR

Powered by the inexorable movements of the earth's crust, a giant escalator has been climbing out of the sea for at least 200,000 years—and it is still moving upward. The staircase, on the northeastern coast of Papua New Guinea, is formed by a series of huge grass-covered coral terraces, some of which are up to 60 miles wide.

In places the escalator has risen to 2,300 feet above sea level, and new coral steps are already breaking through the waves offshore as the land continues to rise. Old coral reefs and lagoons form the staircase's treads, while the risers are made up of outer reef slopes and ancient cliffs that were once underwater. In all, there are 20 major steps in the staircase and innumerable minor ones. The older, higher steps have been severely eroded by rain over the centuries, but the younger, lower steps are more clearly defined.

The movement—of about 0.12 inch per year, or approximately 3.3 feet every 350 years—is caused by a collision between two of the continent-bearing rock plates that make up the crust of the earth. The edge of the Indo-Australian Plate, on which Papua New Guinea and Australia stand, is being lifted as the Pacific Plate slides beneath it at an estimated rate of 4.3 inches per year.

SILVER THREAD TO THE ATLANTIC

The source of the Amazon, the world's mightiest river, is a silver thread of a mountain brook about 17,000 feet high in the snowbound peaks of the Peruvian Andes. From the roof of the South American continent, a mere 120 miles from the Pacific Ocean, the Amazon flows east. Swollen by innumerable torrents and streams, it plunges off the Andes, through gorges and ravines, and flows ever wider, deeper, and slower through its vast basin until it finally disgorges into the Atlantic, some 4,000 miles from its source.

The length of the Amazon has never been precisely calculated, but there is general agreement that it takes second place to the Nile, which is approximately 4,160 miles long. In all other respects the statistical superlatives belong to the Amazon.

For instance, so powerful is the Amazon's outflow that it pushes a fan of yellow-brown silt 200 miles out

ROSE-RED CITY *The 19th-century English poet and clergyman John Burgon extolled Petra, in southern Jordan, as "a rose-red city, half as old as time." Concealed within a ring of hills in the desert, the city can be reached only on foot or, more commonly, on horseback through a dark and narrow gorge known as the Siq. Inside, magnificent facades of temples, tombs, and other buildings are carved into the sandstone cliffs. One of the most spectacular of these buildings is the Khazneh Firaoun, or "Pharaoh's Treasury," which is 92 feet wide and about 100 feet high. It stands opposite the inner mouth of the Siq (below). A large urn near the top (left) was once thought to contain a pharaoh's gold treasure, and it is scarred by rifle bullets fired in the hope of smashing it open. However, the urn is now known to be solid. Petra flourished between the 2nd century B.C. and the 3rd century A.D. as an oasis on the caravan route between the Mediterranean and the Persian Gulf. It declined when a new route was built via Syria.*

to sea. The river has more tributaries than any other (about 1,100 of them), and several—such as the Negro, the Xingu, the Tapajos, the Madeira, and the Trombetas—are more than 1,000 miles long. The Amazon drains a basin of approximately 2.5 million square miles, drawing water from both north and south hemispheres and from six countries: Brazil, Bolivia, Peru, Ecuador, Colombia, and Venezuela. The mouth of the river is 200 miles wide, and from it flows one-fifth of all the river water in the world.

LABOR OF LOVE
Twenty thousand men labored for 22 years to bring the Taj Mahal at Agra, in India, to its final shining glory of perfection beside the Yamuna River. The building, a mausoleum of pure white marble, was built by the Mogul emperor Shah Jahan to house the body of his beloved second wife, Mumtaz Mahal ("The Chosen of the Palace").

She bore him 14 children, and died in childbirth in 1630 at the age of 39.

Originally, Shah Jahan, who ruled India from 1628 to 1658, had planned to build a matching mausoleum in black marble on the opposite bank of the river to house his own body. But the project was never completed. Instead, he was buried beside his wife in the shrine he had built for her.

OVER THE WALL
The Great Wall of China first came into being in about 215 B.C. when the first Chinese emperor, Qin Shi Huangdi, used convict laborers to link up long stretches of much older ramparts. Probably the largest structure ever built, measured by materials used, the wall is 25 to 30 feet high, and a stone roadway about 18 feet across—the width of a modern two-lane highway—runs along the top. The wall was rebuilt and extended many times, and the present one is largely the work of the Ming emperors, who ruled from A.D. 1368 to 1644. But though it stretches for 1,500 miles, the wall cannot be seen from the moon, 239,000 miles away, as has been occasionally asserted. It is not visible from even a fraction of that distance. The theory that the wall could be seen from space was finally exploded in 1969 by the U.S. astronaut Alan Bean. He reported that even when his spacecraft was only a few thousand miles from earth, no trace of human building was visible.

THE LOST GLORY OF ANGKOR
The ancient Khmer Empire reached its peak of wealth and power in the 12th century A.D., and it was the ruler Suryavarman II (1113–50) who directed the construction of its crowning glory: the temple-tomb of Angkor Wat. But the vast, extravagantly carved structure was destined to lie hidden for centuries in the dense jungle of what is now central Kampuchea before being rediscovered by the French naturalist Al-

ANGKOR'S GOD-KING *The rulers of the Khmer Empire in what is now Kampuchea were revered as gods. This giant face, carved on a tower of the Angkor Thom temple complex, is a portrait of Jayavarman VII, who ruled from A.D. 1181 to about 1218. Nearby is the equally famous Angkor Wat temple-tomb. The city of Angkor was designed as a model of the universe and had a vast network of reservoirs and waterways. With the decline of the Khmer Empire, Angkor was all but abandoned. Many of its structures survive today only because Buddhist monks moved in and became caretakers. More recently, military and political strife around Angkor has resulted in some damage; but as great a threat is neglect: the jungle stands ever ready to reconquer the site.*

bert Henri Mouhot in 1860. It was found outside the walls of Angkor Thom, the Khmer capital set in the plain of the Mekong River. Angkor Thom eventually became a huge complex of temples, palaces, lakes, and canals covering some 400 square miles.

Angkor Wat is crowned by five lofty towers, one at each corner and a central pinnacle soaring to 213 feet. It is surrounded by a moat exactly 623 feet wide at every point. The outer walls form a rectangle 5,085 by 4,592 feet.

The Khmers, a Hindu people, built their wealth on rice. They skillfully cultivated three crops a year by irrigation from a system of lakes and canals. Their civilization flourished from the 9th century A.D. until 1431, when the Thais looted Angkor Thom. When the Thais returned later, they found the city abandoned; its 1 million inhabitants had vanished.

NOWHERE NEAR
Cape Three Points, on the Gulf of Guinea near Tokoradi in Ghana, West Africa, is known as The Land Nearest Nowhere. It is the nearest land to a spot in the sea where zero latitude meets zero longitude at zero altitude.

PRINCIPAL LAKES OF THE WORLD

Name and location	Area in square miles (square kilometers)
Caspian Sea (salt), U.S.S.R.–Iran	143,244 (371,002)
Superior, U.S.A.–Canada	31,700 (82,103)
Victoria, Africa	26,828 (69,484)
Aral (salt), U.S.S.R.	24,904 (64,501)
Huron, U.S.A.–Canada	23,000 (59,570)
Michigan, U.S.A.	22,300 (57,757)
Tanganyika, Tanzania	12,700 (32,893)
Baikal, U.S.S.R.	12,162 (31,500)
Great Bear, Canada	12,096 (31,329)
Malawi (Nyasa), Malawi–Mozambique–Tanzania	11,150 (28,878)
Great Slave, Canada	11,031 (28,570)
Erie, U.S.A.–Canada	9,910 (25,667)
Winnipeg, Canada	9,417 (24,390)
Ontario, U.S.A.–Canada	7,550 (19,554)
Balkhash, U.S.S.R.	7,115 (18,428)
Ladoga, U.S.S.R.	6,835 (17,703)
Chad, Africa	6,300 (16,317)
Maracaibo (salt), Venezuela	5,217 (13,512)
Onega, U.S.S.R.	3,710 (9,609)
Eyre (salt), Australia	3,600 (9,324)
Nicaragua, Nicaragua	3,276 (8,485)
Titicaca, Peru–Bolivia	3,206 (8,303)
Athabasca, Canada	3,064 (7,936)
Reindeer, Canada	2,568 (6,651)

RUSSIAN GIANT *In total volume, Lake Baikal is the world's largest body of fresh water. It holds as much water as all five of North America's Great Lakes combined. It is the world's deepest lake—up to 5,315 feet deep in places.*

WELL OF HORROR

Human beings, including children, were hurled into an enormous natural well near the Maya city of Chichén Itzá in Yucatán, Mexico, to placate a rain god. Called the Sacred Cenote, or Well of Sacrifice, it was dedicated to the god Chac. Precious objects of gold, jade, and copper were also thrown into the well, and a rich hoard of these artifacts has been recovered from its depths.

Chichén Itzá dominated the final flowering of the Maya civilization, from A.D. 987 to 1185, after the city was occupied by the Toltec tribe. Then Chichén Itzá was gradually destroyed, probably by internal strife, and abandoned in the 15th century, about 100 years before the Spaniards arrived in Yucatán.

One of the city's best-preserved buildings is a four-sided pyramid topped by a temple. Known as El Castillo ("The Castle"), the pyramid is 78 feet high and has 365 steps, the same number as the number of days in a year. Within the temple is a reclining stone figure holding in its hands a plate, which may have been a receptacle for the hearts and other organs of sacrifice victims.

CASCADING TO NOTHING

The November-to-March rainy season swells the Iguaçu (or Iguassú) River in South America so much that water sometimes pours over its spectacular Iguassú Falls at the rate of 2.8 million gallons per second—enough to fill about six and a half Olympic-size swimming pools every second. But in some years rainfall is so light that the river slows to a trickle—even drying up occasionally, as it did for a month in 1978. There are 275 individual cascades in the falls, which are near the Brazil–Argentina border. The highest cascade plunges more than 200 feet over the crescent-shaped rim, which is 2.5 miles wide.

FALLING BACK

During the past 10,000 years Niagara Falls has been moving upstream at an average rate of about 300 feet per century. But geologists estimate that it will take another 25,000 years at least before the Niagara River cuts its way back to its source, Lake Erie, some 17 miles upstream from the present location of the falls. When that finally happens, most of the lake will drain away—and Niagara Falls will disappear.

DIVERTING SPECTACLE

Victoria Falls, on the Zambia–Zimbabwe border in Africa, will someday be left high and dry. The falls were formed thousands of years ago when the Zambezi River found a vertical crack in the region's rocks at right angles to its course. The river gradually deepened and widened the crack to form the chasm—more than 330 feet deep and 1.25 miles long—into which it now plunges. But these falls are doomed. The water,

flowing at about 1.7 million gallons per second, constantly cuts back the lip of the falls, and each time the lip meets a new crack, another slotlike chasm is formed. The present falls are the eighth to have formed in the last half million years. And the river is gouging out a new crack, known as the Devil's Cataract, into which all of it will one day plunge.

FALLEN ANGEL

American adventurer Jimmy Angel was credited with discovering the highest waterfall in the world after he spotted it from the air in 1935 while prospecting for gold in the Guiana Highlands in Venezuela. Two years later he returned to the area in a single-engine plane and crashed while trying to land on the plateau above the falls.

He survived the crash, and the waterfall was named Salto Angel ("Angel Fall") after him.

But Angel was not the first non-Indian to see the spectacular cascade on the Churún River. The waterfall, plunging 3,212 feet down the side of Auyán Tepuí ("Devil's Mountain"), had been reported by a Spanish explorer, Ernesto Sanchez La Cruz, in 1910.

DEADLY GLOW

An eerie blue glow lights a grotto in the Waitomo Caves, a series of caverns into which the Waitomo stream disappears some 100 miles south of Auckland, New Zealand. The glow emanates from thousands of

PRINCIPAL HIGH WATERFALLS

Name and location	Total height in feet (meters)
Angel, Venezuela	3,212 (979)
Yosemite, Yosemite National Park, U.S.A.	2,425 (739)
Southern Mardalsfossen, Norway	2,149 (655)
Tugela, South Africa	2,014 (614)
Cuquenán, Venezuela	2,000 (610)
Sutherland, New Zealand	1,904 (580)
Ribbon, Yosemite National Park, U.S.A.	1,612 (491)
Great Kamarang, Guyana	1,600 (488)
Northern Mardalsfossen, Norway	1,535 (468)
Della, British Columbia, Canada	1,443 (440)
Gavarnie, France	1,385 (422)
Skjeggedal, Norway	1,378 (420)
Glass, Brazil	1,325 (404)

HIGH JUMP *Yosemite Falls, in California, leaps 2,425 feet, more than four times the height of the Washington Monument.*

ISLAND RIDDLE *Ever since Easter Island (left), a lonely speck of land in the South Pacific, was sighted and named by the Dutch explorer Jacob Roggeveen on Easter Sunday 1722, scholars have argued about the 1,000 or more giant statues that are scattered across the island. Many weigh more than 20 tons, and the largest, some 69 feet tall, tips the scales at 50 tons. Most scholars agree that the statues once stood upright on stone ahus (temple platforms); that they are images of chiefs or spiritual leaders of Polynesians who reached the island from the west about 2,000 years ago; and that they were carved before A.D. 1650, when civil strife rent the island's society. However, some scientists believe that the Polynesians came from the east, and the Norwegian anthropologist-explorer Thor Heyerdahl in 1947 proved this a possibility when he sailed the raft Kon-Tiki from Peru to the Tuamotu Archipelago, west of Easter Island.*

Eight years later Heyerdahl visited Easter Island and conducted two experiments. In one, six natives were asked to rough out the front of a statue on an exposed rock wall, using only stone tools left by the original masons. This they did in 3 days. Asked how long it would take them to complete and polish a free-standing figure, the natives estimated a year. In the other experiment a dozen islanders raised a statue upright onto its ahu by building a platform under the stomach of the prone figure while levering it up with two 16-foot-long tree trunks. (The island, though now treeless, was once forested.) Finally, the Polynesians said that according to tradition, the figures were transported on Y-shaped wooden sleighs pulled by teams of men. None of this proves how the statues came to be, but it does offer a reasonable scenario.

gnat larvae, or grubs, that live on the grotto walls and ceiling. The light helps the larvae trap midges, their basic food supply.

The midges, which breed on the edge of the water in the grotto, find the glow irresistible and fly toward it, but the glowing grubs dangle sticky threads from the ceiling to trap them. Once the grub has caught a victim, it hauls up the line like an angler and sucks the body dry. Tourists have been able to visit Glowworm Grotto, as the cave is known, but the disturbance caused by their presence, combined with silting, is threatening the delicate ecological balance of the underground cavern.

LEAN YEARS
The Leaning Tower of Pisa, in northern Italy, was built as a bell tower for the nearby cathedral. Its top is about 15 feet out of true because the tower's foundations are inadequate. They are only 10 feet deep, though the tower is 180 feet high and weighs almost 16,000 tons. The tower started to settle sideways almost as soon as construction began in 1173, and it was not completed for nearly 200 years. The top tier was built out of line with the rest in a vain attempt to correct the tilt. In 1983 a metal cage was erected around the marble tower as part of a program to strengthen its structure and foundations.

MEN-ONLY MOUNTAIN
No "woman, female animal, child, eunuch, or person with a beardless face" was allowed to set foot on Mount Athos, on a rocky peninsula in northern Greece, according to a special decree issued in A.D. 1060. Only recently has the ban been lifted for clean-shaven men. The others are still barred—even though the mountain is dedicated to a woman. Athos is regarded as sacred by the Eastern Orthodox Church and is dedicated to the Virgin Mary.

The first monastery on Mount Athos was founded in A.D. 963. About 1,400 monks of the order of St. Basil live in monasteries on the 6,670-foot-high mountain and form a self-governing religious community.

SUPERHIGHWAY IN THE SKY
Stretches of the Great Royal Road of the Incas, a superhighway that once ran for over 3,000 miles, are still visible in the Andes in South America. The road was constructed between about 1200 and the coming of the Spanish conquistadores in the 16th century.

The road was about 23 feet wide and had a low stone wall on each side. Like Roman roads, it usually followed the ridges of hills.

BETHLEHEM AS IT WAS
The Church of the Nativity at Bethlehem has been a place of pilgrimage since at least the Middle Ages. Accounts of one visit by pilgrims have survived in documents dating from 1458.

The pilgrims stayed overnight with Franciscan friars, attending mass in the 6th-century church above the underground stable where Christ is thought to have been born. The stable, now an ornate crypt, was originally a hollowed-out cave. One medieval visitor noted the marble manger and its "extraordinary whiteness." The church, now in the Israeli-occupied West Bank, attracts thousands of visitors annually. And the marble-faced manger—originally a trough cut into the wall of the cave, where Christ is said to have been laid after his birth—is still in place.

PEOPLE'S PALACE
During the 18th century ordinary people could roam at will through the splendors of Versailles, the great palace built by the Sun King, Louis XIV, a century earlier. Even the king's bedchamber was on view. Indeed, when the royal births took place, dozens of spectators—nobles and commoners—had the right to be present throughout so that there could be no suspicion about the heir's identity.

Work on the palace, which is 11 miles from Paris, began in 1661, and for the rest of that century and most of the 18th it functioned as both the French court and the seat of government. French aristocrats were compelled to move there—partly so that the king could keep an eye on them—and so were the principal ministries.

The gardens had 1,400 fountains, set in a formal pattern of lawns and walks adjacent to the mile-long Grand Canal. The 240-foot-long Hall of Mirrors was lit by 3,000 candles. In 1919 the Treaty of Versailles between the Allies and Germany was signed in the hall and formally ended World War I.

THE GREATER PYRAMID
A massive pyramid that is believed to be the biggest monument ever built was raised by the fierce Toltec people at Cholula de Rivadabia in central Mexico. It

PRINCIPAL ACTIVE VOLCANOES OF THE WORLD

Name and location	Height in feet (meters)
Lascar, Chile	19,652 (5,990)
Cotopaxi, Ecuador	19,347 (5,897)
Klyuchevskaya, U.S.S.R.	15,584 (4,750)
Colima, Mexico	14,003 (4,268)
Mauna Loa, Hawaii	13,680 (4,170)
Cameroon, Cameroon	13,354 (4,070)
Fuego, Guatemala	12,582 (3,835)
Erebus, Antarctica	12,450 (3,795)
Nyiragongo, Zaire	11,400 (3,475)
Etna, Sicily	11,053 (3,369)
Llaima, Chile	10,239 (3,121)
Iliamna, Alaska	10,092 (3,076)
Nyamuragira, Zaire	10,028 (3,056)
St. Helens, Washington, U.S.A.	9,677 (2,949)
Villarica, Chile	9,318 (2,840)
Ruapehu, New Zealand	9,175 (2,796)
Asama, Japan	8,300 (2,530)
Ngauruhoe, New Zealand	7,515 (2,291)
El Chichon, Mexico	7,300 (2,225)
Hekla, Iceland	4,892 (1,491)
Vesuvius, Italy	4,190 (1,277)
Kilauea, Hawaii	4,077 (1,243)

BLAST-OFF *A contemporary sketch records an eruption that created a new crater on Vesuvius in 1829. The eruption that entombed Pompeii took place in A.D. 79.*

PRINCIPAL ISLANDS OF THE WORLD

Name and location	Area in square miles (km²)
Greenland	840,000 (2,175,000)
New Guinea, Pacific Ocean	305,000 (789,900)
Borneo, Indonesia	290,000 (751,000)
Madagascar, Indian Ocean	227,760 (589,900)
Baffin, Canada	183,810 (476,068)
Sumatra, Indonesia	163,011 (422,200)
Honshu, Japan	88,839 (230,092)
Britain	88,745 (229,849)
Victoria, Canada	80,340 (208,081)
Ellesmere, Canada	77,392 (200,445)
Sulawesi, Indonesia	69,000 (178,700)
South Island, New Zealand	58,093 (150,460)
Java, Indonesia	48,842 (126,501)
Newfoundland, Canada	42,734 (110,681)
North Island, New Zealand	42,218 (109,345)
Cuba	41,634 (107,832)
Luzon, Philippines	40,429 (104,711)
Iceland	39,700 (102,823)

CONE ISLAND *The snow-tipped 8,261-foot summit of Mt. Egmont, one of numerous volcanic peaks in New Zealand, looms over the west coast of North Island.*

CONFINED TO ROOM SERVICE *Toward the end of his life the Spanish king Philip II (1527–98) attended mass without getting out of bed in his room in the Escorial (above) near Madrid. Conveniently, the church was placed just outside his bedroom door. Because of gout, the king found walking difficult, a handicap that he must have found especially galling in this sprawling edifice— with its 84 miles of corridors and courtyards, 86 staircases, and 1,200 doors—that he had built between 1563 and 1584 to commemorate his victory over the French at Saint-Quentin on August 10, 1557.*

STARS OF INDIA *This huge bowl, set in the ground at Jaipur, about 145 miles southwest of the Indian capital of New Delhi, was an astronomical observatory. The black markings on the bowl are slots. Astronomers in an underground room beneath the bowl took sightings through the slots, and noted on the edges of the slots the positions of the stars as they moved into view. The observatory, built in 1728 by an Indian prince named Jai Singh II, includes 12 massive stone instruments, each lined up on a different sign of the zodiac. It also contains a huge sundial, about 90 feet tall, which is known as the Samrat Yantra, meaning the "emperor of instruments."*

PRINCIPAL CAVES OF THE WORLD

Most of the world's most spectacular caves are formed in a kind of terrain known as *karst*. Karst topography is typically limestone with a thin soil cover. Because limestone is water soluble, water seeps through it, forming pits and hollows. Circulating beneath the surface, the water further erodes the limestone, making tunnels and caverns.

The world's caves can be ranked by the depth to which they extend or by the total length of their known passageways. A third criterion is the volume of a cave's interior space. The Big Room at Carlsbad Caverns, New Mexico, is the world's largest known cave chamber. It has a perimeter of 1.75 miles, a floor space of 14 acres, and a ceiling peaking at 370 feet above the lowest point on the cavern floor.

Deepest measured in feet (meters)

Snezhnaya, U.S.S.R.	4,397 (1,340)
Puertas de Illamina, Spain	4,390 (1,330)
Pierre St.-Martin, France and Spain	4,334 (1,321)
Huautla, Mexico	4,067 (1,240)

Longest measured in miles (kilometers)

Mammoth-Flint Ridge, Kentucky	235.6 (379.2)
Holloch, Switzerland	86.9 (139.8)
Jewel, South Dakota	66.6 (107.2)
Greenbrier-Organ, West Virginia	44.7 (72)

WELSH POOL *A rock column rises from an underground lake in Britain's deepest cave: Ogof Ffynnon Ddu, in Wales.*

THE EARLIEST WALLED CITY

The Book of Joshua in the Old Testament tells how the Israelites marched seven times around Jericho before a blast from their sacred trumpets brought the walls tumbling down, after which the Israelites sacked the city. Modern archeology has revealed that Jericho is the oldest known walled city on earth—incredibly ancient even when the Israelites descended upon it sometime between 1400 and 1250 B.C. Remains of walls 9,000 years old have been discovered, but none that date from the time of Joshua. They may have eroded to dust centuries ago, although other archeological evidence points to earlier settlements.

An excavation-riddled mound, 60 feet high and covering an area 839 by 524 feet, is all that remains of old Jericho. It lies alongside modern Jericho just north of the Dead Sea. But within it archeologists have unearthed a succession of cities, each built upon the ruins of the previous one. The oldest walls were found about 50 feet belowground.

OVER THE LINE

Ecuador is Spanish for equator, and in 1936 the nation of Ecuador erected a granite column to mark where the imaginary line of the equator passes near a village 15 miles from the capital, Quito. Unfortunately, the column was in the wrong place. It was a few hundred yards off the line, but that did not stop it from becoming a tourist attraction. Tourists were intrigued by the notion of invariably equal days and nights, and the

stands 210 feet high, less than half the height of Egypt's Great Pyramid of Cheops, but its volume is estimated to be 4.3 million cubic yards, compared with the 3.3 million cubic yards of the Egyptian structure. Known as the pyramid of Quetzalcoatl, it was built between A.D. 900 and 1200 and covers 45 acres—more than three times the area of the Great Pyramid. After the Spaniards found it in the 16th century, they built a Catholic church on the top, a practice they followed with many other native Mexican religious sites.

chance to have one foot in the northern hemisphere and the other in the southern. The monument was finally demolished in the early 1980s, and a new one was built in the right place.

CONDO CHACO

Until the 19th century the largest apartment building in North America was in the shadow of the rock walls of Chaco Canyon in New Mexico. Built in the 11th century by the Anasazi Indians and known as Pueblo Bonito, the multilevel dwelling had almost 700 rooms and at peak occupancy housed as many as 1,200 residents. The Anasazi were skillful masons. They used adobe blocks to fashion the apartments and finished the rooms with a smooth plaster. Pueblo Bonito was abandoned in about 1150, probably because its population was outstripping the area's water and food resources.

SKELETON REEF

The skeletons of countless billions of tiny sea creatures form the Great Barrier Reef, which stretches 1,250 miles along the northeast coast of Australia, almost as far as Papua New Guinea. The largest structure ever created by any living creature, including the human species, the reef is a complex chain of coral reefs and islands rather than a single great wall. There are, however, only two major gaps—Trinity Opening and Grafton Passage, both just north of Cairns. In 1983, in an attempt to row across the Pacific Ocean, Britain's Peter Bird failed to get through the reef and was

rescued just before his boat sank. The distance between the reef and the coast of the Australian continent varies from 5 miles near the northern end to 116 miles at the southern. The Great Barrier Reef covers an area about the size of Kansas. It has taken 12 to 15 million years to form.

THE BIG HOLE

The largest excavation ever dug—the Big Hole at Kimberley, in South Africa—was the work of diamond miners wielding picks and shovels. In the course of 44 years, from 1871 until the mine closed in 1915, they removed about 25 million tons of clay and rock—and 14.5 million carats (about 3 tons) of diamonds. The great mine is now an open-air museum.

IN THE BEGINNING

The oldest examples of human construction still standing are megalithic buildings on the islands of Malta and Gozo in the Mediterranean Sea. Dating from about 3250 B.C. and thought to be ancient temples, they are great slabs of rock arranged in a pattern that somewhat resembles Stonehenge.

TRIPLE-DECKER BRIDGE

The best-preserved Roman buildings in France are in and around Nîmes in southern France. They include one of the most remarkable engineering feats of ancient times: the 1,850-foot-long Pont du Gard, an aqueduct designed to carry not only water but also pedestrians across the Gard River, 12 miles northeast of the town. The enormous aqueduct was built in 19 B.C. The topmost of its three tiers soars 160 feet above the river to carry the water. The 36 small arches of this tier stand upon an 11-arched middle tier, all supported by the six great arches of the lowest tier, which carries the road for people.

BRAKE TO GO

The San Francisco cable-car system, a portion of which is now preserved as a working landmark, flip-flops normal driving reactions. When the driver of a San Francisco cable car wants to go, he puts the main brake on—and releases it when he wants to stop. This is because the car is pulled by a cable that moves at a constant 9 m.p.h. inside a groove in the road. The main brake operates by gripping the cable, so that the car moves with it. Releasing the brake frees the car from the cable, and a second set of brakes, on the wheels, brings the car to a halt. The system was invented by a London-born engineer, Andrew Hallidie, who had emigrated to California. His cable cars have been clanking up and down San Francisco's steep hills since 1873.

MUSIC AT A PRICE

Sydney's dazzling opera house, opened in 1973 after 15 years' work, cost approximately $150 million—14 times the original estimate. But its 2,690-seat main hall is used only for concerts; opera and ballet are staged in the smaller 1,547-seat opera theater. Another peculiarity of the opera house is its lack of convenient parking facilities. A parking garage under the adjoining botanical gardens was planned, but Australian conservationists objected that it would disturb some old trees in a protected area, and construction workers backed them with a strike threat. As a result, concertgoers have to park about a mile away, then ride to the opera house on buses.

SEVEN WONDERS OF THE ANCIENT WORLD

The Greek author Antipater of Sidon, who lived in the 2nd century B.C., was one of several writers to list the greatest monuments and buildings known to the classical world. He settled on seven because that was considered a magic number by the Greeks.

The Egyptian pyramids
Built more than 4,000 years ago, they are the oldest of the ancient wonders and the only ones still surviving. They served as tombs for the Egyptian pharaohs, whose mummified bodies were surrounded by treasures and personal belongings.

The Colossus of Rhodes
A bronze statue of the sun god Helios standing 105 feet high at the mouth of Rhodes harbor. According to legend, the Colossus straddled the harbor and vessels sailed betwe_n its legs. It was built on the Greek island in about 292–280 B.C. and was destroyed in 224 B.C. by an earthquake.

The Hanging Gardens of Babylon
Built in the 6th century B.C. by Nebuchadnezzar II, they consisted of terraces on which flowers and trees were grown. The gardens stretched along the banks of the Euphrates and were watered by irrigation channels.

The Mausoleum at Halicarnassus, Asia Minor
The tomb of Mausolus, a ruler of the city of Caria in the 4th century B.C. Built by his widow, it was destroyed by an earthquake before the 15th century.

The Pharos of Alexandria
The world's first known lighthouse, it stood 400 feet high and had a spiral ramp leading to the beacon. It was built on the island of Pharos, at the entrance to Alexandria harbor in Egypt, in about 280 B.C. By the 15th century it had fallen into ruin.

The Statue of Zeus at Olympia
An imposing figure, 30 feet high, of the supreme Greek god. The body was made of wood and covered with gold and ivory. It was designed in the 5th century B.C. by the Athenian sculptor Phidias and was destroyed by fire in A.D. 475.

The Temple of Artemis at Ephesus, Asia Minor
Built of marble in the 6th century B.C. in honor of the Greek virgin goddess of the hunt and the moon, it was rebuilt in the 4th century B.C. and finally destroyed by invading Goths in the 3rd century A.D. Fragments of the temple are in the British Museum, in London.

SEVEN WONDERS OF THE MODERN WORLD

Advances in science and medicine, and the technology they have fostered, are the wonders of today in the opinion of *Reader's Digest* editors.

Control of diseases
Vaccines and antibiotics have cut the toll in death and misery from many infectious diseases. In the late 1970s, for example, smallpox was declared extinct. And genetic engineering may yield more new weapons against diseases.

Electric power
In little more than 100 years the world has been transformed by the production of energy in a form that can be conveniently used to do all kinds of work.

Space exploration
Age-old dreams, including walking on the moon and close-up looks at other worlds, have come true.

Communications and information processing
Almost any spot on earth is no farther away than the time it takes for a signal traveling at the speed of light to get there; hand in hand with this communications capability is rapid access to huge amounts of information, made possible by the computer.

Organ transplants and artificial organs
Loss of function of a vital organ—whether because of age, accident, or disease—no longer must mean loss of life. Kidney, liver, heart, and marrow transplants, for example, are prolonging people's lives; and the transplanting of brain tissue is under study. There is also progress in creating and implanting completely artificial tissues and organs, e.g. mechanical hearts.

Supermaterials and microtechnology
New kinds of ceramics and plastics can be tailored to have the exact combination of properties desired for new information, communication, and medical technologies. This is made possible through new techniques of engineering at the microscopic and even molecular levels.

Lasers and other optical technology
The use of light to perform tasks requiring pinpoint accuracy, as well as to carry information, has found a place in the modern world in everything from the optical scanners at supermarket checkout counters, to eye surgery, to weapons systems—almost before people learned that laser stood for *light amplification by stimulated emission of radiation*.

Temples and churches

CHIP OFF THE MOON
A tiny slice of moon rock is sealed in a stained-glass window dedicated to scientists and technicians in the Washington Cathedral, Washington, D.C. The rock was brought back by Apollo astronauts in 1969.

SACRED MIRROR
In the Shinto religion the holiest of all objects is a mirror said to have been looked into by Amaterasu, the sun goddess. Millions of pilgrims visit the sacred mirror each year at Ise, the Shinto shrine in Japan. In the past the Japanese imperial family claimed descent from Amaterasu, which is why Japan is known as the

Land of the Rising Sun. Emperor Hirohito formally renounced the dynasty's claim to divinity after World War II.

CLIFF OF TEMPLES
Cave temples are among the earliest forms of religious architecture. Buddhist monks cut 29 such temples out of a riverside cliff face at Ajanta, in central India, between 200 B.C. and A.D. 650. The builders used no scaffolding. They began by finding a small cave or digging a tunnel. Then they cut away the floor, carving the walls as they went, following the formations in the sandstone. The ornate carvings depicted Buddhist symbols and parables.

THE GLORY OF CHARTRES *The stained glass of the Cathedral of Notre Dame at Chartres, France, covers a total area of 22,000 square feet in 176 windows. None is more impressive than the north rose window, 33 feet in diameter, shown above in its entirety, reduced to page size. Angels, doves, kings, and prophets encircle the central image of the Virgin Mary and Christ. The cathedral's most precious relic is a tunic said to have been worn by the Virgin Mary, which was given to the cathedral in A.D. 876 by Charles the Bald, grandson of the first Holy Roman emperor, Charlemagne. There have been, in all, six cathedrals on the site. The first was put to the torch by a French duke in 743; the second was burned down by Danes in 858; and three others were destroyed by fire in 962, 1020, and 1194. The present cathedral, a vaulting masterpiece of medieval architecture lit by the glow from its predominantly blue stained-glass windows, was begun in 1194. The main structure was completed in just 26 years, and the windows were in place by the time the cathedral was consecrated in 1260.*

SLUMBERING GIANT

Few modern cathedrals have taken so long to build as that of St. John the Divine in New York City. Work began in 1892 but stopped during World War II when money ran out. The towers and the interior of the Episcopal church were left half built for nearly 40 years. Construction was resumed only in 1979, by which time New Yorkers had nicknamed the cathedral St. John the Unfinished. It began to be used for services in 1899, although at that time only the crypt had been completed.

In the mid-1980s the towers, the transepts, and part of the roof were still unfinished, and estimates of how long the remaining work would take ranged from 20 to 100 years. However, St. John's is already the world's biggest interior cathedral space: 601 feet from end to end of the nave, long enough to hold two football fields, goal line to goal line; and 124 feet from floor to vaulted ceiling, as high as a 12-story building.

ST. PETER'S THE GREAT

The world's largest Christian church is St. Peter's Basilica in the Vatican City, Rome. It is 611 feet long and at its peak is 458 feet high. The original 4th-century building began to collapse in the 15th century. Rebuilding began in 1506 and ended with the completion of the forecourt and piazza in the 17th century. The quadruple colonnades were designed by the Italian architect Gianlorenzo Bernini.

PLUNDERED SHRINE

Little is left of the cathedral at Canterbury, in England, where Thomas Becket—the Archbishop of Canterbury who quarreled with Henry II on a number of religious matters—was murdered by the English monarch's knights on December 29, 1170. The great Norman building was destroyed by fire 4 years later, and a virtually new cathedral rose in its place. In it, a splendid golden shrine was built for Becket's body, and for three centuries the shrine was visited by thousands of pilgrims. One such pilgrimage was used as the setting for *The Canterbury Tales,* the famed collection of narrative poems by Geoffrey Chaucer (1340–1400).

In 1534, however, Henry VIII made himself supreme head of the Church of England and in 1538 destroyed the shrine, burned the murdered archbishop's remains, and took the gold.

MOUNTAIN OF FAITH

An ancient Buddhist mountain temple, Borobudur, in Java, has been saved from the ravages of time with the help of the modern computer. Borobudur is a vast series of stone terraces built on the sides of a natural earth mound. Circle after circle of small pinnacles climb to a central shrine, or *stupa* (a Sanskrit word meaning "the crown of the head"), at the top of the hill.

The temple was built by migrant Indian Buddhists in the second half of the 8th century A.D. They used thousands of tons of stone quarried from a nearby riverbed. On Borobudur's rising terraces are 504 carved shrines of seated Buddhas, and bas-reliefs cut from the stone recount Buddhist legends.

Over the centuries rainwater drew destructive salts from the soil into the stone temple. Algae, fungi, and lichen began eating away at the terraces. In addition, rain began to wash away the soil beneath the stones, undermining the terraces.

In an 8-year project, organized by the United Nations and the Indonesian government and completed in 1983, more than a million stones were removed from the temple, cleaned with chemicals, and then put back in their original locations. At the same time, the earth beneath was shored up with new foundations, and drains were installed to carry rainwater away from the temple. A computer was used to index every slab, to ensure that each could later be slotted back into its original place.

PRECIOUS UMBRELLA

A gilded and jeweled umbrella erected in 1871 crowns the 2,500-year-old Shwe Dagon Pagoda in Burma. The eight-spoked umbrella, which symbolizes the eightfold path of Buddhism, was presented by King Mindon, founder of Malaya. The pagoda, containing relics of Buddha, is a solid brick spire 326 feet high overlooking the Burmese capital, Rangoon. The spire is covered with 8,688 thin sheets of gold, each measuring about 1 square foot. At mid-1980s prices each of the golden sheets is worth over $5,000.

SACRED STONE

One of Islam's most sacred monuments, the Dome of the Rock, stands in the heart of Jerusalem above a huge stone claimed as sacred by Jews, Christians, and Muslims. Jews and Christians believe that the limestone rock, 60 feet by 50 feet, was the altar on which Abraham was prepared to sacrifice his son, Isaac. Jews venerate it also as the site of Solomon's Temple. Muslims believe that Muhammed ascended to heaven from the rock and point to an indentation in its surface as his footprint. The original dome was built by Arabs between A.D. 684 and 691, on the site of an old Jewish temple.

BUILT-IN HISTORY

Many of the stones used to build the Washington Cathedral, in Washington, D.C., come from sites around the world that have rich historical significance for Christians. A showplace of the Protestant Episcopal Church in the United States, the cathedral is also called the National Cathedral, although its official name is the Cathedral Church of St. Peter and St. Paul. The stones used to make its Jerusalem altar are from the same quarry that yielded the stones for the Temple of Solomon, for example; and its bishop's chair contains large stones from Glastonbury Cathedral, England, founded by St. Joseph of Arimathea in A.D. 43.

The cathedral also houses, among many other religious treasures, a first edition of the King James Bible, which belonged to Henry, the first son of James I of England, and a very early edition of the Book of Common Prayer that predates the official authorization in 1549 for its use by the Church of England.

TOWN THAT STOLE A CHURCH

In 1897 the tiny railway hamlet of Donald in western Canada was condemned to death. The Canadian Pacific Railway, the hamlet's only employer, decided to move its local headquarters 80 miles to Revelstoke to take advantage of a more profitable freight route across the Rocky Mountains.

The church from Donald was supposed to go to Revelstoke too, but many of Donald's residents had already moved to another town named Windermere in anticipation of the closure, and they were furious at the idea. So they stole the church. Dismantling it, they smuggled it by rail and river ferry to their new home. The church reached Windermere safely—except for its bell. That was stolen along the way by a second group of Anglicans from the village of Golden.

Today two churches still bear witness to the thefts. Windermere's church is called St. Peter's the Stolen, and Golden's is known as St. Paul's of the Stolen Bell.

BIBLE BLOOPERS

A number of editions of the Bible have contained unusual translations or printing errors. Some have even acquired special names as a result. In 1560 the "Breeches" Bible was published in Geneva. It got its name because Genesis 3:7 read: *Adam and Eve sewed fig tree leaves together and made themselves breeches.* Traditionally, their clothes were called aprons.

● The "Cider" Bible, in the medieval library of Hereford Cathedral, England, is a manuscript copy made in about 1400 of Wycliffe's Bible—but with one small change. The admonition in St. Luke about strong drink was amended by the copyist to read: *He shall drink ne wine ne cider*—an understandable alteration in an English county renowned for its cider.

● In the "Adulterer's" Bible, which appeared in 1632, the word *not* in the Commandment about adultery was left out, so that it read: *Thou shalt commit adultery.* The London printers Robert Barker and Martin Lucas were fined £300 for the oversight.

● Another 17th-century English printer was fined £3,000 for substituting *a* for *no* in Psalm 14, so that it read: *The fool hath said in his heart there is a God.*

● The "Bathroom" Bible, a modern version originally published by a U.S. firm in 1971, is so called because I Samuel 24:3 was modernized to read: *Saul went into a cave to go to the bathroom.* The Authorized Version of 1611 keeps to the Hebraic euphemism and has: *Saul went in to cover his feet.*

DOME OF FAITH *Sanchi in central India, the site of a group of three enormous stupas, or shrines, is one of the holiest places in the world to Buddhists. This stone carving, on a gateway to the largest of the three shrines, shows the Great Stupa and the gateway surrounded by a crowd of human and mythical worshipers celebrating the Buddha's attainment of nirvana. The stupas were built by order of the Buddhist emperor Asoka, who ruled much of India between about 273 and 232 B.C.—some 200 years after the death of the Buddha, Siddartha Gautama, a Himalayan prince who founded Buddhism.*

STONES THAT SPEAK THE FAITH

The world's great religions have molded not only human thought and behavior, but bricks and stone too. Each faith has inspired a traditional style of building that reflects its central beliefs, and often its history.

BUDDHIST
The typical Buddhist building is a stupa, a circular mound of earth usually covered with bricks and plaster. Relics were often buried in the mound. Most stupas are topped by a small spire, a stylized umbrella or parasol. Parasols were a royal symbol, and they were placed on stupas to signify Buddha's universal dominion. In Korea, China, and Japan the stupa was incorporated into the pagoda. Buddhism's holiest places are: the temple of Borobudur, Java; and the stupas at Sanchi and Bharhut, both in Madhya Pradesh, India.

CHRISTIAN
Most Christian churches are built in the shape of a cross, symbolizing the crucifixion. The altar is usually at the east end of the nave, facing toward Jerusalem. Not all churches follow this pattern, however. Many early ones—including the church of San Clemente in Rome—have their altars at the western end, and some churches are square or circular. Christianity's holiest places are the Church of the Holy Sepulchre in Jerusalem—the presumed site of Christ's crucifixion—and the grave of St. Peter, beneath the altar of St. Peter's Basilica, Vatican City, in Rome.

HINDU
Hinduism, with its thousands of gods, has inspired an architecture characterized by extravagant decoration and a variety of styles. Temple walls are often richly carved with images of gods and mortals of Hindu legend. Hinduism's holiest places are the River Ganges and the holy city of Benares (Varanasi) on its banks.

JEWISH
A synagogue (from the Greek *sunagoge,* meaning "assembly") can be anything from a room in a private house to a grand hall. What makes it a synagogue are two candelabra, an ark, or alcove, to hold the Scriptures, and a platform to read them from. These minimal requirements seem to have grown out of a need to conduct services quietly and sometimes secretly during long periods of persecution. Judaism's holiest places are: Mount Sinai, in the Sinai Peninsula, where God is said to have delivered the Ten Commandments to Moses while the Jews were in the wilderness; and the Wailing, or Western, Wall in Jerusalem, believed to be part of the Temple of Solomon.

MUSLIM
The earliest mosques (from the Arabic word *masjid,* meaning "place of worship") were often open rectangular courtyards surrounded by covered colonnades and were featureless from the outside. Later, the central sanctuaries were usually covered by domes and surrounded by one or more high minarets from which the *muezzin,* or crier, could call the faithful to prayer five times a day. Every mosque has a niche, called the *mihrab,* built into the wall facing Mecca to indicate the direction for worshipers to face while praying. Most also have a fountain or well in the courtyard for ritual cleansing. Decorations are limited to abstract designs or inscriptions from the Koran. The *Hadith,* the Islamic traditions, forbid the representation of living human figures in art, to avoid image worship. Islam's holiest place is the Kaaba shrine in the Great Mosque at Mecca, Saudi Arabia, which is believed to be a replica of God's house in heaven, built on earth by Abraham and Ishmael.

The world's last wildernesses

LIFE IN THE TREETOPS In tropical rain forests most of the animals feed and make their homes in the treetops. Many monkeys and rodents use their tails to help them climb. Other mammals and reptiles have developed winglike skin flaps and broadly webbed toes to help them glide from tree to tree. These have become the so-called flying species of frogs, lizards, snakes, and squirrels. By contrast, some tropical forest birds—such as hornbills, parrots, and touracos—spend much of their lives walking along the branches of trees rather than flying. Plants, too, have adapted to life in the treetops. Lianas, bromeliads, and orchids grow high in trees and are scarce on the ground.

The Southeast Asian jungle tree Adinandra dumosa *takes 2 or 3 years to reach flowering size—and then bears flowers and fruit almost continuously for 100 years or more. It is one of the world's longest-flowering plants. It reaches a height of 50 feet.*

AN INFINITE VARIETY The unique profusion and diversity of plant and animal life in the world's rain forests defy classification or enumeration.

Constant heat and humidity turn rain forests into natural greenhouses, where summer's abundance lasts all year round. In the waters of Amazonia, as the Amazon River basin is called, live 40 percent of all the world's species of freshwater fish. Birdlife is even richer. More than half the world's total of 8,600 species thrive in the great green sanctuary, and 319 different sorts of hummingbird alone have been recorded. Entomologists cannot even guess at the number of insect species that live in rain forests. Estimates range upward from 1 million; but of these, perhaps no more than 25 percent have been cataloged.

RAZOR TEETH The most famed and feared fish of the Amazon Basin are the piranhas. Voracious carnivores, with immensely strong jaws and razor-sharp teeth, piranhas sometimes grow as long as 1 foot. They attack their prey in ferocious packs of a hundred or more.

Amazonia is home to the largest rodent in the world: the web-footed capybara. It is on record that a shoal of piranhas reduced a 100-pound capybara to a skeleton in less than 60 seconds.

INSECTS THAT KILL TREES Attempts to establish forestry plantations in tropical rain forests have often failed disastrously when pests and diseases of epidemic proportions have swept through the plants. For instance, the Ford Motor Company's efforts after 1928 to grow rubber at its testing ground at Fordlandia in Amazonia were thwarted by a leaf blight called *Dothidella ulei,* which infects wild trees.

Other plantations in rain forests around the world have been wiped out by insects that feed on the living timber and destroy its commercial value.

Most trees of the same species in rain forests tend to grow some distance (typically, as much as several hundred yards) from one another. Thus, although any given area may be crowded with hundreds of different species, it usually has only a handful of specimens belonging to the same species. The distance between the trees, scientists believe, is related to the behavior of the very pests that prey on the trees. Detailed analyses of tree distribution have shown that most specimens are just far enough away from their own kind to be beyond the flying range of the pests or disease carriers that attack trees of the same species.

THE WEEPING TREE The Amazonian Indians have been responsible for discoveries of global importance. It is to them, for instance, that the world owes rubber. Columbus was the first European to record that the Indians made balls out of a black vegetable gum. The Indians called the gum and its source *cahuchu,* meaning "the tree that weeps."

The word passed into European languages as *caoutchouc.* The English alternative, *rubber,* may have been coined by the 18th-century English chemist Joseph Priestley (1733–1804), who observed that caoutchouc "rubbed out" pencil marks.

MONOPOLY BUSTER No great demand existed for rubber until after 1839, when U.S. inventor Charles Goodyear (1800–60) discovered a new way of hardening it called vulcanization. This made rubber a suitable material for tires, and demand began to climb. Since raw rubber was then a Brazilian monopoly, Amazonian merchants made fortunes. It was an English botanist, Sir Henry Wickham, who broke the Brazilian stranglehold. In 1876 he chartered a ship to take 70,000 rubber tree seeds from Brazil to England.

Brazilian customs officials allowed Wickham to take the seeds out of the country because he pretended that they were simply botanical specimens for the royal plant collection at Kew Gardens. In fact, once the seeds had been successfully grown in hothouses at Kew, seedlings were sent out to Ceylon (now Sri Lanka) and Malaya, where vast, efficiently managed plantations were established. The wild rubber of Amazonia could not compete in price.

MAJOR RAIN FORESTS *The largest of the world's rain forests is Amazonia, in South America. It covers about 2.5 million square miles—an area larger than Western Europe. Another big rain forest straddles the equator in western Africa. A third marches through southeast Asia, across Indonesia, and into New Guinea and Australia. Vast stretches of rain forest everywhere are being cut.*

THE TROPICAL FOREST'S MANY LAYERS

In a small area of tropical rain forest in South America, covering only 1 square mile, 117 different species of trees, lianas, and flowering plants have been discovered competing in a delicately balanced, multilayered system. The uppermost level (**1**) is the widely spaced tops of the tallest trees—such as the silk-cotton *(Ceiba)*—which tower 135 feet or more into the sky.

Below these is a second layer (**2**) of treetops, 60–80 feet high, forming a continuous canopy. Beneath that is a middle layer of trees (**3**) rising up to 40 feet, with wide, flattened crowns that capture as much of the available light as possible. These are shade-tolerant trees, such as mauritia, orbygnia, and euterpe; many are covered with orchids, ferns, bromeliads, and cacti.

So densely packed are these upper layers that they block out the light almost completely from the lowest levels—a sparser layer of dwarf trees, struggling saplings, palms, and shrubs (**4**) and a ground layer of ferns and nonwoody herbs (**5**). It is a dark world, rich in decaying vegetation.

MIGHTY AMAZON *Great river of the greatest rain forest on earth, fed by a thousand tributaries, the Amazon breaks into many channels as it meanders through its basin, finally pushing a fan of brown silt 200 miles into the Atlantic.*

185

The world's last wildernesses

MOUNTAIN RANGES *The world's longest mountain chain is the Andes, which stretches 4,500 miles. It is followed by the Rockies (3,100 miles), the Himalayas (2,400 miles), and Australia's Great Dividing Range (2,250 miles).*

BOBBING MOUNTAIN Everest, the world's highest mountain, is officially 29,028 feet high, but its summit seems to bob up and down. Surveyors' instruments called theodolites were first used to measure it in 1852, but a mass such as Everest generates its own gravitational pull, so the British surveyors could not be sure that their spirit levels were true—or that their theodolites were level and giving correct readings.

The surveyors made six measurements and took the average: exactly 29,000 feet. This sounded too neat a figure, so they settled for 29,002 feet. Indian and Chinese surveyors have made more recent measurements, and they put the height at 29,030 feet. Changing depths of ice on the peak also alter the mountain's actual height. As Nick Estcourt, a member of the 1975 British expedition, put it: "If Everest is bobbing up and down, we must hope to catch it on a low day."

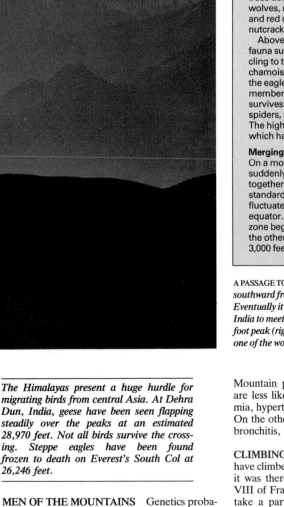

LIFE ON THE SLOPES

Mountainsides are microcosms of the natural world, because the effects of altitude mirror the effects of latitude, but in much shorter distances. A mountain near the equator can be tropical at its base and arctic at its summit, with other climatic zones represented between. And though the species at each level vary in different parts of the world, the patterns of mountainside living are similar everywhere.

In middle-latitude foothills, for example, deciduous and evergreen trees grow, and ferns and flowers flourish. Birds and plant-eating animals—including rabbits, deer, and squirrels—thrive.

Alpine zone

Higher up, the air becomes thinner, and there is more sunlight and wind. Temperatures drop about 3.5°F for every 1,000 feet. Gradually the softer world of the foothills gives way to the alpine zone, where conifer trees dominate. It is a zone of predators. Bears, wolves, martens, and lynxes are found alongside elk and red deer. Woodpeckers, crossbills, and nutcrackers feed on insects and seeds in the firs.

Above the tree line, only the toughest flora and fauna survive. Mosses, saxifrage, and crowberry cling to the rocks. Marmots, mountain goats, and chamois pick at the scanty grazing. The sky here is the eagle's domain. The highest-living mammal is a member of the rabbit family, the collared pika. It survives at 20,000 feet on Mount Everest. Tiny flies, spiders, and springtails are also found at that height. The highest-living bird is probably the alpine chough, which has been found feeding at 26,250 feet.

Merging boundaries

On a mountain there is no cutoff where one zone suddenly ends and another begins. The zones merge together at their edges. Nor are they found at standard heights throughout the world. They fluctuate according to a mountain's distance from the equator. In the European Alps, for instance, the alpine zone begins at about 7,000 feet. In the Himalayas, on the other hand, the same zone begins more than 3,000 feet higher, at about 10,000 feet.

A PASSAGE TO INDIA *The Kali Gandaki River winds southward from the Himalayas in northern Nepal. Eventually it will become the Gandak River and flow on to India to meet the Ganges. Here, 3.5 miles below a 26,810-foot peak (right) called Dhaulagiri, the Kali Gandaki forms one of the world's deepest valleys.*

The Himalayas present a huge hurdle for migrating birds from central Asia. At Dehra Dun, India, geese have been seen flapping steadily over the peaks at an estimated 28,970 feet. Not all birds survive the crossing. Steppe eagles have been found frozen to death on Everest's South Col at 26,246 feet.

OLD MEN OF THE MOUNTAINS Genetics probably play the largest part in longevity, but there is evidence that people can live longer at high elevations than at sea level. At Vilcabamba, a, Peruvian village about 9,000 feet up in the Andes, birth certificates show 9 people out of 819 who are more than 100 years old. In the United States the average is 3 per 100,000.

Mountain people, medical researchers have found, are less likely than lowlanders to suffer from leukemia, hypertension, arteriosclerosis, and heart attacks. On the other hand, they more often get tuberculosis, bronchitis, and pneumonia.

CLIMBING COURTIER The first man known to have climbed a mountain for no reason other than that it was there was Antoine de Ville in 1492. Charles VIII of France ordered de Ville, his chamberlain, to take a party to the top of a 6,880-foot peak near Grenoble. De Ville is said to have been so impressed with the view and his achievement that he stayed up there for 3 days. The first serious alpine climb was made by a geologist named Jacques Balmat and a physician, Michel Paccard. They climbed Europe's highest mountain, Mont Blanc, in 1786.

The world's last wildernesses

SEVEN-YEAR HITCH Mountaineers wanting to climb Mount Everest—named after Sir George Everest (1790–1866), a British surveyor-general in India—have to make reservations up to 7 years in advance. Only two expeditions are allowed to take place at the same time, and each must use a different route. In addition, Himalayan weather conditions dictate that there are only three periods a year when a climb is practicable: in April and May, before the monsoon rains; in October, just after the monsoons; and during the winter in December and January.

Since Sir Edmund Hillary and his Sherpa guide, Tenzing Norgay, first climbed Everest in 1953, almost 150 mountaineers have made it to the top, including 5 who did not use oxygen and 4 women. But by the mid-1980s about 50 climbers had died on Everest.

GRUMPY BEAR Black bears do not go into deep hibernation in their mountain habitats. They doze during winter but rouse themselves from time to time, without eating. In autumn, after fattening themselves up, the bears eat indigestible roots and pine needles, which form plugs in their intestines. They cannot eat until the plugs are passed in spring—which may account for their short tempers at that time of year.

In the Alps the slightest vibration can trigger a disastrous avalanche. In spring, when the risk is greatest, Swiss mountain villagers ban yodeling and forbid their children to shout or even to sing.

BAREFOOT IN THE SNOW Human beings who live at high elevations adjust to the lower level of oxygen in the air by producing more red blood corpuscles, which contain hemoglobin, the substance that absorbs oxygen into the bloodstream. In addition, most mountain dwellers have developed other physical advantages to cope with the thin air and lower temperatures. The Quechua Indians of the Andes in South America, many of whom live at elevations of 12,000 feet, have short, squat bodies that minimize heat loss, and have atypically large hearts and lungs that enable them to carry 20 percent more blood than is normal for their size. Their hands and feet have extra blood vessels, which speed circulation so effectively that the Indians can walk barefoot on ice and snow without getting frostbite.

SKYSCRAPER BLOOMS The world's tallest flower spikes, 15 to 20 feet high, bloom on an Andean plant. *Puya raimondii*, whose trunk has a globe-shaped rosette of spiky leaves, may take up to 150 years to reach its full height of about 30 feet. Then it throws out its spike of blooms, as many as 8,000 on a single stalk.

EMPTY QUARTER *From the air, the dunes of Rub' al Khali ("Empty Quarter")—the southern portion of the Great Arabian Desert that occupies most of the Arabian Peninsula—resemble ripples of beach sand. But some of these dunes are up to 650 feet high, and they can be more than 60 miles long.*
However, dunes cover only 10 to 15 percent of the world's deserts. Much larger areas, known in the Sahara as hammada, *have been worn down to bare rock. Other spots—known as regs or, in Australia, as gibber plains—are covered with pebbles and gravel from which the sand has been blown away.*

CURED BY A JACK During a sandstorm the friction of billions of sand particles hitting each other can raise the air's static electricity to some 80 volts per square yard—high enough to cause a person nausea and splitting headaches. This phenomenon was first recorded by a geographer named van der Esch (first name unknown), who explored the eastern Sahara before World War II. He suffered agonizing headaches during sandstorms until he found that by dragging a conductor—a car jack—behind him on the ground he could rid himself of static electricity.

DEAD BEFORE NIGHTFALL If a man (or woman) were placed without clothes, food, or water in a shadeless part of the Sahara on a hot day, he would be dead before nightfall. To keep his body temperature down, he would have sweated away 4 to 6 pints of water by noon. By the late afternoon he would have lost a total of 1.5 to 2 gallons. Water

would then be lost from his blood, which would thicken and flow more slowly, causing body temperature to rise. Before sunset his temperature would have risen to about 115°F, producing fever, delirium, and eventually death. Even if the man drank 10 pints of water a day, he would last for no more than 5 days. To survive indefinitely in hot and exposed desert conditions, the average adult requires at least 1.5 gallons of water each day.

Of the 250,000 or so flowering plants on earth, only a handful can exist without water in liquid form. One of them, the hairnet plant in Death Valley, California, obtains moisture from mist. The water vapor is absorbed by the plant's roots, which grow up out of the ground and surround the plant like a net.

HOT SPOTS *The world's hot deserts, shown above, can be freezingly cold at night, since there are no clouds to retain the day's heat. In winter, temperatures in the Sahara can plummet to 24°F after dark. The world's hottest place is Azizia in the Libyan Sahara. On September 13, 1922, shade temperatures there reached a record 136.4°F.*

The world's last wildernesses

BEETLE THAT DRINKS FOG An African beetle stays alive in the rainless wilderness of the Namib Desert by drinking fog. About one day in five, thick sea mists roll inland from the desolate Skeleton Coast of Namibia, creating a fog zone that sustains a surprising variety of plant and animal life, including *Onymacris unguicularis*.

This flightless black beetle spends most of its time underground in the sand dunes, where temperatures remain more or less constant. But when thirsty, it emerges, climbs to the crest of a dune, faces the breeze in a prayerlike stance, and allows fog to condense on its body. Droplets then trickle down narrow grooves on the beetle's shell and into its mouth.

SHIPS OF THE DESERT Contrary to popular belief, the camel does not store water in its hump. The hump is a food reserve, composed mainly of fat. Although water is produced when the fat is broken down, the oxygen used in the process causes an additional loss of water through the lungs. This more or less cancels the amount of water gained from the hump. The main advantage of the hump is that the camel's fat is concentrated in a single place, allowing the animal to lose heat freely from the rest of its body.

Another way in which camels conserve water is by retaining the urea that most mammals excrete in their urine. The urea is turned into proteins by bacteria in the camel's stomach.

In addition, camels avoid sweating because their body temperature varies over a greater range than that of any other mammal. Camels do not begin to sweat until their body temperature reaches 115°F, a temperature that would soon kill a human being. After a lengthy period without water, camels will drink up to 40 gallons at a time. They swell visibly in the process, and their blood and tissue fluids are diluted to an extent that would kill most other mammals. Part of the explanation for the camel's prodigious drinking ability may be the unusual shape of its blood corpuscles: they are oval rather than round. When the animal drinks, its blood as well as its tissues can absorb large amounts of water, because the oval corpuscles can swell into spheres without bursting the cell walls.

EMERGENCY RATIONS Spadefoot toads sometimes breed in temporary desert pools that lack sufficient food supplies for their offspring. The toads then supply emergency rations: other tadpoles. The female first lays a large number of small eggs that develop into small tadpoles. The microflora and fauna in the water are usually too sparse to sustain these tadpoles. But ·before they die, the female lays about 10 large eggs, which hatch into large tadpoles. These feed on the smaller tadpoles and grow so rapidly that they gain maturity—and the ability to survive on land—before the pool dries up.

The Pacific Ocean on the edge of Antarctica is covered by an area of ice almost 1,500-feet thick, the Ross Ice Shelf. Using a rocket-powered drill, scientists penetrated the ice shelf—and found crustaceans swimming in the long-hidden oceanic realm below.

MAJOR HOT DESERTS

Scientists define deserts as areas that have less than 10 inches of rain per year. Such areas include not only the hot deserts listed below but also cold deserts, such as Greenland, Antarctica, and northern Russia. A third type of desert, known as edaphic, is an area where, despite adequate rainfall, the soil is too poor to support plants. Edaphic deserts occur on some volcanic islands, in parts of Iceland, and on the Colorado Plateau in the United States. Cold deserts (16 percent) and hot and edaphic deserts (18 percent) together account for just over a third of the world's land surface. The driest spot on earth is the Atacama Desert in Chile. Some parts went without rain for 400 years, from 1570 to 1971.

Depending on the authority, the same desert may be known by a different name, and adjacent deserts may be grouped under a collective name. This list gives commonly accepted names and areas.

Name and location	Area in square miles (square kilometers)
Sahara, North Africa	3,250,000 (8,417,500)
Great Australian	1,000,000 (2,590,000)
Great Arabian, Arabian Peninsula	900,000 (2,331,000)
Gobi, central Asia	500,000 (1,295,000)
Takla Makan, China	125,000 (323,750)
Namib, southwest Africa	120,000 (310,800)
Sonora, U.S.A. and Mexico	120,000 (310,800)
Kara Kum, U.S.S.R.	116,000 (300,440)
Kyzyl Kum, U.S.S.R.	115,000 (297,850)
Kalahari, southern Africa	100,000 (259,000)
Thar, India and Pakistan	80,000 (207,200)
Atacama, Chile	70,000 (181,300)

LANDS OF ICE About one-tenth of the earth's surface, chiefly in Antarctica in the south and Greenland in the north, is permanently covered with ice. If all the ice melted, the sea would rise by about 200 feet and submerge many of the world's largest cities, including London, Tokyo, and New York.

During the last Ice Age, which ended about 10,000 years ago, there was three times more ice than there is today. Almost 90 percent of the world's fresh water was frozen. Average sea level was about 330 feet lower, and there was 8 percent more dry land. Land joined America and Eurasia and linked Ireland, Britain, and France. Venice, now the lagoon city of the Adriatic, was 100 miles from the sea.

The world's longest glacier is the Lambert Glacier in Antarctica, which is at least 250 miles long. The fastest-flowing major glacier, the Qarayaq Glacier in Greenland, has been reported to move forward as much as 80 feet in a day.

SEABIRD SAUSAGE Some of the world's most northerly people, the Eskimo, live in Thule, northwest Greenland, less than 1,000 miles from the North Pole. They augment their high-protein diet of walrus, fish, and seal with a piquant arctic delicacy: a type of sausage. They net little auks, small seabirds that nest in the coastal cliffs, and then stuff them—feathers, legs, beaks, and all—into a sealskin still lined with blubber. The sausage is then sewn up and buried under a rock pile. Six months later the sausage is dug up and eaten. It tastes like oily Camembert cheese.

190

Deserts/Ice fields

HUNTERS IN THE ICE Most polar seals retreat to open water during the winter, but two types have learned to survive on and under the ice all year round: the Weddell seal of the Antarctic, and the ringed seal of the Arctic. Both hunt fish in the rich polar waters beneath the frozen seas. Using their claws or teeth to enlarge cracks in the ice, which is often up to 10 feet thick, the seals make a series of up to 10 breathing holes. They return to these holes to breathe between dives. The seals can stay submerged for up to 10 minutes and swim at 20 m.p.h. down to depths of about 300 feet. The Weddell seal has no land-based

ICE FIELDS *More than 75 percent of the world's fresh water is locked up in permanent ice fields, chiefly in the polar regions. In all, the fields cover about 6,000,000 square miles, or some 10 percent of the world's land surface. If all of this ice melted, many of the world's major cities would be inundated by the rising sea.*

ICE-COLD IN ANTARCTICA *A razor-sharp pinnacle of wind-scoured ice, forced upward by the pressure of surrounding floes, thrusts 25 feet into the air above pack ice off the coast of Antarctica.*

The world's last wildernesses

THREE WAYS ISLANDS ARE FORMED

CORAL Millions and millions of chalky skeletons, deposited by tiny animals that live in shallow tropical waters, lock together to form coral reefs. Coral islands, such as the Maldives in the Indian Ocean and the islands of Australia's Great Barrier Reef, are the tips of reefs built during periods of warm climate, when the polar ice caps were smaller and sea levels higher.

MOUNTAIN Many islands, such as the Hebrides off the northwest coast of Scotland, are the tops of mountains. When rising temperatures ended the last Ice Age about 10,000 years ago, sea levels rose by about 330 feet.

VOLCANIC The huge tectonic plates that underlie oceans and continents meet at various places. At these so-called plate boundaries, weak points occur through which molten rock and ash from deep in the earth can erupt up through the sea. In this manner islands like Surtsey, off Iceland, and Hawaii, in the Pacific, were formed. Once they have cooled, the new islands are colonized by plants and animals.

BIRTH OF A VOLCANIC ISLAND *Molten rock and ash forced up from the seabed form a cone-shaped island, scored with deep gullies and surrounded by vapor from the vent.*

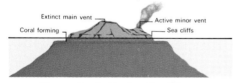

EROSION *Waves eat into the island, eroding cliffs and forming a platform on which, in warm seas, coral grows. The main vent is now extinct, but a lesser one is still active.*

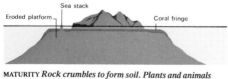

MATURITY *Rock crumbles to form soil. Plants and animals colonize the cooled island. Erosion continues to extend the platform, leaving an occasional offshore stack.*

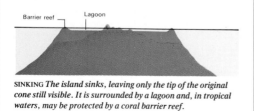

SINKING *The island sinks, leaving only the tip of the original cone still visible. It is surrounded by a lagoon and, in tropical waters, may be protected by a coral barrier reef.*

---

predators, but the ringed seal is hunted by Eskimo and polar bears. The bear waits at a breathing hole until a seal comes up for air, then pounces. The bear may also stop up any nearby breathing holes to increase its chances of a catch.

The most remote island on earth is Bouvet Island, an uninhabited Norwegian dependency in the South Atlantic at 54°26'S, 3°24'E. It is 1,050 miles from the nearest land: an uninhabited island off Antarctica.

HAPPINESS IS ISOLATION The world's most geographically isolated people are the 300 residents of the British dependency of Tristan da Cunha. Their nearest neighbors are 1,320 miles away on St. Helena. After a volcanic eruption in 1961 the Tristan islanders were evacuated to Britain. However, most returned 2 years later, after the danger had passed. Life in Britain, they found, was too hectic for them.

BAROMETER OF THE PAST Weather conditions hundreds of years ago can be plotted by scientists studying coral islands and the reefs that surround them. Marine biologists know that layers of darker-colored corals form when conditions are unfavorable—as a result of cold periods, say, or pollution.

By analyzing such layers in 10-foot cores of Florida coral, which record 360 years of growth, scientists have identified years when there were cold fronts and storms, air pollution, and even—in recent years—radioactive fallout from nuclear weapons tests.

THE LITTLE ISLANDERS Colonies of animals cut off on islands by rising sea levels tend to evolve into smaller species than their continental cousins do. Increased competition for food in a confined space and fewer predators favor the survival of smaller individuals. Dwarf island species that exist today include the key deer of the Florida Keys, the sika deer of Japan, and the dwarf buffalo of the Celebes. Over the past 2 million years miniature elephants and hippopotamuses, now extinct, evolved on Mediterranean islands, and tiny mammoths lived on the Santa Barbara Islands off southern California.

BACK TO NATURE In 1883 the island volcano of Krakatoa exploded, blowing 5 cubic miles of the island into the air. A sterile carpet of ash and pumice rained down on Krakatoa, obliterating all signs of life. Just 9 months later a spider was found spinning its web in the desolation. After 3 years, 11 species of fern and 15 flowering plants were growing on the island. After 10 years there was enough vegetation to hide the scars of the explosion, and in 1908 naturalists counted 263 living species, including 16 species of birds, 2 of reptiles and 4 types of land snails. Forty years after the eruption, Krakatoa, now part of Indonesia, was covered once again with lush forest that supported 1,200 animal species, including pythons, bats, and rats.

The same kind of remarkable comeback was evident after the devastating volcanic eruption of Mount St. Helens, in the Cascade Mountains of Washington, in 1980. In the ash-covered moonscape, "every year there's a marked and measurable increase" in both plant and animal life, a Utah State University biology professor, Jim MacMahon, reported in 1984.

SCIENCE & TECHNOLOGY

Marvels of the human body

MALE OR FEMALE?

Male and female embryos are outwardly identical until 8 to 10 weeks after conception. What happens then depends on whether the chromosomes inherited from the embryo's parents are female—a pattern scientists define as XX—or male, in which case the pattern is XY. The embryo always inherits an X chromosome from its mother, but its father can contribute either another X or a Y chromosome. So it is the father that determines the baby's sex.

Depending on the pattern of chromosomes, either primitive testes (testicles) or ovaries are produced. If testes develop, they secrete a chemical to suppress the so-called müllerian ducts, which would otherwise develop into the female reproductive organs: the fallopian tubes, uterus, and vagina. The testes also produce a hormone called testosterone. This stimulates another set of ducts, the wolffian ducts, to develop into the internal male genital organs and also brings about the development of the external organs.

INHERITED IMBALANCE

Not only do chromosomes determine sex but they influence physical strength and personality traits. If the balance between the chromosomes is abnormal, a baby can develop mixed characteristics. Tests have shown, for instance, that some Soviet women athletes

FACTS AND FIGURES ABOUT THE ASTONISHING BODY

● Doubling a child's height on the second birthday gives a close estimate of his or her final adult height. A boy of 2 has usually grown to 49.5 percent of his adult height; a girl of 2 is 52.8 percent of her adult height.

● Each fingernail and toenail takes about 6 months to grow from its base to the tip.

● During pregnancy a woman's blood volume can increase by 25 percent. Most of the increase is due to the growing fetus and the needs associated with its development in the womb. The augmented blood volume can also aid the mother in case of excessive hemorrhaging during delivery.

● The brain accounts for about 2 percent of body weight. But it uses 20 percent of all the oxygen we breathe, 20 percent of the calories in the food we eat, and about 15 percent of the body's blood supply. It has more than 100 billion (10^{11}) neurons, or nerve cells, and over 100 trillion (10^{14}) synapses, or nerve connections, so that the interconnections in the brain are virtually limitless.

● The adult human body contains approximately 650 muscles, more than 100 joints, and 50,000 miles of blood vessels and capillaries. An adult has 206 bones, nearly half of them in the hands and feet. A baby has 300 bones at birth, but 94 fuse together during childhood.

● For supporting weight, human bone is stronger than granite. A block of bone the size of a matchbox can support 10 tons, or four times more than concrete can.

● A man's testicles manufacture several hundred million new sperm cells a day, enough to double the population of the United States and Canada combined.

● The heart beats more than 2.8 billion times during the average human life span, and in that time will pump around 60 million gallons of blood. Even during sleep, the fist-size heart of an adult pumps almost 80 gallons per hour—enough to fill an average small car's gas tank every 9 or 10 minutes. It generates enough muscle power every day to lift a small car about 50 feet.

● The average pulse rate is 72 beats per minute at rest for adult males and 75 for adult females. The rate can increase to as much as 200 beats per minute during extremely active exercise. Resting pulse rates for athletes can be much slower than the 72 to 75 range.

● The lungs contain about 300 million little air sacs called alveoli. If the alveoli were flattened out, they would cover an area of about 1,000 square feet.

● The body of the average adult contains 79 pints of water, about 65 percent of a person's weight.

● Each kidney contains some 1 million individual filters, and between them the two kidneys filter an average of about 8 quarts of blood every hour. The waste products are expelled as urine at the rate of about 3 pints a day.

● In general, the larger you are, the greater your blood volume. A 155-pound person has about 11 pints of blood. The body's entire blood supply washes through the lungs about once a minute. Human red blood corpuscles are created by bone marrow at the rate of about 2 million corpuscles per second. Each lives for 120 to 130 days. In a lifetime, bone marrow creates about half a ton of red corpuscles.

● The body's largest organ is the skin. In an adult man it covers about 20 square feet; a woman has about 17 square feet. The skin is constantly flaking away and being completely replaced by new tissue about once every 4 weeks. On average, each person sheds about 105 pounds of skin and grows about 1,000 completely new outer skins during a lifetime.

● The smallest human muscle is in the ear; it is a little over 0.04 inch long. The ear also contains one of the few parts of the body that has no blood vessels. Cells in part of the inner ear, where sound vibrations are converted to nerve impulses, are fed by a constant bath of fluid instead of blood. Otherwise the sensitive nerves would be deafened by the sound of the body's own pulse.

● You grow almost 0.3 inch every night when you are asleep but shrink to your former height the following day. During the day the cartilage discs in the spine are squeezed like sponges by gravity while you stand or sit. But at night, when you lie down to sleep, the pressure is relieved and the discs swell again. For the same reason, astronauts can temporarily be 2 inches taller after a long space flight.

● Digestion is a precarious balancing act between the actions of strong acids and powerful bases. The stomach's acids are strong enough to dissolve zinc, but they are prevented from quickly destroying the stomach lining by bases in the stomach. Nonetheless, 500,000 cells of the lining die and must be replaced every minute, and the entire lining is renewed every 3 days.

● The retina at the back of the eye, which covers only about 1 square inch (650 sq mm), contains approximately 130 million light-sensitive cells: about 125 million rod cells for black-and-white vision and 7 million cone cells for color vision.

● In a lifetime the average U.S. resident eats more than 50 tons of food and drinks more than 13,000 gallons of liquid.

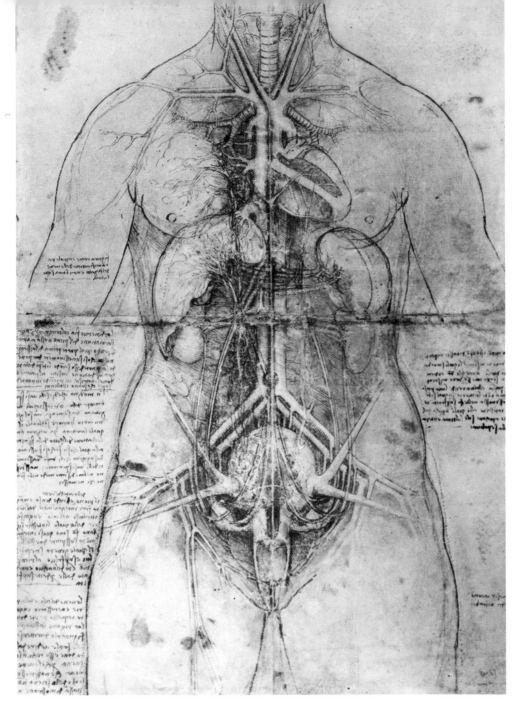

ARTIST'S IMPRESSION *The renowned Italian artist Leonardo da Vinci (1452–1519) learned about the workings of the body by dissecting more than 30 corpses. His sketch (above), though in parts inaccurate, shows the basic anatomy of a woman. By injecting molten wax into human organs, such as the heart and lungs, Leonardo created molds that he could study.*

possess an abnormal XXY chromosomal pattern. In other words, they have inherited a Y chromosome. This helps to give them added physical strength. Men with an extra Y chromosome (an XYY pattern) tend to be taller and more aggressive than the average.

THE RISING SON

People's height depends greatly but not entirely on genetic makeup. What they eat makes a difference too. In 1900 the average height of 12-year-old Japanese children was 4 feet 5 inches. Western diets were a factor in a dramatic change, first in the children of Japanese immigrants to the United States, who ate more proteins—particularly in the form of meat—than did children in Japan. By 1957 these children

were far taller than their homeland counterparts. By the 1970s, however, the Japanese in Japan had caught up with those living in the United States. Japanese men and women now average 5 feet 7 inches and 5 feet 1 inch in height respectively, only slightly less than Britons and Americans.

THE RACE FOR LIFE

The single sperm to penetrate and fertilize the female egg in the womb wins out over as many as 500 million competitors that begin the journey from the testicles. In fact only 300 to 500 survive to reach the area near the fallopian tubes, where fertilization takes place. The distance from the start—in the coiled tubules in the testicles where the semen is created—to the finish is some 24 feet 7 inches. Once the winner has fertilized the egg, the egg's wall becomes impermeable to other sperm. Most of the several hundred losers that are still alive die within the next 24 hours, but some survive within the female body for 3 to 5 days, before dying naturally or being destroyed by the body's cleansing mechanisms.

THE HAIR FACTS

On average, both men and women have about 5 million individual hairs on their bodies. Fair-haired people have slightly more than average, redheads slightly fewer. The only totally hairless areas on the body are the lips, the palms of the hands, the soles of the feet, the sides of the toes and fingers, and the upper part of the ends of the fingers and toes. Though dead from the roots up, the 125,000 or so hairs on the head grow about 0.4 inch per month, slightly more in summer. Cutting does not speed up or slow down the process. Hair thickness varies; redheads have thicker hair than brunettes and blondes. On average, most people lose and replace up to 100 hairs a day, although hairs can remain in place for up to 6 years.

It is not true that normal-colored hair can turn white overnight as the result of a sudden shock. However, shock can cause some colored hair to fall out, and may make obvious white hair that has been concealed by it.

TRANSPLANTS AND THE PIG

As far as transplant surgery is concerned, our best friend is the pig. Pig heart valves, for instance, can be used as replacements for human ones, while, in emergencies, pigskin grafts have been used to cover severely burned human skin. Because pig tissues are the nearest in chemical composition to human tissues, they are not rejected by the defense systems of the recipients' bodies as readily as are tissues from other animals. The only organ that can be transplanted without the risk of rejection is the cornea of the human eye; the cornea does not contain blood vessels, which might otherwise carry white blood cells to the site of the transplant to attack the foreign tissue and destroy the "invading" transplant.

HIGH AND LOW

There is no such thing as a constant, normal body temperature. During the day, it can vary by as much as 2°F on either side of 98.6°F (normal temperature), dropping in the middle of the night and rising during the late afternoon or early evening. The rise and fall does not necessarily indicate illness. It can be brought about by exercise and by the body's own metabolic process of converting food into energy. Women's temperatures vary during the menstrual cycle as well; they

PHYSICAL RECORDS

● The world's tallest man was Robert Wadlow (1918–40) of the United States, who reached a height of 8 feet 11 inches. The world's tallest woman was Zeng Jinlian (1964–82) of China. She was 8 feet 1 inch tall.

● The world's shortest man was an American, Calvin Phillips (1791–1812), whose final height was 26.4 inches. The shortest woman was Pauline Musters (1876–95) of Holland, who was 23.2 inches tall.

● The heaviest man was an American, Jon Minnoch (1941–83). In 1978 he weighed an estimated 1,400 pounds. The world's heaviest woman was also an American, Pearl Washington. She died at the age of 46 in 1972 weighing an estimated 880 pounds.

● The world's oldest person on record as this edition of *Book of Facts* goes to press is Mamie Eva Keith, a retired schoolteacher born in Illinois on March 22, 1873. In 1986 she celebrated her 113th birthday.

PATTERNS OF HEREDITY

Genetic scientists have established that some physical characteristics, known as dominant, are more likely to be passed on to children. Characteristics that are less likely to be passed on are known as recessive.

Dominant	Recessive
Curly hair	Straight hair
Dark hair	Light hair
Non-red hair	Red hair
Normal skin pigmentation	Albinism
Brown eyes	Blue or gray eyes
Near- or farsightedness	Normal vision
Broad lips	Thin lips
Large eyes	Small eyes
Short stature	Tall stature
Nervous temperament	Calm temperament
A or B blood group	O blood group
Rh-positive blood	Rh-negative blood

are higher in the second half of the cycle than in the first. Body temperature also varies depending on where it is taken. Armpit temperatures are 1°F lower on average than mouth temperatures, while rectal temperatures are higher by the same amount.

WHAT HAPPENS WHEN WE GET HICCUPS

Hiccups occur when the diaphragm and the muscles between the ribs suddenly contract. This causes a sharp, uncontrollable inhalation of air, which does not reach the lungs because the muscle spasm has closed the windpipe.

Hiccups usually occur repeatedly in short spasms lasting a few minutes. Most folk remedies, such as holding the breath and counting to some number, have a physiological basis in that they tend to increase the amount of carbon dioxide in the lungs, so triggering the breathing reflex, which opens the windpipe.

Bouts with hiccups have been known to last for decades. Charles Osborne, an American farmer, is said to have hiccupped in 1922 and continued into the 1980s, logging about 7 million hiccups per year.

WHAT HAPPENS WHEN WE SNEEZE

Sneezing is the body's reflex response to the irritation of the nerve endings in the nose by foreign particles or gases. Just as with coughing, a nervous reflex causes a deep breath to be taken. The glottis, near the top of the windpipe, closes off the larynx, so that the pressure in the lungs builds up as a person exhales. The glottis then opens, allowing an explosive rush of air to pass through the nose and blow out particles and mucus at a speed that can exceed 100 m.p.h. The longest fit of sneezing recorded is that of an English teenager, Donna Griffiths. It began in January 1981 when she was 12 years old. She finally stopped sneezing on September 16, 1983, after 978 days.

WHAT HAPPENS WHEN WE COUGH

When we cough, we release an explosive charge of air that moves at a speed of up to 60 m.p.h. The explosion, which works in much the same way as a sneeze, is triggered by the presence of a foreign object, or accumulated mucus, in the main airways to the lungs, and it is designed to dislodge whatever caused the initial irritation.

CONDITIONED HEART

The term *athlete's heart* has been used to describe cardiac abnormalities that were formerly thought to be evidence of serious heart disease. Among these abnormalities are slower heartbeat, enlarged heart, arrhythmias (irregular heartbeat rhythms), and various clicks and murmurs detected by the stethoscope or

THE LIFE THAT LIVES ON US

LITTLE HELPERS *Ball-like cells (left) in the large bowel—here magnified to 3,850 times normal size—support a forest of microscopic life. The strings and the sausage shapes are harmless types of intestinal bacteria.*

DENTAL FLOSS *Fluffy bacilli (above)—magnified here 17,000 times—can, with other bacteria, create plaque, the film that sometimes develops on teeth.*

SPAGHETTI MESS *Threads of the fungus* Trichophyton *(photographed here on skin and magnified 490 times) look like spilled pasta.*

Man is never alone, for he shares his body with hundreds of millions of organisms, most of which are bacteria. More than 600 million individual bacteria live on the skin alone. More than a dozen types of bacteria make their homes on the skin, in the saliva of the mouth, and in the lower part of the digestive system. In addition, several fungi, a virus, and a type of mite share the body of even a healthy person. The bacteria in the bowel do no harm if they stay where they are, and they prevent other, disease-causing bacteria (which may be swallowed accidentally) from multiplying. Some bacteria also manufacture vitamin B_{12}—normally found only in meat—from plant sources. The vitamin helps in the formation of blood cells.

- Four main groups of bacteria live on human skin and can be found almost anywhere on the body. They are known to scientists as corynebacteria (including *Corynebacterium acnes,* which causes acne), micrococci, streptococci, and coliform bacteria.

- Other harmless bacteria live in moist areas, such as the armpits and the groin. They include coagulase-negative staphylococci; gram-positive cocci, and diphtheroids. The skin of the armpits can harbor up to 516,000 bacteria per square inch, while drier areas such as the forearm have only about 13,000 per square inch.

- Saliva contains at least six types of bacteria, some of which can cause dental plaque, tooth decay, and gum disease. They are streptococci, corynebacteria, fusobacteria, *Neisseriae,* bacilli, and spirochetes.

- The large bowel, too, is rich in bacteria. Among the types are coliform bacteria (especially *Escherichia coli*), *Bacteroides,* lactobacilli, clostridia, and streptococci. In the bowel they are harmless. But if they escape to other parts of the body—as a result of an ulcer, say, or a burst appendix—

they can cause peritonitis (an inflammation of the abdominal cavity), blood poisoning, and urinary infections.

- Three main types of yeast commonly live on the skin. *Malassezia furfur* is found mainly on the chest and back. *Candida albicans* is found mainly between the toes; but it is also found in the mouth, where it can cause thrush, an infection especially common in babies. *Trichospora beigelii* lives mainly on the scalp. Skin also harbors two other types of fungus (yeasts are themselves fungi): *Trichophyton* and *Microsporum.* These can cause ringworm and athlete's foot.

- The mite *Demodex folliculorum,* related to the spider family, lives in hair follicles (the cavities containing hair roots) and in the sebaceous glands on most adults' faces, which produce sebum, a fatty lubricant.

- One strain of the virus *Herpes simplex* lives inside the nerve fibers of 90 percent of adults, the only virus known to do so. It is usually dormant but can sometimes erupt on the lips as cold sores when the host's resistance to infection is low. The sores can also be brought on by overexposure to the sun.

197

more sensitive listening instruments. While these symptoms may indicate disease in sedentary people, they are now seen as a sign of health in the well-conditioned athlete and are thought to be an adaptation to conditioning that helps to maintain maximum heart performance.

Low resting pulse rates in the range of 40 to 50 beats per minute are very common in well-conditioned athletes. This compares with 70 to 80 beats per minute in the average adult. Wilt Chamberlain, the former basketball player, was reported to have a resting pulse rate of 38 beats per minute.

REPAIRING THE DAMAGE

Without the protection provided by the body's natural defenses, we might bleed to death from even minor cuts. In normal circumstances, the blood clots to seal a wound within about 2 hours of an injury.

The first line of defense is provided by the platelets, small cells in the blood that clump together to build up a temporary plug at the site of an injury. They also release into the area of the wound a chemical called serotonin, which constricts the damaged vessels, reducing the flow of blood. In addition, the damaged blood-vessel walls themselves release a second chemical called thromboplastin. Thromboplastin enables strands of a protein called fibrin to form a sticky mesh that traps red blood cells, creating a more permanent clot, which hardens into a protective scab.

THE MIGHTY SNORE

The sound of a snore (up to 69 decibels) can be almost as loud as the noise of a pneumatic drill (70–90 decibels). It is caused by the vibration of the soft, mobile back part of the palate, the roof of the mouth, and the arch that sweeps down from this behind the tonsils. In most cases, the nose is partly blocked; so sufferers tend to breathe through their mouths.

Although people sleeping on their backs are more likely to snore, this is not always the case. The best way to stop someone from snoring is to change the snorer's position in bed.

OUTER PROTECTION

Skin is far more than just a protective covering. Five-sixths of the heat produced by the body escapes through the pores, through sweating, conduction, convection, and radiation. These processes are keyed by nerve signals to the sweat glands and to small blood vessels just under the skin. If the pores become blocked so that heat and moisture cannot escape, death results. Heat and moisture travel only one way, however. Externally, the skin—aided by a fatty lubricating substance, called sebum, secreted from the sebaceous glands—is waterproof.

The skin reacts in two ways to the sun's ultraviolet rays. It contains a substance called ergosterol, which reacts with the rays to produce vitamin D. At the same time, the skin protects itself from the burning effects of excessive ultraviolet radiation by producing a dark pigment called melanin, the cause of a suntan.

THE AMAZING INTESTINE

If it were removed from the body, the small intestine would stretch to a length of 22 feet. And if all its internal corrugations were opened out flat, it would cover 360 square yards. In the body, however, the small intestine is compressed like a concertina to a length of a mere 8 feet.

The main business of the small intestine is the absorption of carbohydrate, fat, and protein from food that has first been broken down into molecules by the action of chemicals called enzymes. The absorption can take place in a surprisingly small working part of the intestine, despite the organ's vast potential area. If, for instance, part of the intestine is surgically removed because of disease, the part that remains can function almost as well without it.

TONSILS ON GUARD

Until the 1970s a common childhood trauma in American families concerned the removal of tonsils. Tonsillectomies for children before the age of 7 were encouraged by most doctors, who believed that the surgery reduced the risk of many kinds of throat and respiratory-system infections. However, when antibiotics began to be used successfully against such infections in the 1950s and 1960s, the number of tonsillectomies began to drop. Today most doctors feel that, except in a small minority of cases, there is no health benefit to be derived from the operation—somewhat the reverse, in fact, since any surgical operation carries some risk of death, however small. Tonsils and adenoids are part of the body's natural defenses against disease, standing guard over the entrance to the respiratory and digestive tracts. Some of the cells in their tissues produce antibodies that are effective against invading bacteria, viruses, parasites, and allergy-causing substances. Other cells are capable of destroying invading organisms by swallowing them whole.

THE LIFE-GIVING LUNGS

The lungs are not simply inflatable bags. They are complex structures, containing 300 million air sacs in which oxygen can be absorbed by the blood and carbon dioxide removed from the blood. The area these sacs would cover if spread out flat is about 750 square feet, almost twice the size of a boxing ring.

Because of their extreme elasticity, the lungs are 100 times easier to blow up than a child's balloon. Only about 10 percent of the air in the lungs is actually changed with each cycle of inhaling and exhaling when a person at rest is breathing, but up to 80 percent can be exchanged during deep breathing or strenuous exercise.

SUNTANS IN THE SHADE

It is possible to get a tan or sunburn even on a cloudy day, because about 80 percent of the ultraviolet rays from the sun will penetrate cloud cover.

NO-WIN HORMONE

To gain a competitive edge, professional and even college athletes in many sports have taken anabolic steroids—at great risk to their health and lives. A synthetic form of the male hormone testosterone, anabolic steroids accelerate tissue healing after strenuous exertions or injury, build muscle, and increase aggressiveness. For these gains, the athlete faces both short-term and long-term physiological damage. While taking the drugs, women may acquire deeper voices and more body and facial hair; men may get enlarged prostate glands and breasts and experience reduced sexual potency.

Over the long term, both men and women risk liver damage, intestinal bleeding, disorders in blood chemistry, higher blood pressure, and other pathological symptoms.

Just how many athletes have used anabolic steroids is hard to determine. One clue came from a football player who claimed that 75 percent of the players in the National Football League used the drugs. Their use is banned, and a test is available that will detect amounts as small as one-billionth of a gram in an athlete's bloodstream.

Marvels of the human mind

SHOW OF HANDS

In the great majority of people, speech and language are controlled by the left hemisphere of the brain: 95 percent of right-handed people who have no history of brain damage have their speech centers in the left hemisphere, and right-handers make up 95 percent of the population. The majority of left-handers also have left-hemisphere control of speech, but the percentage drops to 70 percent. About 15 percent of left-handers appear to have speech control in both hemispheres. Doctors use the Wada test, which involves injecting a barbiturate into a patient and noting (among other observations) which arm goes limp first, to check the location of the brain's speech control.

MIND CONTROL

Deep relaxation, if practiced regularly, can strengthen the immune system and produce other beneficial physiological effects, according to new research at Harvard Medical School in Boston, the University of Massachusetts Medical Center (Worcester), and Ohio State University College of Medicine (Columbus). Meditation, yoga, biofeedback, and repetitive prayer are examples of deep-relaxation techniques. All can evoke a physiological state now known as the relaxation response.

The relaxation response seems to counteract the effects of stress, which can be triggered by everyday worries and pressures as well as by threats of physical harm. Under stress, the nervous system causes the release of hormones that elevate the blood pressure,

FACTS AND FIGURES ON THE ASTONISHING MIND

- The weight of the average human brain triples between birth and adulthood, reaching a final weight of about 3 pounds for men and 2.9 pounds for women. By the time a person is 50, though, the brain shrinks slightly, losing about an ounce in weight.

- There is no correlation between brain size and intelligence. A man's brain is usually slightly larger than a woman's, but in both sexes the brain makes up a similar proportion of total body weight.

- Two writers hold opposite records for brain size. The brain of the Russian author Ivan Turgenev (1818–83) weighed 4.44 pounds. The brain of the French writer Anatole France (1844–1924) weighed little more than half that figure: 2.24 pounds.

- The brain is divided into two hemispheres, each a mirror image of the other. In most people the right hemisphere controls the muscles of and receives information from the left half of the body; the left hemisphere monitors and controls the right half of the body.

- In right-handed people—the majority—the left side of the brain is usually concerned with such skills as reading, writing, and talking. The right hemisphere deals with artistic activity and the workings of the imagination. The same is true of most left-handed people, but left-handers are somewhat more likely to have the functions of the two hemispheres reversed.

- The average brain contains about 100 billion neurons—microscopic nerve cells. Each cell has a slender projection called an axon, which links it through a fine connection called a synapse to other parts of the central nervous system. Some axons stretch the length of the spinal cord, more than 3 feet, making them the longest cells in the body. Each neuron is also linked to neighboring neurons by up to 50,000 connections known as dendrites.

- New information reaching the brain from the senses is stored, analyzed, and acted upon by means of electrochemical impulses passing from neuron to neuron through the dendrite connections. Just how complex information is coded into these impulses, or how it is translated back again, is imperfectly understood. But it is known that the brain remains active to some degree around the clock, and that each day it triggers hundreds of millions of impulses—more than all the world's telephone systems put together.

- The thumb is so important in the human scheme of things that it has a special section, separate from the area that controls the fingers, reserved for it in the brain.

- Nerve impulses to and from the brain travel as fast as some racing cars. The fastest impulses recorded, in experiments carried out in 1966, traveled at nearly 180 m.p.h. Nerve impulses move slightly more slowly in elderly people, at up to about 150 m.p.h.

MAPPING THE BRAIN *Scientists can analyze which parts of the brain are most involved in different activities by mapping the varying rates of blood flow. The pictures here, showing flow patterns in the left side of the brain, are computer composites of scans done on several people. In each, the tinted areas show greater than average blood flow, and white shows areas of peak flow.*

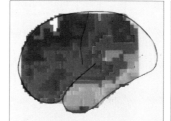

RESTING WITH EYES CLOSED

LOOKING AT A MOVING OBJECT

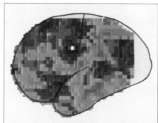

READING SILENTLY

READING ALOUD

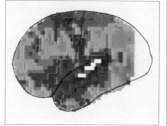

LISTENING TO MUSIC

LISTENING TO WORDS

shift blood flow from limbs to the vital organs, tense the muscles, and accelerate heart and breathing rates. All these reactions can be controlled or reversed by deep relaxation, the new research shows. Furthermore, relaxation may help ward off disease by causing an adjustment in hormone levels that improves the working of the immune system. Finally, the techniques have been effective in lowering high cholesterol levels in some people.

Many hospitals now teach relaxation techniques. Heart patients, asthmatics, and chronic pain sufferers are among those who have been helped. Typically, patients achieve the relaxation response by sitting quietly with eyes closed for 15 minutes twice a day, repeating in their minds a sound, word, or thought (such as a simple prayer).

Meditation, yoga, and other mind-control techniques have been practiced in the East since about 1000 B.C. and have reemerged today as an exciting avenue of medical and scientific research.

IT FEELS NO PAIN

Pain from any injury or illness is always registered by the brain. Yet, curiously, the brain tissue itself is immune to pain; it contains none of the specialized receptor cells that sense pain in other parts of the body. The pain associated with brain tumors does not arise from brain cells but from pressures created by a growing tumor on tissues outside the brain proper.

DREAM MEANINGS

Although the details of dreams tend to vary from person to person, their overall themes and patterns are remarkably consistent. Here are some of the commonest themes and how psychologists usually interpret them:

Falling may indicate a fear of lost status—for example, failing an examination or losing a job.

Flying, if accompanied by a general mood of elation, can be an expression of confidence, a feeling of being on top of the world.

Nudity can reveal a feeling of vulnerability in life. The more embarrassing the circumstances—being naked in a street, say—the more acute the feeling.

Examinations with questions that seem unanswerable suggest a testing situation in real life, at work or at home.

Losing money or valuables may demonstrate a concern for lost values in life; finding them can symbolize confidence.

PHARAOH'S DREAM
Seers in Mesopotamia were studying dreams at least 5,000 years ago. This 13th-century manuscript painting illustrates the Bible story about the pharaoh who dreamed of seven fat and seven lean cattle. Joseph interpreted it to mean that Egypt would have 7 years of plenty followed by 7 years of famine.

DREAMS AND SLEEP

The biological purposes of sleeping and dreaming are as yet imperfectly understood. People deprived of sleep or of the chance to dream for long periods usually become disoriented, lose concentration, and can suffer from hallucinations. A few people, however, are able to do without sleep—and thus without dreams—indefinitely without any ill effects.

Most researchers believe that dreamless sleep is largely a period of physical rest. Blood pressure, body temperature, and heartbeat all drop, and some body tissues—the skin and the internal linings of the stomach and lungs, for instance—regenerate more rapidly than at other times.

Dreaming sleep is thought to be a period of mental restoration during which the mind may sort and store new information acquired during the day.

During a typical 8-hour night, most people spend about 2 hours dreaming, split up into four periods of about 30 minutes each. The first dreaming period usually begins about 60 to 90 minutes after a person falls asleep, the second about 60 to 90 minutes later, and so on through the night.

Dreaming sleep is often known as REM sleep—standing for *rapid eye movement*—because during it the eyes move around behind the closed eyelids as if scanning a picture. It is also called paradoxical sleep because, although the brain is as active as it is in very light sleep, the sleeper's muscles are relaxed, and his responsiveness to external stimuli (noise or a pinprick, say) is as low as in very deep sleep. Dreams can occur during non-REM sleep, but they are not so frequent or vivid. Other warm-blooded mammals, as well as birds, exhibit rapid eye movements during sleep, though for shorter periods—which suggests that these animals also dream.

COVERED IN CONFUSION *A French illustration published in 1867 shows what psychoanalyst Sigmund Freud later called a typical dream: being naked among clothed strangers.*

CALCULATING STRESS

Dr. Thomas Holmes, a professor of psychiatry at the University of Washington in Seattle, has found that four out of every five people whose lives change dramatically in the course of a year can expect a major illness within the next 2 years.

He has helped to devise a rating scale (below) to assess a person's stress risk.

Research showed that 80 percent of those scoring 300 or more and 53 percent of those with 150 to 300 ratings became clinically depressed, had heart attacks, or suffered other serious illnesses. By contrast, two out of three of the people who scored less than 100 did not experience these disorders.

The stress risk is calculated by adding up the points for each fundamental change in the patient's life during the past year, as follows:

Death of spouse, 100; divorce, 73; marital separation, 65; jail term, 63; death of a close family member,

63; personal injury or illness, 53; marriage, 50; being fired, 47; marital reconciliation, 45; retirement, 45.

Change in health of a family member, 44; pregnancy, 40; sex difficulties, 39; gain of a new member in the family, 39; business readjustment, 39; change in financial state, 38.

Death of close friend, 37; change to a different line of work, 36; change in number of arguments with spouse, 35; large mortgage, 31; foreclosure of mortgage or loan, 30; change of personal responsibility at work, 29.

Son or daughter leaving home, 29; trouble with in-laws, 29; outstanding personal achievement, 28; wife stops or starts working, 26; beginning or ending school, 26; change in living conditions, 20; moving to a new home, 20.

Change in schools, 20; change in recreation, 19; change in social activity, 18; small mortgage or loan,

17; change in sleeping habits, 16; change in number of family get-togethers, 15; change in eating habits, 15; vacation, 13; Christmas, 12; minor law violations, 11.

BUILT-IN PAINKILLERS

Athletes who play on despite injury, and soldiers who fight on despite wounds, may not be demonstrating unusual courage. They may simply not notice the pain until the game or the battle is over.

Medical researchers believe that part of the reason may be that the brain creates its own painkillers, known as endorphins and enkephalins, which are capable of blocking the sensation of pain without having any of the undesirable side effects associated with manufactured drugs.

Extreme physical effort and stress both trigger the brain to produce more of the painkillers—hence the players' and the soldiers' temporary immunity.

PIONEERS OF PSYCHOLOGY

The discipline of psychology is little more than a century old. These are some of the people who have played a major part in its development. They are listed in chronological order.

WILHELM WUNDT (1832–1920)
German psychologist, founder of the first laboratory of experimental psychology at Leipzig in 1879. Began to introduce the scientific method to psychology rather than putting forward philosophical theories about the mind, as his predecessors had done.

WILLIAM JAMES (1842–1910)
American philosopher and psychologist who argued that emotions were caused by physical changes: that we feel sorry because we cry, happy because we laugh, and afraid because we tremble, not the reverse.

IVAN PAVLOV (1849–1936)
Russian physiologist and experimental psychologist who demonstrated the development of the conditioned reflex. Pavlov trained dogs to salivate at the sound of a bell by ringing the bell immediately before giving them food. Eventually the dogs became conditioned to salivate at the sound alone. Some psychologists believe that similar conditioning is the basis of all learning in animals and human beings.

SIGMUND FREUD (1856–1939)
Austrian neurologist, founder of psychoanalysis. Believed that the human personality had three parts: the *id*, the unconscious and most primitive part, which aims to satisfy instinctive and biological, primarily sexual, drives; the *ego*, the ordinary social self that deals with the external world; and the *superego*, which incorporates parental and social standards of morality and acts, in part, as the individual's conscience.

ALFRED BINET (1857–1911)
French psychologist who with Théodore Simon developed in 1905 the first reliable intelligence test. A modified version, devised at Stanford University in California and known as the Stanford-Binet test, is still used today to measure intelligence quotient (IQ).

ALFRED ADLER (1870–1937)
Austrian psychiatrist who broke away from Freud in 1911 and founded what is now called individual psychology. Developed the concept of the inferiority complex—feelings of inadequacy and insecurity stemming from real or imagined deficiencies. Believed that human being's main driving force is the desire for power and self-assertion.

CARL GUSTAV JUNG (1875–1961)
Swiss psychologist who broke with Freudianism in 1912. Believed that human behavior largely derives from a general "life urge," not primarily sexual in nature, and that the deepest level of the personality is the "collective unconscious," an inherited part of the unconscious mind found in all members of an ethnic group or species. Introduced

MIND MASTER *A portrait of Freud by the Spanish surrealist painter Salvador Dali.*

personality classifications such as "introvert" (tending to withdraw into oneself) and "extrovert" (tending to be outgoing).

JOHN WATSON (1878–1958)
American psychologist, founder of the school of behaviorism, which holds that people's reactions to given situations—rather than their mental states—are the proper subject of psychological study, since behavior is all that can be objectively measured in others.

WOLFGANG KÖHLER (1887–1967)
Estonian-born psychologist who did much of his work in Germany, then U.S.A. A leading proponent of Gestalt psychology, which argues that behavior and experience must be treated as a whole rather than as a collection of specific behavior patterns or responses to stimuli. In learning theory, Köhler introduced the concept of insight, suggesting that problems were often solved in a flash of insight rather than by trial and error.

ANNA FREUD (1895–1982)
Austrian psychoanalyst (and daughter of Sigmund Freud) who was among the first to study systematically the fears, anxieties, and desires of young children and how the emotional life of the child related to the development of adult neuroses. She summed up her work in *Normality and Pathology in Childhood* (1968).

B. F. SKINNER (1904–)
American psychologist who discovered practical applications for behaviorism in the form of techniques known as behavioral therapy and programmed learning. Both methods provide rewards for good behavior or correct answers to questions—a device known as reinforcement—and punishment (which may merely be the absence of reward) for bad behavior or incorrect answers.

The fight against disease

MODESTY AND THE STETHOSCOPE

The first stethoscope—the instrument that has come to symbolize the practice of medicine around the world—was constructed because a young doctor was shy. It was devised in a matter of moments by the early 19th-century French physician René Laënnec. One day in 1816 Laënnec was consulted by a young woman whose symptoms suggested that she might be suffering from heart disease. Laënnec's modesty prevented him from following the usual practice of placing his ear next to her naked chest to listen to the heartbeat. So he rolled up a newspaper and used that instead. Realizing that the tube magnified the sounds, he went on to construct a 1-foot-long cylinder of wood, the first true stethoscope.

THE FIRST ANESTHETICS

The use of anesthetics to relieve pain in surgery was pioneered by U.S. dentists. The first man to use nitrous oxide as an anesthetic successfully was Horace Wells (1815–48), a Connecticut dentist, who in 1844 performed tooth extractions using the gas. Two years later William Morton (1819–68), a Boston dentist and former partner of Wells, constructed the first anesthetic machine.

Morton's simple device consisted of a glass globe housing an ether-soaked sponge; the patient inhaled the vapor through one of two outlets.

Morton's invention was put to the test on October 16, 1846, in the surgical amphitheater of the Massachusetts General Hospital in Boston. A 20-year-old man was successfully anesthetized so that a tumor on his neck could be removed painlessly.

News of the success spread quickly. Within a year surgeons around the world were using the new technique. Morton, however, did not reap financial benefits from his discovery. When he tried to patent the invention, medical and public opinion judged him greedy and turned against him. He died, rejected, in poverty.

ROYAL EXAMPLE

Even after the introduction of anesthetics into other forms of surgery, some people resisted their use in childbirth because of the biblical statement in the Book of Genesis: "In sorrow shalt thou bring forth children." It took the combination of a Scottish surgeon and a queen to overcome this obstacle.

The surgeon was James Simpson (1811–70), professor of midwifery at Edinburgh University, Scotland, who was the first man to use chloroform to relieve the pain of childbirth. Simpson was dissatisfied with ether, not only because it irritated the eyes, had an unpleasant smell, sometimes caused vomiting, and was highly inflammable, but also because there was no certainty that its use was absolutely safe. In October 1847, however, David Waldie, a friend of Simpson's from their student days, suggested to him that pure chloroform might be worth trying. On November 4, 1847, Simpson experimented with the drug on himself and two of his friends. Five days later he used it while delivering a baby.

The drug was administered simply by being sprinkled on a handkerchief, which was placed over the patient's mouth and nose so that she could inhale the vapors. Delighted by the painless delivery, the mother christened her child Anaesthesia.

Even after this success, it took the seal of royal approval to win the technique complete acceptance. In 1853 Queen Victoria was given chloroform during the birth of her eighth child, Prince Leopold. She found the experience "soothing, quieting, and delightful beyond all measure," and after that her subjects were quick to copy the royal example.

X MARKED A MYSTERY

Wilhelm Konrad Roentgen (1845–1923), the discoverer of X-rays, came across them by chance. Indeed, he initially regarded his research as of merely academic significance and actually resented the immediate interest the public took in his findings.

In November 1895 Roentgen, a professor of physics at Würzburg University in Bavaria, was studying cathode rays when he noticed that the rays were causing a sheet of paper coated with a chemical called barium platinocyanide to glow, even though there was a sheet of cardboard between the source of the rays and the affected paper. The effect continued even when Roentgen took the paper into the next room. Puzzled by this, he embarked immediately on a series of experiments to find out more about the mysterious rays and a month later described his discoveries in a paper, "On a New Kind of Rays," which he read to the Würzburg Physico-Medical Society on December 28, 1895. He christened the new rays X-rays, simply because of their mysterious nature.

The medical and surgical value of X-rays was soon appreciated, and Roentgen won worldwide fame as a result. In 1901 he was awarded a Nobel Prize for his work.

MAGIC MOLD

One of the key discoveries in modern medicine came about by accident. In the autumn of 1928 Alexander Fleming (1881–1955), a Scottish scientist, returned to his laboratory in St. Mary's Hospital, London, after a 4-week holiday. He noticed that, during his absence, a culture plate had not been tightly covered, and the culture of staphylococcus bacteria—the cause of a number of diseases, from boils to pneumonia—had

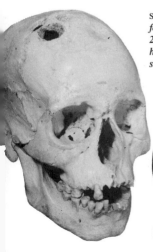

SKULL GAP *Doctors in Jericho bored four holes in this skull (left) in about 2000 B.C. All the holes show signs of healing, proving that the patient survived the surgery.*

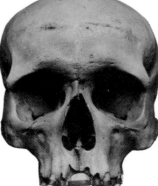

FALSE TEETH *A carved ox tooth served as two front teeth for this Etruscan, who died in about 700 B.C.*

been contaminated by a number of yeasts and molds.

What immediately interested Fleming was that one of the molds, which he identified as *Penicillium notatum,* had killed the staphylococcus in the area of the plate it had infiltrated. On further investigation he narrowed down the reasons for this to the presence of an active ingredient, which he named penicillin after the mold. In 1940 Howard Florey and E. B. Chain managed to isolate penicillin in their Oxford laboratory, demonstrate its antibacterial action, and show that it could be safely administered by mouth or injection, or applied directly to wounds as a powder. All three men were awarded the Nobel Prize in medicine in 1945.

Fleming himself was the first to recognize that chance had played a vital role in his discovery. He later wrote: "There are thousands of different moulds and there are thousands of different bacteria, and that chance put that mould in the right place at the right time was like winning the Irish Sweep."

BLOOD CONFUSION

The Incas in South America were carrying out blood transfusions 400 or 500 years before the technique was successfully achieved in Europe. Because most South American Indians are of the same blood group, O Rh-positive, incompatibility was unlikely, and this may have accounted for the Incas' success.

In Europe attempts at transfusions were made by an Italian physicist, Giovanni Colle, beginning in 1628. Most of his patients died because they received blood from the wrong group, and transfusions were forbidden by the church and the governments of Italy, France, and England in the late 1600s, although some researchers continued their experiments.

Blood transfusions did not become safe until the 20th century, when Karl Landsteiner (1868–1943), a Viennese pathologist, identified blood groups in 1901. This led eventually to the correct matching of the blood of donor and patient. Landsteiner, who became a U.S. citizen in 1929, won the 1930 Nobel Prize in medicine.

TISSUE TREATMENT

The ancient Hindus practiced plastic surgery before A.D. 1000. They worked with steel surgical instruments and used alcohol to dull the senses. One reason for the development of this skill was the common punishment for adultery—cutting off the nose. Surgeons repaired the damage with tissues cut from either the cheek or the forehead, rebuilding the nose around the stump. During the operation the patient breathed through reeds placed in the nasal openings.

World War I, with its attendant disfiguring injuries, was largely responsible for making plastic surgery more widely available in Western medicine.

VICTORY OVER TB

For centuries tuberculosis was one of the most feared of all diseases. This infection, also known as TB and consumption, usually attacks the lungs. At one time TB and its complications played a part in one in five deaths worldwide. Its characteristic lesions—named tubercles in the 17th century—have been identified in Neolithic skeletons in Europe and in mummies of Egyptians who lived in 3700 B.C.

Despite all their efforts, doctors remained powerless against tuberculosis until Robert Koch (1843–1910), a self-trained German bacteriologist, identified the rodlike tubercle bacillus in 1882.

The next advance came in 1922, when an effective vaccine—originally developed in 1906 by two French scientists, Albert Calmette and Camille Guérin—was first given to children. The vaccine was named BCG (bacille Calmette-Guérin), and it is still in use today.

The final step was a treatment that could cure the disease. This came in 1944 with the discovery of streptomycin, the first effective antituberculous drug, by Selman Waksman (1888–1973), a Ukrainian-born scientist who did much of his pioneering research while a professor of microbiology at Rutgers University in New Jersey. For his discovery of streptomycin, derived from soil microorganisms, he received the Nobel Prize in medicine in 1952.

THE HIPPOCRATIC OATH

Medical ethics around the world are often measured against the Hippocratic oath, thought to have been written by the Greek physician Hippocrates (c. 460–370 B.C.). In some medical schools and universities, graduating doctors are still obliged to swear to a form of the oath. Here is a translation of the original oath:

I swear by Apollo the healer, invoking all the gods and goddesses to be my witnesses, that I will fulfill this oath and this written covenant to the best of my ability and judgment.

I will look upon him who shall have taught me this art even as one of my own parents. I will share my substance with him, and I will supply his necessities if he be in need. I will regard his offspring even as my own brethren, and I will teach them this art, if they would learn it, without fee or covenant. I will impart this art by precept, by lecture, and by every mode of teaching, not only to my own sons but to the sons of him who has taught me and to disciples bound by covenant and oath, according to the law of medicine.

The regimen I adopt shall be for the benefit of the patients according to my ability and judgment, and not for their hurt or for any wrong. I will give no deadly drug to any, though it be asked of me, nor will I counsel such, and especially I will not aid a woman to procure abortion. Whatsoever house I enter, there will I go for the benefit of the sick, refraining from all wrongdoing or corruption, and especially from any act of seduction, of male or female, of bond or free. Whatsoever things I see or hear concerning the life of men, in my attendance on the sick or even apart therefrom, which ought not to be noised abroad, I will keep silence thereon, counting such things to be as sacred secrets. Pure and holy will I keep my life and my art.

PORTRAIT OF A DOCTOR *A Byzantine artist's impression of the 5th-century B.C. Greek doctor Hippocrates.*

THE LONELY LEPER

Doctors now know that leprosy is a disease of low infectivity, meaning that it can be transmitted only by close contact over a prolonged period of time. But for centuries lepers were feared and cruelly ostracized. Known to the ancient Hebrews, Greeks, and Romans, leprosy spread to northern Europe in the 6th century A.D. As early as A.D. 583 the church prohibited the free movement of lepers and commanded its priests to segregate lepers from those who did not have the disease.

The unfortunate leper was forced to wear a burial shroud and to lie in a coffin placed before the local church's altar. The priest scattered earth over him and then declared him to be legally dead. From that moment on, the leper was an outcast, obliged to beg for alms to support himself. He had to carry a pointing stick—to point out anything he wanted to buy—carry a bell to warn of his approach, and wear gloves and special fur shoes to protect barefooted travelers walking behind him.

The bacteria that causes leprosy, *Mycobacterium leprae,* was discovered in 1874 by Armauer Hansen, a bacteriologist and physician in Bergen, Norway; but drugs (primarily the sulfones) that are effective against most forms of the disease were not widely used until the 1940s.

RECURRING NIGHTMARE

When bubonic plague—the Black Death—struck Europe in 1347, it was regarded as the greatest single disaster ever to befall mankind. Towns and cities were wiped out. About 30 million people, more than a quarter of the European population, perished. Another 45 million died in Asia. Waves of plague followed at intervals over the centuries. One such epidemic swept Europe in 1664–65. The last major outbreak came in 1910, when 60,000 people died in eastern Siberia in just 7 months.

More than 15 years before, in 1894, a Japanese scientist, Shibasaburo Kitazato, and a French bacteriologist, Alexandre Yersin, had independently discovered that the plague was a bacterial disease carried by infected rat fleas. But it took many years before an effective vaccine could be developed and made available worldwide.

LEGACY FROM THE BLACK DEATH

While the practice of segregating sick people from healthy ones goes back to Old Testament times and probably to prehistory, the modern word *quarantine* comes from a preventive measure taken in Venice in the 1370s in an attempt to prevent a renewed outbreak of the dreaded Black Death sweeping Italy. In 1374 the city appointed three medical officers whose duties were to inspect all ships entering the port and to exclude any they suspected of harboring the plague. Three years later the nearby Dalmatian republic of Ragusa (in present-day Yugoslavia) compelled all suspected sailors, together with their cargoes, to be held in isolation on a neighboring island for *quaranta giorni* ("40 days") to make sure that they were not carrying the disease. The word *quarantine* comes from the Italian for 40. The time was fixed at 40 days because it was believed that all such diseases, like the biblical flood, were limited to that period.

BIRTH OF THE CAESAR

The Romans are thought to have invented the childbirth operation known as cesarean section. According to legend, the name was given to the operation because Julius Caesar was delivered that way.

INFECTION DETECTION

For centuries women feared childbirth—not because of the risks of the birth itself but because of the danger of death afterward from a form of blood poisoning known as puerperal sepsis. It took the zeal of one man, the Hungarian obstetrician Ignaz Semmelweis (1818–65), to introduce the simple hygienic techniques that saved the lives of thousands of women.

In 1846 Semmelweis joined the maternity department of the Vienna General Hospital and immediately became appalled by the death toll in the main ward, where expectant mothers were attended by medical students. However, he also noticed that in another ward, where midwives were responsible for the patients, the death rate was far lower. What, he asked, was the reason for the difference?

Semmelweis refused to accept the official explanation that the deaths were caused by "hospital miasma," or bad air. He concluded that the reason for the difference was that the medical students were

PLASTIC SURGERY *Doctors in India were using tissue from the forehead to rebuild noses in* A.D. *1000.*

READY FOR BIRTH *Soranus, a Greek doctor of the 1st–2nd century* A.D., *made a study of childbirth. This sketch is from a 13th-century edition of Soranus's works and purports to show a fetus in the womb.*

PAINS AND NEEDLES *A Chinese acupuncture chart published in 1679 marks where needles were inserted to treat heart diseases.*

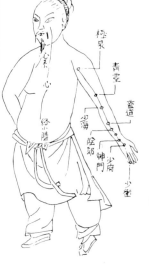

DEATH MASK *17th-century plague doctors wore masks fitted with spice-filled beaks to protect themselves from infection and stink.*

treating their patients after coming from the dissecting rooms and therefore were carrying disease to their pregnant patients. The midwives, on the other hand, were not involved in autopsies.

In May 1847, defying the heated opposition of his colleagues, Semmelweis asked his students to wash their hands in chlorinated limewater and to scrub their fingernails before entering the main ward. The results were dramatic. The death rate had stood at a staggering 12.4 percent. Within 2 months it had fallen to 2 percent.

Semmelweis's fellow doctors, however, could not forgive him for being right. Attempting to extend antiseptic practices, he found himself blocked at every turn, and in 1850 he left the hospital to return to Budapest to carry on his work. In 1865 he died in a lunatic asylum—probably from a form of the same blood poisoning that he had sacrificed his career in Vienna to treat.

THE ELUSIVE HORMONE

For centuries diabetes was a lethal disease. A diabetic had a future life expectancy, on average, of less than 5 years. Most diabetics eventually fell into a coma that led to death. The condition—in which the body is unable to use the sugar it absorbs because the pancreas fails to produce enough of the key hormone insulin—had been described by the Greek physician Aretaeus as long ago as the 2nd century A.D. However, it was not until 1922 that Frederick G. Banting and Charles H. Best, two Toronto-based surgeons, made the discovery that broke the curse of diabetes.

Both men were aware of the research of the British physiologist Edward Sharpey-Schäfer, in which he theorized that the islets of Langerhans—so called after their discoverer, the German pathologist Paul Langerhans—produced a substance that controlled the body's ability to use the carbohydrates it absorbed. In 1913 Sharpey-Schäfer gave the name *insuline* to this theoretical substance.

Banting and Best resolved to track down the elusive hormone. In 1921 they finally succeeded in isolating a watery extract, which they named isletin, after the islets of Langerhans. They then injected a dog in diabetic coma with the extract; within 2 hours the dog's blood sugar level had halved and it was on the road to recovery. In January 1922 the doctors injected their first human patient.

Mass production of the new wonder drug, now known as insulin, was quickly begun. Today, though more than 2 in 100 people in the U.S.A. suffer from diabetes, they usually lead relatively normal lives.

SPRAY THAT SAVED

The introduction of effective anesthetics in the 19th century meant that surgeons were able to perform more complex operations than ever before. Ironically, this advance was accompanied by a substantial drawback: a dramatic rise in the number of postoperative complications. Wounds rarely healed cleanly, and more than half the patients died of blood poisoning. The Scottish obstetrician James Simpson, one of the pioneers of anesthesia, wrote: "A man laid on the operating table in one of our surgical hospitals is exposed to more chances of death than the English soldier on the field of Waterloo." It took the genius of a Quaker surgeon to change this situation. The surgeon's name was Joseph Lister (1827–1912), and his revolutionary innovation was the use of chemicals to prevent surgical infection.

Deeply influenced by the work of the French scientist Louis Pasteur and his germ theory, Lister argued that the risk of infection would be reduced if chemical antiseptics were used to protect wounds against the germs in the atmosphere. His experiments began to gain success and acclaim in 1865, when he used carbolic acid in the form of a spray during operations and on his surgical dressings. For his contribution to the fight against disease, Lister won worldwide fame.

FOOD PERIL

Unexplained attacks of migraine, eczema, stomach pain, diarrhea, nausea, and vomiting could all be cured, some doctors believe, by a simple change of diet. According to a report published in 1983 about the results of tests carried out at Britain's Great Ormond Street Hospital and Institute of Child Health, many of these disorders are caused by allergies.

To prove the point, the researchers took a sample of 88 children, all of whom suffered from frequent severe migraine attacks, and put them on a special diet for 3 to 4 weeks. The diet consisted of lamb or chicken, rice or potato, a single type of fruit, and one vegetable, together with water and vitamin supplements. Other

VACCINE VICTORIES

1796 Edward Jenner, English doctor, makes the first successful smallpox vaccination.

1880 French chemist Louis Pasteur prepares the first anticholera vaccine, followed by vaccines against anthrax (1881) and rabies (1885).

1891 Antitoxins produced to treat diphtheria and tetanus by Emil von Behring and Shibasaburo Kitazato, working with Robert Koch in Berlin.

1922 Tuberculosis vaccine—originally developed in 1906 at the Pasteur Institute in Paris for use with cattle—successfully tested on French schoolchildren.

1953 Polio vaccine developed in Pittsburgh, Pa., by U.S. physician Jonas Salk.

1960 Measles vaccine developed by U.S. bacteriologist John F. Enders.

1962 Rubella (German measles) vaccine developed to protect pregnant women by U.S. physician Thomas H. Weller.

1977 Vaccine against pneumococcal pneumonia developed by scientists at U.S. firm, Merck & Co.

1986 A rising tide of malaria in tropics spurs research in many labs around the world for a malaria vaccine.

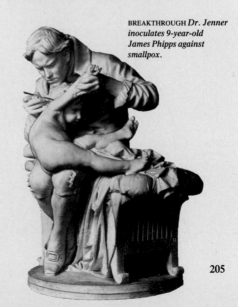

BREAKTHROUGH *Dr. Jenner inoculates 9-year-old James Phipps against smallpox.*

foodstuffs were then reintroduced one at a time at the rate of one per week, so that if the migraines returned, another foodstuff could be substituted. Of the 88 patients, an amazing 78 recovered completely and 4 more were greatly improved. At the same time, the researchers noted that other associated ailments, such as abdominal pain, behavioral disorders, fits, asthma, and eczema, also disappeared.

The suspected foods were then disguised by being mixed with a savory or sweet base, so that the children had no idea if they were eating the suspected food or not. In this further series of tests, 70 of the 88 children became ill again when the suspected foods—these included tea, eggs, milk, rye, and artificial food colorings—were temporarily reintroduced into their diets by the researchers.

WHY YOU ARE SEASICK

Motion sickness—whether on sea, land, or air—has nothing to do with eating or drinking. It is a temporary disorder affecting equilibrium, which is linked to the motion of fluid in the three semicircular canals of the middle ear. What apparently happens is that signals from the eyes and ears get scrambled in the effort to keep the head correctly oriented in the midst of constant swaying and up-and-down motions. Though some people have or develop a natural resistance to the conditions, many do not. Horatio, Lord Nelson, Britain's greatest admiral, was often seasick.

Research to find a cure began during World War II, with the goal of making troops fit for immediate action when they disembarked from ships. Yet even today no drug is fully effective against motion sickness. Most simply sedate the sufferer.

THE KILLERS

Although public health statistics are often unreliable, because reporting criteria vary from country to country, it is safe to say that heart disease, cancer, and strokes kill more people around the world each year than any other illnesses. Heart disease is by far the biggest killer in the Western world. In the United States, for example, 409 out of every 100,000 people die of heart disease each year. In Britain the figure is in the same range; in Australia it is 292. By comparison, lung cancer kills a relatively small proportion of the population each year: 49 per 100,000 in the United States, 32 per 100,000 in Australia, and 72 per 100,000 in Britain. The death rate from strokes in the U.S.A. in 1983 was 67 per 100,000.

ARTIFICIAL HEART
Inventor Dr. Robert K. Jarvik holds a model of the plastic pump that by mid-1986 had been implanted in 19 patients, two of whom lived for more than a year.

In the Third World, such diseases as pneumonia, enteritis, and diarrheal disorders often kill more people than heart disease does. In Ecuador, for instance, enteritis and other diarrheal disorders kill 106 people per 100,000 each year; heart disease kills only two-thirds as many. Moreover, in some of the world's poorest countries, at least one baby in two dies in the first 5 years of life, often from common childhood infections, such as measles, or from disorders associated with birth.

GERM OF AN IDEA

The science of preventive medicine—actually preventing disease, rather than merely coping with its effects—originated with the work of a 19th-century French chemist whose interests at first lay more in wine and vinegar than in human beings. In the 1860s Louis Pasteur (1822–95) was commissioned by France's winegrowers to find out why their products were becoming sour and unsalable in the vats. Pasteur discovered that the unwanted changes were caused by invisible, airborne microbes that were invading the vats. He called the microbes germs.

Pasteur went on to prove that germs were also the cause of human diseases. He argued against the belief, then widely held, that diseases were spontaneously generated within individual sufferers. Diseases, he said, were caused by airborne germs and bacteria that invaded and multiplied in the body. This concept became the foundation of the science of bacteriology and pointed the way to new understanding of the nature of infectious diseases.

Theoretically, the concept was not new. Girolamo Fracastoro, an Italian professor of philosophy, had put forward the first scientific statement of its principles in 1546 in his book *On Contagion and Contagions*. But 16th-century medicine was not advanced enough to prove the theory or make practical use of it.

Pasteur, on the other hand, was able to track down and study germs and bacteria and so develop effective vaccines against them. His two most notable discoveries were vaccines against anthrax (1881) and rabies (1885). His rabies vaccine was the subject of one of his most dramatic demonstrations. In 1885 he saved the life of a 9-year-old German boy, Joseph Meister, with a series of 14 injections after the boy had been badly mauled by a rabid dog.

INDIAN MEDICINE MEN

The first effective treatment for malaria was not devised by doctors, but by Peruvian Indians. It was popularized in Europe in the 1640s by Jesuit monks, who brought the secret of the cure back from South America. The Indians had found that an extract of the bark of the cinchona tree was extremely effective in dealing with the deadly fever. When samples of the bark were distributed in Europe by the Jesuits, its powers were quickly demonstrated.

Two factors, however, stood in the way of the miracle bark's acceptance. Despite the evidence, many physicians at first remained skeptical. In addition, the use of the bark was resisted in Protestant countries because of its Jesuit associations. For example, when Oliver Cromwell, Lord Protector of England, contracted malaria in 1658, he refused to take any "Jesuits' bark" because of this prejudice—and died the same year as a result.

It was not until 1820 that the active ingredient of the bark was isolated and named quinine. But the actual cause of malaria remained a mystery until 1897, when a British doctor in India, Sir Ronald Ross, showed that it was transmitted to humans by the bite of the female *Anopheles* mosquito.

AMAZING ASPIRIN

No home medicine cabinet is complete without aspirin. The drug—properly known as acetylsalicylic acid, Aspirin being the trade name invented for it in the 1890s by the Bayer Drug Company in Germany—is one of the most widely used in the world. More than 33 billion aspirin tablets are swallowed every year in the United States, and another 7 billion in Britain. The world as a whole gulps down about 123 billion aspirins a year, or about 2 pills a month for every man, woman, and child on the planet.

The drug's origins go back to 1758, when an English clergyman, Edward Stone, noticed that the bark of the willow tree had a peculiarly bitter flavor, similar to that of the "Peruvian bark" that had been used since the 1640s to bring down fevers and to treat malaria. When Stone obtained some pulverized willow bark and tested its properties, he found that it, too, was extremely effective in reducing high temperatures and relieving rheumatic aches and pains. In 1763 Stone presented his findings to the British Royal Society, but although he could show what effects the crushed willow had, he could not say what part of the bark caused them. In 1826 two Italian chemists, Brugnatelli and Fontana, found the active chemical to be salicin, the basic ingredient of today's aspirin.

Some remarkable new claims for aspirin have come out of research conducted in the mid-1980s. One study indicated that 5 grains of aspirin a day could reduce the risk of second heart attacks, while another found that a slightly larger daily dose of aspirin could prolong the lives of those suffering from the dangerous heart condition known as unstable angina.

DOCTOR IN THE DAIRY

Measures to deal with the threat of smallpox were devised by the Chinese as early as A.D. 590, when they introduced the first protective vaccinations against the disease. With variations this practice, known as variolation, spread throughout the Orient. It was introduced in England in 1720 by Lady Mary Wortley Montagu, who brought the idea from Turkey, where her husband was British ambassador.

The technique involved inoculating a person with pus taken from victims of a mild form of smallpox. The idea was that, by being infected with the mild form, the patient would acquire immunity to the severe form. But there was a major drawback: the patient risked becoming infected with the lethal form as a result of the treatment.

A much safer method was discovered in the late 18th century. It was the work of Edward Jenner (1749–1823), a British country doctor who, after years of patient research, performed the first successful antismallpox vaccination in 1796. Basing his theory on a chance remark by a dairymaid—"I cannot take the smallpox, since I have had the cowpox" (a similar but mild disease contracted from cows)—Jenner vaccinated a young boy, James Phipps, with an extract taken from a cowpox pustule on the infected hand of a dairymaid. Six weeks later he inoculated Phipps with a mild form of smallpox. No infection developed.

Jenner's vaccination technique—named from the Latin word *vacca,* meaning "cow"—was eventually adopted all over the world. And in 1980 the World Health Organization officially declared the world free of smallpox. It was the first time that human beings had ever eliminated a major disease.

THE CASE OF THE ESCAPING VIRUS

A bizarre minidrama in the conquest of smallpox unfolded in England in 1978, five years after that nation had reported its last case of the disease.

Janet Parker, a medical photographer employed at the University of Birmingham, died from what could only have been smallpox, which was thought to have been conquered in Britain. A few days later, the head of the Birmingham Medical School's microbiology and virology department, Prof. Henry Bedson, cut his throat and died within a week.

The explanation for these grisly events lay in Bedson's lab, where he kept smallpox viruses that he used in his work to eradicate the disease. Directly above his lab was Parker's office. Somehow, one or more of the viruses had escaped into the air and infected Parker, whose mother also contracted the disease but survived. Bedson blamed himself for the tragedy.

A quick sealing off of the building probably averted the further spread of smallpox; but the case remains a grim warning of the dangers involved in working with lethal microorganisms, even in the most modern labs.

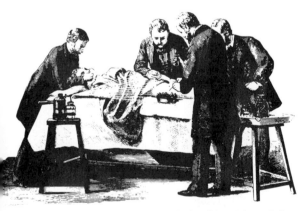

ANTISEPTIC SPRAY *The surgeon Joseph Lister began using carbolic acid in the 1860s to reduce the chances of surgical infections. In this 1882 engraving, a Lister spray gun pumps a fine mist of the antiseptic acid over surgeons and patient during an operation.*

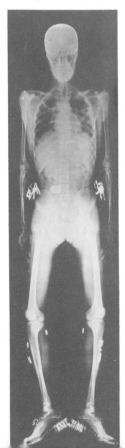

ASPIRIN *The first bottles of Aspirin (below) went on sale in 1899.*

X-RAYS *In the first X-ray of a human body, metal keys and suspenders not visible to the eye show up.*

Food and drink

THE PLANT EATERS
Worldwide, plants provide 88 percent of the calories (primarily as carbohydrates and fats) and 80 percent of the proteins in the human diet. But we have so far domesticated only a tiny percentage of the hundreds of thousands of known plant species, and we still cultivate mostly species that were domesticated by our prehistoric ancestors. Of the some 200 species cultivated today, 15 supply most of the food consumed by human beings. These 15 fall into four major groups: cereals, roots and stems, legumes, and fruits.

Many plant species have been neglected out of ignorance, superstition, or force of habit, but with the world population expected to double within the next 20 or 30 years, such attitudes are likely to change. Among the plants that may become the staples of tomorrow are the amaranth of Central and South America, a hardy herb with showy flowers that grows 5 to 6 feet tall, and the winged bean of Southeast Asia and New Guinea, now under experimental cultivation in more than 70 countries. Both these plants grow quickly with little attention. They are rich sources of protein, and can be eaten leaves, flowers, seeds, stems, roots, and all.

SYNTHETIC FOOD
No great scientific obstacle stands in the way of making food entirely from basic chemicals. Proteins, fats, and carbohydrates can all be synthesized in labs. The questions are how to get people to eat the stuff and, more important, how long-term reliance on synthetic food might affect body systems that have evolved over millions of years to handle food in natural forms. In any event, the future will probably bring an increase in the use of wholly synthetic food supplements.

ACID DIGESTION
The process of digestion begins as soon as food goes into the mouth. Enzymes in the saliva start to break up the food even before it is swallowed. The major digestive organ, though, is the stomach, whose lining contains about 35 million tiny glands. These stomach glands produce some 3 quarts of gastric juices every day, mostly in the form of hydrochloric acid.

TASTING, TASTING
The human tongue distinguishes only four basic tastes. On its surface are thousands of nerve endings, or taste buds. Those at the back sense bitterness; those at the sides sense saltiness and sourness; those at the tip sense all tastes but are most sensitive to sweetness and saltiness. Other taste buds are scattered around the inside of the mouth. The primary tasters of sour and bitter, for instance, are in the roof of the mouth.

All the more complex tastes are made up of combinations of the basic four. Young adults have about 8,000 taste buds, but in older adults, at about 45 years of age, the nerve endings begin to die, so that elderly people normally have only about 6,500. Much of what we perceive as flavor in food is a combination of taste and smell, which is why food seems to lose its flavor when the nose is blocked during a cold.

MIXERS PACK AN EXTRA WALLOP
Alcoholic cocktails made with sweet fruit mixers can impair concentration and judgment faster and perhaps longer than if the same amount of alcohol is taken straight. First, the sugar in mixers accelerates the body's absorption of alcohol. Furthermore, the sugar stimulates the pancreas to produce insulin, which soaks up the excess sugar and stores it. As the remaining sugar is used up to provide energy, the level of sugar in the blood falls.

In ordinary circumstances, this drop triggers other hormones to release the stored sugar or create more. But the alcohol in the drink blocks the triggering process, so that the blood sugar level continues to fall. And since the brain is powered by the energy in blood sugar, mental performance can be seriously affected for several hours.

POPEYE MISLED
The notion that spinach contains extraordinary amounts of iron and therefore promotes strength—an idea made popular by the cartoon character Popeye the Sailor—is based on a mistake. The misconception arose in 1870 when a misplaced decimal point in a set of published food tables made spinach appear to contain 10 times as much iron as other vegetables. In fact, it has no unusual amount. Furthermore, iron does not seem to be especially valuable in building muscles, although it is an essential ingredient in red blood cells and seems to increase a person's resistance to infection and disease.

SALT BINGERS
Nutritionists estimate that the average person needs no more than a tenth of a teaspoon of salt each day. The average North American consumes 20 or 30 times that amount. People who eat too much salt may retain fluids and risk high blood pressure, which predisposes them to more serious problems, such as heart disease.

CLEAN LIVING
Devout Mormons abstain from alcohol, cigarettes, tea, and coffee—and get cancer far less often than other people do. Doctors who have studied the patterns of disease in Utah—home to more than one in three of the more than 2 million Mormons in the United States—have found that American men as a whole are almost three times more likely to get lung

WHY VITAMINS ARE VALUABLE

Vitamins are chemical substances present naturally in most foods and, in synthetic form, in vitamin pills. Both forms are equally nutritious, since the vitamins in each case are chemically identical. The body needs only tiny quantities of them—ranging from about 30 mg (30 thousandths of a gram) a day of vitamin C, for instance, down to 1 microgram (one millionth of a gram) of vitamin B_{12}. Vitamins play no direct part in producing body tissues or energy, but they are essential for the body to function efficiently, just as oil is essential to the running of a car.

Vitamin deficiencies can lead to illness and, in extreme cases, death. The killer diseases scurvy and beriberi are caused by deficiencies of the vitamins C and B_1 respectively. Too little vitamin A in the diet can cause night blindness, and rickets (a childhood disease of the bones) is caused by a deficiency of vitamin D. Anyone who eats a variety of foods, however, is unlikely to run into problems.

cancer than Mormon men. There is a similar reduction in throat cancer among Mormons. And cancer of the large bowel is about 40 percent less common.

FOOD FACTS AND FALLACIES
● An apple a day does not keep the doctor away. A medium-size apple supplies only 0.0004 ounce of vitamin C; an orange has five times as much. Apart from 0.7 ounce of sugar (80 calories), apples contain little else than about 0.07 ounce of dietary fiber.
● Whole wheat bread has more iron, vitamins, and dietary fiber than white bread.
● White eggs are just as nutritious as brown ones. The color of the shell is a characteristic of the breed of chicken. It has nothing to do with nutritive value.
● Margarine is just as fattening as butter, but it is mainly composed of polyunsaturated ("vegetable") fatty acids, while the fatty acids in butter are of the saturated ("animal") type. A diet that replaces saturated fats with unsaturated fats tends to reduce the level of cholesterol in the blood. Lowered cholesterol in turn can reduce the buildup of deposits on the inner walls of blood vessels, and so help to avoid atherosclerosis, which has been implicated as a cause of heart attacks and strokes.
● Carrots can help you see better in the dark. People whose eyesight is normal but whose diets lack adequate vitamin A cannot see in dim light—an ailment known as night blindness. Carrots will cure this condition because they are rich in carotene, which forms vitamin A in the body. However, carrots will not help if the inability to see at night is due to some other cause.
● Honey, often thought to be particularly health-giving, has no exceptional value. It consists mainly of fructose (fruit sugar), glucose (grape sugar), and water. Vitamins are present but in nutritionally insignificant amounts.
● The belief that brown sugar is better for health than white has no scientific foundation. White sugar is 99.9 percent pure sucrose. Brown sugar is 98 percent sucrose and 1 per cent water, and has only minute traces of mineral salts and protein. The difference is therefore negligible.

EATING FOR TWO
The maxim that pregnant women need to eat for two is a fallacy. Expectant mothers do need extra nourishment, but not over the entire 9 months of pregnancy. About 80,000 extra calories are needed over the total 9-month period—roughly the equivalent of 1 month's normal food intake. So the maxim could be rephrased more accurately as: a pregnant woman should eat for one and one-ninth. Moreover, British research published in 1983 suggests that food may be absorbed more efficiently than usual during pregnancy, so that a mother-to-be's normal diet may provide the extra calories without her needing to eat more.

Some women develop bizarre cravings for particular foods during pregnancy. This may be because of variations in hormone levels. Since taste and smell are affected by the level of estrogen hormones, a woman may find she likes things she didn't like before she became pregnant.

POWDERED MILK OF THE MONGOLS
Powdered milk was used as long ago as the 13th century by the cavalry of the Mongol emperor Genghis Khan (c. 1162–1227). The Mongol soldiers dried mare's milk to a powder in the sun to preserve it. Then, at the beginning of each day's journey, they put some of the powder into a water bottle, which was hung on a saddle. The horse's jogging acted as a whisk, turning the mixture into a thin porridge by nightfall.

LIND'S "LIMEYS"
The slang expression *limey,* now used for anyone British—was coined in the early 19th century to describe British sailors. The word came from the Royal Navy's practice of issuing a compulsory daily ration of lemon juice or lime juice to its men to prevent scurvy, a disease caused by a lack of vitamin C.

Scurvy had been a major health hazard for sailors ever since the start of long-distance voyages of exploration in the 15th century. On some voyages three out of four sailors died of it. Yet little was done to check the disease until a Scottish naval surgeon, James Lind, embarked on a program of research to find an effective countermeasure. Lind began his work in 1747 when he sailed as ship's surgeon on H.M.S. *Salisbury* and found that 80 out of the 350-man crew were suffering from scurvy. He took 12 of the scurvy victims and divided them into 6 pairs. For a week he got 5 of the pairs to drink one of five potions each day: cider; an elixir of acidic vitriol; vinegar; seawater; or a mixture of garlic, mustard seed, balsam of fern, myrrh, and barley water. The sixth pair ate a lemon and two oranges. Within 6 days the sailors taking the lemon and oranges were so much better that they could help care for those still suffering from scurvy.

Lind published his findings in his *Treatise of the Scurvy* in 1753. But his prescription was ignored for 42 years. Not until 1795, a year after his death, did the British Admiralty make citrus juice an official part of the naval diet.

COOK'S LIST *A 1768 cargo manifest for the British explorer James Cook includes sauerkraut and malt. Both were thought, wrongly, to help prevent scurvy.*

ESKIMO HEALTH
Eskimos eat more fat than any other people in the world, but heart diseases, which are often caused by a fatty diet, are rare among them.

The reason is that the fats Eskimos get in their normal diet of fish, whale, and seal are of a type known as unsaturated, or more specifically omega-3 fatty acids. These resemble vegetable fats, which are also unsaturated (or polyunsaturated). The fats that can lead to heart disease—because they build up in the walls of arteries, restricting the flow of blood and putting extra strain on the heart—are known as saturated fats, or omega-6 fatty acids. Butter, red meat, and eggs are rich in them.

THE NOT QUITE PERFECT FOOD
A pint of milk a day provides, on average, one-sixth of a person's daily energy requirements, all the calcium, one-third of the protein, about a quarter of the vitamin A, one-fifth of the vitamin B_1, and half the vitamin B_2. Amid all this healthful splendor, milk does contain cholesterol, the substance (also found in

many other foods) that can accumulate in the arteries and lead to heart disease. But a pint of milk contains only about 0.002 ounce of cholesterol—less than a quarter of the amount in one boiled egg. As a rich source of calcium, milk is recommended by many doctors for people suffering from osteoporosis, a degenerative bone disease that affects 20 million Americans, mostly women over 45, and contributes to 1.3 million fractures every year. However, not all doctors agree that osteoporosis is linked to calcium deficiency.

COLD COMFORT
Large doses of vitamin C—the vitamin found in oranges and many other fruits—are no help in warding off colds, according to much research designed to test

CALORIES AND BASIC NUTRIENTS IN COMMON FOODS

In physics one calorie is the heat required to raise one cubic centimeter of water by one degree centigrade. In nutrition calorie defines the energy-producing potential of food. Actually, the calorie unit used by nutritionists is the so-called *large calorie,* or kilocalorie—1,000 calories—but it is customarily shortened to calorie. The body uses the calories in food to provide energy,

including heat, that the body needs to carry on the functions and processes of living. An adult weighing 140 pounds uses up about 1,600 calories a day—even if he or she spends all day in bed. The harder people work and the more they move about, the more calories they burn up. A construction worker, for instance, uses about 4,000 calories a day, an office

Kinds of food	Amount	Food energy (Calories)	Protein (Grams)	Fat (Grams)	Carbohydrate (Grams)
Beverages, milk, fats					
Beer	12 oz.	150	1	0	14
Butter or margarine	1 pat	25	T	4	T
Cocoa	1 cup	245	10	12	27
Cola beverages	12 oz.	145	0	0	37
Cream, half and-half	1 tbsp.	20	T	2	1
Gin, rum, vodka, whiskey	1-1/2 oz.	110	0	0	T
Milk, skim	1 cup	85	8	T	12
Milk, whole	1 cup	150	8	8	11
Oils, salad or cooking	1 tbsp.	120	0	14	0
Wine, table	3-1/2 oz.	85	T	0	4
Yogurt	1 cup	140	8	7	11
Breads, cereals, desserts, pasta, snacks					
Bagel	1	165	6	2	28
Bread:					
White	1 slice	70	2	1	13
Whole wheat, rye	1 slice	60	2-3	T-1	13
Breakfast cereals:					
Bran flakes	1 cup	105	4	1	28
Corn flakes	1 cup	95	2	T	21
Oatmeal	1 cup	130	5	2	23
Shredded wheat	1 piece	90	0	1	20
Brownie with nuts	1	95	1	6	10
Cakes (pieces):					
Angel food	1	135	3	T	32
Devil's food (iced)	1	235	3	8	40
Candy:					
Chocolate, milk	1 oz.	145	2	9	16
Gumdrops	1 oz.	100	T	T	25
Marshmallows	1 oz.	90	1	T	23
Chocolate, baking	1 oz.	145	3	15	8
Crackers, saltine	4	50	1	1	8
Danish pastry (4" diam.)	1	275	5	15	30
Doughnut	1	205	3	11	16
Honey	1 tbsp.	65	T	0	17
Ice cream	1 cup	270	5	14	32
Jams and preserves	1 tbsp.	55	T	T	14
Macaroni, plain	1 cup	190	7	1	39
Macaroni and cheese	1 cup	430	17	22	40

Kinds of food	Amount	Food energy (Calories)	Protein (Grams)	Fat (Grams)	Carbohydrate (Grams)
Muffin	1	120	3	4	17
Noodles	1 cup	200	7	2	37
Pancake (4" diam.)	1	50	2	2	9
Peanut butter	1 tbsp.	95	4	8	3
Pies (1/7 pc. of 9" pie):					
Apple	1	345	3	15	51
Pecan	1	495	6	27	61
Pizza, cheese (avg. slice)	1	145	6	4	22
Popcorn, plain	1 cup	25	1	T	5
Potato chips	10	115	1	8	10
Pretzel (thin twisted)	1	25	1	T	8
Pudding, tapioca	1 cup	220	8	8	28
Roll, frankfurter	1	120	3	2	21
Spaghetti, plain	1 cup	155	5	1	32
Spaghetti, tom. & cheese	1 cup	260	9	9	37
Sugar, white granular	1 tpsp.	45	0	0	12
Waffle (7" diam.)	1	205	7	8	27
Whipped cream	1 tpsp.	10	T	1	T
Fruits and juices					
Apple, raw (3" diam.)	1	80	T	1	20
Apple juice	1 cup	120	T	T	30
Apricots, raw	3	55	1	T	14
Apricots, canned, syrup	1 cup	220	2	T	57
Avocado, raw	1	370	5	37	13
Banana, raw	1	100	1	T	26
Blackberries, raw	1 cup	85	2	1	19
Blueberries, raw	1 cup	90	1	1	22
Cantaloupe, raw	1/2	80	2	T	20
Cherries, canned	1 cup	105	2	T	26
Cranberry juice, canned	1 cup	165	T	T	42
Dates, pitted	1 cup	490	4	1	130
Grapefruit juice	1 cup	95	1	T	23
Grapes, raw	1 cup	70	1	1	16
Lemonade	1 cup	105	T	T	28
Orange, raw	1	65	1	T	16
Orange juice	1 cup	110	2	T	26
Peach, raw	1	40	1	T	10
Pear, raw	1	100	1	1	25
Pineapple, canned, syrup	1 cup	190	1	T	49
Pineapple juice	1 cup	140	1	T	34

the contention of U.S. chemist and Nobel Prize winner Linus Pauling that taking a gram or more a day of vitamin C cuts the incidence and severity of colds. Even so, great numbers of people continue to dose themselves with vitamin C and are convinced that they get fewer colds than before they started the vitamin regimen. One explanation may be the placebo effect: if a person believes a treatment will help, it will.

TEA OR COFFEE CAFFEINE?

A teaspoon of tea leaves contains more of the stimulant drug caffeine than a teaspoon of ground coffee does. But the caffeine in tea is usually more diluted when served. As a result, a cup of tea contains only about 60 percent as much caffeine as a cup of coffee.

BAKER'S LEGACY *This crusty bread was baked more than 1,900 years ago. It was found in an oven in Pompeii, Italy, preserved by ash from the eruption of Vesuvius in A.D. 79.*

worker about 2,500. In terms of some specific activities, the average adult expends calories at about the following rates: running, 19.4 per minute; swimming, 11.2 per minute; bicycling, 8.2 per minute; walking, 5.2 per minute. As long as the calories in what you eat about equal the calories you expend, your weight should remain constant within a few pounds. People who eat more food than they use put on weight—about 1 pound for every 3,500 excess calories. No one ideal diet exists for everybody; the best general rule is to eat with moderation a variety of foods in the different groups listed below. The figures in this chart are based on U.S. Department of Agriculture data. "T" stands for Trace amount.

Kinds of food	Amount	Food energy (Calories)	Protein (Grams)	Fat (Grams)	Carbohydrate (Grams)
Plum, raw	1	30	T	T	8
Prunes, cooked	1 cup	255	2	1	67
Strawberries, raw	1 cup	55	1	1	13
Watermelon, 4" × 8" wedge	1	110	2	1	27
Meat, cheese, eggs, poultry, fish					
Bacon (slices)	2	85	4	8	1
Beef, hamburger	3 oz.	235	20	17	0
Beef, roast (lean)	3 oz.	210	25	12	0
Beef, steak, broiled	3 oz.	220	24	13	0
Bologna (slices)	2	170	6	16	1
Cheese:					
American	1 oz.	105	6	9	T
Blue or Roquefort	1 oz.	105	6	8	1
Cheddar	1 oz.	115	7	9	1
Cottage	1 cup	235	28	10	6
Chicken, broiled	3 oz.	115	20	3	0
Chicken, fried	3 oz.	215	26	10	2
Corned beef (canned)	3 oz.	185	22	10	0
Egg, whole, boiled	1	80	6	6	T
Fish and shellfish:					
Clams, raw	3 oz.	65	11	1	2
Haddock, fried	3 oz.	140	17	5	5
Oysters, raw	1 cup	160	20	4	8
Salmon, canned	3 oz.	120	17	5	0
Tuna, canned	3 oz.	170	25	7	0
Frankfurter (hot dog)	2 oz.	170	7	16	1
Ham, baked	3 oz.	185	25	8	0
Lamb chop, broiled	3.1 oz.	360	18	32	0
Lamb leg, roasted	3 oz.	235	22	16	0
Liver, beef, fried	3 oz.	195	22	9	5
Pork chop	2.7 oz.	305	19	25	0
Pork sausage links	2	120	4	12	T
Salami	3 oz.	450	20	40	T
Veal cutlet	3 oz.	185	23	9	0
Vegetables and nuts					
Almonds, chopped	1 cup	775	24	70	25
Asparagus	1 cup	30	3	T	5

Kinds of food	Amount	Food energy (Calories)	Protein (Grams)	Fat (Grams)	Carbohydrate (Grams)
Beans, green	1 cup	30	2	T	7
Beans, lima	1 cup	260	16	1	49
Beets	1 cup	55	2	T	12
Broccoli	1 cup	40	5	T	7
Cabbage, raw	1 cup	15	1	T	4
Carrot, raw (7" long)	1	30	1	T	7
Cashew nuts	1 cup	785	24	64	41
Cauliflower, cooked	1 cup	31	3	T	6
Celery, raw, diced	1 cup	20	1	T	5
Corn, sweet	1 ear	70	2	1	16
Cucumber, peeled	1	20	1	T	5
Lettuce, iceberg	1 head	70	5	T	16
Mushrooms, raw	1 cup	20	2	T	3
Onion, raw (2-1/2" diam.)	1	40	2	T	10
Peanuts, roasted	1 cup	840	38	72	27
Peas, green, canned	1 cup	150	8	1	29
Pecan halves	1 cup	810	11	84	17
Pepper, green, raw	1 pod	15	1	T	4
Potato, baked	1	145	4	T	33
Potato, french-fry pieces	10	135	2	7	18
Potato, mashed	1 cup	135	4	2	27
Radishes, raw	10	10	T	T	2
Rice, cooked	1 cup	225	4	T	50
Spinach	1 cup	40	5	T	6
Sweet potato, baked	1	160	2	1	37
Tomato, raw (3" diam.)	1	40	2	T	9
Tomato juice	1 cup	45	2	T	10
Walnuts, black	1 cup	785	26	74	19
Sauces, soups, and salad dressings					
Barbecue sauce	1 cup	230	4	17	20
Bouillon cube	1	5	1	T	T
Cream mushroom soup	1 cup	215	7	14	16
Cream tomato soup	1 cup	175	7	7	23
Salad dressings:					
Blue cheese	1 tbsp.	75	1	8	1
French	1 tbsp.	65	T	6	3
Mayonnaise	1 tbsp.	100	T	11	T
Tartar sauce	1 tbsp.	75	T	8	1
Vegetarian soup	1 cup	80	2	2	13

Chemistry—the study of matter

CARBON, THE KEY TO LIFE

If life has formed elsewhere in the universe, it is probably based on molecules of carbon, just as it is on earth. Of all the elements, carbon is the one most likely to form the complex compounds associated with life.

Almost any number of carbon atoms can join together to form stable molecules. As a result, a virtually endless variety of molecular "backbones" can be constructed from carbon. Giant molecules, such as those that make up natural proteins and synthetic plastics, are based on carbon. Very few other elements can form such large molecules, and those that can, such as sulfur, are more restricted as to other elements with which they will combine.

Each carbon atom can link with up to four other atoms, including other carbon atoms. So the number of possible compounds escalates rapidly as the number of carbon atoms in a molecule increases.

Propane, used as bottled gas, has the chemical formula $CH_3CH_2CH_3$, which means that each molecule contains three carbon and eight hydrogen atoms. Butane (C_4H_{10}), a similar gas, has four carbon atoms. The four atoms can be arranged in a single chain, or the fourth carbon atom may form a branch in the middle. These different structural forms give rise to two compounds—known as isomers, from Greek words meaning "the same parts"—that have slightly different properties. The straight-chain form is normal (n-) butane, and the other is named isobutane.

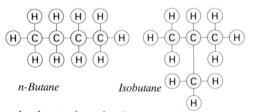

n-Butane   *Iso*butane

As the number of carbon atoms in a molecule increases, more isomeric forms of the same molecule become possible. By the time a molecule has 40 carbon atoms (as do some molecules in crude oil), the theoretically possible number of isomers has risen to 62.5 trillion. So there is a vast array of new compounds whose properties are still being explored.

CAESAR'S LAST GASP

There are at least as many molecules in a single teaspoon of water as there are teaspoons of water in the entire Atlantic Ocean. Even when all the molecules in a single breath of air have been dispersed evenly in the earth's atmosphere, there will still be one or two of the same ones taken into the lungs with every subsequent breath.

Every time you breathe in, you inhale one or two of the same molecules that you inhaled with the first breath you took as a baby. And each breath also contains some molecules from the last gasp of Julius Caesar, Napoleon, and every other person in history.

THE ALCHEMISTS

As the study of chemistry developed in the late Middle Ages in Europe, much knowledge came from the work of Arab alchemists, who had preserved and developed scientific scholarship during the Dark Ages. The word *chemistry* comes from the mystical science of alchemy, from the Arabic *al-kimiya* ("philosopher's stone"), which may be derived from an Arab name for Egypt, *Khemia*. Other chemical terms, such as *alkali* and *alcohol*, are derived from Arabic words too. The prefix *al-* is simply the Arabic word for "the."

PLASTIC BEGINNINGS

Celluloid was the first plastic in the modern sense of the word. It was invented in 1870 by John W. Hyatt and won him a $10,000 cash prize from the New York City firm of Phelan & Collender, which needed an ivory substitute to use in making billiard balls. To make his prizewinning substance, Hyatt hit upon a method of mixing camphor with pyroxylin, a flammable mixture of cellulose nitrates, then molding the stuff under heat and pressure and finally allowing it to cool and harden under normal atmospheric pressure.

After its first use in billiard balls, celluloid was employed in making dental plates, combs, collars, cuffs, and other useful objects. The first completely synthetic plastic, made from the molecules up, was Bakelite. It was invented in 1909 by the Belgian-born U.S. chemist Leo H. Baekeland and named after him.

FOUR ELEMENTS OF ARISTOTLE

For nearly 2,000 years most scholars believed that everything was made up of combinations of just four elements: air, earth, fire, and water. The belief was established by the Greek philosopher Aristotle (384–322 B.C.) and held sway until the 17th century. Then scientists began to insist on direct observation and experiment, rather than abstract philosophy, as the most reliable way to acquire new knowledge.

In chemistry one of the first to challenge Aristotle and the alchemists was the Irishman Robert Boyle (1627–91). In *Certain Physiological Essays* (1661) he defined the modern idea of an element as a substance that cannot be broken down into simpler ones. Boyle also discovered the physical law now named after him, which states that at a constant temperature, the volume of a gas varies inversely with its pressure. If a quantity of gas is compressed into a third of its original volume, for example, its pressure will triple.

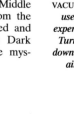

VACUUM FLASK *Robert Boyle used a pump like this in his experiments on gas pressure. Turning the handle dragged down a piston, and so sucked air out of the glass sphere.*

SNOOZE THAT LED TO DISCOVERY

The molecular structure of benzene—the parent of a family of hydrocarbons found in coal tar and known as aromatic compounds because of their pleasant smell—came to a German chemist as he drifted between wakefulness and sleep. The chemist, Friedrich Kekulé von Stradonitz (1829–96), was working as a professor at the University of Ghent, in Belgium, in 1862.

Kekulé knew that the atoms in any molecule are linked by chemical hooks, known as valence bonds. Carbon has four such hooks, hydrogen one. So one carbon atom can link with four hydrogen atoms to form methane. Kekulé also knew that atoms could be joined by double or even triple bonds. In the gas ethylene (C_2H_4), for instance, two carbon atoms are joined by a double bond with each other, and by single bonds with four hydrogen atoms.

In benzene, however, six carbon atoms are linked with six hydrogen atoms. Try as he might, Kekulé could not work out how the atoms could be linked in a chain without leaving some hooks unattached—a chemical impossibility. Then, half awake one night, he saw an animated image of a chain of carbon atoms closing upon itself, like a snake biting its tail.

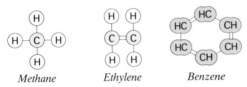

| Methane | Ethylene | Benzene |

Grasping at once what the image implied, Kekulé spent the rest of the night determining the validity of the idea: that the carbon atoms in benzene were arranged not in a chain but in a ring. This discovery was the theoretical basis of the prosperous German dye industry and led to the discovery of toluene, from which the explosive TNT (*trinitrotoluene*) is derived.

THE FIRST FIZZY DRINK

Joseph Priestley, who shares the credit for the discovery of oxygen with the Swedish chemist Karl Wilhelm Scheele, also invented the carbonated drink. In Leeds, England, in the 1770s, Priestley lived near a brewery, and it provided him with abundant carbon dioxide for his experiments with gases. In 1772 he published directions for "impregnating water with fixed air (carbon dioxide), in order to communicate to it the peculiar spirits and virtues of Pyrmont water." Pyrmont was the name of a popular mineral water from a spring near Hamelin, Germany. Priestley hoped that his carbonated water might be effective against scurvy. It was not, but it caught on anyway.

ACID TESTS

Litmus, a dye derived from lichen, turns pink if dipped into acid and blue in an alkali. It is only one of numerous natural pigments that change color depending on acidity. Red cabbage, for instance, turns bright red only when vinegar, which contains acetic acid, is added to the water in which it is cooked. If the acidity is neutralized with an alkali, such as bicarbonate of soda, the red pigment in the cabbage turns blue-green.

Flowers are sensitive to acidity too. Hydrangeas, for example, tend to grow pink in alkaline soil and blue in acid soil—the reaction of litmus in reverse.

TALE OF TWO CHEMISTS

Oxygen is now known to be essential to combustion. But the English clergyman Joseph Priestley (1733–1804), who shared in the discovery of oxygen, died without being convinced of its importance. Priestley subscribed to the phlogiston theory, which held that while burning, objects gave off a substance called phlogiston.

The phlogiston theory began to be discredited soon after the discovery of oxygen when Antoine Lavoisier (1743–94) established in the late 1770s that oxygen was present in the atmosphere and correctly described its role in combustion. Lavoisier, a French chemist, gave oxygen its modern name (Priestley had called it "dephlogisticated air"). Because of his work with oxygen, as well as his quantitative methods of chemical analysis, Lavoisier is regarded as a founder of modern chemistry. A treatise he published in 1787, *Methods of Chemical Nomenclature,* pioneered the custom of naming chemical compounds after the elements they contain. But Lavoisier did not live to see the effect of his ideas. Denounced for his work as a tax collector—one of several important government posts he held—he was guillotined during the French Revolution at the age of 51.

PARTNERS IN SCIENCE
Lavoisier's wife worked closely with him. She took notes on his experiments, and learned English so that she could keep track of British discoveries.

LAVOISIER'S LAB By heating mercury in the retort, which made the water level in the bell jar (far right) rise, Lavoisier showed that a burning object absorbed gas (oxygen) from the air. It did not give off phlogiston, as Priestley believed.

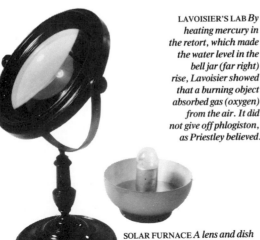

SOLAR FURNACE *A lens and dish used by Priestley in his study of the process of burning.*

ASH THAT MAKES FIRE

Catalysts are substances that help chemical reactions to take place in other substances while they themselves remain unchanged in the process. Catalysts are used widely by industry and in living organisms. Enzymes, for instance, are natural catalysts that speed up by many thousands of times the ability of an animal's body to digest food.

Cigarette ash can also be a catalyst. If a lighted match is held to a sugar cube (placed on a dish for safety), the sugar will char but not burn. If cigarette ash is dropped on the sugar, however, traces of elements in the ash act as catalysts, speeding up the sugar's chemical reaction and causing it to catch fire.

FIRST OF THE SYNTHETIC DYES

Mauveine, the first synthetic dye, was discovered by accident by an 18-year-old English research assistant. William Henry Perkin made the dye from coal tar in his home laboratory during a vacation from his job in London in 1856. He had been trying to make an

THE PERIODIC TABLE

Everything in the universe, living and nonliving, is made up of combinations of a few basic substances: the chemical elements. Each element consists solely of atoms with the same nuclear charge. Of the 108 known elements, 92 are found in nature. The remaining 16—known as transuranium elements—have been created by nuclear bombardment in laboratories since 1934. Atoms differ from one another in the number of protons and neutrons in the nucleus, and in the number of electrons surrounding the nucleus. The number of protons is known as the element's atomic number. Hydrogen, with one proton and one electron, is the simplest of all elements and has the atomic number 1. The most complex naturally occurring element, uranium, has the atomic number 92.

The periodic table was first devised by a Russian chemist, Dmitri Mendeleev (1834–1907), in 1869. A modern table is shown below. Each square represents an element, identified and characterized by its atomic number, chemical symbol, name, and atomic mass. The atomic mass is not usually a whole number, because most elements are a mixture of isotopes—atoms with the same number of protons but different numbers of neutrons—and the figure reflects the isotopes' relative abundance. Any element whose atomic mass appears in parentheses is very unstable, and the mass is of the

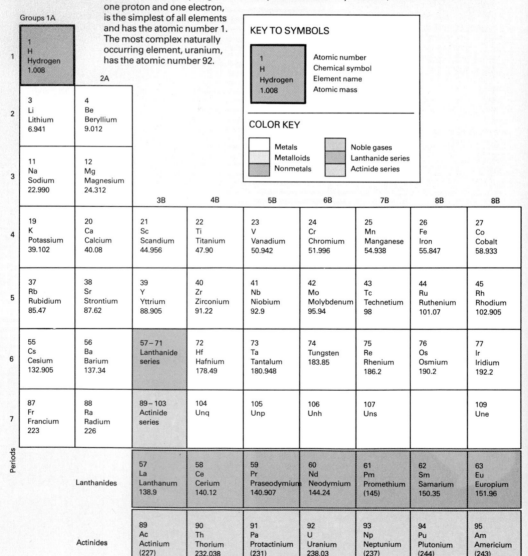

artificial form of quinine, a compound that occurs naturally in cinchona bark and that has been used to treat malaria.

Perkin's discovery was followed by other synthetic dyes, which rapidly put out of business growers of natural dyestuffs, such as indigo and root madder. More than 7,000 synthetic dyes are now in use.

MAN WHO PREDICTED ELEMENTS
Dmitri Mendeleev (1834–1907), the Russian chemist who published the first periodic table of the elements in 1869, deliberately left gaps in the table for three elements that had not yet been discovered, but which he predicted did exist. All subsequent periodic tables, such as the one below, are based on his concepts.

So precise were Mendeleev's groupings of the elements according to their atomic structures and chemical properties that he was able to spell out in detail the nature of "missing" elements years before they were isolated. Mendeleev's gaps were eventually filled by the elements now known as gallium (discovered in 1875), scandium (1879), and germanium (1886).

longest-lived isotope that has been observed. All the isotopes of any element share the same chemical properties but may differ in other ways, such as in their degree of radioactivity.

Each column in the table contains elements with similar properties. For example, the vertical column Group 1A consists of soft metals—lithium, sodium, and so on—that react with water to release hydrogen and form alkaline solutions. From left to right across the table, the elements become less metallic, eventually becoming typical nonmetals, such as carbon, sulfur, and chlorine. The horizontal rows are called periods. The two rows shown separately at the foot of the table have been placed there to make the table more compact and, more importantly, because all the elements in each series (lanthanides and actinides) have almost identical chemical properties and can, in effect, be assigned one position in the table.

Elements with atomic numbers greater than 92 are produced in particle accelerators. The research group that first produces the element gets to name it. Conflicts over priority have arisen. The International Union of Pure and Applied Chemistry (IUPAC) has proposed that, until priority claims are settled, elements should be given names that reflect their atomic numbers. The symbol for such an element consists of the prefix *un*, plus a letter designating its atomic number. The letter is the first letter of the following roots: *nil* for 0, *un* for 1, *bi* for 2, *tri* for 3, *quad* for 4, *pent* for 5, *hex* for 6, *sept* for 7, *oct* for 8, *en* for 9. Thus element 104 becomes Unq; element 105, Unp; and so on.

			3A	4A	5A	6A	7A	0
								2 He Helium 4.003
			5 B Boron 10.811	6 C Carbon 12.011	7 N Nitrogen 14.01	8 O Oxygen 16	9 F Fluorine 18.998	10 Ne Neon 20.183
			13 Al Aluminum 26.982	14 Si Silicon 28.09	15 P Phosphorus 30.974	16 S Sulfur 32.064	17 Cl Chlorine 35.453	18 Ar Argon 39.948

8B	1B	2B						
28 Ni Nickel 58.71	29 Cu Copper 63.54	30 Zn Zinc 65.37	31 Ga Gallium 69.72	32 Ge Germanium 72.59	33 As Arsenic 74.922	34 Se Selenium 78.96	35 Br Bromine 79.90	36 Kr Krypton 83.80
46 Pd Palladium 106.4	47 Ag Silver 107.9	48 Cd Cadmium 112.40	49 In Indium 114.82	50 Sn Tin 118.7	51 Sb Antimony 121.8	52 Te Tellurium 127.60	53 I Iodine 126.904	54 Xe Xenon 131.30
78 Pt Platinum 195.09	79 Au Gold 196.967	80 Hg Mercury 200.59	81 Tl Thallium 204.37	82 Pb Lead 207.19	83 Bi Bismuth 208.980	84 Po Polonium (209)	85 At Astatine (210)	86 Rn Radon 222

64 Gd Gadolinium 157.25	65 Tb Terbium 158.924	66 Dy Dysprosium 162.50	67 Ho Holmium 164.930	68 Er Erbium 167.26	69 Tm Thulium 168.934	70 Yb Ytterbium 173.04	71 Lu Lutetium 174.97
96 Cm Curium (247)	97 Bk Berkelium (247)	98 Cf Californium (251)	99 Es Einsteinium (252)	100 Fm Fermium (257)	101 Md Mendelevium (258)	102 No Nobelium (259)	103 Lr Lawrencium (260)

Physics—the science of energy

THE MAN WHO SHOUTED "EUREKA"

Little is known for certain about the Greek physicist and mathematician Archimedes except his dates (287–212 B.C.) and his home: Syracuse in Sicily. But the extraordinary story of his greatest discovery has survived for more than 2,000 years. It was first recorded in a book on architecture published about 30 B.C. by the Roman architect Vitruvius.

The discovery is said to have resulted when King Hieron II of Syracuse asked Archimedes to find out whether a goldsmith had lied about the purity of the gold used to make the king's new crown. The king suspected that the smith had made the crown out of a mixture of gold and less valuable silver.

Archimedes reasoned that an alloy would be bulkier than the same weight of pure gold, because silver is less dense than gold. But it was difficult to measure the volume of the crown. Inspiration came when, getting into a bathtub, Archimedes slopped water over the side. He realized that anything put into a tub of water would displace its own volume of water. So all he had to do was to compare the amount of water displaced by the crown against the amount of water displaced by an equal weight of pure gold. Elated by his breakthrough, Archimedes is said to have leaped naked from the bath and rushed through the streets of Syracuse shouting the Greek version of "I have found the answer!"—*"Eureka!"*

Back at home, Archimedes found that the suspect crown did displace more water than a gold block of the same weight—proving that the crown was bulkier, and that the king had indeed been cheated. The fate of the goldsmith is unknown.

CONVERSATIONS WITH A DOG

James Clerk Maxwell (1831–79), the Scottish physicist who described the existence of electromagnetic waves 20 years before they were actually observed, used to hold imaginary scientific conversations with his dog, Tobi. Maxwell said that he often worked out his ideas in this way, even during noisy parties.

Maxwell published his theory that light was merely one form of the much wider spectrum of electromagnetic radiation in 1865. Not until the late 1880s did a German physicist, Heinrich Hertz (1857–94), confirm this by producing in laboratory experiments the invisible waves that now carry radio transmissions around the world.

ODD COUPLE OF THE IONOSPHERE

The Kennelly-Heaviside layer—now known as the E region of the ionosphere, an electrically conductive band in the atmosphere that reflects radio waves back to earth—was predicted independently in 1902 by two former telegraph operators, 22 years before the layer's existence was verified.

Both were Englishmen, but Arthur E. Kennelly (1861–1939), after teenage service as a telegraph operator, emigrated to the United States and became Thomas Alva Edison's chief electrical assistant. Acquiring his knowledge of physics and electricity mainly through self-directed study and practical experimentation, Kennelly went on to become a professor of engineering at both Harvard and the Massachusetts Institute of Technology.

No less brilliant than Kennelly, but evidently far more eccentric, was Oliver Heaviside (1850–1925), whose independent prediction of the ionosphere layer trailed Kennelly's by just a few months. At the age of 71, his fame as a scientist secure, Heaviside complained that he was too poor to pay his dues to scientific societies. He often started work at about 10 P.M. and worked through until dawn. And he is said to have startled visitors by dressing bizarrely: on one occasion "with a large blanket over his head, held in place by a rope tied round his neck." Yet Heaviside generously extended his scientific help to all who asked, with the result that his seaside cottage at Torquay, England, became known as "the inexhaustible cavity."

In 1912, when the electron and the nucleus were the only known components of the atom, Heaviside wrote: "As the universe is boundless one way toward the great, so it is equally boundless the other way toward the small. From the atom to the electron is a great step. But it is not finality." Scientists have since discovered more than 100 subatomic particles, and the hunt for still smaller particles continues today.

EDISON'S LOW GRADES

Thomas Alva Edison, the American whose inventions included the phonograph, a practical electric light, the microphone, and "talkie" films, had only 3 months of formal schooling—in 1854 when he was 7 years old. And that ended with his running away after a teacher said that his brain was addled.

Edison later recalled his unhappy 3 months at the Port Huron, Michigan, school run by the Reverend G. B. Engle: "I used never to be able to get along. I used to feel that the teachers did not sympathize with me and that my father thought I was stupid." Edison went on to become one of the greatest practical scientists in history. When he died in 1931, he held almost 1,300 patents, almost one patent for every 3 weeks of his life.

ELECTRICAL HAT TRICK

The dynamo, the transformer, and the direct-current motor used to drive battery-powered machines today were all invented in a single year by one man. The year was 1831 and the man a 39-year-old British scientist, Michael Faraday (1791–1867).

AMPÈRE'S OVERSIGHTS

André Ampère, the French physicist after whom the unit of electrical current (the ampere, or amp) is named, had observed the voltage-altering effect now used in modern transformers in 1820—10 years before Michael Faraday demonstrated it. But he had dismissed the effect as unimportant and ignored it.

Ampère (1775–1836) overlooked another chance in 1832: the chance to develop a modern electrical generator. Faraday demonstrated the principle, in the form of a dynamo, in 1831, and a year later a Frenchman named Hippolyte Pixii built an improved model. Like Faraday's dynamo, Pixii's machine generated

TUG OF AIR *In the Magdeburg hemisphere experiment in 1657, German physicist Otto von Guericke (1602–86) pitted horses against a vacuum created by pumping air from between two fitted copper hemispheres. It took 16 horses to separate them.*

NEWTON'S LAWS OF MOTION

The three laws of motion devised by English physicist Sir Isaac Newton (1642–1727) explain the basic principles that, except under extraordinary conditions or at very high speeds, govern the movements of all objects on the earth and in space. First published in 1687, the laws opened the way for the inventions and calculations that, nearly 3 centuries later, took man to the moon. The laws are:

1. A body continues in a state of rest, or of motion at constant speed in a straight line, except when this state is changed by forces acting upon it.
2. Force is equal to mass multiplied by acceleration. In other words, a given force on a given mass will produce a given acceleration. On twice the mass, it will produce half the acceleration. If the force on a given mass is doubled, however, the acceleration will double too.
3. To every action, there is an equal and opposite reaction.

THE FOUR LAWS OF THERMODYNAMICS

The classical laws of thermodynamics, which grew out of observations of how energy in the form of heat passed from one body of matter to another and deal with the conversion of energy from one form to another, were devised by several scientists during the late 19th and early 20th centuries.

The final law to be worked out was given the name of the zeroth law (bearing the number zero) because, although it was added later, logically it belongs ahead of the other three, which by then had already been given numbers. The four laws in brief:

0. No heat will flow between any two bodies that are at the same temperature.
1. Energy can be neither created nor destroyed. So a body can gain or lose heat (or any other form of energy) only by taking it from or passing it to its environment (or to another body).
2. Heat will not pass spontaneously from a cold body to a hotter one.
3. It is impossible to cool a body right down to the temperature of absolute zero $-273.16°C$ ($-459.67°F$), the lowest possible temperature in the universe, because to do so would require the presence of a still colder body.

All four laws are connected with the concept of entropy, which is a measure of how much useful work can be extracted from a given system. Energy can be extracted from a system only by increasing its degree of entropy.

For instance, a hot-water bottle, filled with boiling water and placed in a cold bed, will pass heat to the bed, losing its own heat. But once bottle and bed are at the same lukewarm temperature, no more useful work can be extracted from the bottle. The dissipated heat cannot be recaptured.

Since the same principle is at work in the universe as a whole, some scientists believe that the energy the universe contains will also, eventually, be dissipated evenly and irrecoverably throughout space. This stage of maximum and universal entropy is known as the "heat death" of the universe.

"alternating" current, a current in which the positive and negative terminals are constantly reversed.

Pixii took his device to Ampère, who said that people would not want current that flowed first in one direction and then the other. For 50 years little use was made of alternating current. But power plants around the world now supply alternating-current electricity generated by machines descended from Pixii's and Faraday's original designs.

HOW BRUSHES GOT THE BRUSH-OFF

The commutator devised by André Ampère to convert alternating current to direct current had a major drawback: brushes. To cancel out the constantly reversing current generated by a dynamo, electrical contacts had to rub, or brush, against the spinning core, just as they do in the traditional generator that recharges the direct-current battery in a car. This constant rubbing meant that the contacts wore out quickly and had to be replaced. Similarly, motors that required direct current had to have brushes.

The man who eventually discovered how to do away with the inefficient brushes was Nikola Tesla (1856–1943). Tesla was born in Croatia (now part of Yugoslavia) but emigrated to the United States in 1884 and became an American citizen.

A compulsive worker, Tesla never married and had few close friends because he thought they would interfere with his studies. As a young man, rather than accept the distractions of a regular job, he would dig ditches from time to time to earn money, then retreat to his laboratory once more to continue his quest for a brushless motor. Finally, in 1888, Tesla received a patent on his big breakthrough, an alternating-current motor that he declared would "dominate the world of electric drives."

It did. About 95 percent of the power of all the world's electric motors—from washing machines and kitchen mixers to giant industrial motors—can be traced to Tesla's design. Tesla patented his design in 1888 and later sold the rights to the Westinghouse Electric Company for $1 million. But he plowed the money back into his work, and by the mid-1890s there was nothing left.

NAME OF FEAR

A 20th-century German physicist had a morbid fear of a name—the name, ironically, of one of the world's greatest physicists, Sir Isaac Newton. The German, Professor Philipp Lenard (1862–1947), was born more than a century after the British scientist died; yet he could not stand to speak Newton's name, or even to see or hear it. In lectures at the universities of Heidelberg and Kiel, where he worked, Lenard would turn his back if Newton's name had to be mentioned. A student would then write it on the blackboard, and it would have to be rubbed out again before Lenard could continue. Lenard's phobia was linked with a passionate dislike of Britain in general and of British scientists in particular. In 1914, in one of his books, he accused all British scientists of plagiarizing the successes of German physicists. Such delusions later led him to become an ardent supporter of the Nazi cause and a rabid critic of "Jewish" science.

Nevertheless, Lenard was a pioneering researcher in the study of cathode rays and the structure of the atom, and in 1905 he won the Nobel Prize in physics.

Nuclear physics

ACCIDENTAL DISCOVERY

Uranium's radioactive properties were not discovered through research, but accidentally. In 1896, inspired by the discovery of X-rays, the French scientist Henri Becquerel, an expert on fluorescence—the ability of some substances to give off visible rays—was trying to discover whether other substances gave off invisible rays (radiation) after exposure to sunlight. In the course of his experiments, Becquerel left a sample of pitchblende, a mineral containing uranium, in a drawer on top of an envelope containing an unexposed photographic plate. When he developed this plate, it was fogged. Becquerel quickly realized that radiation from the mineral was responsible for this, and hence that the substance was radioactive.

THE ATOMIC AGE IN BRIEF

1895 Discovery of X-rays by German physicist Wilhelm Roentgen (1845–1923).

1896 French physicist Henri Becquerel (1852–1908) discovers radioactivity.

1897 British physicist Sir Joseph Thomson (1856–1940) discovers the electron.

1898 Physicists Pierre and Marie Curie (1859–1906 and 1867–1934) discover radium.

1905 German-born Albert Einstein (1879–1955) suggests mass can be converted to energy.

1911 New Zealand physicist Ernest, Lord Rutherford (1871–1937) discovers the atomic nucleus.

1913 Danish physicist Niels Bohr (1885–1962) describes the structure of the atom.

1919 Rutherford splits the atom.

1932 American chemist Harold Urey (1893–1981) discovers deuterium.

1932 English physicist Sir James Chadwick (1891–1974) discovers the neutron.

1932 U.S. physicist Carl Anderson (1905–   ) discovers the positron.

1932 Britain's Sir John Cockcroft (1897–1967) and Ireland's Ernest Walton (1903–   ) use a particle accelerator to split lithium into two alpha particles.

1938 Austria's Lise Meitner (1878–1968) and Germany's Otto Hahn (1879–1968) and Fritz Strassmann (1902–80) discover nuclear fission.

1940 Austrian-born Otto Frisch (1904–79) and German-born Rudolf Peierls (1907–   ) calculate critical mass of uranium 235 and tell British government about a possible superbomb—the atom bomb.

1941 U.S. chemist Glenn Seaborg (1912–   ) isolates plutonium, the key element in a nuclear bomb.

1942 Italian-born physicist Enrico Fermi (1901–54) builds the first nuclear reactor (below) as part of the Manhattan Project, U.S. effort to produce an atomic bomb.

1945 First nuclear explosion, at Alamogordo, N.M. U.S.A. drops atomic bombs on Japanese cities of Hiroshima and Nagasaki.

1949 First Soviet nuclear test.

1951 First nuclear electricity generated from AEC's experimental breeder reactor in Idaho.

1952 Hydrogen bomb, employing thermonuclear fusion of deuterium, detonated by U.S.A. at Eniwetok atoll, Marshall Islands, in the western Pacific.

1953 European Center for Nuclear Research (CERN) founded near Geneva.

1956 Calder Hall, world's first commercial-scale nuclear power plant, established in England.

1964 The omega-minus elementary particle, predicted by theory, is discovered at Brookhaven National Laboratory (Upton, N.Y.), launching the search for more elusive subatomic particles.

1979 Accident at Three Mile Island (Pa.) nuclear power plant releases radioactive material.

1980s While threat of accidents slows nuclear power development in U.S.A., other nations accelerate development. Accident at Chernobyl plant, in the Ukraine, U.S.S.R., April 1986, raises new concerns in European nations about increasing dependence on nuclear energy. Meanwhile, nuclear disarmament remains an elusive goal of world powers.

CHICAGO PILE *A contemporary sketch of the world's first nuclear reactor. Built in a squash court beneath a Chicago football stadium, it ran for a few minutes on December 2, 1942, proving that nuclear power was feasible.*

SAVED BY A DRAFT

The life of the Polish physicist and Nobel Prize winner Marie Curie (1867–1934) was probably saved by the drafty conditions in the Paris loft where she and her French husband, Pierre, were attempting to isolate the element radium. The drafts prevented her from inhaling lethal quantities of radioactive dust.

The mysterious element was successfully isolated in 1898, together with another element that Marie named polonium, after her native Poland. She continued to investigate the properties of radioactive materials until she died in 1934 of leukemia caused by the radiation from the elements she was studying. Pierre had died in 1906 when he was run over by a cart in a Paris street.

BREAKING DOWN THE ATOM

The New Zealand–born physicist Ernest Rutherford (1871–1937) was the first to show that the atom is not the smallest unit of matter. He proved this in the early 1900s with an ingeniously simple particle detector that he built himself in his laboratory in Manchester, England. The instrument allowed him to observe the flashes of what he termed alpha particles, one form of the radiation produced by radioactive decay.

By counting the flashes, Rutherford found that the particles could be deflected, nearly reversed, by a thin metal sheet placed in their path. This astonished Rutherford. It was as if bullets were bouncing back from a piece of tissue paper.

In 1911 Rutherford concluded that all atoms must have a central, positively charged nucleus. It was these nuclei that were massive enough to repel the positively charged alpha particles hitting the metal sheet. The nucleus, he also concluded, was surrounded by negatively charged electrons, circling the nucleus in the way that planets orbit the sun. For these and other discoveries, Rutherford has been called the father of nuclear science.

INFINITE SPACE

An atom is almost entirely empty space, since more than 99.9 percent of its mass is contained in its infinitesimal core, the nucleus. The word *nucleus* itself comes from a Latin word meaning "little nut." If an atom were the size of a soccer ball, its nucleus would still be invisible to the naked eye. If the nucleus were magnified to the size of a tennis ball, its nearest electron would be nearly half a mile away.

RADIATION BLOCKS

Radioactive elements decay in different ways, giving off particles or combinations of particles with very different properties. Some elements emit alpha particles, each particle containing two protons and two neutrons. Some give off beta particles—fast-moving electrons with either a negative or a positive electrical charge. Other elements emit neutrons or gamma radiation—a high-energy version of X-rays. Still others give off neutrinos, particles that have no electrical charge and virtually no mass.

The material required to block any of these types of radiation varies hugely. A sheet of paper is enough to stop an alpha particle. A sheet of tinfoil will stop beta particles. Gamma rays and neutrons, however, can penetrate 7 feet of concrete. And neutrinos can pass right through the earth.

RADIOACTIVE PEOPLE

Every human is naturally radioactive. This is because the body normally contains elements that have radioactive isotopes. Potassium, an essential constituent of

ATOM TRACKS *Like the vapor trails of jets, white lines of water droplets mark the paths of unseen atomic particles in a laboratory cloud chamber. These tracks, photographed in 1932, record the splitting of nitrogen nuclei—the first splitting of the atom—by physicist Ernest Rutherford.*

DEATH CLOUD *A vast mushroom cloud rises over the Japanese city of Nagasaki. The atomic blast, pictured here seconds after the detonation on August 9, 1945, killed or wounded about 75,000 people and leveled a third of the city. Yet by today's standards the bomb was small: 20 kilotons, or one-fiftieth of a megaton.*

body tissues, includes a tiny amount of the radioactive isotope potassium 40. Another example is radioactive carbon 14, which is produced in the atmosphere by the action of cosmic rays on carbon compounds and is absorbed by living organisms.

NATURAL REACTOR

The world's longest recorded nuclear chain reaction—successive splitting of uranium nuclei, as in a nuclear reactor—started spontaneously in what is now the African country of Gabon about a billion years ago and continued for more than 100,000 years. The reaction occurred because of uranium deposits there.

Evidence of the prehistoric chain reaction came to light in 1972. French scientists noticed that the concentration of the fissile isotope uranium 235 in ore from a mine at Oklo was as low as 0.29 percent, compared with 0.72 percent in natural uranium, suggesting that the uranium's natural rate of decay into other isotopes and other elements had been speeded up by a spontaneous nuclear reaction.

Such a chain reaction would be impossible today because the ever-decreasing concentration of uranium 235 in natural ores is now too low. At least 1 part per 100 is necessary to trigger a spontaneous reaction.

NUCLEAR COURT

A disused squash court under Stagg Field football stadium at the University of Chicago was chosen as the site of the world's first man-made nuclear reactor in 1942. The reason was security; it was thought that the reactor would attract less attention there than in a new building. The reactor itself was built by a team of scientists under the Italian physicist Enrico Fermi (1901–54). It was operated for only a few minutes, to show that a nuclear chain reaction was possible.

Chicago Pile No. 1, as it came to be called, consisted of a honeycomb of 57 layers of machined graphite bricks. The bricks were drilled with holes—22,000 in all—into which balls of uranium metal and compressed uranium oxide were inserted. The total amounts involved were about 40 tons of uranium and 400 tons of graphite. Because so much graphite dust was released during construction, the pile was built inside an airtight balloon, which was deflated when the pile was completed.

The pile was activated on December 2, 1942. Control rods made of cadmium, a neutron-absorbing material, were slowly withdrawn until there were enough free neutrons for the chain reaction to become self-sustaining.

SCRAM FOR SAFETY

The main emergency safety device in Chicago Pile No. 1 was a shutdown control rod hanging from a rope—and a scientist with an ax. If the chain reaction seemed to be becoming uncontrollable, the scientist was supposed to chop through the rope and let the cadmium control rod drop into the pile. Ever since, the emergency shutdown of a reactor has been called a scram, standing for *safety control rod ax man*.

UNDERGRADUATE A-BOMB

In 1976 John Aristotle Phillips, a 21-year-old senior at Princeton University, designed an atomic bomb in 4 months using information he obtained entirely from unclassified sources. In a 34-page thesis, the physics major presented plans for a plutonium device packing a charge about one-third as powerful as the A-bomb exploded over Hiroshima. Although he did not actually build one, Phillips thought his bomb would weigh 125 pounds and cost about $2,000.

"I wanted to show that any undergraduate with a physics background could do it," Phillips explained, "and therefore that it is reasonable to assume that terrorists could do it too."

In fact, two foreign governments contacted Phillips for information. He refused their requests and alerted the Central Intelligence Agency, which then classified Phillips's thesis as secret. Undaunted, the young man began to lecture on the perils of nuclear proliferation while writing a book about the fleetingness of the fame his project had brought him. He was screen-tested for a movie based on his book that was never made, ran for Congress and lost in 1982, and in 1984 made news for designing computer software meant to help candidates win political elections.

THE WORLD'S MOST EXPENSIVE WATER

The so-called heavy water used in many nuclear reactors to slow down fast neutrons and control chain reactions is the world's most expensive water. It costs about $1,500 per gallon to produce. The main differences between it and ordinary water are that it is about 10 percent denser, and it is poisonous.

The variation in density stems from a difference in the hydrogen atoms both types of water contain. The nucleus of an ordinary hydrogen atom contains one proton only. But one atom of hydrogen in every 5,000 has a neutron in its nucleus as well, making it twice as massive. This type is called heavy hydrogen, or deuterium. It is expensive because it has to be separated out from ordinary water by a laborious process of repeated extractions and purification.

NOW YOU SEE IT . . .

It is impossible to record the movement of nuclear particles accurately.

Everyday objects are visible because light beams bounce off them into the observer's eye. The objects remain unaffected. Nuclear particles, however, are so small that the energy contained in a ray of light is enough to knock them off course or out of position. Thus, though a scientist can "see" where a particle was at the moment the ray hit it, there is no way of knowing where the particle is afterward or how it is moving.

The difficulty was summed up in 1927 by the German physicist Werner Heisenberg (1901–76). Heisenberg's uncertainty principle asserts that it is impossible to know simultaneously where a particle is and how it is moving. The more accurately its position is measured, the less accurately its momentum can be known, and vice versa.

THE MULTIMEGATON BLAST

The most powerful man-made explosion ever detonated was a 58-megaton hydrogen bomb set off in the atmosphere at a Soviet test site on the Arctic island of Novaya Zemlya in October 1961. The explosion was the equivalent of about 65 million U.S. tons (58 million long tons) of TNT—nearly 3,000 times more powerful than the atomic bomb that devastated the Japanese city of Hiroshima in August 1945.

THE STRAIGHTEST LINE

The Stanford linear accelerator in California, which went into operation in May 1966, boosts electrons along a 2-mile track so straight that its supports are of different heights to compensate for the curvature of the earth.

The accelerator is capable of boosting electrons to more than 99.9 percent of the speed of light.

Weapons and warfare

GREEK FIRE

The first people to use a form of napalm—the highly inflammable petroleum jelly used in flamethrowers and bombs—were the Byzantine Greeks. The chief ingredient of "Greek fire" was probably a naphtha compound now known as naphthene palmitate. It is the main constituent of napalm, which takes its name from the compound (*naphthene palmi*tate).

Greek fire was used in two ways: as a missile hurled from a catapult and in flamethrowers. It burned when it came into contact with water and was a favorite weapon on Byzantine war vessels. Greek fire may have changed the course of history. Thanks to the fireballs, the Byzantine rulers of Constantinople (present-day Istanbul) were able in A.D. 716–18 to destroy the wooden fleets of the Muslim Arabs who were besieging the city, and this blocked the spread of Islam into Europe.

The exact formula used by the Byzantine Greeks is not known. But it probably involved combinations of naphtha, sulfur, petroleum, bitumen, turpentine, charcoal, quicklime, and potassium nitrate (saltpeter). Similar concoctions have been used many times since in war and sabotage.

BACON AND GUNPOWDER RECIPE

The first European recipe for gunpowder—seven parts saltpeter (potassium nitrate) to five parts charcoal and five parts sulfur—is attributed to the 13th-century English monk and scientist Roger Bacon. No one knows who invented the explosive, although the

ARROWS TO ATOMS: THE HISTORY OF WEAPONS

B.C.

500,000 Sharpened poles, the first spears, used in Europe.

250,000 Stones shaped into axes in Africa, Asia, and Europe.

45,000 Spears with stone heads used in Europe.

30,000 Bow and arrow invented in Africa.

3000 First metal swords and shields (bronze) made in Mesopotamia and southeastern Europe. War chariot, the first fighting vehicle, invented.

2000 First known armor, of bronze scales, made in Mesopotamia.

c. 700 Galleys—warships powered by oars—invented by Phoenicians and Egyptians.

500 Catapults and giant crossbows used by Greeks and Carthaginians.

By 200 Hand-held crossbows in use in China.

A.D.

300 Stirrups used in China, revolutionize effectiveness of cavalry.

950 Gunpowder used by Chinese for fireworks and signaling devices.

1250–1300 Bronze and iron cannons probably used by Chinese. First European record of cannon is 1326.

1495 First known muzzle-loading rifles made for Holy Roman Emperor Maximilian I.

1585 Floating mines used by the Dutch at siege of Antwerp.

By 1650 Bayonets first used in Europe by the French.

1800 Submarine, *Nautilus,* demonstrated by U.S. inventor Robert Fulton.

1833 Breech-loading bolt-action rifle designed by Prussian inventor Johann Dreyse.

1849 Austrian Army balloons drop bombs on Venice.

1861 H.M.S. *Warrior,* first ironclad warship, launched in England.

1862 Hand-cranked, multibarreled Gatling gun, invented in U.S.A. by Richard Gatling. A five-barreled model fired 700 rounds a minute.

1867 Dynamite invented by Swedish chemist Alfred Nobel.

1884 Fully automatic machine gun invented by American-English engineer Hiram Maxim.

1906 H.M.S. *Dreadnought,* first steel-plated, turbine-propelled battleship, launched in England.

1911 Aerial bombs, cans of nitroglycerin, dropped by Italians from airplanes on Ain Zara, Libya.

1915 Fighter aircraft, wooden-framed biplanes, used by Germany and Britain. First modern flamethrowers used by Germany.

1916 First use in warfare of tanks, by British in World War I, France.

1939 First turbojet, the Heinkel He178, tested in Germany.

1942 First jet fighter, German Messerschmitt Me 262, flown; later sees action in World War II.

1943 V-1 flying bomb launched in Germany.

1944 Germany's V-2 (A-4) rocket used against London and Antwerp.

1945 First atom bomb used in warfare; a 20-kiloton device dropped on Hiroshima, Japan, by U.S.A.

1952 First hydrogen bomb, a 10-megaton device, detonated by the U.S.A. at Eniwetok atoll, western Pacific.

1957 First intercontinental ballistic missile (ICBM), the SS-6, tested by the Soviet Union.

1969 Strategic Arms Limitation Treaty (SALT) talks, aimed at reducing U.S. and Soviet nuclear arsenals, begun at Helsinki, Finland.

1977 Neutron bomb, which kills people but leaves buildings intact, developed in U.S.A.

1981 U.S.A. steps up development of laser weapons.

1983 First Trident missiles installed in U.S.A. Ground-launched cruise missiles installed in Europe.

1984 U.S.A. funds research for new defense system, dubbed "star wars" by press, which uses lasers and particle-beam weapons to destroy incoming hostile missiles.

AXMAN
In drawing
c. A.D. 1300,
barefoot English
soldier goes
into battle
armed with only
a huge ax.

Chinese were using it in the 10th century A.D. for signals and fireworks. By 1300 the Arabs were using it to propel arrows from guns. And in 1326 the Council of Florence in Italy made the earliest authenticated European reference to guns and gunpowder in a document ordering a consignment of iron bullets.

TWENTY-NINE-YEAR SIEGE
The longest known siege is one recorded by the Greek historian Herodotus in the 5th century B.C. Toward the end of the 7th century the Egyptians had kept up an assault on the town of Azotus (now Ashdod, in Israel) for 29 years before it surrendered.

THE CASTLE THAT SETTLED A DEBT
In France in 1365 the duke of Burgundy paid for the loan of some cannons with a castle. The duke had borrowed the cannons from the town of Chartres to use in his assault on the nearby castle of Camrolles. The cannons soon destroyed the castle walls, and the fall of Camrolles marked the end of traditional medieval fortifications. The duke then presented the battered castle to the townspeople of Chartres to discharge his debt to them.

The first documented use of cannons in Europe took place 19 years earlier when Edward III of England defeated the French at the Battle of Crécy, in northwest France. But that victory had less to do with the new weapon than with the superior range of the English longbowmen.

CANNONS CAST ON THE SPOT
For 1,000 years the triple walls of Constantinople presented an impregnable defense against invaders. Each wall was some 30 feet high and about 16 feet thick. But in 1453, in the space of just 55 days, the Turks captured the Byzantine city with the use of some 70 pieces of artillery. Twelve of the bronze cannons used weighed over 20 tons each. They were cast on the spot and pulled into position by a team of 140 oxen and 200 men. Each piece was 16 feet long, with a 26-inch caliber and could fire an 800-pound shot 1 mile. The maximum rate of fire, however, was extremely slow: seven rounds a day.

None of the original Constantinople cannons survives. But an identical copy, cast in the Dardanelles in 1465 and last used in 1807—when it blasted a hole in the British frigate *Active,* though it did not sink her—is kept in the Tower of London.

EXPLOSIVES FOR PEACE
Alfred Nobel (1833–96), the Swedish chemist and inventor of dynamite (1867), believed that his explosives would bring peace to the world. An ardent pacifist, and founder of the Nobel Peace Prize, he thought his inventions would form the basis of strong national defense systems and so act as deterrents against warlike countries.

SEEING IN THE DARK
A regular diet of carrots so improved the eyesight of Britain's night-fighter pilots in World War II that they were able to sight and shoot down bomber after German bomber. That, at least, was the story put out by the British Air Ministry, and the one that was widely believed by German intelligence. There was a grain of truth in it: Carrots contain a substance called carotene, which is converted by the body into vitamin A. And vitamin A, in turn, aids the formation of visual purple, a pigment in the eyes that is essential for good vision in poor light. But other foods, including milk, butter, and green vegetables, also contain vitamin A. So extra carrots make little difference to anyone who is already on a balanced diet. The wartime story, however, served to hide the truth about why British fighter pilots were so successful.

The real reason was a chain of radar masts along the south and east coasts of England. The 350-foot-high masts could detect a German bomber up to 100 miles away, giving the Royal Air Force plenty of time to get its night fighters into the air and after the invaders.

Ironically, radar had first been successfully demonstrated in 1934 by Rudolf Kuhnold, head of the German Navy's signal research division. But 5 years later, at the outbreak of the war, Germany still had not produced an effective radar system, and Britain had.

FINAL CHARGE
The last full-scale cavalry charge took place during World War II. In November 1941 a division of Mongolian cavalry thundered across no-man's-land toward a German infantry division dug in near Muscino, a village not far from Moscow. The attack was a disaster. About 2,000 cavalrymen died in the charge—and not a single German infantryman.

NAZI STRONGHOLD THAT NEVER WAS
In March 1945, in the final weeks of World War II in Europe, the Allied drive eastward to Berlin received a piece of startling news. Joseph Goebbels, the German propaganda minister, let it be known that the Nazis had built a huge "National Redoubt" on the alpine border of Austria and Bavaria. Allied intelligence chiefs may have suspected the report was a hoax (which it was), but they passed it on to Gen. Dwight Eisenhower, the Allied supreme commander, with the warning that, if true, details of the fortress were too alarming not to be taken seriously.

Under Hitler's personal command, so the story went, armaments were being manufactured in bombproof factories, food and equipment stored in vast caverns, and a whole underground army trained to liberate Germany from the occupying forces. As a result of the hoax, some Allied divisions were diverted toward the nonexistent redoubt, slowing Eisenhower's Berlin offensive and perhaps allowing Soviet troops to win the race to enter the German capital.

"Not until after the campaign ended," wrote Gen. Omar Bradley later, "were we to learn that this Redoubt existed largely in the imagination of a few fanatical Nazis. . . . I am astonished that we believed it as innocently as we did. But while it persisted, this legend of the Redoubt was too ominous a threat to ignore."

SURPRISE VERSUS SURPRISE
The Japanese surprise attack on December 7, 1941, on U.S. naval forces at Pearl Harbor was answered just over 4 months later by U.S. bombers that slipped in from the sea to bomb Tokyo and other Japanese cities on April 18, 1942. This raid, little remembered in the grand strategy of World War II, was a big boost to American morale in the days when the Japanese advance across the Pacific seemed unstoppable.

In all, 16 B-25 bombers and 80 airmen, led by U.S. Army Col. James H. Doolittle, former test pilot and barnstormer, took part in the raid. Many of the bomb-laden B-25s barely made it off the short, heaving deck of the aircraft carrier U.S.S. *Hornet,* a takeoff that even for much lighter planes would have been extremely risky. Moreover, the flight plan had called for the carrier to be hours closer to the Japanese mainland when the planes took off; but the sighting of a Japanese ship had forced the Americans to send the bombers off prematurely in the hope of preserving the secrecy of the mission. That left some grim figures: the fuel that had been carefully measured for the planned flight now had to suffice for a longer flight to safety at friendly Chinese airfields.

When it was all over, Tokyo had been bombed but little damaged. While no U.S. bomber was downed by enemy fire, most of the planes ran out of gas and crashed in China. Eventually, 71 of the 80 airmen made it back to the United States, some painfully crippled and near death. After the raid the Japanese army officer in charge of Tokyo's defenses committed suicide, and President Franklin D. Roosevelt hailed "the beginning of a great offensive"—although it would be almost a year before the Japanese defeat at Guadalcanal signaled the beginning of a sustained U.S. offensive in the Pacific.

WHITTLED REVOLVER

The first model of the "gun that tamed the West" was whittled in wood aboard ship by a young man who had run away to sea at the age of 16. Five years later, Samuel Colt (1814–1862) patented a working model of his gun, which had a cartridge cylinder rotated by cocking a hammer. After the outbreak of the Mexican War in 1846, Colt's guns became so popular that "Colt" was synonymous for a time with "revolver."

SCALPING: A WHITE MAN'S CUSTOM

The Indians of North America did not invent scalping. Indeed, some historians believe that the custom was actually introduced by the white man. Cutting off all or part of the scalp of an enemy as proof of victory was first described by the Greek historian Herodotus. Writing in the 5th century B.C., he attributed the custom to the Scythians, a warlike people of southern Russia.

The custom may have been practiced by a few eastern Indian tribes in North America before the arrival of Europeans, though not all historians accept even this. What is certain, however, is that the practice was spread west across the continent by the colonial governments of France and Britain. Officials of both governments encouraged their settlers to kill others by offering a cash reward for each death. The only proof required was a scalp. By the early 18th century, in what is now the United States and Canada, the French were paying bounties for British scalps, the British were paying for French scalps, and each was paying for scalps of the other's Indian allies.

Scalps were usually cut from the dead. But prisoners could be scalped alive and then killed. And sometimes victims, once they had been scalped, were allowed to return home alive as a dreadful warning or challenge to their fellows.

BAREFOOT IN THE STIRRUPS

The introduction of the metal stirrup in Europe in the late 8th or early 9th century A.D. revolutionized the nature of warfare. Together with the saddle, known in Europe since the 4th century B.C., the stirrup gave horsemen greater stability and allowed them to use their spears underhand, so that they could put their whole weight behind a thrust without getting pushed off the horse. Before, cavalrymen had been limited to a weaker overhand stabbing technique.

The stirrup was first used by barefoot Hindu warriors in the late 2nd century B.C., as a loop that fitted around the rider's big toe. In the 4th century A.D. the stirrup was adapted by the Chinese, who fitted it around a booted foot, the form in which it appears today. Military historians have compared the impact of the stirrup on warfare with that of the tank, which was first used in battle during World War I.

BOOMERANGS THAT DON'T

The popular image of the boomerang—as a V-shaped wooden weapon that, if thrown properly, stuns or kills an animal and then returns to the hurler—is part fantasy. The so-called returning boomerang has long been used by the aborigines of Australia, but it is too light and thin to serve as an effective weapon and is used mainly for games. It probably developed from nonreturning boomerangs, throwing sticks or clubs used for hunting animals and even in warfare.

FLEET PROTECTOR *The Aegis, a computer-controlled weapons system built into cruisers of the U.S.S.* Ticonderoga *class (inset), is the United States' answer to missiles and aircraft that could knock out the U.S. Navy's aircraft carriers. Named for the shield of Zeus, Aegis is meant to spot and destroy anything thrown at U.S. fleets.*

Mathematics—the numbers game

EDWARD'S ACRE

Before the reign of England's Edward I, an acre was the amount of land a yoke of oxen could plow in a day; the word comes from the Latin *ager,* meaning "field." But since the performance of oxen could vary widely, Edward fixed the acre at an area 40 rods long by 4 rods wide, each rod being 16.5 feet long. That measurement has survived unchanged.

FIRST FOOT

As the term implies, a foot was originally the length of a man's foot from heel to big toe. The Romans divided it into 12 *unciae*—the word from which are derived both "inch" and "ounce" (an ounce was once a twelfth of a pound). The 12-inch foot was not universally accepted, though. In the 17th century the Dutch foot was divided into only 11 inches.

The English king Henry I established the yard early in the 12th century as the distance from the tip of his nose to the tip of his outstretched thumb. Edward I redefined it as 3 feet in 1305.

HOW NUMBERS DEVELOPED

The numeral system that is almost universal today was probably invented by the Hindus. It simplified calculations by making the value of a number depend on its position as well as the number itself. In the number 444 the single figure 4 represents 400, 40, and 4, and the whole number is the sum of these values. By contrast, the Romans used symbols whose values were the same whatever their position.

Modern systems, known as place-value systems, can be based on numbers other than 10. The Babylonians based their system on 60. Modern computers use the binary system, based on 2.

The Hindu system, which included a zero, was adopted by the Arabs and may have reached Europe as early as the 10th century, though it was some time before it replaced Roman numerals. The man credited with popularizing Arab notation is the Italian mathematician Leonardo Fibonacci (c. 1170–1240), who advocated its use in his *Book of the Abacus,* published in 1202.

The decimal point is thought to have been a European invention. Its inventor is not known, but its use was first popularized by a Flemish mathematician named Simon Stevin (1548–1620) in a book called *De Thiende (The Tenth),* published in 1585. Until the development of decimals, numbers smaller than 1 had to be expressed as fractions.

Babylonian	𒁹	𒈫	𒐈	𒐉	𒐊	𒐋	𒐌	𒐍	𒐎	𒌋	
Egyptian	𓏺	𓏻	𓏼	𓏽	𓏾	𓏿	𓐀	𓐁	𓐂	𓎆	
Greek	Α	Β	Γ	Δ	Ε	F	Ζ	Η	Θ	Ι	
Roman	I	II	III	IV	V	VI	VII	VIII	IX	X	
Ancient Chinese	一	二	三	四	五	六	七	八	九	十	
Maya	𝋡	𝋢	𝋣	𝋤	𝋥	𝋦	𝋧	𝋨	𝋩	𝋪	𝋠
Hindu	१	२	३	४	५	६	७	८	९	१०	०
Arabic/European 15th century	1	2	3	4	5	6	7	8	9	10	0
Modern Arabic/European	1	2	3	4	5	6	7	8	9	10	0
Digits designed for computer printing	1	2	3	4	5	6	7	8	9	10	0

POWER OF SUGGESTION

On the face of it, an attempt to predict someone else's choice of a number between 5 and 10 would be wrong five times out of six. But it is possible to improve the odds. Write the number 7 on a piece of paper and conceal it. Then ask someone to respond rapidly to the following: "Five times five? Six times six? Name a color. Name a number between 5 and 10." For their final answer, most people will come up with 7, the number you wrote down. Why the trick works is not clear. Perhaps the mind is drawn unconsciously to numbers in the center of a given range (5 to 10 in this case), and the first two questions help to create a mental sequence: 5, 6 . . . 7. Asking for a color merely diverts the subject's attention away from numbers so that he or she does not spot, and therefore avoid, the next number in the sequence.

NOAH'S MARK

The cubit, the unit that Noah used to build his ark, was, like most early measures, based on the human body. It was the length from the elbow (*cubitum* in Latin) to the tip of the middle finger. The cubit's precise length varied. The Egyptians made it equal to about 21 inches. In biblical times it was closer to 22 inches; but by the time of the Roman Empire the cubit had shrunk to about 18 inches.

FROM FURROW TO FURLONG

The word "furlong," now used mainly in racing parlance, has its origin in the plodding of oxen. "Furlong" comes from the phrase "a furrow long," meaning the length of a furrow in a standard square field of 10 acres. By the 9th century the furlong was regarded as the equivalent of a Roman *stadium,* a unit that was one-eighth of a Roman mile. It was later defined as one-eighth of a statute mile, or 220 yards.

MILES AND MILES

The Romans invented the mile. For them it meant a thousand paces (*mille* being Latin for "one thousand"), in which each pace was two steps, or 5 feet, long—making a total of 5,000 feet. In medieval times the 220-yard furlong was the main unit of length in common use, and so the length of the mile was adjusted to make it equal to 8 furlongs: 1,760 yards, or 5,280 feet. The new length was fixed in England by an act of Parliament in the 16th century, which created the statute mile.

The nautical mile—still used by ships and planes—is a much later unit, invented to make it easier for navigators to work out from their position how far they have traveled or vice versa. Each nautical mile along the equator, 6,082.66 feet, represents one-sixtieth of a degree of longitude. So a ship that sails 300 nautical miles along the equator in a day will be exactly 5 degrees away from her previous position. However, because the earth is not a perfect sphere,

COMMON FORMULAS

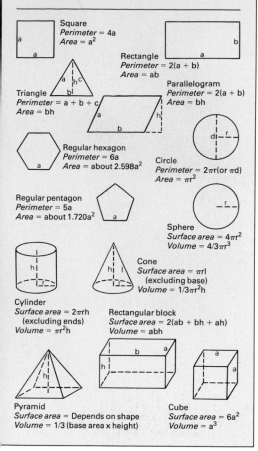

Square
Perimeter = 4a
Area = a^2

Rectangle
Perimeter = 2(a + b)
Area = ab

Triangle
Perimeter = a + b + c
Area = bh

Parallelogram
Perimeter = 2(a + b)
Area = bh

Regular hexagon
Perimeter = 6a
Area = about $2.598a^2$

Circle
Perimeter = $2\pi r$ (or πd)
Area = πr^2

Regular pentagon
Perimeter = 5a
Area = about $1.720a^2$

Sphere
Surface area = $4\pi r^2$
Volume = $4/3\pi r^3$

Cone
Surface area = πrl
(excluding base)
Volume = $1/3\pi r^2 h$

Cylinder
Surface area = $2\pi rh$
(excluding ends)
Volume = $\pi r^2 h$

Rectangular block
Surface area = 2(ab + bh + ah)
Volume = abh

Pyramid
Surface area = Depends on shape
Volume = 1/3 (base area x height)

Cube
Surface area = $6a^2$
Volume = a^3

then simply defined as being 10 times larger or smaller than their neighbors. Since then, the meter has been redefined three times with ever greater precision. The definition now accepted internationally was adopted in 1983. It defines the meter in terms of time: the distance traveled by a beam of light in a vacuum in a period lasting 1/299,792,458 second.

THE SUM THAT'S ALWAYS THE SAME
Take any three-figure number in which the first digit is larger than the last—say, 725. Reverse it (here making 527), and subtract the smaller from the larger, making 198. Now add the result to the same number reversed, 891. The answer is 1,089. It will be 1,089 whatever number you start with. Even if the result of the subtraction is two digits rather than three (221 minus 122, for instance, comes to 99), simply put a zero on the front before reversing it, to make the sum of 099 plus 990—and the answer again is 1,089.

THE UNPYTHAGOREAN THEOREM
The theorem named after the Greek philosopher and mathematician Pythagoras (c. 582–507 B.C.) was not discovered by him. The theorem—which states that in any right-angled triangle the sum of the squares on the two shorter sides equals the square of the hypotenuse, or longest side—was used by ancient Egyptian surveyors, and it was known to the Babylonians (though probably not rigorously proved by them) at least 1,000 years earlier.

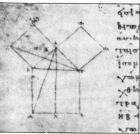
GREEK (C. A.D. 800)

LATIN (C. 1120)

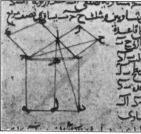
ARABIC (C. 1250)

FRENCH (1564)
perpendiculaire à la bafe, le de l'vne ft efgal du cofté part de aufsi par u'auons propo- ctangle

the correlation is not precise in all parts of the world, and an average figure is usually used. The United States uses the international nautical mile, a unit of 6,076.1033 feet. Britain uses the Admiralty mile of 6,080 feet.

The maritime measurement of speed in knots—one knot being equal to one nautical mile per hour—comes from the days when sailors used a knotted rope to determine their speed at sea. A float was tied to the end of the rope, which was knotted at regular intervals, and tossed overboard. As the float bobbed past the sailor holding the rope, an hourglass was turned over, and the rope was let out freely while the sand ran through. When the sand stopped flowing, the boat's speed was figured by counting the number of knots that had been let out.

THE REVOLUTIONARY METER
Twelve French scientists invented the metric system during the French Revolution, partly to standardize the bewildering variety of local measurements then in use and partly as a symbol of defiance against traditions they had come to regard as oppressive. It was the first comprehensive system of measurement to be based on something other than the human physique. The scientists, who were appointed by the French National Assembly in 1791, based the system on the circumference of the earth measured on a line through Paris and both the Poles. To give themselves a convenient-size unit, they divided the line by 40,000,000 and called the result a meter (from the Greek word *metron,* meaning "measure"). All the other units of length—kilometers, millimeters, and so forth—were

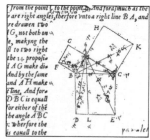
ENGLISH (1570)

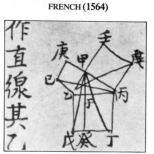
CHINESE (1607)

WORLD FIGURES *By the 17th century Pythagoras's theorem was known all over the world. The picture at top left is from a copy of the works of the Greek mathematician Euclid. The others are translations of the same text.*

BEAUTIES OF THE GOLDEN RATIO

Many paintings as well as some of the world's most beautiful buildings, including the Parthenon in Athens, derive much of their artistic appeal from mathematics. In particular they make use of rectangular shapes based on a proportion of height to width known as the golden ratio, or the golden mean. Each rectangle has its sides in the proportion of 1 to 1.618033989. Like the number pi (π), which expresses the mathematical relationship between the diameter of a circle and the circle's circumference, this golden ratio number—often denoted by the Greek letter *phi* (ϕ)—is a never-ending decimal. It also has some remarkable properties.

If a golden ratio rectangle is divided into a square and a rectangle, the smaller rectangle repeats the same proportion. If the smaller rectangle is divided again, the same is true of the yet smaller rectangle, and so on. If corresponding points on the rectangles are joined in the way pictured below, the result is what mathematicians call a logarithmic spiral—exactly the same spiral as the shell of a snail.

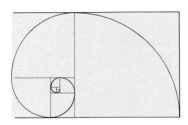

Uniquely, too, the golden ratio is the only number that can be squared by adding 1 to it ($\pi^2 = \pi + 1$) and the only number that can be turned into its own reciprocal ($1/\pi$) just by subtracting 1 (that is, $1/\pi = \pi - 1$).

FIBONACCI'S MAGIC NUMBERS

The arithmetical sequence now known as the Fibonacci series was invented in A.D. 1225 by the Italian mathematician Leonardo Fibonacci (c. 1170–1240) to solve a puzzle about the breeding rate of rabbits. Each number in the series—which begins 1, 1, 2, 3, 5, 8, 13, 21, 34—is, after the first two figures, merely the sum of the previous two numbers. Yet this simple sequence has links with other mathematical relationships and with the world of nature.

If, for instance, you examine any plant that sends out individual leaves from a single stem, find two leaves directly above each other, and then count one of the pair plus all the intervening leaves, the total will always be a Fibonacci number. Similarly, if you count the clockwise spirals of seeds on the head of a sunflower, and the counterclockwise spirals on the same flower, the figures will always be not only Fibonacci numbers but consecutive Fibonacci numbers. The largest such numbers of sunflower spirals on record are 144 and 233.

Perhaps even more curious is the ratio of successive terms in the Fibonacci series. The numbers 144 and 233, for instance, are in the ratio of 1 to 1.61805; and 233 and the following Fibonacci number, 377, are in the ratio 1 to 1.6180257. Successive ratios in the series converge ever more closely on the number 1.618033989—which is the golden ratio known to mathematicians since at least 300 B.C.

COUNTING THE COUNTLESS

The British astronomer Sir Arthur Eddington (1882–1944) once estimated that the total number of fundamental particles in the entire universe came to only 10^{89}—the number 1 followed by 89 zeros. However, mathematicians have devised names for even larger numbers. The number 10^{100}, for example, was named a googol by the U.S. mathematician Edward Kasner (1878–1955) at the suggestion of his young nephew.

The largest named number is 10 to the googol power—that is, 10 multiplied by itself a googol number of times. The name for such a number is googolplex.

COUNTING, COUNTING

If a person counted at the rate of 100 numbers a minute, and kept on counting for 8 hours a day, 5 days a week, it would take a little over 4 weeks to count to 1 million—and just over 80 years of nonstop counting to reach 1 billion.

NUMBERLESS

The Nambiquara, an Indian people who live in the Brazilian state of Mato Grosso, on the fringes of the Amazon jungle, seem to use no system of numbers at all. The closest the Nambiquara get is a verb meaning "to be two alike."

CHINESE SQUARE

One of the world's oldest "magic" squares—a pattern of consecutive numbers in which every row adds up to the same total—is described in the Chinese book of

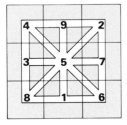

divination called the *I Ching*. Thought to have been written in about the 12th century B.C., the book refers to a magic square (pictured at left) made up of the numbers 1 to 9. Every row, every column, and both diagonals add up to 15.

DOUBLE FIGURES

A simple mathematical trick can enable you to discover any number a person thinks of—and find out his or her age as well. Ask the person to pick a number of any size, double it, add 5, and multiply the result by 50. Next, tell the person to add 1,737 (this key number changes every year; for 1988 the number rises to 1,738, and so on for each subsequent year). Then ask the person to subtract the year in which he or she was born. The last two digits in the final answer will tell you the person's age on his or her birthday this year; the others will be the number first thought of.

POLYGON PI

The Greek mathematician Archimedes (287–212 B.C.) is credited as the first to calculate the ratio between a circle's diameter and its circumference, the number now known as pi (π)—so named because it was the first letter of the Greek word *perimetros*, meaning "perimeter" or "circumference." Archimedes drew two polygons, many-sided figures, just inside and just outside the circle and then measured the length of the polygons' perimeters. By this means, he established that π was approximately 22/7.

Later mathematicians, using polygons with more and more sides so that they followed ever more closely the shape of the circle, gradually improved on Archimedes' figure. But the process was agonizingly cumbersome. In 1610, for instance, a Dutchman named Ludolph van Ceulen completed a calculation of π based on a polygon with more than a million million million sides. The mathematics occupied him for much of his life, yet it established the value of π to only 35 decimal places.

In 1961, in contrast, a computer was able to calculate and print out the value of π to 100,000 places in just 8 hours, and in 1981 a computer in Japan took only a little over 5 days to calculate its value to no fewer than 2 million places. However, the value of π is usually approximated to 3.14159 or 3.142.

MEASURE FOR MEASURE

The table below shows how to convert standard U.S. measurements to their metric equivalents and vice versa. As well as giving precise equivalents, it shows useful approximations.

Standard U.S. units

Length

		Precise equivalent	Approximate equivalent
	1 in	25.4 mm	25 mm
12 in	1 ft	304.8 mm	300 mm
3 ft	1 yd	0.9144 m	1 m
1,760 yd	1 mi	1.6093 km	1.5 km

Area

		Precise equivalent	Approximate equivalent
	1 sq in	645 mm²	650 mm²
144 sq in	1 sq ft	0.0929 m²	0.1 m²
9 sq ft	1 sq yd	0.836 m²	1 m²
4,840 sq yd	1 acre	0.405 ha	0.5 ha
640 acres	1 sq mi	259 ha	250 ha

Volume (solid and liquid)

		Precise equivalent	Approximate equivalent
	1 cu in	16,387.1 mm³	15,000 mm³
1,728 cu in	1 cu ft	0.028 m³	0.03 m³
27 cu ft	1 cu yd	0.765 m³	1 m³
16 fl oz	1 pt (liquid)	0.473 L	0.5 L
2 pt	1 qt (liquid)	0.946 L	1 L
4 qt	1 gal	3.785 L	4 L

Weight

		Precise equivalent	Approximate equivalent
	1 oz	28.3495 g	30 g
16 oz	1 lb	0.4536 kg	0.5 kg
2,000 lb	1 ton (short ton)	0.907 tonne	0.9 tonne
2,240 lb	1 long ton	1.016 tonne	1 tonne
2,204.6 lb	1 metric ton	1 tonne	1 tonne

Metric units

Length

		Precise equivalent	Approximate equivalent
	1 mm	0.03937 in	0.05 in
10 mm	1 cm	0.39 in	0.5 in
1,000 mm	1 m	39.37 in	3 ft 3 in
1,000 m	1 km	0.62 mi	0.5 mi

Area

		Precise equivalent	Approximate equivalent
	1 sq mm	0.0016 sq in	0.001 sq in
100 mm²	1 sq cm	0.155 sq in	0.2 sq in
10,000 cm²	1 sq m	10.76 sq ft	10 sq ft
10,000 m²	1 ha	2.47 acres	2 acres
100 ha	1 sq km	0.386 sq mi	0.5 sq mi

Volume (solid and liquid)

		Precise equivalent	Approximate equivalent
	1 cu cm	0.061 cu in	0.05 cu in
1,000 mm³	1 cu cm	0.061 cu in	0.05 cu in
1,000 cm³ (cc)	1 cu dm	61.024 cu in	60 cu in
1,000 dm³	1 cu m	35.31 cu ft	35 cu ft
		1.308 cu yd	1 cu yd
1,000 cm³ (cc)	1 L	1.76 pt	1.5 pt

Weight

		Precise equivalent	Approximate equivalent
	1 g	0.035 oz	0.05 oz
1,000 g	1 kg	2.2046 lb	2 lb
1,000 kg	1 tonne	1.1023 short tons	1.1 short tons
		0.9842 long tons	1 long ton

How to convert units of measurement

Standard U.S. to metric

To convert	into	multiply by
Length		
inches	millimeters	25.4
inches	centimeters	2.54
feet	meters	0.3048
yards	meters	0.9144
miles	kilometers	1.6093
Area		
square inches	square millimeters	645.16
square feet	square meters	0.093
square yards	square meters	0.836
acres	hectares	0.405
square miles	square kilometers	2.58999
Volume		
cubic inches	cubic millimeters	16,387
cubic feet	cubic meters	0.0283
cubic yards	cubic meters	0.7646
gallons	liters	3.78
Weight		
ounces	grams	28.35
pounds	kilograms	0.45359
short tons	tonnes	0.9072
long tons	tonnes	1.016

Metric to customary U.S.

To convert	into	multiply by
Length		
millimeters	inches	0.0394
centimeters	inches	0.3937
meters	feet	3.2808
meters	yards	1.0936
kilometers	miles	0.6214
Area		
square millimeters	square inches	0.00155
square meters	square feet	10.764
square meters	square yards	1.196
hectares	acres	2.471
square kilometers	square miles	0.386
Volume		
cubic millimeters	cubic inches	0.000061
cubic meters	cubic feet	35.315
cubic meters	cubic yards	1.308
liters	gallons	0.264
Weight		
grams	ounces	0.0352
kilograms	pounds	2.2046
tonnes	short tons	1.1023
tonnes	long tons	0.984

Temperature: degrees Celsius (centigrade) and degrees Fahrenheit
Exact conversion $F° = (C° × 1.8) + 32$ $C° = (F° − 32) ÷ 1.8$ *Approximate conversion* $F° = (C° × 2) + 30$ $C° = (F° − 30) ÷ 2$

WHAT METRIC PREFIXES MEAN

Prefixes—syllables added to the name of a unit to signify multiples or fractions of it—simplify the use of large and small quantities. Their most familiar use is in the metric system of measurements. One thousand meters, for example, is simply one kilometer, and a thousandth of a meter is a millimeter. The prefix symbols shown here are used with the abbreviation for the basic unit, so kilometer is shortened to km and millimeter to mm.

Prefix	symbol	Meaning	Factor by which unit is multiplied
tera	T	one trillion	$10^{12} = 1,000,000,000,000$
giga	G	one billion	$10^{9} = 1,000,000,000$
mega	M	one million	$10^{6} = 1,000,000$
kilo	k	one thousand	$10^{3} = 1000$
hecto	h	one hundred	$10^{2} = 100$
deka	da	ten	$10 = 10$
deci	d	one-tenth	$10^{-1} = 0.1$
centi	c	one-hundredth	$10^{-2} = 0.01$
milli	m	one-thousandth	$10^{-3} = 0.001$
micro	μ	one-millionth	$10^{-6} = 0.000,001$
nano	n	one-billionth	$10^{-9} = 0.000,000,001$
pico	p	one-trillionth	$10^{-12} = 0.000,000,000,001$

Computers—marvels in miniature

5,000 YEARS OF COMPUTING
The abacus is the earliest form of mechanical computer. Invented more than 5,000 years ago, probably in China, it consists of a wooden frame with wires that are strung with beads. The beads represent units: tens, hundreds, and so on. Calculations are made by moving the beads up and down.

The abacus is still used in the Far East and in the Soviet Union, and a skilled operator can make calculations on it at least as quickly as on a pocket calculator. As recently as 1983 more than 2 million abaci were being produced each year in Japan, where they are known as sorobans.

ACE IN THE HOLE
The punched cards used in computing were developed by French weavers in 1801.

In that year Joseph Jacquard invented a loom for the manufacture of elaborate patterned fabrics. The pattern was coded on a loop of cards with holes punched in them. The holes allowed needles to pass through and lift corresponding threads of the warp. The Englishman Charles Babbage adopted a similar system of punched cards for his computer in 1834.

THE FIRST DIGITAL COMPUTER
Charles Babbage (1792–1871), an English scientist and mathematician, drew up the first plans for a programmable digital computer in 1834, but he never saw it completed. His "analytical engine"—a version of an advanced adding machine he had invented 20 years earlier—was to have been programmed by punched cards, make calculations with the aid of a memory bank, print out the answers, and operate at the then remarkable speed of one addition per second.

The British government invested about $75,000 in the engine, and Babbage added $25,000 more, but the precision required to produce the engine's thousands of parts was beyond the capabilities of the manufacturers consulted.

Government support was withdrawn in 1842 after the astronomer royal, George Airy, said the project was worthless. Babbage struggled on unsuccessfully, in the hope of completing the machine, until his death almost 30 years later.

OUTLAWS WHO HELPED A CENSUS
Efforts to trap 19th-century train robbers in the American West became the inspiration for the first electronic computer. To identify outlaws posing as passengers on U.S. trains, researchers proposed recording the physical characteristics of each passenger on his or her ticket. When a ticket was purchased, holes could be punched next to the appropriate characteristics, such as mustache and hair color. Then, if a robbery took place, the idea was that the ticket records could be matched against passengers who remained on the train after the theft—and missing passengers could be described.

The idea was never widely adopted, but an American statistician, Herman Hollerith, realized that the method could be adapted for processing census information, and for the 1890 U.S. census he produced a tabulating machine.

Census information was recorded on punched cards which were "read" by feelers. The feelers could detect a hole and then generate a corresponding electric signal. The result was that complete analysis of the 1890 census took less time than the 1880 census did—despite an increase in the national population from 50 to 63 million.

In 1896 Hollerith founded the Tabulating Machine Company, which 28 years later became the basis of what is now the world's largest computer firm, International Business Machines Corporation (IBM).

COMPUTER MILESTONES

1642 Blaise Pascal, French mathematician and philosopher, invents the first adding machine.

1834 Charles Babbage, English scientist, draws up the first plans for a programmable digital computer.

1890 U.S. statistician Herman Hollerith invents a tabulating machine used for the 1890 U.S. census.

1930 U.S. scientist Vannevar Bush develops a large electromechanical analog computer.

1942 First electronic digital calculator constructed at Iowa State University by Prof. John Atanasoff and Clifford Berry.

1946 ENIAC (*electronic numerical integrator and calculator*), the first fully electronic computer, built at the University of Pennsylvania.

1946 John von Neumann at the Institute for Advanced Study, Princeton, N.J., designs a computer that stores information and uses binary numbers.

1948 First successful stored program computer operated at Manchester University in England.

1951 The first mass-produced computer, Univac 1 (standing for *uni*versal *a*utomatic *c*omputer), built by the Eckert–Mauchly Computer Corporation in Philadelphia, Pa.

1953 IBM introduces its first commercial computer, the 701, which uses valves.

1956 FORTRAN, a logical and algebraic language for programming computers, introduced.

1960 Transistors are used to replace valves in commercial computers by the Digital Equipment Corporation in the U.S.A.

1961 Time-sharing computer introduced at Massachusetts Institute of Technology, Cambridge, Mass.

1965 Silicon chip introduced in the U.S.A.

1971 Pocket calculators introduced. In the U.S.A. the Intel Corporation patents the microprocessor, an entire computer processor on a single silicon chip.

1975 Personal—and affordable—computers begin to appear, launching another computer revolution that brings the machines into homes and schools, as well as into every aspect of business.

1980s U.S.A. and Japan, as well as other nations, compete for leadership in computer technology, seeking workable designs for superfast machines having millions of processors working in parallel. Such research spawns talk of "artificial intelligence."

BUILT-IN TRANSLATOR

Despite the proliferation of special computer languages, such as BASIC, COBOL, and so on, all computers can essentially understand only two symbols: 1 and 0. But to avoid having to use this cumbersome binary notation, computers usually have a built-in translation program, or "compiler," which can take a coded language, almost like a real language, and convert it into binary notation.

The most common coded language presently in use is BASIC—or, to give it its full name, *beginner's all-purpose symbolic instruction code*. Other languages include COBOL (*common business oriented language*), which is used for general and commercial purposes; FORTRAN (*formula translation*), for scientific use; and ALGOL (*algorithmic language*), which is designed for scientists, engineers, and mathematicians.

THE ONE-MINUTE BOOK

In the early 1980s electronic printers could reach speeds of 450 lines a second and, at that rate, turn out a 225-page book in 1 minute.

WHIZ KIDS

Computer success seems to favor the young. In 1975, as a freshman at Harvard, William Gates began writing software. Within a year he dropped out of Harvard to establish the Microsoft Corporation. In 1986 the company went public and Gates, the majority shareholder, found himself worth over $200 million in terms of the market value of his Microsoft stock.

COUNTING IN TWOS

Human beings count in tens (the decimal system) because we have ten digits on our hands. A computer, however, recognizes just two possibilities: either an electric current is passing a point in its circuitry or it is not. The computer therefore counts in twos (the binary system).

The binary system uses only two symbols, 1 and 0, standing for current and no current. Moving a symbol one place to the left has the effect of doubling its value. Thus, the value of 1 as it is doubled becomes 2,

4, 8, 16, 32, 64, 128, and so on. The value of 0 always remains zero. Using the binary system, the notation for the numbers 1 to 10 is 1, 10, 11, 100, 101, 110, 111, 1000, 1001, 1010.

FIVE GATES OF WISDOM

Since individual circuit elements in computers can be only on or off, a method of combining the output from the elements is needed to perform logical calculations. This is achieved by using gates—simple pieces of circuitry that have two input wires and one output wire. An electrical pulse is sent along the output wire only when a particular pattern of pulses is received on the input wires. The names of the five types of gate describe the output each produces:
- An OR gate produces an output if it receives a pulse on either input wire.
- A NOR gate produces an output only when it does not receive a pulse.
- An AND gate produces an output only if pulses are sent through both input wires at the same time.
- A NAND ("not and") gate supplies an output unless it receives a pulse on both input wires.
- NOT gates, or inverters, have only one input and, as the name implies, the output is always the opposite of the input.

More complex steps are dealt with by arranging the gates in sequence or in parallel combinations.

MEMORIES ARE MADE OF THIS

Computer memories are defined by the number of bytes of information they can store. Each byte is a combination of binary numbers—usually eight of them—and stands for an ordinary number or letter. In one method, for instance, the series 01000001 is the byte standing for the letter *a*.

Each of the binary numbers—always either a 1 or a 0, corresponding to the presence or absence of electric current in a section of circuitry—is known as a bit, from the term "binary dig*it*."

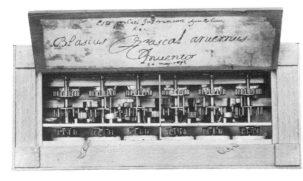

WHEELS WITHIN WHEELS *Blaise Pascal (1623–62), the French philosopher and mathematician, was 19 years old when he invented this adding machine in 1642. A train of cogwheels enabled numbers to be carried automatically and allowed subtractions to be performed as well.*

TOO HARD TO BUILD *Charles Babbage, who designed the first programmable computer in 1834, never saw it built, because Victorian engineers could not make the parts with sufficient precision. This model (right) was built from his drawings in the late 19th century, years after his death.*

More than 64,000 bytes can be stored on a single fingernail-size silicon chip, and a memory of this size is often described as a 64K memory. The K stands for kilobytes. Technically a kilobyte is 1,024 bytes (equivalent to 2^{10}, or in binary notation, the figure 1 followed by 10 zeros), so that a 64K memory can actually hold 65,536 bytes. For most practical purposes, though, a kilobyte is regarded as 1,000 bytes.

There are also mass storage systems that can hold up to 472,000 million bytes, equivalent to 472,000 megabytes. This is enough to hold a 100-letter record for every person in the world or to store as many words as there are on 27 million pages of a daily newspaper. Even such a large memory bank does not have a large physical size. Some storage systems that are "read" by laser beams can store on a disk the size of an ordinary long-playing record up to 12.5 billion bytes of information—more than enough to hold the entire 30 volumes of the *Encyclopaedia Britannica*.

KEYBOARD CRIMINALS

One of the problems with combating computer crime is that while it is easy to prove that money has been stolen, it is more difficult to discover who typed the instructions into the computer to carry out a theft, such as transferring funds from one account to another. By far the most common computer crime is theft of computer time from an employer. In a 1984 survey by the American Bar Association, 72 U.S. corporations and government agencies reported that computer thieves were costing them annual estimated

HERMAN'S HARDWARE *An 1890 magazine cover illustrates the first processing of census information by tabulating machines—the first electric computers. Invented by U.S. statistician Herman Hollerith, the machines cut the time for the job by two-thirds and helped Hollerith to found a business that in 1924 became the heart of IBM, the world's largest computer firm.*

losses of $2 million to $10 million each, mostly to crafty programmers on the payroll. Experts say most computer crime goes unreported, but losses may run as high as $4 billion in the United States alone.

THE SILICON CHIP

In its pure form, silicon is an insulator, but when it is fractionally impure it will allow a feeble current to pass and so becomes a semiconductor, the basis of a silicon chip. Silicon processed to 99.9999999 percent purity is drawn into cylindrical bars about 4 inches thick. The bars are sliced into disks 0.02 inch thick. Each disk provides material for up to 250 chips.

Miniaturized circuits are photographically printed and etched onto the disk, and layers of such substances as phosphorus, boron, and aluminum are then deposited on the surface to form transistors, resistors, capacitors, and diodes—the electronic circuitry that controls and guides the current.

COMPUTERCIDE

Increasing reliance on the computer to solve all kinds of problems has fostered a countervailing belief that when things go wrong, the computer is to blame. The result has been a new form of violence called "computer kill." One of its chroniclers is Donn Parker, a computer expert at SRI International, a California consulting firm. Parker knows of at least five cases of people shooting computers with guns, and of other computers that have been "burned up with gasoline and plastic explosives, stabbed with screwdrivers, attacked, in one case, with the heel of a woman's shoe, and shorted out with a metal key."

PROGRAM IN A POCKET

Until the 1980s, most computer programs were stored on tapes or disks. But in 1983, an American researcher named Jerome Dexler devised a pocket-size program device no larger than a credit card. In the device, programs are recorded on cards in the form of minute black holes, each one about 0.002 inch in diameter, on a silvery surface.

Each card can carry 16 million bits of information that can be read by a laser scanner when the card is inserted into a specially equipped computer. The cards can be produced more cheaply than an equivalent silicon chip and are easier to carry than other forms of program, such as cassette tape.

ELECTRONIC BRAINS

Present-day computers are not electronic equivalents of human brains. They cannot think, nor are they creative. But the day of the true electronic brain is slowly inching closer. In the early 1950s researchers in the United States began work on programs to make computers simulate the behavior patterns of humans in their approach to problems.

This means that the computer has to work on a trial-and-error basis, which results in the computer's developing its own programs.

In order to work more like the human brain, computers of the future will require a million or more processors working in parallel. Programs will be designed that will make analogies, reorganize information, and draw inferences from raw data.

HOW A PROGRAM WORKS

Without a program to tell it what to do and how to do it, a computer is unable to function. If, for example, you wanted to know how many times the word *the* appears in this paragraph, or in a whole book, it would not be enough merely to put the text into a computer and then ask it how many times the word appears. For the computer to accomplish the calculation, it must be told what to do in simple steps. The instructions might be:

1. Search the text for a space followed by *T* or *t*.
2. If the next letter is not *h,* go back to Step 1.
3. If the letter is *h,* is the next letter *e*?
4. If not, go back to Step 1. If it is, go to Step 5.
5. If *e* is followed by a space, add 1 to the total.
6. Go back to Step 1.

A full computer program for this operation would need to be broken down into even simpler steps, but a series of such programs could enable a computer to analyze any amount of text in detail.

COMPUTER PROGRESS
The earliest and largest of the digital machines in the 1940s was the ENIAC (*e*lectronic *n*umeral *i*ntegrator *a*nd *c*alculator). It was built at the University of Pennsylvania and used by the U.S. Army to calculate firing angles for new artillery weapons, taking into account range, the type of shell, and weather conditions. ENIAC contained 18,000 valves, occupied several rooms, consumed enough power to drive a locomotive, and could perform 5,000 additions per second.

Today a microprocessor—the silicon chip at the heart of a microcomputer—can cost as little as $5, can fit on a child's fingernail, consumes the same power as an electric light bulb, and can perform 400,000 operations per second.

SUPERCOMPUTERS
The race is on to develop a new generation of supercomputers for the 1990s. In 1985 there were about 75 supercomputers in the world, and they were mainly in national laboratories solving complex scientific problems and used in industry for weapons design, oil and mineral exploration, and aircraft design. The fastest can do 100 million operations per second. The next supercomputers—being developed chiefly in Japan and the United States—will be capable of more than 1 billion calculations per second. Such speeds can be multiplied by hooking supercomputers together.

The speed at which computers can work is astonishing, even when compared with the human brain. The brain contains about 100 billion nerve cells, each one capable of working 100 times a second. But inside a microprocessor, speeds are measured in nanoseconds. A nanosecond is one billionth of a second. For comparison, a nanosecond is to a second what a second is to 31.7 years.

Superfast, however, does not mean superintelligent. The dream of "artificial intelligence" will remain elusive until scientists can construct parallel circuits whose interactions are as intricate, yet as effective, as those of human brain cells.

COMPUTERS THAT TALK
Computers can now be used to read to blind people, with a synthetic speech. In 1982 Raymond Kurzweil, a student at the Massachusetts Institute of Technology, designed a machine containing a minicomputer that will read almost any typeface and then convert print into speech, using digitally stored sounds.

It is capable of learning the characteristics of an unfamiliar typeface and is claimed to make fewer mistakes than a human reader. The synthetic voice pauses as called for by punctuation.

ELECTRONIC GUINEA PIGS
U.S. scientists are developing electronic animals to take the place of real ones in laboratory experiments. Computer models are being devised of the rats, rabbits, dogs, and other animals now sacrificed every year in scientific laboratories. The models will allow chemists to test the effect of new drugs without harming real creatures, and will allow medical students to practice surgery.

One program invented at the University of Pennsylvania enabled student vets to carry out simulated dissections simply by punching keys on a computer terminal. The model even included the sound of heartbeats and nerve impulses to add realism to the electronic surgery.

The electronic guinea pigs will not, scientists believe, completely remove the need for experiments on real animals. But they could save the lives of many of the 60 million animals now used in scientific research each year in the United States alone.

SILICON CHIP *The rectangular chip (shown actual size and enlarged) can handle the payroll computing system for a sizable company. Its complex circuitry, which consists of five major subcircuits, was miniaturized photographically before being etched onto the chip.*

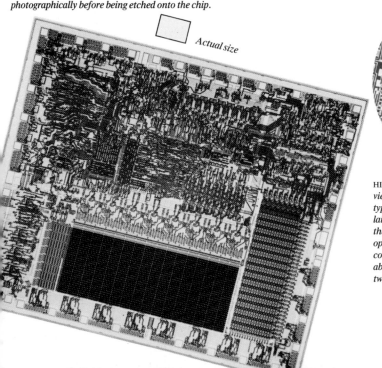

Actual size

HIGH-SPEED CHIP *The magnified view above shows part of an advanced type of chip in which the silicon is laid on sapphire, a technique that multiplies speed of operation. The three black components (top center) are each about 0.01 inch across, or about twice the thickness of a hair.*

Business and trade

BIGGER THAN BELGIUM

Exxon, the giant U.S. oil company, has for years ranked at or near the top of the world's companies in annual sales. In 1985 Exxon raked in $86.7 billion. However, that was only good enough for the number 2 spot, because it was a mediocre year for oil but a good year for automobiles: General Motors was tops with $96.4 billion. Only the world's 23 richest nations had gross national products that exceeded the gross of GM. Belgium, for example, has a GNP of about $85 billion.

Neither Exxon nor GM was first in net income in 1985. That distinction went to International Business Machines Corporation, which earned $6.5 billion. Measured by assets, banking corporations, led by Citicorp with $173 billion, dominated the top 10.

The world's largest public employer is the state-owned rail system of the Soviet Union. Its workers number some 2 million.

BUDGET BREAKERS

The dubious distinction of being the world's greatest budget breaker could belong to one of several candidates. A clear winner is difficult to determine.

One strong contender is Indiana's Marble Hill nuclear power plant, reputed to be the most expensive project ever dropped. The original cost estimate in 1978 was $1.4 billion, but when the project was scrapped, half finished, in 1984, it had already cost $2.5 billion. If the plant had been completed, the eventual price tag would have totaled $7.7 billion. Another nuclear power facility, at Shoreham on Long Island, New York, was budgeted at $261 million. By 1986 the cost had reached $4.6 billion, more than 15 times the original estimate. Studies by New York State indicate that residents will not need electricity from Shoreham until the year 2013, but the utility says the area's energy needs cannot be met without Shoreham or a new power plant.

The Concorde, paid for by French and British taxpayers, was forecast in 1962 to cost between $400 and $460 million for a production run of 16 jets. By 1978, when the last of the 16 came off the production line at the British Aircraft Corporation's Bristol works, the cost had soared to more than 13 times as much: a total of $4.28 billion, or nearly $267 million for *each* of the 11 Concordes now in service.

THE GREAT SILVER SPREE

In 1973 the Hunt brothers, a pair of Texas multi-millionaires, began accumulating silver as a hedge against inflation. They bought so heavily that by early 1974 silver prices had doubled, to $6.70 from $3.27 per troy ounce. The brothers continued their buying spree until 1980—amassing in their personal vaults some 63 million ounces of silver—by which time the silver markets were in chaos. Silver rose to $50.05 per troy ounce in January 1980. Then the bubble burst and the metal fell to $10.80 two months later. The Hunts escaped ruin in the debacle, but many small investors were badly hurt.

THE FIRST COMPANY

Which company is the world's oldest depends largely on definition; the concept of corporations as independent entities was not formalized legally until the 19th century. Nevertheless, the merchant venturers' companies of the golden age of exploration have a claim to the distinction. Among them were such pioneering outfits as the Russian, or Muscovy, Company, founded in England in 1553 as The Mystery and Company of Merchant Adventurers for the Discovery

---

ECONOMIC "LAWS"

The study of economics, founded as a separate academic discipline in the 18th century, remains an inexact science—largely because it deals with complex patterns of human behavior that resist simplification. This has not stopped economists from propounding, sometimes with more than a trace of irony, generalities such as the following.

Law of Diminishing Returns That if one factor of production—staff, say—is continually increased while the others remain constant, eventually each new unit of increase brings a smaller addition to production than the previous one. In a car cruising around a test track, for instance, each sustained increase in speed is achieved by burning more gasoline in the same time frame. But not so obvious is the fact that each additional gallon of gasoline burned produces a smaller and smaller increase in speed, so that if the test car cruised at 100 m.p.h., it could be expected to burn more than twice as much gasoline as a car traveling at 50 m.p.h. Also called Law of Variable Proportions.

Gresham's Law That bad money drives out good. For example, debasing the metal content of coinage lowers the value of money, since owners of unadulterated coins then tend to hoard them or melt them down to buy a greater number of debased coins. Attributed to Elizabeth I's financial adviser, Sir Thomas Gresham, but probably first stated by the Polish astronomer Nicolaus Copernicus.

Iron Law of Wages That if wages rise above subsistence level, they produce a rising birthrate and population, which in turn forces wages down again. Popularized by British economist David Ricardo, but of French origin. Not now accepted.

Parkinson's Law That work expands to fill the time available to do it, or that the amount of work done varies inversely to the number of people employed. Humorously (yet also seriously) published by the British economist Cyril Northcote Parkinson in 1958.

Peter Principle That in any organization every employee rises to his or her level of incompetence. All valuable work is therefore done by people who have not yet reached that level. Another satirical law, published in 1969 by Canadian-born professor Laurence J. Peter.

Say's Law That every rise in the supply of goods produces an increase in demand for them. Stated by the French economist Jean-Baptiste Say in 1803. True only of barter economies, but generally believed until the Great Depression.

Law of Supply and Demand That competition between consumers and producers brings the supply of goods and the demand for them into balance. Cardinal law of free-market economic theory. Overproduction lowers prices, increasing demand; overconsumption raises prices, decreasing demand.

MAJOR ECONOMISTS

1723–90 Adam Smith Scottish economist, chief founder of classical economics. Based theories on the premise that if every man pursued his own self-interest, a guiding "invisible hand" ensured that the general result was in the best interest of society. Argued for free-market competition, free trade between nations, and freedom of commerce and industry from government intervention—a view known as *laissez-faire,* meaning "let [people] do [as they choose]." First economist to advocate the division of labor, each worker specializing in making one part of a complex product in factory production.

1766–1834 Thomas Robert Malthus English economist. Contended that poverty and its associated miseries were unavoidable, since human population increases by geometric ratio but means of subsistence increase by arithmetic ratio; thus population growth alternated with population-reducing forces such as famine, disease, and war.

1772–1823 David Ricardo English economist. Developed the labor theory of value: that the value of any product is roughly equal to the value of the labor that has gone into producing it.

1818–83 Karl Marx German economist. Theoretical founder, with Friedrich Engels, of Communism. Interpreted history as being chiefly determined by economic forces and the struggle between social classes. Invented the notion of surplus value—that although the value of a product depends on the amount of labor embodied in it, only part of the value is paid to the laborer. The "surplus" is retained by the owner or employer in the form of profit, dividends, or rent, and hoarded as capital.

1883–1946 John Maynard Keynes English economist. Most famous of the Cambridge school of economists, who between the two world wars attacked classical economics. Argued that unemployment was reduced not by cutting wages but by increasing purchasing power to stimulate demand. Advocated heavy state investment in public works to provide jobs and increase purchasing power.

1908– John Kenneth Galbraith Canadian-born U.S. economist. Believes that obsession with growth—in national income, consumer expenditure, jobs, and capital investment—leads to the production of waste: goods and services that people do not really need. Attacked such waste in his book *The Affluent Society,* published in 1958, calling for government intervention to control it.

1912– Milton Friedman American economist. Chief member of the Chicago school of economists. Anti-Keynesian. Advocates tight control of the money supply—a doctrine known as monetarism—on the grounds that government spending in excess of income produces inflation and leads to higher levels of unemployment.

definition still used in British law means "before 1189." But the exact foundation date is not known.

WAGES AND THE COST OF LIVING

American and Canadian workers are the highest paid in the world, earning three times as much as their Greek counterparts, the lowest paid workers among industrial nations outside the Communist bloc. Per capita annual incomes in the United States ($14,200) and Canada ($12,800) are also among the highest in the world. The real value of earnings depends on a number of factors, including the cost of living.

In the United States the cost of living is reflected in two indexes: consumer prices for commodities and services; and producer prices, which cover both farm and industrial products. The U.S. Department of Labor has assigned the arbitrary index figure of 100 to both consumer and producer prices in the year 1967. By 1986 the index had risen by more than three times in every category except farm prices, which were about 2.4 times greater than in 1967. After a period of relative stability in the mid-1980s, U.S. living costs were expected to push upward again.

SIGN OF THE THREE BALLS

The traditional symbol of pawnbrokers—three golden balls—may have been derived from the coat of arms of the Medici family, which ruled the Italian city of Florence during the 15th and 16th centuries. The symbol was spread by the Lombards—Italian bankers who set up businesses in medieval London.

TREE OF MONEY *There are about 140 stock exchanges in the world, and the two largest—in New York and London—had humble births. While London's present exchange traces its roots to a noisy 18th-century coffeehouse, stockbrokers in New York began in 1792 to trade beneath a buttonwood tree (above), long since vanished, which is thought to have stood outside what is now 60 Wall Street. The street got its name from a boundary stockade, or wall, built in 1653 by Dutch colonists to protect the settlement against attacks by English colonists and Indians. The origin of stock exchanges goes back to medieval France, where 13th-century stockbrokers traded bills of exchange—IOUs issued in return for loans. At about the same time, Belgian merchants in Bruges began to gather outside the house of the mercantile family Van der Buerse, whose name gave Paris's stock exchange its title, the Bourse.*

of Regions, Dominions, and Places Unknown. Its first governor was the Venetian Sebastian Cabot, whose father, John Cabot, discovered Newfoundland in 1498.

In Europe the Bayerische Staatsbrauerei ("Bavarian State Brewery") was established near Munich in A.D.1040, while the firm of Urquell of Pilsen, founded in 1295 in what is now Czechoslovakia, lives on in the word *pilsner,* or just *pils,* for any strong lager.

Perhaps the most curious claim to the title of the world's oldest company is made by the Faversham Oyster Fishery Company of Kent, in England. An act of Parliament passed in 1930 referred to the fishery's existence "since time immemorial"—which under a

233

Communications—linking the world

BEACONS IN SPACE

In the 11th century B.C. the Greeks lit dozens of hilltop bonfires to send news of the fall of Troy. The news reached Argos, 500 miles away, in just a few hours. Today just three communications satellites are enough to link any two places in the world at the speed of light. The space beacons are parked in what are called geostationary orbits 22,300 miles up, where their speed keeps them fixed above the same spot on the earth as it spins on its axis.

The first such globe-spanning satellites were the Intelsat 2 series, launched from Cape Canaveral, Florida, in the late 1960s. The first of the series took up its position in space in October 1966.

WIRES THAT TRAPPED A KILLER

The world's first public telegraph line, installed in Britain in May 1843, helped to catch a murderer. Used mainly to control train movements, the line was set up along an 18.5-mile stretch of railway track from London to West Drayton, Middlesex.

The system, invented by two Englishmen, William Cooke and Prof. Charles Wheatstone, had five wires connected to five needles. Sending electric currents down any two of the wires simultaneously would deflect the corresponding needles to identify individual letters.

In 1845 a murder suspect named John Tawell was spotted boarding a train at Slough. It was too late to stop the train, but news of the sighting was telegraphed ahead to London, and Tawell was arrested near Paddington Station. He was later tried, convicted, and hanged.

THE CRIPPEN FACTOR

When the Italian Guglielmo Marconi (1874–1937) invented wireless telegraphy in 1895, only shipowners and navies were quick to catch on to the advantages of the new system over the established network of wires and submarine cables.

A crime helped to change public opinion. In 1910 Capt. Henry Kendal of the SS *Montrose*, bound for Quebec from Liverpool, thought he recognized a wanted British murderer, Dr. Hawley Harvey Crippen, and his mistress, Ethel LeNeve, among the passengers. He telegraphed his suspicions to England. Chief Inspector Walter Dew of Scotland Yard caught a faster boat to Canada and arrested Crippen and LeNeve as they disembarked. Crippen was subequently hanged for the murder of his wife.

TERSE CODE

The lead type used by printers helped U.S. inventor Samuel Morse (1791–1872) in about 1838 to design the Morse code. He used the numbers of each letter in a printer's tray of type as a guide to how frequently the letters were used in English. Then he assigned the shortest signals to the commonest letters. So *e* has the shortest code—a single dot—and *j*, *q*, and *y*, which are rarely used, have the longest codes: combinations of three dashes and a dot.

PUZZLED GENIUS

The Scottish-born American inventor of the telephone, Alexander Graham Bell (1847–1922), claimed that he never really understood the principles of electricity—crucial to the device that, on March 10, 1876, first successfully transmitted human speech. Even in his later years, when the telephone was being widely used, Bell said he still did not understand how someone speaking in Washington could be heard by someone in Paris.

SMART NUMBER *This phone of the 1890s was custom-built for the wealthy Rothschild family. To call the operator, the user had to wind the handle. Public as well as private telephone systems spread rapidly around the world. Berlin had a city network in 1877, only a year after Bell's invention was patented.*

BIRTH OF A NEW ERA *On April 6, 1965, the world's first commercial communications satellite was launched into orbit from Cape Canaveral, Florida. Called the Early Bird, the 85-pound device resembled a bulky table lamp (scale model at left). President Lyndon Johnson used the satellite to make a telephone call to six European leaders, marking the first commercial satellite transmission. Launched by the Communications Satellite Corporation (Comsat), Early Bird increased by nearly two-thirds the transatlantic telephone capacity— to 240 simultaneous calls—and was the only mode of live transatlantic television.*

"HOY, HOY!"

U.S. inventor Thomas Alva Edison (1847–1931) held some 1,300 patents, but a lesser known contribution to modern life may have been his suggestion about using the telephone. He advised people to answer the telephone with a simple "Hello." The telephone's inventor, Alexander Graham Bell, liked "Hoy, hoy!"

MISSED OPPORTUNITY

A Canadian businessman missed a chance to share in the industry founded on the most valuable patent ever granted: number 174,465, Bell's original U.S. patent for the telephone. A Toronto-based publisher, George Brown, was offered exclusive Canadian and British Empire rights to the telephone in the late 1870s for just $150. Brown turned the offer down; he did not think the rights were worth it. For 1982, the last year before its court-ordered break-up into smaller companies, the firm that was built on the patent, American Telephone and Telegraph, was one of the world's largest in terms of assets and staff. It had assets of $148 billion and some 1 million employees. After the breakup AT&T was left with assets of $39.8 billion.

"CUSS-LESS" TELEPHONE

An undertaker in Kansas City invented the automatic telephone exchange because he suspected that telephone operators were being paid by rival undertakers not to connect his calls. Almon Brown Strowger set about inventing a "girl-less, cuss-less, out-of-order-less, wait-less telephone," and in 1891 patented an automatic switchboard whereby callers selected the number by pressing a combination of three buttons. The first automatic exchange was set up in La Porte, Indiana, in 1892. American Bell, the largest U.S. telephone company, adopted the new system—which by then had been modified to use a dial instead of buttons—in 1919.

HELLO . . . HELLO

The time delay in many international telephone conversations is caused by the vast distances the signals must travel. Even at the speed of light (186,000 miles per second) the signals take about one-eighth of a second to reach a geostationary satellite and a similar time to bounce back.

In a two-way telephone conversation using two satellites (between Britain and Australia, for instance) the delay can be more than a second, long enough for a speaker to start talking again in the belief that the original remark has gone unheard.

SIGNALS UNDER THE SEA

Submarine communications cables have been in use since 1851, when the first underwater telegraph cable was laid on the bed of the English Channel between Dover and Calais. Before long it was severed by a fisherman's anchor. Eight years later a cable 2,326 miles long was laid under the Atlantic between Ireland and Newfoundland. Half the cable was towed out from each side, and it was spliced in mid-ocean. That connection lasted only a month.

The first one-piece transatlantic cable was laid by the *Great Eastern*, a giant steamship designed by the British engineer Isambard Kingdom Brunel in 1866; and the first undersea telephone cable linked England and France in 1891.

Not until 1956 was the first transatlantic telephone cable laid, when a reliable "repeater" was developed to amplify the signals over the long distances involved. The cable contained 102 repeaters and carried only 36 conversations at a time.

COMMON CODES

Alphabetical codes are used to transmit messages when other methods are impracticable. Semaphore has a long history in military signaling. Finger spelling is used by the deaf and dumb. Morse was invented in about 1838. Braille, used in books for the blind, was devised by Louis Braille (1809–52), a blind Frenchman. Phonetic alphabets are used to clarify individual letters in radio messages.

	Semaphore	Finger spelling	Morse	Braille	Phonetic
A			.-		Alpha
B			-...		Bravo
C			-.-.		Charlie
D			-..		Delta
E			.		Echo
F			..-.		Foxtrot
G			--.		Golf
H			....		Hotel
I			..		India
J			.---		Juliet
K			-.-		Kilo
L			.-..		Lima
M			--		Mike
N			-.		November
O			---		Oscar
P			.--.		Papa
Q			--.-		Quebec
R			.-.		Romeo
S			...		Sierra
T			-		Tango
U			..-		Uniform
V			...-		Victor
W			.--		Whiskey
X			-..-		X-ray
Y			-.--		Yankee
Z			--..		Zulu

Engineering 1: tunnels and mines

FROM PALACE TO TEMPLE

The earliest successful underwater passage was built before 2000 B.C. at Babylon, in Mesopotamia. The Euphrates River was diverted during the dry season so that engineers could build a brick-lined 2,950-foot channel in the riverbed to connect the royal palace with a temple on the opposite bank

Once the channel was completed, it was roofed and sealed with waterproof bitumen, and the river was returned to its normal course. This building method, known as cut-and-cover, is still used.

A THOUSAND UNDERGROUND SHRINES

Carthaginians, Greeks, Egyptians, and Romans all built catacombs in which to inter their dead, but few were as complex as the Indian temples built during the 5th to 13th centuries. At Ellora, in the Indian state of Maharashtra, archeologists have found a thousand underground shrines and 6 miles of tunnels carved out of rock with hand chisels.

CARRYING THE WATER

The Romans used tunnels extensively for the aqueducts they built to carry water to their towns and cities. The Appia, the first aqueduct to supply Rome (312 B.C.), ran as a tunnel for about 10 miles.

The longest tunnel of any kind in the world today serves the same purpose. It is the 105-mile tunnel carrying water from the West Branch of the Delaware River to New York City.

BIRTHDAY GREETING

Isambard Kingdom Brunel, the 19th-century English engineer, gave himself a unique birthday greeting when he designed the Box railway tunnel in Wiltshire in the late 1840s. By altering the alignment of the tunnel entrance slightly from its agreed specifications, he ensured that on April 9 each year the rising sun flooded the tunnel with light. That day was Brunel's birthday.

INSPIRED BY A MOLLUSK

In 1818, after observing the action of the wood-boring mollusk *Teredo navalis,* the French-born engineer Marc Isambard Brunel (father of Isambard Kingdom Brunel) designed the first successful machine for tunneling beneath riverbeds. The mollusk, scourge of wooden-hulled ships, bores into timbers, gnawing the wood with its powerful jaws and supporting the borehole with its hard tubular shell.

So Brunel built a box-shaped iron casing, or shield, that could be pushed through soft ground by means of screw-operated jacks. The men dug through shuttered openings in the face of the shield while behind them the tunnel was lined with bricks.

THE BIGGEST HOLE *The "Big Hole" at Kimberley, South Africa, is the world's deepest open-cast mine. During the 44 years the mine was open, between 1871 and 1915, some 25 million tons of earth was removed from it, mostly by laborers with picks and shovels. The hole, which is a mile around and about 4,000 feet deep, has yielded 14.5 million carats of diamonds.*

The machine drove the world's first underwater tunnel beneath the River Thames from Wapping to Rotherhithe in London. The tunnel was opened in 1842, and 22 years later it was being used as a railway tunnel, as it still is today.

POP GOES THE WORKER
Builders of underwater tunnels in the second half of the 19th century often worked in pressurized chambers called caissons. The air inside the caissons was pressurized in order to hold water back while the tunnel was dug. Similar chambers were used to dig the foundations for bridges.

In 1905 a tunneler working in a caisson under the East River in New York had a lucky escape when the side of the pressure chamber collapsed. The enormous pressure fired him upward through 5 feet of riverbed silt, like a cork from a champagne bottle. He shot to the surface and was rescued—shaken but not seriously hurt—by the crew of a passing tug.

TUNNELING THROUGH THE ALPS
Four railway tunnels cut into the Alps reduced the traveling time through Europe's largest land barrier by up to 70 percent. The Fréjus, St. Gotthard, Simplon, and Lötschberg railway tunnels were completed in the late 19th and early 20th centuries.

During the construction of the Fréjus Tunnel (1857– 71) pneumatic power, now commonplace in industry, was used for the first time to drive tools.

Altogether, some 400 workmen died while working on the tunnels, many in floods and avalanches. At the Simplon Tunnel alone there were 5,000 casualties, including 133 people permanently disabled.

THE TUNNEL THAT NOBODY WOULD BUILD
In the 19th century a French eccentric called Thomé de Gamond spent about 40 years and his personal fortune in trying to promote a tunnel beneath the English Channel. His ambition was to span the 20 miles that separate France from England—an idea that for over 200 years has never failed to capture headlines and then fall flat. In Gamond's case, both France and England thought that the cost would be too great and that, politically and economically, it was best that the two countries remain apart.

Gamond's main supporter was his daughter Elizabeth, who rowed the boat from which he descended to the seabed for rock samples. After all his money had gone, she taught music and gave him her earnings so that he could continue his life's work. But the tunnel remained a dream, and Gamond died penniless and humiliated in 1876.

As with Gamond, government disinterest and lack of financing have doomed subsequent Channel tunnel schemes. But in 1986 President François Mitterand of France and British prime minister Margaret Thatcher announced support for a privately financed 30-mile double railway tunnel between Dover and Calais. Scheduled for completion in 1993 at a $7-billion cost, the rail tunnel would be paralleled later by a separate one for automobiles.

LUCKY ACCIDENT
During World War I a cleaner in an electric lamp factory in Berlin accidentally created the material used for modern drilling bits: tungsten carbide. At the time, there was a shortage of the industrial diamonds used to make light filaments, and the factory's scientists were trying to produce a material to replace the diamonds. They were about to give up when the cleaner spilled some iron filings on the engineers' work. As a result, the new material hardened and formed the metallic compound now called tungsten carbide.

At first the tungsten compounds were used only for making light filaments. But during World War II tungsten began to be used to make the tips on armor-piercing shells, and since 1945 it has been used in drill bits that bore through rock, in preference to the more expensive industrial diamonds.

LIFE SENTENCE, DEATH SENTENCE
Forced labor in mines seems to be a punishment favored by tyrants. In ancient Egypt prisoners of war, criminals, and entire families who had displeased the authorities were sentenced to work underground in gold mines for the rest of their lives. Two thousand years later Charles IX of Sweden (1550–1611) ordered the overseers in his silver mines to torture and execute any Polish prisoners of war sent underground who refused to work there. If the overseers failed in this, they themselves were executed.

COOLING OFF
A refrigerating plant with the cooling capacity of 2,750 tons of ice is installed in the world's deepest mine: the Western Deep Levels gold mine at Carletonville, South Africa. Without the cooling plant, the temperature at the lowest levels, over 12,000 feet down, would be as high as 131°F.

MINING TECHNIQUES

Today three main mining techniques are in use: open-cast, drift, and deep underground mining. A fourth technique, known as panning, is still used by amateur prospectors around the world.

Panning In the 19th century, panning methods— known since the time of the ancient Egyptians— were used by prospectors to find minerals, particularly precious metals and gems that had washed down ancient river courses and settled in pockets in the bedrock. The prospectors' basic equipment consisted of a shovel and a sieve, or pan, into which the mineral-rich gravel was scooped. The miners who thronged to California, the Klondike, and Australia in the gold rushes mostly used panning. But panning has been replaced by geochemistry, which traces deposits back to their source by analyzing soil, stream sediments, and plant material.

Open-cast mining Used to get ores lying close to the surface. Excavators strip off coverings of soil or clay (thus the less precise term *strip mining*), and ore-bearing rock is then broken up by blasting and removed. Alternatively, water is used to flush the ore-rich rock from unwanted material. Because the ore is "open"—on the surface—giant excavating machinery can be used, making the mining quick and relatively cheap.

Drift mining Used for deposits fairly near the surface, but not so near as to make open-cast mining economical. Large shafts, or "drifts," are driven into the ground—often a hillside—more or less horizontally. This enables conveyor belts and trucks to move ore directly from the working face to the surface. Sometimes called gloryhole mining.

Deep underground mining Used to reach seams hundreds or thousands of feet below the surface. It is the most expensive technique because long vertical shafts and tunnels have to be driven to reach the ore, the ore must be moved a considerable distance to reach the surface, and the size of the tunnels restricts the use of large excavating machinery.

Engineering 2: bridges and dams

THE ARCH BREAKTHROUGH

The use of the arch by the Greeks and Romans as a building technique became as important to bridge building as the silicon chip has been to electronics. Before the arch, most bridges, like other buildings, made do with the post-and-lintel system of vertical pillars supporting horizontal beams.

Only wood could be used for the longer spans, but it was a fire risk and eventually rotted. The first known use of the arch was in mud-brick constructions in about 4000 B.C. At Mohenjo-Daro in Pakistan between 3000 and 2000 B.C. arches were used to span small drains and culverts. And in about 1400 B.C. the Egyptians built what was then the largest known arch span, in a grain store at Thebes. The span was 13 feet wide.

HANGING ON

Stone Age people probably used simple suspension bridges some 10,000 years ago—crossing streams by means of two vines tied to trees on each bank. The trick was to walk on one vine while holding the other.

LONDON BRIDGE IS STAYING UP

There has been a bridge on the site of London Bridge since at least before the middle of the 10th century A.D. The Romans, who occupied Britain in the 1st century A.D., may also have put a bridge across the Thames at the same site, but no evidence of it remains. The first known bridge was a wooden structure, and it was replaced by a 19-arch stone bridge, which was completed in 1209. The new bridge, built by an engineer called Peter of Colechurch, was London's only fixed crossing of the Thames for more than 500 years. It was joined by Westminster Bridge in 1750.

London Bridge became much more than a roadway. It was crowded with houses, shops, taverns, chapels, and a fort. The children's song, "London Bridge Is Falling Down," which dates from the 18th century, refers to the frequent collapse or demolition of these often ramshackle buildings, not to the bridge itself.

Peter of Colechurch's bridge was finally pulled down and replaced by a five-arch design in 1831. It was this bridge—known as Rennie's Bridge after its designer, John Rennie—that was sold to Lake Havasu City in Arizona for $2,460,000 and rebuilt there in the 1970s. Its successor, the present bridge, which has only three arches, was opened in 1973.

DISASTER ON THE HIGH GIRDERS

Thomas Bouch, the 19th-century British engineer who built the first railway bridge over the River Tay in Scotland, was knighted for his engineering achievements at the same ceremony in June 1879 as Henry Bessemer, who invented the Bessemer steelmaking process in 1855.

Six months after the ceremony, on the night of December 28, Bouch's bridge collapsed in a storm, killing 75 people. The bridge, which was largely made of wrought iron, was so buffeted by gusting winds that its 13 central girders were blown 160 feet into the river below, taking a train with them. A subsequent government inquiry blamed the disaster on faulty design and construction. Had the Tay bridge been made of Bessemer's steel, modern engineers believe, it could have survived the storm. But steel bridges were illegal in Britain at the time because steel was regarded as an experimental metal.

WHEEL OF FORTUNE

The family of a Dutch engineer still earns an income from a waterwheel that does not exist. In 1580 the engineer, Pieter Morice, was granted a license allowing him to set up a waterwheel under an arch of London Bridge to provide power for pumping fresh

BRIDGE DESIGN

The earliest type of bridge was a beam bridge: logs or slabs of stone laid flat across a stream. Box-girder bridges, made of metal, are a modern form. In a cantilever bridge the supporting beam is in at least two parts joined by a hinge, a design that reduces the strain at the center of the span. In an arch bridge the weight of the roadway is carried by an arch to the foundations on each bank; in some modern designs the arch is partly above the roadway. A suspension bridge is essentially an inverted arch, with its roadway hung from a curving cable.

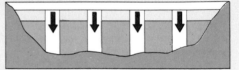

BEAM BRIDGE *Straight slabs or girders carry the roadway in a beam bridge. The spans have to be relatively short, and the load (shown by the arrows) is borne by the piers.*

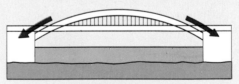

ARCH BRIDGE *The 1,650-foot-long Gladesville Bridge spans the harbor at Sydney, Australia. Its roadbed carries two rail tracks, eight car lanes, and a footpath.*

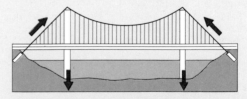

SUSPENSION BRIDGE *The world's longest bridges are now all suspension bridges. In this design the bulk of the load is carried on cables anchored to the banks.*

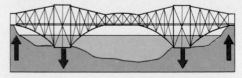

CANTILEVER BRIDGE *The central span pushes down through the piers and pulls up at each end. The longest cantilever, the Quebec Bridge in Canada, is 3,239 feet long.*

water to neighboring houses. At the time, the bridge was an ideal site because its 19 arches so constricted the river's flow that there was a difference of up to 5 feet between the water levels on either side. When the bridge was replaced in the 19th century, there was no longer a suitable arch under which Morice's heirs could operate the waterwheel. Since the license had been granted for 500 years, Morice's descendants were awarded compensation. They still get $3,750 a year from the Thames Water Authority.

A BRIDGE THAT WENT TOO FAR
Many 19th-century engineers believed that the key to longer suspension bridges was to keep the structure light so that cables did not have to be made stronger to support longer and longer spans.

The fate of the Tacoma Narrows Bridge in the state of Washington in 1940 proved that this logic had its limits. Four months after the slender and spectacular bridge opened to carry traffic on a single 2,800-foot span across Puget Sound, the span collapsed. Designed to be safe in winds of up to 120 m.p.h., the bridge was destroyed by a wind of only 42 m.p.h. The wind started the bridge deck moving in wavelike up-and-down oscillations that eventually reached 30 feet from crest to trough.

After 3 hours the deck started to twist back and forth through 90 degrees until some of the suspending cables broke and sent first the middle and then the whole of the span plunging into the water of Puget Sound. No lives were lost, because the bridge had been closed in time.

HUMBER HIGHWAY
The Humber Bridge in northern England—currently the world's longest suspension bridge—has a deck with a curved underside, like an upside-down airplane wing, so that the stronger the wind, the more firmly it holds itself in place. In addition, the cables that hold the roadway are set at an angle rather than vertically in order to damp down vibrations at low wind speeds. The bridge's central span is 4,626 feet long, and the towers are so far apart that they are 1.4 inches out of parallel to allow for the curvature of the earth.

Work on an even larger bridge began in 1978 in Japan. The Akashi–Kaikyo Bridge, due to be completed in 1988, will be a double-decker, carrying a roadway on one level and a railway on the other. Its main suspension span will stretch 5,840 feet—more than a mile.

THE FIRST DAMS
The earliest dams in the world were modest affairs, built to create reservoirs for irrigation or for potable water in dry times. The earliest known dams, made of earth faced with stone, were built in about 3200 B.C. at Jawa in the north of present-day Jordan.

SEEDS OF SUCCESS
A pioneer in making reinforced concrete—without which it would be impossible to build modern dams or bridges—was a French commercial gardener. Joseph Monier wanted to make flowerpots larger than was possible with clay, so in 1849 he had the idea of

FACTS ABOUT
SCIENCE & TECHNOLOGY

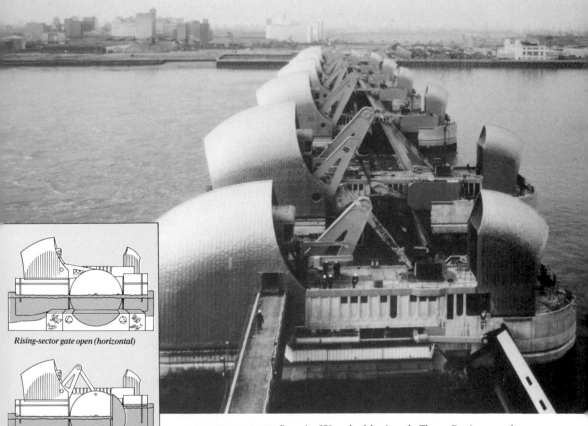

Rising-sector gate open (horizontal)

Rising-sector gate closed (vertical)

TAMER OF THE THAMES *Spanning 570 yards of the river, the Thames Barrier, opened in 1984, protects London from surge-tide floods. When not in use, the bow-shaped steel gates lie in sills on the riverbed, out of the way of ships.*

239

making them from wire netting covered in concrete. He soon realized that the principle could be extended to other sorts of construction, and patented the idea of casting concrete around crisscrossing iron bars. The combination created a material that was stronger than either of its elements alone, and in addition the cement covering prevented the iron bars from rusting.

A DAM THAT DID NOT LAST

Ancient Egypt depended on the Nile to irrigate its crops. But although the Egyptians built an elaborate network of irrigation canals, they built only one dam. Constructed between 2950 and 2750 B.C., it contained more than 100,000 tons of earth faced with masonry; it sprawled for about 350 feet across a watercourse called Wadi el-Garawi, to the south of Cairo. At its base the dam was 276 feet thick.

The dam was used to trap rainwater for nearby quarries. But despite its size, it lasted only a few years before being breached by the weight of the water behind it. All that remains are the stubs of the wall on either side of the watercourse.

. . . AND TWO THAT DID

Two irrigation dams built by Roman engineers in the 2nd century A.D. in Mérida, Spain, are still in use. The only major maintenance work they have needed in the past 1,800 years has been the renewal of their stone facings, which was done in the 1930s.

THE SANDHOGS

Caissons were used experimentally in Europe to build underwater foundations in the mid-19th century, but the technique did not become famous until the great piers for the Brooklyn Bridge were built in the late 1860s. The caisson is simply a sunken box, as watertight as possible, that enables men to first excavate and then build on a riverbed as they breathe compressed air forced down from above water.

The men in the caissons became known as sandhogs, an apt description for workers digging in the muck on the bottom of a river. The caisson was a great engineering advance, but it also introduced the dreaded caisson disease, or "bends," a painful and crippling condition that results from passing too quickly from the pressurized atmosphere of the caisson into normal atmospheric pressure. The disorder is caused by release of gas bubbles in the victim's tissues.

RECORD BREAKER

For more than 3,000 years the Great Pyramid of Cheops in Egypt was the world's largest structure, with a total volume of more than 3.3 million cubic yards. It was surpassed only after the 10th century A.D. by a Mexican pyramid, now known as the Quetzalcoatl, which has a volume of about 4.3 million cubic yards. Then, in 1942, both records were overtaken by the Grand Coulee Dam across the Columbia River in Washington State. The concrete dam, which holds back a reservoir 150 miles long and whose turbines can generate more than 2 million kilowatts of hydroelectric power, is 550 feet high—only about 65 feet taller than the Great Pyramid. But its volume is more than three times greater, at 10.6 million cubic yards.

Newer dams have been built that are still larger and higher. An earth-fill dam at New Cornelia Tailings, Arizona, is more than 20 times larger, with a total volume of 274 million cubic yards. The Grand Dixence Dam in Switzerland, completed in 1962, is nearly twice as high, at 935 feet. Dwarfing all is a Soviet dam built in the 1980s across the Vakhsh River; it is 1,099 feet high.

MOVING A BOAT UPHILL

Before canal locks were invented, boats could be moved past such obstacles as hills or rapids only by being portaged—physically carried.

The Vikings, for instance, are known to have portaged their longships on rollers across more than 10 miles of land to get from the Baltic to the North Sea and bypass the dangerous waters of the Skagerrak. The Kiel Canal, first built as the Eider Canal in 1784, now follows much the same route.

Flash locks
The first types of lock were stanches, or flash locks, which were used to reduce gradients on rivers and raise the water level in shallow stretches. They were usually single barriers built across gaps in weirs. To allow passage, the barrier was opened, and a boat either rode through on the surge, or flash, of water or was hauled through against it.

The Chinese installed two of these flash locks about 250 feet apart on the Grand Canal in A.D. 984, and some scholars argue that they represent the first true lock, known as a pound lock. But there is no evidence that the gates were used in sequence in the way that the much safer pound lock is.

Pound locks
Pound locks consist of two sets of gates set close together so that they enclose, or impound, a short stretch of water. They made it possible to build canals up steeper and higher slopes. Boats passing upstream enter the pound through the lower gates, which are then closed. Valves are opened in the upper gates, allowing the water in the lock to rise. When the level in the lock matches the level upstream, the upper gates are opened and the boat sails on. Boats traveling downstream go through the reverse procedure.

Inclined planes
To supplement particularly busy locks, inclined planes were sometimes built beside them. In one type, boats were floated onto movable docks; then the docks, which ran on rails, were winched up or down the slope and lowered into the water again. Such a lock was built at Foxton on Britain's Grand Union Canal between 1896 and 1900, but it was abandoned in 1911. Few inclined planes remain in use.

HOW A POUND LOCK WORKS *Valves in or beside the gates at each end of a pound lock allow the water level inside to be raised or lowered to match the level outside.*

DROWNED WATERFALL

The world's largest waterfall has been drowned by a dam. The lake created by the dam is so big and so deep that the site of the falls, 118 miles upstream, is now just an underwater cliff. The drowned waterfall is the Guaíra Falls, on the Paraná River between Paraguay and Brazil. The falls were about 130 feet high, far lower than several other waterfalls. But the volume of water flowing over them was more than double the flow over Niagara Falls.

The dam that has drowned the falls is the Itaipu Dam, completed in November 1982. The installation of giant turbines to generate electricity is still going on. By 1988 the dam is scheduled to produce 12.6 billion watts of electricity, which would make Itaipu the world's largest power station.

THE GRANDEST CANAL

The first canals were built in about 4000 B.C. to improve navigation on the shallow, silty rivers of Mesopotamia. The longest canal in the ancient world, however, was built in China. Called the Grand Canal, it was begun in the 6th century B.C. as a series of short sections linking stretches of navigable rivers. By A.D. 1327 it had grown into a waterway 1,107 miles long, stretching from the Chinese capital, Beijing (Peking), to Hangzhou (Hangchow). When work was at its height during the early 7th century A.D., the work force is estimated to have been 5 million.

The Grand Canal is still in use but has been overtaken in length by Russia's Volga–Baltic Waterway, opened in 1964. This incorporates 1,850 miles of artificial waterway and links the Black Sea to the Baltic via Leningrad.

THE MISSING ARCH

Although the Romans mastered the principle of the arch for bridges at least 200 years before the birth of Christ, they did not think of applying it to dams until the 6th century A.D. Modern dams derive much of their strength from their shape, which curves against the weight of the water behind them like an arch laid on its side, with the crown of the curve jutting upstream into the lake. The first dam known to have used the principle was the Daras Dam. It was built on the Persian frontier for the Byzantine emperor Justinian, between A.D. 527 and 565, and was described by the Byzantine historian Procopius in 560.

ONE FAMILY'S FATEFUL BRIDGE

The Brooklyn Bridge took the life of the man who designed it and almost killed his son as well.

In the summer of 1869 John A. Roebling, the bridge's designer, was surveying the site from an East River piling when his foot slipped and he was severely injured by a docking ship. Carried to his son's nearby house in Brooklyn Heights, the elder Roebling died from tetanus 3 weeks later. The son, Col. Washington A. Roebling, took over his father's work, but in 1872 was permanently and painfully disabled by caisson disease as he worked beside his men digging the foundation for one of the great piers that would anchor the bridge. Voiceless as well as crippled, the younger Roebling continued to direct the building of the bridge, observing the work through field glasses from his sickroom in Brooklyn Heights. His wife, Emily, carried his instructions to the bridge site, and in 1881 walked across the bridge on temporary planking. Two years later the bridge formally opened with tremendous fanfare. Washington Roebling died at 89 in 1926, outliving Emily by 23 years.

THE FIELD BUSTER

Although it improves the irrigation of thousands of acres of land, Egypt's Aswan High Dam—364 feet high, nearly 2.5 miles long, and built across the Nile in the 1960s with Soviet money and expertise—is turning fields hundreds of miles away into desert. For centu-ries farmers in the lower Nile delta near the Mediterranean have depended on the fertile silt washed down the river valley in the annual floods. But now that the river has been bottled up in Lake Nasser (known as Lake Nubia in its southern portion in Sudan), the floods have stopped—and the desert is creeping in. Still, it is unlikely whether these losses will cancel out the tremendous gains in irrigated land made possible by the dam.

DESERT LAKE *Inset map shows location of Lake Nasser behind Aswan High Dam. The lake spreads back 2,000 square miles into southern Egypt and northern Sudan. Rectangle on map indicates area covered by aerial photograph of lake's main body and arms.*

Transportation

STIFF PARKING FINE The first paved roads were processional ways leading to the great temples and festival sites in the cities of the Babylonians and Assyrians, and over them were carried idols of the gods of these early Mesopotamian civilizations. The Assyrians were the first to make a state business of road building. Rules of the road were strict. King Sennacherib, who ruled Assyria in the early 7th century B.C., decreed that anyone putting up a building or parking a chariot alongside the processional way in his capital, Nineveh, would face death by impaling.

The word coach *derives from the Hungarian town of Kocs, where in about A.D. 1500 a comparatively smooth-riding horse-drawn vehicle was designed.*

The carriage was slung between the axles on leather straps, and the front wheels were smaller than the rear ones to make steering easier.

ALL ROADS LEAD TO ROME Road construction was one of the great triumphs of the Roman Empire. By the time the empire fell in the 5th century A.D., its road system included more than 50,000 miles of roads in Europe and the Middle East.

Not until the great age of railways in the 19th century was the Roman network surpassed in scope—or in speed of travel. At their peak, Roman highways allowed a traveler from Rome to reach London in 6 days. For 1,500 years that traveling time between the two cities was rarely bettered.

Gunpowder was proposed as fuel for the first internal-combustion engine, which was suggested in the 17th century by the Dutch mathematician Christiaan Huygens (1629–95). He is better known for inventing, in about 1656, the first working pendulum clock.

QUICK START It was the development of the electric starter that finally made gasoline the fuel choice for the automobile. A British Arnold car was the first to be fitted with an electric starter in 1896.

By 1912 the Cadillac Company in the United States had introduced the system into production models. Until then 40 percent of cars were steam-powered, 38 percent used electric batteries, and only 22 percent used gasoline. The electric starter meant that cars could start up at once—unlike those with steam power, which took time to heat to the required pressure. And gasoline-driven cars could be refueled more easily than electric cars could.

English coachmen in the late 19th century despised the newfangled machines competing for road space: bicycles. Especially hated were "penny-farthings," bikes with big front wheels and small rear wheels. In 1876 one coachman was fined for whipping a cyclist who was overtaking him.

ACCIDENT PIONEER A huge steam-powered gun carriage invented by a French artillery officer, Nicholas Joseph Cugnot, was the world's first self-propelled

THE CHANGING SHAPE OF THE CAR

1885 German engineer Karl Benz put a gasoline engine in a vehicle that looked like a motorized tricycle and was steered by a tiller. Benz's engine produced less than 1 horsepower.

1886 The German Gottlieb Daimler's converted phaeton fitted with a gasoline engine was a true "horseless carriage." A later model, built in 1889, could run twice as fast as Benz's pioneer. It also had a clutch and gears, setting the pattern for the car of the future.

1891 Two French toolmakers, René Panhard and Émile Levassor, were the first engineers to put the engine at the front of a car. This gave better balance and made the car easier to steer.

1891–92 Early Peugeots had their engines in the rear. They were light, weighing only around 900 pounds. Oddly, they had no radiators. Instead, the water used to cool the engine was itself cooled by being circulated around the metal frame.

1893 Duryea brothers, Charles E. and J. Frank, built first successful gasoline-powered automobile in the U.S.A.

1896 British engineer Frederick Lanchester introduced a car with a system of epicyclic gears that could be preselected. The design was a forerunner of modern automatic transmissions.

1901 A new Daimler model combined into one machine for the first time all the vital features of the modern automobile: a powerful four-cylinder engine, a pressed-steel chassis, a honeycomb radiator, and a recognizably modern gear stick moving in a "gate." The model was named Mercedes, after the daughter of an Austrian, Emil Jellinek, who was the Daimler representative in Nice, France.

1908 Henry Ford's Model T, the Tin Lizzie, was the first everyman's car. It not only brought motoring to the masses but was the first mass-produced car and became a cornerstone of 20th-century U.S. prosperity.

1922 The bull-nosed Morris launched the family car in Britain. In the 1920s this popular line could be bought for as little as $775, at $115 down and about $9 per week. Also in 1922, the Austin Seven became the first of the family runabouts. It had all the big-car characteristics contained in a small design. Top speed was 45–50 m.p.h., and it averaged 40 miles on a gallon of gasoline.

1938 The Volkswagen (German for "people's car"), launched in the late 1930s in Germany, went on to rack up worldwide sales of more than 40 million. In the early 1980s the Beetle was still being made in South America.

1948 The Rover Company in England brought out the revolutionary go-anywhere Land-Rover. This was a peacetime version of the American Willys Jeep—standing for GP, or general-purpose vehicle. The jeep was also a versatile four-wheel-drive vehicle that did all the U.S. Army's donkeywork in World War II.

1959 The Austin Mini was introduced in Britain. It became hugely popular. It was small enough to squeeze through city traffic, easy to park, cheap to run, yet big enough for four adults.

1983 Austin Rover in Britain introduced the Maestro, with a "talking dashboard" designed to alert the driver to engine problems, the latest in a line of electronic systems added to cars since the 1960s.

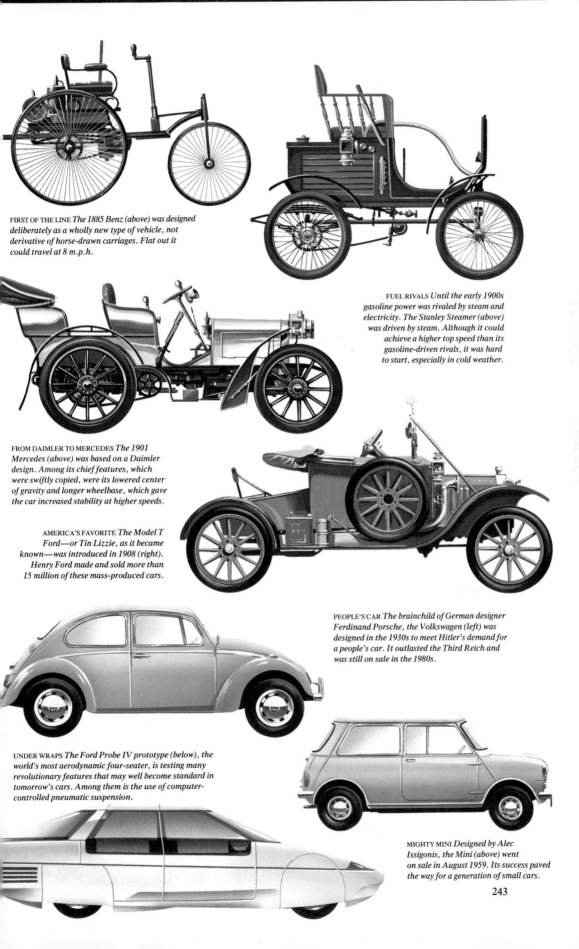

FIRST OF THE LINE *The 1885 Benz (above) was designed deliberately as a wholly new type of vehicle, not derivative of horse-drawn carriages. Flat out it could travel at 8 m.p.h.*

FUEL RIVALS *Until the early 1900s gasoline power was rivaled by steam and electricity. The Stanley Steamer (above) was driven by steam. Although it could achieve a higher top speed than its gasoline-driven rivals, it was hard to start, especially in cold weather.*

FROM DAIMLER TO MERCEDES *The 1901 Mercedes (above) was based on a Daimler design. Among its chief features, which were swiftly copied, were its lowered center of gravity and longer wheelbase, which gave the car increased stability at higher speeds.*

AMERICA'S FAVORITE *The Model T Ford—or Tin Lizzie, as it became known—was introduced in 1908 (right). Henry Ford made and sold more than 15 million of these mass-produced cars.*

PEOPLE'S CAR *The brainchild of German designer Ferdinand Porsche, the Volkswagen (left) was designed in the 1930s to meet Hitler's demand for a people's car. It outlasted the Third Reich and was still on sale in the 1980s.*

UNDER WRAPS *The Ford Probe IV prototype (below), the world's most aerodynamic four-seater, is testing many revolutionary features that may well become standard in tomorrow's cars. Among them is the use of computer-controlled pneumatic suspension.*

MIGHTY MINI *Designed by Alec Issigonis, the Mini (above) went on sale in August 1959. Its success paved the way for a generation of small cars.*

243

Transportation

road vehicle. On its first run in 1769 the three-wheeled monster averaged less than 1 m.p.h. The following year an even larger successor is said to have created the world's first motor vehicle accident by overturning on a Paris street.

THE BELLS WERE RINGING The bicycle won its right to the roads of Britain in 1888. Parliament passed an act classifying it as a carriage. Under the law, every bike had to be fitted with a bell, which had to be rung nonstop while the machine was in motion.

A three-wheeled vehicle powered by dogs was invented in the 1880s by a Monsieur Huret of France. Inside the two huge rear wheels were treadmills driven by the animals. An outcry by animal lovers led to the idea's being scrapped.

WORLD-BEATER A round-the-world car race was staged by the French newspaper *Le Matin* in 1908, with the aim of boosting the French car industry—but no French car finished. First home over the 13,500-mile westward course from New York to Paris was a German Protos, which took 165 days but suffered a 15-day penalty for traveling part of the way by train. The winner, in 170 days, was an American car, a Thomas.

BORN IN A SHED Henry Ford, founder of the Ford Motor Company, made his first car in a backyard shed at his home in Detroit, Michigan, in 1896. Twelve years later he began production of the Model T. Its 1908 price tag was $850, which by 1916 had dropped to $400, thanks to Ford's adoption of mass-production methods. From 1908 to 1927, when Ford replaced the Model T with the Model A, half the automobiles that Americans bought were Ford's Model T's—over 15 million of them.

Henry Ford did not invent the assembly line. What he did was set assembly lines in motion. Stationary lines had been in use for years.
Ford first used the moving assembly line idea in 1913 to speed production of magnetos, the dynamos that produced ignition sparks, for the Model T. By the end of 1914 he had installed a chain-driven conveyor to handle chassis construction in the same way. This cut assembly time from 12 hours to 1 hour per chassis.

THE STORY OF THE ROAD

Ceremonial boulevards in the ancient cities of Mesopotamia, paved with stone 4,000 years ago, were the first roads in the modern sense. Later, Roman roads formed a huge network in Europe and the Middle East, and Roman techniques were still being copied by Napoleonic engineers as late as the 19th century. Only with the introduction of tar, asphalt, and concrete in the past 150 years have road-building techniques shown significant improvement over Roman methods.

ROMAN The roads on which the Roman legions tramped across Europe were simple, but lasting, in construction. The roads were founded on tightly packed earth covered with pebbles set in mortar. This was overlaid with a hard filling, cambered so that the water would run off each side. Some roads were paved on top with stone slabs.

MACADAM In this 19th-century technique, a convex foundation of tightly packed earth formed the road base. It was covered with two 4-inch courses of carefully graded stones. These were overlaid with pebbles, which were ground to a fine dust by the wheels of horse-drawn coaches. Later, tar was added to the top layer, creating the surface called tarmac.

MODERN The highways of the 20th century are built on a base of pebbly material over which a layer of concrete is laid. Above this is a layer of tar or asphalt. The surface is often smoothed with rolled asphalt, though sometimes concrete slabs alone are used.

FIRST EASY RIDERS An inflatable tire with a rubber inner tube was invented by a Scottish engineer, Robert Thomson, in 1845. Made of canvas, with leather treads around the inner tube, it gave a comfortable ride, but there were so many manufacturing and fitting problems that Thomson dropped the idea. In 1888 a Belfast veterinary surgeon, John Dunlop, invented a pneumatic tire with rubber treads for his 10-year-old son's tricycle. The following year he helped to form a company that would produce his invention—which eventually grew into the Dunlop Rubber Company.

A limousine built in 1968 for the official use of the president of the United States cost $500,000. The car, a Lincoln Continental Executive, weighed 5.5 tons, including over 2 tons of steel plate. No less speedy and responsive than the standard limo, it was designed to travel at 50 m.p.h. even with all its tires shot away.

DEATH ON THE ROAD Two people died in automobile accidents in the United States in 1899. Seventy years later there were more than 60,000 fatalities in a single year—more Americans than were killed in the entire Vietnam War.

Already in this century more than 25 million people have been killed on the world's roads. By the year

HOBBYHORSE *The 18th-century forerunner of the bicycle was propelled by the rider's feet.*

PEDAL POWER *The first front-wheel-drive bicycle came out in 1861.*

HIGH RIDE *The first penny-farthing—the name comes from the wheel arrangement—was built in 1870.*

BICYCLE FEVER *By the 1890s new models had helped to make bicycling a craze.*

2000 the car will probably have claimed more victims than World War I and World War II combined—an estimated 45 to 50 million lives.

SMOOTHER ROADS Tarmac, the most widely used road surface in the world, gets its name from a Scottish engineer who did not really invent it. The engineer, John Loudon McAdam (1756–1836), invented a road-building technique called macadamizing in the early 19th century. Over a bed of large tightly packed rocks, McAdam put a dry layer of smaller stones. This he topped with fine gravel or crushed slag to make a smoother surface. The idea for binding the surface together with tar was devised only in 1854, 18 years after McAdam's death, by a Nottingham surveyor named E. P. Hooley, who named the new surface tarmacadam (later shortened to tarmac) in McAdam's honor.

After 1900, with the increase in auto traffic, concrete roads became more popular. The first concrete road in the United States was laid in 1894 in Bellefontaine, Ohio.

POTTERY ENGINE In 1983 Japanese engineers claimed a breakthrough in making a workable engine out of pottery. The pottery engine, developed by researchers at the Asahi Glass Company, is made from carbon silicon and nitrogen silicon ceramics that are almost as strong as steel but conduct much less heat. Researchers hope that ceramic engines will operate safely at much higher temperatures. This would increase their efficiency, cut pollution, and allow the use of almost any fuel to power them.

DANGER SIGNALS The world's first traffic lights were installed near the House of Commons in London in December 1868—and soon injured a policeman who was operating them. The red and green gas-lights were set in a revolving lantern perched atop a cast-iron pillar some 23 feet high. A manually operated lever changed the lights and extended and lowered the signal arms. One night in January 1869 the gas exploded, blowing gravel into the eye of the constable manning the lever. Despite the accident, the lights were used at night for the convenience of members of Parliament until 1872, when they were removed. Not until 1926 did traffic lights reappear in London.

SILENT SPIRIT In 1958 David Ogilvy, the Scottish founder of the U.S. advertising agency Ogilvy and Mather, devised one of the automobile industry's most memorable selling lines: "At 60 miles per hour the loudest noise in this new Rolls-Royce comes from the electric clock." When Ogilvy presented the ad to Rolls-Royce, however, the chief engineer was not impressed by its pithiness. He simply shook his head sadly, Ogilvy recalled later, and said, "It's time we did something about that damned clock."

In 1980 the company did. Its new Silver Spirit model was fitted with a soundless digital clock.

INTERNATIONAL AUTO REGISTRATION MARKS

A	Austria	LB	Liberia
ADN	South Yemen	LS	Lesotho
AFG	Afghanistan	M	Malta
AL	Albania	MA	Morocco
AND	Andorra	MEX	Mexico
AUS	Australia	MS	Mauritius
B	Belgium	MW	Malawi
BD	Bangladesh	N	Norway
BDS	Barbados	NL	Netherlands
BG	Bulgaria	NZ	New Zealand
BH	Belize	P	Portugal
BR	Brazil	PA	Panama
BRN	Bahrain	PAK	Pakistan
BRU	Brunei	PE	Peru
BS	Bahamas	PL	Poland
BUR	Burma	PNG	Papua New
C	Cuba		Guinea
CDN	Canada	PY	Paraguay
CH	Switzerland	RO	Romania
CI	Ivory Coast	RA	Argentina
CL	Sri Lanka	RB	Botswana
CO	Colombia	RC	Taiwan
CR	Costa Rica	RCA	Central African
CS	Czechoslovakia		Republic
CY	Cyprus	RCR	Congo
D	West Germany	RCH	Chile
DDR	East Germany	RI	Indonesia
DK	Denmark	RIM	Mauritania
DY	Benin	RL	Lebanon
DZ	Algeria	RM	Madagascar
E	Spain	RMM	Mali
EAK	Kenya	RN	Niger
EAT	Tanzania	ROK	South Korea
EAU	Uganda	ROU	Uruguay
EC	Ecuador	RP	Philippines
ES	El Salvador	RSM	San Marino
ET	Egypt	RU	Burundi
F	France	RWA	Ruanda
FJI	Fiji	S	Sweden
FR	Faroe Islands	SD	Swaziland
GB	Britain	SF	Finland
GBA	Alderney	SGP	Singapore
GBG	Guernsey	SME	Suriname
GBJ	Jersey	SN	Senegal
GBM	Isle of Man	SU	Soviet Union
GBZ	Gibraltar	SY	Seychelles
GCA	Guatemala	SYR	Syria
GH	Ghana	T	Thailand
GR	Greece	TN	Tunisia
GUY	Guyana	TR	Turkey
H	Hungary	TT	Trinidad and
HK	Hong Kong		Tobago
HKJ	Jordan	USA	United States
I	Italy	V	Vatican City
IL	Israel	VN	Vietnam
IND	India	WAG	Gambia
IR	Iran	WAL	Sierra Leone
IRL	Ireland	WAN	Nigeria
IRQ	Iraq	WG	Grenada
IS	Iceland	WL	St. Lucia
J	Japan	WV	St. Vincent
JA	Jamaica	YU	Yugoslavia
K	Kampuchea	YV	Venezuela
L	Luxembourg	ZA	South Africa
LAO	Laos	ZRE	Zaire
LAR	Libya	ZW	Zimbabwe

LADY'S RIDE For women who caught bicycling fever, divided skirts and other new fashions made riding easier.

INTO THE FUTURE *An experimental Italian racing bicycle has lightweight carbon fiber disks instead of spokes, and the rear wheel is larger than the front wheel. Rider wears helmet to cut wind resistance.*

Transportation

THE FIRST RAILWAY DEATH The inaugural run of the world's first railway passenger service, in Britain in 1830, also caused the first railway death. Ironically, the victim was one of rail travel's staunchest supporters. William Huskisson, a former president of the Board of Trade, was a guest of George Stephenson (1781–1848), who with his son Robert had designed and built the *Rocket* locomotive. The *Rocket* was then the fastest engine in the world, having attained 35 m.p.h. without a train in 1829.

Wanting to enlist support for the development of railways, the Stephensons had arranged for eight trains to carry various dignitaries, including the prime minister (the duke of Wellington) between Liverpool and Manchester as a publicity exercise. When the first train pulled off on a siding to give the prime minister a better view of the other trains in action, several people got off.

Huskisson, who was standing on the main line, misjudged the speed of an approaching train and was run over. During the frantic dash to get the fatally injured Huskisson medical attention, the locomotive *Northumbrian* reached a speed of 36 m.p.h.

STATED SAFE SPEED In 1825 the British railway pioneer George Stephenson deliberately misled an inquiry by members of Parliament into the safety of trains. He told the government committee to expect train speeds of 12 m.p.h., even though he expected them to reach 20 m.p.h.

Stephenson played down speed in order to allay public fears of the new mode of travel. Political opponents had claimed that it could seriously damage passengers' health. Trains traveling at more than 12 m.p.h., they had insisted, would cause mental disorders and would expose passengers to the risk of being suffocated, because the speed would suck all the air from their lungs.

IN THE GROOVE The idea of using wheels on rails predates the existence of trains. As early as 3000 B.C. the ancient Greeks began using grooves about 6 inches deep and 3 to 5 feet apart to move heavy loads on wagons.

European mines were equipped with hand-propelled trucks on wooden rails in about the 15th century. The existence of such a railway in Germany was documented in 1430. The first all-iron rails were laid in Leicestershire in England in 1789, although iron plates had been used to cover wooden rails since the 1690s.

The longest stretch of straight rail track in the world crosses part of Australia's Nullarbor Plain just north of the Great Australian Bight. The rails run straight as an arrow for 297 miles.

THE FIRST SUBWAY The trains used on the world's first underground railway, which opened between Paddington and the City of London in 1863, were powered by steam, not electricity. The original tunnels still form part of London Transport's Metropolitan Line. By use of a cut-and-cover technique, which involved excavating a trench and then constructing a brick tunnel inside, the line was built to relieve traffic congestion on the roads. Smoke and steam from the engines escaped through ventilators and open-roofed sections. Electric trains began to replace steam only in

TIMETABLE OF WORLD RAILWAY HISTORY

1779 First steam engine capable of rotating a shaft built for a Birmingham button manufacturer, James Pickard.

1789 First iron rails laid in Leicestershire, England.

1803 Richard Trevithick, English engineer, constructs the first steam locomotive.

1815 First rail track laid in U.S.A.

1825 Stephenson's Stockton and Darlington Railway, the first public steam railway, opens; carries freight from a colliery to a river port.

1827 Baltimore & Ohio Railroad, first U.S. railway system, chartered.

1829 George and Robert Stephenson's *Rocket* locomotive sets a new speed record of 35 m.p.h.

1830 World's first regular railroad passenger service started, between Liverpool and Manchester. Widespread railroad construction begins in Britain, soon to spread to Europe and North America.

1850 U.S. Congress makes first land grant for development of railroads.

1857 Steel rails first used in Britain.

1863 World's first underground railway opened in London. Scotsman Robert Fairlie invents an engine with pivoting axles that allow trains to negotiate tighter bends.

1865 George Pullman's sleeping car, the *Pioneer*, introduced in Chicago.

1869 U.S. inventor George Westinghouse patents the air brake, making high-speed train travel feasible and safe. Transcontinental railway, linking the Atlantic to the Pacific coasts, completed in the U.S.A.

1879 First electric railway demonstrated in Berlin.

1883 First public electric railway opened at Brighton in England. Orient Express goes into service.

1891 Construction begins on the 5,787-mile Trans-Siberian Railway, the longest in the world—between Moscow and Vladivostok in Russia. Construction completed in 1904.

1892 Rudolf Diesel patents the diesel engine in Germany.

1895 Baltimore & Ohio Railroad introduces electric mainline service in Baltimore.

1898 First U.S. subway system opens in Boston.

1964 "Bullet train" service between Tokyo and Osaka in Japan opened; trains average speeds of 130 m.p.h.

1976 Britain introduces diesel high-speed trains (HSTs), with average speed of 125 m.p.h.

1981 Advanced passenger train (APT) developed in Britain. Prototypes had a cruising speed of 125 m.p.h. (top speed 156 m.p.h.). Automatic tilting suspension allowed the train to corner smoothly at high speeds.

1983 French TGV (*Train à Grande Vitesse*) sets new world speed record for passenger trains, completing the 264-mile Lyons–Paris run at an average speed of 132 m.p.h. (top speed 170 m.p.h.).

1987 Japan and West Germany testing prototype trains with top speeds up to 250 m.p.h.

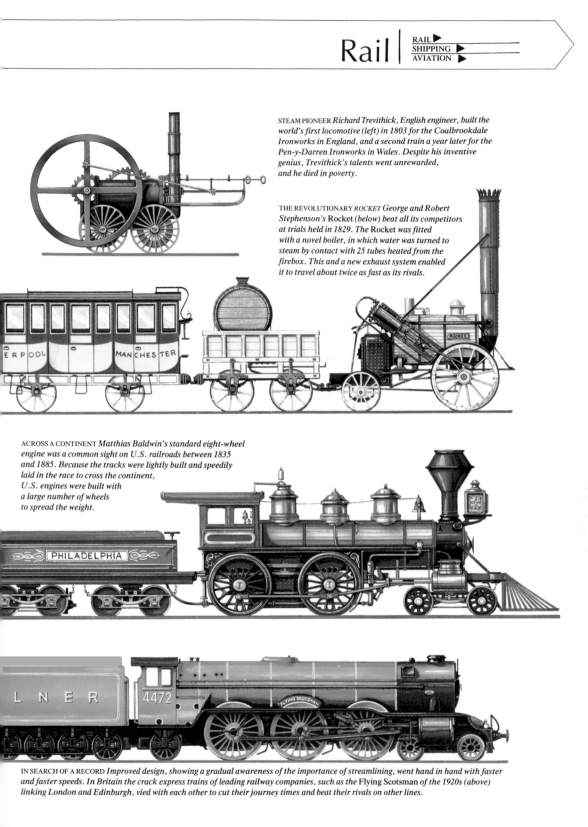

STEAM PIONEER *Richard Trevithick, English engineer, built the world's first locomotive (left) in 1803 for the Coalbrookdale Ironworks in England, and a second train a year later for the Pen-y-Darren Ironworks in Wales. Despite his inventive genius, Trevithick's talents went unrewarded, and he died in poverty.*

THE REVOLUTIONARY *ROCKET George and Robert Stephenson's Rocket (below) beat all its competitors at trials held in 1829. The Rocket was fitted with a novel boiler, in which water was turned to steam by contact with 25 tubes heated from the firebox. This and a new exhaust system enabled it to travel about twice as fast as its rivals.*

ACROSS A CONTINENT *Matthias Baldwin's standard eight-wheel engine was a common sight on U.S. railroads between 1835 and 1885. Because the tracks were lightly built and speedily laid in the race to cross the continent, U.S. engines were built with a large number of wheels to spread the weight.*

IN SEARCH OF A RECORD *Improved design, showing a gradual awareness of the importance of streamlining, went hand in hand with faster and faster speeds. In Britain the crack express trains of leading railway companies, such as the Flying Scotsman of the 1920s (above) linking London and Edinburgh, vied with each other to cut their journey times and beat their rivals on other lines.*

WORLD-BEATER *France's electric-powered TGV became in 1983 the world's fastest train in regular service. On straight stretches of its Lyons – Paris run, its speed reaches 170 m.p.h. In 1987 both Japan and West Germany were at work on faster trains.*

the 1890s, when a new line running below ground level was opened, part of it beneath the River Thames. Electric power was used on the new line because of the difficulty of ventilating such a deep tunnel adequately.

The world's first escalator was installed in Coney Island, N.Y., in 1896. A man with a wooden leg, known as "Bumper Harris," was employed to ride up and down Britain's first escalator, installed in a London subway station in 1911, to show that if a one-legged man could manage it, the public need not fear the new moving staircase.

The world's longest escalator is in the U.S.S.R. Part of Leningrad's subway network, it carries passengers a vertical distance of nearly 195 feet.

GETTING THE TRAINS TO RUN ON TIME The introduction of railways changed the timekeeping habits of a nation. Before the railway age British time was kept on a local basis, so that time throughout the country could differ by as much as 15 minutes. Even within London there was a variation of 2 minutes between the eastern and western ends of the city.

The system meant that the railway companies could not issue reliable timetables. By 1850 the railways nationwide had adopted London Time, but that merely added to the confusion. Some towns in the mid-19th century even installed clocks with two minute hands—one for local time, the other for railway time.

Pressure for change grew after a court case in Dorset on November 24, 1858. At 10:06 a.m. on that day by Dorset clocks a Dorchester judge ruled against a man involved in a land battle because he was late for the 10 a.m. hearing. Two minutes later the man arrived and claimed he was on time—by the station clock in his hometown of Carlisle.

The case had to be retried, and in 1880 Parliament ended the confusion by ordering the whole country to set its clocks to Greenwich Mean Time.

Wild West souvenir hunters disconnected North America's first transcontinental railway almost as soon as it was completed. When the Union Pacific and Central Pacific railways met at Promontory, Utah, in 1869, after 6 years of construction, the occasion was celebrated by linking the last section of track with two golden spikes.

However, fearing that the spikes would be stolen, the builders removed them after the ceremony and replaced them with conventional steel spikes. This failed to deter the souvenir hunters, and within a few days 12 spikes, 6 ties, and 2 pairs of rails had disappeared from the spot.

STATION ON THE ROOF OF THE WORLD The world's highest standard-gauge passenger railway runs between Lima and Huancayo in the Peruvian Andes. A meter-gauge line in Bolivia ascends slightly higher, but it is mainly a freight line, carrying few passengers. The highest station along the Peruvian route is at Galera, 15,686 feet above sea level. Between Galera and Ticlio the track reaches an elevation of 15,689 feet above sea level.

In about 4 hours the train climbs from Lima at sea level to Galera. The change in altitude is so rapid that some passengers find it difficult to breathe, and attendants join the train near the highest point to administer oxygen to anyone who feels faint.

The track is laid on gradients that reach 1 in 25, and on steep slopes where there is no room for the line to curve back and forth across the mountainside, track is laid out in zigzag sections known as switchbacks. At the end of each section is a short siding, so that the train alternately steams forward and reverses across the slope as it climbs.

When the construction of the Moscow Metro—the Soviet capital's subway system—fell behind schedule in the 1930s, 80,000 extra laborers were drafted to help the project catch up, under the supervision of the future Soviet premier, Nikita Khrushchev. Most of the drafted "volunteers" were not paid.

The system's 22-station core, on which work started in 1931, was opened by Joseph Stalin on May 15, 1935. It is now the world's busiest underground system, moving up to 6.5 million passengers a day. The longest subway system is in London, with 260 miles of routes, but New York's system has the most stations: 458 to London's 277.

SLIPUP FOR A QUEEN But for the bad phrasing of a question, the transatlantic British liner *Queen Mary*—now a floating hotel in California—would have been known by another name. Shortly before the ship's launch in 1934, Sir Thomas Royden, a director of the Cunard line, met King George V, intending to get his permission to name the ship *Queen Victoria*.

Royden asked if the vessel could be christened "after the greatest queen this country has ever known." The king replied, "That is the greatest compliment ever paid to my wife. I'll ask her." Naturally, Queen Mary assented, which meant that Cunard had to conceal its original plan.

PHARAOH'S ROYAL SHIP The 4,600-year-old royal ship of the Egyptian pharaoh Cheops is the oldest surviving vessel in the world. Originally buried in separate pieces near the Great Pyramid of Cheops at Giza, the ship has now been reassembled and is housed in a special museum near the pyramid.

Tons of silica gel, which is distributed in bags throughout 158-foot-long hull, help to preserve the ship. The gel absorbs moisture given off by the hull during the heat of the day. At night the process is reversed, ensuring that the ship's ancient timbers are kept at a constant level of humidity.

CHINESE NAUTICAL GENIUS The hinged sternpost rudder, the magnetic compass, multiple masts, and watertight compartments were all invented by Chinese sailors before they were widely taken up in the West. The rudder, which began to replace the steering oar in Europe during the 13th century A.D., had been known in China since the 1st century B.C.

MAYDAY, MAYDAY

The internationally recognized distress signal Mayday (from the French phrase *m'aidez,* meaning "help me") is used only when a ship is in grave and imminent danger and requires immediate assistance. A ship urgently needing help but not in imminent danger uses the signal Pan Pan (from the French *panne,* meaning "breakdown"). Pan Pan is also the signal for "Man overboard."

Under the International Convention for the Safety of Life at Sea there are a number of other recognized ways of calling for help. A ship's captain who sees any of these distress signals is legally obliged to respond to them.

- Gun or other explosive signal fired at intervals of about a minute.
- Continuous sounding of a fog signal, such as a foghorn.
- Rockets or shells throwing red stars fired one at a time at short intervals.
- Morse Code SOS (three dots, three dashes, three dots) transmitted by any means available.
- International Code flags NC (flag N above flag C).
- A square flag with above or below it anything resembling a ball.
- Flames on a vessel (for example, burning tar or oily rags).
- Red parachute flare or red hand flare.
- Orange smoke.
- The slow raising and lowering of outstretched arms.

An additional sign—a piece of orange canvas with a black square and circle—can be used to attract the attention of aircraft. The British Navy's red ensign flown upside down has been used as a distress signal, but it is not internationally recognized under the convention.

Multiple masts were in common use in China by the 3rd century A.D., and the compass by the 11th century. Watertight compartments, which prevent extensive flooding when a vessel is pierced, were being fitted in Chinese ships by the end of the 13th century, 600 years before they were adopted in Europe.

NAVIGATING WITH KNOTS By the 8th century A.D. Arab seamen on the Red Sea and the Indian Ocean had an instrument for finding latitude, their distance north or south of the equator. Called the *kamal,* from the Arabic for "guide," it was accurate to within about 30 miles. The device consisted of a hand-size rectangular board with a knotted cord attached to its center. Each knot represented the known latitude of a port.

With the appropriate knot in his teeth, the navigator held the *kamal* out before his eyes until it filled the space between the North Star and the horizon, with the board's bottom edge at the horizon. The height of the polestar is the same at any given latitude; it is almost directly overhead at the north pole, and just on the horizon at the equator. So when the star appeared above the top edge of the *kamal,* it meant that the boat was too far north and had to sail south to reach the desired port. When the star was below the top of the *kamal,* the boat altered course and sailed north. Modified *kamals* are still used today by Arabs on the sailing ships known as dhows.

THE 3,000-YEAR-OLD WRECK A Turkish sponge boat captain's casual remark about an underwater wreck led to the discovery in 1960 of one of the world's oldest shipwrecks, a Bronze Age cargo vessel that sank in about 1200 B.C.

The captain had mentioned to American journalist and diver Peter Throckmorton in 1958 that he intended to dynamite the wreck to sell its cargo of bronze for scrap. Throckmorton, intrigued by the reference to bronze, persuaded the captain to delay his plan, then used the time to pinpoint the wreck—90 feet down, off Cape Gelidonya in southwest Turkey. He persuaded the University of Pennsylvania to sponsor an expedition.

George Bass, the 27-year-old American appointed to lead the expedition, was a classical archeologist. So he took the then unusual step of learning to dive and went on to pioneer the first academically disciplined underwater excavation.

Curiously, the wreck's discovery helped to improve the translation of the *Odyssey,* Homer's epic poem, which is set in the 13th century B.C.—about the time the wreck went down. In one section the poet tells how Odysseus "spread out a lot of brushwood" on his ship. Baffled translators had interpreted this to mean

HAPPY HEADLINE *Reporters for the New York Evening Sun had every reason to believe that a great tragedy involving the "unsinkable Titanic" had been averted. They had listened in on telegraph messages clattering in from the North Atlantic and misinterpreted information on the start of a rescue effort to mean that the ship was still afloat and all aboard were rescued. Not until days later was the true toll known: more than 1,500 dead and 705 saved by the liner Carpathia after the Titanic hit an iceberg and sank on the night of April 14–15, 1912. Almost from the day she went down, there was talk of finding, salvaging parts of, or even raising the Titanic. It was just talk until the night of August 31–September 1, 1985, when a team led by Robert Ballard of the Woods Hole (Mass.) Oceanographic Institution and French ocean explorer Jean-Louis Michel located the Titanic 13,000 feet down on the bottom of the Atlantic in the Grand Banks area off Newfoundland. Using remote-controlled submersibles guided from their ship, Knorr, Ballard and Michel obtained photos of the great liner.*

Transportation

LANDMARKS IN MARITIME HISTORY

30,000 B.C. Aborigines reach Australia aboard seagoing craft.

8000–7000 Reed boats developed in Mesopotamia and Egypt. Dugout canoes used in northwest Europe.

4000–3000 Square-rigged sailing ships used on Nile River in Egypt.

2500–1500 Egyptian reed ships reach Crete and Somalia.

1200 Phoenicians develop keeled sailing ships, with planked hulls. The keels formed the ships' backbones, to which the frames were attached.

c. 100 Rudder invented in China.

By 200 Chinese junks have more than one mast.

800–900 Square-rigged Viking longships carry first raiders and colonists across the North Sea to the British Isles, the Faroes, and Iceland.

A.D. 200–300 Fore-and-aft sailing rig invented by Arab sailors; allows boat to sail across the direction of the wind as well as with it.

By 1090 Chinese navigators are using magnetic compass.

By 1300 Chinese ships have watertight bulkheads.

1400–1500 Three-masted ship developed in western Europe, making possible major voyages of discovery.

1620 Submarine invented by Dutch physicist Cornelis Drebbel.

1776 Buoyancy tanks and torpedoes invented for hand-propelled submarine, the *Turtle,* by U.S. engineer David Bushnell.

1783 In France the marquis Claude de Jouffroy d'Abbans builds and sails first paddle-driven steamboat on Saône River.

1807 The *Clermont,* built by Robert Fulton, begins run between New York City and Albany on Hudson River, initiating world's first commercially successful passenger steamboat service. About 20 years earlier, American engineer John Fitch had introduced steam ferries on the Delaware River, but the venture failed.

1836 Englishman Francis Pettit Smith patents a screw propeller. Swedish engineer John Ericsson patents a screw propeller in the U.S.A. 6 weeks later.

1838 British engineer Isambard Kingdom Brunel's *Great Western,* first steamship built specially for transatlantic service, sails from Bristol to New York in 15 days.

1845 Brunel's *Great Britain,* first transatlantic screw-driven iron ship, makes maiden voyage to New York. Donald McKay's *Rainbow,* first true clipper ship, launched in Boston.

1852 American-built clippers begin to smash speed records, with ships of Canadian-born Boston shipbuilder Donald McKay leading the way. His *Sovereign of the Seas* (built 1852) set the all-time sailing-ship record between New York and Liverpool of 13 days 14 hours; and his *Champion of the Seas* (1854) covered 465 miles in 24 hours, a record that steamships could not beat for 25 years.

1863 France's *Plongeur,* first mechanically driven submarine, uses engine powered by compressed air.

1908 Gyroscope compass produced by German engineer Hermann Anschutz-Kämpfe. Once set to point north, the gyrocompass remains stable, despite a ship's pitching and rolling.

1955 U.S. Navy builds the *Nautilus,* first nuclear-powered submarine.

1955 Hovercraft design patented by British engineer Christopher Cockerell.

1959 Soviet icebreaker *Lenin,* first nuclear-powered surface ship, commissioned.

1980 Japan launches 1,750-ton tanker *Shin-Aitoku-Maru,* first sail-assisted commercial ship in 50 years.

1983 Hinged ship invented by German engineer Ortwin Fries. Ship designed to bend into V-shape and suck up oil spills into its twin hulls.

IN ANCIENT EGYPT *Wooden sailing ships, with a single mast set well forward and carrying a single rectangular, or "square," sail, were sailing on the Nile as long ago as 4000 B.C. The sail's position meant that the ship could move only before the wind—that is, with the wind behind it.*

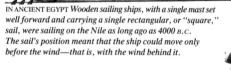

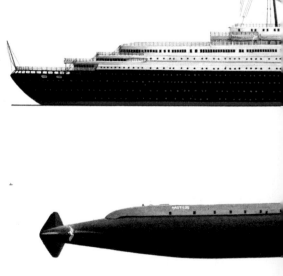

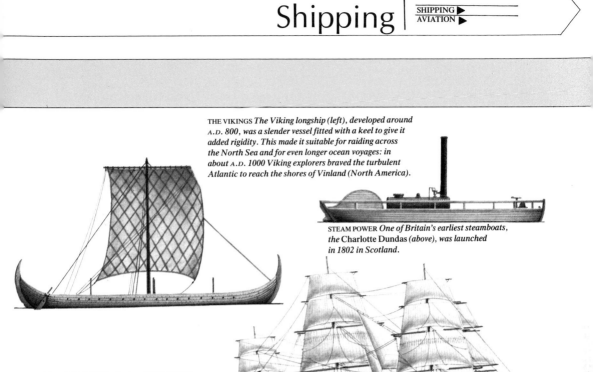

THE VIKINGS *The Viking longship (left), developed around* A.D. *800, was a slender vessel fitted with a keel to give it added rigidity. This made it suitable for raiding across the North Sea and for even longer ocean voyages: in about* A.D. *1000 Viking explorers braved the turbulent Atlantic to reach the shores of Vinland (North America).*

STEAM POWER *One of Britain's earliest steamboats, the* Charlotte Dundas *(above), was launched in 1802 in Scotland.*

AGE OF THE CLIPPER *The Boston clipper* Flying Cloud *(right) lived up to her name with all sails set. Despite the engineering achievements of the Industrial Revolution, it took many years for steam to replace sail. Until the second half of the 19th century the bulk of the world's most valuable cargoes were carried in graceful clippers. Their sculpted hulls were designed to allow speeds of up to 20 knots. The merchandise they carried included the first of the new season's growth of China tea, and tea races became an annual event.*

A QUEEN OF THE OCEAN *The great age of the ocean liner occurred before World War II, when France's* Normandie *(left) and Britain's* Queen Mary *and* Queen Elizabeth *all competed on the transatlantic run. Interned after the fall of France in 1940, the* Normandie *was destroyed by fire in New York harbor in 1942.*

ATOM POWER *The world's first nuclear-powered submarine, the* Nautilus *(left), was built for the U.S. Navy in 1954. In her first 2 years of service she traveled 62,000 miles without refueling. By 1965 she had traveled about 330,000 miles, mostly underwater. During that time she used a total of three reactor cores—about 12 pounds of fuel.*

HOVER REVOLUTION *British engineer Christopher Cockerell patented his amphibious hovercraft design in 1955. The first craft "sailed" in 1959. It rides on a cushion of air; the air is forced down by fans and retained by a flexible skirt.*

Transportation

that he built a wattle fence around the gunwales to keep out high seas and spray. But it now seems clear from the evidence found in the wreck that brushwood was actually laid out over the bottoms of boats to protect their thin hulls from damage caused by shifting cargo, just as Homer's words had implied.

BLOODY PUNISHMENT European navies in the days of sail were notorious for their brutal penalties. Keelhauling—dragging a man under the ship's bottom—had been in use for about 300 years when it was phased out early in the 18th century. Keelhauling involved trussing the offender to a line and dropping him from one yardarm into the sea; he was then dragged under the keel and hoisted to the opposite yardarm. Many sailors drowned in the process.

Flogging with the cat-o'-nine-tails—a rope or wooden handle with nine knotted cords, each about 18 inches long—was first described in 1702. Officially, captains in Britain's Royal Navy were forbidden to order more than a dozen strokes without special written permission, but the regulation was usually ignored. Use of the cat was finally suspended in the Royal Navy in 1879.

The letters SOS were adopted as an international distress signal in 1912 because the Morse code for them—three dots, three dashes, and three dots—was easy to remember. One of the first ships to send the new call sign was the British liner **Titanic**, *which struck an iceberg and sank on her maiden voyage to New York in April of that year. The letters did not stand for anything. "Save Our Souls" was a definition invented later.*

LIGHT THAT FAILED Lighthouses have been used as an aid to navigation for more than 2,000 years. But the modern lighthouse started with the efforts of a British engineer, Henry Winstanley, to erect a structure on the dangerous Eddystone Rocks, in the English Channel 14 miles out to sea from Plymouth. It was a daunting task. At high tide only one rock was exposed; its surface was just big enough for the base of the lighthouse. Winstanley's stone and wood structure, 80 feet high, took 2 years to build. It went into operation in November 1698, burning a candelabra of 60 candles. Two years later the tower was raised to a height of 120 feet.

The present Eddystone Lighthouse was built in 1882.

NOBLE FAILURE *Henry Winstanley's Eddystone Lighthouse shone for only 5 years before it was swept away in a storm in November 1703, with its inventor inside.*

A screw propeller was invented by an English farmer whose hobby was building models. In 1835 Francis Pettit Smith, a farmer in Kent, devised a model boat with a propeller drive. He patented it in 1836 as an alternative to paddle wheels for full-size ships.

PADDLE VERSUS SCREW A bizarre tug-of-war to determine which was more efficient, paddle wheels or screw propellers, was staged in 1845 by the British Admiralty. The contest was between two 900-ton frigates: H.M.S. *Alecto*, which had paddle wheels, and H.M.S. *Rattler*, which was driven by a propeller. The ships were tied stern to stern, and both captains ordered full speed ahead. *Rattler* won easily.

TURBINE DASH To win government approval, the world's first turbine vessel, *Turbinia*, made an unmannerly appearance at the Spithead naval review in 1897, which was being held as part of Queen Victoria's diamond jubilee celebrations. Designed and built by Sir Charles Parsons (1854–1931), a British marine engineer, the 50-ton *Turbinia* cut through the anchored fleet at the unprecedented speed of 34.5 knots (about 40 m.p.h.). Naval chiefs were so impressed that they commissioned the turbine-driven destroyer *Viper*, which went into service 3 years later.

Rum was introduced into Britain's Royal Navy in 1687, when Samuel Pepys, the renowned diarist, was secretary of the navy. It was abolished in 1970 after the Admiralty finally decided that rum rations were not compatible with modern standards of efficiency. Grog (rum diluted with water) was first issued by Admiral Edward Vernon in 1740, at a time when the daily ration for each sailor was 1 pint of neat spirits. The name was derived from the admiral himself, who was called Old Grogram because he wore a cloak made of a fabric called grogram (grosgrain).

SOLDIERS AND SAILORS LAST Where the code of "women and children first" originated is not known for certain, but it has had no more courageous observance than in the wreck of a British troopship, the *Birkenhead*, on February 26, 1852. In January the 2,000-ton *Birkenhead*, one of the world's first

---

PORT AND STARBOARD

Looking toward the bow (front) of a ship, port is the left-hand side, starboard the right-hand side. When under way at night, all vessels are obliged to display a red sidelight to port, a green one to starboard, and a white masthead light.

Starboard is so called because the right-hand side of a boat was the side ("board") where the steering oar, or "steer," was set in the days before central, sternpost rudders were used.

Port is so named because ships in harbor always tied up on that side so that the steering oar would not be crushed against the dock. The same terms are now used in exactly the same way by air pilots.

BIRDMAN *Flying has always captured the human imagination. In a Greek legend, the inventor Daedalus built wings of wax to escape from imprisonment on Crete.*

ironclads, had sailed from Ireland headed for South Africa. She was laden with reinforcements, including 476 soldiers, for a campaign against Xhosa tribesmen. Also on board was a large group of civilians, including 20 women and children.

Probably because of a navigational error, the ship hit rocks near Cape Agulhas, Africa's southernmost point. Of the eight lifeboats, only three proved seaworthy, and these were boarded by the civilians. With the ship breaking up, the master, Capt. Robert Salmond, ordered the assembled redcoats: "Save yourselves. All who can swim, jump overboard and make for the boats."

But the soldiers' commander, Lt. Col. Alexander Seton, seeing that the lifeboats would be swamped in the scramble for safety, quickly countermanded the instruction. "Stand fast, I beg you," he shouted to his platoons. "Do not rush the boats carrying the women and children."

Seton drew his sword, ready to cut down the first man who disobeyed, but the threat was unnecessary. The soldiers remained steady, even while the ship broke in two. Of those on board, 454 lost their lives, including Seton and Salmond.

The first man to sail solo around the world could not swim. He was a Nova Scotia–born U.S. sea captain named Joshua Slocum. In his 37-foot sloop, Spray, he set out from Boston in 1895 at the age of 51 and returned 3 years later. He financed the journey by giving lectures at the ports along his route. After settling down in Martha's Vineyard, he continued to take solo cruises. In November 1909 he set sail for the West Indies. Neither he nor the Spray was ever seen again.

MAINLY DEADWEIGHT The largest modern supertankers, known as ultra-large crude carriers (ULCCs), are not as heavy as they seem. They are usually described in terms of their deadweight, which is not the weight of the ships themselves but of how much cargo they can carry. Empty, the ships usually weigh only a fraction of the deadweight tonnage.

The world's largest ship in the early 1980s was the oil tanker *Seawise Giant,* completed in Japan in 1981 for a Liberian company. The ship itself, which is almost a quarter mile long—long enough to hold four football fields end to end (with four end zones)—weighs just under 90,000 tons, not much more than the 75,000 tons of the liner *Queen Elizabeth 2.* But its deadweight is just over 620,000 tons. Fully loaded with crude oil, therefore, it weighs a total of around 710,000 tons.

In heavy seas, ships of this size can bend more than 3 feet from stem to stern. And they may take more than 4 miles to stop.

WHO KILLED THE RED BARON? Nobody knows for certain who shot down Baron Manfred Freiherr von Richthofen, who with 80 unofficially attributed kills was among the most successful air aces of the First World War. On April 21, 1918, his red Fokker triplane was pursuing a Sopwith Camel close to the ground when he was himself attacked by another Camel flown by Capt. A. Roy Brown, a Canadian. Some Australian machine gunners on the ground fired at Richthofen, who was nicknamed the Red Baron, as Brown attacked. Richthofen's guns are said to have jammed, and he tried to break off the fight, but he was hit. The Fokker landed intact, and Richthofen's body was found with a bullet wound in the chest. Brown was credited with the victory, but it remains uncertain who fired the fatal shot.

A VIEW OF MONS: GARNERIN'S BALLOON AND PARACHUTE
HIGH JUMP *By the late 18th century, hot-air balloons had made flight practical, if sometimes perilous. André Garnerin gave the first public demonstration of how to escape from a balloon by parachute in Paris in 1797.*

Transportation

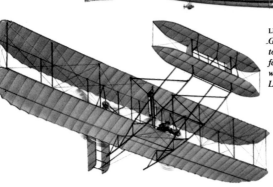

LIGHTER THAN AIR *Pioneered by Ferdinand von Zeppelin in Germany, airships, held aloft by hydrogen gas, were intended to become the ocean liners of the skies. But passengers lost faith in them after 35 people died when the Hindenburg—the world's largest airship—burst into flames as it landed at Lakehurst, New Jersey, on May 6, 1937.*

INTO HISTORY *The American inventors Orville and Wilbur Wright stepped into the history books in 1903 when their biplane, Flyer 1 (left), made the world's first powered heavier-than-air flights in a series of hops totaling 97 seconds. Their aircraft was the product of intensive research and preflight testing with kites and gliders.*

THE MONOPLANE *Some early aircraft designers distrusted the single-wing monoplane, arguing that it lacked stability. German engineer Hugo Junkers proved otherwise in 1915 with his all-metal Junkers J1 (right).*

THE HELICOPTER *Though the first model helicopter was demonstrated in 1784, the first manned version was not devised until 1936. Heinrich Focke, one of the designers who took up the challenge, might never have done so had not the Nazis forbidden him to design conventional aircraft because of his "political unreliability."*

JET PIONEER *Britain's de Havilland Comet (above) was the first pure jet airliner to go into commercial service. It made its maiden flight in 1949 and its first commercial flight in 1952. Two years later, however, after two fatal crashes, all flights were discontinued. Though the metal fatigue that had caused the crashes was eventually detected and cured, the Comet lost its lead over its competitors.*

1783 A Frenchman, Sébastien Lenormand, was the first person to use a parachute when he jumped from the tower of Montpellier Observatory in southern France. The first public exhibition jumps were given in Paris in October 1797 when André Jacques Garnerin—a former balloon inspector in the French Army—jumped from a balloon. He made his descents from heights of several thousand feet.

The parachutes of the late 1790s were rib-supported canvas umbrellas about 195 feet across. In the 1880s the modern limp-canopy type was invented in the U.S.A., where the first exhibition jumps with rip-cord parachutes took place in 1908.

1852 The world's first airship flight took place in France when an engineer, Henri Giffard, steered his steam-powered craft for 17 miles, landing near Versailles. But the airship did not become practical until the gasoline engine and lightweight aluminum (for the structure) were introduced in the 1880s. These were used by a former German army officer, Count Ferdinand von Zeppelin, who built his first dirigible in 1900.

The prototype zeppelin was driven by two 16-horsepower Daimler engines and contained about 400,000 cubic feet of hydrogen in 17 gastight bags. The first commercial zeppelin service started in 1910, and the airships made bombing raids over Britain in World War I. In the 1930s airship travel became fashionable. The longest scheduled flights were from Frankfurt to Rio de Janeiro, which took 5 days as against 5 weeks by ship.

1903 On December 17 the American aviation pioneers Wilbur and Orville Wright made the world's first powered, controlled, and sustained flights in their 12-horsepower biplane *Flyer 1.* Orville was the

STRAIGHT UP *The Rolls-Royce thrust measuring rig (above), nick-named the Flying Bedstead, became the world's first vertical takeoff (VTO) jet in 1954. It is the direct ancestor of modern VTO aircraft, such as Britain's Harrier "jump jet."*

FASTER THAN SOUND *The Anglo-French Concorde, with its streamlined fuselage and pointed nose, was the world's first supersonic airliner to go into passenger service, bringing London within 3 hours of New York. A rival project in the United States was abandoned because of cost.*

first to take to the air near Kitty Hawk, North Carolina. The fourth and final flight, with Wilbur as pilot, lasted 59 seconds and covered 852 feet.

1909 The first airplane sea crossing, across the English Channel, took place on July 25 when the Frenchman Louis Blériot took off in his 25-horsepower Blériot XI monoplane. The 23-mile trip from Calais to Dover took 36 minutes.

1911 The first single-shell (or monocoque) fuselage was introduced in the wooden Deperdussin racing plane from France. Another advance in aeronautical design was the appearance in 1915 of the Junkers J1 monoplane, made by a German company in Sweden. It was an all-metal aircraft with cantilevered wings that needed no external wires or struts.

1919 In June the first nonstop transatlantic crossing was made by the British aviators John Alcock and Arthur Whitten Brown. Their Vickers Vimy twin-engined biplane took 16 hours 27 minutes to make the flight—from Newfoundland to western Ireland.

1927 The first solo flight across the Atlantic occurred in May when a 25-year-old U.S. airmail pilot, Charles Lindbergh, flew nonstop from New York to Paris, winning $25,000 for his feat. His single-engined monoplane, *Spirit of St. Louis,* covered the 3,600 miles in 33 hours 39 minutes at an average speed of 107.4 m.p.h.

1937 Lindbergh flew in an unpressurized plane, which meant that he could not fly above bad weather. Ten years passed before the first fully pressurized aircraft, the experimental Lockheed XC-35, was introduced in the U.S.A. The first pressurized airliner to go into commercial service was the Boeing 307 Stratoliner, which made its maiden flight on December 31, 1938.

1947 The invention of the jet engine in the late 1930s meant that planes would eventually be able to fly faster than the speed of sound (almost 761 m.p.h.). The first plane to do this was Bell Aircraft's rocket-powered X-1, piloted by Capt. Charles Yeager. The British de Havilland Comet—the first commercial jetliner—went into service in 1952.

1970 The era of the jumbo jet began with the introduction by the Boeing Company of its wide-bodied 747, which can carry up to 490 passengers. Part of the 747's height—more than 63 feet, as tall as a 6-story building—consists of an upper deck in the nose. In 1986 Boeing announced plans for a 1,000-seat superjumbo that would cross the Pacific nonstop.

1976 The Anglo-French Concorde made its first test flight in 1969. It entered service 7 years later. It carries comparatively few passengers—up to 100—at speeds of more than 1,000 m.p.h., and crosses the Atlantic in less than 3 hours. The plane's long nose is pointed downward when the plane lands so that the pilot can see ahead.

1985 A "hypersonic passenger transport" was proposed to the U.S. Congress by officials of the Defense Department and the National Aeronautics and Space Administration, who said all that was needed was money to build an airliner that would exceed speeds of Mach 10 (about 7,410 m.p.h.) and even climb into a low earth orbit. Dubbed the Orient Express because of its projected Los Angeles–Peking flying time of 2 hours, the plane could be airborne by the early 1990s, the officials said.

Transportation

WRIGHTS WRONGED Although the first flights by the Wright brothers in December 1903 had been publicly recognized as the first true manned flights by 1908, for many years the prestigious Smithsonian Institution in Washington, D.C., labeled another plane, Samuel Langley's *Aerodrome,* as "the first airplane capable of sustained free flight with a man."

The *Aerodrome* had twice been launched by catapult from a houseboat on the Potomac River, in October and December 1903. But on both occasions it plunged into the water because it lacked sufficient power and was structurally weak.

Because of the Smithsonian's view, the Wright *Flyer 1* in 1928 found a home abroad at the Science Museum in London. But in 1943 the Smithsonian acknowledged that the Wrights' plane had flown successfully before Langley's, and *Flyer 1* was returned to the United States in 1948 after a 20-year exile.

The first living creatures to be transported by air were a sheep, a rooster, and a duck. The Montgolfier brothers—Frenchmen whose hot-air balloon made the first manned flight in November 1783—had sent the animals up from Versailles 2 months previously to see if the creatures would be harmed by the rarefied air. The animals survived unharmed except that one of the rooster's wings was damaged, probably by a kick from the sheep.

WITHOUT A PARACHUTE In World War I no Allied pilot was ever equipped with a parachute, though by 1918 parachutes were regularly saving the lives of German pilots. The reason was that a parachute that the user could open had not been invented, and the type then used was stowed separately from the pilot and hauled from the aircraft by the pilot's weight as he jumped. In certain circumstances—if, say, the airplane was in a spin—the line or the parachute might foul some part of the plane. So rather than have a parachute that could not always be relied on, the Allied authorities preferred to have none.

THE WINDMILL PLANE In 1925 the Spanish inventor Juan de la Cierva demonstrated a new "wonder" flying machine: the autogyro. It had a freewheeling overhead rotor, which was designed to provide extra lift and so eliminate a then serious problem of planes' stalling on take-off.

Ironically, Cierva was killed in December 1936 by the very fault his invention had tried to eliminate. An airliner in which he was a passenger stalled and crashed while taking off from Croydon in England.

TROUBLE IN THE AIR Helicopters were not perfected until decades after the orthodox airplane because designers faced two apparently insurmountable problems. First, the spinning rotor that lifted a helicopter tended to make the body of the machine spin faster and faster in the opposite direction. Second, as soon as a helicopter moved forward, the rotating blades moving in the direction of the flight generated more lift than those moving toward the rear. This was because the speed of the "advancing" blades was added to the speed of the aircraft itself. And the effect was to make the helicopter roll over.

The two problems were finally solved by two independent inventors: a Spaniard who never built a helicopter and a refugee from the Russian Revolution of 1917. The Spaniard, Juan de la Cierva, whose main interest was in autogyros, invented in 1922 a flapping hinge that allowed the angle of the rotor blades to vary as they were spinning and so equalize the degree of lift. In 1941 Russian-born Igor Sikorsky, then living in the United States, perfected the use of a small, vertically mounted tail rotor to counter a plane's tendency to spin in the opposite direction to its main rotor.

As a child, Charles Lindbergh—the American aviator who in May 1927 made the first solo flight across the Atlantic—had a morbid terror of heights.

FATHERS OF THE JET Ideas for applying some form of jet propulsion to aircraft date back to the 19th century. But it was not until the late 1930s that the first practical jet engines were developed. The first jet to be given a test run, in March 1937, was the centrifugal-compressor engine developed by the German Hans von Ohain and financed by the Heinkel aircraft company. The following month saw the first runs of the centrifugal engine developed by the English engineer and pilot Sir Frank Whittle.

Ohain's engine first flew on August 27, 1939, in the Heinkel He 178, but the Whittle W1 engine did not fly until May 1941, when it powered the Gloster E.28/39. By then, Hugo Junkers in Germany and Dr. A. A. Griffith in England had evolved the more complicated axial-compressor jet engine. Britain adopted the Whittle engine and installed it in the Gloster Meteor fighter, but the Germans chose the axial unit and fitted it in the Messerschmitt Me 262. Both aircraft entered combat service in 1944.

Although the Whittle type of engine was dominant in the postwar years, it did not have the thrust potential of the axial type, which is now used to power modern jet aircraft.

ANIMALS & PLANTS

The origins of life

LIVING BUILDING BLOCKS

All living things, plant and animal, stem from a single cell. Most cells are too small to see, a mere few ten-thousandths of an inch across. A few single-celled organisms, such as the freshwater protozoan *Spirostomum,* can be up to 0.12 inch long and thus visible to the naked eye.

Each cell consists of a thin membrane holding a liquid called cytoplasm, which contains fats, proteins, acids, and carbohydrates. In the center of the cytoplasm is a nucleus. The nucleus holds the genetic code that determines how an organism devel-

FROM CELL TO ANIMAL

Biologists see a parallel between evolution and the development of an animal in its mother's womb. This analogy was stated over a century ago as "Ontogeny [the development of an embryo in the womb] . . . repeats in brief . . . phylogeny [the evolutionary history of the species to which the organism belongs]." The fertilized egg is a single cell, as the earliest forms of life on earth are assumed to have been. But within hours it begins to divide: into 2, then 4, 8, 16 cells, and so on. For some time all the cells produced are similar. Each cell has the capacity to become any specialist cell in the adult creature.

Then this cluster of undifferentiated cells gradually forms into a hollow ball with two layers, the inner endoderm and the outer ectoderm. Next, a third layer, the mesoderm, develops between them. Once these changes take place, no new cell can give rise to "daughter" cells of the other two types.

Growing specialization
As an embryo continues to develop and grow, its cells gradually become more specialized. The ectoderm cells become skin or nerve tissue, for instance. Endoderm cells can become parts of the digestive system or lungs. Mesoderm cells may develop into muscle and bone. All the while, the embryo recalls the species' evolution.

A 4-week-old human embryo, for example, has slits in the region of the neck that resemble the gills of a fish. At 6 weeks, when the embryo is half an inch long, its shape is still that of a marine animal, but the slits, known as branchial arches, have begun forming into the upper and lower jaws. At 7 weeks the developing baby has the attributes of a primate. It has a clearly visible tail, and the arms are longer and stronger than the legs—proportions that will be reversed in the born human.

Human characteristics
By 9 weeks after conception the embryo has human features. The eyes have become part of the front of the face, and the ears and jaws are prominent. The tail has vanished into the growing buttocks.

After 12 weeks the ears have risen to eye level, the eyelids have shut, and nails have begun to form. The limbs are jointed, but the head is still disproportionately large. In the next 4 weeks the face will become recognizably different from that of other human fetuses of the same age.

After 28 weeks all the main characteristics have formed, but the baby is red and wrinkled, with a dried-up appearance. In the next 10 weeks it fills out, the lungs develop, and it will be ready, after an average 266 days, to enter the world.

ops. Plants and animals grow by the division of their cells. The form taken by the completed organism is decided by chemical messages contained in DNA, short for deoxyribonucleic acid. DNA is a mixture of sugars and phosphates that form a spiral ladder of molecules inside the cell nucleus.

Each time a cell divides, the ladder splits in two down the middle. Half the ladder joins each new nucleus. In the newly formed cell, each half-rung projecting from the spiral is able to link up only with the same chemical partner it had in the original cell. As a result, the ladder is "repaired" exactly as it was before, and the genetic code it contained is faithfully copied in each new generation of cells.

CRACKING THE CODE

The secret of the DNA code of life was finally unraveled at Cambridge University, England, in 1953 by an American, James Watson, then 25, and a 37-year-old English biologist, Francis Crick. They knew that DNA consisted of a chain of sugars and phosphates held together by four compounds known as nucleotides. Each nucleotide contained a different organic base. There were two large bases, guanine and adenine, and two small ones, thymine and cytosine. But how did the bases fit together?

Biking from the railroad station to the college one day after a trip to London, Watson decided to experiment with a two-link structure. He and Crick made cutout models of the shapes of the four molecule bases and began trying to fit them together.

Watson recorded their moment of triumph. "Suddenly I became aware that an adenine-thymine pair . . . was identical in shape to a guanine-cytosine pair." The bases linked in pairs, each pair forming a single rung in the DNA ladder, and each base determined what its partner could be. The two sides of the spiral ladder fell into place.

HIGH-SPEED COPIER

A DNA molecule is an awesomely complex and extremely fast copier. It may consist of hundreds of thousands of coils containing millions of nucleotide "rungs." When a cell divides, the molecule has to untwist, and all the new nucleotides necessary must be assembled in the right order and be joined together by enzymes. Yet all this has to be done—in a bacterium, for example—in the time it takes a cell to divide: less than 20 minutes. The spiral must uncoil at the rate of several hundred turns a second, a speed that would tear apart any car engine, and the new chain must be assembled at the rate of several thousand nucleotides per second.

DIVIDE AND MULTIPLY

The enormous diversity of plant and animal life became possible only after the development of sexual reproduction. The first organisms to use this method were green algae, plant masses formed by groupings of primitive cells, which about a billion years ago began to reproduce by fusing with each other.

Until then all reproduction had been by cell division, the process known as cloning. Each organism was identical to its parent. Sexual reproduction, however, enabled a greater variety of organisms to evolve, because the new life could take different combinations of traits from the parents.

THE SCATTERING SEED

The first plants to colonize the land about 420 million years ago were flowerless mosses, horsetails, and ferns. They reproduced by throwing out spores—minute organisms that carried the genetic blueprint for the plant. Although spores can germinate centuries after they have been cast off, their survival rate is low because they carry no food store.

Ferns began bearing seeds about 345 million years ago. Unlike a spore, a seed has a built-in food store, making its survival chances greater. The most primitive seed-bearing plants still found on earth are the cycads, plants that resemble palm trees. They have existed for some 160 million years.

HALF AND HALF

There are 46 chromosomes in the living cell of a human being, and these chromosomes carry the genetic information that decides how a person will develop—whether he or she will be dark or fair, short or tall, blue- or brown-eyed. But the sex cells, the female egg and the male sperm, have only 23 chromosomes each. They fuse at conception to make a cell containing 46 chromosomes, half from each partner, and it is this mixing of two sets of characteristics that creates the diversity of human life.

Other species that reproduce sexually also have chromosomes, but the numbers vary widely. A garden pea, for instance, has 14 chromosomes, a potato 48, and a crayfish 200.

SYNTHETIC LIFE

In 1953 an American scientist, Stanley Miller, attempted to reproduce the atmosphere and weather conditions of earth at the very dawn of life. He passed an electric charge through a mixture of hydrogen, methane, and ammonia gases for 20 hours in an enclosed water bath. In the process, he formed some organic compounds, including amino acids, the basic building material of living cells. In 1979 at the University of Texas, researchers Allen J. Bard and Harald Reiche produced amino acids by exposing to sunlight a solution of ammonia, methane, and water that contained particles of platinum and titanium oxide.

These experiments in laboratory-made life suggest that life began as the result of the sun's rays and violent electrical storms acting on the gases present in the young earth's atmosphere.

MINI-METHUSELAHS

In the arid White Mountains of California, stunted bristlecone pines—the world's oldest trees—cling to a tenuous life and still grow very slowly in the occasional rainfall after 4,600 years of life. But they are not the oldest living things on earth.

In sandstone rocks in a dry valley of Antarctica lives a colony of tiny lichens, primitive partnerships of plant and fungus. American scientists have calculated these lichens to be at least 10,000 years old.

HOW A SEED BECOMES A PLANT

Whether cast by the wind, dropped from its parent, or planted by human hand, a seed germinates when air and water seep through its outer coat.

An embryo root, called the radicle, pushes out of a seed fallen to soil and grows downward seeking moisture and nutrients. One or two seed leaves, called cotyledons, emerge from the seedpod and begin providing food for the baby plant. A shoot called a plumule, which will eventually push its way into the air, grows upward from the seedpod.

A stem, called the hypocotyl, carries the plumule out into the daylight, bringing with it, in most plants, the seed leaves. As the stem grows upward, new leaves open out from it. Belowground the root spreads, pushing minute hairs through the soil to collect water and minerals. Finally, the seed leaves die and fall away as new leaves take over their role.

FACTS ABOUT ANIMALS & PLANTS

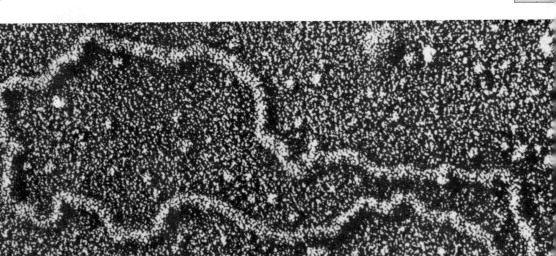

PIONEER GENETIC ENGINEERING *This ropelike molecule of DNA, here magnified more than 170,000 times, was the subject in 1973 of the first successful attempt at genetic engineering. The rope consists of two spiral strands twisted together and joined like the rungs of a ladder—a double helix. Scientists at Stanford University severed the loop (taken from* Escherichia coli *bacteria found in the human gut) and spliced it to another piece of DNA from the same species. They introduced the new genetic combination into a living cell and encouraged the cell to multiply. The new cells had properties derived from both original pieces of DNA, proving that the splice had worked.*

How plants are classified

THE PLANT KINGDOM

Plant classification
All plants are grouped into a number of broad categories, according to their common characteristics. This chart includes examples of each of the major plant divisions, classes, and orders, as well as representative members of the leading families. Numerous genera and species occur within each family.

ANGIOSPERMAE *Angiosperms*	Division
DICOTYLEDONEAE *Dicotyledons*	Class
Magnoliales	Order
Magnoliaceae	Family

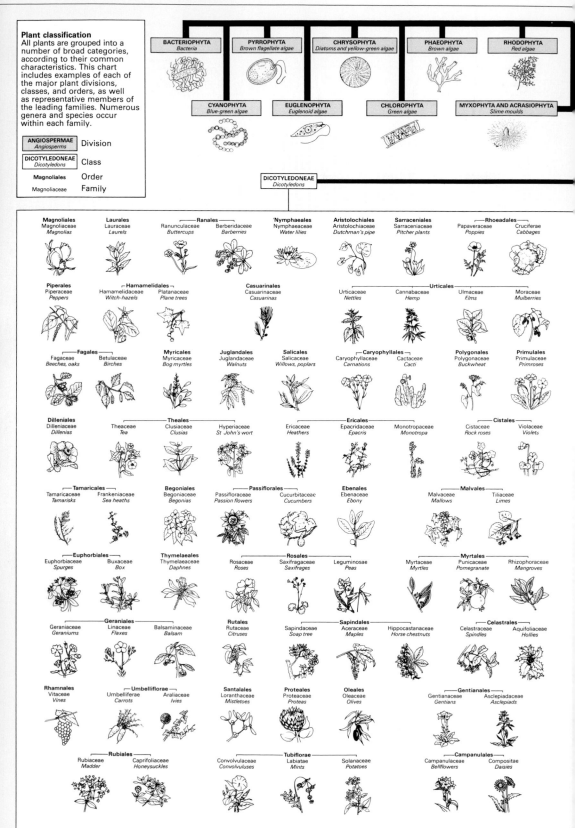

The basic classification unit for plants, as for animals, is the species. This chart shows how botanists group related species into larger units: the genus, family, order, class, and division. The chart includes fungi, but some scientists classify the 80,000 or so species of fungus as a separate kingdom, alongside plants and animals. Other organisms that are arguably neither plant nor animal, such as most bacteria, some algae, and viruses, may be assigned to other kingdoms: Protista, for example, or Procaryota.

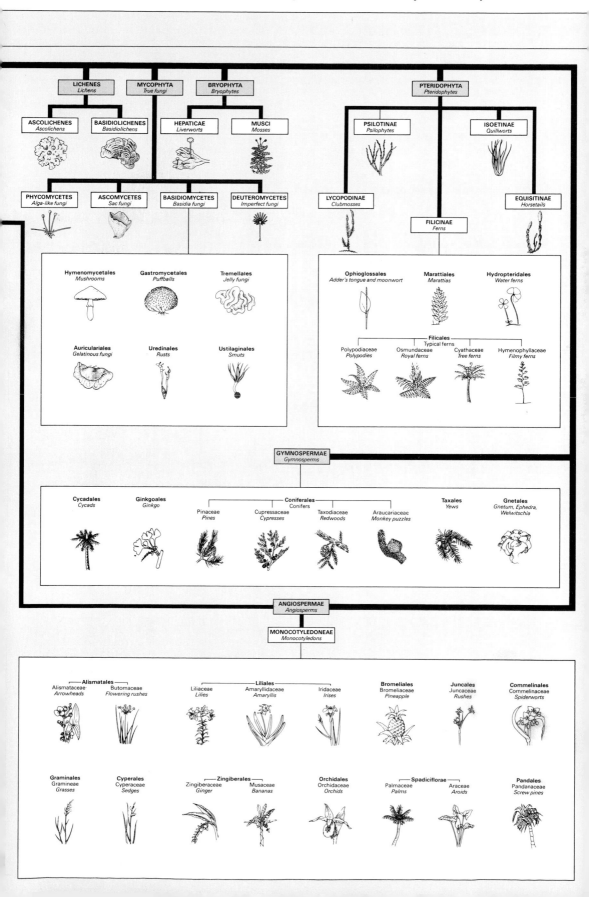

Flowering plants and fungi

FIRST AND LAST

The first land plants appeared at least 400 million years ago. They had forked stems but no true leaves, flowers, or seeds. A few similar plants still exist: the whisk ferns, which are native to tropical and subtropical regions, and the *Tmesipteris* group of ferns in New Zealand, Australia, and Polynesia.

TIME CAPSULE

The oldest known living seed came from a North American arctic lupine. It was found in 1954 buried in frozen silt near Miller Creek in the central Yukon, Canada, by a mining engineer named Schmidt. Scien-

tists determined it had been there for about 10,000 years. Yet when the scientists planted it, a lupine grew that was identical to the modern plant. Today seed banks keep stocks of seeds in similarly cold, dry conditions so that rare and endangered plant species are assured of a future.

BUILT-IN GREENHOUSE

The windowed plant, *Fenestraria*, makes a private greenhouse that protects it from the harsh sun of southern African deserts. Most of the plant grows underground, and only a small transparent window is exposed above the surface. The window, composed of translucent cells, has two layers. An outer layer blocks the most damaging ultraviolet rays of the sun, and an inner layer cuts down and diffuses the light to a safe level for the green photosynthetic tissue of the buried plant.

PATTERN FOR A PALACE

The Crystal Palace—a vast structure of glass and iron, built in Hyde Park, London, to house the Great Exhibition of 1851—was inspired by the pattern of a water lily. The designer, Sir Joseph Paxton, had been head gardener to the duke of Devonshire at Chatsworth and had successfully grown, for the first time in Europe, the giant South American water lily, *Victoria amazonica*. The plant's leaves are up to 7 feet across, and the arrangement of their ribs gives them such strength that they can support a child. Paxton studied the pattern of the ribs and, years later, used a similar pattern of ribs and struts to support the roof of his iron and glass palace. The building, which was moved to south London after the exhibition, was destroyed by a fire in 1936.

UNDERGROUND BLOOMS

Two Australian species of orchid spend their entire lives buried in the earth. The only part that ever emerges is a cluster of capsules, which is pushed above the surface to disperse the dustlike seeds. Both species feed on decaying plant material in the soil, breaking it down with the aid of fungi. One of the two orchids, *Rhizanthella gardneri*, was discovered in 1928 by a J. Trott, who plowed it up by accident on a farm in Corrigin, Western Australia. The second, *Cryptanthemis slateri*, was discovered by an E. Slater in 1931 at Alum Mount in New South Wales. Very little is known about either species because very few specimens have ever been found.

CORPSE FLOWER

Rafflesia, a parasitic plant named after the founder of Singapore, Sir Stamford Raffles, grows in the forests of Southeast Asia and has the largest and perhaps the smelliest flower in the world. The bud, which looks like a wrinkled brown cabbage, opens into a huge purplish or reddish-brown flower 1 to 3 feet across. The bloom weighs up to 15 pounds and is covered with irregular warts. Looking and smelling like a hunk of blood-encrusted and decaying carrion, the flower is visited by vast swarms of flies, which pollinate the flower while crawling over it.

RIDDLE OF THE COCONUTS

The largest seeds in the plant kingdom are also the most mysterious. The seeds—which belong to the double coconut, or coco-de-mer, *Lodoicea maldivica*—

POLLEN: GRAINS OF LIFE

Pollen refers to the minute grains, borne by the male stamens of a flower, that fertilize the female egg cells to create the seed of a new plant. Although all pollen may look the same to the naked eye—tiny, usually yellow particles—each type is different, as these much-magnified examples indicate.

Insect-pollinated plants, such as apple and blue chicory (succory), have rough and often sticky pollen grains that cling to insects, and the flowers are usually bright and scented to attract insects.

Wind-pollinated plants, such as pine, have smooth grains, and the flowers are much less conspicuous.

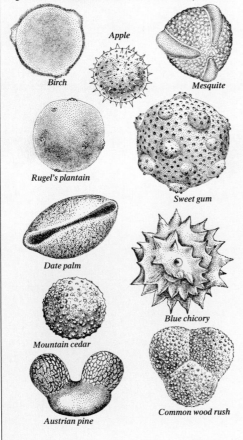

Apple

Birch

Mesquite

Rugel's plantain

Sweet gum

Date palm

Blue chicory

Mountain cedar

Common wood rush

Austrian pine

HOW SEEDS ARE DISPERSED

Evolution has provided plants with ways of scattering their seeds so that young plants grow far enough away from their parents to prevent competition between generations. Many seeds are carried by wind, animals, or water. Some plants have fruits that are eaten by animals, which then deposit the seeds in their droppings. Other plants have pods that burst, scattering their seeds. Many plants are lavish in the production of seeds. Orchids, for example, hold up to 20,000 in a single capsule. Sizes of seeds vary from those of orchids, which are about 0.01 inch long and so light that a million of them weigh only 0.01 ounce, to the giant double coconut of the Seychelles, which weighs up to 45 pounds.

Traveler's-joy

Dandelion

Maple

WIND-BORNE SEEDS *A dandelion seed has a fluffy parachute. Clematis—including the wild species traveler's-joy—has a feathery tail. Maple has a papery curved wing.*

Mistletoe

Wood avens

Blackberry

SPREAD BY ANIMALS *Birds rub sticky mistletoe into tree bark. Blackberry seeds are contained in edible fruits. The hooked seeds of wood avens cling to animal fur.*

Poppy   *Water lily*   *Geranium*

SHAKEN AND STIRRED *A poppy capsule sprinkles seeds like a salt shaker. Water lilies have floating fruit. The geranium's capsule splits, throwing out seeds.*

leaf edges form a cage around the insect, trapping it. The plant then floods the trap with digestive juices. These dissolve the unfortunate insect's body and extract the nitrogen it contains.

RISE OF THE ROSE

More than 8,000 varieties of rose have been developed for garden cultivation, yet all of them are descended from a mere handful of wild species. Roses have been cultivated for almost 5,000 years and were known to the Persians, Greeks, and Romans, but until the end of the 18th century only four or five species were grown. They included the dog rose, musk rose, and red Provins rose, which became the emblem of the Lancastrians during the 15th-century Wars of the Roses in Britain. The white rose of York was probably a form of dog rose.

Modern varieties, such as hybrid tea roses (single-flowered) and floribundas (cluster-flowered), began to be bred only around 1900, after the European species were crossed with cultivated oriental species imported from China.

MINIATURE BLOOM

The floating *Wolffia* species, members of the duckweed family, are among the world's smallest flowering plants. *Wolffia arrhiza,* which occurs on freshwater ponds and lakes in most continents, is a rootless green blob as small as 0.02 inch across.

PLANTS IN MEDICINE

Many plant species produce drugs that are invaluable in modern medicine. The foxglove is the source of the drug digitalis, used to treat heart disease. But fox-

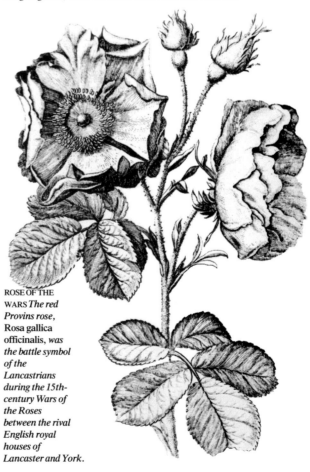

ROSE OF THE WARS *The red Provins rose,* Rosa gallica officinalis, *was the battle symbol of the Lancastrians during the 15th-century Wars of the Roses between the rival English royal houses of Lancaster and York.*

take up to 10 years to develop before they are ready to grow into a new palm tree. They look like two coconuts joined together and can weigh up to 45 pounds each.

In the wild they usually grow on hilltops in the remote Seychelles islands. What baffles scientists is how the seeds got on island hilltops. Since the seeds are so heavy, the trees might be expected to spread downhill as each generation of seeds falls from its parents. But how could the seeds travel uphill to colonize a new peak? No native animal or bird would be capable of carrying them, and since the seeds sink in water, they cannot have been carried up by the sea.

TRAPPER IN WAITING

Venus's-flytrap, *Dionea muscipula,* which grows in nitrogen-poor bogs in the eastern United States, has developed a natural trap to collect the nitrogen it needs. Its leaves, which are hinged along the spine, are colorful and sweetly scented to attract insects. As soon as an insect touches down, sensitive hairs on the leaf trigger a sudden expansion of cells in the hinge base, causing the halves of the leaf to snap shut. Curved spines along the glove was used in folk medicine long before the medical profession recognized its value and began extracting the drug in the late 18th century.

Deadly nightshade, *Atropa belladonna,* yields atropine, a drug used to dilate the pupils so that an optician, say, can more easily see the retina at the back of the eye. Opium, morphine, and heroin, which are powerful painkillers, come from a type of poppy, *Papaver somniferum.* And the ergot fungus, *Claviceps purpurea,* yields lysergic acid, from which many drugs are produced to treat psychiatric disorders. Use of such drugs can cause psychotic symptoms.

RISING FROM THE ASHES
South Africa's national flower, the protea, can survive a forest fire. Indeed, it cannot survive without one. When the seeds of the sugar-bush *Protea repens,* for example, have been fertilized, tough bracts close around the flower head containing the seeds, creating a protective shell that can last for up to 20 years.

The bracts—containing asbestoslike fibers that are fireproof—will not open again until they have been scorched by fire, and they begin to open only when the fire has passed. The fluffy seeds, which have been protected by the bracts, then emerge unscathed—and the wind blows them away to ground newly cleared by the fire.

INVASION FROM ARGENTINA
More than 175 South African protea species—over half the number in the region—face extinction because of an invasion by South American ants. To propagate, these beautiful plants depend on the indigenous African ant, which collects the seeds, takes them underground, and feeds on the sweet, oily growth carried on the seed capsule. The ants then leave the seeds underground, in effect planting them.

However, the Argentine ant—which probably arrived at the turn of the century in provisions imported for the British armies fighting in the Boer War—has been supplanting the local ant. Argentine ants, too, have a taste for the sweet growth on the capsule, but they eat it on the surface of the ground; so fewer and fewer seeds get buried. Furthermore, the more aggressive South American ants destroy any of their African relatives they chance to meet, thus compounding the risk to the plants.

SUSPENDED ANIMATION
The bird's-nest club moss, *Selaginella lepidophylla,* which is found in North America, can survive for several months without water. In a drought it rolls up to form a tight ball so as to minimize the area exposed to drying winds and sun, and it turns pale as water is lost from the cells. The plant remains in this state of suspended animation until it is dampened. Then, within about 15 minutes as the water is absorbed, the plant unfurls and becomes green again.

AND MOTHER CAME TOO
Seeds normally leave their parent plant behind when they are dispersed to a new site. But the rose of Jericho, *Anastatica hierochuntica,* is different. In this plant, which grows in desert regions from Iran to Morocco, the parent travels with the offspring—though the parent dies before it starts the journey.

The fruit containing the seeds ripens at the onset of the dry season. As the drought continues, the dying branches curl protectively around the fruit, and the roots wither until desert winds blow the plant away. The branches open to release the seeds only when the rains come, by which time the plant may be tens of miles from its original site.

NONSTOP LEAVES
The leaves on most plants grow to a maximum size and then stop. But the leaves of *Welwitschia mirabilis* never stop growing. The plant, a native of the Namib Desert of southern Africa, consists of a single woody stump and just one pair of leaves, and it takes about 100 years to reach full size.

Throughout that period, the leaves grow constantly. But since the desert winds fray them at their ends almost as fast as they grow, the leaves never get longer than about 7 feet. This has a beneficial effect. The leaves' frayed edges act like nets, collecting droplets of water from the sea mists that roll across the Namib and keeping the plant alive through droughts that can last for years.

BALLOON TRAVELERS
So efficient are pines in their reproductive methods that it is quite possible for a pine tree in Scotland to be pollinated by another in Norway, on the other side of the North Sea. Pine pollen is able to travel such huge distances on the wind because each pollen grain is buoyed up by two microscopic balloons.

WATER-BOTTLE HOME
The Pima Indians, who made their home in the arid regions of the southwestern United States before Europeans arrived, had a simple and ingenious way to carry water on their journeys across the desert. They simply filled up natural water bottles made by the massive, candelabralike saguaro cactus.

Left on its own, the cactus does not produce the bottles. But when the desert-dwelling gila woodpecker hollows out a nest for itself in the fibrous flesh, the cactus responds by lining the hole with a tough, corky layer of tissue, which remains long after the cactus has died and rotted.

TOP OF THE POPS
The *Sphagnum* mosses found in peat bogs use a battery of natural air guns to disperse the dustlike spores that are their offspring. In the last stages of ripening, the spore capsules shrink to about a quarter of their original size, compressing the air inside, and become shaped like tiny gun barrels, each with its own airtight cap. Each barrel is only about 0.1 inch long.

Eventually the cap breaks away and the trapped air escapes with an audible pop, firing the packet of spores inside as far as 7 feet.

THE TERRIBLE PALM
Rattans are the longest, though not the tallest, plants in the world. The tallest are the giant redwoods of California, which have been measured at 360 feet and are still growing. But the rattan palm, which winds its snakelike way through trees in the tropics, can be far longer. One Malaysian specimen measured 555 feet.

The palm climbs up to the highest part of the canopy of its native rain forest using sharp, backward-pointing barbs on whiplike extensions of its long leaves. Once a barb has dug into something, it is like a fishhook, extremely difficult to remove. The barbs have earned one South American species the local name of *Jacitara,* meaning "the Terrible."

JAPANESE LANTERNS
Like fireflies and some fish, there are plants that glow in the dark. The fungus *Mycaena lux-coeli,* for instance, which grows on the Japanese island of Hachijo, can be seen in the dark from 50 feet away, gleaming like a diminutive lantern. A bay near Parguera, Puerto Rico, is called Phosphorescent Bay be-

cause of the glow from millions of tiny marine plants called *Pyrodinium*, a type of plankton.

All plants and fungi that have this ability seem to make use of a biological clock, for they produce the enzymes responsible for the phosphorescence only at night. Luminous animals are thought to glow in order to attract mates or warn off predators, but scientists have not yet decided why the same faculty should be of any value to plants.

SNAP AND CRACKLE
The stinkhorn fungus *Dictyophora*, of tropical Brazil, is one of the world's fastest-growing organisms. It pushes out of the ground at the rate of an inch every 5 minutes, and grows to full size in about 20 minutes. Its growth is water powered. When the fungus is ready to grow, chemical changes in its cells allow them to absorb water rapidly. The growth is so fast that a crackling can be heard as the water swells and stretches the tissues of the fungus.

During the growth, a delicate netlike veil forms around the fungus—the origin of its other common name, "the lady of the white veil." As soon as the fungus reaches full size, it starts to decompose at the tip. Flies are attracted by the strong odor of decaying flesh and they crawl over the surface, collecting spores on their feet, thereby ensuring that the fungus's offspring are carried to new homes.

THE CREEPING BLOB
The slime mold usually lives on rotting wood and eats bacteria and decaying vegetation. When it is ready to reproduce, thousands of neighboring mold cells coalesce to form a single organism about 2 inches across.

The new organism resembles a slug or a patch of slimy mud. And unlike any of the original mold cells, it can move. In its few hours of life, the blob moves on a layer of slime—often toward light—as far as 1 foot. This mobility makes it more likely that the next generation of molds will find a favorable home, thus increasing chances of survival.

At the new location, a stalk starts to sprout, lifting some of the cells from the blob. Spores form on the stalk and are dispersed by the wind to develop into colonies of new, stationary mold cells. When the spores have gone, the mobile parent, its function completed, dies.

THE FUNGUS THAT REFRESHES
Alcoholic drinks would never have been invented without a fungus. The fungus is a family of yeasts called Ascomycetes. These yeasts are solely responsible for fermenting all alcoholic drinks because they feed on sugar and turn it into alcohol and carbon dioxide, the gas that bubbles from fermenting liquids. Members of the same fungus family also cause bread to rise, create the veins in blue cheese, and produce such antibiotics as penicillin and streptomycin.

BURIED ALIVE
Mushrooms are far bigger than they look. The fruiting body—the part that is picked and eaten—represents only about 10 percent of the fungus. The rest, hidden underground, is a network of tiny strands called hyphae, which spread through the earth to feed on plant debris. Some species of mushroom derive nutrition from the roots of trees, and in turn help the tree to soak up vital minerals from the soil. The truffle, for example, often grows alongside the roots of hazel and beech trees. It is so well adapted to its underground life that even the fruiting body—which is collected as a prized delicacy—remains below the surface of the soil and can be found only by its smell.

LIKE FATHER, UNLIKE SON

Almost every member of the plant kingdom has a pattern of reproduction very different from that of animals. Most adult animals look like their parents. But plants, while not necessarily looking like their parents at all, always resemble their grandparents.

In flowering plants and conifers, this difference between parent and offspring is obscured because part of the offspring generation remains hidden within the flower head of the parent plant. The hidden offspring then gives rise to a second generation, which does resemble the original plant.

Alternation of generations
In ferns, however, both forms are clearly visible. The familiar woodland fern plant has two sets of genetic codes (chromosomes) in its cells. Scientists call this form diploid, from the Greek *diplous,* meaning "double." But its offspring—produced from spores—looks quite different: a half-inch-long green plant, roughly heart shaped. This plant has only one set of chromosomes in its cells, and is known as haploid, from the Greek word *haplous,* meaning "single." The haploid plant produces both female egg cells and male sperm cells, and when fertilization takes place between them, the product is a new diploid fern.

Scientists call this two-stage reproduction—common to all plants except fungi and some algae—the alternation of generations.

MUSHROOM MOUTHFUL *Despite an unappealing appearance, the shaggy inky cap fungus,* Coprinus comatus, *is edible.*

Trees—the green giants

HOPE FOR THE ELM
The elm tree's habit of sending out suckers from its roots has contributed to the spread of Dutch elm disease, which has devastated the species in North America, Europe, and Asia. But the same habit may also save the elm.

Dutch elm disease is a fungus carried by bark beetles (*Scolytidae*). In a woods several trees may be connected underground, all of them having started out as suckers from one tree. When any one of the trees is infected, the disease travels throughout the root system, killing one tree after another.

But though the trees die, their root buds, which produce the suckers, survive underground, enabling the elms to push out new suckers years after their death. The bark on the new suckers is too thin for the bark beetle to eat or bore into, and the new suckers seem to be able to hold the fungus at bay.

TALKING TREES
Certain trees appear to be able to communicate—at least with others of their kind. Evidence for this startling claim comes from a study carried out in 1982 by two U.S. biologists, Dr. Gordon Orians and Dr. David Rhoades, of the University of Washington. They placed swarms of predatory caterpillars and webworms on the branches of willows and alders in a deliberate experiment to find out how trees defend themselves against attack.

Within hours of the assault, the scientists found, the chemical composition of the leaves began to change. Quantities of chemicals known as terpenes and tannins were produced, making the leaves less palatable. At the same time, the protein content of the leaves changed, making the protein indigestible. The result was that the insects starved and began dying from protein deficiency.

The scientists' most remarkable discovery, however, was that nearby trees, which were not themselves under attack, began to produce the same chemical defenses—suggesting that the trees were somehow passing information to each other. The trees were far enough apart to have no physical contact between their branches, and there were no underground connections between their root systems. A separate U.S. study of sugar maple trees came up with the same findings, and some biologists now suspect that this ability may be common to many plant species.

How the warnings are transmitted is not known for certain, but scientists believe that as a defense mechanism the trees may release scented airborne chemicals, known as pheromones, that alert their neighbors.

GIANTS OF THE FOREST
Trees, not whales, are the largest organisms alive on earth today. In volume, the biggest of all is the giant sequoia *(Sequoiadendron giganteum)* "General Sherman," in California. It is 280 feet tall. Native to the western United States, giant sequoias can have trunks 36 feet thick and weigh over 6,000 tons—more than 30 times as much as the largest known blue whale.

Trees are also enormously strong. Some tropical forest giants carry a tangle of vines, creepers, and epiphytic plants (which grow on the tree but do not feed off it) whose total weight is more than twice that of the tree.

The world's tallest tree—as distinguished from the largest, the giant sequoia—is also a western U.S. species, *Sequoia sempervirens,* the redwood (also called California, or coast, redwood). The tallest specimen is in Redwood Creek Grove, California. Its tip, which is slowly dying back, reaches 362 feet.

DEATH IN BLOOM
The largest florescence of any flowering plant is produced by a tree—the talipot palm, *Corypha umbraculifera*—found in Sri Lanka and other tropical lands. This palm lives for 40 to 70 years and flowers only once in its lifetime. But its blossoming is unforgettable: a spectacular branched head up to 20 feet tall and 30 to 42 feet across. After the display the palm bears up to 60 million fruits, each about an inch across. In about a year the fruits ripen and the seeds they contain are mature. Then, having done its best to create a new generation, the palm tree dies.

INSTANT TIMBER
The world's fastest-growing tree is a tropical member of the pea family, *Albizzia falcata*. One tree in Sabah, Malaysia, grew 35.2 feet in 13 months. Another, also planted in Sabah, reached 100 feet in 5 years, 4 months. The tropical gum tree *Eucalyptus deglupta* is a speedy grower too. One specimen reached 150 feet in just 15 years.

Although some species of bamboo can grow faster than these trees, bamboo is not classified by botanists as a tree but as a type of woody grass. Unlike trees and flowering plants, which grow from the tip, bamboos and other grasses grow from the base, pushing out of the ground like toothpaste from a tube. This is why trees and flowering plants usually die if they are cut down, but grasses can survive close grazing and regular mowing indefinitely.

HYDRAULIC MARVELS
Trees have been called the most effective pumps in the world. Silently and without any moving parts, a medium-size oak tree can raise as much as 140 gallons a day to supply its needs. And in a day even a 5-foot sapling may lift 10 gallons—enough to fill a small car's gas tank.

A suction pump can raise water up a pipe to a maximum height of about 33 feet. Beyond that height the weight of the water is sufficient to counteract the force of atmospheric pressure, and the column breaks. But a tree's natural pump can lift water more than 10 times as high without difficulty.

A tree's pump is powered by the sun. As molecules of water are evaporated from the leaves, others move up the sapwood of the tree to take their place, in a process known as osmosis. The tubes up which the water moves are so tiny that the wood acts more like blotting paper than like a group of pipes, and this helps the tree overcome the 33-foot height limit of a suction pump.

NO LONGER DEAD AS A DODO
A tree once kept alive by the dodo is flourishing again—thanks to turkeys. Stanley Temple, a U.S. biologist working in the Indian Ocean island nation of Mauritius in the late 1970s, noticed that the fertile

HOW A TREE GROWS

Almost all the wood that makes up a tree is dead. Even on a large, mature tree, all growth occurs in a few tiny areas—at the tips of the shoots and roots, and in a thin layer of cells known as the cambium. The cells on the tips allow shoots and roots to grow upward, outward, and downward. The cambium layer is responsible for the thickening of the trunk, branches, and roots.

The main cambium tissue forms two types of food-carrying cells: phloem tissue on its outer side to carry sugars from the leaves around the tree; and xylem tissue, or sapwood, on its inner side to carry soil water from roots to leaves. A subsidiary layer of cambium tissue produces corky bark.

Every spring the cambium produces large, thin-walled cells to carry water and nutrients needed for the peak growth period. Each summer it produces denser, thick-walled cells. Together the cells produce a regular pattern of light (spring) and dark (summer) rings in the trunk, which form a diary of the tree's life. Each pair of rings represents a year's growth, and the thickness of the rings from year to year can reveal past events and conditions. In years of drought, for instance, growth is slower and the rings thinner.

As xylem cells age, they become impregnated with lignin, a chemical related to cellulose. Eventually they become dense heartwood, the dead core that gives a tree structural strength. As phloem cells age, they become part of the bark. The cortex in the outer layers contains additional storage cells and strengthening fibers.

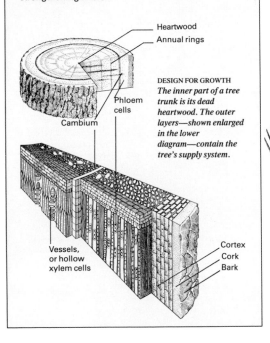

Heartwood
Annual rings

Phloem cells

Cambium

DESIGN FOR GROWTH
The inner part of a tree trunk is its dead heartwood. The outer layers—shown enlarged in the lower diagram—contain the tree's supply system.

Vessels, or hollow xylem cells

Cortex
Cork
Bark

seeds of *Calvaria major*, a species of tree indigenous to the island, were not germinating. In fact, none had apparently germinated for 300 years, the age of the youngest specimens of the tree still growing.

Impressed by the coincidence between this date and the known time of the dodo's extinction, and noting that some large, tough calvaria seeds had been found in the gizzards of semifossilized dodos, he concluded that the strong digestive system of the long-gone bird had been an essential part of the tree's propagation. In an attempt to recreate the dodo's role, he fed some of the seeds to domestic turkeys, collected the seeds when they had been

through the birds' digestive mill, and planted them. For the first time in three centuries *Calvaria major* germinated, producing healthy new plants.

SHED AND SURVIVE

The shedding of leaves each autumn is a survival technique evolved by deciduous trees that helps them survive the cold season. In winter much of the water in the soil turns to snow and ice, which trees cannot draw up into their tissues. Since the leaves need, and lose, more water than other parts of a tree, their absence in winter allows the tree to conserve moisture. An area of trees in leaf of about 100 square yards needs more than 20 tons of water a day to thrive. The same area of trees without leaves needs only a fraction of this amount.

Coniferous evergreen trees such as pines can survive the winter without shedding their greenery because their narrow needles have a much smaller surface area and so lose less water through evaporation. In addition, the leaves of evergreen trees are often covered with a glossy layer that acts like a sheet of plastic, preventing escape of moisture.

HARDWOOD, SOFTWOOD

The timber industry's terms *hardwood* and *softwood* have nothing to do with the hardness or density of a tree's wood. Hardwood comes from broad-leaved deciduous trees—those that lose their leaves in winter. Balsa, for instance, is classified as a hardwood because it comes from a broad-leaved tree, even though the wood is very soft. Softwood comes from coniferous trees, such as pines and spruces. Yew is classified as a softwood even though the wood is strong and very durable.

PINE GLORY
Like other conifers, pines carry their seeds in cones. This is the maritime pine (Pinus pinaster), a Mediterranean species.

Crops and agriculture

FISHING FARMERS
Stone Age fishermen may have been the first farmers. The reason: farmers need to live in permanent settlements while their crops grow—unlike hunters, who must wander in search of game. So Middle Eastern fishermen, who were among the first to build permanent settlements on the edges of lakes or the sea, may have been among the first to grow crops as well. Some of the ancient world's most sophisticated inland farmers lived in what is now southern Turkey. At the settlement of Catal Huyuk, which dates from about 6700 B.C., modern archeologists have found traces of no fewer than 14 different crops, including wheat, barley, peas, lentils, and vetch.

HARVEST TIME
People were harvesting wheat in its wild forms long before they learned to grow it. Wheat was first cultivated by farmers in the Middle East around 8000 B.C., but archeologists have found in the same region crude sickles, used to harvest the wild forerunners of the cereal, dating from about 10,000 B.C.

THE THAILAND CLAIM
Agriculture may have originated in present-day Thailand, rather than in the Middle East as archeologists have long believed. Remains of crop plants, including peas, beans, cucumbers, and peppers, were found in a cave in northeast Thailand in the early 1970s and have been dated by carbon-14 tests to about 9700 B.C.— several centuries earlier than the first known farming in the Middle East.

PLOWING AHEAD
The plow has been the farmer's most important tool for nearly 5,000 years. Invented in the Middle East in about 3000 B.C., it enabled early farmers to turn over the topsoil, burying weeds and thus giving crops a chance to grow without competition. Originally a crude instrument consisting of a forked branch with one prong sharpened to cut through the soil, the plow later acquired a specially shaped wooden frame and was fitted with bronze, and then iron, blades. Oxen were first harnessed to plows by the Egyptians in about 1500 B.C.

CIVILIZING CEREALS
The world's great civilizations have all been based on the cultivation of cereals. For without an abundant and reliable source of food, villages cannot grow into cities, nor cities into empires. The civilizations of Mesopotamia, Egypt, Greece, and Rome were all based on wheat. Rice was the staple food in ancient India, China, and Japan, and maize in the Inca, Aztec, and Mayan empires of the Americas.

DEADLY FOOD
Cassava, one of the tropical world's staple food crops, contains an extremely dangerous poison. Unless the plant's raw roots are thoroughly washed and cooked they yield prussic acid, which is fatal to humans even in small quantities. The starchy cassava, *Manihot esculenta*, is used to make tapioca.

CHEWING-GUM TREES
Chewing gum is derived from the latex of the chicle (or sapodilla) tree, *Achras zapota*. Native to Central America, the chicle grows wild, and each tree may be several miles from its nearest neighbor. Local Indians, known as *chicleros*, harvest the milky latex by cutting V-shaped incisions in the bark and letting the juice ooze out. The latex is collected and boiled to provide the gum base for chewing gum. Since the late 1940s chicle latex has been partly replaced by synthetics in gum manufacture.

BREAD'S FAMILY TREE

Modern wheat hybrids have an ancestry going back to the chance crossing in western Asia of wild einkorn with a related wild grass more than 10,000 years ago. The cross produced wild emmer, which under cultivation gave rise to emmer, durum, and other mutant forms. Wild emmer also crossed with a second wild grass to produce spelt. Bread wheat, which has been cultivated for about 4,500 years, is descended from a cross between emmer and the second wild grass. It probably developed first in what is now eastern Turkey and western Iran as a spontaneous hybrid in fields of cultivated emmer where the wild grass was growing as a weed. Modern hybrids are often complex crosses of bread wheat (used for its food quality) with durum and spelt (used for their resistance to disease).

In the future, scientists may be able to manipulate the genetic structure of wheat plants directly to create varieties that can extract nitrogen from air, as peas and beans do, and thus grow well without the need for expensive fertilizers.

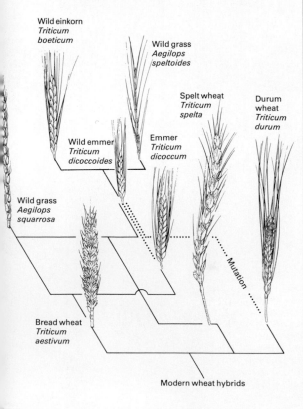

Wild einkorn
Triticum boeticum

Wild grass
Aegilops speltoides

Spelt wheat
Triticum spelta

Durum wheat
Triticum durum

Wild emmer
Triticum dicoccoides

Emmer
Triticum dicoccum

Wild grass
Aegilops squarrosa

Mutation

Bread wheat
Triticum aestivum

Modern wheat hybrids

MILK TREE

Venezuelans collect milk from a herd that never moves. The South American milk tree, *Brosimum utile*, belongs to the fig family and produces a sap that looks, tastes, and is used just like cow's milk.

MONOPOLY-BUSTING PIGEONS

A lucrative Dutch spice monopoly was broken by pigeons. Until the late 18th century, nutmeg trees grew only on the Dutch-owned Indonesian islands of Banda and Amboina (Ambon) because earlier traders had deliberately destroyed nutmeg trees elsewhere to maintain control of the supply. As a result, Dutch merchants were able to demand artificially high prices for the spices derived from the tree. By 1900, though, island-hopping pigeons that fed on nutmeg seeds had carried them to neighboring islands not under Dutch control. Once the new trees grew, the Dutch monopoly crumbled and prices fell. The nutmeg tree, *Myristica fragrans*, actually produces two spices. Its hard seeds yield nutmeg, used to flavor cakes and milk dishes; and a red fleshy structure surrounding the seed produces mace, used in chutneys and pickles.

REVENGE OF THE PLANTS

Two modern garden insecticides used to protect vegetables and flowers from predatory insects are derived from plants. Rotenone is produced from the root of a Southeast Asian pea, *Derris elliptica*, and pyrethrum comes from a type of daisy, *Chrysanthemum cinerariaefolium*. These plant-derived pesticides are regarded by botanists as safer than earlier synthetic insecticides, such as DDT, because they are much less poisonous to mammals, including human beings, and do not accumulate in animal tissues.

UNDERGROUND NUTS

The peanut, a relative of the garden pea, buries its own seeds and so assures the survival of the next generation. After fertilization, the pods branch downward from the peanut's flower and force their way into the soil, allowing the peanut, which is the plant's seed, to ripen underground. In this way the seeds are protected from predators. Contact with the moister soil beneath the surface also enables the seeds to soak up more efficiently the water they need for germination. Most plants, by contrast, grow upward, toward the light, and release their seeds aboveground.

CROPS AROUND THE WORLD: HOW THEY BEGAN

Barley First grown in Egypt in about 4000 B.C. Modern varieties are descended from the strain *Hordeum spontaneum*. Now grown mostly in Europe, North America, and Australia for cattle fodder and to make malt, used in distilling and brewing.

Beans Family of plants now very widely grown, and thought to have been first cultivated in about 6000 B.C. String, kidney, and lima beans originated in Central and South America. Mung and soya beans were first cultivated in Asia, broad beans in Europe.

Maize First cultivated in Mexico in about 5000 B.C. Introduced to Europe from the Americas by Christopher Columbus in the late 15th century. Modern varieties are descended from the original cultivated plant that was crossed with a 15th-century hybrid called teosinte.

Millet First cultivated in China in about 2700 B.C. Now grown mostly for cattle fodder in the U.S.A. and U.S.S.R., but because of its resistance to drought is also used as food in tropical Africa.

Oats Probably originated as a weed growing with other cereals, such as wheat or barley. Domesticated about 2,500 years ago in Asia and Europe. The most widely cultivated form is *Avena sativa*, derived from a western Asian wild grass, *Avena fatua*. Predominantly used as cattle food, but also used in breakfast cereals.

Potato First known to have been cultivated in the Peruvian and Bolivian Andes in about A.D. 200. Introduced to Europe by the Spaniards in the late 16th century. More than 150 varieties are now grown.

Rice First known to have been cultivated in India in about 3000 B.C., later spreading to China, Japan, and Southeast Asia, now the main producers. About 25 varieties are grown, all descended from an original wild species, *Oryza sativa*.

Rye Originated as a weed growing among other cereals. First cultivated in southwest Asia in about 1000 B.C. and now used as flour in rye bread or as food for cattle.

Sorghum Probably originated in Africa in about 3000 B.C. It is now grown for human and animal consumption in Africa, India, China, and the U.S.A.

Wheat Probably the earliest domesticated cereal, developing from chance hybridizations of wild grasses more than 10,000 years ago. It was grown by the early civilizations around the Mediterranean Sea and the Middle East, and was being baked into bread in Mesopotamia as early as 8000 B.C.

CROP OF AGES
Sorghum, now grown around the world, probably grew first in Africa some 5,000 years ago.

Fruits and vegetables

BREADFRUIT AND THE *BOUNTY*
The mutiny on the *Bounty* happened during a vegetable delivery. In 1789 Capt. William Bligh set sail from Tahiti on board the *Bounty* with a cargo of breadfruit plants for the West Indies. The aim was to introduce them as a new crop to provide cheap food for slaves on the islands.

The mutiny interrupted the voyage, and the breadfruit plants did not reach their destination then. But 4 years later Bligh completed the mission aboard another ship. Ironically, the breadfruit was not welcomed in the Caribbean. The slaves and native islanders preferred their traditional fruit, a type of banana known as a plantain.

YES, TREES HAVE NO BANANAS
Banana trees are not trees at all. Although banana plants resemble small palm trees, they are in fact giant herbaceous plants—that is, they lack a tree's typical woody tissues. The plant's "trunk" is not wood; it is formed from tightly wrapped leaf bases. As contrasted with such types as plantains, which are usually cooked and eaten as vegetables, banana varieties developed for eating as uncooked fruit have lost the ability to reproduce. They have no viable seeds; all that remain of the seeds are the soft black specks in the core of a banana. So the stock of plants has to be renewed from cuttings, clones genetically identical to the parent. By contrast, the seeds of wild bananas are the size of peas and are extremely hard.

Fibers from the leaves of other relatives of the banana yield Manila hemp, which is used to make water-resistant ropes for the fishing industry, twine, hammocks, hats, and table mats.

EDIBLE FLOWERS
Western gardeners and cooks regularly ignore one of the tastiest parts of summer squashes such as zucchini: the flowers. Male flowers—those without the basal swelling that grows into the vegetable—can be cooked with a little butter or coated in batter and lightly fried.

The leaves make a useful herb for cooking; and the seeds, which yield an edible oil, can be roasted, salted, and eaten.

The vegetable marrow family, which includes squashes, gourds, and pumpkins, is largely composed of varieties of a single and originally Mexican species, *Cucurbita pepo,* cultivated by man for at least 5,500 years.

TUBER TRAGEDY
The Irish potato famine of the late 1840s happened because of the way potatoes are grown in cultivation. New crops are raised by planting potatoes, not seeds, so that each new generation of potato plants is a clone, genetically identical to the previous year's plants. Because all the plants are identical, if one plant is susceptible to a disease, all the plants can fall to it. The cause of the famine was a fungus disease, potato blight, which swept over Ireland and wiped out the entire potato harvest for 4 consecutive years from 1847 to 1850.

Had the crops been grown from seeds and thus had a variety of genetic patterns, the disease would not have had such a devastating effect. More than a million people starved to death, and hundreds of thousands fled to the United States. Before the famine the population of Ireland was more than 6.5 million. By 1851, the year after the famine ended, it had dropped to 5.1 million, and it has never recovered. In the early 1980s the population of Eire and Ulster combined was only 4.9 million.

Ironically, the Irish population had grown vastly in the previous two centuries partly as a result of the introduction from South America of the potato—a cheap, easily grown, and popular staple crop. Blight-resistant strains were later imported from South America. Britain, one of the world's potato-eating champions, now consumes over 15,000 tons a day—enough to give everyone in the country a 10-ounce helping.

WHY CHILIES ARE HOT
Even the most fiery chili pepper gets all its heat from no more than 0.1 percent of the fruit. The burning taste comes from a chemical called capsaicin (capsicin), of which only a trace is needed to cause an unwary diner to grab for water.

Chilies are the berries of a species of the potato family, *Capsicum annuum.* The species includes both the small hot types, such as the red tabasco pepper, and the large red and green sweet peppers. Hot peppers dried and crushed yield cayenne pepper. Sweet peppers are used to make paprika.

The species is native to the Americas, but the largest crops by far are now grown in India.

CHANGE FOR THE BETTER
Many crops perform much better in new homes than in their own. The coffee plant, for instance, *Coffea arabica,* is native to Ethiopia. But most coffee now comes from Central or South America. Cocoa (*Theobroma cacao*) originated in South and Central America, but Ghana is now the world's main exporter. Citrus fruits, once native to Southeast Asia, and soya beans from northern Asia now grow best in the Americas. One of the major reasons for the better performance of the expatriate plant is that the migrant is free, even if only temporarily, from the pests and diseases that evolved alongside it in its original home.

JACK THE GIANT FRUIT
The jackfruit tree of southern Asia, *Artocarpus heterophyllus,* bears massive fruits weighing up to 110 pounds—the world's largest tree fruits. Up to 250 fruits are produced by a single tree each year, and the sweet pulp is eaten fresh or preserved in syrup, particularly in India and Sri Lanka.

SCRUB UP WITH A SQUASH
The bathroom sponges known as loofahs were edible at an earlier stage of their existence. They are the fruit of a tropical relative (*Luffa cylindrica*) of summer squash and have nothing to do with sea sponges. The young cooked fruits taste something like squash.

To make bathroom loofahs, the ripe fruits are immersed in running water until the outer wall disintegrates, and the fibrous remains are then cleaned and bleached. Loofahs have also been used as filters in steam and diesel engines; in mats, shoe soles, and gloves; and as padding in the steel helmets used before World War II by the U.S. Army.

THE APPEAL OF F1 HYBRIDS

Most fruits and vegetables grown around the world are hybrids—varieties created, often artificially, from interbreeding two or more separate strains. Over generations of selective breeding and cross-fertilizing, hybrid plants can be tailored to have almost any set of characteristics: for instance, consistently larger fruit, faster growth, or greater resistance to pests and diseases.

The perils of inbreeding
Farmers and gardeners also make use, however, of another property peculiar to the earliest generations of a new hybrid. Plants that have been bred selectively for generations so that they always grow true to type tend to lose their vigor. They grow feebly because of inbreeding. But if two true-breeding varieties are crossed, the first resulting generation—known as Filial 1, or F1 for short—has the dominant qualities of its parents, plus vastly increased vigor. As a result, F1 seeds can produce more abundant crops than either of their parent varieties.

The generation descended from the F1 has almost as much vigor as the F1, but less uniformity, because about one plant in four will display what are called recessive characteristics, derived from the original varieties but submerged in the F1 generation. These second-generation plants—known as F2 hybrids—are also widely grown because no laboriously controlled cross-pollination is needed, and so the seeds are cheaper to produce.

Generations later than F2 can be grown, but are usually sold only as mixtures because their genetic structure is by then so scrambled that few of the resulting plants grow true to type.

A monk's experiments
The principles used by modern plant breeders to create hybrids, including F1 and F2 strains, were discovered by an Austrian monk named Gregor Mendel (1822–84). He published his results, based on experiments with garden peas, in 1866; but his work was ignored until confirmed by other researchers in 1900, 16 years after his death. Mendel found that all genetic characteristics, in animals as well as plants, are carried in pairs. He also found that where two opposed characteristics—such as tallness and shortness—are carried by the same plant, one of the factors will consistently dominate. This explains why plants grown from F1 seeds are so uniform.

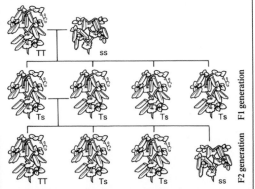

HEREDITY PATTERN *When two true-breeding varieties (top two plants in diagram) are crossed—one carrying a pair of dominant genes (say, for tallness, TT in diagram) and the other a pair of recessive opposites (for shortness, ss)—all of the resulting F1 seeds grow into tall plants because each carries a dominant T gene. When F1 plants are crossed with each other, however, only three of the four possible genetic combinations in the resulting F2 generation contain the dominant tallness (T) gene. The fourth has only the recessive genes and thus grows into a short plant.*

QUEEN OF THE GREENS
Cabbages, broccoli, cauliflowers, brussels sprouts, kohlrabi, and kale are all varieties of a single Mediterranean species, *Brassica oleracea*. Over thousands of years, farmers have developed the different vegetables by selecting from originally wild plants and their cultivated progeny those with the densest flower heads (for cauliflowers and broccoli), those with the best rosettes of winter leaves (for cabbages), those with the largest buds (for brussels sprouts), and those with the thickest stems (for kohlrabi).

TASTY AND SMELLY
The durian, a Southeast Asian fruit from a plant known to botanists as *Durio zibethinus*, is rated by many gourmets as the world's most delicious food. There is just one problem: it smells awful. Critics groping for a description of its qualities have labeled it "onion-flavored custard." The wild plants are a favorite food of elephants and orangutans.

FALSE FRUIT
The strawberry is technically not a fruit at all. In botanical terms, fruits are seed-bearing structures that grow from a flower's ovaries, and a strawberry is merely the swollen base of the strawberry flower. The plant's true fruits are the small, hard, nutlike pips embedded around the outside of the flesh. The pips contain the seeds. Strawberries came originally from the Americas. Garden varieties were first bred in 18th-century France from spontaneous hybrids between a North American species, *Fragaria virginiana*, and a Chilean species, *F. chiloensis*.

TASTE TEST *Some gourmets rate the durian of Southeast Asia as the world's most delicious fruit—despite its pungent smell. Critics call it "onion-flavored custard."*

How animals are classified

THE ANIMAL KINGDOM

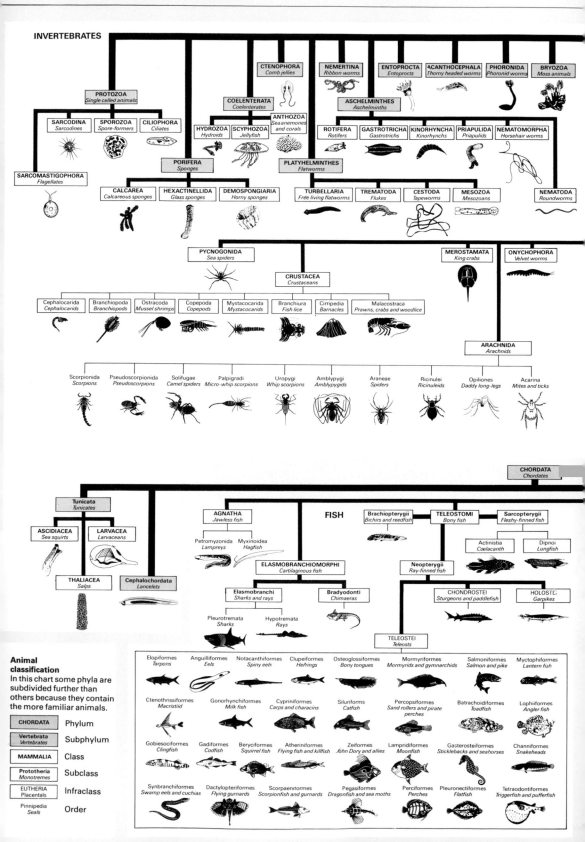

Animal classification

In this chart some phyla are subdivided further than others because they contain the more familiar animals.

CHORDATA	Phylum
Vertebrata / *Vertebrates*	Subphylum
MAMMALIA	Class
Prototheria / *Monotremes*	Subclass
EUTHERIA / *Placentals*	Infraclass
Pinnipedia / *Seals*	Order

Nature confirms only one way of grouping animals. It is the species, animals that can interbreed in the wild and produce fertile offspring. To show how animals are related through evolution, however, zoologists classify them further—into genera, families, orders, classes, and phyla. The system of identifying each animal by a two-part Latin name made up of the genus and species was devised by a Swedish naturalist, Carl von Linné (1707–78), known by the Latin name he gave himself, Carolus Linnaeus.

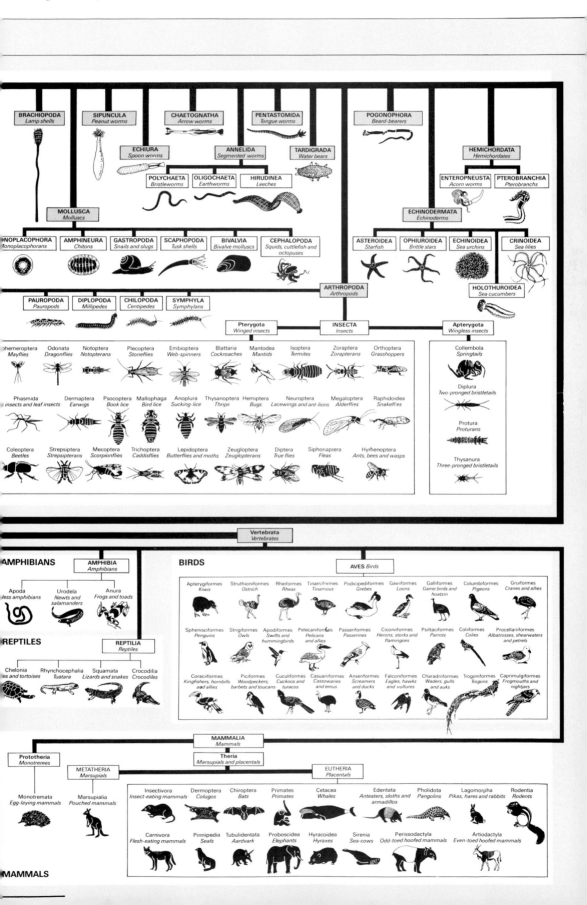

Animals without backbones

SECONDHAND STING

Sea slugs have no shell to protect their soft, rippling bodies and no natural defenses. But they eat weapons. The sea slug *Glaucus,* for instance, eats the sting cells of the *Porpita* jellyfish but does not digest them. Instead, the cells are passed intact to the slug's skin, ready for use against a predator.

Another slug eats the stinging buds of anemones, to which it is immune. The buds are swallowed intact. Then the sea slug's body guides them through the intestinal wall to the back, where they nestle under the skin. If triggered, the stings shoot out at an enemy or attacker.

DEADLY MEDLEY

The Portuguese man-of-war is not one animal but many, all living in lethal four-part harmony. This bobbing, slimy horror, a type of jellyfish, whose toxic tentacles can kill human beings, consists of four different types of animal, totaling perhaps 1,000 individuals. Each type has its own specialized job—floating, catching food, digestion, or reproduction. All work together well and none could live on its own. Between them, these primitive individuals form the crew of a killing machine with a poison almost as powerful as a cobra's.

For small fish, contact with the man-of-war's trailing tentacles, which can be 60 feet long, means instant oblivion. For humans a bad sting means severe pain, a rapid drop in blood pressure, shock, and sometimes death. Luckier victims will carry for days the angry red welts that the tentacles leave. There is no known antidote for the stings, but ordinary vinegar seems to neutralize some of the poison's effects.

TREE-CLIMBING CRABS

A giant relative of the hermit crab finds food not in the water but in the trees. The purse crab, *Birgus latro,* lives on the islands of the southwest Pacific and Indian oceans. When young it lodges in an empty shell, like the hermit crab, but a mature purse crab can be as long as 18 inches.

Its enormously powerful pincers and long walking legs enable it to climb coconut palms as efficiently as a lumberjack with climbing irons. Once at the top, the crab snips off young coconuts and then returns to the ground to eat them.

GIANTS OF THE DEEP

The world's largest invertebrates—animals without backbones—are squids of the genus *Architeuthis.* Nobody knows how large these monsters may grow in their home in the ocean's abyss, but occasional specimens come to the surface. One measured in New Zealand in 1887 was 57 feet long, including nearly 50 feet of tentacles. Another washed up in New Zealand in 1933 was 70 feet long. A squid of this size weighs well over a ton and has an eye 16 inches across, the largest eye in the animal kingdom.

Squids many times larger than these may exist. The suckers of a 50-foot squid leave round scars on a sperm whale—the traditional enemy of squids—that are 4 inches across. But sperm whales have been found with scars 18 inches across—more than four times as large.

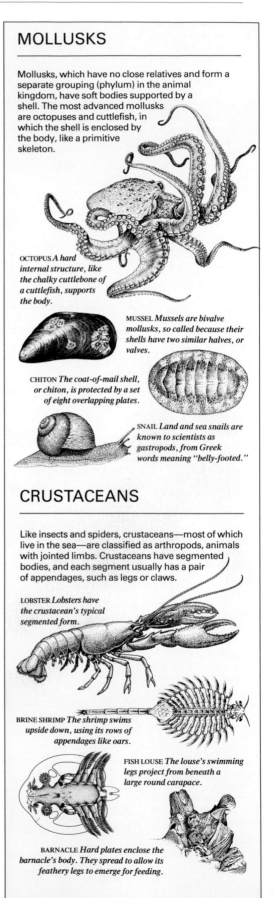

MOLLUSKS

Mollusks, which have no close relatives and form a separate grouping (phylum) in the animal kingdom, have soft bodies supported by a shell. The most advanced mollusks are octopuses and cuttlefish, in which the shell is enclosed by the body, like a primitive skeleton.

OCTOPUS *A hard internal structure, like the chalky cuttlebone of a cuttlefish, supports the body.*

MUSSEL *Mussels are bivalve mollusks, so called because their shells have two similar halves, or valves.*

CHITON *The coat-of-mail shell, or chiton, is protected by a set of eight overlapping plates.*

SNAIL *Land and sea snails are known to scientists as gastropods, from Greek words meaning "belly-footed."*

CRUSTACEANS

Like insects and spiders, crustaceans—most of which live in the sea—are classified as arthropods, animals with jointed limbs. Crustaceans have segmented bodies, and each segment usually has a pair of appendages, such as legs or claws.

LOBSTER *Lobsters have the crustacean's typical segmented form.*

BRINE SHRIMP *The shrimp swims upside down, using its rows of appendages like oars.*

FISH LOUSE *The louse's swimming legs project from beneath a large round carapace.*

BARNACLE *Hard plates enclose the barnacle's body. They spread to allow its feathery legs to emerge for feeding.*

FLOATING KILLER

The sting of the box jellyfish, or sea wasp, a kind of jellyfish with a dome-shaped bell only 10 inches high, contains one of the world's most potent poisons. It can cause a victim to develop a fierce temperature, gasp for breath, and die, all in the space of a few minutes. In the past 100 years at least 65 people have died from sea-wasp stings while swimming off Queensland, Australia. An antidote to the poison does exist, but the poison acts so quickly that the victim has little chance of getting treatment in time.

BIRD-EATING SPIDERS

Spiders large enough to tackle birds—and win—live in holes and under fallen trees on the forest floors of South America, Asia, and Africa. Some species found in South America have a body as much as 3 inches across—the size of a man's palm—and a leg span of 8 inches. Often called bird-eating spiders, they have been known to catch small birds, but the bulk of their diet consists of small mammals and insects. Like other spiders, the giants do not chew their food. Instead, they inject digestive juices into the prey and then suck out the fluids from its body.

SHELL SHOCK

The Indian and Pacific oceans, home of many of the world's most poisonous sea creatures, house one of the most beautiful killers in the cone shell snail, a relative of the harmless whelk. Its shell is so highly prized by collectors that a single good specimen can fetch $500 or more.

But the animal that lives inside this marvel owns a horrifying, and loaded, living syringe—a trunklike tube that it can whip against the body of an attacker. In the tip of the trunk are minute needle teeth through which the snail injects a paralyzing fluid. At least 10 people have died from its effects, generally within a few hours of the pinprick sting.

WORM ANESTHETIC

Leeches, which are related to earthworms, have their own built-in anesthetic so that they can feed in peace. The leech clamps itself to its victims with suckers at each end of its body. At the center of the front sucker is the mouth. The leech makes a Y-shaped wound with its three sharp-toothed jaws and then sucks the blood.

Anesthetic in the leech's saliva numbs the wound so that the victim does not feel its attacker and brush it off. Leeches also secrete a substance that causes blood vessels to dilate, increasing blood flow, and an anticoagulant substance to prevent blood from clotting.

COURTING DANGER

Because scorpions are not immune to their own poison, even mating is a risky business for them. As a result, the desert hunters, which normally live alone, have evolved a cautious courtship ritual.

The male seizes the female's pincers in his own, and the pair then shuffles backward and forward, sometimes with the stinging tails carefully entwined to keep them away from the scorpions' bodies. The male deposits a packet of sperm on the ground and pushes and pulls the female until she is over the packet and can take up the sperm to fertilize the eggs.

After the dance the scorpions go their separate ways. The fertilized eggs develop and hatch within the mother's body. Then the young clamber out and stay on her back for a couple of weeks until they are old enough to fend for themselves.

SPIDER MATING STRATEGIES

Hazardous though the mating of scorpions may be, at least the partners are of equal size. In most species of spider, the male is many times smaller than his mate, and runs a real risk of being eaten. Before courting, the male spider spins a tiny pad of web into which he deposits sperm from his abdomen. He then sucks the sperm into a specialized leg known as the pedipalp. To mate successfully, he must approach the female closely enough to plunge the pedipalp into the genital opening on the front of her abdomen.

In one spider species, *Pisaura listeri*, the male hands the female a gift of a fly wrapped in silk as he approaches. Only when the female has her mouth full does he dart in to mate.

SHARPSHOOTING SHRIMP

Amid the coral reefs of tropical waters lurks a tiny bandit, the 2-inch-long pistol shrimp. The pincers on its large right claw form a matching peg and hole.

When a small fish wanders into the ambush spot, the shrimp scuttles out, aims this "pistol," and snaps the peg into the hole. The resulting shock wave in the water stuns the fish for a few seconds and gives the shrimp time to close in for the kill.

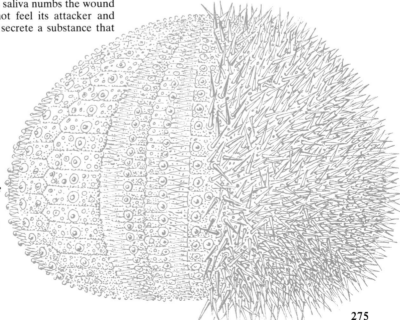

LIVING PINCUSHION *The common sea urchin,* Echinus esculentus, *is one of about 800 species of these spiky, ball-shaped creatures. They are related to the starfish. This cutaway drawing shows the patterned shell that encloses the body but is normally hidden by the jutting spines. Sea urchins, which are eaten as a delicacy in many parts of the world, feed through a mouth at the base of the shell. The mouth area is their only vulnerable point.*

HEADSTRONG BARNACLES

Barnacles spend their entire adult lives standing on their heads. The larvae of these crustaceans, which live on coastal rocks around the world, are free-swimming. But when a larva finds a suitable rocky surface, it glues itself to the rock by means of a gland on its head. The barnacle then changes shape, secreting shell plates around its body to protect it for its immobile adult life. When the tide covers it, the barnacle opens the plates, and feathery appendages emerge to kick food particles into the mouth.

Some parasitic barnacles undergo even stranger transformations than their nonparasitic relatives. *Sacculina* barnacles make their homes inside crabs. The larva settles headfirst on a crab and throws off its body and legs. It then produces a dart-shaped organ, which it thrusts into the crab's body and through which it injects itself as a formless mass of cells.

Settling by the crab's intestine, the larva sends out branches through its host, hindering the crab's development. Finally, the barnacle becomes adult as little more than a bag of sex organs below the crab's abdomen. It has both male and female sexual organs and reproduces itself by shedding sperm and eggs into the surrounding water.

REWARDS OF RESISTANCE

Pearls, treasured throughout the world as jewelry, are the product of a fight against an invader. Mollusks with double shells, such as clams, oysters, and mussels, lay down pearl as the inner layer of their shells. The mother-of-pearl, as it is called, consists largely of thin layers of calcium carbonate, the chemical of which chalk is composed.

When some foreign matter, often a parasitic larva, gets into its body, the mollusk forms a small sac around the foreign matter, isolating it, and then builds layer upon layer of calcium carbonate around the sac, imprisoning the invader forever and creating a pearl. Cultivated pearls are produced by inserting an artificial irritant, usually a bead of mother-of-pearl, into the body of an oyster.

Natural pearls are rare. Only one oyster in a thousand contains one. The freshwater pearl mussel, once widely cultivated in Europe, might take 6 years to build up a pearl, and only 1 in 3,000 mussels examined is likely to contain one. However, with luck the rewards can be considerable. The largest pearl ever found, the Pearl of Laotze, weighs 14 pounds 1 ounce and is 9.5 inches long. This football-size pearl was found in the Philippines, inside a giant clam.

WORMS, WORMS EVERYWHERE

The world's 10,000 species of roundworm have learned to make their homes almost anywhere—in the earth, in fresh water, in the sea, even in the bodies of other animals and plants. They are so abundant that a mere handful of garden soil will contain about 1,000.

Many roundworms are small or microscopic, but some grow to 3 feet. Some are phenomenal breeders. Females of one species—the 14-inch-long intestinal parasite known as *Ascaris lumbricoides*—can lay 200,000 eggs a day.

THE LONG AND THE SHORT OF IT

The world's longest insect is the giant stick insect, *Pharnacia serratipes,* of Indonesia. Females of the species can be up to 13 inches long. For sheer bulk, combining length and width, the champion insect may be the South American Hercules beetle, *Dynastes her-cules,* measuring as much as 7.5 inches long and 2 inches wide. By contrast, some of the tiny species of *Alaptus,* fairy flies that develop as parasites inside the eggs of other insects, are only 0.01 inch long when fully grown.

OLDEST INHABITANT

The longest-existing species inhabiting the earth is a deep-sea snail, *Neopilina galatheae.* It was found living at a depth of 11,400 feet off Costa Rica in 1952, and fossil remains show that it has not changed at all in 500 million years.

LONGEST REACH

The Arctic jellyfish of the northwest Atlantic has the longest reach of any animal. One of these creatures, which was washed up on a Massachusetts beach in about 1865, had a body 7.5 feet across and tentacles 120 feet long, giving it a total possible span of more than 240 feet.

LONGEST WORMS

Ribbon worms—named for their flat, ribbon-shaped bodies—far exceed any other kind of worm in length. The bootlace worm, *Lineus longissimus,* is a type of ribbon worm that lives around British coasts. It commonly grows to over 15 feet. Some, however, have topped 100 feet, and a specimen washed ashore in Scotland in 1864 measured more than 180 feet—the longest worm and the longest animal, end to end, ever found.

GARDENING UNDERGROUND

The workers of the tropical American leaf-cutting ants tend their own food-producing gardens in their underground nests, which measure as much as 33 feet across and contain some 500,000 ants. First the workers collect pieces of leaves and bear them like flags to the nest. They then tear the pieces up, and on this compost they grow a crop of fungus, which is eaten by the ants.

DOUBLE-HEADED DECEIVERS

Some insects appear to have a head at both ends of their bodies. Many hairstreak butterfly species, for example, have protuberances on their hind wings that look like frontal antennae when the insect rests with its wings folded. As soon as the butterfly lands, it turns rapidly so that its head is facing the way it has just come. The quick change of direction and the false head deceive predators. Birds rely on knowing which is the head end so that, when they pounce, they can anticipate and allow for the victim's movement. But the hairstreak moves off in the direction its true head is facing—which is usually the opposite direction from that expected.

SILKEN THREADS

Most moth and butterfly caterpillars make silk. They produce it from salivary glands and use it to construct supporting threads and cocoons, which protect them while they change from larva to adult. Most species usually produce silk in short lengths, which are glued and woven together in the cocoon, and the threads are too short to be commercially useful.

But the mulberry silkworm, *Bombyx mori,* spins single threads up to 3,900 feet long—a talent that has made the caterpillar so valuable that almost all of them are now domesticated for silk production.

The silk is retrieved by softening the cocoon in hot water—incidentally killing the pupa inside—then unwinding the thread. The discovery of how to rear silkworms on mulberry trees was made more than 4,000 years ago in China.

HOW INSECTS FLY

Airplanes, like most birds, derive their ability to fly largely from the specialized shape of their wings: a rounded leading edge, flattened underneath and bulging on top, tapering away to a slender trailing edge. The wings of insects, however, do not have this typical airfoil shape. Instead they are roughly the same thickness throughout.

As a result, insect wings are used in the air in much the same way that oars are used in water. They push downward to help the insect climb, backward to move it forward, and scull horizontally when the insect hovers.

Many insects also use what scientists call a clap-fling mechanism: the wings are clapped together at the end of each beat, then flung apart at high speed, hurling turbulent rings of high-pressure air below and behind them. This action helps to thrust the insect up and forward.

Some insects, like the larger butterflies and moths, are capable of gliding, twisting their wings slightly to ride the air currents. Most insects, however, and particularly the smaller ones, rely on the sheer speed of their wingbeats to keep them up.

HOW FAST THEY FLY

Larger insects, such as dragonflies, have relatively slow wingbeats but are swift fliers. Tiny insects, such as mosquitoes, beat their wings very rapidly but fly fairly slowly. The buzzing sound made by insects is caused by their wing movements and by air turbulence. The faster the wings vibrate, the higher in pitch is the buzz. The table below shows how many complete up-and-down wingbeats each insect carries out each second in flight, and shows how fast it usually flies.

	Wingbeats per second	Flight speed (m.p.h.)
White butterfly	8–12	4–9
Damselfly	16	2–4
Dragonfly	25–40	16–34
Cockchafer beetle	50	17
Hawkmoth	50–90	11–31
Hoverfly	120	7–9
Bumblebee	130	7
Housefly	200	4
Honeybee	225	4–7
Mosquito	600	0.6–1.2
Midge	1,000	0.6–1.2

WHY CLEAN AIR IS KILLING A MOTH

A type of peppered moth, *Biston betularia*, has evolved in response to a changing industrial environment. The moth is normally colored a pale, speckled gray. This camouflages it against lichen on the tree trunks where it rests by day. But in about 1860 a black variety—a natural mutation—appeared in increasing numbers in industrial areas. The black moth had a great advantage over the gray one because its dark color blended in with the soot-covered trees, and so the black moths were less easily spotted by predators. By 1900, in industrial areas, the black form of the peppered moth far outnumbered the pale form.

The black form is still the dominant type in industrial areas today, but researchers who have been studying it since the 1950s have discovered that its numbers are dwindling. The reason: modern clean-air regulations have cut down the amount of grime in the atmosphere and on trees—and are tipping the survival advantage back toward the pale moth.

MANNA FROM BUGS

The manna eaten by the Israelites on the flight through the Sinai from Egypt may have been the sticky honeydew that comes from the mealybug, *Trabutina mannipara*. The bug, which feeds on the evergreen tamarisk in the deserts of the Middle East, passes the honeydew through its intestines. The honeydew then falls to the ground as shining scales and is eaten today by the nomadic tribes of the desert.

COLD LIGHT

The light that is chemically produced by tropical *Photinus* fireflies is the most efficient light known. Up to 90 percent of the energy it uses is turned into light. By contrast, only 5.5 percent of the energy used to power a household light bulb emerges as light; the rest is wasted as heat.

The glow of a firefly contains only 1/80,000 of the heat that would be produced by a candle flame of equal brilliance. Fireflies are, in fact, beetles. Some tropical species provide spectacular nighttime displays in which thousands of males flash their light in unison from trees. The flickering spots of light, which are used to attract females, can be seen hundreds of yards away.

SPRAY GUN

The bombardier beetle, *Brachinus frumans*, drives off attackers by spraying them with a hot caustic liquid. The beetle keeps the basic elements of the liquid—hydrogen

ATTACK AND DEFENSE *Among honeybees, as among other bees, wasps, and ants, only females (like the worker bee shown here) have stings. The male drones are harmless. The peacock butterfly (pictured on the right) relies on eyespots on its wings for defense. When suddenly displayed, the spots confuse and frighten off insect-hunting birds.*

peroxide and chemicals called hydroquinones—in a gland in its abdomen. When threatened, it passes the liquid into a heat-resistant combustion chamber with a spout-shaped opening. At the same time, it releases enzymes that make the liquid explode, producing water, caustic quinones, oxygen, and heat. The explosion makes the liquid shoot through the opening at about 212°F, the boiling point of water.

The beetle itself, which can swivel its rear end in almost any direction to aim the spray at its attacker, remains unhurt by either the heat or the corrosive power of the liquid. Up to 20 of the burning sprays can be fired in quick succession, each giving a gunlike pop. The sprays have a range of about 2 inches—four times the beetle's length.

BORN TO SLAVERY
The British blood-red ant, *Formica sanguinea*, finds slave workers by raiding the nests of another ant species, *Formica fusca*. After killing any worker ants that resist, the blood-red ants carry off dormant pupae—ants that are changing from larvae to adults inside cocoons—to their own nests. There the newborn abducted ants become slaves of their captors. The blood-red ants have their own workers and are only partly dependent on such slave labor. But the European Amazon ant, *Polyergus rufescens*, is totally dependent upon ant slaves, which excavate the Amazons' nests and take care of their young.

AN ANT THAT EATS ITSELF
The queen of the black garden ant, *Lasius niger*, feeds partly on its own wing muscles. After mating in midair in the summer, the queen returns to earth and bites off its wings for food. Meanwhile, the males, having fulfilled their sexual role, fall to the ground and crawl away to die. The queen finds a crevice for a new nest, where she lives on her fat reserves and on the nutrients contained in the now useless wing muscles. The queen begins to lay eggs the following spring. The first eggs hatch only into larvae that develop into wingless female workers. The workers feed the queen while she lays more eggs—until in the summer winged queens and winged males are born, take to the air to mate, and begin the cycle all over again.

FLEA FEATS
The human flea, *Pulex irritans*, can jump as far as 13 inches and as high as 8 inches—or 130 times its own height. This is the equivalent of a human being jumping to a height of about 780 feet—enough to reach the roof of a 70-story building. The flea achieves this athletic feat by flexing an elastic pad beside its hind legs and then suddenly releasing it, propelling itself into the air like an arrow with a built-in bow. Each time a flea jumps, it is subjected to a gravitational force 200 times stronger than normal, a sudden and tremendous strain that would kill most human beings.

PIGGYBACK PARASITE
The human warble fly, *Dermatobia hominis*, of North and South America does not, despite its scientific name, attack human skin directly. Instead, it seizes mosquitoes and flies and attaches its eggs to their bodies. Then it releases the insect. When the mosquito or fly later lands on a human to bite and feed, the warmth of the victim's body causes the dermatobia egg to hatch. The newly emerged larva bores beneath the skin to feed and grow. A boil forms at the site.

Only when the larva is fully grown does it leave the human victim's body—dropping off to pupate in the soil, become an adult, and begin in its turn the hunt for a free ride for its eggs.

HOW INSECTS EAT

The first primitive insects had biting mouthparts like those of modern ants, beetles, grasshoppers, cockroaches, and praying mantises. But many other types of insects have changed their feeding habits in the course of evolution to include sucking or licking as well as chewing.

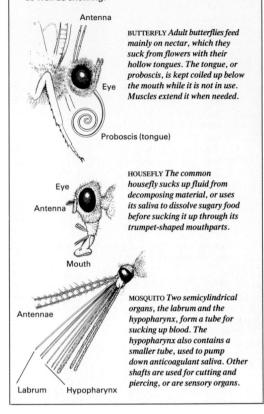

Antenna

Eye

Proboscis (tongue)

BUTTERFLY *Adult butterflies feed mainly on nectar, which they suck from flowers with their hollow tongues. The tongue, or proboscis, is kept coiled up below the mouth while it is not in use. Muscles extend it when needed.*

Eye

Antenna

Mouth

HOUSEFLY *The common housefly sucks up fluid from decomposing material, or uses its saliva to dissolve sugary food before sucking it up through its trumpet-shaped mouthparts.*

Antennae

Labrum   Hypopharynx

MOSQUITO *Two semicylindrical organs, the labrum and the hypopharynx, form a tube for sucking up blood. The hypopharynx also contains a smaller tube, used to pump down anticoagulant saliva. Other shafts are used for cutting and piercing, or are sensory organs.*

BLOODSHOT
Some conspicuous slow-moving insects—among them the oil beetle, the bloody-nosed beetle *(Timarcha tenebricosa)*, and the common ladybug—"bleed" not when they have been hurt, but in order to *prevent* injury. When alarmed, they release drops of a reddish or yellowish bitter-tasting liquid from their mouths and from pores at their joints. The caustic flavor repels attackers before the insect is seriously harmed.

FLIGHT OF THE HONEYBEE
A queen honeybee lays and fertilizes at least 600,000 eggs during her 3- to 5-year reign. She does so after her one and only mating flight, on which she mates with four or five males, or drones, in succession. She keeps the collected sperm in an internal reservoir and goes on laying until she is succeeded by one of her royal daughters. The deposed queen then flies off with half the workers and starts a new hive elsewhere. Fertilized eggs produce female bees, queens or workers, and unfertilized eggs produce males. But how the queen controls which eggs are fertilized—and thus the proportion of workers and drones in the hive—is not known.

A PLAGUE OF LOCUSTS
Throughout the ages swarms of locusts—a type of grasshopper—have devastated plants and crops as they migrate up to thousands of miles through the

tropics in search of food. A typical swarm can be more than 30 miles long, 5 miles wide, and contain an estimated 500 billion insects. Such a swarm—a vast black cloud, often blotting out the sun—weighs about 100,000 tons and can eat each day the weight of food that could meet the daily nutritional requirements of 20 million people. The migrations seem to be triggered by population explosions of locusts in the desert areas where the insects breed.

LIFE SPANS
Adult mayflies, of the order Plectoptera (Ephemeroptera), often live for only 4 to 5 hours in their winged stage—or at most a few days. However, mayflies are not really so ephemeral, having previously lived for 2 or 3 years in their larval stage.

The insect with the longest life is the queen termite, which usually lives for 15 to 20 years. Most insects have an active adult life of only a few weeks.

PLANET OF THE INSECTS
An acre of average pastureland contains an estimated 360 million insects, of which springtails—wingless leaping insects—are the most common. About 1 million species of insects have so far been classified. At least three-quarters of the known animal species in the world today are insects, and there are more than a million insects for every man, woman, and child. Together, the world's insect population weighs about 12 times as much as the total human population.

LARVA THAT LIVES IN OIL
The larva of the California petroleum fly, *Psilopa petrolei*, lives in pools of crude oil seeping from the ground in oil fields. The larva's skin and intestinal lining are adapted to withstand the oil, which permanently fills its gut and surrounds its body, but which would kill most other forms of life. The fly feeds solely on other insects that become trapped in the oil. The larva, which lives submerged in the oil, rises to the surface when it is fully grown and undergoes the metamorphosis to adult form. When the transformation is complete, the fly takes to the air. But it stays near the oil field, laying its eggs in the pools to start the cycle again.

SURFACE SKIMMERS
Some rove beetles skim effortlessly over water, pulled by the surface tension of the water ahead of them. They lower the surface tension at the rear of their bodies through a glandular secretion at the ends of their abdomens. This results in giving the surface tension at the front a driving force. Much the same principle drives the camphor-powered boats that were once popular as children's toys.

EARLY WORM CATCHES THE FLY
Most caterpillars are sluggish creatures that feed on plants. But a group of about 20 known species found on the Hawaiian islands have become hunters of flies. The caterpillars, known locally as inchworms, ambush the flies when they land. Lunging out with six tiny claws, the caterpillar dispatches the fly in as little as one-twelfth of a second.

The caterpillars lie in wait among forest leaves. Their five pairs of eyes are rudimentary. So, to detect their prey, they rely on sensitive hairs along their backs. When a fly brushes against the hairs, the caterpillar strikes, devouring the fly—wings, legs, and all. The caterpillars, which grow to about an inch long, are called inchworms because they move with a curious looping step, drawing the tail up to the head, then stretching out again, so that they seem to be measuring as they crawl along.

INSECT LIFE CYCLES

There are two distinct types of insect life cycle. Beetles and moths, for instance, undergo a complete transformation from a grub or caterpillar (the active, larval, or immature stage), through a passive stage (known as the pupal or chrysalis stage) to the very different shape of the adult, known as the imago. In other insect species, such as the dragonfly, the immature insect more closely resembles the shape of the adult and is called a nymph. The nymph molts several times, its wing pads enlarging with each molt until it reaches adult size.

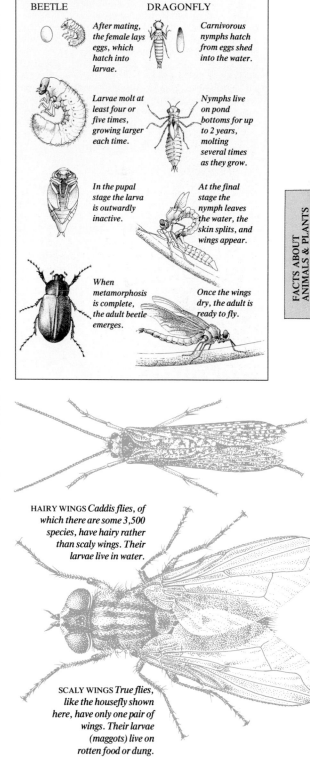

BEETLE

After mating, the female lays eggs, which hatch into larvae.

Larvae molt at least four or five times, growing larger each time.

In the pupal stage the larva is outwardly inactive.

When metamorphosis is complete, the adult beetle emerges.

DRAGONFLY

Carnivorous nymphs hatch from eggs shed into the water.

Nymphs live on pond bottoms for up to 2 years, molting several times as they grow.

At the final stage the nymph leaves the water, the skin splits, and wings appear.

Once the wings dry, the adult is ready to fly.

HAIRY WINGS *Caddis flies, of which there are some 3,500 species, have hairy rather than scaly wings. Their larvae live in water.*

SCALY WINGS *True flies, like the housefly shown here, have only one pair of wings. Their larvae (maggots) live on rotten food or dung.*

Fish—the gilled marvels

MAN-EATER

The great white shark, which grows to 36 feet or more, is probably the most dangerous of all sharks. Also known as the white pointer, it is most aggressive when hungry, and its teeth, up to 2 inches long, can sever a human limb with one bite. Ten or so shark species—including the mako (or blue pointer), the tiger, and some types of hammerhead—have been cited in attacks on human swimmers and divers, but most sharks are thought to avoid human contact.

Some bizarre objects have been found in shark stomachs. One dissected gray shark contained the hindquarters of a pig, the front half of a dog, 300 pounds of horsemeat, and eight sheep legs.

FISH OUT OF WATER

The mudskipper, a small fish that inhabits mangrove swamps and mud flats on the coasts of tropical Africa, spends much of its time out of water. Using its pectoral fins, which are flexed in the middle rather like legs, it walks or hops for short bursts of a few minutes in search of food. The fish has no lungs to enable it to breathe air. Instead, it keeps its gill chamber full of oxygenated water, occasionally gulping water from pools to replenish its supply. It also absorbs oxygen through the throat and the roof of its mouth. The mudskipper's eyes are right on top of its head and can be swiveled in all directions. To keep them moist and working, the fish "blinks" by pulling the eyes down and wiping them on its moist cheeks.

Many species of catfish can live out of water for several days, thanks to a lunglike organ that supplements their gills. The fish uses this ability to move home in the dry season, wriggling overland between stretches of water. But how it knows which way to go is still a mystery to scientists.

AQUATIC ARCHER

The Southeast Asian archer fish shoots down its prey with a jet of water. Firing from beneath the water's surface, it can hit insects about 3 feet above the surface by squirting water up a tube formed between the palate and the tongue.

THE FOUR-EYED FISH

Tropical America is home to a fish with four eyes. The four-eyed fish swims at the surface of the water, searching for its insect food. An eye projects above the top of the head on each side, and each eye is divided into two by a horizontal bar that coincides with the water level. The upper part is adapted for vision in air and the lower part for vision in water. The lens of the eye is shaped so that it can focus in both air and water simultaneously on two distinct retinal areas. So the fish sees four images, enabling it to home in on prey above and below the water.

CHANCE IN A MILLION

Because most fish breed by shedding their eggs and sperm directly into water, fertilization is a risky business. A medium-size female cod may lay more than 6 million eggs at each breeding session—sometimes laying several hundred thousand in a day—but on average only one or two will grow into adults. Most fertilized fish eggs or young fish are eaten by other creatures. This is particularly true for sea fish that lay their eggs in plankton, where they are eaten in vast quantities by whales and other browsing animals.

To compensate for this high casualty rate, most fish species lay large numbers of eggs. Female turbots have been found with up to 9 million eggs in their ovaries; and a ling fish, a large relative of the cod, once yielded 28 million eggs.

SHELLFISH NURSERY

The bitterling, a small European member of the carp family, uses a mussel as a living nursery. During the breeding season the female bitterling grows a long tube from its genital opening.

Using the tube, she inserts her eggs within the shells of a freshwater mussel so that they develop inside the mussel's gill chamber. The male then releases sperm into the water near the opening through which the mussel breathes. The sperm is drawn in with the water, and the eggs are fertilized

---

HOW FISH BREATHE

The gills that a fish uses to breathe underwater are more efficient than the lungs used by air-breathing animals. Up to 80 percent of the oxygen that passes over the gills is absorbed into the fish's blood—four to five times as much as is absorbed from the air by most mammals. The gills—a series of membranes that allow air, but not water, to pass through—are arranged so that the blood in capillaries immediately under the membrane runs in the direction opposite to the water passing over them. As a result, oxygen-rich water starting its passage over the gills meets blood with a fairly high oxygen concentration. Water that has almost finished passing over the gills, and given up most of its oxygen, encounters blood coming into the gills that is deficient in oxygen. Because of the two-way flow, the blood at any point always has less oxygen than the water directly opposite it, so that oxygen is absorbed into the blood across the whole width of the gills.

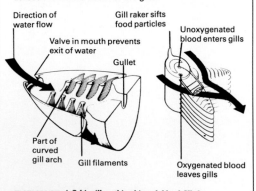

Direction of water flow

Gill raker sifts food particles

Unoxygenated blood enters gills

Valve in mouth prevents exit of water

Gullet

Part of curved gill arch

Gill filaments

Oxygenated blood leaves gills

FLOW OF LIFE *A fish's gills—thin-skinned, blood-filled filaments—are arranged rather like the heat-losing fins on a car engine and are supported by rigid gill arches. Blood is carried to and from the filaments (shown enlarged on the right) by veins running through the arches.*

inside the shellfish. After hatching, the larvae may remain inside the mussel for a month, existing on the remains of their egg yolks before emerging to start life outside. The mussel benefits from the relationship. Its parasitic larvae attach themselves to the young bitterlings' gills, and are carried away when the bitterling larvae leave.

FISH WITH A ROVING EYE
Some adult flatfish, including flounder, sole, and halibut, have both eyes on one side of the head. Although they start life with symmetrical heads, one eye moves over the top of the head to the other side as they grow. The two-eyed side (usually the right) develops a camouflage coloring, which in some species changes to match different backgrounds, while the other side remains white.

The reason for the lopsided growth is that flatfish spend most of their adult lives lying on their sides on the sea bottom, sometimes burying themselves in sand with only their eyes protruding while they wait for their next meal.

AIRBORNE FISH
Flying fish do not actually fly. They glide. Propelled by their tails, they leap into the air at speeds of up to 20 m.p.h. and use their wide pectoral fins as wings. They usually glide close to the ocean's surface, where a flick of their tails against the water can produce extra thrust. Flying fish have been known to soar as high as 20 feet and travel as far as 1,300 feet in one glide through the air.

MOTHER DAD
Sea horses are one of the few species in the animal world in which the male gives birth to the young. The male has a special brood pouch on its abdomen into which the female lays her eggs. The eggs are not only fertilized in the pouch; they hatch and develop there until the young begin to resemble a miniature version of their parents. The male then goes into labor and gives birth, jettisoning the young sea horses in a series of convulsive contractions that can last for several hours.

LIVING JAVELINS
Throughout the world's tropical waters there is an extraordinary breed of living spears. Called needlefish, these nocturnal surface-feeders can be 5 feet long, yet weigh only about 10 pounds because they are so slender. When disturbed or frightened, they can swim fast enough to leap out of the water. Their aim in doing this, it seems, is not to attack; it is probably an evasive tactic. But a panicky needlefish can be a terrifying experience for anybody unlucky enough to get in its way. One sailor, Capt. William Gray of the Miami Seaquarium in Florida, was pinned to his boat when a needlefish that his boat had startled leaped up and ran him through the leg.

Most other victims have been people fishing at night with lights. Many naturalists believe needlefish can be attracted or frightened by light. But daytime divers and swimmers have never been known to be hurt by one. In the water and unbothered by lights, needlefish dart around obstacles.

LIVING LIGHTS
Life in the deepest ocean has taken extraordinary twists to cope with eternal darkness, cold, and pressures hundreds of times greater than at the surface.

More than half the inhabitants of the lowest depths are luminous, an adaptation that usually serves as a mating signal or to attract prey. Some deep-ocean species act as hosts to colonies of glowing bacteria that light up parts of the hosts' bodies from within. The Indian Ocean fish *Photoblepharon* has a large spot under each eye that is full of blood vessels and packed with such bacteria. And these glowing spots have "curtains" too—black skin folds that the fish can raise to shut off the light when danger threatens.

The bathysphere fish—so called because the pale-blue, glowing spots on its sides resemble the portholes of a diving bell—has lights in its teeth to lure prey, for many fish seem drawn to light. But the hatchet fish has greenish lights that look like teeth and may serve the opposite purpose: to deter enemies while the hatchet fish feeds on plankton.

MOUTHS WITHOUT BODIES
Some deep-sea fish have developed huge mouths to help them make the most of any food that comes their way. In the abyss, food is scarce, for there are no plants to start the food chain. Instead, tiny shrimps eat the scraps and waste that rain slowly down from the surface waters; and the shrimps in turn provide food for bigger hunters. Some of these hunters, like the swallower and the gulper fish, are little more than tooth-filled mouths attached to elastic stomachs so that they can eat fish several times their own size.

Gulpers can grow to a length of 6 feet; but most of this is simply a whiplike tail. The rest is a gaping, cavernous mouth.

ANGLING FOR FOOD
Down below 2,000 feet lives the bizarre angler fish. A long fin like a fishing rod grows from its head, and the angler can bend this forward so that the tip hangs just in front of its mouth. On the end is the bait, a wormlike luminous growth that wriggles convincingly. When fish try to take the bait, the angler strikes,

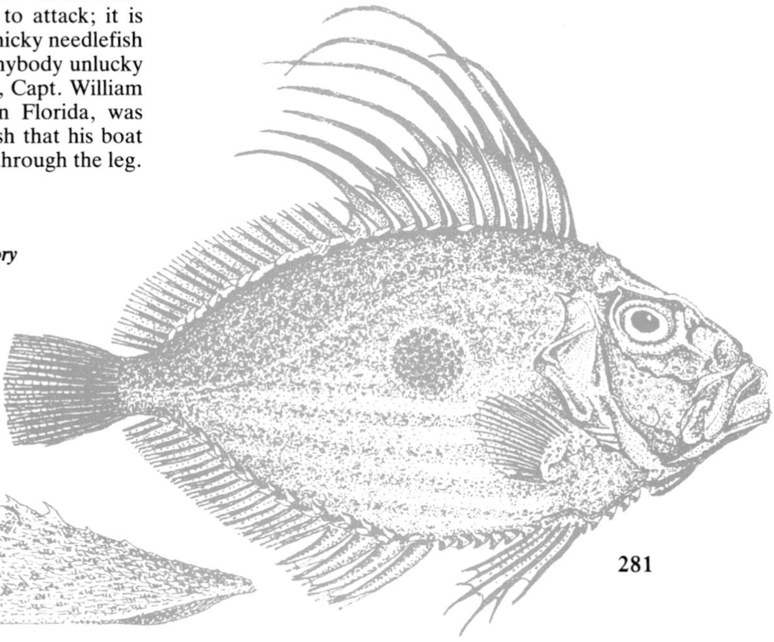

SKELETON KEY *Most fish, like the John Dory shown on the right, have a skeleton made entirely of bone. The 3-foot-long thornback ray, below, has a more primitive skeleton made of cartilage reinforced with bony plates.*

281

swallowing the catch whole. The angler's method of reproduction is even odder. In the black, sparsely populated depths, it is difficult to locate a mate. So when a pair do meet, the 6-inch-long male—whose weight may be only a tiny fraction of that of a fully grown, 3-foot-long female—makes certain that they will not lose each other. He sinks his teeth into the female's body and hangs on, sometimes for the rest of his life. In some types of angler fish, the male's mouth and jaw gradually fuse to the female's body. His eyes fade, his internal organs stop working, even his circulatory system hooks up with his mate's so that he is fed by her blood. Effectively, he dies as an individual and becomes merely a part of her body.

His only function then is to fertilize the eggs the female spawns before they float away to begin life.

PREHISTORIC RELIC

After it disappeared from the fossil record 70 million years ago, the coelacanth was thought by scientists to be extinct. But in 1938 a 5-foot-long coelacanth was caught off the South African coast, and since 1952 nearly 100 specimens have been caught around Comoros in the Indian Ocean. This primitive fish has a simple heart, and its kidneys are positioned away from the backbone, unlike those of other animals with backbones. Female coelacanths have also been found with eggs the size of tennis balls inside them, but it is unknown whether they hatch inside or outside the mother.

PYGMIES AND GIANTS

Fish vary enormously in size. Among the smallest is the dwarf pygmy goby, a freshwater fish found in the Philippines, which can be less than 0.3 inch long when fully grown. At the other extreme is the whale shark, which can be more than 60 feet long. It weighs about 5 billion times as much as the goby, but the whale shark is a placid animal that feeds on plankton. Whales themselves are not fish but mammals, the same group of animals as human beings.

A MOUTHFUL OF BABIES

Many fish of the cichlid family, such as the Mozambique mouthbreeder, carry their eggs in their mouths after the eggs are laid and fertilized. There the eggs are safe from predators and have a constant stream of oxygen-rich water. After hatching, the young fish remain in the mouth until they have absorbed their egg yolks. Then they venture out to feed for short periods, though never far from their parent's mouth, where they return at night or if threatened.

Brooding may last up to 5 weeks, and during this time the parent eats nothing at all in order to avoid swallowing its offspring by accident. Usually the female broods, but in some species of cichlid— which are found throughout tropical Africa, Asia, and America—the male broods.

The brooding instinct encourages fertilization in some cichlid species. In these species the male's anal fin is marked with an egg-shaped and egg-colored spot. When the female tries to catch the decoy egg, she gulps in some sperm from the male and so fertilizes the real eggs in her mouth.

LIVE-IN GUESTS

Some pearlfish seek shelter inside sea cucumbers, backing into the sausagelike animal via its anus. After finding the cucumber's opening, the pearlfish (so named for its pigment-dotted transparent body) inserts its tail and then wriggles its whole body inside. Several pearlfish individuals may share the same cucumber. The fish get shelter from the arrangement.

They also get food, since they sometimes eat the sea cucumber's internal organs. But though the sea cucumber is not normally killed in the process, because it has the ability to regenerate these organs, it seems to derive no benefit from its live-in guests.

NESTLED FISH

Some fish are born in nests. Members of the labyrinth fish family, such as the air-breathing fighting fish, build nests from mucus-coated air bubbles. The bubbles are blown by the male and used to form a raft.

The eggs are laid in the water, then caught by the adults in their mouths and spit into the underside of the raft. After the eggs hatch, the young stay on the raft for a time under the protective eye of the father.

Another nest builder, the male three-spined stickleback, collects pieces of aquatic plants, then glues them together with a cement secreted from his kidneys. He assembles the plant mass in a small pit under the water and then creates a burrow inside before luring a female in for egg laying.

PERILOUS BEAUTY

Lionfish are among the most beautiful fish in the sea. But among the fragile finery of their plumage lurk weapons: 18 venom-tipped spines, in fact. Usually, lionfish swim lazily around coral reefs, but when frightened they stop and swing around to point the spines at the enemy.

This is a sign of extreme danger for human swimmers and divers. In one case, in 1960, a 38-year-old man got two of the delicate spines in his fingers while skin diving off the Marshall Islands in the Pacific Ocean. The pain knocked him out, and his blood pressure dropped dangerously. Only emergency medical aid, say doctors, saved his life.

KILLING BY PAIN

Some experts rate the stonefish as the most dangerous fish of all. Squat, warty, and slime-covered, this grotesque creature is found around the coasts of the Pacific and Indian oceans from the Red Sea to northern Australia. Wherever they are known, stonefish are greatly feared. Their stone-colored lumpy bodies make them almost impossible to spot against the rock and coral where they live.

Even disturbances in the water only inches away will not make a stonefish budge. It remains motionless, its venomous spines raised until it is too late for its victim.

Stonefish use their spines only for protection, though. When feeding, they wait until a fish wanders too close; then they lunge in a blur of speed.

Every human being who has been stung by a stonefish and has lived to tell the tale emphasizes one thing: maddening, excruciating pain that can last as long as 12 hours. The pain becomes so intense that the victim froths at the mouth and may bite convulsively even at people who come to help.

Australian doctors who have dealt with cases of stonefish poisoning report that it generally takes three or four strong men to get a stonefish's victim to shore without his drowning in the grip of the agony. Most of those who die are victims of drowning; the pain is so unbearable that they double up in the water and can think of nothing else.

On shore the simplest antidote to the poison is to apply heat, generally in the form of near-scalding water. Also, an antivenom has been developed by marine researchers. But early medical help is vital. Swimmers who get treatment fast can expect to walk again in a month or two. Less fortunate victims can die within 6 hours.

Amphibians and reptiles

TOO CLUMSY TO LIVE ON LAND

The largest amphibian is the giant salamander, *Andrias japonicus,* which grows to a length of 6 feet. Ungainly on land, it lives mainly in mountain streams, feeding on snails, crabs, and sometimes fish. It leads an inactive life and surfaces to breathe at irregular intervals. It may also be the longest-lived amphibian; one is on record as living for 55 years. Some Japanese consider its cooked flesh a delicacy.

GROWING UP SMALLER

Instead of becoming bigger as it grows up, the "paradoxical" frog, *Pseudis paradoxa,* becomes smaller. It lives in tropical South America, and the tadpole grows to as much as 10 inches in length. But when the tadpole turns into a frog, a considerable shrinkage occurs. As with other frogs, the tail is absorbed into the body. And when the process is complete, the adult is never more than 3 inches long.

GOLIATH OF A FROG

The world's largest frog is the Goliath frog of West Africa, *Rana goliath.* It can weigh 7 pounds and be 3 feet long, but only one-third of its length is taken up by its head and torso. The rest is taken up by its 2-foot-long hind legs. Despite their size, the frog's legs are not favored by gourmets.

SMALL FROG, BIG EGG

The shortest amphibian and the smallest frog is the Cuban *Sminthillus limbatus.* Fully grown, it is only half an inch long. It produces a single large egg, rather than many small eggs at a time as most frogs do.

WHEN THE RAIN COMES

On the very rare occasions when it rains in the deserts of central Australia, the water-holding frog, *Cyclorana platycephalus,* emerges from its underground den and absorbs so much water—as much as 50 percent of its own weight—that it resembles a small balloon. This keeps it alive during long droughts. Rainstorms also encourage the frogs to feed voraciously on insects and to mate. The eggs are laid in pools and hatch quickly, starting the tadpoles on a race against the sun for survival. To win, the tadpoles have to grow into young frogs and so become able to breathe air before their pond dries up. Within a few weeks—faster than most species of frog—the tadpoles grow into little froglets.

As the rainwater dries up, the adult frogs and their young burrow underground and make a small living chamber for themselves. Once inside, they secrete a membranelike envelope around their skins, complete with breathing hole, to stop any of the body-stored water from escaping. The frogs then wait without moving, possibly for as long as 5 or 6 years, until the rain comes again.

DROPPING OUT OF SIGHT

The spadefoot toad, *Pelobates fuscus,* is named after the "spade" (a flat, sharp-edged bone) on each of its hind feet. By using each spade in turn, it can dig so rapidly through the dry, sandy soil in the arid areas

LIFE CYCLE OF A FROG

The development of the common frog, *Rana temporaria,* is typical of most frogs. Each female lays 3,000–4,000 eggs in spring, creating the clumps of spawn seen on lakes and pools. But predators such as fish, newts, and ducks ensure that few eggs survive to become adult frogs.

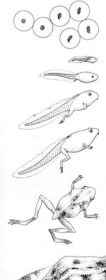

Each egg consists of an embryo protected by layers of jelly. The eggs hatch in about a week.

Newly hatched tadpoles attach themselves to plants. They start to swim 1–3 days later.

At about 3 weeks a tadpole is swimming vigorously. At 7–8 weeks its hind legs are visible and it has begun to feed on insects.

At 9–10 weeks lungs have begun to replace gills and the tadpole gulps air from the surface.

At 10–12 weeks the tail shortens and is absorbed into the body. The front legs develop and the tadpole resembles the adult.

Fully grown, the young frog leaves the water. It feeds on small insects and will not reproduce for at least a year.

FIRST ASHORE *Amphibians are the most primitive class of vertebrates—animals with backbones—on land. They were the first group to adapt to life out of water. Yet most of them, like this African clawed toad, still need water, at least for breeding.*

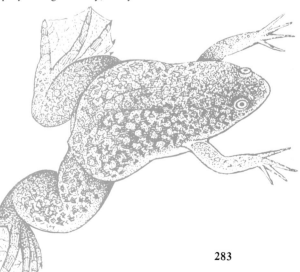

where it lives that it appears to sink vertically into the ground. The spadefoot and its relatives are found in Europe, Asia, North Africa, and the United States.

The spadefoot toad spends most of its life in an underground burrow to avoid excessive loss of water. Even so, it loses 50 percent of its body weight during prolonged dry periods.

When it rains, the animals surface to top off their water supply. As well as drinking, some species can absorb water through the undersides of their bodies. The bellies of these species have a thin skin covered with blood vessels, so that the frog's bloodstream and tissues can soak up water more directly.

USING THEIR HEADS
Some Mexican tree frogs use their heads to survive—literally. The frogs, known as helmet frogs, have bony crests or bumps on the top of their skulls and use them as doors on their homes. The frogs ensure their survival during droughts by moving into the trunks of trees or into holes in bromeliads—plants of the pineapple family that often grow high up in trees.

Once inside the hole, the frog seals the entrance with its head and sits out the drought. The helmet loses little water, and the seal ensures that the chamber—and the frog—remain comfortably moist.

NATURAL-BORN JUMPERS
Frogs are superb jumpers, and the small North American frog *Acris gryllus* can jump up to 6 feet—36 times its own 2-inch length. If a human being could match this feat, the world's long-jump record would be around 215 feet—more than seven times longer than it actually is. Another frog species, Europe's *Rana dalmatina,* can also jump as far as 6 feet, or 24 times its own length. And even the common North American bullfrog can jump up to 10 times its own body length.

For jumping, frogs use their long back legs, which can be folded into three sections and suddenly extended by powerful muscles to provide the impetus. The short front legs act as shock absorbers on landing.

SECRET OF STAYING YOUNG
As long as it lives in water, the axolotl salamander of Mexico keeps its youthful appearance for life, retaining its feathery external gills and larval tadpolelike shape. It can even breed in this form.

But if the lake in which it lives dries up for any reason, the axolotl, known to scientists as *Ambystoma mexicanum,* can change into an adult form of salamander, with lungs in place of gills. It normally grows about 8 inches long.

CARING FOR THE YOUNG
Most amphibians lay up to 4,000 eggs a year in water and then abandon them, resulting in huge losses of eggs and young. Indeed, only a tiny fraction of the young survive to breeding age. Some amphibians, however, make special arrangements for the care of their eggs and young. These more protective species tend to produce fewer eggs.

For instance, some tropical tree frogs make foam nests for their eggs. The male and female mate

under a branch or leaf overhanging the water. As the eggs are laid, the slime surrounding them is beaten into a thick froth by the frogs' hind legs. (Some species even stick leaves to the outside of the frothy slime.) The inner part of the foam then breaks down into a little protected pond for the developing tadpoles. Eventually the tadpoles drop from the foam nest into the water below to complete their development.

Some South American tree frogs dig a nest pit in the bank of a pond or stream, so that water seeps into the pit. This creates a natural incubator in which the young can be kept warm. At the same time, the incubator protects the young from predators—such as fish or crocodiles—that might lurk in larger, more open areas of water.

Other tree frogs in the tropical American forests lay their eggs in pockets of water that collect at the leaf bases of bromeliads high in trees. So the young frogs have a safe nursery and often spend most of their lives in the bromeliad, coming to earth only when they are fully grown.

GUARDIANS OF THE EGGS
Some species of frogs and toads have special ways of looking after their eggs. In the case of the midwife toad, for instance, the male—not the female—cares for the babies. He gathers up the strings of eggs after they are laid and winds them round his hind legs. He periodically dips his legs into a pool or stream to dampen the eggs, and so keep them alive. He returns to the water for the hatching of the young, which takes place after about 3 weeks.

In the marsupial frog, the female has a pouch under the skin of her back in which the eggs are carried. The tadpoles usually leave the pouch as soon as they hatch. But some stay there until they have developed into little frogs.

The Surinam toad, *Pipa pipa,* lives permanently in water, and the female hatches up to 60 eggs on her back after they have been fertilized by the male. The eggs stick to the skin, which then grows up around them, so that each egg is contained in its own protective pocket. The young develop in these homegrown cradles until they emerge about 12 weeks later as miniature adults.

GROWING UP IN FATHER'S THROAT
The eggs of the Darwin's frog of South America, *Rhinoderma darwini,* are laid in moist ground, and the male parent sits on guard until there is a sign of life inside them. The father then swallows from 5 to 15 of the eggs and keeps them in the croaking sac in his throat. The eggs remain in this protected environment until the young are hatched.

The father then lets the froglets hop out of his mouth, and they go off to lead their own lives.

The frog is named after Charles Darwin, the 19th-century British naturalist, who was the first scientist to describe it.

ADULTS IN MOM'S CARE
Some female amphibians have solved the problem of protecting eggs and young by carrying them inside their bodies. The Alpine salamander, for example,

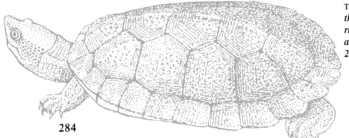

TURTLE *Tortoises and turtles, like this 12-inch-long Central American river species, have existed almost unchanged for some 200 million years.*

passes through all the stages from egg to tiny adult inside its mother's body. These animals live in low temperatures, and it takes 2 to 3 years before the litter, of just two salamanders, is born. The young are able to live on land and breathe air immediately. Fire salamanders also grow in their mothers' bodies, but they are born in water and have gills.

A few frogs also produce live young with a built-in food supply. The larvae of these species are nourished while they are growing from an egg yolk that is born with them. In the African toad, *Nectophrynoides vivipara,* the embryos take their nourishment directly from the mother. They feed on secretions from the inside walls of the oviduct—the tube through which the eggs leave the ovary—before being born as tiny replicas of the adult.

POISON FROM THE SKIN
A deadly venom obtained from the skin glands of the arrow-poison frogs of South America is still used by Indian hunters to kill small mammals and birds. The frogs, of the genus *Dendrobates,* are roasted over a fire, and the venom that drips from their skin is applied to the tips of the hunters' arrows. The frogs secrete the venom to protect themselves from predators, such as lizards and snakes. And their brightly colored skins—brilliant mosaics of red, yellow, orange, and blue—seem to warn predators of the danger.

The skin of all amphibians is liberally scattered with glands. Most of these produce mucus to keep the animal's skin moist, but other glands, like those of the arrow-poison frog, can secrete foul-tasting or poisonous substances. The majority of the glands are too small to be visible without a microscope. But some of them are large and obvious, such as the bulging parotid glands behind the eyes of the common European toad.

BREATHING THROUGH THE SKIN
Most amphibians breathe with gills when they are larvae in the water, and with lungs when they become adults and live on land. But there are also land-living, cave-dwelling, and tree-climbing species that breathe through neither lungs nor gills, but through their moist skins. For instance, frogs of the genus *Telmatobius*—which live underwater in the high Andes—can absorb enough oxygen from the cold water through their skins alone. They have no lungs or gills. Some telmatobius species that live on the muddy bottoms of deep lakes have evolved a special baggy skin to breathe in the oxygen-poor water.

The hairy frog of the Cameroons also seems to make use of its skin to help it breathe. During the mating season, the males grow thin, hairlike pieces of skin on their flanks and hind legs. Scientists believe that the extra skin surface helps the frogs to absorb more oxygen during peak activity.

TENTACLES FOR EYES
Among the least-known amphibians are about 170 species known as apoda. They live in the tropics, and are rarely seen and very difficult to study because most of them burrow underground. Many of the apoda species are almost completely blind. They seem to feel their way by means of a thin tentacle that protrudes from a pit on each side of the face.

Unlike other amphibians, apoda, which resemble earthworms, have small reptilelike scales embedded in the skin. They have no legs, shoulders, or hip-bones. Most of them are less than 0.10 inch long when fully grown. But one species, *Caecilia thompsoni,* can grow to 4 feet long.

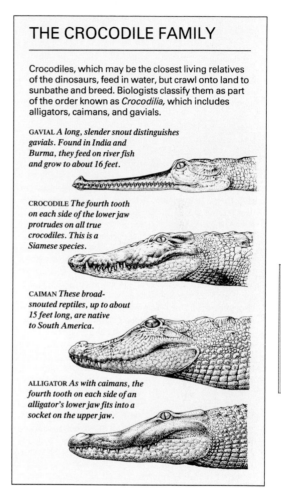

THE CROCODILE FAMILY

Crocodiles, which may be the closest living relatives of the dinosaurs, feed in water, but crawl onto land to sunbathe and breed. Biologists classify them as part of the order known as *Crocodilia,* which includes alligators, caimans, and gavials.

GAVIAL *A long, slender snout distinguishes gavials. Found in India and Burma, they feed on river fish and grow to about 16 feet.*

CROCODILE *The fourth tooth on each side of the lower jaw protrudes on all true crocodiles. This is a Siamese species.*

CAIMAN *These broad-snouted reptiles, up to about 15 feet long, are native to South America.*

ALLIGATOR *As with caimans, the fourth tooth on each side of an alligator's lower jaw fits into a socket on the upper jaw.*

SNAKE *The grass snake,* Natrix natrix, *found in parts of Africa and Asia, can grow up to 6 feet long, but it is harmless. A smaller subspecies,* Natrix natrix helvetica, *is common in Britain and Europe.*

LIZARD *This 15-inch-long spiny South African lizard lies flat when disturbed, to guard its more vulnerable underside.*

Birds—conquerors of the sky

FLYING GIANTS

The largest flying creatures in history were the pterodactyls, a group of reptiles that lived more than 70 million years ago alongside the dinosaurs. Unlike birds, these reptiles had wings made of leathery skin, not feathers. Some had awesome wingspans.

The 70 million-year-old *Pteranodon,* for instance, measured as much as 23 feet from wingtip to wingtip. But it lacked strong wing muscles and seems to have glided, rather than flown, in search of its prey. In the 1970s, fragments of an even larger pterodactyl, with a probable wingspan of 49 feet, were found in Texas.

THE EARLIEST BIRD

Scientists have long searched for irrefutable fossil evidence of the evolutionary link between man and ape. They take hope from the fact that an extremely important "missing link" of a similar kind was found in fossil form by German quarrymen working near the village of Solnhofen, Bavaria, in 1861. The link, which proved that birds evolved from reptiles, was a species now known as *Archeopteryx* (meaning "ancient bird"). It lived about 150 million years ago.

Archeopteryx had feathers and a wishbone, typical of true birds. But its significance as the earliest bird was not recognized at first. Its reptilian features—teeth, a long tail, and claws on its wings—were so strong that one fossilized skeleton languished among the small dinosaurs in a museum in Eichstädt, West Germany, for 20 years because the faint impressions of its feathers in the rock were overlooked.

BORN TO FLY

The bones of modern birds are so completely adapted to the need to conserve weight in flight that a bird's feathers usually weigh more than its entire skeleton. The bones are more or less hollow, braced by internal struts and honeycombed with air sacs. During flight, air flows into these sacs and then to the lungs, increasing the supply of oxygen to body tissues. Even the beak is modified to save weight. Instead of being made of heavy bone, like human jaws, the beak is made of lightweight horn. And it contains no teeth.

The resulting design is so light that a golden eagle—which can have a wingspan approaching 8 feet—weighs a total of less than 9 pounds.

 WEIGHT SAVING *The bones of a bird are honeycombed for strength and lightness.*

FASTEST AND TWO OF THE RAREST

The fastest-moving animal is the peregrine falcon, clocked at 217 m.p.h. in a dive on prey.

One of the world's rarest birds is the dusky seaside sparrow: only five are known to exist—they are in captivity in Florida, and all are male. Scientists hope to crossbreed the birds with females of a closely related type.

The world's rarest bird in the wild is uncertain because in many places no reliable count has been made. But one of the rarest must be a Hawaiian honey eater known as Bishop's ooaa, *Moho bishopi.* A single specimen was sighted in 1982—the first glimpse of the species in 78 years.

LARGEST EGG

The largest egg among extant birds is laid by the ostrich. However, although the egg weighs 3 pounds, it is small by comparison with its parent, totaling only 1.4 percent of the ostrich's average weight of 220 pounds. Generally, smaller birds lay proportionately larger eggs. The egg of the tiny goldcrest, for instance, is 14 percent of the bird's body weight. Proportionately, one of the largest eggs is laid by the kiwi, the flightless bird of New Zealand. Its single egg may be 5 inches long and can weigh more than a pound —20 percent of the mother's weight.

COMPOST INCUBATOR

Most birds use body heat to incubate their eggs, but the mallee fowl, one of the brush turkey family found in Australia and on many Pacific islands, keeps its eggs warm by burying them in a compost heap of rotting vegetation.

The male bird tends the eggs, testing the incubator's temperature with its bill and adding or removing a covering of sand so that the inside of the mound remains almost constantly at 91°F. The eggs, which are laid one by one over a period of up to 6 months, hatch singly, but the care lavished on the eggs is not extended to the chicks. Once hatched, the chicks are ignored by their parents and forced to fend for themselves immediately.

UNDERGROUND ECHOLOCATION

The oilbird of Trinidad and northern South America nests in underground caverns that may be more than 1,000 yards from open air. As an adaptation to the lack of natural light in such caves, the oilbird has evolved an echolocation system of navigation similar to the one used by bats. During flight, it emits a series of clicks, finding its way in the blackness of the caves by listening to the echoes. So sensitive is the system that the bird can distinguish its own echoes from the clicks, squawks, and screeches of other birds.

The oilbird feeds chiefly at night on fatty fruits, such as oil-palm nuts, which are also used to make commercial oil. This diet gives the oilbird its oily flesh, from which Indians extract a cooking and lighting oil. The oilbird is also noteworthy because it appears to use its nose to find food, unlike other birds, which generally have a poor sense of smell.

DARWIN'S WOODY WOOD FINCH

On the Galapagos Islands in the Pacific lives a group of bird species, all of which are believed to be descended from a single South American ancestor. They are named Darwin's finches after the English naturalist Charles Darwin, because their different responses to the island environment helped to sugest to Darwin his theory of evolution.

Each species has adapted itself to a different diet, developing a beak to suit its particular food. One finch has adopted the role of woodpecker, evolving a powerful beak to chip through bark and get at insects. However, unlike the woodpecker, it lacks an elongated barbed tongue with which to spear its prey. To compensate for this disadvantage, the finch has developed a special trick of its own. It breaks off a spine from a nearby cactus and uses this as a probe to extract the insects.

NESTING PATTERNS

Nest building has survival value: it protects eggs and young from weather and predators. The most elaborate nests are built by members of the weaverbird family.

One weaverbird species, the sociable weaver, builds the largest nests. Up to 300 pairs weave individual nesting chambers under a single massive woven roof. By contrast, emperor penguins—which breed in Antarctica, far from any vegetation—make no nests at all.

SOLITARY CONFINEMENT *The male hornbill seals its mate behind a mud wall during incubation, to deter predators. The male feeds her, and later the chicks, through a hole. When the chicks are older, she breaks out to help in the feeding.*

KNOT NEST *The Baya weaverbird—one of several weaver species—sews, ties, and weaves its nest onto a branch, fashioning an entrance tunnel at the bottom. Each species builds its own distinctive style from grass and leaves.*

NIGHT STARVATION *Emperor penguins breed in the cold and dark of the Antarctic winter. The male incubates the egg on his feet for 64 days, during which time he cannot feed or even move. He keeps the egg warm under a flap of skin below his belly. The female returns after the egg hatches.*

IN THE PINK

Flamingos, the family of large, long-legged wading birds that live in many parts of the world, owe their distinctive pink coloring to their diet. All flamingos have some pink in their plumage, and one, the rosy flamingo, is entirely pink. The color is derived from carotenoid pigments—also present in carrots—that are contained in the microscopic plants and animals flamingos eat. Without this natural food, the birds' pink plumage fades and their breeding behavior can be affected.

WHY SEABIRDS HAVE RUNNY NOSES

Seabirds face a special environmental health hazard arising from their feeding habits: salt, which in large doses is poisonous, leading to dehydration and an overload on the kidneys. Yet seabirds absorb large quantities of salty water while feeding. The excess is disposed of by special salt-processing glands in the head. The glands discharge a highly concentrated salt solution into the nostrils, from where it drips back into the sea. With this built-in desalinization plant, seabirds never need to drink fresh water. They extract all they need from seawater.

LIGHT MEAL

Fishermen who use lights to attract their catch at night have a flying counterpart: skimmers, ternlike birds that appear to use minute marine creatures in the same way. The skimmer usually hunts in coastal waters during the evening and on bright nights, flying just above the water with the tip of its lower beak—which is much longer than the upper beak—skimming the surface to catch insects, shrimps, and small fish.

As it forages to and fro over the water, it often leaves a phosphorescent wake of disturbed microorganisms, and marine biologists believe that this light may help attract more fish within range. After catching its prey, the skimmer's beak snaps shut and the knifelike edges hold the food, which is swallowed in flight. The skimmer has a carefully controlled method of flight on its hunting flights just above the water. Unlike most birds, it has wings that never dip below the horizontal, so no noisy splashes alert the fish in its path.

LOCKING UP FOR THE NIGHT

The perching birds, which make up the majority of bird species, use a lock to stay on their perches. Tendons pass from the muscle at the back of the bird's leg, down around the back of its ankle, to the inside of the toes. When a bird settles its weight on a branch, the legs bend, tightening the tendons so that its toes automatically grip the perch. Even when the bird falls asleep, it is in no danger of slipping from the branch. As soon as it straightens its legs or jumps from the perch, however, the tendon relaxes and the grip of the toes is released.

PROUD PERCHER *Fierce and possessive, a great eagle owl grasps its prey against a branch. The bird is found in Europe, Asia, and Africa.*

Mammals—the milk-fed class

BABY IN WAITING

The female red kangaroo of Australia, *Macropus rufus*, has an extraordinary internal production line, which enables it to produce babies (known as "joeys") or to stop producing them, depending on external conditions. It can speed up the development of a fetus if an existing baby dies. Or it can reverse the development, reabsorbing the fetus, if drought makes the baby's survival unlikely.

Like other marsupials, the female red kangaroo produces tiny young. The baby, born less than 1 inch long, crawls to its mother's pouch, attaches itself to a teat, and remains there for about 6 months, feeding on milk and growing. Meanwhile, the female mates again, usually within a few days of the birth. After about 200 days the young joey begins to explore the outside world but keeps returning to the pouch for shelter. By 230 days the joey has no further need of its mother's shelter, but continues for a while to put its head back into the pouch to feed on milk.

During this whole time another baby remains in a state of suspended growth inside the mother. A fertilized egg has begun its development but waits at the blastocyst stage—as a minute sphere of cells —until the way is clear for its further development. This may happen in one of two ways. When the first joey starts to leave the pouch, the embryo restarts its development and is born about the time the joey leaves permanently.

Alternatively, if the joey in the pouch dies through accident or through malnutrition in time of drought, the embryo begins developing at once. A baby is then born some 35 days later, replacing the joey that has died.

BIRTH OF A JOEY *A baby kangaroo—less than an inch long at birth (left)—climbs through the mother's fur to her pouch (center), then attaches itself to a teat for about 6 months (right) to complete its early development.*

DOUBLE MILK

The red kangaroo can produce two different kinds of milk at the same time from adjacent teats. While a tiny joey is attached to one of the teats, the other teat is available to feed a joey that has left the pouch. The elder of the two is given milk with a higher proportion of protein (33 percent higher) and a much higher proportion of fats (400 percent higher).

MAJOR MINER

The Russian mole rat, *Spalax microphthalmus*, is one of the world's champion burrowers. In its search for the underground bulbs, roots, and tubers on which it feeds, it excavates long tunnels, punctuated by mounds of earth aboveground. Belowground these tunnels contain resting chambers, food storage chambers, and latrines. Special chambers are constructed for breeding. Scientists excavated one tunnel system in the U.S.S.R. and

measured its length at 1,180 feet. It was calculated that this system, a relatively short one, represented approximately 2 months' work. The longest-known burrow had 114 interconnected mounds. The rat is blind and carves out its tunnels with its teeth, not its claws. It rams its blunt head into the soil to loosen it as it chews out new tunnels.

USELESS TEETH

The numbat, or banded anteater, has 52 permanent teeth—more than any other land mammal. Yet it needs none of them. Its diet consists largely of termites and ants, which it swallows whole. A marsupial found in western Australia, the numbat gathers its prey with its long, thin tongue, which can be extended 4 inches or more from the mouth. It spends much of its time in search of food, eating up to 20,000 small termites a day. The numbat's teeth, which are small and widely separated, are thought by some scientists to be an evolutionary legacy from an ancestor that needed teeth to catch and cut up tougher insect prey.

ONE OF A KIND

One species of hedgehoglike mammal known as a tenrec is probably the world's rarest land creature. The species, *Dasogale fontoynonti*, is known only from a single specimen, which was found in eastern Madagascar and whose body is now preserved in a museum in Paris. Nobody knows whether or not any others still exist in the wild.

MIDGET WITH A GIANT HUNGER

The Etruscan shrew, which lives around the Mediterranean Sea and in Africa, is one of the world's smallest mammals. Fully grown, it weighs only about 0.07 ounce—less than a 0.094-ounce U.S. dime—and its maximum length, including tail, is just over 3 inches. But, like other shrews, it has a giant-size appetite. Because they are so tiny, shrews have a large surface area compared to their body volume and lose heat very fast. To compensate, they eat almost continuously and cannot survive for more than a few hours without food. If they lack suitable prey, they will eat each other, including their own young. Some eat up to three times their own body weight in a day.

The smallest of all mammals is a rare type of bat, *Craseonycteris thonglongyai*, which is found only in Thailand. Although an adult has a wingspan of more than 6 inches—twice the length of the Etruscan shrew— it weighs less: about 0.06 ounce.

THE DAM BUILDERS

North American beavers are prodigious dam builders. Their biggest dams can be 2,000 feet long and contain hundreds of tons of timber. Even a fairly average dam is more than 65 feet long. Beavers build their homes in the ponds created by the dams, and the homes, known as lodges, can themselves be huge structures up to 6 feet high and 20 feet across. Like a moat, the pond protects the lodge from predators and also floods the surrounding area, allowing the beavers to gather more food in safety from the drowned forest. The animal's front teeth are so powerful that a group of beavers can fell a tree 20 inches thick in just 15 minutes. Each dam and lodge is made by a colony of beavers working together. Their structures do not seem to be the product of intelligent cooperation, but rather the cumulative result of the instincts of the colony's members. For example, the trigger that starts beavers building a dam is the sound of running water, and construction stops when the water is no longer heard.

BUILT-IN CHOPSTICKS
The aye-aye, a rare lemur from Madagascar, has on its front paws middle fingers so thin and elongated that they resemble chopsticks. Indeed, the aye-aye uses them to eat with, dipping them one at a time into the pulp of fruits, lifting the finger to its mouth and sucking off the juice. It drinks water the same way. The aye-aye's main food is wood-boring insects. It finds them by listening at the bark of trees with its big ears, then gnawing away the bark until it can insert its chopstick finger and extract the prey.

QUADS ALL THE TIME
The female of the nine-banded armadillo, *Dasypus novemcinctus,* regularly bears a litter of identical quadruplets, and all four of the babies come from the same egg. The armadillo's egg splits during development and produces identical quads, so that the whole litter is invariably of the same sex. The advantages of this arrangement, if any, are not clear. But it serves the armadillo well enough for it to be a relatively common species across a region from the southern United States to southern Brazil.

SLOW-MOTION LIVING
Sloths are the slowest of mammals. They spend almost their entire lives upside down in the trees of Central and South American tropical forests, feeding on leaves and fruit. Their limbs are well adapted as climbing hooks, but they have a top speed of only about 1 m.p.h. as they inch along through the trees. Their bodies work slowly, and they have a lower and more variable body temperature than other mammals—from 75° to 91°F in the two-toed sloth. Even their fur is adapted for an upside-down existence; it grows from the belly up around the back, instead of the other way around, as in most mammals.

The sloth's apparently slothful way of life is the product of a perfect adaptation to its environment. Its characteristic posture—hanging immobile and upside down from a branch—guards it from the attention of predators. And its thick, coarse coat, naturally brown or grayish white, is camouflaged green by the presence of microscopic green algae.

The U.S. naturalist William Beebe (1877–1962) once followed a sloth through the forest for a week. He found that it spent 11 hours feeding, 18 hours moving very slowly about, 10 hours resting—and 129 hours sleeping.

THE BIG SLEEP
The North American woodchuck spends as much as 8 months each year asleep. All its activity is packed into the warmest months. The mechanisms used in its hibernation are typical of most true hibernators. As the days shorten, the woodchuck eats far more than usual, and this extra food is converted to fat, in particular a nutrient-rich reserve known to biologists as brown fat.

When this fat has built up to a critical level (about one-seventh of the woodchuck's body weight), the animal retreats into its burrow and becomes torpid, allowing its body temperature to drop with that of the surroundings until it may be within a few degrees of freezing point. The brain temperature is still kept up, however, and the temperature sensors still work. If there is a danger of freezing, some brown fat can be used to raise the body temperature rapidly. Then, when spring arrives, the brown fat reserves are used to bring the body temperature back to normal.

TEETH OF LIFE
An elephant's tusks are specialized front teeth. Yet it can do without them. More important than tusks to the elephant's survival are its 24 molar teeth, used for grinding up food. Unlike the permanent teeth of most mammals, which all develop at about the same time, the elephant's molars appear in succession. When the animal is young, the first two teeth on each side of the upper and lower jaw are in use, but successive teeth grow and move forward from the rear, coming into use as the previous ones are worn down and lost.

By the time an elephant is 45 years old, the last four teeth are in full use and the rest of the teeth have gone. These last teeth are massive. They weigh about 9 pounds apiece, are 12 inches long, and have big ridges to help grind the food. But an elephant may eat more than 500 pounds of tough plant food a day, wearing away even these teeth eventually, so that by the time an elephant is 65 or 70 it faces starvation through a simple inability to chew.

FERTILITY SYMBOL
Their breeding capabilities have made rabbits a symbol of fertility. Females can start to breed at the age of 4 months and can produce a litter of up to nine young after a gestation period of about 30 days. They can become pregnant again almost directly after giving birth, and can produce up to six litters during spring and summer.

If a pair of rabbits and its progeny bred to their maximum capacity and if there were no losses among the offspring, a family of more than 33 million animals could result within 3 years. Given this potential, the rabbit has been surprisingly rare

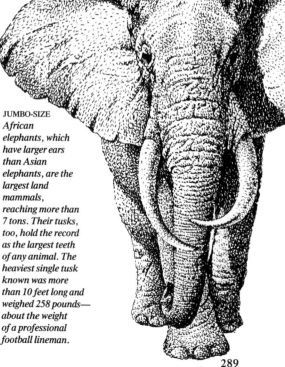

JUMBO-SIZE *African elephants, which have larger ears than Asian elephants, are the largest land mammals, reaching more than 7 tons. Their tusks, too, hold the record as the largest teeth of any animal. The heaviest single tusk known was more than 10 feet long and weighed 258 pounds— about the weight of a professional football lineman.*

for much of its history. For one thing, up to 90 percent of the young are killed by predators. The rabbit's fecundity has often led it into trouble. Prized for their meat and fur, and sometimes as pets, European (or Old World) rabbits traveled with settlers to many parts of the world, including Australia and South America. (The native American rabbit, or cottontail, already occupied North America.) In some of these new habitats there were no predators, and the European rabbits underwent population explosions and became pests and constant threats to crops. When a disease called myxomatosis began to decimate the imported rabbits of South America, farmers there were delighted and rabbit-plagued farmers around the world took note. In 1950 the South American disease was introduced to Australia to control a plague of rabbits. Four years later the British unleashed myxomatosis and killed 99 percent of Britain's rabbits. In some areas of Britain rabbits are common again, but cyclical outbreaks of the disease keep the population from getting out of control.

THE LONG MARCH
The barren ground caribou of Canada make the longest migrations of any land mammal. They move to the Arctic high tundra for the summer, where the young are born, and return south in the autumn to the northern edge of the forest region—a round trip of about 1,400 miles. The animals migrate in giant herds of up to 20,000 individuals. The trek enables the caribou to feed on the richest pastures available at each season of the year, and so helps to support larger herds than would otherwise be possible.

EVOLUTIONARY U-TURN
The ancestors of whales were once land animals. Scientific examination of whale skeletons indicates that they have a vestigial pelvis or hipbone, proving that whales once possessed legs. The ancestors of whales, like the ancestors of all animals, originally came from the sea. But the whale line, after occupying the land, returned to the sea about 70 million years ago, and through thousands of generations lost many characteristics of land mammals.

Their front legs changed into flippers, their rear legs disappeared, their bodies acquired a thick insulating layer of blubber, and their nostrils moved from the snout to the top of the head to become a blowhole. The ancestors of whales may have returned to the sea because food was more plentiful there or because enemies were fewer.

TALKING UNDERWATER
Although dolphins have no vocal cords, they can communicate with one another, navigate, and hunt for prey by making distinctive underwater sounds. By forcing air past valves and flaps located immediately below their blowholes, dolphins can emit at least 32 different sounds, including whistles, groans, barks, clicks, and squeals. Besides making sounds to "talk" to other members of their school, dolphins navigate and hunt by using an echolocation technique like those used by bats and oilbirds.

Whales, too, converse with one another by making whistles and chirps. The male humpback whale, for example, produces a long and complex song that may last for 30 minutes. These sounds are sometimes extremely loud. Blue whales have emitted whistles that reach 188 decibels—louder than a jet plane. In one case, the moans of fin whales seem to have been picked up by other whales more than 100 miles away.

TAIL FIRST
Whales and dolphins (porpoises) are born tail first. Unlike land mammals, which are born into air and can breathe air as soon as the head is out of the birth canal, whales are born underwater, and their backward form of delivery keeps them from drowning during the time it takes to be born. Like all mammals, whales have lungs, not gills, and must breathe air.

Immediately after birth the whale calf is helped to the ocean's surface by its mother—and sometimes by other attendant whales—to take its first breath of air. The calves are enormous. At birth a blue whale may be 25 feet long and weigh 2 tons—nearly as heavy as some adult elephants. Each day, the calves suck 100 to 150 gallons of milk, which contains about 50 percent fat, and they can double their weight in a week, growing faster than any other mammal. Each day, a baby blue whale grows longer by about 1.5 inch and gains up to 200 pounds. After 7 months it can weigh 25 tons.

WHALE OF A BRAIN
Sperm whales have the heaviest brain of any animal. It can weigh more than 20 pounds, six times larger than an average human brain. Fully grown, sperm whales can weigh 60 tons and grow up to 65 feet in length, making them the largest of the toothed whales and the world's biggest carnivores.

The whale's head, which can be one-third the length of its entire body, contains up to 500 gallons of pure oil. Until the development of refined mineral oils, sperm oil was in great demand as one of the finest lubricants known. Early hunters wrongly believed the fluid to be the animal's sperm.

THE DOLPHIN'S ENEMY
Although dolphins (porpoises) are mammals and sharks are fish, the two animals share some traits. Both live in all the seas of the world. Both are superbly adapted for life and speed in water. Both live on fish—but dolphins never eat sharks, while sharks sometimes do eat dolphins.

For millions of years sharks have occasionally preyed on solitary dolphins that have become separated from their school. But in a group, dolphins can outwit, terrify, and even kill their archenemy. Dolphins at sea have been spotted chasing a shark, closing in on it from different directions to force it well away from the school. In some aquariums dolphins have been known to kill sharks by butting them to death with their pointed "beaks."

One such gang attack was made by a group of dolphins that had been sharing a large tank with a shark. Just before one of the female dolphins was about to give birth, the dolphins coolly lined up at the far end of the tank from the shark, then raced through the water one at a time, each smashing its beak into the shark's side. After only a few minutes of this battering-ram punishment the shark was dead, its internal organs pounded to pulp.

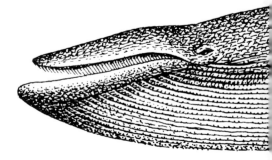

In another case, dolphins are thought to have thrown a shark out of the tank. Its body was found the next day, 30 feet from the edge of the pool.

THE BIGGEST MEETING
The greatest gathering of a single species of mammal takes place annually on the Pribilofs, an island group in the Bering Sea off Alaska. Each year an estimated 1.5 million Alaskan fur seals assemble there to breed, producing some 500,000 pups.

WHY SEALS CRY
Seals on land often look miserable, with tears trickling down their cheeks. In fact, the tears have nothing to do with their emotional state. As with some other aquatic creatures, the tears, produced naturally by seals to lubricate the eyes, wash off into the water when the animals swim. There is no need for the duct running from eyes to nose that is found in land mammals, including the human species. In seals the duct has disappeared, so when a seal is on land, there is nowhere for the tears to go except down the face.

BEHIND THE MERMAID LEGEND
The source of mermaid legends may be mammals of the order Sirenia, collectively known to science as sirenians (sirens). Commonly referred to as sea cows, these creatures—which include the dugong and the manatee—are about the same size as a human being and from a distance look somewhat like a woman with the tail of a fish.

Female sea cows have prominent breasts on the front of their bodies near the forelimbs, and a flattened, sometimes forked tail. Close up, the resemblance to a storybook mermaid vanishes. A sea cow has a chubby, rounded face with small eyes, a cleft upper lip, and a bristly mustache.

TOOTHLESS GIANTS
Although the baleen whale family includes the world's largest creature, the blue whale, the mammals feed on very small marine organisms. They are unable to hunt larger prey because, except during their embryonic stage, they lack teeth. Baleen whales are named after their bonelike baleen plates, also called whalebone and once used as the stays in women's corsets. The plates, between 3 and 10 feet long and up to 12 inches wide, grow from the upper gums and enable the whales to strain the krill (tiny larvae and shrimplike crustaceans) out of plankton masses in the sea. Krill is the main food of baleen whales.

The whale feeds by swimming with its mouth open, trapping the krill on the frayed insides of the baleen plates and using its huge tongue to help swallow the catch. Baleen whales strain several tons of ocean plankton each day, and the blue whale may consume 4 tons of nourishing krill daily. The largest blue whale known was landed on the South Atlantic island of South Georgia in the early 20th century. It was 110 feet 2 inches long.

MARSUPIAL AND PLACENTAL MAMMALS

The two main groups of present-day mammals are the marsupials, or Metatheria, and the placentals, or Eutheria—the group that includes man. Marsupial females have a pouch in which their young develop. In placentals, the young develop inside the mother. Marsupials now live only in Australia, New Guinea, and the Americas. Despite the biological differences, many pouched animals fill the same ecological niches as their placental relatives, and often resemble them.

TREE DWELLERS *Marsupial phalangers (right) glide between trees by using membranes stretched between arms and legs. They resemble flying squirrels (left).*

TUNNELERS *The southern marsupial mole (right) has a leathery pad on its nose, and it digs with clawed forefeet—like the Cape golden mole (left) of Africa.*

SCAVENGERS *Marsupial Tasmanian devils (right) and the Eurasian wolverine (left) have powerful teeth and claws. Both feed largely on carrion.*

HUNTERS *The slope-backed marsupial wolf (right) looks much like an Old World wolf (left). Both are adapted to pulling down prey and tearing flesh.*

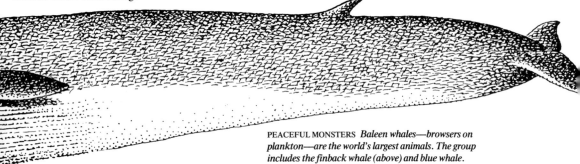

PEACEFUL MONSTERS *Baleen whales—browsers on plankton—are the world's largest animals. The group includes the finback whale (above) and blue whale.*

Farm animals and pets

OUR FIRST FRIEND
The ancient Egyptians used dogs for hunting 8,000 years ago, and Stone Age tribes may have had hunting dogs before 10,000 B.C. The ancestors of the dog were probably the lighter-built southern Asian races of the wolf, but other wolf races may have figured in the dog's ancestry.

About 5,000 years ago people began to develop breeds of dogs that had qualities desired by human owners. Eventually these experiments led to such breeds as the short-legged dachshund for hunting badgers, and the sheepdog for herding flocks.

All dogs—from a Mexican chihuahua weighing 2 pounds to a huge Saint Bernard of more than 200 pounds—are members of the same species. In biological terms, this means that any dog can potentially breed with any other dog, although differences in size can make this unlikely in some cases. And there is no genetic barrier between dogs and wolves either, despite dogs' long domestication.

GIVE A DOG A NAME
● The German shepherd surged in popularity because of World War I, when British and American soldiers brought home stories of the dogs' courage and devotion in war service for the Germans. But anti-German feeling in many countries after the war led to the dogs' being called Alsatians—a name that arose from a questionable notion that the breed originated in Alsace-Lorraine. In the United States, movies starring German shepherds named Strongheart (1922) and Rin Tin Tin (beginning 1923) added hugely to the breed's fame and popularity.
● Doberman pinschers get their name from a German tax collector. Aware of the unpopularity of his job, Ludwig Dobermann, of Apolda in Thuringia (East Germany), developed in the 1880s an especially fierce breed of hunting dog (pinscher) to help him on his rounds. Today Dobermans are widely used as guard dogs.
● Chihuahuas are named after the state of Chihuahua in Mexico. They are believed to have been the sacred dogs of the Aztecs, and were sometimes eaten by the Indians in religious ceremonies.
● Labradors do not come from the Canadian region of Labrador but from the neighboring province of Newfoundland, where they helped fishermen haul in nets.
● The cocker spaniel originated in 14th-century Spain. The first half of its name comes from its use by hunters to flush out woodcock; the second half, from the name of its home country.
● The first Pekingese in Europe were five dogs brought from China after they had been taken by the British from the women's apartments in Peking's Summer Palace during the Boxer Rebellion (1898–1900). Before this, the breed had been monopolized by the Chinese royal family, and theft of a Peke carried the death penalty.
● The King Charles spaniel is not a British breed. It was a pet in Japan as early as 2000 B.C. It got its

English name (in the U.S.A. it is often known as the English toy spaniel) after it became fashionable at the 17th-century court of Charles I.

THE FIRST GUIDE DOG
The idea of using dogs to help blind people grew out of a chance incident at a German hospital during World War I. A doctor walking in the grounds with a blinded soldier was called away and left his pet German shepherd (Alsatian) to look after his patient. Impressed by its response, the German doctor began training dogs to guide the blind.

In the early 1920s a wealthy American, Dorothy Eustis, had set up a kennel in Vevey, Switzerland, to breed and train German shepherds for the army and police. Hearing of the German experiments, she hired former German Army dog trainers and eventually set up the Seeing Eye center in New Jersey, where German shepherds and other breeds learned to guide the blind. After shepherds, the breeds most used as seeing-eye dogs are Labrador retrievers, golden retrievers, and boxers.

CALL ME MOTHER
All pet hamsters are descended from a single female wild golden hamster found with a litter of 12 young in Syria in 1930. The species had been named in 1839, when a single animal was found in Syria near the city of Aleppo, but no hamster had been seen by scientists for nearly a century. Selective breeding has now produced several color varieties.

AT HOME ON THE RANGE
The word "maverick"—meaning a rogue animal or a person who does not conform—comes from a Texas lawyer and rancher, Samuel Maverick (1803–70), who did not bother to brand his cattle.

PIG IN THE MIDDLE
In 1859 the United States and Britain almost went to war over a pig. It belonged to an Englishman, Charles Griffin, who lived on San Juan Island in Puget Sound between Vancouver Island and what was then the Territory of Washington. The pig kept straying onto the potato patch of Lyman Cutler, an American. Cutler shot the pig. Griffin demanded that the British arrest Cutler, and troops from both sides rushed in.

The pig's aimless foraging had thrust to the fore an ambiguity in the 1846 treaty that established part of the U.S.–Canadian boundary. At the western end, said the treaty, the border ran along the 49th parallel of latitude to "the middle of the channel" separating Vancouver Island from the mainland. There the border turned south. But that channel was divided into several smaller channels by a cluster of islands that includes San Juan—and the two nations could not agree on which channel was meant. The

PRZHEVALSKI'S HORSE *All modern horses are thought to be descended from this wild species, now found only in Asia.*

DINGO *A forerunner of the domestic dog, the dingo was taken to Australia by aborigines some 8,000 years ago.*

JUNGLE FOWL
The wild red jungle fowl of Malaya and India is the bird from which domestic chickens were bred.

"Pig War" dragged on for 13 years. No shots were exchanged, but British and U.S. troops remained at opposite ends of San Juan Island. The dispute was settled through arbitration by the German kaiser, Wilhelm I, who awarded San Juan and adjacent islands to the United States in 1872. They are now part of the state of Washington.

PIGGY PADDLE
In the Tokelau Islands of the South Pacific, pigs have learned to find their own food in the sea. They wade and swim through the shallow reef waters, ducking under the surface to catch sea slugs and shellfish.

WITH A GUAU GUAU HERE...
Animals do, it seems, speak different languages—at least as far as their countries' written word is concerned. Sheep do not "baa" in Germany; they say *mäh* (pronounced as a drawn-out "may"). And in Spain they say *bee* (pronounced "bay"). Norwegian dogs say *vov vov*, not "bow wow" or "woof woof." French dogs say *whou whou*, and Spanish ones *guau guau*. In France ducks say *coin coin*, not "quack quack," and turkeys say *glou glou*, not "gobble gobble." In Italy hens say *ko-ko-day*, not "cluck-cluck," and the roosters greet the dawn by shrieking, not "cock-a-doodle-doo," but *chicchirichi* (pronounced "kee-kee-ree-kee").

TABBIES AND THE CASBAH
Tabby cats are thought to get their name from Attab, a district in Baghdad, now the capital of Iraq. There, according to an Arab observer writing in the 12th century, "are made the stuffs called *Attabiya*, which are silks and cottons of divers colors." Brought to the Western world in its abbreviated form, the word was originally applied to striped silk taffetas, and the association with striped cats followed.

COWS AS BIG AS ELEPHANTS
Scientists at Ohio University are working on a project that could result in enormous livestock. By juggling with the genetic structures of animals—adding and subtracting genes, including genes from other species—they hope to create new breeds that will make traditional farm animals look dwarfish. So far, they have bred what is probably the world's largest mouse.

Known only by its laboratory number, 178, it is two and a half times larger than a normal mouse but eats no more. The leader of the project, Dr. Thomas Wagner, has predicted that in a few years it will be possible to use the same techniques on larger animals, so that scientists could breed cows weighing 5 tons—only slightly less than an elephant—and pigs the size of hippos.

THE FIRST ROUNDUPS

Dates when animals were first domesticated are not precise. These dates, however, are widely accepted by historians and biologists:

Dog by 10,000 B.C.	Donkey 3000 B.C.
Goat 8000 B.C.	Cat 2000 B.C.
Cattle 5500 B.C.	Chicken 2000 B.C.
Sheep 5000 B.C.	Duck 1500 B.C.
Pig 3000 B.C.	Goose 1500 B.C.
Horse 3000 B.C.	Rabbit A.D. 1000

DOMESTICATED CATTLE *One ancestor of major European and American breeds is thought to be the wild urus, or aurochs. Although the last one was seen in Poland in 1627, a German biologist, Heinz Heck, created a look-alike in 1932 by crossbreeding varieties (above) that included Highland and Holstein-Friesian blood.*

TOP DOGS

The popularity of dog breeds varies from country to country and time to time. In numbers registered, these were the most popular in the U.S.A. in the mid-1980s, according to the American Kennel Club.

1 Cocker spaniel
2 Poodle
3 Labrador retriever
4 German shepherd
5 Golden retriever
6 Doberman pinscher
7 Beagle
8 Miniature schnauzer
9 Shetland sheepdog
10 Dachshund
11 Chow chow
12 Yorkshire terrier
13 Lhasa apso
14 Shih Tzu
15 English springer spaniel
16 Pomeranian
17 Siberian husky
18 Collie
19 Basset hound
20 Boxer

WILD BOAR *Farm pigs are descended from the wild boar, which was crossed with Far Eastern breeds around the end of the 18th century.*

MOUNTAIN GOAT *Native to the northern Rockies, this wild species is related to the chamois of Eurasia.*

MOUNTAIN SHEEP *Also called the bighorn, this wild Rocky Mountain denizen is closely related to domesticated sheep.*

Animal behavior

GUARD DUTY Caterpillars of the imperial blue butterfly of Australia have their own special escort—a band of black ants. Each morning, as the caterpillars leave their nests on black wattle trees to feed on leaves, the ants join them. The ants use their huge jaws to drive off any potential predators while the caterpillars feed. As payment for their guard duty, the ants suck a sugary secretion from the caterpillars' backs. The ants—which nest underground and climb up the trees each day to join the caterpillars—even watch over the insects in their pupa stage, when there is no sweet reward for their work.

The small fish Nomeus *spends its life among the dangerous tentacles of the Portuguese man-of-war, and apparently shares the food caught by its lethal host. If a nomeus is injured, however, the protection ceases. A wound triggers the predatory instincts of its host, which then eats the lodger.*

BODY BAIT One species of assassin bug, *Salyavata variegata,* uses the bodies of dead termites as bait to capture fresh victims. It captures its first termite by camouflaging itself with pieces of carton—the pasteboardlike material containing chewed vegetable matter that termites make to build nests—and then snatching a termite that wanders too close.

Once it has sucked the body dry, the bug dangles the carcass in an entrance hole. Termite workers try to clear it away, but when a worker grasps the body, the bug hauls the body and the worker from the nest. The diligent worker then becomes the bug's next meal, and its body becomes the bait for the next victim.

Among the coral reefs of the Indian and Pacific oceans, fish of all kinds make use of the services of cleaner fish, which relieve them of parasites and damaged skin. One such cleaner—there are more than 40 species—is the 4-inch-long striped sea swallow, a kind of wrasse. Its clients, including large predators such as moray eels, do not eat the cleaner and are quiet under its attentions, even allowing it to browse inside their mouths.

HOME GUARD Birds use stinging insects as an unwitting army to protect their nests. Some seed-eating African weaverbirds build their nests above the homes of fierce paper wasps. The rufous woodpecker of India and Southeast Asia tunnels into the football-size nests of stinging tree ants and lays its eggs there. Though woodpeckers eat ants, and the aggressive tree ants will attack any intruder near their nest, the two animals call a truce at the woodpecker's breeding time. The woodpecker benefits from the protection provided for its nest by the ants, and the ants gain by not being eaten by the woodpecker during the rearing season.

MOBILE BODYGUARD The hermit crab lives inside an empty shell, on which a sea anemone often rides as a "bodyguard." The anemone's stinging tentacles deter predators, and in return it gains mobility and

TYPES OF TOGETHERNESS

Biologists divide partnerships between living organisms into four main categories: symbiotic, parasitic, commensal, and epizoic.

Symbiotic A word meaning literally "living together." Symbiosis is a mutually beneficial relationship between two different organisms. Lichens, for example, are a symbiosis of two organisms—a fungus and one of the primitive plants known as algae.

Parasitic A close and one-sided relationship in which an organism lives off its host, harming it in the process. Flatworms, for example, thrive in the blood vessels of their human hosts.

Commensal A close and one-sided relationship in which one organism benefits, but not at the expense of its partner. Many microorganisms, for example, benefit from living in the human digestive tract but cause no harm.

Epizoic A close relationship in which one partner dwells on the body of another—or is carried or towed about by it. The remora "sucker" fish, for example, attaches itself to a larger fish by means of a suction disk on its head.

---

thus a wider feeding range, as well as scraps of the crab's food. Hermit crabs use abandoned mollusk shells as protection, and move to larger ones when they outgrow them. But they do not leave their bodyguards behind. When about to move, the crab gives the anemone a warning tap so that it relaxes its hold on the shell. Then the crab uses its claw to lift the anemone to the new shell.

THE BADGER'S SCOUT The ratel, or honey badger, of tropical Africa has a flying partner—a small bird that guides the ratel to its favorite food: honey. The bird—the honey guide, *Indicator indicator*—gives a special call when it has found a beehive that alerts any nearby honey badger. Then the bird leads the badger to the hive. The badger, whose tough skin is impervious to stings, breaks in with its sharp claws and eats its fill of honey. Meanwhile, the bird picks through the debris of the nest for its own favorite food: larvae and insects. The bird, which is unable to break into a beehive by itself, thus gets food it could not otherwise reach; and the ratel is drawn to food that it might not notice.

FROM HOST TO HOST Most parasites live off only one host, but there is a group of parasites that need two hosts in order to survive. They are the threadlike flatworms that spread the wasting disease of bilharzia through much of Africa and parts of Asia and South America. Of the four species of bilharzia worm, two—*Schistosoma hematobium* and *Schistosoma mansoni*—depend almost entirely on man himself as the definitive host.

The worm's life cycle is highly complicated. The newly hatched worms, born in rivers and pools, are microscopic and have just 24 hours to find their first host: the egg of a tiny but hardy freshwater snail.

If the worms fail to find a snail host within 24

hours, they die. If they succeed, they develop inside the snail and eventually return to the water as barely visible young worms. These, in turn, have 72 hours at most to find a human host.

The young worms can penetrate the skin of a swimmer or paddler at any point, travel through the veins to the heart and thence through the lungs to the liver. There they grow into fully fledged worms 0.4 to 1 inch long. Once in the adult stage, the worms migrate to the gut and bladder, where they can remain for up to 25 years. Their eggs are discharged into rivers and pools in the urine and feces, and so the cycle continues.

More than 200 million people in over 70 countries have bilharzia, whose symptoms include listlessness, diarrhea, and blood in the urine and bowels.

LOBSTERS IN LINE Every autumn off the Bimini Islands, in the Bahamas, thousands of spiny lobsters migrate from reefs to deeper water. During this journey they often form a marching column of up to 50 lobsters to cross open areas.

Each hooks one pair of its front legs around the tail of the animal in front, or flicks its antennae to maintain contact. In this way, each lobster's vulnerable belly and tail are protected by the armored legs and antennae of the one behind while the column scuttles across the seabed as fast as a man can swim.

SENTRY TO A SHRIMP The 6-inch goby fish, *Cryptocentrus coeruleopunctatus*, acts as a sentry for a tiny shrimp with which it shares a burrow on the seabed. Whenever the entrance to their burrow becomes littered with rubble, the shrimp—known as the snapping shrimp—emerges to clear the rubble, using its claws like a mechanical digger. While it is at work, the goby stands guard, with one of its antennae touching the shrimp. The moment the goby discerns any danger, it wriggles its body. The shrimp, alerted by the movement of its companion's antenna, at once jumps back into the safety of the burrow—immediately followed by the goby.

HOME SHARP HOME Several Central American species of ants have evolved a remarkable living arrangement—with a tree. The ants make their homes in the sharp, fleshy spines of swollen thorn acacias. They burrow into the base of the trees' thorns, eating the pulp and hollowing out a nest at the same time. Once established, the ants—species of the genus *Pseudomyrmex*—feed on special protein-rich nodules that grow on the tips of the acacias' leaves.

The trees thrive because the ants protect them from all other predators, such as other insects, birds, and small animals. When the ants find any such predator on their trees, they quickly close in, biting and stinging, until the invader is driven away.

FOSTER CHILD OF THE BUFFALO South Africa's giant Kruger National Park is the home of an elephant that thinks it is a buffalo. In the early 1970s five baby elephants that had been the subject of a veterinary experiment were released in the park, close to a herd of buffalo. Later, game rangers reported that one of the young elephants had joined the herd and was adopting buffalo habits. In 1980 a park visitor saw the 10-year-old elephant and its "family" of 20 buffalo trumpeting and bellowing in an effort to drive eight lions away from a waterhole.

By the mid-1980s the elephant still seemed at home with the buffalo. As one park ranger, Ted Whitfield, reported: "I've seen him drinking when a herd of elephant arrives. The buffalo take off, and so does he."

FACTS ABOUT
ANIMALS & PLANTS

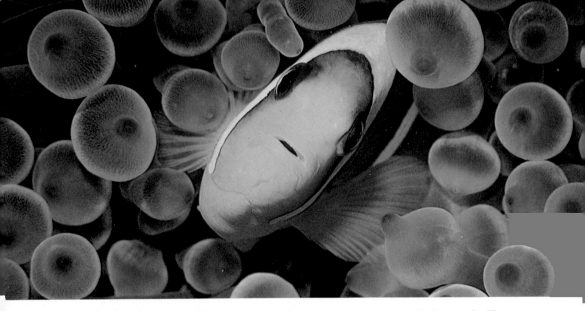

BARBED RETREAT *The clown fish protects itself from predators by taking refuge among an anemone's stinging tentacles. The fish, which is about 2 inches long, secretes a coat of mucus that counteracts the poisonous discharge from the anemone's stinging cells. The anemone seems to benefit because the clown fish lures other species into the tentacles, and the fish benefits by eating up leftover scraps of the anemone's food.*

Animal behavior

SHOCKING TAIL The electric eels of South America have enough power in their tails to light a dozen household bulbs—or to kill a man on contact. The eels can release a shock of about 500 volts at 2 amperes. The biggest discharge on record is 650 volts. The surge of current is generated chemically from thousands of linked battery cells—modified muscle tissues that take up four-fifths of the eel's 6-foot length. The electric charge can be released in a fraction of a second, but it takes the best part of an hour for the eel to recharge its batteries for another shock.

Despite its name, the electric eel is not an eel at all. It is a type of freshwater fish related to carp and minnows. The fish uses its extraordinary ability to protect itself from predators and to stun prey. Adult eels also use weak "radar" pulses from their battery cells as an aid to navigation, since they live in murky swamps and backwaters.

The Southeast Asian spider Cyclosa mulmeinensis *makes dummies of itself. It wraps up parts of its prey in silk until they are the same size as the spider, then plants the dummies in strategic spots on its web. Spider-hunting birds are quite likely to select one of the decoys instead of the spider.*

HOLDING THE RING The musk oxen of Canada, Alaska, and Greenland defend themselves from wolf attacks by forming a defensive ring. Females and the young gather in the center of the circle, and the males form a wall around them, with their horns pointing outward. If a wolf ventures too close, it risks being caught on a pair of horns and tossed over a male's back into the circle, where it will be trampled to death by the females.

CARBON COPIERS Many animals protect themselves by imitating others. They usually do it in one of two ways.

In Batesian mimicry—named after the 19th-century British naturalist Henry Bates—harmless or edible animals imitate the appearance of poisonous or inedible ones, which predators avoid. The harmless wasp beetle, for example, flaunts the bright warning colors of the wasp and even apes its flight patterns to fool beetle-eating predators.

In Müllerian mimicry—named after Fritz Müller, a 19th-century German zoologist—poisonous or inedible species imitate each other, a habit also known as economy of coloration. The mechanism cuts down the number of different warning patterns that predators need to remember, and so reduces the numbers eaten by accident.

BLUFFING IT OUT For survival in nature, sometimes the next best thing to being fierce is looking fierce. When alarmed, the Australian frilled lizard, which is about 3 feet long, raises a frill that normally lies flat along the neck. The frill stands out in a disk up to 2 feet across. The lizard adds to this alarming increase in apparent size by opening its mouth to reveal a bright yellow interior, then hisses loudly. In the face of all this, a potential predator can hardly be blamed for not realizing that the lizard is harmless.

STICKY END Tropical termites use a natural quick-setting glue to defend their nests from marauding ants. Termite soldiers belonging to the genus *Nasutitermes* can fire jets of the glue from an aperture on their heads across a distance of an inch or more. The glue rapidly becomes very sticky, immobilizing the assailants, while its smell attracts other soldiers to the nest's defense. Soldier termites of the genus *Coptotermes* produce a similar glue, but they are unable to discharge it at a distance. As a result, both the termite and the ant become entangled. Nevertheless, even if the defender dies, its suicidal mechanism helps to preserve the rest of the nest.

The sea cucumber, or bêche-de-mer, of the Pacific can disembowel itself to escape capture. When frightened, it contracts its sausagelike body violently and expels a tangled mess of its own internal organs. But far from dying in the process, it leaves the organs as a meal for its attacker and slithers away to grow a new set within a few weeks.

The sea cucumber, which may grow to more than 2 feet long, can also eject a bunch of sticky white threads, resembling an untidy web of spaghetti, to entangle small fish and shrimps that disturb it.

EVASIVE ACTION Moths use a dramatic free-fall tactic to evade pursuing bats. Bats detect their prey by means of an echolocation system, bouncing sounds off objects in their path. But because the moth can pick up the bat's high-pitched squeaks from 100 feet away, it has an edge over its faster adversary, which

---

HOW LONG THEY LIVE

Most animals die through violence, disease, or accident, not from old age. As a result, the maximum life spans of animals in the wild are not known with certainty. Most scientists believe that marine animals are generally capable of living longer than land animals because their bodies, permanently supported by water, are not worn down or worn out so quickly by the effects of gravity. In addition, many cold-blooded animals, such as reptiles, seem to have no fixed adult size and go on growing until they die. Theoretically, some scientists believe, such animals could live forever.

Practically, however, few animals live much longer than the normal life expectancy of a human being. These are the longest recorded life spans, in years, for a variety of animals:

152	Marion's tortoise	50	Lobster
100	Deep-sea clam	40	Cow
90	Killer whale	35	Domestic pigeon
90	Blue whale	34	Domestic cat
90	Fin whale	29	Dog (Labrador)
80	Freshwater oyster	28	Budgerigar
70	Cockatoo	20	Sheep
70	Condor	18	Goat
70	Indian elephant	18	Rabbit
62	Ostrich	10	Golden hamster
62	Horse	6	House mouse
50	Chimpanzee	0.2	Housefly
50	Termite		

has a detection range of only about 20 feet. When a moth intercepts signals from a bat, it takes evasive action by suddenly dropping to the ground in mid-flight.

The maneuver does not always work, though, because the bats can sometimes track the moths as they fall and catch them before they reach the ground. As a result, some moth species have evolved new tricks that restore their advantage in the dogfight. They resort to aerobatics in an attempt to shake off the bat. Some tiger moth species have even developed a jamming device—an ultrasonic sound that throws the bats off course.

LEAPING FOR LIFE Antelopes and gazelles usually rely on their speed to escape from such predators as lions, cheetahs, and hyenas. But African impalas and springbok have an even quicker form of evasive action; it is called pronking. The animal arches its back and leaps repeatedly 10 feet straight up in the air. The repeated jumps can disconcert a predator about to spring, giving its intended target an opportunity to bound away.

BATTLESHIP ON LEGS Some species of millipedes have developed a deadly form of chemical warfare to protect themselves against predators: they release clouds of lethal hydrogen cyanide gas through minute vents like gunports along the sides of their bodies.

Laboratory study of the millipedes, which are slow-moving and feed only on plants, shows that they are capable of controlling the broadside so that the gas spurts only from the vents nearest an attacker. At least one African species, *Apheloria corrugata,* can also fire broadsides from both sides at once—if it is handled, say, or attacked by an army of ants. Then it crawls ponderously away, leaving behind a cloud of the poisonous gas.

MASTERS OF DISGUISE *The shape of an insect's body has sometimes adapted to its need to hide. This Costa Rican bush cricket has even developed a two-tone color scheme, so that it resembles a decaying leaf. Similarly, stick insects resemble twigs, and some South American moths look, at rest, just like bird droppings.*

THE EYES HAVE IT *The North American owl butterfly,* Taenaris phorcas, *frightens attackers away by exposing a pair of startling eyes on its wings. The owllike false eyes even include a glint of light to complete the illusion.*

WARNING SIGNS *Poisonous animals—like the South American arrow-poison frog pictured on the left—often have brightly colored bodies to remind predators to keep clear. Indians skewer and roast such frogs to obtain a liquid poison that, delivered on an arrowhead, will paralyze and kill monkeys and birds almost instantly.*

297

Animal behavior

EYE OF THE SQUID The eyes of squids and octopuses (cephalopods) are similar to human eyes, and in some ways superior. A cross section of an octopus eye reveals a cornea, lens, iris, and retina, just as in a human eye. But cephalopods can distinguish polarized light, and they have no blind spot because the optic nerve linking eye and brain starts behind the retina rather than directly on it, as in the human eye. In addition, the eyes of some cephalopods have twice as many light-sensitive cells as human eyes in the retinal area, where vision is sharpest. This may mean that, given equal brightness, some squids and octopuses can perceive finer detail than humans can. In the murky depths of the sea an ability to see clearly in dim light could give a valuable advantage to the cephalopods.

HEAT-SEEKING SNAKES Pit vipers, the family of snakes that includes the North American rattlesnake, can "see" infrared radiation. This heat radiation, invisible to human eyes, is given off by living creatures. Two pits—which give the family its name—lie between the eye and nostril on either side of the snake's head. Each pit contains a thousand or more heat-sensitive cells that enable the snake to tell the direction and distance of an animal several yards away, even in complete darkness. Pythons have a similar detection mechanism in pits around their lips.

THE NOSE KNOWS Although most dogs have poor eyesight, they have a superb sense of smell. Dachshunds have about 125 million smell-sensitive cells in their noses, compared with a human's meager 5 million. A German shepherd dog has 220 million smell cells, which makes its nose about a million times more sensitive than a human being's. A bloodhound's sense of smell is on a par with a German shepherd's.

Experiments carried out in 1885 by British biologist George Romanes showed that a skilled tracker dog failed only when it came to the scent of identical twins. The dog could distinguish the twins' scent from all others. But it could not distinguish their individual scents from one another.

Dogs also have superb hearing. They can detect high-pitched sound frequencies of up to 40,000 vibrations a second, as against 20,000 vibrations per second heard by human ears.

Some insects can apparently see light through their skins. Experiments with the caterpillars of moths and butterflies show that even with their eyes covered, they are still sensitive to light.

COLOR VISION Contrary to popular belief, all animals are not color-blind. Dogs, horses, and sheep can distinguish some colors—though not as well as humans can—while the primates, especially chimpanzees and rhesus monkeys, have color vision equal to that of humans.

On the other hand, experiments seem to show that it is the movement of the matador's cape, not its red color, that excites a bull in the ring. But a

SIGHT LINES

Many creatures see the world very differently from the way humans do, because their eyes have adapted to suit their particular way of life.

Buzzard Soaring birds of prey, such as hawks and buzzards, need especially keen eyesight to pick out small animals on the ground. In the fovea, the most sensitive part of the eye's retina, a buzzard has about 1 million light-sensitive cells per square millimeter—five times as many as a human. As a result, the images it sees are much sharper.

Cat Although a cat has poorly developed color vision—seeing the world largely in black, white, and gray—it can see far better in the dark, thanks to a crystalline layer in the retina that enables it to absorb 50 percent more light than human eyes. By day the cat's irises contract into slits to keep out excessive light.

Bee Sensitivity to ultraviolet light, which is invisible to humans, enables bees to spot special honey-guide markings on many flower petals. Such markings point the way to nectar and pollen. The same sensitivity allows bees to "see" the sun, even on a cloudy day, so that they can find their way back to the hive.

Spider Most spiders have 8 simple eyes, known as ocelli, arranged on the head so that they can see in all directions at once. In species such as the jumping spider, which stalks its prey rather than simply waiting for it, two of the eyes at the front are better developed than the rest, allowing the spider to gauge distances accurately for its final pounce.

Sandpiper Many foraging birds, such as chickens and shorebirds, have eyes set on the sides of their heads, so that each eye sees a different scene. The resulting wide field of vision allows them to spot danger from almost any direction, but limits their ability to judge distances. Shorebirds such as sandpipers compensate for this lack of stereoscopic vision by bobbing their heads up and down and sideways to view an object from several angles against its background.

Butterfly Like other adult insects, butterflies have compound eyes made up of numerous separate eyes—up to 28,000 in a dragonfly but as few as 9 in some ant species. Each mini-eye is equipped with its own minute lens, so that insects see objects as a mosaic of overlapping points of light, rather like a badly tuned television picture. Compound eyes are unable to focus sharply, but they are good at spotting movement.

HOW THE BEE SEES *The flowers of the fleabane,* Pulicaria dysenterica, *appear yellow (left) to human eyes, but blue (right) to bees, whose eyes are sensitive to ultraviolet light. Many flowers have special ultraviolet markings that act like beacons, pointing the way to nectar and pollen.*

relative of fighting bulls, an Indian buffalo called the zebu, has been found to have some color vision, so the proverb "like a red rag to a bull" may not be entirely meaningless.

SILENT AS DEATH Some owls, such as the barn owl, can catch their prey even in complete darkness, thanks to their remarkable hearing. Many temperate-zone owls can hear sounds 10 times softer than a human ear can pick up.

The tufts on the top of many owls' heads are not their ears. The ears are on either side of the head just behind the flattened face feathers. In some species—the long-eared owl, for example—the right ear is half again as large as the left and is set higher on the head, an arrangement thought to help the owl to zero in on prey by sound alone. Most victims get little warning of the owl's approach: its wings are fringed with soft feathers that make its flight almost silent.

In the eyes of most creatures the lens focuses light from objects onto a layer of light-sensitive cells called the retina. But Copilia quadrata, a shrimplike creature in the Mediterranean Sea, sees on a different principle. The animal has one lens in the front of its head, but no retina. Behind the lens is a single light-sensitive spot that darts about, building up an image as a system of dots, rather like a cathode ray builds an image on a television screen. The "receiving equipment" where these images are sensed is located in the creature's waist.

BIRD SHADES Seabirds such as gulls, terns, and skuas have built-in sunglasses. The retinas of these birds contain minute droplets of reddish oil that have much the same effect as holding a sheet of red translucent plastic before one's eyes. The droplets' effect is to screen out much of the sun's blue light before it reaches the light-sensitive cells in the retina, and so to cut down the glare from the sea and sky.

FEET MADE FOR TASTING Although taste is usually associated with the mouth, blowflies can detect sugars through their feet. The flies' feet are covered with special sweet-sensitive taste buds that can detect traces of sugar millions of times more efficiently than can the human tongue.

Unlike most birds, which hunt by sight or hearing, the flightless New Zealand kiwi uses its sense of smell to find food. The kiwi has nostrils at the tip of its 6-inch beak, the only bird that does. It uses them to sniff out food at night, plunging its beak into rotten wood or the ground to find worms and grubs.

GYPSY LURE Male gypsy moths are attracted by the scent of female moths as far as 7 miles away. At such a distance there is probably no more than one molecule of scent per cubic yard of air. The males detect the scent through feathery antennae. By comparing the strength of the scent reaching each antenna, they can home in on the source. The female moths have scent-producing glands at the end of their abdomens. Virgin female moths send out a particularly strong smell—so potent, in fact, that males can be attracted to an empty container that once held a virgin female moth.

PRECISION DRILLING The ichneumon fly, *Rhyssa persuasoria*, can hear and smell through its feet. The female runs up and down trees, hunting the sound and scent of wood wasp larvae chewing their way beneath the bark. When the ichneumon fly finds a larva, it drills through the bark into the tree with its 1.5-inch-long ovipositor, or egg-laying duct. Then it lays an egg on top of the tunneling larva, which later serves as food for the fly's offspring.

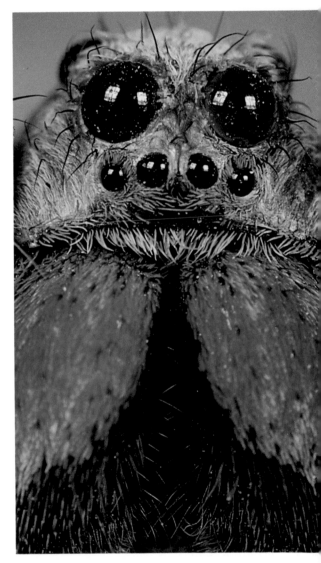

EYES FRONT...AND BACK *The South African wolf spider has a total of eight eyes, allowing it to see in all directions at once. Two of the front eyes—the larger ones here— are better developed than the rest, allowing the spider to judge the range accurately when it pounces on prey.*

Animal behavior

SILENT SERENADE The huge left pincer of the tropical fiddler crab may look terrifying to an enemy—but its only job is to attract a mate; it is not even used for feeding. At breeding time, the brightly colored male crab pumps the giant claw back and forth in a sawing motion similar to that of a violinist.

This silent serenade mesmerizes the less colorful female crab, which has no big claw. She then sidles into the male's burrow to mate.

UNTOUCHING LOVERS In the spring, newts dive into a pond for an aquatic courtship dance in which they mate, often without touching one another. The male, his colors brightened and with a prominent new crest along his back and tail, swims around the female, luring her to the bottom of the pond. There the male deposits his sperm on the pond bed, and the female squats on it to fertilize her eggs.

FAN DANCER The strutting peacock, with its spectacular train, or tail display, is one of the most colorful of courting males. When seeking a mate, the bird, a native of southern India and Sri Lanka, lifts and opens its train to form a fan that often spans 5 feet.

It then calls in a loud, rasping shriek to draw the attention of the demurely plumaged female to its spectacular display of feathers.

REMOTE-CONTROL MATING Two nights of mass courtship make up the breeding season of the palolo worms, little marine bristleworms that live in Pacific coral reefs. Yet the mating takes place without the worms themselves being present. On two nights of the last quarter of the October–November moon, the rear end of each worm, called an epitoke, becomes detached from the body and surges to the surface with millions of other epitokes.

At sunrise the epitokes release sperm and eggs into the sea to unite. The worms themselves remain in their coral homes.

A similar palolo worm native to the Caribbean swarms in the same way during the first and third quarters of the July moon.

The madness of March hares chasing, leaping, and boxing each other in the spring is not as silly as it looks. It is all part of the animals' courtship display; the show-off males are trying to impress the females.

PERFECT TIMING Fireflies flash their lights to one another in precise and split-second codes to attract a mate of the same species. The male black firefly of North America flashes every 5.7 seconds when flying. When he gets within 10 to 15 feet of a female on the ground, she flashes back exactly 2.1 seconds after he does. In another family, the male gives two flashes 1.5 seconds apart, and the female responds 1 second later. Some males flash orange when in flight and green on the ground.

FALLING FOR EACH OTHER There can be no more unusual courtship than the acrobatic, midair love dance of the great gray slug of Western Europe. A pair of these astonishing hermaphrodites will circle each other on a tree branch or a wall for up to 90 minutes, forming as they move a mass of sticky mucus. Suddenly, they launch themselves into space and hang, locked together and suspended by the sticky rope they have made. There they will mate, each fertilizing the other, in a slow process that can take from 7 to 24 hours. Then one slug will climb back up the rope; the other will drop to the ground.

The male mole cricket sends out his mating call in hi-fi stereo through homemade speakers. He burrows out an underground nest with a twin-tunnel entrance. Then he sits underground at the junction of the tunnels and, by rubbing his forewings together, emits a trilling song that is amplified by the tunnel shape and attracts passing females.

ALL TOGETHER, BOYS Contrary to the children's rhyme, the frog rarely does a-wooing go. Instead, the male normally sits down with other males in a stream or pond, blows up his cheeks, and croaks. The sound guides female frogs to the trysting spot. Many frogs call in chorus, and some species even appear to have a chorus master who leads the croaking.

HONEYMOON SUITE The bowerbird of Australia and New Guinea does not call out for a mate. The male lures the female with a distinctive work of art: a bower of love. These hutlike structures are erected in small clearings. Colored with a mixture of plant juices and saliva, they are decorated with flowers or berries, shells or bones, and are sometimes even surrounded with gardens of moss, twigs, and stones.

Each species of bird builds its own model of bower. Some bowers have thousands of twigs and hundreds of decorations. Many take days to build. After mating, most bowerbird species abandon their honeymoon suites. The hens fly off to build new nests in the trees, where they lay their eggs.

The female praying mantis is such a ruthless huntress that she often eats her smaller partner immediately after mating. Sometimes she even begins her meal while they are still copulating.

MASTER WEAVERS Weaverbirds do not learn about nest building from their parents. The knowledge is part of their genetic blueprint. In southern Africa the lesser masked weaver's nest is a complex protective structure of twisted and knotted vegetation, ball shaped and suspended from the end of a branch or a twig. Its construction is something of an architectural phenomenon. The male bird gathers strands of grass, and by threading, pulling, and twisting, knits them into a tough, tightly knotted, enclosed basket that is almost impervious to predators.

To find out how much of this ability was instinctive, a team of scientists reared five generations of the weavers in captivity, denying nesting materials to all but the fifth generation. The results of the experiment were reported in France in 1974. The great-great-grandchildren of the original birds were given the necessary grass and twigs and, despite never having seen a weaver's nest nor having had any contact with any bird that had, they built a perfect home.

THE GENTLEMAN WAS A LADY One of the most unusual of all male-female relationships exists among the brightly colored cleaner wrasse, *Labroides dimidiatus,* of the Great Barrier Reef off the northeast coast of Australia. The pugnacious 4-inch male fish vigorously defends his territory, and a group of up to 16 females, against other male cleaners. But this is not easy, since in addition to patrolling his borders he must keep the females under his control. One of these females usually dominates the others, and the male is particularly aggressive toward her, since she threatens to assume his dominance—and even his gender.

Only hours after his death, in fact, this female begins to take on his former responsibilities. She/he now presides over the harem and assumes characteristic male behavior. Within a month the dominant female actually becomes a fully functional male. In turn, the death of this new male will result in the next dominant female's taking over the male role, and so on.

FLIGHT OF THE CUCKOO The young of the shining bronze cuckoo, abandoned by their parents and with no adult bird to guide them, set out each March on a 4,000-mile migration from their breeding grounds in New Zealand. They accurately follow the path of the parent flock over 1,250 miles of open sea

SONG AND DANCE ROUTINES

Spectacular displays by animals and birds in their springtime courtship rituals are basically identification parades to ensure that each species mates only with its own kind. The songs and dances of the mating season help each to pick the right partner. Most birds and animals go into season as spring's longer days and extra sunshine trigger hormones that start ovulation in the female and sperm production in the male. Alerted by mating calls, males and females then go into recognition rituals that can take days to complete.

Strong elements of aggression are involved. A male may make instinctive threatening gestures when a female, drawn by his call, enters his territory, and he is placated only by a correct defensive response. Many animals cannot mate until they have been stimulated by the correct sequence of call, color, and movement. A female rock dove, for instance, does not ovulate until she has seen her mate's courtship ritual. This inborn behavior makes it probable that the female of the species will not waste her period of fertility by mating with the wrong partner.

LEAPING FOR LOVE *Crested cranes go through an elaborate dance as a prelude to mating. The ritual starts with the birds stretching out their wings and strutting around each other. Often the performance reaches a climax with an ecstatic leap into the air. One species, the sandhill crane of North America, may jump as high as 20 feet.*

FACTS ABOUT ANIMALS & PLANTS

Animal behavior

to Australia, then turn north to Papua New Guinea and the Bismarck Archipelago. One mistake could be fatal: the birds cannot swim.

THE LAWBREAKER Every autumn the tiny, ruby-throated hummingbird seems to defy the laws of physics as it propels its tiny body—a mere 0.1 ounce in weight—on a nonstop 500-mile flight from North America across the Gulf of Mexico to South America.

Metabolic tests suggest that the bird is simply too small to store enough energy for the task. But it does, and it makes the return trip in the spring.

The very small animals that form the plankton in the upper reaches of the ocean waters migrate not horizontally but vertically. They rise near the surface at night, then sink back down into deeper water by day. No reason has been found for the movement.

THE SUN SEEKER The sun-loving Arctic tern makes the longest known migration: from the top of the world to the bottom and back. It lives its whole life where the days are longest, breeding in the almost unbroken daylight of the Arctic summer, then flying south with the sun to feed in the nearly endless day of the Antarctic summer. Its flying round trip covers about 22,000 miles each year.

Flocks from Canada, Greenland, and Iceland migrate, year after year, along set routes down Europe and the African coast or along the Pacific coast of the Americas. They travel fast, too. One tern banded in Northumberland, England, on June 25, 1982, was caught 11,000 miles away in Melbourne, Australia, just 115 days later. It had averaged almost 100 miles of flying a day.

A DATE FOR THE BIRDS Every year the short-tailed shearwaters that breed on islands in the Bass Strait between Australia and Tasmania set out on a 5-month, 20,000-mile tour of Pacific lands, including visits to the coasts of Japan, Alaska, Canada, and Fiji. Unfailingly they arrive back in the Bass Strait in the last few days of September.

They go off at once to feed, returning within a day or two of November 20 to begin breeding. Then, in mid-April, the whole flock, young and old, sets out on its annual trip once more.

Using their own wing power, many species of butterflies can travel up to 600 miles without a refueling stop. Some have even been known to fly right across the Atlantic Ocean from North America to Europe, backed by the driving force of the prevailing westerly winds.

MASS TRANSFORMATION The origin of the swarming brown locusts, which devastate all vegetation in their path, was a mystery for centuries. Then, in 1921, British scientist Sir Boris Uvarov discovered that the pest was nothing more than an altered version of a green grasshopper, common in Africa and Asia.

The insect changes its color and character when population explosions cause overcrowding. The transformed insects then migrate in a swarm to find another home. In 1958 one plague of locusts in Somalia covered 400 square miles.

GIFT FROM GRANNY AND GRANDPA Every autumn monarch butterflies, born in summer in the northern United States and southern Canada, fly off on a 2,000-mile journey into the past. With no guide and no apparent means of finding their way, they go south, precisely to the spot where their ancestors two or more generations back—not their parents—wintered 12 months before.

An inborn migratory instinct is handed down through generations that never make the journey. In summer the monarch lives for about 6 weeks, so three or four generations span the northern warm season. Only the grandchildren or great-grandchil-

dren survive to migrate as the autumn cold closes in. The butterflies' winter quarters range over a wide area, including spots in the southern United States and Mexico. Millions of monarchs crowd into these sites, which are seldom larger than 10 acres. In spring the insects head north again for another summer of breeding.

MUNCHERS ON THE MARCH The voracious army ants of the Americas march in almost perpetual migration. Workers carry eggs, larvae, and food. They are flanked by soldier guards, which also protect the queen. When on the move, the whole army bivouacs at night in a huge ball formed of the ants' bodies, with the queen, eggs, and young in the center. Where food is abundant, they may stay for up to 3 weeks, sending out foragers that pick clean the surroundings—eating up plants, vermin, spiders, even household pets or animals that get in their way. When an area's food is exhausted, the ants send out scouts to find a new site, and the army begins marching again.

DYING FOR A MEAL The panic migrations of the lemmings, small volelike animals of northern Norway, are triggered by a hiccup in the food chain. In years of abundance the female will have up to four litters of eight young in a season, instead of the normal two litters of five. The resultant population explosion turns the food glut into a shortage.

Huge groups of lemmings then dash off in search of food such as roots and grasses. Most die on the journey. Heedless of danger, they plunge over cliffs into rivers, and some of them even dive into the sea in their uncontrolled drive to find food.

WHY ANIMALS MIGRATE

Food and climate are the great driving forces of migration. Swallows and martins breeding under eaves in the European spring must be back in North Africa before the winter frosts, which would kill both them and the insects they feed on. Many whales feed in the rich polar seas and swim to the warmer waters of the tropics to breed. Elk, moose, and caribou wander in huge circles, seeking forage.

For most migrating animals, to stay put would mean to die. But some move without apparent reason: the Arctic tern, for instance. Some scientists have speculated that the migratory patterns of some creatures may have been established as foraging expeditions when the continents were closer together—and that the enormous distances now traveled by salmon and eels, for example, were once far shorter, having grown almost imperceptibly from one generation to the next as the oceans widened.

MIGRATION SECRETS

It is still not certain how most animals, particularly birds, find their way on long migrations. Experiments have shown that many birds use the sun to navigate, making automatic allowances for its movement across the sky. The pecten, a frondlike projection from the retina of a bird's eye, is believed to be the sextant that guides birds through a clear sky. Yet overcast weather does not stop them from reaching their destination.

In 1977 Charles Walcott, a biologist at New York State University, discovered particles of magnetic iron oxide in the skulls of pigeons and other migratory birds. It seems that these particles act as a built-in compass that responds to the earth's magnetic field, enabling the birds to navigate.

But how some first-year birds find their way unaided to ancestral migratory quarters is still a mystery, probably locked up in the genetic code.

MASSED MONARCHS *Huddled for warmth, monarch butterflies cling to a tree after one of their instinct-guided migrations. Millions congregate each winter in a few remote sites—so many that their weight bends tree branches to form a domed blanket, which protects them from frosts that could otherwise be fatal.*

Animal behavior

HUNT AN OTTER, KILL A COW In the mid-18th century, American, Russian, and Canadian hunters on the Pacific coast of North America almost wiped out the sea otter in order to collect the pelts, which fetched prices as high as $1,000 apiece.

Because of the hunting, there was an increase in the number of sea urchins, a staple in the otters' shellfish diet. As a result, urchins destroyed large areas of kelp (seaweed). This in turn devastated the habitat of many animal species—including the Steller's sea cow, a manateelike creature that browsed on kelp. Extensive kelp beds were a matter of survival for this huge mammal, said to have reached 25 feet in length and weighed 9,000 pounds.

A 1911 international treaty to protect the sea otter and efforts to control sea-urchin populations began the regeneration of the sea otter and the kelp beds. But the change came much too late for the Steller's sea cow. Slaughtered to feed otter hunters and its main food ravaged by urchins, the species vanished, its last individual seen in 1770.

THE SUN NEVER SETS ... ON KITTY The 19th-century British biologist Thomas H. Huxley (grandfather of *Brave New World* author Aldous Huxley) once explained, only half in jest, why the British empire owed its power to the love of elderly spinsters for pet cats. His argument resembled one used in all seriousness by Charles Darwin, a founder of the theory of evolution, and it illustrates the complex links between different forms of life. It went like this:

Because spinsters liked cats, they often kept them as pets. The cats kept down the numbers of field mice, thus reducing the mice's raids on the nests of bees, the only insects that pollinate red clover. As a result, red clover grew abundantly in the pastures around farming villages and provided British cattle with a nutritious diet. The plentiful supply of high-quality beef kept British sailors strong and healthy, thus improving the fighting quality of the Royal Navy, which guarded and extended the British empire around the world.

In the spring many algae breed rapidly as a result of warmer temperatures, abundant food, and little competition. This occurs in all parts of the world. But the population increase can be catastrophic if it involves certain dinoflagellates, because these organisms are poisonous to animals. Like some biblical plague, they can turn the water into a blood-colored soup, with as many as 6,000 dinoflagellates in a single drop. Called a red tide, the infested water can kill millions of fish and other animals that swim through it. They die as the poison swamps their bodies' defenses and paralyzes their nervous systems.

A PLAGUE OF RABBITS Homesick settlers in Australia got a small shipment of rabbits from Britain in the mid-19th century, and triggered one of the world's most devastating ecological disasters. Two dozen of the rabbits were released on a livestock farm near Geelong in Victoria in 1859. Within 3 years they had outgrown the ranch, and for the next two decades they spread out across the southern part of the continent, advancing their range at the rate of 70 miles a year. By the end of the century the rabbit population had reached plague proportions. Native shrubs and grasses that had provided lush forage for sheep—then the mainstay of the Australian economy—were destroyed on a huge scale.

Thousands of square miles of pastureland turned into dust bowls, hastening the extinction of other browsing species, such as Australia's jumping mice and rabbit bandicoots. Many of the marsupial species of Australia and Tasmania were wiped out.

Ranchers tried vainly to halt the rabbits' advance. Some tried to set up fences to keep them away. But the waves of rabbits came in such numbers that, as one rancher put it, "the whole ground seemed to move." When the rabbits reached a fence, those behind simply clambered on top of the ones in front, smothering them but creating within minutes a ramp of bodies that enabled the rest to swarm over the fence.

The plague was halted only in 1950 when a rabbit disease called myxomatosis was introduced. And as the rabbits died, the grasses returned.

THE CHAINS OF LIFE

All life on earth is bound together in complex associations between what is eaten and what eats it, between the hunter and the hunted. Scientists call these associations food chains or food webs. All food webs start with plants, the primary food producers, which use the sun's energy to convert chemicals into food. Plants are eaten by primary consumers: plant-eating animals such as cattle. These are eaten in turn by secondary consumers: meat eaters such as lions and people. At each level, waste material, such as dung and dead organisms, is broken down by bacteria and fungi and returned to the soil to be absorbed by plants again.

The extermination of a single species in any food chain can drastically affect all the others. When myxomatosis was introduced into England in 1954 to kill rabbits, for instance, weeds previously eaten by rabbits spread rapidly; and mice and beetle populations dropped sharply because, deprived of rabbits, foxes began to eat more of them.

Food, meat, and energy
At each link in a food chain, most of the energy contained in the food is used to keep the eater alive and active. Only a small proportion is converted to extra meat for the next predator in the chain. Some animals, such as the pig, convert as much as 20 percent of their food to meat, but most convert only about 10 percent. So for a man to gain 2 pounds in body weight, he would need to eat 20 pounds of food such as, say, fish. To gain that much weight, the fish would have to eat 200 pounds of animal plankton, which in turn would need to consume a ton of plant plankton, the primary producers.

The only way to make this process more efficient—and thus to make a given area of the earth support more people—is to shorten the food chain by cutting out some of the intermediate links. If fish, say, ate plant plankton directly, and animal plankton were left out of the food chain, a given quantity of plant plankton could support about 10 times as many fish—and thus 10 times as many people—as at present. Man can eat plant foods himself, but most are very low in vital protein. One exception, however, is soybeans, which are 50 percent protein, making them one of the richest protein sources of any food.

THE ARTS & ENTERTAINMENT

Architecture

BEND OF HUMILITY
Many Gothic cathedrals, including Notre-Dame in Paris, have a slight kink in their main axis so that the nave does not line up exactly with the center of the altar. According to some scholars, medieval cathedral architects built the kink in deliberately as a humble expression of man's imperfections and as a reminder to worshipers that God alone is perfect. Other researchers, however, believe that the kinks may simply be the result of mistakes by builders.

GHOST TRAP
Sarah Winchester, 19th-century heiress of the Winchester Repeating Arms Company, built an enormous house—as a ghost trap. Doors opened onto blank walls, and staircases led nowhere. All were designed to confuse the ghosts that she believed were haunting her. Her obsession began after the death of her husband—the son of the company's founder, Oliver Winchester—in 1881, and of her month-old baby daughter, Annie. Mrs. Winchester visited a spiritualist with the aim of trying to make contact with her lost family and was told that she was being haunted by the ghosts of countless rifle victims.

In 1884 she began to build her mansion in San José, California, constructing a wild profusion of rooms, doors, windows, and staircases in the belief that the ghosts would get lost in the building's maze. By the time she died, in 1922, the house had spread over 6 acres and contained a total of some 160 rooms, 2,000 doors, and 10,000 windows.

PALE REFLECTIONS
To modern eyes, ancient Greek temples derive much of their grandeur from their simple lines, their disciplined elegance, and the white austerity of their stones. But the Greeks saw them differently.

Scholars now know that originally the temples were almost gaudy. Brilliant paints—blues, reds, and yellows—were splashed on many of the stones and turned columns, friezes, roofs, and sculptures into a riot of color. There was nothing restrained about the use of the color. Since the pigments were expensive, their lavish use was simply an ostentatious display of wealth. The temples' present whiteness is the result of time and the bleaching, paint-flaking power of the Mediterranean sun.

BEAUTY AND THE BEAST
The exquisite dome that crowns the Taj Mahal in India owes its shape to one of the most blood-soaked leaders in history. In 1401 Tamerlane, a 14th-century Mongol warlord who was responsible for hundreds of thousands of deaths, set fire to Damascus, Syria, and sacked the Great Mosque. Those inside it at the time, according to a contemporary historian—30,000 women, children, priests, and refugees—were put to death.

Far from wishing to forget this act of carnage, Tamerlane had the unique bulging dome of the mosque copied at Samarkand for his own magnificent tomb, the Gur Amir, parts of which still stand.

From there the style spread northward (where it evolved into the onion shape characteristic of the domes on Russian churches as well as on the palace of the Kremlin) and southward across the Himalayas. It caught on in India after one of Tamerlane's descendants, Baber, overthrew the Sultan of Delhi in 1526 and founded the Mogul Empire. It was one of Baber's dynasty, Shah Jahan, who built the Taj Mahal. The shape of the glittering white dome, completed in 1648, derives directly from the mosque that Shah Jahan's ancestor had looted nearly 250 years before.

REACH FOR THE SKY
On a clear day a visitor to the observation platform at the top of the Empire State Building in New York can see for 80 miles. For more than 40 years the 102-story Empire State was the tallest building in the world at 1,250 feet. It was surpassed in 1972 by the twin-tower World Trade Center, also in New York, which is 1,350 feet tall.

Today the tallest building in the world is the Sears Tower in Chicago built in 1973–74, which has 110 stories and rises 1,454 feet.

Thirty people have leaped to their deaths from the Empire State Building since it opened in 1931. But extraordinarily, at least two would-be suicides have survived. On December 22, 1977, a 26-year-old man named Thomas Helms jumped from the observatory on the 86th floor. But because he did not jump far enough outward from the building, he fell only about 20 feet onto a 3- to 4-foot-wide ledge on the 85th floor. Although Helms was knocked unconscious for half an hour by the fall, he was not seriously hurt.

On December 2, 1979, twenty-nine-year-old Elvita Adams jumped from the same level. She seems to have jumped farther outward, but was saved by a strong gust of wind that blew her onto the same ledge. She escaped with a broken hip.

GOING UP
Modern cities owe their characteristic skyline, bristling with skyscrapers, in great part to the invention of the elevator. In 1854, at the American Institute Fair in New York, Elisha Otis, a mechanic, demonstrated his new invention—a safe elevator. Otis had himself hauled up with some freight. As a stunned crowd watched, the lift rope was cut. Otis and the freight remained motionless—protected by an automatic locking system. Two years later the first passenger elevator was installed in a five-story Broadway china shop.

From then on, tall buildings sprouted where, before, people's reluctance to climb stairs had restricted most buildings to fewer than six stories. Modern elevators, which move fast enough to make passengers' ears pop with the changing air pressure, can reach the top of even the tallest building in less than a minute. The world's fastest passenger elevator is in Tokyo. Installed in a 60-story building in 1978, it operates at speeds of up to 22 m.p.h.

SUPER HANGAR
The most capacious building in the world is the Vehicle Assembly Building at Cape Canaveral, Florida. Built between 1963 and 1965 for the construction of Apollo spacecraft and Saturn V moon rockets, it encloses a volume of 129,482,000 cubic feet. St. Peter's in Rome would fit inside with plenty of room to spare. The steel-frame building is 525 feet high, 716 feet long, and 518 feet wide. The four doors are the largest in the world; each is 456 feet high.

MICHELANGELO'S DOME *The great dome of St. Peter's in Rome, spanning 137 feet, was largely designed by the Italian artist Michelangelo. The base is prevented from splaying outward under the dome's weight by an encircling iron chain. This revolutionary idea, which did away with the need for massive buttressing, was first used by the architect Filippo Brunelleschi (1377–1446) on the dome of Florence Cathedral. According to an old story, Brunelleschi used a trick in winning a competition in 1417 to design the dome. Rather than reveal his plans in advance, he persuaded the judges to decide by asking the competitors to stand an egg on its end on smooth marble. After the others failed, Brunelleschi, in an early example of lateral thinking, neatly smashed one end, then stood the egg upright easily.*

PILLARS OF FOLLY

Sir Christopher Wren (1632–1723), the man who designed the vast dome of St. Paul's Cathedral in London, was once ordered to modify a much smaller roof. In 1689, when Wren designed the interior of Windsor Guildhall, he built a ceiling supported by pillars. But after the city fathers inspected the finished work, they decided that the ceiling would not stay up as it was—and ordered Wren to add more pillars.

Wren did not believe that the ceiling needed any extra support, so he put up four sham pillars that serve no structural purpose at all. They do not even reach the ceiling. The illusion fooled the city fathers, though. The phony pillars still stand—and Wren's 300-year-old ceiling shows no signs of falling down.

307

ARCHITECTURE DOWN THE AGES

Western architecture traces its descent from the major public buildings of ancient Greece. Some earlier structures were built with an eye for proportion and striking decoration, but they had little influence on the evolution of building design.

These two pages show the significant periods of Western architectural development, identify the distinctive features and types of building, and list some major surviving examples, along with the dates they were built. Each period had its own particular building needs, levels of building knowledge and skill, and range of available material and labor. These factors led to styles of architecture, such as Norman, Gothic, or Baroque. But buildings designed in the styles of a particular period can be found in places far from the source of the style. Such buildings are often interpretations or revivals of earlier architectural forms and have been given local names, such as Venetian Gothic.

GREEK (750–30 B.C.)
Main types of building: temples; stoas, or covered colonnades; theaters and amphitheaters. Temples were built in marble and limestone, replacing earlier timber temples but retaining the post-and-lintel construction of the wooden originals. Temples had painted decoration and low-pitched wooden roofs. Columns had ornamental capitals—the top of the column—in one of three designs, known as orders. The simplest, Doric, consisted of columns with plain molded capitals and no base. Ionic capitals were decorated with a pair of scrolls, known as volutes. Corinthian capitals were decorated with an inverted bell-shaped arrangement of acanthus leaves.
Examples Parthenon, Athens (447–432 B.C.); Erectheum, Athens (421–405 B.C.); theater, Epidaurus (350 B.C.).

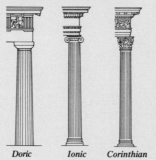
Doric   *Ionic*   *Corinthian*

ROMAN (100 B.C.–A.D. 365)
Wide-scale building program included temples, baths, basilicas, theaters, amphitheaters, bridges, aqueducts, and triumphal arches. Brick, stone, and concrete replaced marble and limestone. Romans developed the arch, and devised two other classical styles for columns, adding to the three used in ancient Greece: the Tuscan order, a plain style derived from the Greek Doric order, and the Composite order, combined Ionic scrolls with Corinthian leaves.
Examples Pont du Gard, Nîmes, France (19 B.C.); Colosseum, Rome (A.D. 70–82); Baths of Caracalla, Rome (A.D. 211–17).

Tuscan   *Composite*

BYZANTINE (330–1453)
Combination of Roman and Eastern influences. Characterized chiefly by the dome. Exterior surfaces were plastered. Interior surfaces were flat but brightly colored and elaborately decorated with marble, mosaic, or frescoes.
Examples San Vitale, Ravenna, Italy (526–47); Hagia Sophia, Istanbul, Turkey (532–37); St. Mark's, Venice, Italy (1063–85).

San Vitale

ROMANESQUE (c. 850–c. 1200)
Roman semicircular vaults and arches were reintroduced in stone to build churches and fortifications. Massive piers and thick walls were used. Ornament was sparse and geometrical. Also known as Norman architecture, from early examples in Normandy.
Examples Tower of London Keep (1086–97); Durham Cathedral nave, England (1093–1130); Worms Cathedral, West Germany (11th and 12th centuries); St.-Sernin Cathedral, Toulouse, France (1080–1120).

Worms Cathedral

GOTHIC (c. 1150–c. 1550)
Pointed arch and ribbed vault replaced semicircular Romanesque forms. Strong vertical lines, most noticeable in churches. Pillars were slenderer. Flying buttresses were used to support walls of high naves on the outside. Windows were large and divided into panels by slim stonework tracery.

In Britain the Gothic period is divided into three stages:
Early English (1189–1307)
Pointed arches, slim lancet windows, simple tracery.
Decorated (1307–77)
Elaborate geometric tracery and carving; S-shaped ogee curve often used in windows and doors.

Early English

Perpendicular (1377–1485)
Characterized by large windows broken into more rectangular, round-topped panels.
Examples Notre-Dame, Paris (1163–1250); Lincoln Cathedral, England (1192–1235); Rheims Cathedral, France (1211–90); Doge's Palace, Venice (1309–1424); Milan Cathedral, Italy (c. 1386–1485); Westminster Hall, London (1397–99); King's College Chapel, Cambridge, England (1446–1515).

Decorated

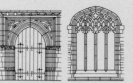
Perpendicular

RENAISSANCE (c. 1420–c. 1900)
Revival and adaptation of Greek and Roman designs. Gothic vaulting and spires were replaced by domes, columns, and pilasters (rectangular columns usually embedded in a wall).
Examples St. Peter's, Rome (1506–1626); Château de Chambord, Blois, France (1519–47); Escorial, Madrid (1563–84); Longleat House, England (1567–80).

Window (left) and column detail (above) on the Château de Chambord.

BAROQUE (c. 1600 – c. 1780) Buildings designed with flowing curves and extravagantly decorated with plasterwork, sculptures, gilt, paint, and marble. Style known as rococo is similar to baroque but generally lighter and less formal; rococo decoration often includes a shell motif.
Examples Versailles, France (1661 – 1756); St. Paul's Cathedral, London (1675 – 1710); Vierzehnheiligen Church, Bavaria, West Germany (1744 – 72).

A shell motif tops a detail from a rococo panel at Versailles.

St. Paul's Cathedral

PERIOD OF REVIVALS
Neoclassical (c. 1775 – c. 1900) Revival of Greek and Roman styles of architecture. Generally solid and severe, with restrained decoration. In England this period includes Georgian architecture.
Examples Petit Trianon, Versailles, France (1762 – 68); U.S. Capitol, Washington (1793 – 1867); British Museum, London (1823 – 47); St. George's Hall, Liverpool, England (1840 – 54); Houses of Parliament, Melbourne, Australia (1856 – 80).

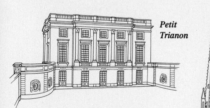

Petit Trianon

Neo-Gothic (c. 1775 – c. 1900)
Revival of Gothic style of architecture. Used particularly in churches and public buildings.
Examples Houses of Parliament, London (1836 – 68); Trinity Church, New York City (1839 – 46); Dominion Parliament buildings, Ottawa, Canada (1861 – 67); Royal Courts of Justice, London (1871 – 82); Town Hall, Manchester, England (1869 – 77).

Trinity Church

INDUSTRIAL REVOLUTION (c. 1850 – c. 1914)
Multistory factories and huge glass-covered areas, such as markets, railroad stations, and greenhouses. Progressive use of wrought iron, cast iron, steel, and reinforced concrete.
Examples Palm House, Kew Gardens, London (1845 – 47); St. Pancras Station, London (1863 – 67); Carson, Pirie, Scott & Co. Building, Chicago (1899 – 1904).

Palm House, Kew Gardens

ART NOUVEAU (c. 1875 – c. 1914) Slender proportions and long, undulating lines. Designs often asymmetrical. Decorative shapes and ornamental motifs derived from natural forms, such as flowers, flames, and waves, and from geometric patterns.
Examples Sagrada Familia Cathedral, Barcelona, Spain (begun 1882); Samaritaine Store, Paris (1905); School of Art, Glasgow, Scotland (1897 – 1909).

Sagrada Familia Cathedral

ART DECO (1920s and 1930s)
Bold geometric style with unfunctional decoration inspired by tribal art and Egyptian motifs. Synthetic materials, such as glass, plastic, and steel, used.
Examples Chrysler Building, New York City (1929 – 32); Broadcasting House, London (1932).

Chrysler Building

MODERN ARCHITECTURE (1918 – present day) Design stems from current needs, site, economics, and new technology rather than from styles of the past. Early modern buildings were usually rectangular, with simple walls and windows. Steel-and-concrete frameworks and cores replaced load-bearing walls, allowing large areas of glass, often in horizontal bands, and open-plan interiors. A developed and refined version of this "international style" makes up much of modern architecture.
Examples Bauhaus Building, Dessau, East Germany (1925 – 28); Daily Express Building, London (1931); Falling water, Bear Run, Pennsylvania (1936); Unité d'Habitation, Marseilles (1946 – 52); Seagram Building, New York City (1956 – 58).

Bauhaus

POSTMODERNISM (c. 1957 – present day) Reaction to the anonymous simplicity of much modern architecture. Use of variety of structural and decorative features intended to give a new richness and personality to buildings while avoiding revivalism.
Examples Piazza d'Italia (which includes a lake in the shape of Italy), New Orleans (1978); TVAM Building, London (1981 – 82); A.T. & T. Building, New York City (1978 – 82).

A.T. & T. Building

Painting and sculpture

MAJOR PAINTING STYLES

Gothic Religious painting with Christian themes that flourished between the 12th and 16th centuries. The stylized figures were usually clad in flowing drapery.

Renaissance Style developed in Europe in the 15th and 16th centuries often with classical Greek and Roman subjects, and known for realistic detail and perspective.

Baroque Extravagant and highly decorative style. It was popular mainly in Catholic European countries from about 1600 to 1780.

Rococo Florid 18th-century style of decoration using light colors, scrollwork, and irregular curves.

Pre-Raphaelite Highly symbolic style adopted by group of mid-19th-century London artists, including Dante Gabriel Rossetti, who were inspired by the brightly colored pictures produced in Italy before the time of the Renaissance artist Raphael (1483–1520).

Romanticism Sensational or sentimental style, often depicting mythological themes. Romanticism reached its peak in France in about 1830.

Impressionism Late-19th-century style used largely by French painters—including Claude Monet, Camille Pissarro, Auguste Renoir, and Edgar Degas—who concentrated on the effects of light and pure color.

Postimpressionism Turn-of-the-century style that aimed to show the spiritual significance of objects. Its main exponents were the Frenchmen Paul Cézanne (1839–1906) and Paul Gauguin (1848–1903).

Expressionism Twentieth-century style of artists—including the Norwegian Edvard Munch (1863–1944)—who expressed their emotional themes through distorted shapes and violent colors.

Fauvism Style of painting featuring distorted shapes, violent colors, and disregard of perspective. The French painter Henri Matisse (1869–1954) was a leader of the school, whose members were known as *les fauves,* meaning "the wild beasts."

Cubism Geometric style invented by the French painter Georges Braque (1882–1963) and the Spaniard Pablo Picasso (1881–1973). It emphasized the mind's perception of an object rather than attempting to reproduce actual appearance.

Abstract Art Nonrepresentational styles of the 20th century. There are two major categories: "pure" abstract art, as in the geometric works of the Dutch painter Piet Mondrian; and highly subjective treatments of recognizable objects, such as the Cubist canvases of Braque and the sculpture of Henry Moore.

Realism Works that show scenes as they really are, and that often have a social or political message.

Surrealism French movement dating from the 1920s that uses dreamlike effects to explore the subconscious mind. Exponents include Salvador Dali (1904–85) and René Magritte (1898–1967).

Action Painting Modern technique of splashing, throwing, and pouring paint on canvas, and allowing it to form its own shapes. It was invented by the U.S. painter Jackson Pollock (1912–56).

Pop Art Style that emerged in the late 1950s and early 1960s. It made use of comic strip cartoons, advertisements, and images of movie stars (for instance, Marilyn Monroe), often enormously enlarged and garishly painted. Its main exponents included David Hockney (1937–), Eduardo Paolozzi (1924–), Andy Warhol (1930–), and Roy Lichtenstein (1923–).

TREASURE OF THE GOLDEN HOUSE

A vast treasure palace that Nero built in the center of Rome after the great fire of A.D. 64 inspired an artistic style 1500 years later in Italy. The palace—called the Golden House, because its facade was reputedly clad in gold—was designed by Nero's court painter, Famulus. But after Nero's fall from power and his suicide in A.D. 68, much of the palace was demolished.

Some buried rooms, however, were rediscovered in the late 15th century, their florid style of decoration—using a combination of human and animal forms, flowers, foliage, and shells—came to be called "grotesque," from the Italian *grotta* ("cave"). The style influenced a number of Italian artists, including Raphael, who were let down into the rubble-strewn apartments by rope. Raphael, like his fellow painters, left his own mark on the Golden House. He scratched his signature on one of the ceilings.

DESTITUTE IN HAARLEM

Despite receiving many well-paid commissions, the Dutch painter Frans Hals was rarely out of financial trouble. When his first wife died in 1615, she was buried in a pauper's grave, and Hals was twice taken to court for failing to support his children. He was also sued for not paying local tradesmen. In 1617 he mar-

PORTRAITS OF THE ARTIST *In almost 100 ruthlessly honest self-portraits, the Dutch painter Rembrandt van Rijn (1606–69) created a pictorial chronicle of his life, from early success to lonely old age. The three portraits here show him at the age of 23 (above), in fancy dress about 5 years later (center), and as a disillusioned man of nearly 60 (right).*

ried an illiterate young woman, Lysbeth Reyniers, who gave birth to a daughter 9 days later. She subsequently had eight more children, and added to her husband's problems by being brought before Dutch magistrates several times for brawling.

In his last years Hals, who died in 1666, was destitute, and the city council of Haarlem gave him a yearly pension and fuel. But the artist spent most of his annual allowance on alcohol and was said to have been drunk every night. Despite his troubles, he created in 1624 one of the world's most famous portraits of cheerfulness, "The Laughing Cavalier."

THE DOME THAT IS NOT THERE

Andrea dal Pozzo's most remarkable artistic achievement—a spectacular but illusory dome—arose from a financial crisis during the building of the Church of St. Ignazio in Rome. The church is dedicated to the founder of the Jesuits, of which Pozzo was a lay brother, and it was meant to have the biggest dome in Rome after that of St. Peter's. The building was complete except for the dome when money ran out, and in 1691 Pozzo, famed for his illusionist work, was called in. A master of perspective, he painted a dome on the flat ceiling of the church. Seen from the church's entrance and nave, the dome appeared to be real, and visitors stopped to admire it.

Pozzo's dome was meant originally to be only a temporary measure until money was raised to build a real dome. But the dome that did not exist became more famous than many that do. Pozzo's illusory dome can still be seen today, together with his fresco the "Triumph of St. Ignazio," which covers the nave.

SEVENTY PICTURES IN SEVENTY DAYS

Although his "Landscape With Rising Sun" fetched $9.9 million at a New York auction in 1985, the 19th-century Dutch painter Vincent van Gogh made little money painting. But this did not affect his prolific output. In 15 months at Arles, in southeast France, from 1888 to 1889, he produced over 200 pictures. And, in a feverish burst of creativity, he painted a picture a day in the last 70 days of his life.

The son of a pastor, Van Gogh was by turns a missionary in a Belgian coal-mining district, a tramp, and then a painter whose genius was not fully recognized until after his death. For almost all his life, he suffered from mental illness—marked by alternating rages, depressions, and periods of incredible creativity—that finally approached insanity. After one particularly violent quarrel with his friend and fellow artist Paul Gauguin, during which he threatened Gauguin with a razor, Van Gogh cut off his own right ear and sent it to a cousin with whom he was in love. In 1889 he became a voluntary inmate of the asylum of St.-Rémy, near Arles. His mental condition seemed to improve, and in May 1890 he went to live under medical supervision near his brother Theo at Auvers-sur-Oise, north of Paris. But in July 1890 Vincent became overwhelmed by depression and shot himself.

Six months later, Theo, who had always financially supported Vincent, died of what his doctor called "overstrain and sorrow." He left behind the 750 letters that Vincent had written to him, which reveal the painter's artistic philosophy and aims and give a vivid account of his mental turmoil.

FAMILY TRAGEDY *In 1634—about the time this portrait was painted—Rembrandt married Saskia van Uylenburgh and set up home with her in Amsterdam. The marriage was a happy one. But three of their children died in infancy, and in 1642, the year Rembrandt painted his masterpiece, "The Night Watch," Saskia died soon after their fourth child was born.*

DOGGED BY DISASTER *After Saskia's death, nothing went right for Rembrandt. A love affair with his son's nurse ended in the courts in 1649. In 1657 he went bankrupt, and his house and furniture were seized. His second common-law wife died in 1663, about 3 years before this last, sad portrait, and his only son, Titus, died in 1668. Rembrandt died a year later.*

SUICIDE BID IN THE JUNGLE

In 1882 Paul Gauguin gave up his prosperous position as a Paris stockbroker to become a full-time professional painter. He broke with his family and spent the rest of his life traveling—first to Brittany, then to Martinique and Panama, and later to Arles, in southeastern France, where he stayed with Vincent van Gogh. Seeking what he called "the natural life," Gauguin made two visits to the South Pacific, and the Polynesians and the islands were the subjects of some of his finest paintings.

But the artist's canvases did not sell, and on New Year's Eve 1897—starving and ill—he went into the jungle in Tahiti and swallowed a large dose of arsenic. The suicide attempt failed. After a short sleep, he agonizingly vomited most of the powder. The next morning he dragged himself back to the coast.

Gauguin remained in the South Seas and was in continual conflict with the civil and religious authorities because of his bohemian ways and his siding with the natives. His last years were dominated by sickness and poverty, and on his death in the Marquesas Islands in 1903 the island's French bishop wrote: "The only noteworthy event here has been the sudden death of a contemptible individual named Gauguin, a reputed artist but an enemy of God and everything that is decent!" In 1980 one of Gauguin's oil paintings, "The Guitar Player," painted in Tahiti in 1892, was sold at Sotheby's in London for £380,000.

GENIUS IN A WHEELCHAIR

In 1912 the French Impressionist painter Pierre Auguste Renoir had to choose between walking again and painting. At the time, he had been crippled by rheumatoid arthritis for 6 years and was confined to a wheelchair in his home in southern France. He consulted an eminent physician, who put him on a special diet to build up his strength. Four weeks later the 71-year-old painter was lifted from his chair and managed to struggle a few painful steps. Then, still standing, he turned to the doctor and said: "I give up. It takes all my willpower, and I would have none of it left for painting. And if I have to choose between walking and painting, I'd much rather paint." He then sat down and never walked again.

But Renoir continued to paint. With a brush tied to his misshapen hands, he produced at least two masterpieces, "The Judgment of Paris" and "The Women With Hats." He even took up sculpture, which he achieved by guiding an assistant's hands over the clay with a stick and telling him what to add and remove. By his death in 1919, Renoir had masterminded two of Europe's best-known and most acclaimed sculptures: his large "Venus" and "Woman Suckling Her Baby."

THE LITTLE CRIPPLE

The Brazilian sculptor and architect Antonio Lisboa went on working after he had lost the use of his arms and hands. After contracting an unknown but crippling disease in his mid-thirties, Lisboa worked with his hammer and chisel strapped to his arms. He was nicknamed Aleüadinho, meaning "Little Cripple," and a granite form of rococo architecture is now called *Aleijadinho* after him. He was born in about 1738 and produced his masterpiece, 12 large stone figures known as "The Prophets," between 1800 and 1805. The statues still stand today in the open air in the Brazilian town of Congonhas do Campo.

STATUE THAT BECAME A GALLOWS

The equestrian statue of the Roman emperor Marcus Aurelius—the largest bronze Roman sculpture in existence—was once used as a gallows. Pope John XIII used it in A.D. 965 to hang a rebellious city prefect by his hair. It is the only Roman bronze equestrian work to survive from more than 20 that were still standing as late as the 4th century. The 16-foot-high statue was mistakenly thought to be of Constantine, the first Roman emperor to be baptized (although only on his deathbed), and because of that belief it was revered throughout the Middle Ages.

In 1347 the tribune Cola di Rienzo, to celebrate a festival, temporarily converted the horse into a fountain, with wine flowing from one nostril and water from the other. In 1539 Michelangelo designed a plinth for the statue in Campidoglio Square in Rome. He is said to have been so impressed by the horse's

DWARF OF THE LEFT BANK Henri de Toulouse-Lautrec, famed for his vivid posters of Paris night life (below and below right) was left permanently stunted after breaking his legs as a child.

THEATRE ROYAL
DES
Galeries Saint-Hubert
SAMEDI 8 JUILLET

aristide BRUANt dans son cabaret

DIVAN JAPONAIS
75 rue des Martyrs

DISSIPATION'S TOLL By the end of the 1890's, Lautrec was a broken man. He died in 1901 at the age of 36-killed by acute alcoholism and syphilis.

PAINTING TERMS: WHAT THEY MEAN

Aquatint Form of etching in which varying degrees of tone are produced by dipping the plate repeatedly into acid; different parts of the plate are covered with varnish before each dipping.

Cartoon Full-size preparatory drawing for a painting.

Chiaroscuro Strong contrasts of light and shade in a painting.

Diptych Two-paneled hinged altarpiece.

Engraving Drawing by means of lines cut on blocks or plates of metal or wood. The lines retain the ink, which is spread over the surface before printing. Paintings are traditionally reproduced in this way. Other engraving methods include drypoint, linocut, woodcut, and etching.

Etching Form of engraving in which a resin-coated copper plate is drawn on with a stylus and then dipped in acid. The acid eats into the metal through the lines in the resin. Thereafter the printing process is the same as in line engraving.

Gouache Opaque watercolor paintings, in which the colors are mixed with a white base.

Impasto Thickly applied oil paint.

Intaglio Carving sunk into the surface of a hard material, such as stone or gem.

Lithograph Picture reproduced from a design marked out with an oily crayon on a flat stone or metal plate. When the design is printed, the stone is dampened. The greasy lines absorb ink, and the wet areas repel it.

Mezzotint Engraving process, popular during the 18th century, in which a metal plate is first scored with a network of dots. The dots are later smoothed out to give a variety of tonal effects.

Mural A painting applied directly to a wall.

Plastic In a painting, conveying a sculptured effect through the modeling and lines of the figures.

Still life Study of an arrangement of inanimate objects, such as fruit or flowers.

Tempera Powdered paint mixed, or "tempered," with egg yolk and thinned with water. It was widely used until the invention of oil paints in the 15th century.

Triptych Three-paneled hinged altarpiece.

---

lifelike beauty that he commanded it to walk. The statue was originally covered with gold. And according to another legend, if the gold ever reappears, the end of the world is at hand, and the Last Judgment will be announced by a voice coming right out of the horse's mouth.

WRONG WAY UP
In 1961 the Museum of Modern Art in New York put on display "Le Bateau" ("The Boat"), a canvas by the French Fauvist painter Henri Matisse (1869–1954). The painting, measuring 56 inches by 44 inches, was hung upside down—and the mistake was not discovered for 47 days.

PARIS'S STATUE OF LIBERTY
The Statue of Liberty—officially called "Liberty Enlightening the World"—which dominates the approaches to New York harbor, is a scaled-up copy of an identical statue that still stands on the banks of the Seine River in Paris. The Paris original, carved by the sculptor Frédéric Auguste Bartholdi (1834–1904), is 9 feet tall. The New York version is constructed of copper sheets over an iron and steel framework, which was engineered by Gustave Eiffel, the builder of the Eiffel Tower. It is 152 feet tall and stands on a granite and concrete pedestal of about the same height, so that the whole statue measures 305 feet from ground level to the tip of the torch flame.

The statue, a gift from France to commemorate the birth of the United States, was officially handed over on Independence Day, July 4, 1884, and reassembled in New York 2 years later. In 1986 a long-overdue refurbishing of the statue was completed, followed by a lavish celebration of the statue's centennial in New York City over the July 4th weekend.

MATCHBOX COLLECTION
The Swiss sculptor Alberto Giacometti (1901–66) was so obsessed with refining the human form to its bare essentials that he often kept chipping away at his sculptures until there was nothing left of them. He worked mainly in France, but between 1942 and 1946 he sought refuge from World War II in neutral Switzerland. When he returned to Paris, he took back with him the entire production of those 4 hardworking years—in six matchboxes. Giacometti's distinctive "thin man" bronze figures gradually became famous, however, and his work is now represented in major collections throughout the world.

ART BEGINS AT 76
Although most critics give the American primitive artist Grandma Moses (1860–1961) low marks esthetically, few fail to be charmed by the enthusiasm for life that permeates her paintings. Born Anna Mary Robertson, she left home at 12 to work as a live-in housemaid until she married Thomas Salmon Moses in 1887. They had 10 children, 5 of whom died in infancy. To supplement their farming income, Anna Moses made potato chips and butter and sold them to neighbors. She did not begin to paint until she was 76, after arthritis had so crippled her hands that she could no longer embroider. Grandma Moses then proceeded to turn out more than 1,000 pictures before her death at the age of 101 in Hoosick Falls, New York, less than 25 miles from her birthplace in Greenwich, New York.

AGAINST HER WISHES
One of the most original and acclaimed American painters, Georgia O'Keeffe (1887–1986) did not give permission to display her work at the show that launched her on the road to fame. The 29-year-old O'Keeffe was working in 1916 as head of the art department at West Texas State Normal College in Canyon, Texas. As a way of keeping in touch with an old friend, a fellow art student and former roommate in New York City, she wrapped up some of her recent drawings and mailed them off, imploring her friend to show them to no one else. The friend promptly showed them to Alfred Stieglitz (1864–1946), a pioneer in photography as a creative art and a highly influential sponsor of modern art. Without asking O'Keeffe, Stieglitz hung her drawings in his next show at his well-known gallery. When word of her friend's perfidy and Stieglitz's presumption reached O'Keeffe, she was incensed at them both.

By 1918, however, Stieglitz's unremitting admiration for her work had cooled her anger, and she came to New York to paint full time. She and Stieglitz were married in 1924. After Stieglitz's death in 1946, O'Keeffe made her home in New Mexico.

SLIM LINE
"Standing Woman," sculpted by Giacometti in 1958–59.

313

Music and drama

COMPOSERS ROYAL

Many of the royal patrons of music have also been performers, and a few wrote music themselves. Among the most notable were Henry VIII of England, who wrote two masses (now lost), and several surviving short pieces, including an arrangement of a song for three voices, *Pastyme with good companye.* He is also reputed to have written the music for *Greensleeves.*

Henry V composed church music under the name of "Roy Henry." Frederick the Great of Prussia was a skilled flutist who wrote numerous flute sonatas and concertos. In the 19th century, Albert, Queen Victoria's prince consort, was an accomplished organist and composer of church music. At Victoria's two jubilees, anthems of his were sung in Westminster Abbey.

RIOT AT THE BALLET

The normally sedate world of classical music and dance became the setting for a full-blown riot at the world premiere of the ballet *The Rite of Spring,* with music by the Russian-born composer Igor Stravinsky. The ballet, organized by the Russian impresario Sergei Diaghilev (1872–1929), was performed on May 29, 1913, to mark the opening of the new Théâtre des Champs-Élysées in Paris.

The protests at the so-called barbarism of the music and the erotic nature of the dancing began in the gallery and quickly spread to all parts of the house. Protests by Stravinsky's supporters followed, and fighting broke out. One critic of the time described the score as "the most dissonant and the most discordant composition yet written." But today the music no longer sounds so controversial and has a secure place in the orchestral repertoire.

EARLY STARTERS

One of the most outstanding musical prodigies was the English composer William Crotch, who at the age of 2 years and 3 months could play the national anthem on a homemade organ. The son of a carpenter, he gave his first public organ recital in his hometown, Norwich, shortly before he was 3. The following year, 1779, he gave daily organ recitals in London.

Crotch was hailed as "the English Mozart," because Mozart was another early starter. Mozart was composing short piano pieces by the age of 6 and was only 12 when he wrote his first opera, *Bastien and Bastienne,* about a pair of pastoral lovers.

Mozart had an astonishing musical memory too. At the age of 14 he heard Gregorio Allegri's *Miserere*—a setting of Psalm 50—performed in the Sistine Chapel in Rome, and after that one hearing wrote down the full score from memory.

HEIGHT OF FASHION *Russian-born designer Léon Bakst (1866–1924) stunned Paris with the sets and costumes he created for Sergei Diaghilev's ballet company in the early 1900s. From left to right are Bakst's costumes for the productions of* La Péri, The Firebird, *and* Le Dieu Bleu. *Of these, only* The Firebird, *with its colorful music by Igor Stravinsky, is still regularly performed today. Though* Le Dieu Bleu *was based on a story by Jean Cocteau, a leading young French writer, it flopped at its first performance in 1912.*

HOW DID MOZART DIE?

On a rainy day in December 1791 Wolfgang Amadeus Mozart—Europe's most renowned composer—was given a pauper's burial in an unmarked mass grave in St. Mark's cemetery, Vienna. Only a few of his close friends attended the ceremony, and today no one knows exactly where his bones lie. Three months earlier Mozart's last opera, *The Magic Flute,* had been a huge success following its Viennese premiere—but he did not live to enjoy the financial rewards.

For some time before he died, Mozart is said to have been tormented by premonitions of death. He declared that his last work—his *Requiem,* which was completed after his death by his former pupil Franz Sussmäyr—had been commissioned by a mysterious man in a black cloak. He regarded this as an omen that he was about to die. Scholars subsequently discovered that the mysterious cloaked figure was, in fact, a messenger from an Austrian nobleman who wanted to commission the *Requiem* secretly in the hope that the work would be taken for his own. There is also an air of mystery over the cause of Mozart's

Title role in La Péri

death. Some say that he died of a high fever; others ascribe his premature death—he was only 35—to a combination of kidney disease and overwork.

However, in 1825 the Italian composer Antonio Salieri—who was a rival of Mozart's in Vienna—stated on his deathbed that he had poisoned Mozart. A mediocre musician, Salieri was jealous of Mozart's genius, but there is no proof that he murdered him. It is thought that his confession was a desperate bid to gain some kind of lasting fame, which he knew that his own compositions would not provide.

DISTANT ADMIRER

In 1877 the Russian composer Peter Ilyich Tchaikovsky received a letter from a wealthy, middle-aged widow with 11 children, Nadezhda von Meck. She wrote to tell him how much she admired his music and offered to pay him a generous annual allowance on one condition: that they never met. She did not want to run the risk of meeting her idol in the flesh and possibly being disillusioned—and this suited Tchaikovsky, who, although married, was ill at ease in female company.

For the next 14 years—until Mme. von Meck became gravely ill with tuberculosis—the couple frequently corresponded but kept their vow not to meet. However, they sometimes attended the same concerts in Moscow, when they would surreptitiously observe each other. On one occasion they came face to face,

and Tchaikovsky politely doffed his hat to his patroness. She turned scarlet with embarrassment and became speechless.

This made Tchaikovsky equally flustered, and they both hurried off in different directions.

DEADLY BEAT

The Italian-born composer Jean Baptiste Lully died as the result of a self-inflicted injury sustained while conducting. In 1687 he was directing a Te Deum (a Latin hymn of thanksgiving to God) in Paris when he accidentally struck himself on his foot with the heavy, long staff that he was beating on the floor to indicate the tempo. An abscess developed, rapidly followed by gangrene, and Lully—director of music at the court of Louis XIV—died of blood poisoning at the age of 54.

The baton—the lightweight stick used by modern conductors to mark tempo—was introduced at a London rehearsal in 1820 by the German conductor and composer Louis Spohr.

THERE AND BACH

In the autumn of 1705 the 20-year-old Johann Sebastian Bach, then the church organist at Arnstadt in central Germany, was given 4 weeks' leave to visit Lübeck to hear the great Danish-born organist and composer Dietrich Buxtehude. Because Bach was short of money, he walked the 220 miles between the two German towns. On arriving at Lübeck he found

*Title-role costume
for* The Firebird

*Costume for a young
rajah in* Le Dieu Bleu

that the 68-year-old Buxtehude was ready to retire. Bach was offered his job as organist—on one condition: he had to marry Buxtehude's 30-year-old daughter. Bach turned it down, just as another young composer, George Handel, had done 2 years earlier. Bach walked back to Arnstadt and arrived 12 weeks late, which earned him a severe reprimand from the church authorities.

MAD ABOUT WAGNER

The music of Richard Wagner so impressed the 18-year-old Ludwig II (1845–86), king of Bavaria from 1864, that he decorated a castle—Neuschwanstein—with huge scenes from the composer's operas. He also put Wagner on his payroll and gave him the money to start the annual Bayreuth Festival, which is still held today. Only Wagner's works are performed at the festival.

Always eccentric, Ludwig became known as Mad Ludwig and ended his days under restraint as a madman. He drowned himself in 1886, three years after Wagner's death.

THE ORPHANS AND THE RED PRIEST

The Pio Ospedale della Pietà in Venice, a music school for orphaned or illegitimate girls, was the workplace in the early 18th century of the priest and master violinist Antonio Vivaldi. In 1723 his contract as music master specified that he had to write two concertos a month, and if he was away he had to send them on to the orphanage at his own expense. Altogether, Vivaldi—known as *Il Prete Rosso* ("the Red Priest"), because of the color of his hair—wrote more than 450 concertos, including the set called *The Four Seasons* for violin and orchestra.

MIXED REVIEWS

The power to arouse both bitter scorn and wild praise has belonged to many avant-garde artists, among them Meredith Monk (1942–). Actor, dancer, singer, choreographer, writer, composer, filmmaker, and producer of multimedia shows starring herself, Monk is known for works like *Juice,* a piece that takes 3 nights to perform, at three different locations, sepa-

THE MEANINGS OF MUSICAL TERMS

Absolute pitch (perfect pitch) Ability to identify from memory a musical sound, note, or key or to sing any given tone without the aid of an instrument or tuning fork.

Adagio Slow tempo; a composition or movement written to be played at this pace. Literally "at ease."

Allegretto Short, lively piece of music played not quite so fast as allegro.

Allegro Lively and fast, literally "merry."

Alto Male form of female contralto voice, now usually applied to boys; an abbreviation for contralto.

Andante Played at a moderate, or "walking," pace or tempo.

Aria Solo song usually part of an opera, oratorio, or cantata.

Baritone Middle-range male voice, between tenor and bass.

Baroque Heavy, ornamental music of the 17th century and first half of the 18th century.

Bass Lowest male singing voice. The lowest note of a chord or the lowest vocal or instrumental part of a composition.

Cadenza Short, brilliant passage at the end of a concerto movement or aria; although usually prepared beforehand by the composer or performer, it is intended to have an air of spontaneity.

Canon Composition in which a voice or instrument is imitated by another (or several others) starting later and overlapping it.

Cantata Extended choral work with or without soloists and generally with orchestral accompaniment.

Castrato Male singer who has been castrated to allow his voice to develop powerfully in the soprano or contralto range.

Chord Combination of two or more notes.

Coloratura Florid, virtuoso singing using runs, trills, and rapid-scale changes. **Coloratura soprano,** female singer with a light voice trained in such a style.

Concerto Work for solo instrument or instruments, with orchestra, usually in three movements.

Contralto Lowest female singing voice.

Crescendo Gradually becoming louder.

Diminuendo Gradually becoming softer.

Etude Study or solo instrumental piece aimed at improving a student's technique. Some composers, notably Chopin, also wrote études for public performance.

Falsetto Artificial form of singing in which males reach notes above the normal range of their voices; sometimes used to imitate women's voices or for comic effect.

Fortissimo Very loud.

Fugue Vocal or instrumental composition in which the instruments or voices enter in close succession and repeat or imitate each other.

Intermezzo Instrumental piece played between the acts or scenes of an opera or other dramatic work; short concert piece, usually for piano.

Larghetto Slow and dignified tempo slightly faster than largo.

Largo Very slow and dignified—literally "broad."

Lento Slow.

Lieder Songs for solo voice and piano. Term is the plural of German *Lied,* meaning "song."

Madrigal Composition for two or more unaccompanied voices.

Mezzo Middle, or medium, neither loud nor soft. **Mezzo piano,** "half soft." **Mezzo forte,** "half loud." **Mezzo soprano,** female voice between soprano and contralto.

Nocturne "Night piece," or melancholic, reflective work for one or more instruments.

Obbligato Obligatory accompaniment played by a specific instrument—as in "song with violin obbligato."

Opera Drama generally sung throughout with orchestral accompaniment. **Grand opera,** very dramatic and emotional large-scale work. **Opera buffa,** comic opera. **Opera seria,** serious opera (including grand opera).

Operetta Light opera with songs interspersed with spoken dialogue.

Opus Work (usually abbreviated as Op.). For instance, *Op. 2* is the second work published by a composer—but not necessarily the second one he has actually written.

rated by weeklong "intermissions." In 1969 Clive Barnes of the *New York Times* found her work "mildly tedious," but by 1971 he attacked her as a "disgrace to the name of dancing." A decade later another *Times* critic, John Rockwell, praised her as "the archetypal multimedia artist," and he marveled at her ability "to emit amazing varieties of sounds rarely heard from a Western throat, full of wordless cries and moans, a lexicon of vocal coloration."

DREAM OF THE DEVIL
The Italian violinist Giuseppe Tartini (1692–1770), threatened with arrest for eloping with a 15-year-old girl, Elisabetta Premazore, sought shelter with the Franciscan friars at Assisi. One night in the monastery Tartini dreamed he had sold his violin to the devil, who in return played a violin sonata of incredible beauty.

Tartini later tried to recapture the sonata he had heard in his dream. The result, "The Devil's Trill" sonata, was, he felt, only a shadow of the dream music. But violinists ever since have felt that the sonata, with its intricate trill in the last of its four movements, deserves its name—if only because it is fiendishly difficult to play.

PIGTAIL PRANK
One day in November 1749 a 17-year-old choirboy in St. Stephen's Cathedral in Vienna took out his scissors and snipped off the pigtail of the boy in front of him. This prank resulted in his instant dismissal from the choir school. In the years of hardship that followed, the former star pupil scraped a living by teaching and by playing the violin in the streets of Vienna.

But the boy's musical genius as a composer gradually asserted itself, and in 1755 he published the first batch of his 84 string quartets. By the end of his long and prolific career (he died in 1809 at the age of 77) he had written 104 symphonies, numerous piano sonatas and chamber works, and two popular oratorios, *The Creation* and *The Seasons*. Had the boy stayed with the choir, he might have had a very different musical career—and the world might not have so much of Joseph Haydn's music to enjoy.

Oratorio Religious musical composition for soloists, chorus, and orchestra.

Overture Orchestral music generally composed as the introduction to an opera, oratorio or play.

Pitch Relative highness or lowness of a note. **Concert pitch,** the pitch to which orchestral instruments are tuned: 440 vibrations per second for the A above middle C. It is also called international pitch.

Pizzicato Notes plucked with the fingers on the strings of a bowed instrument.

Presto Fast.

Prima donna Main female singer in an opera.

Rallentando Slowing down.

Recitative Speechlike singing, frequently used in operas, oratorios, and cantatas.

Rhapsody Romantic, lyrical work, usually in one movement.

Ritornello Recurring passage or section.

Rococo Term used to describe light, decorative music written during the 18th century.

Rondo Composition in which one particular section or passage recurs intermittently.

Rubato Performed at slightly faster or slower tempos than those marked, and so allowing more expressiveness.

Serenade Light music to be played outdoors in the evening; music played or sung by a lover outside his sweetheart's window.

Sinfonia Symphony. **Sinfonia concertante,** term used mainly in the time of Haydn and Mozart for a concerto for two or more instruments.

Sinfonietta Short symphony.

Sonata Work in three or four movements for one or two instruments—such as a violin or cello with major accompaniment by a piano.

Sonatina Short sonata.

Soprano Highest female singing voice; also describes boy singers, who are often called trebles.

Suite Light instrumental piece in several loosely connected movements.

Symphony Large-scale orchestral work, usually in four movements, although some shorter symphonies are in one movement. Passage in vocal work for instruments alone.

Tempo Musical time or speed.

Tenor Highest common male singing voice. **Countertenor,** higher than tenor but using artificial falsetto.

Toccata Keyboard composition that displays the performer's virtuosity, particularly on the organ.

MASTER OF SONG *Franz Schubert, composer of some of the world's finest lieder, accompanies a singer at a musical evening.*

GROWTH OF THE SYMPHONY ORCHESTRA

The average modern symphony orchestra has from 90 to 120 players. But at the beginning of the 18th century orchestras were much smaller—in about 1715, for instance, Handel composed his *Water Music* suite for an orchestra of two oboes, two horns, bassoon, harpsichord, and strings. To do justice to the larger-scale music of the Romantics, such as that of Berlioz, the orchestra had to grow. By the beginning of the 19th century it numbered between 40 and 50 players, and by 1900 it had doubled in size again.

The modern orchestra has balanced sections of strings, brass, woodwind, and percussion. The string section consists of some 30 violins—usually split into groups of 16 and 14—about 12 violas, 10 cellos, and 8 double basses.

The brass section includes eight French horns, three trumpets, three trombones, and a bass tuba. The percussion section has a variety of instruments, including drums, cymbals, triangle, chimes, gongs, tambourines, castanets, rattles, and a xylophone. The woodwind section normally has two clarinets, three oboes, three flutes, two bassoons, and sometimes an English horn, piccolo, and double bassoon. In addition, some works call for a harp or a piano, which are specially provided.

Percussion instruments
All percussion instruments are played by being hit or struck with a beater or the hand.

SNARE DRUM *Wires across the drum's bottom give a rattling effect.*

BASS DRUM *The largest of the drum family, it can be operated by foot.*

Brass instruments
Valves and the player's lips help to control the pitch of the notes.

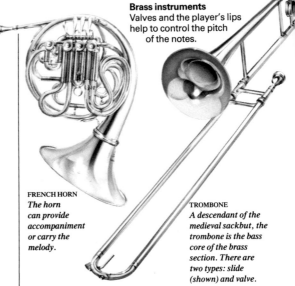

FRENCH HORN
The horn can provide accompaniment or carry the melody.

TROMBONE
A descendant of the medieval sackbut, the trombone is the bass core of the brass section. There are two types: slide (shown) and valve.

FAST WORKERS
George Frideric Handel composed his oratorio *Messiah* in just 24 days, from August 22 to September 14, 1741. He wrote it for a festival in Dublin in aid of various charities, including "poor and distressed prisoners for debt"—and all other performances in his lifetime were in aid of charities of Handel's choice.

Handel's speed of composition was approached by two later composers, not of oratorios but of comic operas: Gioacchino Rossini, who in 1816 wrote *The Barber of Seville* in 19 working days, and his fellow Italian Gaetano Donizetti, who composed *The Elixir of Love* in 1832 in less than a month. Rossini put his speed of composition down to laziness, saying that he could not be bothered to write music for longer.

An even more urgent case of fast work occurred in Prague in 1787, two days before Mozart's opera *Don Giovanni* was to receive its first performance. The manager of the Czech opera house realized to his horror that there was no overture to start the opera, and in desperation he asked the composer what could be done about it. "Don't worry," replied Mozart airily. "I have it all in my head!" He spent the intervening time writing the overture, had it copied as quickly as possible—and the conductor and orchestra received it only 30 minutes before curtain time.

SHORTEST AND LONGEST
The 20th-century French composer Erik Satie probably holds the record for a composition that is the shortest—and the longest—in the world. His piece for piano called *Vexations* lasts for just under a minute. However, Satie states in the score that it should be played 840 times in succession—a nonstop playing time of 14 hours.

SEEN BUT NOT HEARD
Ludwig van Beethoven began to lose his hearing in 1798 when he was only 28, and by 1824—when his Ninth Symphony, the "Choral," received its premiere in Vienna—he was completely deaf. However, this did not stop him from helping the conductor, Michael Umlauf, to direct the work.

Beethoven stood before the orchestra during the performance and indicated the tempo at the beginning of each of the four movements. At the end of the symphony the audience rose and applauded vigorously. Feet were stamped, hands clapped above heads, and there were loud cries of "Bravo!" But Beethoven was unaware of all this. He had to be turned around by one of the soloists to see the ovation he could no longer hear.

SOUNDS OF SILENCE
The quietest piece of music ever written is *4'33"* by the American avant-garde composer John Cage. It is usually performed by a pianist, who sits at his instrument for 4 minutes and 33 seconds, indicating by gestures that the work is in three movements but playing nothing. The score, "composed" in 1952, is blank and can be played on any instrument or group of instruments. The music consists of any sound from inside or outside the hall that the audience can hear.

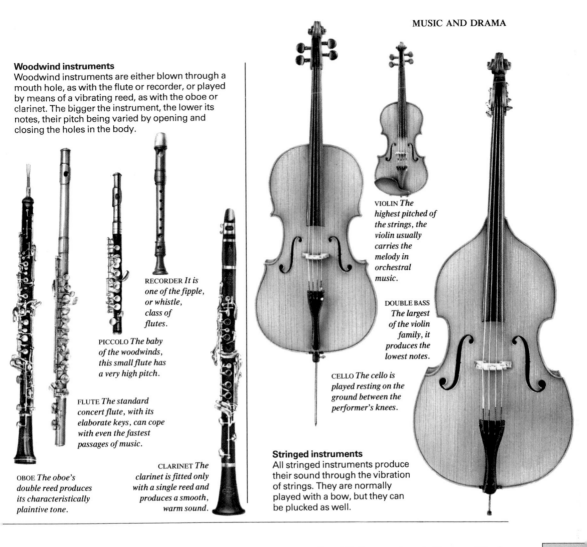

Woodwind instruments

Woodwind instruments are either blown through a mouth hole, as with the flute or recorder, or played by means of a vibrating reed, as with the oboe or clarinet. The bigger the instrument, the lower its notes, their pitch being varied by opening and closing the holes in the body.

RECORDER *It is one of the fipple, or whistle, class of flutes.*

PICCOLO *The baby of the woodwinds, this small flute has a very high pitch.*

FLUTE *The standard concert flute, with its elaborate keys, can cope with even the fastest passages of music.*

CLARINET *The clarinet is fitted only with a single reed and produces a smooth, warm sound.*

OBOE *The oboe's double reed produces its characteristically plaintive tone.*

VIOLIN *The highest pitched of the strings, the violin usually carries the melody in orchestral music.*

DOUBLE BASS *The largest of the violin family, it produces the lowest notes.*

CELLO *The cello is played resting on the ground between the performer's knees.*

Stringed instruments

All stringed instruments produce their sound through the vibration of strings. They are normally played with a bow, but they can be plucked as well.

LOUD AND SOFT

The pianoforte, or piano, gets its name from the Italian words for "soft" and "loud," *piano* and *forte,* words still commonly used in music. It was introduced in 1709 by its inventor, the Florentine harpsichord-maker Bartolomeo di Francesco Cristofori, who described it as a *gravicembalo col piano e forte* ("harpsichord with soft and loud"). Gradations of tone can be produced on a piano, because the strings are struck by felt-covered hammers. The harder the keys are hit, the harder the hammers strike and the louder the notes. A harpsichord, on the other hand, in which the strings are plucked mechanically by plectra, keeps a constant volume of tone.

BAKED IN A PIE

The English nursery rhyme "Sing a Song of Sixpence," which goes on to describe "four and twenty blackbirds baked in a pie," may have described a medieval banquet in France.

In 1454 members of the Order of the Golden Fleece—an order of knighthood founded in France by Philip the Good, duke of Burgundy—held a sumptuous feast at which there was an enormous baked pie. Inside the pie were more than 20 musicians, who emerged to serenade the guests.

FROM RUSSIA, WITH LOVE

Irving Berlin, the songwriter who composed the unofficial national anthem of the United States, *God Bless America,* was born in Russia. Berlin, whose real name was Israel Baline, was born in Tyumen, Siberia, in 1888. When he was 4, he and his family emigrated to the United States and settled in New York City.

KILLED BY A TORTOISE

The Greek dramatist Aeschylus (525–456 B.C.) was once told by a prophet that he would die of "a blow from heaven." The prophet's words came true when, according to a popular story, an eagle dropped a tortoise on the playwright's bald head, mistaking it for a stone, and killed him outright. Aeschylus was buried in an austere tomb at Gela, in Sicily; there was no mention of his dramatic works. The inscription simply stated that he had been a soldier at the Battle of Marathon in 490 B.C., when the Greeks repelled the invading Persians.

Of Aeschylus's 90 plays, only 7 have survived, including *Seven Against Thebes, The Suppliants,* and the trilogy known as the *Oresteia* (458 B.C.), a grim tale of guilt and vengeance. Aeschylus changed the form of Greek drama by adding a second actor to the customary solo actor and chorus—and thus invented dramatic dialogue.

PASSION AND THE PLAYWRIGHT

The world's most prolific playwright was the Spaniard Lope de Vega (1562–1635), who wrote about 1,800 plays and religious dramas (*autos sacramentales*). Of his work, some 426 plays and 42 *autos* have survived. His best-known drama, *Fuenteovejuna,* based on a true story about rape and revenge in a village community, is still staged. After a series of passionate love affairs, de Vega became a priest in 1614, but this did not prevent him from embarking on yet another affair with a married woman. In later life he suffered greatly from guilt, and the walls of his monastic cell were splashed with blood from his weekly self-scourgings.

SUICIDE OF A STOIC

The Roman playwright and philosopher Seneca (c. 4 B.C.–A.D. 65) was as calm about his own death as he had been about life. Seneca spent much of his later career instructing the emperor Nero in the art of politics and in Stoic philosophy, which held that people should control their emotions and calmly accept everything that happened to them as part of the natural order. When Nero came to power in A.D. 54, Seneca was one of his most trusted confidants and

advisers. Eight years later, however, he fell out of favor with the emperor for reasons now unknown and retired from court politics.

In A.D. 65 Seneca was allegedly involved in an unsuccessful conspiracy to assassinate Nero and was commanded by the emperor to kill himself. He accepted the verdict of his former pupil stoically. He had his veins opened and slowly bled to death.

During his time in Rome the Spanish-born dramatist wrote nine tragedies, of which the most sensational was *Thyestes*. In it, a father unknowingly has his children served to him as the main course in a banquet. By 1581 all of Seneca's plays had been translated into English, and their themes of horror and revenge fascinated the early English dramatists. The plays were imitated by, among others, the young William Shakespeare in his play *Titus Andronicus*.

BIRDS IN THE LAND

The English playwright William Shakespeare (1564–1616) is indirectly responsible for the presence of starlings in North America. The species did not exist there until, in the 1890s, a wealthy New Yorker named Eugene Scheifflin (1827–1906) released 100 birds in the city's Central Park as part of a project to bring to the United States all the birds mentioned in Shakespeare's works.

THE DEADLY DUEL

Ben Jonson (1572–1637), a former London bricklayer turned clergyman who became England's first poet laureate, was once jailed for murder. It happened in 1598 when Jonson, who was appearing on the London stage, quarreled with a fellow actor named Gabriel Spencer. In the rapier duel that followed, Spencer was fatally wounded.

Jonson was arrested. He pleaded guilty to a charge of murder, but escaped the gallows by claiming "benefit of clergy"—that is, that as a clergyman he could not be hanged. He did, however, lose all his property and, as a convicted murderer, was branded on his left thumb with a capital *T*, standing for Tyburn, the gallows near London's Hyde Park.

Jonson was jailed again in 1604 for making fun of James I's fellow Scotsmen in a court entertainment that he had helped to write. He and his two coauthors were sentenced to have their ears and noses cut off, but they secured their release unharmed through the help of some powerful friends.

Jonson regained the king's favor when his comic play *Volpone* ("The Fox") was produced in 1606, and in 1616 he was made poet laureate.

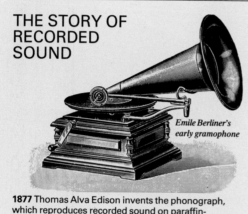

THE STORY OF RECORDED SOUND

Emile Berliner's early gramophone

1877 Thomas Alva Edison invents the phonograph, which reproduces recorded sound on paraffin-soaked strips of paper using a steel stylus.

1878 Edison markets his phonograph, with the paper strips replaced by thin sheets of tinfoil.

1886 Edison develops cylindrical wax records to replace tinfoil.

1888 First flat phonograph record, 7 inches in diameter, introduced in the U.S.A. by Emile Berliner, a German-born immigrant.

1892 Berliner develops the master disc, from which several copies of a record could be made on vulcanized rubber. Before then, singers had to repeat a song for each copy of a recording.

1895 Shellac discs replace those made of rubber.

1925 High-quality sound-recording techniques developed by Joseph P. Maxfield and others at Western Electric Co. The first electrically produced disc is released by the Victor Talking Machine Co.

1948 First plastic, long-playing disc marketed in U.S.A.

1958 First practical stereo records marketed in Britain and U.S.A.

1971 Quadraphonic sound, with four separate sound signals, introduced in Britain and the U.S.A.

1981 First videodisc, combining pictures and sound, marketed in the U.S.A.

1983 First compact disc (CD)—4.7 inches across, made of aluminum and largely unaffected by static, scratches, or dust—marketed in Britain and the U.S.A. The disc is played with a special laser stylus, which does not touch the surface.

STOLEN THUNDER

The English playwright and critic John Dennis (1657–1734) may have devised a new means of producing the sound of stage thunder and given a new phrase to the English language. Stage thunder in the early 18th century was created by rolling iron balls around inside large bowls. Dennis was able to generate a more realistic sound by rolling the balls down long wooden troughs instead. He first used the troughs, or "thunder runs," when his play *Appius and Virginia* was produced in London at the Drury Lane Theater in 1709. However, the thunder effects were the production's only success; the play itself closed after only a few nights.

Not long afterward, Dennis visited the Drury Lane to see a production of Shakespeare's *Macbeth*. From his seat at the front of the pit he realized that his thunder runs were being employed. He jumped up, turned to the audience, and shouted: "That is *my* thunder. The villains will play my thunder but not my plays."

Poetry and prose

THE HOMER MYSTERY

The earliest known European poems are the *Iliad* and its sequel, the *Odyssey,* thought to have been compiled around 800 B.C. These Greek epics—the first deals with the Trojan War, the second with the journey home of Odysseus from the war—are widely credited to the authorship of Homer, who is thought by many to have been a blind bard from either Smyrna (in present-day Turkey) or the Aegean island of Chios.

Some scholars, however, assert that the epics are the work of a number of poets over many years, and that the works were memorized and added to by wandering bards long before they were written down. Homer, in other words, may have been the last in a chain of authors. Another theory is that Homer was a woman, an argument advanced by the British authors Samuel Butler and Robert Graves, among others.

EARLY POET OF THE FARM

The first European poet for whom there is indisputable documentary evidence is Hesiod, a Greek farmer who lived in Ascra, on the slopes of Mount Helicon in central Greece, in the 8th century B.C. He wrote *Works and Days,* which, in the course of accusing his brother of stealing most of their inheritance, gives a poetical treatment of the ages of man and an account of a year in the life of a farmer.

VERGIL OVERRULED

The first Roman emperor, Augustus (63 B.C.–A.D. 14), who founded the empire in 27 B.C., became a dedicated patron of the arts, giving financial help to the poet Vergil, among many others. Before Vergil died in 19 B.C., he seriously considered leaving instructions that his epic on the founding of Rome, the *Aeneid,* be destroyed if it remained unfinished at his death. But when Vergil died, Augustus insisted that the finished portion be published—and Vergil's reputation as the most important poet of classical Rome grew from there.

SMITTEN TO CREATE A MASTERPIECE

The Italian poet Dante Alighieri (1265–1321) was inspired to write two of his finest works, *The Divine Comedy* and *The New Life,* by a fair-haired, blue-

C. BRONTE:
not all
sweetness.

BROOKE:
buried
in Greece.

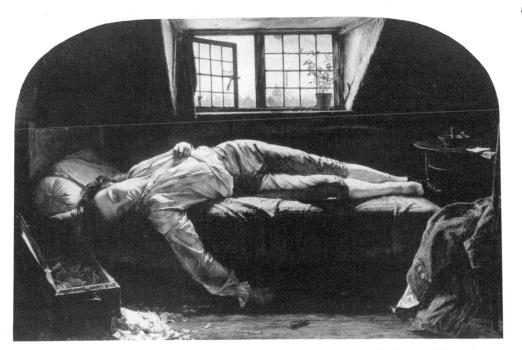

DEATH IN A GARRET *One of the most remarkable literary forgeries of all time—the poems of an imaginary 15th-century monk called Thomas Rowley—was perpetrated by a 16-year-old lawyer's apprentice, Thomas Chatterton. Born in Bristol, England, Chatterton was obsessed with medieval documents even as a child. He created his own antiquated vocabulary and spelling, and sent one of his fabricated poems,* The Ryse of Peyncteynge yn Englande *("The Rise of Painting in England"), to the connoisseur, collector, and historian of art Horace Walpole (1717–97) in London. At first Walpole, whose special interest was English art history, believed the poem to be geniune and praised it highly. Chatterton moved to London and found lodgings in a garret. He hoped to make a living as a journalist and poet in his own right. But his Rowley poems were viciously attacked as frauds by Walpole's old friend, the poet Thomas Gray, and Chatterton soon found himself penniless and starving, without work. On the evening of August 24, 1770, when he was still 17 years old, he proudly refused his landlady's offer of a meal and locked himself in his room. There he drank some arsenic he had acquired and died during the night in agonizing convulsions. His death and the promise shown in his poems later led the poet William Wordsworth—who was 4 months old when Chatterton committed suicide—to write of him as ". . . the marvelous boy / The sleepless soul, that perished in his pride." This highly romantic view of the dead Chatterton, sprawled across his bed as dawn breaks over the hazy dome of St. Paul's Cathedral, was painted by the English artist Henry Wallis in 1855–56.*

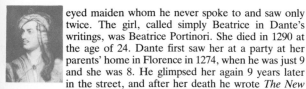

BYRON:
"dangerous to know."

CARROLL:
inspiration on a boat.

CERVANTES:
jailed for debt.

CICERO:
hunted down.

DANTE:
puppy love at nine.

DICKINSON:
poems housebound.

DOSTOEVSKI:
condemned to death.

eyed maiden whom he never spoke to and saw only twice. The girl, called simply Beatrice in Dante's writings, was Beatrice Portinori. She died in 1290 at the age of 24. Dante first saw her at a party at her parents' home in Florence in 1274, when he was just 9 and she was 8. He glimpsed her again 9 years later in the street, and after her death he wrote *The New Life (La Vita Nuova)*, in which he describes his ideal love.

Beatrice also appears in *The Divine Comedy (La Divina Commedia)*, an epic poem in three sections. She is the symbol of faith who guides Dante through the final section, *Paradise*. The first two sections, in which she does not appear, are *The Inferno* and *Purgatory*. *The Divine Comedy* was completed in 1321, the year of Dante's death in Ravenna.

● Probably the most familiar quotation from Dante's *The Divine Comedy* is "Abandon hope, all ye who enter here." But it is an imprecise translation. A more correct version of the quotation (part of the inscription above the gates of hell described in *The Inferno*) is "Abandon *all* hope, you who enter."

MURDERER, THIEF, AND POET

The poem that made François Villon famous—his 2,000-line *Le Grand Testament*—is a revealing portrait of the poet as a vagabond, beggar, and thief. Born in Paris in 1431, Villon was a brilliant student but in his teens and twenties got into one drunken brawl after another and eventually killed a priest with his sword. For this he was banished from Paris in 1455, but he received a royal pardon the following year.

Returning to Paris and a life of debauchery, Villon was constantly in and out of prison for theft and fighting. He was sentenced to death after being involved in another street brawl in which someone was killed. However, his friends succeeded in having his sentence reduced to one of 10 years' exile. He left Paris in 1463 and was not heard from again.

Villon—whose poetry gives an unrivaled picture of criminal life in medieval France—may have died of the effects of alcoholism, or he may have been murdered in yet another brawl. But despite his dissipated ways, Villon was capable of such memorable lines as *"Mais où sont les neiges d'antan?"* ("But where are the snows of yesteryear?").

SWEETNESS AND SPITE

Of the ill-fated Brontë children, Charlotte (1816–55), author of *Jane Eyre,* was the longest-lived. She died at 38 from complications of pregnancy. Her brother, Branwell, died at 31; her sister Emily (1818–48), author of *Wuthering Heights,* at 30; a third literary sister, Anne (1820–49), at 29; and two other sisters in their teens. The Brontë family's curse was tuberculosis, then called consumption.

Perhaps because of their early deaths, the Brontës are often viewed through a haze of sentimentality that tends to obscure their strong wills and outspoken views. Charlotte, for one, displayed a flair for acid literary criticism. In dedicating the second edition of *Jane Eyre* to the English novelist William Thackeray (1811–63), she could not resist a vicious swipe at another English writer, Henry Fielding (1707–54): "They say he [Thackeray] is like Fielding. . . . He resembles Fielding as an eagle does a vulture: Fielding could stoop on carrion, but Thackeray never does."

"MAD, BAD, AND DANGEROUS TO KNOW"

"I awoke one morning and found myself famous," wrote Lord Byron shortly after the publication in 1812 of the first two cantos, or sections, of his epic narrative poem *Childe Harold's Pilgrimage.* The poem was a portrait of himself as a melancholy, romantic hero traveling alone through Europe, fleeing from a life of dissipation and idle pleasure.

One of Byron's mistresses, Lady Caroline Lamb, called him "mad, bad, and dangerous to know." Byron spent much of his short life living up to the description—and trying to live it down. His unfinished satirical masterpiece, *Don Juan,* includes long digressions that are Byron's views on society, money, power, poetry, and the state of England.

In 1823 Byron joined the Greek revolutionary committee for the liberation of Greece from the Turks. He arrived at the Greek town of Missolonghi in January 1824 and attempted to resolve quarrels between the Greek patriot leaders. Three months later he caught what was apparently malaria and died in Greece at the age of 36.

FAMILY PROBLEMS

No poet came from a more eccentric family than did Alfred, Lord Tennyson (1809–92), the poet laureate of Victorian Britain. His father, a parson in Lincolnshire, England, terrified the neighborhood and was once barely restrained from murdering his son Frederick with a gun and a knife. Of the parson's 12 children, two were insane, one was a drug addict, one was an alcoholic, one was subject to outbursts of rage almost as bad as the father's, and all had bouts of depression alternating with various forms of religious mania.

Depite this background, Tennyson produced some of the most popular poems of the 19th century. They included *The Charge of the Light Brigade* and *The Idylls of the King,* which was based on the legend of King Arthur. His masterpiece, *In Memoriam,* was written after the death of his fellow poet and close friend Arthur Hallam, who had been engaged to Tennyson's sister Emily.

RESURRECTED LOVE POEMS

One night in February 1862 the London-born poet and painter Dante Gabriel Rossetti returned home to find his wife, Lizzie, dying of an overdose of laudanum, a tincture of opium. She had had consumption for years and had apparently decided to end her life.

Overcome with grief, Rossetti placed the only manuscript of his lyrical poems in Lizzie's coffin. "I have often been working at these poems when she was ill and suffering and I might have been attending her," he told two friends. "And now they shall go!"

He had been married to Lizzie for less than 2 years, but she had long been his model and inspiration. Then, 7 years after her death, Rossetti claimed that her spirit had visited him in the form of a songbird called a chaffinch. She told him to reclaim his poems. On the night of October 4, 1869, Rossetti had Lizzie's remains dug up and retrieved his poems.

Published in 1870, the first edition of the *Poems* sold out in 2 weeks. By the end of the year, six more editions had been printed, bringing Rossetti royalties of more than £800.

BAD FOR EACH OTHER

An explosive friendship between two 19th-century French poets, Paul Verlaine and Arthur Rimbaud, culminated in Verlaine's shooting Rimbaud in 1873 and being jailed for 2 years. The two met in 1871 when the 17-year-old Rimbaud arrived in Paris from the countryside. Verlaine, who was 10 years older than Rimbaud, deserted his wife and traveled with the young poetic genius to England and Belgium. But the pair indulged in fierce, drunken quarrels. After the shooting incident, the wounded Rimbaud completed

FAMOUS PEN NAMES

Many authors have published some or all of their works under a pseudonym, or *nom de plume* (pen name). The pen-name signatures of five of the authors listed here—Charlotte Brontë, Charles Dickens, Samuel Clemens, Charles Dodgson, and Charles Lamb—appear below.

Pen name, *Real name*
Acton Bell, *Anne Brontë (1820–49)*
Currer Bell, *Charlotte Brontë (1816–55)*
Ellis Bell, *Emily Brontë (1818–48)*
Nicholas Blake, *Cecil Day Lewis (1904–72)*
Boz, *Charles Dickens (1812–70)*
Lewis Carroll, *Charles Lutwidge Dodgson (1832–98)*
Elia, *Charles Lamb (1775–1834)*
George Eliot, *Mary Ann Evans (1819–80)*
Maxim Gorky, *Aleksei Peshkov (1868–1936)*
O. Henry, *William Sydney Porter (1862–1910)*
John le Carré, *David Cornwell (1931–)*
George Orwell, *Eric Blair (1903–50)*
Ellery Queen, *Used by the coauthors Frederic Dannay (1905–82) and his cousin Manfred B. Lee (1905–71)*
Saki, *Hector Hugh Munro (1870–1916)*
George Sand, *Amandine Dupin (1804–76)*
Stendhal, *Marie Henri Beyle (1783–1842)*
Mark Twain, *Samuel Langhorne Clemens (1835–1910)*
Voltaire, *François Marie Arouet (1694–1778)*
Mary Westmacott, *Agatha Christie (1890–1975)*

front, but he never reached his destination. He became ill after being bitten by a mosquito, and acute blood poisoning set in. Never a strong person, Brooke died on April 23, 1915, at the age of 27. He was buried in his own "corner of a foreign field," in an olive grove on the Greek island of Skyros.

HIDDEN ASSETS
Only seven of Emily Dickinson's poems were published during her lifetime. Most of the rest—some 1,770 poems and fragments—were found after she died in 1886, in the old family house she shared with her sister, Lavinia, in Amherst, Massachusetts.

FACING THE FIRING SQUAD
The Russian novelist Feodor Dostoevski wrote his best works after facing his own execution. On the morning of December 22, 1849, Dostoevski was one of 20 political prisoners marched out to face a firing squad in Semenovsky Square, St. Petersburg (now Leningrad). The first three condemned men were blindfolded and tied to posts, and the second group of three—which included Dostoevski—was moved forward. The execution squad took aim, but at the last moment an officer rode forward with a white flag and announced that the death sentences had been commuted to imprisonment in Siberia. The reprieve came too late for the well-being of one of the three men bound to the posts: he had gone out of his mind.

Dostoevski (1821–81) had been condemned to death for allegedly plotting against the czar and for setting up a secret printing press for socialist propaganda. The writer served 4 years' hard labor in a camp at Omsk, and after his release wrote about his prison experiences in *The House of the Dead* (1861). Dostoevski's views on the criminal mind are set out in his most famous book, *Crime and Punishment*, published in 1866.

MARK MY WORDS
The writer Mark Twain was born in 1835, the year of Halley's comet. Twain—author of *The Adventures of Tom Sawyer* and *The Adventures of Huckleberry Finn*—remarked that as he had come into the world with the comet, so he would pass from the world with it. Halley's comet returned in May 1910, and Twain died in April of that year at 74.

Twain's real name was Samuel Clemens. He took his pen name from a cry of Mississippi boatmen, with whom he worked for a time as a river pilot. "Mark twain" was the call, from a sailor sounding the shallows, for a depth of 2 fathoms.

FLOWERS ON THE PILLORY
Daniel Defoe, the author of *Robinson Crusoe*, was once put in a London pillory for libeling the church. But instead of being abused and pelted with filth and rotten fruit (which was what normally happened to someone in the pillory), he was protected by his supporters. They formed a guard to shelter him, covered the wooden framework with flowers, and defiantly drank his health. At the same time, copies of a poem hastily written by Defoe, *Hymn to the Pillory*, were sold among the crowd.

Defoe (1660–1731) had been born plain Daniel Foe. But in 1700, in an attempt to improve his image and his debt-ridden finances, he changed it to the more aristocratic-sounding Defoe. The change was of limited value. Despite a prolific literary output, which included the bawdy novel *Moll Flanders*, he died in poverty in cheap lodgings in the East End of London at the age of 71.

JOHNSON:
writing for mother.

PUSHKIN:
shot in a duel.

RIMBAUD:
poet and gunrunner.

his prose poem *Une Saison en Enfer* ("A Season in Hell"), what he called a "spiritual biography," at the age of 19. He then renounced literature and spent the rest of his life traveling the world. He became involved with the slave trade in North Africa and ended up as a gunrunner. At Marseilles in May 1891 Rimbaud had his right leg amputated, because of a tumor, and died later that year.

Verlaine died in 1896 in the lodgings of one of his mistresses in the Latin Quarter of Paris.

FOR EVER ENGLAND
"If I should die, think only this of me/That there's some corner of a foreign field/That is for ever England." These lines from "The Soldier," by the young English poet Rupert Brooke, were written in 1914, the year World War I began in Europe. The following year, as a naval officer, he sailed for the Dardanelles

BIBLICAL BANKRUPTCY

The Gutenberg Bible, the first work to be printed in Europe with movable type, bankrupted its creator, the German printer Johann Gutenberg. To exploit his new type, Gutenberg had joined forces with Johann Fust, a lawyer and goldsmith, from whom he borrowed money. But in 1455, the year in which the Bible appeared, Gutenberg was unable to repay the loan and the partnership was dissolved.

Fust took over the press and its types, and set up a successful business with his son-in-law, Peter Schoeffer, who was also a printer. Gutenberg himself died destitute and forgotten in Mainz in 1468, at the age of about 70. Some 48 copies of his Bible survive from the original printing of about 200. Today a Gutenberg Bible can be worth as much as $1 million.

A NIGHTMARE OF A BOOK

Robert Louis Stevenson (1850–94) threw the first version of his macabre masterpiece, *The Strange Case of Dr. Jekyll and Mr. Hyde,* on the fire and burned it. This followed a quarrel with his American wife, Fanny, who violently disliked the work.

The idea for the novel came to the Scottish writer in a nightmare on a winter's night in 1885. His cries of terror frightened Fanny, who woke her husband, only to be told: "Why did you wake me? I was dreaming a fine bogey tale!"

The next morning Stevenson set to work on the story. He wrote nonstop, in bed at his home in the English seaside resort of Bournemouth, for 3 days and nights. He then read his tale to Fanny and, in the row that followed, destroyed the manuscript. However, Stevenson soon regretted his hasty action and spent a further three days rewriting the 30,000-word book. This time Fanny made no objections, even though the story was virtually the same, and *Dr. Jekyll and Mr. Hyde* was published as a "shilling shocker" in 1886.

WET WONDERLAND

The story of *Alice in Wonderland* was first told by the English writer and mathematician Lewis Carroll (1832–98) to a group of four friends while they rowed up the Thames from Oxford to Godstow for a midsummer picnic. One of the party was 9-year-old Alice Liddell (the model for the fictional Alice), and she and her companions remembered what Carroll called the "golden afternoon" for the rest of their lives. But meteorological records show that the day in question, July 4, 1862, was not particularly golden at all. Far from being a day of cloudless sunshine, the weather for the Oxford area was cool and somewhat wet.

A VERY JAMESIAN FRIENDSHIP

Born to wealth and social prominence in New York City, married to a Boston banker at 23, an expatriate in France for the last 30 years of her life, divorced at 51 from her mentally ill husband, Edith Wharton (1862–1937) might have been a heroine in a novel by Henry James (1843–1916). In fact, James was her literary hero, and they became close friends during the last 12 years of James's life. Superficially the relationship was that of master and pupil, with Wharton often reading aloud to James from her work in progress.

Yet it was not so simple. Wharton chafed under some critics' praise that she was James's cleverest protégé. As for James, he was acutely aware of the irony that Wharton's "Jamesian" stories were surging in popularity while the sales of his own books sagged. In a twist that could have occurred in the fiction of either, James was dismayed to discover, 3 years before his death, that Wharton was secretly trying to raise money for him. However, their friendship survived, and together they collaborated in compiling an anthology whose proceeds aided World War I refugees. It was one of James's last acts before his death in England, his adopted home, in February 1916. Partly to show his support for Britain's entry into World War I, he had become a British subject in 1915.

DUEL IN THE SNOW

The Russian poet Alexander Pushkin (1799–1837) anticipated his own death—in a duel that took place in the snow—in his novel in verse form, *Eugene Onegin,* published in 1831. In the book the shallow and cynical Onegin, tired of social life in St. Petersburg (now Leningrad), visits a country estate, where he rejects the advances of a teenage girl who falls in love with him. Bored and seeking excitement, he challenges a

---

FIGURES OF SPEECH

Alliteration Use of two or more words with the same initial letters: *I sing of brooks, of blossoms, birds, and bowers* (Robert Herrick, *Argument of His Book*).

Antithesis Placing together of sharply contrasting ideas: *They died that we might live.*

Aphorism Terse, witty, pointed statement on a general principle: *Anybody who hates children and dogs can't be all bad* (W. C. Fields).

Bathos Sudden descent into the ridiculous, often for comic effect: *He's a gentleman: look at his boots* (George Bernard Shaw).

Climax Series of statements in rising order of intensity: *I came. I saw. I conquered* (Julius Caesar).

Euphemism Polite or inoffensive way of saying something unpleasant: *Euphemisms such as "slumber room" . . . abound in the funeral business* (Jessica Mitford).

Hyperbole Exaggerated statement used for emphasis: *A horse! A horse! My kingdom for a horse!* (William Shakespeare, *Richard III*).

Innuendo Indirect or subtle implication, usually unpleasant: *I'll be delighted to attend his funeral.*

Irony Saying one thing but meaning the opposite: *For Brutus is an honorable man* (William Shakespeare, *Julius Caesar*).

Litotes An ironical understatement in which an affirmative is expressed by the negative of its opposite: *This is no small problem.*

Metaphor Figure of speech in which something or someone is said to be that which it only resembles: *When it comes to fighting, he is a tiger!*

Oxymoron Figure of speech in which opposites are combined for effect: *His honor rooted in dishonor stood/And faith unfaithful kept him falsely true* (Alfred, Lord Tennyson).

Simile Figure of speech in which one thing is compared to another, usually with the word *like* or *as: When the evening is spread out against the sky/Like a patient etherised upon a table* (T. S. Eliot, *The Love Song of J. Alfred Prufrock*).

Zeugma Using the same word, in different senses, to govern two or more other words: *He took his leave and my umbrella.*

romantic young poet named Lenski (closely modeled on Pushkin) to a duel and kills him. The fictional situation was echoed in Pushkin's own life. In 1831 he married a frivolous 17-year-old, Natalia, who became infatuated with a guards officer, Baron Georges d'Anthes. Beside himself with jealousy, Pushkin insulted the officer and his family—and this led to a pistol duel in January 1837, in which Pushkin was mortally wounded by the baron.

WINGS OF FAME
The literary fame of the Russian-born American writer Vladimir Nabokov (1899–1977) rests on his satirical novel *Lolita,* published in 1955. But Nabokov—a keen butterfly collector—considered his greatest achievement to be the discovery of several species of butterfly, which now bear his name. His own favorite was Nabokov's Pug (*Eupithecia nabokovi*), which he discovered in Utah one night in 1943.

MYSTERY OF THE MOVING WOUND
Dr. Watson, colleague of the fictional Baker Street detective Sherlock Holmes, was given a bullet wound by their creator, the Scottish novelist Sir Arthur Conan Doyle (1859–1930). But Sir Arthur does not seem to have been able to make up his mind where the wound should be.

In the first book about the pair's adventures—*A Study in Scarlet,* published in 1882—Watson has the wound in his shoulder, and it is said to be a result of his military service in India. But in *The Sign of Four,* published eight years later, Watson's wound has mysteriously moved to his leg.

NAILED TO THE ROSTRUM
The verbal brilliance of the Roman orator Cicero (106–43 B.C.) resulted in his head and right hand being cut off and nailed to the public rostrum from which he had made some of his greatest speeches. At the age of 62, Cicero was rash enough to challenge the supremacy of his former friend, the soldier and political leader Mark Antony, who was in control of Rome after the assassination of Julius Caesar.

Cicero attacked Antony in a series of speeches known as the Philippics—a term that derives from the speeches of the Greek orator Demosthenes against Philip of Macedon in the 4th century B.C.

In response, Antony declared Cicero an outlaw, and when the orator tried to escape to Greece, he was captured and killed by a gang of bounty hunters. On Antony's orders, Cicero's head and hand were brought back to Rome and displayed on the rostrum of the Forum—a grisly fate for the head that had thought and spoken against Antony and the hand that had written against him.

LORD JOZEF
The novelist Joseph Conrad (1857–1924), now recognized as a master of English for such books as *Lord Jim* and *Nostromo,* did not speak a word of the language until he was 19 years old. He was born in Poland, and his real name was Teodor Jozef Konrad Walecz Korzeniowksi. He learned English after becoming a mariner aboard British merchant ships in the 1870s and published his first novel, *Almayer's Folly,* in 1895 when he was 38 years old.

FUNERAL COSTS
Dr. Samuel Johnson (1709–84), the creator of the first modern English dictionary, wrote his only novel in order to pay for his sick mother's medical expenses. Mrs. Johnson became ill in January 1759 at the age of 90, and her son—who was short of cash—wrote *Ras-*

selas, Prince of Abyssinia, in just 7 nights. Mrs. Johnson died soon after the book's completion, so the £100 Johnson earned from it went to pay her debts and the cost of her funeral. The 40,000-word novel tells how an innocent young prince leaves his home in the Happy Valley to explore the world.

Rasselas was published in 1759, and 3 years later Dr. Johnson's financial troubles were ended when he was awarded a state pension of £300 a year.

WORDS AND SENTENCES
Some of the world's most enduring literary works—including fiction, autobiography, philosophy, and poetry—were written or begun while their authors were in prison.

● The Spanish novelist and dramatist Miguel de Cervantes (1547–1616) began his comic novel *Don Quixote* (published in 1605) in a Seville prison after he was jailed for debt in 1597.

● The English courtier, explorer, poet, and historian Sir Walter Raleigh (c. 1552–1618) was sentenced to death in 1603 on a trumped-up charge of treason against the new king, James I. He was reprieved, but not pardoned, at the last moment. Imprisoned in the Tower of London, he wrote his *History of the World.* The unfinished work appeared in 1614—while Raleigh was still in prison. He was released on parole in 1616 to lead an expedition to find gold in South America. But he was forced to turn back empty-handed after his men clashed with Spanish troops. On his return to England, Raleigh was arrested again on the earlier treason charge, and executed in 1618.

● The English writer and preacher John Bunyan (1628–88) was jailed in 1675 for his Nonconformist religious teachings. During his 6 months in the Bedford county jail he wrote much of his religious allegory *Pilgrim's Progress,* which was published in two parts in 1678 and 1684.

● The English writer John Cleland (1709–89) was put in Newgate Prison in London for debt in 1749. While in jail, he was offered 20 guineas by a publisher named Drybutter to write a licentious novel. The result was *Fanny Hill, or the Memoirs of a Woman of Pleasure* (1750), and the money Cleland received for it secured his release.

● The French satirist Voltaire (1694–1778) was jailed in 1717 for writing poems that ridiculed France's dissolute regent, the duke of Orleans. During his 11 months in the Bastille, in Paris, Voltaire started work on his epic poem *La Henriade* (1723), an attack on religious fanaticism and political intrigue.

● The American short story writer O. Henry (1862–1910) served 3 years and 3 months in the federal penitentiary in Columbus, Ohio, for embezzling funds while he had been a teller with the First National Bank. He wrote some of his best stories in his cell, including the collection he published in 1908 under the title *The Gentle Grafter.*

● The British philosopher and mathematician Bertrand Russell (1872–1970) was jailed for 6 months in London during World War I for his pacifist writings. During his confinement he wrote *An Introduction to Mathematical Philosophy* (published in 1919). In the book Russell gave a simplified account of his classic work *Principia Mathematica* (1910–13), which had been written with the British mathematician and philosopher A. E. Whitehead.

● The Nazi dictator Adolf Hitler (1889–1945) started his autobiography, *Mein Kampf* (*My Struggle*), in jail. After the Munich beer hall putsch, an unsuccessful bid to seize power in 1923, he was jailed for 9 months in Landsberg Fortress and there dictated the first part of the autobiography to his disciple Rudolf Hess.

VERLAINE:
shot his friend.

VILLON:
killed a priest.

WHARTON:
befriended her hero.

FACTS ABOUT THE ARTS & ENTERTAINMENT

Newspapers and advertising

COMIC TWIST

The word *cartoon* originally meant a full-size working drawing for a painting or tapestry. But in 1843 the English satirical magazine *Punch* published its own entries for a competition for murals in the newly built Houses of Parliament in London. The magazine's drawings, which caricatured the genuine entries, were labeled "Punch's Cartoons," and so the word came to be used first for pictorial jokes about politics and later for any comic drawing.

THE FIRST ADVERTISING AGENCY

The world's first advertising agency was founded by a British businessman named William Tayler in London in 1786. The first American agency was established in Philadelphia 55 years later by Volney B. Palmer. One of Palmer's more eccentric practices was to demand from newspapers a 25 percent commission for any advertising placed by anyone who was—or had ever been in the past—his client. Astonishingly, it seems that he got it.

FRONT-PAGE NEWS *The* Avisa Relation oder Zeitung *(left) was one of the world's first two newspapers. Both were weekly journals first published in Germany in January 1609, and both folded in the 1620s. Since then, news styles and the speed at which news is flashed around the world have changed radically. The Times *of London, for instance, trumpeted Nelson's victory at Trafalgar on November 7, 1805—two weeks after the battle. But pictures taken on the moon in 1969 by the* Apollo 11 *astronauts Neil Armstrong and Buzz Aldrin were on the front pages of newspapers all over the world within hours of being released.*

FLIGHT OF FACT

Reuter's, now one of the world's biggest news agencies, began in 1850—with pigeons. German bankers needed prompt information on Paris stock-exchange prices, but the French telegraph system went only to the Belgian capital, Brussels, and the German system went from Berlin to Aachen.

Paul Julius Reuter (1816–99), a German bank clerk, organized a pigeon-post service to bridge the gap of 100 miles. His birds beat the fastest mail train, which took up to 9 hours, by 7 hours. In 1851, using new submarine cable between Dover and Calais, he extended his stock prices service to London. He became a British citizen and soon started supplying news as well as prices. Today the network he founded flashes changing stock and commodity prices all over the world electronically within minutes or even seconds of the event.

PARTY LINE

The leading daily newspaper in the Soviet Union, *Pravda,* has a circulation of about 7 million. It is the official organ of the Communist Party, and so has more influence than the Moscow paper *Izvestia* (*"News"*), although *Izvestia*'s circulation is about a million higher. *Pravda* is Russian for "truth."

EAGER READERS

More than 8,000 daily and weekly newspapers are published around the world, about a quarter of them in the United States. But readership levels vary widely in different countries. According to international statistics published in 1983, the country with the most eager readers was Bulgaria. Some 624 copies of its daily newspapers were sold each day for every 1,000 people in the country.

In Britain the daily figure for sales of newspapers was 410 copies per 1,000 people; in Australia it was 336, and in New Zealand 310. The U.S. figure was 282. The countries with the lowest circulation figures—less than 2 copies per 1,000 people—were Benin, Chad, Sudan, and Burkina Faso.

PRIZE JOURNALIST

Joseph Pulitzer (1847–1911), the Hungarian-born American who established the Pulitzer Prizes, originally had a burning ambition to be a soldier. He went to the United States in 1864 only because he had been rejected by the Austrian, French, and British armies, owing to his poor physique and weak eyesight. In America, however, his skill on horseback gained him a place as a cavalryman in the Union Army toward the end of the Civil War. After the war he settled in St.

Louis and became a journalist. In the 1880s he made a fortune with the St. Louis *Post-Dispatch* and the New York *World*. In his will he left $2 million to Columbia University to set up a school of journalism, and part of the money went to establish the Pulitzer Prizes. The prizes have been awarded annually since 1917 to outstanding U.S. journalists, literary writers, and composers. There are 18 categories, each with a $1,000 prize. Pulitzer Prize winners include playwright Tennessee Williams, and Carl Bernstein and Robert Woodward of the *Washington Post* for their reporting on the Watergate scandal.

BIRTH OF THE BAFFLERS
The first newspaper crossword puzzle was published in 1913 in a Sunday supplement to the New York *World*. Compiled by an Englishman, Arthur Wynne, it contained 32 clues, which were mainly simple word definitions. Since then, other types of crossword have been developed, among them the cryptic crossword, in which the solution is hidden in an obliquely worded clue. Three of the more baffling clues, authorship unknown, are:

  1 Gegs (9,4).
  2 (8).
  3 HIJKLMNO (5).

The answers? 1 Scrambled eggs (*gegs* is an anagram). 2 Clueless. 3 Water (H to O: H_2O).

THE TESTIMONIALS BUSINESS
The practice of paying celebrities to endorse products began in the late 1870s when the actress Lillie Langtry allowed her name to be used in soap advertisements. However, not all celebrities were regular users of the products they endorsed, and some never used them at all. Fake testimonials were finally discredited in the 1950s by the film star Grace Kelly, who later became Princess Grace of Monaco. At the time, she was appearing in Lux soap commercials, and the advertisers attributed her delicate complexion to the use of their product. However, when she was asked by a Chicago reporter how any soap could achieve her dewy freshness, she replied briskly: "Soap of any kind, Lux or otherwise, never touches my face."

FACE AND FORTUNE Actress Lillie Langtry, renowned for her beauty and her friendship with Edward VII, endorsed a soap brand in the 1870s—and founded an advertising technique that is still in use.

WHO SPENDS WHAT

A survey of 85 countries carried out by the International Advertising Association and published in 1983 showed that, in 1981, the countries spent a total of 118.4 billion in U.S. dollars on advertising. The United States and Canada spent $64.8 billion, Europe $28.8 billion, Asia $13.2 billion, Latin America $6.9 billion, Australia and New Zealand $2.7 billion, and the Middle East and Africa $1.9 billion.

The survey found the major individual spenders to be the United States, with an advertising budget of $61.3 billion—or 52 percent of the world's total—Japan with $11 billion, Britain with $6 billion, West Germany with $5.5 billion, and France with $4.5 billion. By contrast, poorer countries spent much less. Nepal's total amounted to $1.1 million.

The amount of money spent on advertising per head also varied enormously. The average figure for each person in the countries polled was $43.68. But at one end of the scale, advertisers in the United States spent $266 per person, and at the other, in Nepal, the figure was the equivalent of 7¢.

Expenditure on print advertising far exceeded that spent on other sorts. On average, the countries spent almost twice as much on advertising in newspapers, magazines, catalogs, and handbills as they did on television commercials, and nearly seven times as much as they did on radio ads.

Despite inflation, the proportions spent by each country are likely to be much the same today.

BILL STICKERS *The first known printed advertisement was distributed in Strasbourg, then in Germany, in 1466. By the 1840s, when this London street scene was painted, posters and handbills were almost everywhere. Outdoor advertising remains a relatively cheap and effective device.*

Movies and television

HOW OSCAR GOT HIS NAME

The Academy of Motion Picture Arts and Sciences, which awards the annual Oscars, was born on May 4, 1927. It was then that more than 30 leading figures in the U.S. film industry met to establish a nonprofit organization to improve the artistic quality of the medium. The group included such stars as Mary Pickford and Douglas Fairbanks and art director Cedric Gibbons, who on a tablecloth at a banquet in Hollywood's Biltmore Hotel, sketched the design for a golden statuette. His design became the model for the academy's trophies, and the first were presented in May 1929.

At first the trophy was known simply as the Statuette. It was not until 4 years after the inaugural banquet that Oscar was christened. In 1931 Margaret Herrick, then the academy's librarian, spotted a copy of the statuette on an executive's desk. "Why," she exclaimed, "he looks like my Uncle Oscar!" Her off-the-cuff remark was repeated around the academy—and the name stuck.

MOVIE MILESTONES

● The first practical motion-picture camera was invented by a French scientist, Étienne Jules Marey, in 1882. His device recorded a sequence of pictures around the edge of a sensitized glass disc. When the pictures were looked at in rapid succession, they created the illusion of movement.

The disc meant, however, that only very short sequences could be shown at a time. So in 1887 Marey replaced the discs with rolls of film—2 years before roll film was introduced for still pictures in George Eastman's Kodak camera. In 1893 Marey patented a film projector, enabling his films to be seen on a screen.

● The first commercial showing of a film was in the converted basement of the Grand-Café in Paris on December 28, 1895. The films, of everyday life in the French capital, were made by the brothers Louis and Auguste Lumière. Each reel of film lasted about a minute.

● The first motion pictures in color were shown in a London theater in 1909. But the films showed only two-color pictures, and it was not until 1930 that a full-color film was developed by the American firm Technicolor. The new process was first used in Walt Disney cartoon shorts.

● The first commercial sound-on-film production was *Der Brandstifter ("The Arsonist")*, a German film made in 1922. But talkies did not supersede silent films until after the release and enormous success in 1927 of *The Jazz Singer,* starring Al Jolson.

FLIGHT INTO THE FUTURE

The first film that realistically portrayed space travel—and also featured the first use of the countdown to zero that marks a rocket launch—was *Die Frau Im Mond ("The Woman in the Moon")*, made in Germany in 1928 by director Fritz Lang. One of his technical advisers was an engineer named Hermann Oberth, who in the late 1930s and early 1940s helped to design the "flying bombs," the V-1 and V-2, that brought death and destruction to London. The shape of the rocket in Lang's film so much resembled the German rocket bombs that Nazi dictator Adolf Hitler later demanded that all prints of the film be seized as a threat to military security.

Lang successfully predicted the future of spaceflight by showing his rocket ship as having several stages that fired in succession—just like the Saturn rockets that took man to the moon. And the scene in which the craft is trundled out of a hangar on tracks leading to the launching pad heralded the real-life activities at Cape Canaveral a generation later.

BIRTH OF THE "TALKIES"

The film industry changed from "silents" to "talkies" in the late 1920s, after the success in 1927 of *The Jazz Singer,* starring Al Jolson. Overnight, films without

MOVIE MASTER *The Russian director Sergei Eisenstein (1898 – 1948) was an undisputed master of film. His films include* October *(right),* **Ivan the Terrible** *(lower right), and* **Alexander Nevsky** *(below).*

spoken dialogue were converted into those with speech. And one of the first directors to make the change was Alfred Hitchcock—whose *Blackmail,* in 1929, became the first British talkie. The film had originally been made as a silent, but Hitchcock—who had shrewdly kept most of the sets intact—reshot it entirely with dialogue.

His greatest problem concerned his leading lady, Anny Ondra, a Czech whose fractured English was impossible to understand. Her voice had to be dubbed. Later that year the silent version was released for those theaters not yet converted to sound.

The Times of London was in no doubt about which of the two versions was better. In a leading article on August 14, 1929, the paper declared: "The comparison is much in favor of the silent version." The paper was also in no doubt about the future of films with dialogue. "The talkie is an unsuitable marriage of two dramatic forms," it declared in the same article. "We cannot believe that it will endure."

MOVIE RECORD HOLDERS

● The world's most prolific film industry is no longer in Hollywood but in Bombay, India. In 1979—a boom year for the Indian cinema—714 feature films were produced, each lasting at least an hour. In the same year, Japan produced 335 films, France 234, Turkey 195, the Philippines 170, and the United States 167. Only 38 films were made in Britain.

● The world's most perennially popular author among filmmakers is William Shakespeare. There have been almost 300 film productions of his major plays, including 41 versions of *Hamlet* alone.

● Sherlock Holmes has been portrayed on screen more often than any other fictional character. Sir Arthur Conan Doyle's detective has been played by 62 actors in 177 films. The next most portrayed character is Count Dracula, with 133 film appearances, followed by Frankenstein's monster (91 films), Tarzan (83), Hopalong Cassidy (66) and Zorro (66).

● The longest commercially made talking film seen at one screening is *Lawrence of Arabia.* It was made by the British director David Lean in 1962 and stars Peter O'Toole. It runs for 3 hours 41 minutes—1 minute longer than *Gone With the Wind.*

● The longest film ever made was a British underground movie called *The Longest, Most Meaningless Movie in the World.* In its original version, which was premiered at a Paris theater in October 1970, it ran for 48 hours.

● The world's most expensive film was *War and Peace,* made by the Russian director Sergei Bondarchuk between 1963 and 1967. The 8-hour-long film, which is screened over three to four evenings, is reported to have cost more than $40 million. It was shot on 168 different locations—the biggest total for any film—and included a cast of 120,000 extras from the Red Army.

● The first film to be shown to airline passengers in flight was a silent version of Sir Arthur Conan Doyle's *The Lost World.* It was screened during an Imperial Airways flight from London in April 1925.

● The largest makeup budget for any film was $1 million for the 1968 American production *Planet of the Apes;* the sum took up 17 percent of the film's total production costs. The longest makeup job was the "tattooing" used on Rod Steiger in the 1969 film *The Illustrated Man.* It took nine men about 20 hours to apply the imitation tattoos all over his body.

● The most financially disastrous film ever made was United Artists' *Heaven's Gate,* a western. It cost an estimated $36 million, and on its opening day in New York and Toronto, in November 1980, it did such poor business that it was withdrawn immediately. The film was reedited from 219 minutes to 147, and released throughout North America in April 1981. By the autumn of 1982 it had earned less than 5 percent of its outlay and had caused the downfall of United Artists, which was sold to MGM for $380 million. At one stage during filming, the director, Michael Cimino, insisted that the set of an entire western town be shifted back 3 feet, at a cost of $1 million.

SHOOTING ACCIDENTS

Despite persistent legends about the lethal chariot scene in *Ben Hur,* the only deaths that occurred during either version of the film—made in 1925 and 1959—involved horses, not people.

Three horsemen did die, however, during the shooting of a cavalry charge in the 1941 American film *They Died With Their Boots On.* One of the three, an actor named Bill Mead, was riding beside the film's star, Errol Flynn, when his horse stumbled. As the horse went down, Mead hurled his sword forward in an attempt to avoid falling on it. But the sword stuck in the ground hilt down, and Mead impaled himself on the blade.

THE SECOND JAMES STEWART

The real name of the British actor Stewart Granger (1913–) was James Stewart. He changed it in the mid-1930s to avoid confusion with the Hollywood star James Stewart (1908–). The American's name is his real one.

CINEMA CENSORSHIP

Belgium is the only Western country never to have imposed censorship on films for adults. Denmark, known for its liberal outlook, banished censorship for adult audiences in 1969, followed by Austria and Portugal in the 1970s. Film censorship was abolished in Russia by the short-lived Kerensky government in March 1917. However, the Bolsheviks brought it back in 1922—and under Stalin, Soviet film censorship became the strictest in the world. At the end of World War I, Germany also abolished censorship. But the subsequent torrent of silent sex films brought the return of the censor soon afterward in 1920.

PAID AUDIENCES

The first audiences in Hong Kong had to be paid to watch movies. Chinese people were frightened of the potential evil power of the "moving spirits" on the screen in the first film for Chinese inhabitants, and refused to enter. For 3 weeks in the early days of the

HOLLYWOOD STARS *Groucho, Chico,* and *Harpo Marx (right)* and *King Kong (below).*

silents, the English owner hired audiences by the day, paying them for their attendance until their superstitions were shown to be without foundation. His policy paid off, and by 1913 he had 10 theaters in the colony

TOP DOG

Rin-Tin-Tin, the German shepherd dog who became the world's most popular animal film star, was discovered as a shell-shocked puppy in a German trench in World War I by a U.S. serviceman, Lt. Lee Duncan. He took the dog to Los Angeles with him and trained him for a film career. For several years Rin-Tin-Tin provided his studio, Warner Brothers, with its main source of income, and the dog was duly given top billing above that of his human costars.

At the time of Rin-Tin-Tin's death in 1932, his fan mail was running at about 2,000 letters a week—the same as that of Douglas Fairbanks Sr.

MOUSE WITH A MILLION FANS

Walt Disney's most popular cartoon figure, Mickey Mouse, made his first sound cartoon in November 1928 in *Steamboat Willie*. Disney (1901–66), a former commercial artist, used his own voice for Mickey's high-pitched tones. Within a year Mickey Mouse clubs had sprouted across the United States, and by 1931 they had a million members. In London, Madame Tussaud's immortalized Mickey in wax. In 1933, according to Disney, Mickey received 800,000 fan letters—an average of more than 2,000 a day and a total that still stands as a record for movie fan mail.

"A TOP-HOLE PRESENT"

The first person to be interviewed on television anywhere in the world was the Irish actress Peggy O'Neil. On April 29, 1930, she appeared on a televisor, as the sets were then known, at Britain's Ideal Home Exhibition in Southampton, wearing a Baird Television sweater. "Television is certainly very fascinating," she gushed. "This is the first time I have been interviewed by television. . . . To say the least, it's very wonderful. And what a top-hole present a televisor would make—there's a new idea!"

BOMBED-OUT GERMAN TV

In 1935 Germany became the first country to have a regular television service—named *Fernseh*, meaning "far-seeing." Broadcast from Berlin, the filmed pro-

STARS WHO CHANGED THEIR NAMES

Screen name	Real name
Fred Astaire	Frederick Austerlitz
Theda Bara	Theodosia Goodman
Dirk Bogarde	Derek Jules Gaspard Ulric Niven Van den Bogaerde
Charles Bronson	Charles Buchinsky
Michael Caine	Maurice Micklewhite
Cyd Charisse	Tula Ellice Finklea
Joan Crawford	Lucille Le Sueur
Tony Curtis	Bernard Schwarz
Doris Day	Doris Kappellhoff
Kirk Douglas	Issur Demsky
Judy Garland	Frances Gumm
Cary Grant	Archibald Leach
Laurence Harvey	Larushka Mischa Skikne
Rita Hayworth	Margarita Carmen Cansino
Rock Hudson	Roy Fitzgerald
Boris Karloff	William Pratt
Danny Kaye	David Daniel Kaminsky
Dean Martin	Dino Crocetti
Walter Matthau	Walter Matasschanskayasky
Marilyn Monroe	Norma Jean Baker
Mickey Rooney	Joe Yule
Robert Taylor	Spangler Brough
Rudolph Valentino	Rodolpho Alfonso di Valentina d'Antonguolla
John Wayne	Marion Morrison

grams were shown 3 days a week at a definition of 180 lines, and the German actress Ursula Patzschke became the world's first television announcer.

In 1936 live pictures of the Berlin Olympics were transmitted, but with only partial success. Broadcasting continued until the transmitter was hit during an Allied bombing raid in 1943.

JUNIOR WATCHERS

By the time U.S. children reach the age of 18, it is estimated that, on average, each has watched more than 17,000 hours of television—a record total of 710 continuous days and nights of viewing. In that time each will have seen almost 360,000 commercials and witnessed more than 15,000 screen murders.

CORONATION FEAT *The 1953 coronation of Queen Elizabeth was the first major international TV transmission. It was seen live in France, the Netherlands, and West Germany as well as Britain.*

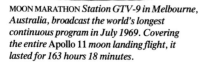

MOON MARATHON *Station GTV-9 in Melbourne, Australia, broadcast the world's longest continuous program in July 1969. Covering the entire Apollo 11 moon landing flight, it lasted for 163 hours 18 minutes.*

HOW TELEVISION WAS INVENTED

1897 The cathode-ray tube—the component that displays television pictures—was invented by the German physicist Ferdinand Braun. But it was a Russian professor, Boris Rosing, who first realized that the bright spot of light the ray threw onto the screen could be made to form a picture. He experimented with this idea in St. Petersburg (now Leningrad) between 1907 and 1911 and managed to produce crude reproductions of simple shapes.

1908 A Scottish electrical engineer named Alan Campbell Swinton put forward the idea of a completely electronic television system. Addressing the Röntgen Society of London in 1911, he proposed that the cathode-ray tube should be used not only as a receiver but also to transmit pictures.

1923 The first electronic camera tube was developed by Vladimir Zworykin, who had studied electrical engineering under Professor Rosing. By the end of 1923 he had produced a cathode-ray tube that could display a crude television picture.

1926 The world's first public demonstration of television was given in January by the Scottish inventor John Logie Baird in his laboratory in London. He had been working on his own largely mechanical system, with electronic amplification, which he called a "televisor"—and his invited audience included members of the prestigious scientific organization the Royal Institution. Overnight Baird became a national figure.

1929 Although Baird had experimented with color television as early as 1928, it was in 1929 that an American team led by a Bell Laboratories engineer, Herbert Ives, demonstrated the first fully engineered color system. It transmitted three separate pictures in red, green, and blue—thereby using three transmission channels—and needed clumsy receivers to combine them into a single image. This drawback was not overcome until the 1950s.

 Baird opened the world's first television studio in London. The crude, jerky pictures were made up of only 30 scanning lines on the screen—and because they contained so little visual information, they could be broadcast from an ordinary radio transmitter.

1931–36 In the United States, Vladimir Zworykin produced the first practical version of his iconoscope electronic camera, and in England a similar tube, the emitron, was developed by a research team at EMI headed by Isaac Shoenberg. The EMI team progressed from mechanical scanning to an entirely electronic system, and in 1935 worked with the Marconi Electrical and Musical Instruments Company—formed by Guglielmo Marconi, the inventor of radio—to produce a high-definition service.

 In November 1936 the BBC started a high-definition service from Alexandra Palace in London. For 3 months both Baird's system and that of Marconi-EMI were used alternately in competition

with each other. Baird had improved the definition of his early 30-line pictures to 240 lines, but he did not have a satisfactory electronic camera, and the programs had to be filmed. In addition, Baird's camera had to be bolted to the floor to damp down vibrations caused by the speed at which the machinery turned—and gallons of water were needed to keep it from overheating. The Marconi-EMI system provided a better picture with 405 lines. The electronic camera was also mobile and silent, and so it was chosen over Baird's mechanical system.

1939 The U.S.A.'s first fully electronic service was started by the National Broadcasting Company.

1950 A meeting of European broadcasters advocated the use of a common picture standard of 625 lines. This was adopted in all but two countries: Britain, which was using its prewar 405-line service, and France, which had already opted for 819 lines. Britain and France did not adopt 625 lines until the 1960s. Today, most nations use the 625-line standard, with the exception of the U.S.A., Japan, and a few others, which have adopted the U.S. 525-line standard.

 The color television camera was perfected in the United States in the early 1950s with two key inventions. By using a coding system, studios were able to broadcast a color TV signal on the same transmission channel as had previously served for black and white. And the Radio Corporation of America's "shadow mask"—a color separation process—enabled a single cathode tube to show a color picture.

1956 The first practical videotape recorder was made in Redwood, California, by the Ampex Corporation. It was originally meant for use by broadcasters so that they could record programs for later transmission without loss of quality. But the machines were large, complex, and expensive—and it took some 15 years before the size and price of videotape recorders had shrunk so that home viewers could tape programs.

1960 Transistors made it possible to construct very small television sets. The Japanese firm of Sony developed the first all-transistor portable television in 1960. The minitelevision had an 8-inch screen. TV screens are measured diagonally.

1962 Until the introduction of satellite communications, there were no intercontinental television links. Then, in 1962, the Telstar satellite began relaying transatlantic programs. The first official program exchange was on July 23, when U.S. transmission began with a baseball game in Chicago. Later that night American viewers saw a special Eurovision program introduced from London by Richard Dimbleby. It opened with a shot of Big Ben. Today, programs can be relayed from almost anywhere in the world via orbiting satellites, and TV companies plan to use satellites to transmit programs directly to viewers—eliminating the need for expensive antennas.

1979 In Japan the Matsushita Electric Industrial Company took out the first patent for a flat-screen pocket television set, with a liquid crystal display as a screen. In 1983 another Japanese company, Sony, introduced a black-and-white cathode-tube model about the size of a paperback book and costing around $300. TV engineers had already developed flat-screen sets no larger than a pocket calculator and capable of producing full-color images.

1980s Commercial network television companies, long the driving force in the U.S. industry, face stiff challenge from subscriber-paid TV programs, as well as from home video cassettes, which are shown on TV sets.

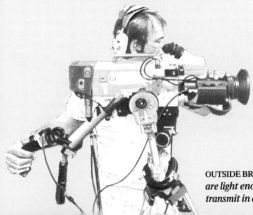

OUTSIDE BROADCAST *Modern TV cameras are light enough to be carried and can transmit in almost any conditions.*

331

BEATEN TO BASE The all-American game of baseball—usually said to have been adapted from an old children's game by a New Yorker, Abner Doubleday, in 1839—had a direct ancestor in England called rounders. A vicar in Kent wrote disparagingly in 1700 about the game being played on Sundays.

The English author Jane Austen refers to "base ball" in her novel *Northanger Abbey*, written in 1798. And the diamond-shaped field and the rule that says that a batter is out if he misses the ball three times are similar to those set out in a boy's book that was published in England in 1829 and reprinted in the United States soon afterward.

DOUBLY GREAT No other baseball player has ever been both so good a hitter and so good a pitcher as George Herman ("Babe") Ruth, who joined the Boston Red Sox as a 19-year-old left-hander in 1914 and twice won 20 games before being sold to the New York Yankees in 1920. His 714 career homers stand second to Henry Aaron's 755, while as a pitcher Ruth won a total of 94 games.

BASEBALL BY THE RULES Whether or not Abner Doubleday invented baseball, a surveyor named Alexander Cartwright seems to have organized the first game played under rules like today's. On June 19, 1846, he set up a game in Hoboken, New Jersey, between the New York Nine and the Knickerbockers. The bases were 90 feet apart, each team had three outs per inning, there were nine men on a team, and Cartwright forbade "soaking"—hitting a runner with the ball as he ran toward first base. After four innings, the Nine led by 23–1. Cartwright pronounced the game over, and the losing Knickerbockers bought everybody dinner.

Today's huge salaries in sports are mainly attributable to income from television networks, who get their money from selling commercial time or billing viewers, or both. Sports telecasts were a direct outgrowth of radio broadcasts, and the first-ever radio coverage of a major league baseball game was by station KDKA of Pittsburgh on August 5, 1921. Fans heard announcer Harold Arlin describe the Pittsburgh Pirates' 8–5 win over the home team Philadelphia Phillies.

As far as is known, neither owners nor players received as much as a penny from the broadcast.

A RECORD EVER YOUNG One baseball record that seems well out of reach is Denton True ("Cy") Young's career total of 511 pitching victories, which he ran up over 22 years (1890–1911) with a total of five teams in the American and National leagues. Well behind Young in second place is Walter Johnson, active from 1907 to 1927, who had 416 victories over 21 years.

Young's record amounts to winning an average of more than 20 games a season for 25 years, or 25 games for 20 years. In fact, the incredibly durable right-hander won more than 30 games in five seasons. He won no fewer than 20 games over 14 consecutive seasons, from 1891 to 1904.

Of pitchers active in 1986 with more than 300 wins, all were nearing the end of their baseball careers, and none was thought to have a good chance of reaching even 350 wins. The pitchers were Steve Carlton, Phil Niekro, Tom Seaver, and Don Sutton.

On the other hand, none of these pitchers was likely to break a less enviable record held by Cy Young: 315 career losses.

HIGH HEROICS Baseball has had its share of hard drinkers and high livers, and not all of them have tried to hide their habits. Ralston Burdett ("Rollie") Hemsley, a catcher who played with seven major league teams over 19 seasons, beginning with the Pittsburgh Pirates in 1928, was said to be seldom sober on or off the field. With the Cleveland Indians from 1938 to mid-1942, he once tried to steal second base and was hit on the head by a ball rifled from the catcher. As Hemsley lay stunned, the Cleveland trainer, Lefty Weisman, ran out to help him off the field. His eyes clearing somewhat, Hemsley recognized Weisman and pushed him away. "Heck, Lefty," he said, "leave me in. I've *started* games when I was dizzier than this."

BASEBALL

WORLD SERIES CHAMPIONS SINCE 1955

Year	Winning team's margin in games	
1955	Brooklyn (N) 4	New York (A) 3
1956	New York (A) 4	Brooklyn (N) 3
1957	Milwaukee (N) 4	New York (A) 3
1958	New York (A) 4	Milwaukee (N) 3
1959	Los Angeles (N) 4	Chicago (A) 2
1960	Pittsburgh (N) 4	New York (A) 3
1961	New York (A) 4	Cincinnati (N) 1
1962	New York (A) 4	San Francisco (N) 3
1963	Los Angeles (N) 4	New York (A) 0
1964	St. Louis (N) 4	New York (A) 3
1965	Los Angeles (N) 4	Minnesota (A) 3
1966	Baltimore (A) 4	Los Angeles (N) 0
1967	St. Louis (N) 4	Boston (A) 3
1968	Detroit (A) 4	St. Louis (N) 3
1969	New York (N) 4	Baltimore (A) 1
1970	Baltimore (A) 4	Cincinnati (N) 1
1971	Pittsburgh (N) 4	Baltimore (A) 3
1972	Oakland (A) 4	Cincinnati (N) 3
1973	Oakland (A) 4	New York (N) 2
1974	Oakland (A) 4	Los Angeles (N) 1
1975	Cincinnati (N) 4	Boston (A) 3
1976	Cincinnati (N) 4	New York (A) 0
1977	New York (A) 4	Los Angeles (N) 2
1978	New York (A) 4	Los Angeles (N) 2
1979	Pittsburgh (N) 4	Baltimore (A) 3
1980	Philadelphia (N) 4	Kansas City (A) 2
1981	Los Angeles (N) 4	New York (A) 2
1982	St. Louis (N) 4	Milwaukee (A) 3
1983	Baltimore (A) 4	Philadelphia (N) 1
1984	Detroit (A) 4	San Diego (N) 1
1985	Kansas City (A) 4	St. Louis (N) 3
1986	New York (N) 4	Boston (A) 3

(A) American League team.

(N) National League team.

The color barrier that had kept major league sports white-only did not fall in baseball until 1947, when Branch Rickey of the Brooklyn Dodgers brought up Jackie Robinson from the minor leagues. Facing down prejudice and hostility with dignity and superb play, Robinson was named Rookie of the Year, and the way was opened for the black athletes who have since enriched professional sports.

THE MAN CALLED IRON HORSE One of the great endurance feats in any sport is Henry Louis Gehrig's playing of 2,130 consecutive games for the New York Yankees. His streak began on June 1, 1925, and the first baseman did not miss a game until May 2, 1939. Just over 2 years later Gehrig died of what has come to be known as Lou Gehrig's disease, a form of neuromuscular paralysis (amyotrophic lateral sclerosis).

FOUR BALLS AND OUT FOREVER The smallest player ever to appear in a major league baseball game was Edward Carl Gaedel, who stood 3 feet 7 inches tall and weighed 65 pounds. He was hired by the legendary baseball impresario Bill Veeck to bring some excitement to the lineup of the hapless St. Louis Browns. In 1951, wearing the number ⅛ on his uniform, Eddie Gaedel strode to the plate to pinch-hit against the Detroit Tigers and was promptly walked on four pitches by the unamused Tiger pitcher, left-hander Robert Max ("Sugar") Cain. Gaedel was then removed from the game for a pinch runner.

The next day, Gaedel's major league career came to an end when the American League barred him. Furious and hurt, the 26-year-old midget was reported to have spent most of that day in a bar, where he was arrested after abusing a policeman.

The same year Bill Veeck briefly brought midget Eddie Gaedel to the St. Louis Browns, he also signed one of the greatest pitchers of all time, Leroy Robert ("Satchel") Paige, in the hope of drawing larger crowds to the Browns' always nearly empty ballpark. Paige admitted to being 45 years old—an age that many said was years younger than his actual age—and though he was still a crafty pitcher, was well past his prime in 1951. Paige had spent his best years, as had so many other great black athletes of his era, in the so-called Negro leagues. The saga of Satchel Paige did not end after his 3 years with the St. Louis Browns. In 1965, at the self-professed age of 59, he pitched 3 shutout innings for the Kansas City Athletics.

FOOTBALL WITH PITCHERS The first team to claim the professional football championship of the United States was the Philadelphia Athletics, managed by Connie Mack (1862–1950). The year was 1902.

Mack's name is indelibly associated with the Philadelphia Athletics baseball team, which he managed for 50 years beginning in 1901, winning nine American League pennants and five world series. But besides being a shrewd judge of baseball talent and tactics, Mack also had an entrepreneurial flair, and in the first years of the century fielded a football team stocked with his star baseball players.

Apparently the idea appealed to other baseball teams too. Mack claimed the 1902 professional football championship on the basis of a 12–6 victory by his football Athletics, starring Rube Waddell, over a Pittsburgh team powered by a fullback named Christy Mathewson, who had been a superb college back at Bucknell.

Both Mathewson and Waddell, outstanding pitchers, were later elected to the baseball Hall of Fame.

TIGER STARTED IT Princeton claims credit for having the first football team widely known by a nickname, the Tiger. Bestowed in about 1887, the name stemmed from the two-tone uniform first sported by Princeton players against Pennsylvania in 1876: knee-length black tights, black stockings, black jerseys with orange stripes, and an orange *P* on the chest.

Sports

THE FIRST FORWARD PASS The earliest description of an officially allowed, completed forward pass appears in an account of the Yale–Princeton game of November 30, 1876. The play involved two Yale men: Walter Camp—then playing his first season, who became famous as a football player and coach at Yale—and O. D. Thompson. Because of his role in organizing football and systematizing its rules, Walter Camp is called the father of American football. He named the first All-American team in 1889.

In the 1876 game Camp, running with the ball, was about to be brought down by Princeton tacklers and threw the ball forward to Thompson, who caught it and galloped toward the goal line. Assuming that the catch would be ruled illegal and the play would be called back, the Princeton players simply let Thompson run. He scored easily.

The Princeton team appealed hotly to the referee to disallow the touchdown, but the official persuaded the teams to let the toss of a coin decide. The coin came down on Yale's side, and Thompson's score stood.

It was later reported that the name of the referee was C. B. Bushnell, a Yale undergraduate.

THE FIRST PRO GAME There is considerable controversy over when and where the first professional U.S. football game was played—where, in other words, athletes were first paid to play a game closely resembling football as it is played today in the United States and Canada. Many authorities cite Latrobe, Pennsylvania, where the Latrobe YMCA team beat a team from nearby Jeanette 12–0, on August 31, 1895.

But West Racine, Wisconsin, also has adherents, who say that the first pro game was played there between the Racine Athletic Association and a squad sponsored by the Chicago Banker's Club. This match is said to have been played in October 1894 and resulted in a scoreless tie. If so, the Racine AA must have felt especially proud because the well-heeled Chicago bankers had recruited some of the era's best college players, already famous for their exploits on Ivy League teams and other powerhouses back east. One of these stars was the lineman William "Pudge" Heffelfinger of Yale, selected for Walter Camp's All-American teams in 1889, 1890, and 1891.

> *In the years since the legendary Walter Camp first made his gambling, desperate toss, the forward pass has come to dominate the offensive play of U.S. football teams, both professional and college. In a 1986 game between the New York Jets and the Miami Dolphins, the teams rushed for a combined total of 182 yards on the ground, but passed for 884 yards, a new National Football League record. In the 51–45 contest, won in overtime by the Jets, 10 touchdowns were made by forward passes.*

UPSET POET One of the great upsets in professional football history was the New York Jets' 16–7 humbling of the Baltimore Colts in the Super Bowl on January 12, 1969. The Colts, who were favored to win

SUPERCOACH *Vince Lombardi, shown here being carried off the field by the victorious Green Bay Packers after the 1968 Super Bowl, brought a stern, evangelical zeal to coaching professional football. His dedication to winning was absolute and won the respect of players and fans. A college player and then coach, Lombardi took over a hapless Green Bay franchise in 1959 and made it a powerhouse, a success story that fueled a tremendous surge in popularity for pro football.*

PROFESSIONAL FOOTBALL

SUPER BOWL WINNERS

The Super Bowl game originated in 1967 as a contest between the championship teams of two rival leagues, the older and more established National Football League (NFL) and the American Football League (AFL). After Super Bowl IV in 1970 the leagues merged into one National Football League, which has two main divisions, the National Football Conference (NFC) and the American Football Conference (AFC). The Super Bowl has since been played between the AFC and NFC champions.

Year	Teams and score	
1967	Green Bay (NFL) 35	Kansas City (AFL) 10
1968	Green Bay (NFL) 33	Oakland (AFL) 14
1969	New York (AFL) 16	Baltimore (NFL) 7
1970	Kansas City (AFL) 23	Minnesota (NFL) 7
1971	Baltimore (AFC) 16	Dallas (NFC) 13
1972	Dallas (NFC) 24	Miami (AFC) 3
1973	Miami (AFC) 14	Washington (NFC) 7
1974	Miami (AFC) 24	Minnesota (NFC) 7
1975	Pittsburgh (AFC) 16	Minnesota (NFC) 6
1976	Pittsburgh (AFC) 21	Dallas (NFC) 17
1977	Oakland (AFC) 32	Minnesota (NFC) 14
1978	Dallas (NFC) 27	Denver (AFC) 10
1979	Pittsburgh (AFC) 35	Dallas (NFC) 31
1980	Pittsburgh (AFC) 31	Los Angeles (AFC) 19
1981	Oakland (AFC) 27	Philadelphia (NFC) 10
1982	San Fran. (NFC) 26	Cincinnati (AFC) 21
1983	Washington (NFC) 27	Miami (AFC) 17
1984	Los Angeles (AFC) 38	Washington (NFC) 9
1985	San Fran. (NFC) 38	Miami (AFC) 16
1986	Chicago (NFC) 46	New Engl.(AFC) 10

by 18 to 20 points, represented the established National Football League, while the Jets, led by the brash quarterback Joe Namath, belonged to the upstart American Football League. "Broadway Joe," as he was dubbed by sportswriters, had audaciously "guaranteed" a Jets victory before the game. An adoring Colts fan, the humorous poet Ogden Nash, told how it felt to be on the losing side of the upset in these lines from his poem "Prognostications Are for the Birds; Lay Off Me, Please, While I Eat My Words":

> So Broadway Joe, like great Achilles,
> Declared the Colts were only fillies.
> Less modest than Caesar in his claim,
> He bragged of conquest *before* he came.
> Some figured that he'd outgrown his pants
> To count his chickens in advance.
> Spectators came prepared to cackle
> And hoot in glee at Joe's debacle.
> Debacle indeed the record shows.
> But whoever it was, it wasn't Joe's.

DOCTOR'S ACCOMPLICE In the late 19th century the YMCA Training School in Springfield, Massachusetts, not only had the inventor of basketball—Dr. James Naismith—on its faculty but also a man who was to become one of the most famous football coaches of all time, Amos Alonzo Stagg. The "grand old man of football," who as a Yale undergraduate had been named to the first All-American team, Stagg went on to coach football at the University of Chicago for 41 years, from 1892 to 1932. He ended his coaching career at Susquehanna University in 1953 at the age of 91, and lived to 102.

When the football teams of the universities of Chicago and Wisconsin trotted out on the field for a game in 1913, the fans were witnesses to a significant turning point in sports watching. The players wore identifying numbers on their jerseys.

BREAKING THE COACH BARRIER It was not until 1966 that a black man became coach of a major U.S. professional sports team, and he quickly demonstrated that the move was long overdue. The man was Bill Russell, and the team was the Boston Celtics of the National Basketball Association. In 1968 and 1969 the Celtics won the NBA championship with Russell as player-coach. As a full-time player, the 6 foot 9 inch center had led the Celtics to eight straight NBA championships from 1959 to 1966, and he was voted the league's most valuable player five times.

UNREMEMBERED RENAISSANCE Two teams dominated professional basketball in the 1920s and 1930s, one black and one white. The white team was the Celtics of New York, now often called the Original Celtics to distinguish them from the Boston Celtics.

COLLEGE FOOTBALL

TEAMS RANKED NO.1 BY POLLS SINCE 1970

Since 1936 the Associated Press (AP) has annually polled sportswriters (and later, broadcasters) for their choice of the best college football team. In 1950 United Press International began doing the same with college football coaches. The polls are taken after the regular season ends, before the postseason bowl games. The National Collegiate Athletic Association (NCAA) recognizes both polls.

Year	AP selection (by press)	UPI selection (by coaches)
1970	Nebraska	Texas
1971	Nebraska	Nebraska
1972	Southern Cal.	Southern Cal.
1973	Notre Dame	Notre Dame
1974	Oklahoma	Southern Cal.
1975	Oklahoma	Oklahoma
1976	Pittsburgh	Pittsburgh
1977	Notre Dame	Notre Dame
1978	Alabama	Southern Cal.
1979	Alabama	Alabama
1980	Georgia	Georgia
1981	Clemson	Clemson
1982	Penn State	Penn State
1983	Miami	Miami
1984	Brigham Young	Brigham Young
1985	Penn State	Penn State

The black team, the New York Renaissance, was vilified on the court and refused lodging on the road because of the open prejudice of the time. Just how good a team the "Rens" were became clear when they met the heavily favored Celtics in a six-game series in the winter of 1926–27. The teams played dead even, splitting the series three games to three.

DOCTOR'S BRAIN WAVE Modern basketball was invented in 1891 by a Canadian-born teacher, Dr. James Naismith, at the International YMCA Training School (now Springfield College) in Springfield, Massachusetts. In 4 years it had swept across the United States, and it is now played in 150 countries by 100 million people. Early players had to wait after a score while the ball was retrieved from the half-bushel fruit baskets first used, until an unknown genius had the simple idea of cutting the bottoms off the baskets so that they became hoops.

The first woman to play in a men's professional basketball league was Nancy Lieberman. The 28-year-old averaged 11 minutes a game for the Springfield Fame in the United States Basketball League in 1986, before she was forced to end her season because of an injury. As a college player at Old Dominion University and on the U.S. Olympic team, she had captured national attention and done much to increase the popularity of women's basketball.

In 1986 another professional basketball team, the comic, crowd-pleasing Harlem Globetrotters, hired Lynette Woodward. She was the first woman Globetrotter in the team's 60-year history.

WONDER BOYS A group of 14-year-olds from the east side of Buffalo, New York, got together in 1895 and formed a basketball team they called the Buffalo Germans, a name they chose because most of them were of German extraction. For the next two decades, at home and on tour, the Germans were the wonder team of American basketball, winning 792 games and losing a mere 86; at one time they won 111 straight. For a guarantee of $500 a game, they played teams

OVER THE TOP *Shown here executing his trademark "skyhook" shot, which opposing players have called "unstoppable," Kareem Abdul-Jabbar at the end of the 1986 season had scored more points, blocked more shots, and won more most-valuable-player awards (six) than any other player in the history of the National Basketball Association. In perhaps the most physically punishing of team sports, his 7'2" body had held up without serious injury for more than two decades, including his starring years as Lew Alcindor at the University of California, Los Angeles.*

PROFESSIONAL BASKETBALL

NATIONAL BASKETBALL ASSOCIATION CHAMPIONS SINCE 1953

Year	Championship series winner in games	
1953	Minneapolis 4	New York 1
1954	Minneapolis 4	Syracuse 3
1955	Syracuse 4	Fort Wayne 3
1956	Philadelphia 4	Fort Wayne 1
1957	Boston 4	St. Louis 3
1958	St. Louis 4	Boston 2
1959	Boston 4	Minneapolis 0
1960	Boston 4	St. Louis 3
1961	Boston 4	St. Louis 1
1962	Boston 4	Los Angeles 3
1963	Boston 4	Los Angeles 2
1964	Boston 4	San Francisco 1
1965	Boston 4	Los Angeles 1
1966	Boston 4	Los Angeles 3
1967	Philadelphia 4	San Francisco 2
1968	Boston 4	Los Angeles 2
1969	Boston 4	Los Angeles 3
1970	New York 4	Los Angeles 3
1971	Milwaukee 4	Baltimore 0
1972	Los Angeles 4	New York 1
1973	New York 4	Los Angeles 1
1974	Boston 4	Milwaukee 3
1975	Golden State 4	Washington 0
1976	Boston 4	Phoenix 2
1977	Portland 4	Philadelphia 2
1978	Washington 4	Seattle 3
1979	Seattle 4	Washington 1
1980	Los Angeles 4	Philadelphia 2
1981	Boston 4	Houston 2
1982	Los Angeles 4	Philadelphia 2
1983	Philadelphia 4	Los Angeles 0
1984	Boston 4	Los Angeles 3
1985	Los Angeles 4	Boston 2
1986	Boston 4	Houston 2

from Kansas to New York City. The Germans finally disbanded in 1920 but reunited as mostly 51-year-olds for one last exhibition game in 1931, which they won.

Probably no other player could take charge of a basketball game quite as decisively as 7 foot 1 inch "Wilt the Stilt" Chamberlain, whose professional career began with the Philadelphia Warriors in 1959 and wound up in 1972 with the Los Angeles Lakers, who won the NBA championship that year. His unprecedented 100-point game against the New York Knicks on March 2, 1962, remains a basketball landmark.

COLLEGE CRAZE From the 1930s until the 1950s college basketball was king of U.S. spectator sports. At Madison Square Garden in New York City, a

promoter named Ned Irish began staging college doubleheaders in 1934. They were an immediate success, even though the winning teams rarely scored more than 40 points.

The first college to have a men's basketball team (in 1893) was Vanderbilt University in Nashville, Tennessee. The first basketball game between two colleges pitted Minneapolis–St. Paul School of Agriculture against Hamline University of St. Paul, Minnesota. The School of Agriculture overwhelmed Hamline. The final score was 9–3.

COLLEGE BASKETBALL

NCAA AND NIT CHAMPIONS SINCE 1953

Supremacy in U.S. college basketball is determined at the end of the season by two tournaments in which the nation's best teams participate. They are the National Invitation Tournament (NIT) and the National Collegiate Athletic Association (NCAA) tournament. In general, each attracts different teams, and the NCAA field is the stronger.

Year	NCAA	NIT
1953	Indiana	Seton Hall
1954	La Salle	Holy Cross
1955	San Francisco	Duquesne
1956	San Francisco	Louisville
1957	North Carolina	Bradley
1958	Kentucky	Xavier (Ohio)
1959	California	St. John's
1960	Ohio State	Bradley
1961	Cincinnati	Providence
1962	Cincinnati	Dayton
1963	Loyola (Chicago)	Providence
1964	University of California, Los Angeles (UCLA)	Bradley
1965	UCLA	St. John's
1966	Texas Western	Brigham Young
1967	UCLA	Southern Illinois
1968	UCLA	Dayton
1969	UCLA	Temple
1970	UCLA	Marquette
1971	UCLA	North Carolina
1972	UCLA	Maryland
1973	UCLA	Virginia Tech
1974	North Carolina State	Purdue
1975	UCLA	Princeton
1976	Indiana	Kentucky
1977	Marquette	St. Bonaventure
1978	Kentucky	Texas
1979	Michigan State	Indiana
1980	Louisville	Virginia
1981	Indiana	Tulsa
1982	North Carolina	Bradley
1983	North Carolina State	Fresno State
1984	Georgetown	Michigan
1985	Villanova	UCLA
1986	Louisville	Ohio State

Sports

CHAOS ON ICE The frozen ponds of long, cold Canadian winters were a natural birthplace for a game that involves ice skaters attempting to push a small object past a goalie. In fact, in the mid-1800s, before rules and organization came to ice hockey, everybody in town wanted to play in the winter, and usually did. Early Canadian hockey games featured as many as 30 players on a side. By the 1880s, signs of order began to appear. Students at McGill University in Montreal, Quebec, drew up a set of rules. Leagues were formed in Kingston, Ontario, and Montreal; and a Montreal company started manufacturing hockey sticks. Then, in 1893, a governor-general of Canada, Baron Stanley of Preston, initiated a tradition that endures to this day. In recognition of the fast-growing popularity of hockey, he announced that he would award a "cup" to the team that won the amateur hockey championship of Canada. The ornate 2-foot-high trophy, which cost the baron $48.50, was first won by the Montreal Amateur Athletic Association.

Today the Stanley Cup is awarded every year to the professional team that wins the final best-of-seven series in the National Hockey League playoffs at the end of the season.

Both Johns Hopkins and Yale universities claim to have been the host for the first organized ice hockey game played in the United States. The date is also uncertain—sometime in 1893, 1894, or 1895.

FAMILIAR STORY When the Montreal Amateur Athletic Association beat the Ottawa Capitals for the Stanley Cup in 1894, a reporter for an Ottawa newspaper described the scene in terms that seem strikingly familiar almost 100 years later. "There were fully 5,000 persons at the match, and tin horns, strong lungs, and a general rabble predominated. The ice was fairly good. The referee forgot to see many things."

THE TAMER GAME How to control violence, both by players on the ice and by fans in the stands, has become a perennial hot issue in hockey. But in the early part of the 20th century, ice hockey was looked upon as a relatively tame event. In Canada a riot at a Toronto lacrosse game in 1911 sent scores of people to hospitals. Thereafter fans began to desert the lacrosse fields for the safer confines of the hockey rink, and hockey began to supplant lacrosse as Canada's national game.

UNCHANGING FANS Sports fans were misbehaving in the 1st century A.D., when the Roman historian Tacitus reported battles in Pompeii's amphitheater between the hometown crowd and visitors from neighboring Nuceria. Shouted insults led to stone throwing and fighting with weapons. There was such carnage in the stands that the emperor Nero forbade similar gatherings for 10 years.

GROWTH SPORT No professional sport has experienced faster growth than that of ice hockey in the late 1960s and 1970s. In 1965 the National Hockey League consisted of just six teams, as it had for years. They were the Boston Bruins, Chicago Black Hawks, Detroit Red Wings, Montreal Canadiens, New York Rangers, and Toronto Maple Leafs. Then, in 1966–67, the league doubled in size, to 12 teams. Four more teams were added in the next 5 years, and then 5 more, to make a total of 21 teams by the 1980s. Two developments fueled the expansion. The first was the lure of television dollars; the other was the threat from a new professional league, the World Hockey Associ-

PHENOMENON Any debate over the abilities of Wayne Gretzky comes down to whether he is the greatest ice hockey player of all time or merely the greatest of his own time. In every one of his first 7 years in the National Hockey League, the Edmonton Oilers' center was named the league's most valuable player, and he was the scoring leader (total of goals plus assists) in all but his first season, 1978–79. He has been dubbed The Great Gretzky and The Great One, but admiring fans and players sometimes call him just The Kid (he turned 26 midway through the 1986–87 season).

HOCKEY

STANLEY CUP WINNERS SINCE 1953

Year	Cup series winner in games	
1953	Montreal 4	Boston 1
1954	Detroit 4	Montreal 3
1955	Detroit 4	Montreal 3
1956	Montreal 4	Detroit 1
1957	Montreal 4	Boston 1
1958	Montreal 4	Boston 1
1959	Montreal 4	Toronto 1
1960	Montreal 4	Toronto 1
1961	Chicago 4	Detroit 2
1962	Toronto 4	Chicago 2
1963	Toronto 4	Detroit 1
1964	Toronto 4	Detroit 3
1965	Montreal 4	Chicago 3
1966	Montreal 4	Detroit 2
1967	Toronto 4	Montreal 2
1968	Montreal 4	St. Louis 0
1969	Montreal 4	St. Louis 0
1970	Boston 4	St. Louis 0
1971	Montreal 4	Chicago 3
1972	Boston 4	N.Y. Rangers 2
1973	Montreal 4	Chicago 2
1974	Philadelphia 4	Boston 2
1975	Philadelphia 4	Buffalo 2
1976	Montreal 4	Philadelphia 0
1977	Montreal 4	Boston 0
1978	Montreal 4	Boston 0
1979	Montreal 4	N.Y. Rangers 1
1980	N.Y. Islanders 4	Philadelphia 2
1981	N.Y. Islanders 4	Minnesota 1
1982	N.Y. Islanders 4	Vancouver 0
1983	N.Y. Islanders 4	Edmonton 0
1984	Edmonton 4	N.Y. Islanders 1
1985	Edmonton 4	Philadelphia 1
1986	Montreal 4	Calgary 1

ation, which began play in the 1972–73 season. By the end of the decade the NHL had absorbed the WHA and its most successful teams.

REASON TO SING THE BLUES The St. Louis Blues were a happy bunch in 1968 when they reached the Stanley Cup playoffs. One of the teams created in the NHL's first wave of expansion the year before, the Blues faced the most successful franchise in hockey, the lordly Montreal Canadiens.

Although they failed to win a game in the 1968 Cup series, the Blues lost three games by a single goal, twice forcing the Canadiens into overtime, and lost the fourth and deciding game by just two goals.

The next year the Blues again fought their way to the Stanley Cup finals, and again faced Montreal. This time the games were not quite so close, and St. Louis again failed to win a game.

In 1970 the Blues reached the Stanley Cup playoffs for the third straight year. This time things were a little different: their opponent was the Boston Bruins, who,

in sweeping the four games, outscored the Blues by a total of 20 goals to 7.

The Blues did not reach the Stanley Cup finals the next year—nor in the next 15 years through 1986. Their record of 12 consecutive losses in the Stanley Cup series has not been equaled before or since.

A RARE BREED Goalies are generally looked upon as a breed apart, not subject to the rules of conduct governing most other human beings, on or off the ice. Their job is to stop a hard rubber disc whistling at them from all angles at speeds that can be in the neighborhood of 100 m.p.h., while opposing skaters try relentlessly to knock them out of position in front of the net. Before protective face masks became acceptable gear, no professional goalie had more than a few of his own teeth left in his head. Now, some goalies retain more of their teeth.

Lorne "Gump" Worsley, a goalie who played mainly with the New York Rangers in the 1950s and 1960s, explained, "Look, you don't have to be nuts to be a goalie, but it helps." Another goalie, Samuel James "Sugar Jim" Henry, who played for several teams in the 1940s and 1950s, was once asked what he thought about his 9-year-old son's dream of following in his father's footsteps. "I don't know if he's serious," said Henry. "But if I ever catch him with a big stick in his hands, I'll hit him over the head with it."

The Olympic custom of carrying a flaming torch from Greece to the site of the Games was not started until 1936. Dr. Karl Diehm, of the German Olympic Organizing Committee, proposed the idea of having an international team of runners carry a torch across Europe to Berlin for the opening of the 1936 Games.

BONESHAKER The first town-to-town bicycle race, a forerunner of the Tour de France, was organized by a French magazine and took place in the early summer of 1868. The some 100 competitors rode "boneshaker" bicycles, so called because of their iron-rimmed wheels. (Pneumatic tires were not invented until 1888.) The race, over a 76-mile course from Paris to Rouen, was won by an English doctor, James Moore, who averaged just 7 m.p.h.

The Tour de France, a 23-day, 2,500-mile test of speed and endurance, began in 1903. It was won in 1986 for the first time by an American, Greg Lemond.

FIDDLER ON THE WHEELS The first known pair of roller skates was constructed by a Belgian musician, Joseph Merlin, who wanted to impress guests at a masked ball held in London in 1760. Merlin made his entry on the skates, playing a violin—with shattering effect. Unable to stop or change direction, he shot across the ballroom and crashed into an ornate full-length mirror, breaking the mirror and the violin and badly injuring himself.

Roller skating became widely popular after 1823, when a London fruitseller, Robert Tyers, demonstrated a pair of five-wheeled skates. The modern, four-wheeled skate design was patented in 1863 by a New Yorker named James L. Plimpton. Ball-bearing wheels were introduced in 1884, and plastic wheels (which give a faster, smoother, safer ride) were first marketed in the United States in the 1970s.

Sports

PRESENT WITH A FUTURE Bjorn Borg, the Swede who won the Wimbledon men's singles championship a record five times in a row, from 1976 to 1980, might never have played tennis but for a childhood gift. After winning a table tennis tournament at the age of 9 in 1965, Borg was asked by his father to name a prize. The boy asked for a tennis racket, and the gift prompted him to lose interest in what had been until then his favorite sport: ice hockey.

HOW KING TURNED THE TABLES When Bobby Riggs, a 55-year-old former U.S. tennis great of the 1930s and 1940s, challenged the top women players of 1973 to "battles of the sexes," nobody could have predicted that the outcome would be of tremendous benefit to women's tennis and to women's sports in general. In the first match in May against the Australian Margaret Smith Court, Riggs won handily, seeming to make good his boast that a man of any age could always beat the best women athletes. Then in July, in the atmosphere of a carnival extravaganza at the Houston Astrodome before 30,472 spectators and a nationwide TV audience, he took on Billie Jean King—who beat him in three straight sets. King, already a tireless promoter of women's tennis, used the publicity to drum up more coverage, bigger crowds, and

MARTINA *Always a gifted player, Martina Navratilova undertook a rigorous physical and mental conditioning program that carried her to the top of women's tennis in the 1980s.*

TENNIS

U.S. OPEN: Men's Singles Since 1975

Year	Name	Nationality
1975	Manuel Orantes	Spain
1976	Jimmy Connors	U.S.A.
1977	Guillermo Vilas	Argentina
1978	Jimmy Connors	U.S.A.
1979	John McEnroe	U.S.A.
1980	John McEnroe	U.S.A.
1981	John McEnroe	U.S.A.
1982	Jimmy Connors	U.S.A.
1983	Jimmy Connors	U.S.A.
1984	John McEnroe	U.S.A.
1985	Ivan Lendl	Czechoslovakia
1986	Ivan Lendl	Czechoslovakia

WIMBLEDON: Men's Singles Since 1975

Year	Name	Nationality
1975	Arthur Ashe	U.S.A.
1976	Bjorn Borg	Sweden
1977	Bjorn Borg	Sweden
1978	Bjorn Borg	Sweden
1979	Bjorn Borg	Sweden
1980	Bjorn Borg	Sweden
1981	John McEnroe	U.S.A.
1982	Jimmy Connors	U.S.A.
1983	John McEnroe	U.S.A.
1984	John McEnroe	U.S.A.
1985	Boris Becker	West Germany
1986	Boris Becker	West Germany

larger prizes for all women's sports events. One indication of King's success is that in her day, a top woman tennis player might hope to earn as much as $100,000 a year. In the mid-1980s top-ranked Martina Navratilova was making over $2 million a year in prize money.

Table tennis was originally played with balls made from champagne corks and paddles made from cigar-box lids. It was invented in the late 1880s by James Gibb, an English engineer who wanted a game he could play to get some exercise indoors on wet weekends. It was first marketed, with celluloid balls replacing the corks, under the name Gossima. Its popularity soared in 1901 after the British manufacturer of the equipment renamed the game Ping-Pong.

WIVES KEEP OUT On pain of death, married women were not allowed even to watch, let alone compete in, the ancient Olympics. The Greeks believed that the presence of wives at Olympia would defile Greece's oldest religious shrine there, although young girls were allowed in. Ironically, the shrine that

U.S. OPEN: Women's Singles Since 1975

Year	Name	Nationality
1975	Chris Evert	U.S.A.
1976	Chris Evert	U.S.A.
1977	Chris Evert	U.S.A.
1978	Chris Evert	U.S.A.
1979	Tracy Austin	U.S.A.
1980	Chris Evert Lloyd	U.S.A.
1981	Tracy Austin	U.S.A.
1982	Chris Evert Lloyd	U.S.A.
1983	Martina Navratilova	U.S.A.
1984	Martina Navratilova	U.S.A.
1985	Hana Mandlikova	Czechoslovakia
1986	Martina Navratilova	U.S.A.

WIMBLEDON: Women's Singles Since 1975

Year	Name	Nationality
1975	Billie Jean King	U.S.A.
1976	Chris Evert	U.S.A.
1977	Virginia Wade	U.K.
1978	Martina Navratilova	Czechoslovakia
1979	Martina Navratilova	Czechoslovakia
1980	Evonne Goolagong Cawley	Australia
1981	Chris Evert Lloyd	U.S.A.
1982	Martina Navratilova	U.S.A.
1983	Martina Navratilova	U.S.A.
1984	Martina Navratilova	U.S.A.
1985	Martina Navratilova	U.S.A.
1986	Martina Navratilova	U.S.A.

standard method of awarding first place to the racer with the best time. There was no timekeeping system, and crossing the finish line first was no guarantee of victory. Rhythm, style, and grace were considered to be at least as important as beating opponents. After each event, judges would deliberate, often for several minutes. Then each would cast a secret vote.

The ancient Olympic Games—held every 4 years as part of a 5-day religious festival—lasted for more than 1,100 years, from 776 B.C. to A.D. 393. In that year they were outlawed by Theodosius I, the Christian emperor of Rome, on the grounds that they were pagan. The Games were not held again until 1896, when the custom of staging them every 4 years resumed. Except for breaks during the World Wars, the 4-year cycle has prevailed since.

METEORIC TEENAGER Nobody has more poignantly demonstrated the fragility of a top athlete's career than Tracy Austin, who in 1979—at the age of 16 years 8 months—became the youngest woman ever to win the U. S. Open tennis championship by beating Chris Evert Lloyd. In the next 2 years Austin went on

was off-limits to married women was dedicated to a woman, the fertility goddess Rhea, who was the mother of the supreme god, Zeus.

The penalty for women who broke the rule was to be thrown from a nearby cliff. Only once is a grown woman known to have watched the Games and lived. She was a widow named Callipateira, who dressed up as a male judge in order to watch her son, Pisdorus, compete. When he won, she was so overjoyed that she threw off the judge's robes. She was not condemned to death, because her father, brothers, and sons had all performed gloriously in successive Olympics. Instead, a new law was passed requiring all judges to appear like some of the athletes: naked.

The seven gold medals won by U.S. swimmer Mark Spitz at the Munich games in 1972 are a world record—but not worth their weight in gold. Olympic "gold" medals are made of gilded silver.

FINISHING FIRST WASN'T EVERYTHING Winning a victor's crown in the ancient Olympics had more in common with an election than with today's

CHRIS *Two years older than Navratilova, Christine Marie Evert Lloyd dominated women's tennis in the middle and late 1970s. Her epic matches with Navratilova became media events and won fame for both players.*

Sports

to beat Lloyd several more times and to win her second U.S. Open title in 1981, besting Martina Navratilova in the final. Then a sciatica problem flared up painfully, and since 1982 pain and injuries have thwarted Tracy Austin's efforts to regain top form.

ROUGH JUSTICE Golf, the game said to have been given to the world by Scotland, was banned several times in that country in the 15th century—as a military precaution. The game was so popular that it was distracting men from archery practice at a time when England was embroiled in the Wars of the Roses (1455–85) and it seemed that the fighting might spill over the border. The game's earliest mention was in a Scottish law passed in 1457, which decreed that "goff be utterly cryit doune and not usit." The ban did not last for long, however. By the early 1500s the game was back in favor, and even Scottish kings—including James VI, who introduced the game to England when he became James I—are known to have played it.

QUEEN'S FANCY With a following wind, racing pigeons have been clocked at speeds of up to 110 m.p.h. in races ranging from 100 miles to 1,000 miles. The most famous pigeon fancier is Britain's Queen Elizabeth II, who keeps a loft of about 150 birds near her Sandringham estate.

LIGHTNING RETURN The Mexican-born U.S. golfer Lee Trevino is one of the few people in the world to have been struck by lightning and survive. A bolt lifted him bodily nearly a foot and a half into the air, knocked him out, and scorched his left shoulder at Chicago during the 1975 Western Open tournament. Trevino and two others were taken to hospital after the strike, but none was seriously hurt.

However, Trevino has suffered from back trouble ever since, and in 1980 was awarded a special trophy for not allowing the injury to interfere with his game.

THE GOLDEN BEAR *Jack Nicklaus was called the best golfer ever—even before he won the 1986 Master's at age 46.*

GOLF

U.S. WOMEN'S OPEN CHAMPIONS SINCE 1970

Date	Name	Nationality
1970	Donna Caponi	U.S.A.
1971	JoAnne Carner	U.S.A.
1972	Susie Maxwell Berning	U.S.A.
1973	Susie Maxwell Berning	U.S.A.
1974	Sandra Haynie	U.S.A.
1975	Sandra Palmer	U.S.A.
1976	JoAnne Carner	U.S.A.
1977	Hollis Stacy	U.S.A.
1978	Hollis Stacy	U.S.A.
1979	Jerilyn Kaye Britz	U.S.A.
1980	Amy Alcott	U.S.A.
1981	Pat Bradley	U.S.A.
1982	Janet Alex	U.S.A.
1983	Jan Stephenson	Australia
1984	Hollis Stacy	U.S.A.
1985	Kathy Baker	U.S.A.
1986	Jane Geddes	U.S.A.

U.S. MEN'S OPEN CHAMPIONS SINCE 1970

Date	Name	Nationality
1970	Tony Jacklin	U.K.
1971	Lee Trevino	U.S.A.
1972	Jack Nicklaus	U.S.A.
1973	Johnny Miller	U.S.A.
1974	Hale Irwin	U.S.A.
1975	Lou Graham	U.S.A.
1976	Jerry Pate	U.S.A.
1977	Hubert Green	U.S.A.
1978	Andy North	U.S.A.
1979	Hale Irwin	U.S.A.
1980	Jack Nicklaus	U.S.A.
1981	David Graham	Australia
1982	Tom Watson	U.S.A.
1983	Larry Nelson	U.S.A.
1984	Fuzzy Zoeller	U.S.A.
1985	Andy North	U.S.A.
1986	Raymond Floyd	U.S.A.

HOW SOCCER GOT ITS NAME   Although the first official rules for soccer were drawn up in 1848, Association Football—the original formal name of soccer—continued for most of the 19th century to be a rough-and-tumble affair. Most matches took place without referees. Tripping, elbowing, and shirt-pulling were all regarded as acceptable ways of slowing down opponents and getting or keeping the ball.

The name *soccer* was coined in England by Charles Wreford Brown in 1863. At that time, students at Oxford University were fond of turning colloquial words such as "swot" (for bookworm) and "togs" (for clothes) into "swotter" and "toggers." Brown took the third, fourth, and fifth letters of Association and added the suffix *cer* to create "soccer"—which made a neat but distinctive counterpart to "rugger," the colloquial name for rugby.

Ten-pin bowling was invented as a ruse to evade the law. An ancient German version of the game, using nine pins, was brought to the United States by Dutch settlers in the 17th century, but it was banned by a number of state legislatures in the 1840s because bowling alleys had become the focus of widespread betting and attracted criminals. Promoters added the tenth pin to get around the ban.

NEWS THE OLD-FASHIONED WAY   The modern marathon was inspired by a professional courier named Pheidippides, who is said to have carried the news of the Athenians' victory over the Persians at Marathon in 490 B.C. from the battlefield to Athens. He ran the 22 miles without stopping. On arriving in the city, he gasped, "Rejoice, we conquer!"—and dropped dead, possibly of heat exhaustion.

Earlier, when the Persian Army first landed at Mar-

SOCCER

WORLD CUP WINNERS SINCE 1934

Year	Championship final	Host
1934	Italy 2, Czechoslovakia 1	Italy
1938	Italy 4, Hungary 2	France
1950	Uruguay 2, Brazil 1	Brazil
1954	W. Germany 3, Hungary 2	Switzerland
1958	Brazil 5, Sweden 2	Sweden
1962	Brazil 3, Czechoslovakia 1	Chile
1966	England 4, W. Germany 2	England
1970	Brazil 4, Italy 1	Mexico
1974	W. Germany 2, Netherlands 1	W. Germany
1978	Argentina 3, Netherlands 1	Argentina
1982	Italy 3, W. Germany 1	Spain
1986	Argentina 3, W. Germany 2	Mexico

MR. SOCCER *Brazilian star Edson Arantes do Nascimento got his nickname of Pelé from his skill at pelada, a rough-and-tumble form of soccer he played in the streets as a child. In a career total of 1,363 matches, Pelé scored 1,281 goals.*

GOLF

MASTERS GOLF CHAMPIONS SINCE 1970

Date	Name	Nationality
1970	Billy Casper	U.S.A.
1971	Charles Coody	U.S.A.
1972	Jack Nicklaus	U.S.A.
1973	Tommy Aaron	U.S.A.
1974	Gary Player	South Africa
1975	Jack Nicklaus	U.S.A.
1976	Ray Floyd	U.S.A.
1977	Tom Watson	U.S.A.
1978	Gary Player	South Africa
1979	Fuzzy Zoeller	U.S.A.
1980	Severiano Ballesteros	Spain
1981	Tom Watson	U.S.A.
1982	Craig Stadler	U.S.A.
1983	Severiano Ballesteros	Spain
1984	Ben Crenshaw	U.S.A.
1985	Bernhard Langer	West Germany
1986	Jack Nicklaus	U.S.A.

Sports

athon, Pheidippides completed an even longer run. He was sent from Athens to ask Sparta for help against the invaders, and he covered the 150 miles between the cities in an astonishing 2 days. However, the Spartans were celebrating a religious festival and refused to leave until it was over. By the time they and Pheidippides arrived in Marathon, the Athenians had already routed the Persians—and Pheidippides was sent off on the run that killed him.

THE LURE OF LONG-DISTANCE RUNNING Top men runners can cover the marathon distance in less than 2 hours 10 minutes. And the top women long-distance runners—who competed for the first time in an Olympic marathon in 1984—can cover the 26 miles 385 yards in less than 2 hours 25 minutes.

But the appeal of marathons has also attracted tens of thousands of part-time runners, who submit happily to the rigors of marathon races around the world. Many of these runners' achievements have nothing to do with speed. Texan Bucky Cox recorded a time of 5 hours 29 minutes in a 1978 marathon—at the age of 5. And in 1976 a Greek runner named Dimitriou Yordanidis covered the route from Marathon to Athens in 7 hours 33 minutes. He was 98.

MARATHON FIT FOR A KING The distance of the modern marathon, 26 miles 385 yards, was arranged for the benefit of a British monarch. Although the race had been included in the Olympics since the modern Games were introduced by the Frenchman Baron de Coubertin in 1896, the length of the course was not standardized.

Then, in the London Games of 1908, the organizers planned the race to be run from Windsor Castle to the White City stadium, a distance of 26 miles. The extra 385 yards were added so that the race could end in front of Edward VII's royal box—and that distance, whose metric equivalent is 42.195 kilometers, was adopted as the international standard in 1924.

In the 1908 race, an Italian, Dorando Pietri, reached the stadium well ahead of the field but reeling from heat exhaustion. He fell three times and had to be helped to his feet. Finally he was helped across the finish line, and was disqualified for receiving aid. Pietri spent 2 days in the hospital after the race, and the gold medal went to a U.S. runner, Johnny Hayes.

U.S. sprinter Jesse Owens (1913–80) was christened James Cleveland Owens. He became known as Jesse from the sound of his initials: J. C.

OWENS VERSUS THE NAZIS Jesse Owens, the son of a black Alabama cotton picker, upstaged Adolf Hitler at the 1936 Olympic Games. Nazi leaders had contemptuously dismissed the competitive abilities of Owens and the nine other blacks on the U.S. team; but the 10 beat the cream of Nazi youth to collect a total of seven gold, three silver, and three bronze medals.

Owens alone won four golds, in the 100- and 200-meter sprints, in the long jump, and in the 400-meter relay. In the 1984 Los Angeles Games, another black U.S. athlete, Carl Lewis, matched Owens by picking up four golds in the track-and-field events.

ALIAS SUGAR RAY Sugar Ray Robinson—five times world middleweight champion between 1951 and 1960—got his ring name by accident. He took part in one of his first fights, an amateur flyweight bout, as a stand-in for another boxer. Since he had no official registration card of his own at the time, he used the card of an inactive fighter named Ray Robinson. He won the bout and never bothered to acquire a card in his own name of Walker Smith. U.S. sportswriter Jack Case added the nickname Sugar after he heard a woman at ringside yell it during a fight. It was appropriate, Case said, because Robinson was such a "sweet mover" in the ring.

NOBLE TRADITION Boxing with fixed rules, with gloves, and in a roped-off ring started in 1743, the heyday of bare-knuckle contests.

Boxing gloves were introduced by British fighter Jack Broughton, known as the father of boxing, who reigned as English champion for 21 years. The gloves, called "feather bedders," came into use after aristocratic boxing fans in England asked for a chance to

PACESETTER
Women's running was a little-noted sport when Norwegian Grete Waitz entered her first marathon in 1978 at age 25. Her inspiring, record-setting performances in several New York City marathons pushed Olympic Games officials to add a women's marathon, the first of which was won by U.S. runner Joan Benoit at Los Angeles in 1984.

spar with famous professional boxers but requested that gloves be worn to minimize the risk of damage to noble noses and eyes.

The Marquess of Queensberry rules, which form the basis of modern boxing regulations, were not devised by him alone. The rules—which made the marquess's name a byword for fair play—were drawn up in 1867 by a committee that included at least two other men. The marquess (1844–1900) gave his name to them because he was the group's chairman. The rules were first adopted for London fights.

BOX ON . . . AND ON AND ON The longest recorded gloved fight was between two American fighters, Andy Bowen and Jack Burke, in New Orleans in 1893. It lasted for more than 7 hours. After 110 rounds the fight was declared a draw because the pugilists were too exhausted to continue.

BOXING

HEAVYWEIGHT CHAMPIONS SINCE 1919
In the mid-1980s three different groups named boxing champions. They were the International Boxing Federation (IBF), World Boxing Association (WBA), and World Boxing Council (WBC). No single champion had been named since Leon Spinks in 1978.

Champion	Reign
Jack Dempsey	1919–26
Gene Tunney	1926–28
Max Schmeling	1930–32
Jack Sharkey	1932–33
Primo Carnera	1933–34
Max Baer	1934–35
Jim Braddock	1935–37
Joe Louis	1937–49
Ezzard Charles	1949–51
Jersey Joe Walcott	1951–52
Rocky Marciano	1952–56
Floyd Patterson	1956–58, 1960–62
Ingemar Johannson	1959–60
Sonny Liston	1962–64
Cassius Clay (Muhammad Ali)	1964–67, 1974–78
Jimmy Ellis	1968–70
Joe Frazier	1970–73
George Foreman	1973–74
Leon Spinks	1978

International Boxing Federation

Larry Holmes	1983
Michael Spinks	1986

World Boxing Association

Muhammad Ali	1978–79
John Tate	1979–80
Mike Weaver	1980–82
Mike Dokes	1982–83
Gerrie Coetzee	1983–84
Greg Page	1984–85
Tony Tubbs	1985–86
James Smith	1986

World Boxing Council

Ken Norton	1978
Larry Holmes	1978–83
Tim Witherspoon	1984
Pinklon Thomas	1984–86
Trevor Berbick	1986
Mike Tyson	1986

"I'M THE GREATEST" Such blithe self-assessments helped make Muhammad Ali one of the most loved and hated of boxing champions. His glory years began when, as 22-year-old Cassius Marcellus Clay, he knocked out heavily favored Sonny Liston (left) in 1964.

Collectibles

CHERRY TREE TIME

Clocks with movements carved from cherry wood and oak were made in the United States in the mid-18th century, because brass was then both expensive and difficult to obtain in North America. The wooden clocks were invented by two brothers, Benjamin and Timothy Cheyney, clockmakers from East Hartford, Connecticut. In 1806 another clockmaker named Eli Terry, of Plymouth, Connecticut, made 4,000 wooden clocks by fitting standard parts together on an assembly line. In 1836 cheaper brass spelled the end of wooden time, and few such clocks now survive. They were not very accurate, and the parts wore quickly.

A SILVERSMITH TO REVERE

History remembers Paul Revere for his midnight ride in 1775 from Boston to Lexington, Massachusetts, to warn the armed American patriots, the Minutemen, that British troops were on the march. But he had already assured himself a lasting reputation for his skill as a silversmith, and his finely engraved work still generates high bids in the world's auction rooms.

HOW COINS ARE GRADED

Coin collectors have a language of their own. They use, for instance, a series of precise definitions to describe the condition of coins and medals.

Fair means that a coin can just about be identified. *Good* means very worn, but the outline of the design is still visible. *Very good* means the design shows clearly, but the detail is worn away. *Fine* shows signs of wear.

Very fine shows slight wear. *Extra fine* is almost perfect. *Uncirculated* is in mint condition, apart from marks caused by coins rubbing together. *Proof* coins, the highest grade of all, have a mirrorlike finish and are struck from polished dies especially for collectors. As a rough guide, the condition of contemporary coins is usually extra fine, but any coin minted more than 50 years ago is generally no better than fine.

Revere also cast bells and cannons, built America's first mill for rolling sheet copper, and engraved the printing plates for the first paper money in Massachusetts. Revere was the son of a French Huguenot refugee, Apollos Rivoire, who changed his name to Revere, "so that the bumpkins could pronounce it easier."

CONVICT'S CREATION

German alchemist Johann Böttger (1682–1719) was imprisoned in Albrechtsburg fortress in 1703 by Augustus the Strong, elector of Saxony, because he had failed in his promise to make gold. Böttger won his freedom by promising to make porcelain instead. At that time porcelain had to be imported at great cost; only the Chinese knew the secret of its manufacture. Böttger succeeded in 1710, and began producing high-quality, marketable porcelain at Meissen, near Dresden. The town, now in East Germany, remains to this day a center for the production of porcelain. The most valuable Meissen pieces, dating from the early years of production, now fetch up to $200,000 or more.

WILLOW OF THE WEST

The popular Chinese-style willow-pattern china came from Staffordshire in England, not China. It may have originated with Thomas Minton (1765–1836), who invented a simple design of a Chinese scene with willow trees in the 1780s. The standard willow pattern started to appear in the first decade of the 19th century and is still produced. An early willow-pattern plate can now be worth between $30 and $400.

The legend that the willow picture tells of a lovely Chinese girl running away with her father's impoverished secretary, pursued by the angry father, has nothing to do with China either. It was invented in England sometime in the 19th century.

THE CRAFTSMEN'S GUIDE

Sheraton furniture is known for its elegant design, yet Thomas Sheraton—the man after whom it is named—may never have made a stick of it himself. Sheraton, born in Stockton-on-Tees, England, in 1751, was the son of a cabinetmaker. He spent the early part of his life traveling the country in his father's trade. He arrived in London in about 1790 and became a shopkeeper, author, and drawing master. His elegant designs were published in *The Cabinet-Maker's and Upholsterer's Drawing Book* (published in four vol-

PORCELAIN PAIR *This Harlequin typifies Meissen's products. The Columbine (right) is from Nymphenburg.*

KING OVER THE WATER *Eighteenth-century Jacobite loyalists pledged allegiance to the exiled Stuarts with glasses decorated with portraits of Bonnie Prince Charlie.*

PENNIES PLUS *Staffordshire pottery figures were sold at Victorian fairs— hence their name of fairings—for pennies. Some now fetch up to $600.*

umes in 1791–74) and *The Cabinet Directory* (1803), and were copied by scores of enthusiastic cabinetmakers. But there is no evidence that Sheraton ever had a workshop in London or made any of the beautiful pieces of furniture that he designed. He died, poverty-stricken, in 1806. In the early 1980s, a set of six 19th-century chairs that followed the original Sheraton designs fetched over $15,000.

A POTTED PORTRAIT
The common toby jug is thought to immortalize a legendary drinker, Harry Elwes, who was said to have downed 16,000 pints of beer without eating in between. An unlikely tale, perhaps, but when Elwes died in 1761, Staffordshire potter Ralph Wood began making portrait jugs. He named the jugs Toby Fillpot, which may have been Elwes's nickname and is a character in the ballad "Little Brown Jug." The true toby jug was a fat old man seated on a chair and holding a pint pot. Now there are hundreds of varieties with portraits of famous people, such as Winston Churchill and Benjamin Franklin.

CRYSTAL-CLEAR SECRET
The secret of clear crystal glass was locked up for most of the 16th century on the islets of Murano in the Lagoon of Venice. But money talks, and by the early 17th century, renegade Venetians had sold the secret—the use of manganese and skilled blowing to produce colorless glass—abroad. Other countries, especially Bohemia, started setting up rival glassmaking industries, and soon they were outstripping the Venetians with better techniques. By the 18th century the Venetian industry had fallen so far behind that in 1730 a Venetian named Briati disguised himself and worked for 3 years in a Bohemian glassworks to learn again the secrets his city had lost. Today a Venetian glass goblet of the 17th century in good condition might fetch between $40,000 and $50,000.

ONE FOR THE POT
Tea was so expensive when it was first brought to Europe in the early 17th century that it was kept in locked wooden boxes. These were called caddies, from the Chinese *catty*—a unit of weight, usually about 1.3 pounds. Veneered wood, silver, and even papier-mâché were used to make caddies, which today sometimes fetch more than $100 at auction.

A BAG OF GOLD
Two disappointed sailors in the English port of Plymouth walked one day in 1863 into a small stamp shop owned by Stanley Gibbons (1840–1913), founder of a world-famous London stamp dealing firm, and

dumped on the counter a bag containing thousands of triangular stamps issued in the Cape of Good Hope between 1853 and 1863.

They explained disgustedly that they had won the stamps in a raffle in a South African pub and just wanted to get rid of them. They were delighted when Gibbons gave them £5 for the bag. Gibbons went on to sell the stamps at about ninepence a dozen, making a profit of £500. Today the stamps are valued at from $20 to $100,000 each.

WALL FURNITURE
The beautiful, simple furniture made by the Shaker religious sect in New England was designed so that it could be hung on pegs around the walls. Every evening the Shakers tidied up in this way in case the night should be disturbed suddenly by the Second Coming of the Lord. Only the larger pieces of furniture, such as chests and tables, were left on the floor.

FACE OF FORTUNE
The vanity of a king helped to make his stamps a favorite target of collectors. Ferdinand II (1810–59), the ruler of Sicily, was so vain that when postal officials suggested Sicily should issue its own postage stamps, he agreed only on condition that his portrait was never to be disfigured by a franking mark. Anyone who disobeyed, he decreed, would be guilty of treason. To placate the king—who became known as King Bomba after he ordered an artillery bombardment of rebellious subjects in Palermo and Messina in the late 1840s—fearful officials designed a special franking mark that fitted as a frame around his head.

Today, the franked stamps can be worth several hundred dollars apiece, partly because of their curiosity value but mainly because of their rarity. Largely as a result of delays caused by the king, the new stamps were not issued until January 1, 1859—and their issue was halted less than 5 months later, on Ferdinand's death.

THE ONE AND ONLY
The world's most valuable stamp is a one-cent black-on-magenta British Guiana (now Guyana) printed in the capital, Georgetown, in 1856, when supplies from Britain failed to arrive. Yet the young colonial collector who found the only known copy among some old stamps in 1873 sold it for the equivalent of a few pennies because he thought it was dull and uninteresting. In 1934 it fetched $32,000, and in 1980 it fetched $850,000 at auction.

The stamp is now thought to be unique; but there is a story that while it was in the possession of British-born American millionaire Arthur Hind, in the early

MODELS ON THE MARCH
The history of model soldiers goes back 4,000 years, to ancient Egypt. They became widely popular in the late 19th century, when hollow-cast lead figures began to be made in Europe. These modern models show German officers in World War I.

years of the 20th century, a British merchant seaman called on him with another genuine black-on-magenta. Hind is said to have paid the seaman a huge sum for the second stamp—and then burned it, telling friends as he did so: "Now there is still only one."

ANONYMOUS FAME
The world's first stick-on, prepaid stamps were introduced in Britain on May 6, 1840. Only two denominations were issued: the penny black and the twopenny blue. Since they were not intended for overseas use, neither stamp carried the name of the country on them, and the tradition remains to this day.

DYING FOR A STAMP
A Paraguayan stamp printed in 1932 helped to start a war. The stamp showed a map in which the Chaco territory between Bolivia and Paraguay, claimed by both sides, was labeled Chaco Paraguayo. In addition, the stamp bore the provocative legend *Ha sido, es, y será* ("Has been, is, and will be"). On June 15, 1932, Bolivian troops attacked Paraguay. The war dragged on until June 12, 1935, by which time 100,000 men had died. In the end the two countries signed a peace treaty in 1938 under which Paraguay gained 90 per cent of the disputed territory.

AN EMPRESS'S CURRENCY
The autocratic head of Maria Theresa, ruler of the Austrian empire from 1740 to 1780, still appears on the Austrian one-thaler coin—a silver coin that is no longer used in Austria. During Maria Theresa's reign the coin became so respected in countries bordering the Red Sea that traders would often accept no other coins. After the empress died, the coin continued to be minted in several European countries, and it is still used in parts of the Middle East. Such coins are all dated 1780, whatever year they were minted. In 1986 an average specimen was worth about $5.

TOGGLE ARTISTRY
Some of the smallest items valued by collectors are netsuke (pronounced net-ski). These button-size toggles were used by the Japanese to hold the drawstrings on the purses that they hung from their belts as part of their traditional dress. Netsuke were made for hundreds of years and reached their peak as an art form

BUBBLE GUM BONUS *Mickey Mantle, from the rare 1952 Topps Chewing Gum set of baseball cards, was priced by dealers in 1986 at $2,450. There are an estimated 200,000 serious collectors.*

between the 17th and 19th centuries. Usually made of wood or ivory, they were carved in a great many shapes, the one proviso being that they should not have any sharp points to catch on clothing. More than 2,000 artists made signed netsuke, and there are many more unsigned ones. Since the mid-19th century, fake netsuke have also been made. The price of genuine articles reached a peak in 1980–81, when one collector reputedly paid $250,000 for a single netsuke. Since then prices have come down.

LITTLE PERFORATIONS
The world's smallest stamps were issued in Bolivia between 1863 and 1866. They measured a mere .31 inch by .37 inch.

TWO BITS OF TREASURE
The nickname "two bits" for a U.S. quarter comes from the days of the pirates on the Spanish Main—and from their favorite coins, known as pieces of eight. Spanish silver dollars, mostly minted in Spain's silver-rich Mexican empire, were called *pesos de ocho* (meaning "pieces of eight") because each was worth eight *reales*. The dollars were cut into wedge-shaped portions, like a cake. An eighth portion, or "bit," was worth one *real;* a half portion, or "four bits," was worth four *reales;* and a piece worth two *reales* was a quarter portion, or "two bits."

LICK THAT
The most worthless stamp ever issued—taking only face value into account—was a 3,000-pengö stamp issued in Hungary on February 5, 1946. At the time of issue, one U.S. cent would have bought 25 billion of the stamps.

COLLECTIBLES ON THE HOOF
A well-bred foal can appreciate by its second birthday into one of the most expensive animals on earth. Beginning in the 1970s, fueled in part by Arab oil money, the price of yearlings skyrocketed. In 1985 one sold for $13.1 million, eight for over $2 million each, and 24 for over $1 million at the trend-setting Keeneland Select Sales auction in Lexington, Kentucky. Prices softened a bit in 1986, but even so, the Maktoum family of oil-rich Dubai laid down $40.2 million for 57 yearlings.

MECHANICAL BANK *Designed to make saving fun for children, these cast-iron toys were manufactured in the U.S.A. between about 1860 and 1935. Originals now fetch as much as $20,000, but newer versions—such as this Betsy Ross bank made for the U.S. Bicentennial—are relatively inexpensive. Pressing a lever makes Betsy turn to her sewing basket.*

ENGLISH AND AMERICAN FURNITURE STYLES

SAXON AND NORMAN (before 1272)

Chairs were heavy, boxlike in design, square, and simply carved—and only for the head of the household or important visitors. Chests had elaborate decorations and were put to a variety of uses in addition to storage. Because such chests were portable, they could double as chairs, tables, and even beds.

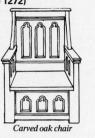

Carved oak chair

MEDIEVAL (1272–1553)

By medieval times, the chest, now raised off the floor on short, strong legs, had become an early cupboard. Chairs were still boxlike, but their carving was more delicate and elaborate.

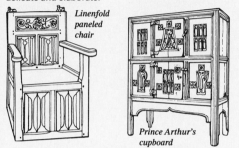

Linenfold paneled chair

Prince Arthur's cupboard

ELIZABETHAN AND JACOBEAN (1553–1660)

Round legs, turned on a lathe, transformed the previously square-cut lines of cupboards and chairs. Rich merchants began to use different rooms for different functions, and it was no longer necessary to stack tables away between meals. Beds were heavy and draped to keep out drafts, and the chest on legs had become a carved oak cupboard.

Jacobean carved oak bedstead   *Turned 17th-century chair*

RESTORATION (1660–1714)

Royalist nobles returning with Charles II from exile in France brought with them a taste for Continental elegance—high-backed chairs with curved legs and serpentine stretchers. Cupboards were decorated with veneers and marquetry, while the diarist Samuel Pepys chronicled the construction of the first known bookshelves in 1666. The 12 surviving shelves, or presses, are at Magdalene College, Cambridge. Walnut became fashionable, ending the dominance of oak furniture.

Chimneypiece

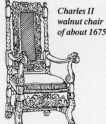

Charles II walnut chair of about 1675

GEORGIAN AND REGENCY (1714–1837)

This was the classic age of English furniture. The designer Thomas Chippendale (1718–79) set new styles in mahogany, with ladderback chairs, claw-and-ball feet, and tripod table stands. Robert Adam (1728–92) decorated furniture with classical medallions and brightly painted panels. George Hepplewhite, who died in 1786, perched chairs on slender saber legs with scrolled arms and shield backs.

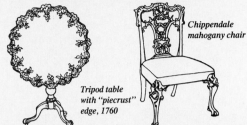

Chippendale mahogany chair

Tripod table with "piecrust" edge, 1760

FEDERAL (1783–1815)

Independence from Britain marks the beginning of the federal period in the former American colonies. The style shows the influence of all the great recent English designers—Sheraton, Adam, Hepplewhite, even Chippendale—combined into something uniquely American. A mahogany chest-on-chest had extensive decoration, veneering, inlay, and fine urn-finials. Eagles were favorite further embellishments.

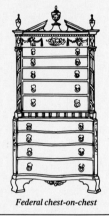

Federal chest-on-chest

VICTORIAN (1837–1901)

Mahogany was still the popular wood, but design became heavy and ornate. Chunky chests of drawers were topped with swirling, carved or molded flowers and leaves, and large mirrors. Chairs and settees were padded with horsehair and covered with leather or buttoned upholstery in rich colors.

Balloon-back dining chair

Circular four-seat ottoman of about 1840

MODERN (1901–present day)

Contemporary furniture has been influenced by new materials as well as by demands for convenience and economy. The dominant designer after World War II was the American Charles Eames (1907–78). His lounge chair and ottoman have rosewood-and-leather seat units mounted on aluminum bases.

Eames chair and ottoman, 1956

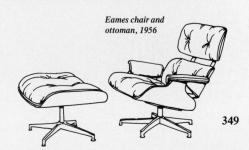

Games and gambling

GAMBLER'S GUIDE

The first practical guide for gamblers was written more than 400 years ago by an Italian doctor and mathematician named Geronimo Cardano (1501–76) in his *Book of Games and Chance*.

Cardano worked out the laws of chance governing games of cards and dice, and explained in his book the most profitable strategies to use at each stage of the games. Cardano's calculations still hold good. For example, he worked out correctly the likelihood of throwing any particular number with one, two, or three dice.

THE MAN WHO BROKE THE BANK

Charles de Ville Wells, the gambler whose exploits were celebrated in the song "The Man Who Broke the Bank at Monte Carlo," emptied the Monaco casino's cash reserves not once but six times over 3 days during an extraordinary run of luck in July 1891. Playing roulette and using a version of the Martingale system, in which a gambler doubles his stake every time he loses a bet, the 50-year-old London businessman turned his inital $400 into $40,000. Later that year he won another $10,000 at the same casino.

Wells was later jailed for fraudulently misrepresenting his English business ventures and lost his fortune and reputation. He is said to have died poor in 1926.

HELLO, DOLLIES

During the 1920s the Dolly sisters, Jennie and Rose, two Hungarian-born cabaret performers who became famous in the United States, had unlimited credit at the fashionable Deauville and Le Tourquet casinos in France. The reason: Jennie was being courted by Gordon Selfridge, the wealthy owner of one of London's largest department stores. Selfridge bought a sizable interest in both casinos so that the twin sisters could gamble his money away—and he could get most of it back through the casino's winnings.

DEAD MAN'S HAND

A poker hand consisting of two black aces, the two black eights, and the queen of hearts is known to professional poker players as a "dead man's hand." The hand got its name after the murder of the U.S. frontier scout, town marshal, and gunfighter Wild Bill Hickok (1837–76). Hickok was holding those five cards when he was shot in the back during a poker game in a saloon at Deadwood, in the Dakota Territory, in August 1876.

He was the last of four players to be seated, and it was the only time that he had been known to sit with his back to a door. Hickok asked his fellow gamblers to change places with him, but they refused to do so because of a superstition that it might spoil their luck. Hickok's killer was an old enemy of his, Jack McCall, who the previous day had lost $500 to Wild Bill in a poker game. Hickok is buried in Mount Moriah cemetery in Deadwood, now in South Dakota.

BIRTHDAY BETTING

The laws of chance worked out by the 17th-century French scientist and philosopher Blaise Pascal have a number of curious and apparently implausible consequences. One of them concerns birthdays: the chances of at least two people in a random group of six having birthdays in the same month. On the face of it, this seems to be an evens bet, because there are six people and 12 months.

But the odds are in fact much better, because the chances of three, four, five, or all six people having birthdays in the same month must be added in as well. The result is that the chance of all six having birthdays

ORIENTAL KING *Indian cards, the earliest of which date from around 1527, are circular, hand-painted, and lacquered. The Mir of Surkk ("King of Sun") is one of only two court cards in the 98-card pack.*

JACK *The model for the jack of spades is thought to be Ogier the Dane, a fictional hero of French medieval literature. This card is 18th-century.*

QUEEN *Britain's Queen Anne is depicted in all her regal splendor in a 1707 version of the queen of clubs.*

BATTLE IN BLACK AND WHITE

Chess is derived from Chaturanga, an Indian war game that dates from before the 6th century A.D. The earliest known reference to it is in a 6th-century Persian document, but in 1972 two ivory figurines—thought to be chessmen and possibly dating from A.D. 200—were found in Russia.

The game passed by way of Persia to the Arabs and reached Europe in about the 10th century. Its English name comes from the Persian title *shah*, meaning "king" or "ruler." Chess is now international, but several Eastern countries retain their own versions of the game. In China it is known as Xiang-qi, and in Japan it is called Shogi.

● The term *checkmate* comes from the Persian *shah mat*, meaning "The king is dead."

● In Japanese chess, captured pieces change sides and are dropped back on the board in positions chosen by the player.

● The name *rook,* for the piece sometimes known as the castle, is a corruption of the Persian word *rukh,* meaning "chariot." Later the chariot came to be replaced by a piece resembling a howdah, or platform, on an elephant's back—and the rook's modern shape is derived from the howdah.

● One of the earliest sets of European chess pieces in existence was found in a sandbank on the Isle of Lewis in the Outer Hebrides in 1831. They date from the 12th century and are carved in walrus ivory. Now known as the Lewis chessmen, they are probably of Icelandic or Norwegian origin.

● In 12th-century Japan a type of chess known as Tai-Shogi had a board with 625 squares and 354 pieces.

● In the Middle Ages, chess was thought by some to be too easy, so more complicated versions of the game were introduced. Tamerlane's chess, played at the court of the 14th-century Mongol conqueror, had a board of 110 squares, and the pieces included camels and giraffes.

in *different* months works out at just over 1 in 5, which means that the odds of at least two of the six people sharing a month are nearly 4 to 1.

RAKE'S LOTTERY
The first successful French lottery was set up by an Italian. He was history's most famous womanizer, Giovanni Giacomo Casanova. The lottery was started after Casanova, then 33, promised a French government minister that he would help to raise money for a new military academy—without costing the impoverished French crown a single franc. In the system he used, customers bought a share in one or more of 90 numbers. In each draw five numbers were picked as winners, and the prize money for each number was split between the winning ticket holders.

In an extra Casanova-like twist, he gave each number the name of a deserving young girl, and the five winning girls each got a bonus prize of 200 francs.

In April 1758 the first draw raised 2 million francs, of which the government took 600,000, Casanova kept 20,000, and the rest was distributed in prizes. By the end of 1759 there had been 14 more draws, establishing the lottery as an effective fund-raiser and a fashionable amusement, and enriching Casanova. He died in 1798 at the age of 73, in bed—alone.

FIRST BOARD GAMES
The earliest game boards and pieces that can be positively identified were discovered during excavations at the ancient Mesopotamian city of Ur by the British archeologist Sir Leonard Woolley in 1926–27. They date from about 3000–2500 B.C.

It is not known for certain how these games were played, but the evidence suggests that they were race games with rules not unlike those of pachisi. Boards and their pieces have also been found in Egyptian tombs and depicted on wall paintings, mostly dating from about 2000 B.C. onward.

NERO'S GAME
Backgammon has always been a favorite game of gamblers. The Roman emperor Nero is said to have played a very similar game for extremely high stakes.

GUILLOTINED Court cards were discarded in the French Revolution. The jack of hearts (left) became a gardener, the queen of spades a symbol of press freedom.

TELLING A MORAL Many playing cards have carried moral, educational, or political messages. This card—one of a British set urging proper goals for youth—dates from 1788.

Crowns are Ambitious gilded toys
As blefsings never meant,
Know' that the greatest Joys on Earth
Are Plenty, & Content.

LIBERTÉ DE LA PRESSE

PASCAL'S TRIANGLE

The laws of probability that govern all random events, including those on which bets are made, were first worked out systematically by the French scientist Blaise Pascal (1623–62). He realized that while individual random events could not be predicted, it was possible to predict their pattern statistically if the events were repeated a large number of times. Thus, although one throw of a die cannot be predicted accurately, it is possible to predict that in a large number of throws, each number will appear on average once in six throws.

Working out the odds
This number triangle gives the probabilities of each outcome when several coins are tossed together. The first and last number in each row is 1. Each other number is the sum of the two above. If six coins are tossed, consult the "6 coins" row. The sum of the numbers in that row, 64, is the total number of possible outcomes. In one case, there are six heads and no tails. The probability of this is 1 in 64. In six cases, there are five heads and one tail; the probability is 6 in 64. Similarly, there are 15 chances in 64 of four heads and two tails, and so on.

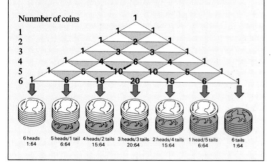

Nunmber of coins

6 heads	5 heads/1 tail	4 heads/2 tails	3 heads/3 tails	2 heads/4 tails	1 head/5 tails	6 tails
1:64	6:64	15:64	20:64	15:64	6:64	1:64

The origin of backgammon is unknown. It probably evolved from early race games played in Egypt and the Middle East long before the Christian era. It is probably the oldest dice game still played.

MONOPOLY: MAKING A MINT
In 1975 twice as much Monopoly money was printed in the United States as real money. And in most years the Monopoly output, on face value, comfortably beats the U.S. Treasury's. The commercial success of the board game is unrivaled, with nearly 100 million sets sold in its first 50 years. An out-of-work heating engineer, Charles Darrow of Philadelphia, invented Monopoly in the early 1930s, and it made him a millionaire, though not immediately. Darrow first tried to sell his idea to Parker Brothers, a Massachusetts firm that was America's leading games manufacturer. But the firm turned it down on the ground that it was too complicated. Parker Brothers changed its mind only in 1935 after Darrow had 5,000 sets made privately and proved, by selling them, that the game had wide appeal.

WORD-PERFECT
The highest known scores in Scrabble are 1,961 points for a single play (Ron Jerome, England, 1974) and 4,454 points for a complete game (Jeff Grant, New Zealand, 1981). Both these scores were worked out, however, with the letters face up so that the most advantageous combinations could be constructed. In competitive games, the highest known score for a single play—achieved in Britain in 1982 by Dr. Saladin Khoshnaw—is 392 for "caziques," a word meaning "Indian chiefs." For a player's game total, the world record is 792; it was set by Diane Dennis of Britain in March 1984.

CASH AND CARDS
The first mention of European playing cards was in 14th-century Italy. The cards were probably adapted from those used by the Mameluke sultans, who ruled Egypt for some 300 years from the middle of the 13th century. The Arabs, in turn, may have been inspired by Chinese playing cards. The Chinese cards are thought to have been based on paper money issued during the Tang Dynasty (A.D. 618–907).

The design of the standard 52-card pack of the West is originally French. The spades replaced the French pikes (*piques*), and the club suit gets its shape from the French trefoil symbol.

The joker in a pack of cards is derived from the Fool, one of the cards in a tarot pack—of which the 22 face cards are used for fortune-telling. The tarot pack was originally used in an old game called tarok in central Europe, played with the 22 face cards plus 40, 52, or 56 numbered cards.

THREE FOR THE POT
The origin of billiards is not known, but the first known reference to it was made in France in 1429.

The game has been known in Britain since 1591. Only three balls are used: two white cue balls, one for each player, and a red. Points are scored by sinking in a pocket (as in pool) either of the other balls with the cue ball (though it is considered bad form to sink your opponent's cue ball); by going "in off" (that is, sinking the cue ball off one of the other balls); or by making the cue ball hit both the other balls. A pocketless variation of the game on an oval table is also played.

BORED WITH BILLIARDS
Snooker was invented in 1875 at Ootacamund, in southern India, by British Army officers who were bored with playing billiards. The name was probably taken from the term *Snookers,* applied to first-year cadets at the Royal Military Academy, London. The game is played with a white cue ball and 21 colored balls on a billiard table. The game, or "frame," ends when all the colored balls are sunk in the table's pockets. A sequence of successful strokes is called a "break." The highest possible theoretical score for clearing all the balls in one break is 155.

SQUARING UP
Though games experts have worked out complex strategies for most games, one of the simplest of all—the children's game of Boxes—is governed by pure skill, and no satisfactory strategy has ever been devised for it. The game is played by drawing a grid of dots on a sheet of paper. Each player in turn joins two adjacent dots with a line, with the aim of completing as many boxes as possible.

SQUOPPING THE WINK
Tiddlywinks has a language all its own. The aim of the game, which is played internationally, is to flick small counters, known as winks, into a central pot. But in the early part of the game, players also try to cover an opponent's wink with their own to prevent it from being played—a technique known as squopping.

Players flick the winks by pressing down on the counter's edge with a larger counter called a squidger, and keen players have their own squidgers specially made to their personal design.

THE EARTH

The structure of the earth

ROCK-UNSTEADY

When the German meteorologist Alfred Lothar Wegener (1880–1930) put forward in 1912 the idea that the continents move over the face of the earth—the theory of continental drift—he was largely ignored by other scientists. The idea that anything as large as an entire continent was less than rock-steady seemed ludicrous to many. Wegener was right, but it was not until some 40 years later—more than 25 years after he died on an expedition to Greenland—that his theory won widespread acceptance.

Wegener was trying to explain several geological puzzles. He knew from fossil evidence that tropical plants once grew in colder regions, such as Alaska. And rock formations indicated that glaciers once covered parts of tropical Africa. Moreover, as early as 1620, the English philosopher Francis Bacon (1561–1626) had pointed out the jigsawlike fit between the west coast of Africa and the east coast of South America.

Conclusive evidence for Wegener's theory, however, emerged only when scientists began to study the magnetism in rocks in the 1950s and 1960s. They found that within rocks formed at different times in a single continent magnetic deposits were lined up in different directions, as though the North Pole had once been near the equator and had moved over the ages to its present position. Since scientists knew that the poles had always been roughly aligned with the earth's axis of rotation, the only explanation was that the rocks themselves had moved after they were formed—and that the underlying continents had moved with them.

PLANET EARTH *Clouds swirl across the ocean below the tip of Africa in a photograph taken 90,000 miles above the earth. The picture was snapped by U.S. astronauts on their way back from the moon aboard* Apollo 17 *in December 1972.*

SUPERCONTINENT

An astronaut looking down on the earth 200 million years ago would have seen a single giant landmass. Geologists today call it Pangaea (from the Greek words for "all earth"). The vast ocean that covered the rest of the earth they have named Panthalassa (from the Greek words for "all sea"). Between 180 and 200 million years ago Pangaea began to split into two sections: Laurasia, which consisted of present-day North America, Europe, and Asia; and Gondwanaland, which consisted of Africa, South America, India, Antarctica, and Australia.

As these continents drifted, they continued to split up. The resulting parts—each on a giant raftlike plate of rock—slowly took up their present positions. The two Americas linked. Arabia separated from Africa and became part of Asia. And India plowed into southern Asia, producing enough pressure over time to push up the giant Himalayas.

PARTING OF THE WORLDS

Every year the New World moves about 1.2 inches farther away from the Old, pushed apart by the widening bed of the Atlantic Ocean. A chain of underwater mountains, known as the Mid-Atlantic Ridge, runs down the center of the Atlantic. Along its length molten rock constantly wells up and cools, forming new crust and driving apart the continent-bearing plates on either side. The combination of the widening rift and molten rock is making Iceland, which sits astride the ridge, a little bigger every year. In a million years the Atlantic Ocean will be wider by about 25 miles.

BACK TO THE MELTING POT

Where one plate's edge dips below another, in what scientists call subduction zones, deep ocean trenches are formed. Among them is the deepest trough in the oceans, the Marianas Trench, which drops to 35,808 feet below sea level.

Some scientists have suggested that these trenches could be used in the future as a way of getting rid of long-lived nuclear waste. Dropped into a trench, the waste would eventually be swallowed up and its radioactive elements returned to the melting pot from which they originally came.

MAN OVER MATTER

Man may soon be able to control earthquakes—with water. It is known that if water is pumped into the ground in unstable areas, accidentally or deliberately, it may trigger an earthquake by lubricating the rocks beneath, allowing them to slip more freely past each other. Geologists are working on plans to release tension in unstable zones by pumping water into the ground deliberately, thereby causing a series of small, controlled quakes in place of a single large one.

POLE REVERSAL

The earth's magnetic field sometimes flips, reversing polarity, so that north becomes south. The change seems to happen about every 500,000 years, but short-lived flips may also occur, lasting only a few thousand years. During the changeovers, the force of the earth's magnetic field gradually lessens until it is very weak. The field then reestablishes itself the other way

PROSPECTING BY REMOTE SENSING *Geologists, who once prospected for minerals on foot with little more equipment than a rock hammer, can now use satellite photographs to help track down mineral deposits anywhere in the world. This sparklingly clear picture, whose colors have been enhanced by a computer to make analysis easier, was taken from an altitude of 580 miles over South America. It shows a slice of northern Chile more than 100 miles long. The gray area in the lower center is a salt flat known as the Salar de Atacama, in the Atacama Desert. The flat lies in a barren Andean basin, in a region that has been mined for centuries for its copper and nitrates. Sapphire-blue lakes glisten at the upper right of the picture, northeast of the salt flat, behind a row of snow-capped volcanic peaks that mark the Bolivian border. Rainfall is rare, but some evidence of erosion gulleys can be seen in the hills east (right) of the basin.*

around. A compass needle that once pointed north then points south. Evidence for this phenomenon is seen in rocks. Many record the direction of the earth's magnetism at the time they were formed, because they contain traces of iron, which reacts to magnetism. For the same reason, ordinary bricks record the magnetic field prevailing at the time they were baked. The last known reversal, which took place about 30,000 years ago, was dated through the remains of a clay fireplace built by Australian aborigines. The cause of the magnetic reversals remains unknown.

SHORT WAY AROUND
Britain's Transglobe Expedition became in 1982 the first to circle the earth via both poles. This is the short way around, though not the easy one. Because the earth is slightly flattened at the poles, a journey around the planet via the poles is about 42 miles shorter than if the same transglobal journey is made along the equator.

CHANGE OF BIRTHDAY
In 1656 James Ussher, archbishop of Armagh, announced that the world had been created at precisely 10 A.M. on October 26, 4004 B.C. He calculated the date by working back through the generations and the ages of the biblical patriarchs listed in the Old Testament. Today, by working back from the ages of rocks, scientists believe that the earth came into being about 4.6 billion years ago.

ROCK OF AGES
The oldest known rocks on the earth's surface are estimated to be no more than 4.2 billion years old—several hundred million years younger than the planet itself. The rocks from the earth's first few hundred million years are thought to have been lost through erosion or by being pushed into the molten interior by the shifting of the continents. The oldest known rocks were found in Western Australia in 1983. Their age was calculated from measurements of the decay of radioactive elements they contained.

THE RINGING EARTH
Major earthquakes can set the whole world ringing like a giant bell. The frequencies are too low for the human ear to detect, but they can be measured by sensitive seismographs (instruments used for measuring earthquakes). After a Chilean earthquake in May 1960—which had a magnitude of 8.3 on the Richter scale and an intensity of 11 on the Mercalli scale—the world reverberated for a month.

WARM SPOTS IN THE DARK, COLD DEEP
In the endless blackness of the ocean deeps, far from the warmth of the sun, some forms of life owe their survival to the heat of the earth. Temperatures at the bottom of the oceans' abysses are usually near freezing and support very little life. But where there are cracks in the earth's crust, the heat from the core escapes to warm the water.

One such hot spot was discovered by explorers aboard the scientific submarine *Alvin* in 1977. About 500 miles west of Ecuador—and about 8,000 feet down—they found a densely populated colony of earth-heated life forms, including bacteria, crabs, clams, fish, and 10-foot-long worms.

HOT AS THE SUN BENEATH OUR FEET
At an estimated 9,000°F, the molten core of the earth is as hot as the surface of the sun. At the core of the sun, however, the temperature is far higher: around 27 million °F.

PROTECTIVE POISON
The earth's atmosphere not only provides people with air to breathe—it gives vital protection. Without it, ultraviolet radiation from the sun would destroy life on earth. The deadly rays are largely absorbed by a poisonous form of oxygen called ozone, which is most abundant in the atmospheric layer known as the stratosphere, between about 10 and 30 miles up. The radiation that does pierce the stratosphere and reach the ground is what causes people to tan or burn.

Only a small proportion of ozone is needed to lower the ultraviolet radiation to a safe level. If all the ozone were collected at sea level, it would form a layer no more than 0.16 inch thick.

HIGH-LIFE WEIGHT LOSS
The quickest way to lose weight is to move to a mountaintop on the equator—and run eastward. Because the force of gravity diminishes the farther away you are from the center of the earth, you weigh less standing on a mountaintop than you would at sea level. Similarly, you weigh less at the equator than you would at either pole, because the earth bulges at the equator and the poles are slightly flattened.

The running helps because the earth's rotation sets up a mild centrifugal force, which counteracts the

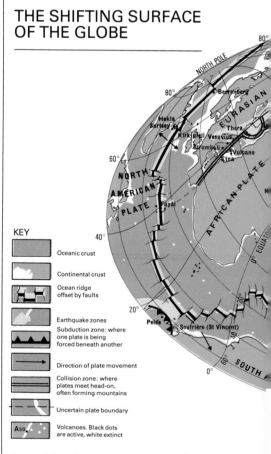

THE SHIFTING SURFACE OF THE GLOBE

KEY

	Oceanic crust
	Continental crust
	Ocean ridge offset by faults
	Earthquake zones
	Subduction zone: where one plate is being forced beneath another
	Direction of plate movement
	Collision zone: where plates meet head-on, often forming mountains
	Uncertain plate boundary
	Volcanoes. Black dots are active, white extinct

The earth's surface—the land and the seabeds—is a patchwork of giant plates. The plates form the lithosphere (from the Greek *lithos*, "stone"), in which are embedded the continents. The lithosphere in turn rides on a layer of plastic, partially molten rock called the asthenosphere (from the Greek *astheneia*, "weak" or "soft"). Beneath mountains, such as the Himalayas, the plates can be 50 miles thick, but beneath oceans they average about 3 miles thick.

effect of gravity, just as water will stay in a bucket that is swung around on a rope in a complete vertical arc. Running eastward, in the direction of the planet's spin, increases the centrifugal effect, so that you weigh fractionally less than you would standing still. Running westward against the spin, you would weigh slightly more. The faster you run, the greater the difference.

In a large object, such as a ship, the difference in weight can be considerable. A 20,000-ton ship steaming east at 20 knots along the equator (where the centrifugal effect is greatest) weighs about 3 tons less than it would if it reversed its course and headed west.

THE WATERY SOUTH

Only 29 percent of the earth's surface is dry land. The Southern Hemisphere is especially watery. There, the proportion of water to land is approximately 4:1, compared with 3:2 in the Northern Hemisphere.

LAND TIDES

The seas are not alone in responding to the tidal pull of the sun and the moon. Land is affected as well. Twice daily, as the surface of the oceans rises and falls, the continents rise and fall too, sometimes by as much as 6 inches when the moon is directly overhead and exerts its greatest effect.

THE PLANET'S HEART

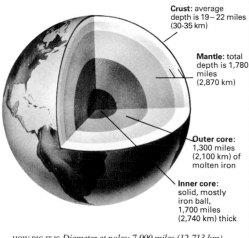

Crust: average depth is 19–22 miles (30-35 km)

Mantle: total depth is 1,780 miles (2,870 km)

Outer core: 1,300 miles (2,100 km) of molten iron

Inner core: solid, mostly iron ball, 1,700 miles (2,740 km) thick

HOW BIG IT IS *Diameter at poles: 7,900 miles (12,713 km). Diameter at equator: 7,926 miles (12,756 km). Surface area: 196,885,000 square miles (510,066,000 km²). Land area: 57,294,000 square miles (148,429,000 km²). Sea area: 139,591,000 square miles (361,637,000 km²).*

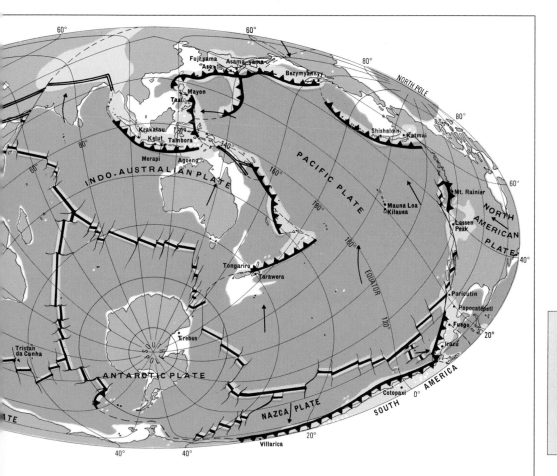

Where the plates meet, massive forces are released in the form of volcanoes and earthquakes. The theory of plate movement—known as plate tectonics, from a Greek word meaning "structure"—was devised in the 1960s by a number of scientists, among them a Canadian named J. Tuzo Wilson, who used the term *plate* for the raftlike structures on which the continents ride.

The diagram above shows the major plates. Along the Mid-Atlantic Ridge, the plates are moving apart—the Americas are moving away from Europe and Africa at the rate of about an inch a year. Molten rock constantly wells up through the cracks between the plates and cools to form new crust. Elsewhere equal amounts of crust are being destroyed. In the Pacific Ocean, at so-called subduction zones, sections of seabed plates are being slowly forced under the edges of adjacent plates and returned to the earth's molten interior. As a result, South America is getting closer to New Zealand.

Riches from the earth

THE WORLD'S MOST VALUABLE GEMSTONES

For thousands of years men and women have worn precious stones for decoration and as talismans to protect them from ill health and misfortune. The stones are treasured for their color, translucence, durability, and monetary value. The Egyptians were probably the first to cut and polish gems to increase their beauty. The four gemstones most prized today are diamonds, sapphires, rubies, and emeralds.

DIAMOND The hardest and most lustrous gem, it retains its brilliance and polish for generations. It is said to make people lucky in love as well as strong and courageous.

Diamonds are a form of carbon that has been crystallized under great pressure and very high temperatures. South Africa and Australia are two major sources of the gems.

SAPPHIRE After the diamond, it is the hardest stone. Commonly blue, it also occurs in purple, green, white, pink, gold, and orange. Its supposed mystical qualities include the promotion of peace and the purification of the mind.

The stone is formed from a variety of the aluminum oxide, corundum. Sri Lanka is a notable source of sapphires of all colors.

EMERALD A brittle gem, it tends to chip and is rarely flawless. The stone's rich green is caused by the presence of chromium, a hard white metal. In ancient times powdered emerald was believed to cure fever and the plague.

The stone is formed from a combination of three main minerals: silicon (the chief constituent of sand and quartz), aluminum, and beryllium. Colombia is the source of the finest emeralds.

RUBY The rarest of the gems. Its prized pigeon-blood red color also comes from chromium. Rubies were thought to promote good health and to keep people looking young. In addition, they were said to guard fruit trees from disease.

Some of the world's highest-quality rubies are quarried from gravels in Burma.

BILLION-DOLLAR LOSER

The man who discovered South Africa's vast Witwatersrand gold deposits sold his claim for less than $50. In an affidavit to Pretoria's Mines Department in July 1886, a part-time prospector, George Walker, reported finding a "payable gold field"—and launched one of the world's biggest gold rushes.

Fortune hunters from around the globe converged on the bleak, windswept southern African interior. Within 3 years 630,500 ounces of gold had been dug from the vein. And Johannesburg, then a 3-year-old shantytown of tents and wood-and-iron shacks, was on its way to becoming one of Africa's most important cities.

A 50-mile-long rocky outcrop, the Witwatersrand (meaning "ridge of white waters") provided the bulk of the world's gold output for the next few decades. Since then, six other huge fields, stretching in a 300-mile arc between the provinces of Transvaal and the Orange Free State, have been discovered. Together they produce more than 800 tons of refined gold a year, nearly 70 percent of the world's supply.

Of George Walker, the billion-dollar loser, there is no further trace. He may have gone back to his old work as a handyman, just another prospector who had sold out too cheaply and too soon.

FOOL'S GOLD

Many early prospectors mistook chunks of pyrite—a gold-colored iron ore—for gold. The ore became known as fool's gold and was considered worthless. Today, however, it does have a real value: it is used in the large-scale production of sulfuric acid, which is essential in the manufacture of drugs, fertilizers, detergents, and many other goods.

GOLD-PLATED COFFINS

The ancient Egyptians often plated their coffins and monuments with gold hand-beaten to a thickness of 1/50,000 inch, a fraction of the thickness of rice paper.

Modern techniques can do even better. Gold is so malleable that in its finest form (24 karat) an ingot measuring 2 cubic inches, about the size of a matchbox, can be beaten or rolled out into enough gold leaf to cover a tennis court. Such a leaf would be less than 1/250,000 inch thick.

ALUMINA MINERALS
Ruby and sapphire are gem varieties of corundum, a natural aluminum oxide. Aluminum is the most abundant metal in the earth's crust, but it does not occur in its free state—only as compounds with other elements.

CORUNDUM *After the diamond, it is the hardest mineral. Opaque varieties, mixed with magnetite and other impurities, are used as abrasives.*

SAPPHIRE *Corundum gemstones of any color except red are classified as sapphires. These are Sri Lankan gems.*

RUBY *Large rubies are among the most precious of jewels. The pigeon-blood red stones here are from Burma.*

DOWN-UNDER GOLD DIGGERS

The Australian gold rush of 1851 gave the Australians one of their nicknames: "diggers." Within a few months 370,000 immigrants, mostly from Britain, had arrived in Australia. The population in the state of Victoria more than doubled. But its capital, Melbourne, emptied of adult men. Business halted, schools closed, and ships lay idle in Port Philip Bay, deserted by their gold-hungry crews.

The rush had been started by an Australian miner, Edward Hammond Hargraves, who was convinced by his experiences in California during the gold rush of 1848–49 that he could find gold in his own country. In February 1851 he panned out gold from a creek near Bathurst, New South Wales, and found more gold in another river. These finds won Hargraves a job and a cash award of £10,000 from a grateful government.

RICHER THAN FORT KNOX

The largest hoard of gold in the United States is not at Fort Knox, Kentucky. It is in the vaults of the Federal Reserve Bank of New York, parts of which lie 85 feet beneath the streets of Manhattan.

Fort Knox contains the bulk of U.S. gold reserves, which in the mid-1980s amounted to almost 9,000 tons, worth in excess of $90 billion. But the Federal Reserve Bank of New York holds almost 14,000 tons.

The gold belongs to around 40 nations, which have chosen to leave part of their wealth in New York City. Four men working in two shifts are charged with transferring gold from one nation's vaults to another's as international deals are made.

BEANS MEANS "VALUABLE"

The terms *karat* and *carat* (which measure the purity of gold and the weight of gems, respectively) come from the Greek word *keration,* meaning "carob bean." Beans were once used in Greece as weights.

Pure gold is 24 karats. Gold with a lower karat number may mean that it has been mixed with other metals to produce a desired color or hardness. For example, 18-karat gold consists of 18 parts of gold mixed with 6 parts of another metal, usually copper or silver. In diamonds and other gemstones the carat is used as a measure of weight. Five carats are equal to 0.035 ounce. So a stone weighing 1 ounce would be about 142 carats.

WHY DIAMONDS MAY NOT BE FOREVER

The soft gray graphite used in pencil lead and sometimes as a lubricant consists of the same substance as diamond, the hardest substance in nature. Both are forms of carbon. The difference between graphite and diamond lies in the way their atoms fit together.

If the carbon atoms are linked in flat planes, the result is graphite, because the planes slide readily over each other. But if the atoms form a rigid three-dimensional network, the result is a diamond. Some scientists argue that all the diamonds that miners have taken from the earth could one day turn into flaky graphite. The scientists say that diamonds are inherently unstable because, once brought to the surface, they are no longer subject to the enormous pressures that created them. As a result, these scientists believe, diamonds will revert slowly to the low-density form of

BERYLLIUM MINERALS

Beryllium is used in alloys with copper, nickel, and aluminum because it is light and strong and resists corrosion. It is also used in X-ray tubes and in nuclear reactors. The element is extracted commercially from beryl. Aquamarine and emerald are gemstone varieties.

BERYL *Crystals of beryl can weigh as much as 25 tons. These are from Mozambique.*

EMERALD *Grass-green gems rank with diamonds in value. These are Colombian stones.*

AQUAMARINE *This sea-green stone was mined in Brazil.*

CARBON MINERALS

Diamond and graphite are both naturally occurring crystalline forms of carbon. Coals are largely noncrystalline forms of the same element. Hydrocarbons, such as crude oils and tars, are formed from combinations of carbon with hydrogen.

DIAMOND *Most stones are found in kimberlite, a gray ore named after Kimberley, South Africa.*

COAL *Long used as a fuel, coal is also a source of petrochemicals. This bituminous type is mined in Appalachia.*

GRAPHITE *The "lead" in pencils is made of graphite. This piece was mined in South Korea.*

FACTS ABOUT THE EARTH

carbon: graphite. The reversion process is extremely slow, however, and could take many billions of years. The diamonds-to-graphite theory is not universally supported. Other scientists assert that diamonds will revert to graphite only if they are heated.

FOR LOVE OF MARY
The first diamond engagement ring was made in 1477 for the 18-year-old archduke Maximilian, son of the Hapsburg Holy Roman emperor Frederick III. Maximilian was engaged to marry Mary, daughter of Charles the Bold, duke of Burgundy. To mark the coming wedding, the people of Germany showered Maximilian with silver and gold.

Counselors at Frederick's court advised Maximilian to have some of the gold made into a ring and to set it with diamonds in the shape of the letter *m*. Maximilian did so and gave the ring to Mary at her home in Ghent. By marrying her, he gained the vast Burgundian estates in the Netherlands; and the giving-of a diamond engagement ring from a man to his future wife became a tradition.

BRILLIANT DISPLAY
The French statesman Cardinal Jules Mazarin invented in about 1650 the shape known as a brilliant, in which a diamond or other gem is cut in precisely angled facets. He had 12 large diamonds cut in this shape to display their glitter and brilliance. The brilliant—which both reflects and splits light—is still the choice of most jewelers as the best cut for showing off a precious stone's fire.

LUCKY STRIKE
In 1903 a Canadian blacksmith, Fred La Rose, of Cobalt, Ontario, threw his hammer at a marauding fox, missed—and struck silver. The hammer landed on what turned out to be the world's richest vein of silver. La Rose sold his claim for $30,000, and by 1913 the vein had yielded silver worth $300 million.

BURYING MANHATTAN
In most modern gold mines, miners have to dig tons of rock to find ounces of gold, and mountains of waste rock are generated in the process. If the nearly 60 million tons of waste from just one gold mine, the Randfontein, near Johannesburg, South Africa, were spread out evenly, it would bury the whole of New York's Manhattan Island, an area of 22 square miles, to a depth of 8 feet.

GEOLOGICAL TREASURE ISLAND
In digging foundations for new buildings in New York City, construction workers have found some of the world's finest garnet crystals. One find was a 12-inch fragment of a huge garnet, uncovered during construction at the Columbia-Presbyterian Medical Center near the northern end of the island of Manhattan. Beryl and tourmaline crystals have also been found in the city's construction holes.

And for tourists who would prefer to stay out of construction pits, Manhattan offers a free, street-level, 24-hour-a-day display of the world's geological riches—on the facades of its elegant buildings. For example, 375-million-year-old coral fossils can be found on the main doorway of Saks Fifth Avenue; Tiffany's windows are framed in Spanish Alhambra marble; and a rare gneiss covers the check-in counter of a midtown hotel.

MINIMINERS
Microbes are now being used throughout the world to leach minerals from rocks. One of the most widely used microbes is *Thiobacillus*, which has successfully extracted sulfur, copper, and nickel. When placed in a bath of crushed rock and liquid, the microbes trigger a series of complex reactions that dissolve the metal. In its liquid form, the metal can then be extracted from the bath by conventional chemical processes.

A similar technique has been applied to recover

THE SCRATCH TEST

One way geologists identify and classify minerals—including gemstones—is by the Mohs scale of hardness, which was devised by a German mineralogist, Friedrich Mohs (1723–1839). It has 10 grades, each represented by a standard mineral. Minerals at each grade will scratch all those of lower grades, and will be scratched by all higher grades.

The 10 grades and minerals, in order of increasing hardness, are: 1, talc; 2, gypsum; 3, calcite; 4, fluorite; 5, apatite; 6, orthoclase feldspar; 7, quartz; 8, topaz; 9, corundum; and 10, diamond.

On the same scale, most gold ores have a hardness of 2.5–3. Silver is 2–3; platinum, 4–4.5; sapphire and ruby, 9; and emerald and aquamarine, 7.5–8.

A sampling of other gemstones' hardness ratings: amber, 2–2.5; amethyst, 7; garnet, 6.5–7.5; jadeite (a type of jade), 6.5–7; lapis lazuli, 5.5; malachite, 3.5–4; moonstone, 6; opal, 5.5–6.5; tiger's eye, 4; tourmaline, 7–7.5; turquoise, 6.

For comparison, graphite—pencil "lead"—has a hardness of 1–2, about the same as a human fingernail. A U.S. penny is about 3; a pocketknife blade, 5; window glass, 6; and a steel file, 7.5.

GOLD *One of the few metals that can be found in pure form, gold has been prized by human beings since the Stone Age. This nugget is from South Africa.*

PLATINUM *Platinum is usually found with related metals, such as palladium. These pieces come from the Soviet Union. Palladium and platinum are used as chemical catalysts as well as in jewelry.*

SILVER *Most of the world's silver is used to make photographic film. Silver deposits are often mixed with ores of lead, zinc, and copper. But, like this Mexican nugget, they may also contain white quartz.*

uranium from ores in Portugal, Canada, France, Sweden, and South Africa. At present the miniminers are used only to work low-grade ores and ores that are unworkable, or uneconomic to recover, by ordinary means. But it seems likely that use of the microbes for the extraction of minerals and metals will grow as biologists find more and better ways of putting the miniminers to work.

BAMBOO OIL DRILLS
Crude oil was drilled in ancient China. The Chinese philosopher Confucius recorded in the 6th century B.C. that his countrymen drove hollow bamboo rods into the ground in search of brine to provide salt for cattle. In the process they also came across natural gas and flammable petroleum, which they used themselves or sold for fuel.

HELLFIGHTING
In the 1950s and 1960s Paul Neal "Red" Adair was almost always called in to help put out big fires in the world's oil and gas fields. Capping or otherwise quelling such infernos was the specialty of this daring troubleshooter from Houston, Texas, whose exploits were the subject of the Hollywood film *Hellfighters,* starring John Wayne. The world's biggest gas fire, which raged at Gassi Touil in the Algerian Sahara from November 1961 to April 1962, was finally put out by Adair and his team. Flames from this fire shot 450 feet above the desert. After weeks of preparation Adair set off 550 pounds of dynamite to choke the blaze. His reported fee for the job: $1 million.

THE FIRST GUSHER
The first oil strike in modern times occurred when a drill operated by Col. E. L. Drake struck oil at 69.5 feet near Titusville, Pennsylvania, in August 1859. It sparked off an oil rush similar to the California gold rush a decade earlier. Cities rose like mushrooms as hordes of adventurers began drilling. Immense fortunes were made by those who struck oil, while others lost their chance of riches when their wells ran dry as suddenly as they had begun to flow.

Before 1890 Illinois, Indiana, Kentucky, and Ohio joined Pennsylvania as important oil-producing states. The chief petroleum product was kerosene for lamps. Gasoline, too explosive for use in lamps, was often just poured into the nearest river.

ISLAND IN THE STORM
Since oil was discovered there in the late 1960s, drilling rigs have sprouted like a chain of concrete-and-metal islands from the storm-tossed waters of the North Sea. The largest rig, about halfway between Britain and Norway, is the jointly owned Statfjord B, which weighs 900,000 tons. Built at a cost of more than $2 billion, it is the largest structure ever moved by human beings. The storage tanks in its base can hold 1.9 million barrels of crude oil.

The rig was towed into position by a flotilla of tugs. Then its legs were flooded to set it on the seabed some 500 feet below the waves. Statfjord B, which went into production in November 1982, is so massive that to bring it to a halt from a towing speed of about 2 knots took the tugs more than 20 miles.

UNDERSEA WELLS OF METALS
The water in several deep basins at the bottom of the Red Sea is superrich in dissolved salts and is much hotter than the overlying ocean. Sediments in these basins contain abundant copper, iron, zinc, lead, and other metals. Apparently, these compounds are welling up from beneath the sea floor through rifts caused by spreading of the bed of the Red Sea.

At many other undersea locations, there is evidence of rich mineral deposits at rift points on the ocean bottom. With advancing technology, these spots may become the mining centers of the future.

URANIUM MINERALS
All atom bombs and all nuclear power plants require uranium. In nature the element occurs as chemical compounds in more than 150 minerals.

PITCHBLENDE *Both uranium and radium are extracted from pitchblende.*

TORBERNITE *Copper, uranium, and phosphorus combine to form green crystals of torbernite.*

COPPER MINERALS
Gold and copper—the first metals used by man—occur naturally in fairly pure form, and both are easy to work. Copper, now used widely in electronics and to make such alloys as bronze and brass, is found in more than 160 minerals.

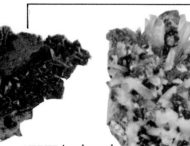

AZURITE *A carbon and copper compound. This sample is from Zaire.*

CHALCOPYRITE *The most common ore of copper. Here, the yellow ore is mixed with quartz.*

MALACHITE *This green rock, from Zaire, is formed from copper carbonate.*

Alternative energy

POWER SOURCE

Nearly all the world's energy comes, directly or indirectly, from the sun. Even the winds are largely driven by the sun's heat. And the energy contained in oil and coal was originally collected by plants from sunlight millions of years ago. The exceptions are geothermal energy (heat from the earth's interior) and tidal

power, which is caused mainly by the moon. The sun's total energy output is the equivalent of 3.8 sextillion (3,800,000,000,000,000,000,000) megawatts of electricity (and 1 megawatt equals 1 million watts). But the earth intercepts only about 1/2,000,000,000 of this energy—about 1.9 trillion megawatts. As little as 1 percent of this fraction—about 1.9 billion megawatts—would be enough to supply all human energy needs if it were harnessed.

SUN, WIND, AND TIDE: THE TRIPLE CHOICE

The appeal of what are known as "alternative" energy sources is that—unlike oil, gas, coal, and nuclear power—they are inexhaustible and virtually free of pollution. The technology for harnessing them effectively, however, is still in its infancy and relatively expensive. Three major alternative energy sources are being explored by scientists around the world: the sun, the wind, and the tides.

SUN

A huge amount of solar energy reaches the earth's outer atmosphere, far more than all the electrical and other sorts of power now generated for human use. However, despite its abundance, solar energy is thinly spread, and collecting it is difficult and expensive. Even so, many houses are at least partially heated by means of rooftop solar panels, which capture the radiant energy of the sun. The first solar cells, which turn sun power directly into electricity, were made at the Bell Laboratories in New Jersey in 1954. Similar cells now provide spacecraft with lightweight and reliable power sources.

WIND

Sailboats have always used the wind for power; and the wind was being used as a power source on land 1,300 years ago in Persia, when the first windmill drove a wheel that turned a millstone. Modern windmills are often designed to spin at high speeds so that they can generate electricity. One type—known as a Darrieus, after the French scientist G. J. Darrieus, who designed it in the 1920s—has a vertical axis, like the earliest Persian windmills. The advantage of this arrangement is that it needs no second set of bearings to swivel the vanes toward the wind. It works equally well regardless of wind direction. Other types look like enormous propellers.

TIDE

Water mills have used the power of the tides for about 1,000 years. Incoming tides are trapped behind a dam across a bay or estuary; then the water is allowed to flow out and drive waterwheels as the tide ebbs. In the 20th century more efficient turbines have been developed that can make use of water flowing in either direction to generate electricity. Despite the potential of tidal power, only one large tidal-power plant has so far been built: on the estuary of the Rance River in Brittany, France. It was completed in 1968 with a dam nearly 2,500 feet long. The dam channels the water to 24 turbines, each capable of generating 10 megawatts, or enough power to light a town of about 40,000 people. Tidal power plants are most effective where the rise and fall in the tide is 20 feet or more. But since there are relatively few such places in the world, it is unlikely that tidal power will be a major contributor to world energy supplies in the foreseeable future.

GETTING MORE OUT OF MUCK

Cow dung can be used to produce a substitute for fuel oil. At one experimental plant near Munich, West Germany, it was shown that the dung from 1,000 cows can be converted into the equivalent of about 450 gallons of fuel oil every day. The dung is sealed inside giant fermenters and, as it decomposes, it gives off the flammable gas methane, which can be used to replace the fuel oil in boilers and generators. In addition, the residue left behind after the gas has been collected makes a rich and odor-free fertilizer.

The system could make large farms self-sufficient in energy. But so far the high cost of the fermenters has discouraged most farmers from using them.

STICKY BOTTOM LINE

Not all the schemes that have been tried for turning organic material into fuel have been successful. In 1982, for instance, a Kenyan company abandoned a $100 million project designed to turn molasses (made from sugar cane) into an alcohol-based fuel. It became clear that the process required more energy than it produced.

COLLECTION POINT

The trouble with much renewable energy—such as the heat of the sun or the power of the wind—is that it arrives in relatively small amounts spread over large areas. Before it can be used on a large scale, it must be collected and concentrated. But to concentrate, say, enough power to equal the output of a medium-size 2,000-megawatt power station requires an array of solar cells covering 27 square miles, or 1,000 giant windmill generators covering 310 square miles.

Since few countries have so much spare land available—and since such large systems would be enormously expensive—most researchers believe that wind and solar power are better used on a small scale, to supplement the energy needs of individual homes rather than of whole towns.

Another trouble with renewable energies such as solar, wind, and wave power is that they cannot be switched on and off when they are needed. By contrast, the energy contained in a car's gas tank is available at the turn of the ignition switch. Surprisingly, there is as yet no very good way to store electricity efficiently. (Batteries are inefficient because they are very heavy for the amount of power they contain.) Thus, electricity has to be generated as it is used.

One answer is to convert electricity into potential energy—the energy contained in any object at a height. In Britain in 1975 engineers began hollowing out a Welsh mountain near Llanberis to build a giant pumped-storage station. The power station, known as Dinorwig, went into operation in the early 1980s. It consists of two lakes at different heights linked by huge tunnels. The tunnels guide water to turbines set in a vast artificial cavern, which is as large as a football field and high enough to hold a 16-story building. When other power stations generate surplus electricity, the Llanberis station uses it to pump water up the tunnels to the upper lake. When a sudden burst of power is needed, the water is allowed to run back down through the turbines and return the electricity to the national grid.

CALIFORNIA WIND POWER
Almost 13,000 wind turbines have been set up in California. By the summer of 1985 they had produced the energy equivalent of a million barrels of oil. The turbines have a combined power output of about 600 million kilowatt-hours, or 1 percent of the state's energy needs. Such turbines can be connected to established power grids or supply electricity for individual homeowners.

FIRST SOLAR PANEL
The simplest way to tap the sun's power is to collect its heat. In the 18th century the Swiss scientist Horace Bénédict de Saussure (1740–99) designed the first solar heating panel. A simple wooden box with a glass top and a black base, it worked on the principle that sunlight penetrating glass will be absorbed by a dark surface on the other side, and be trapped as heat. This is the reason why greenhouses become so much hotter than the air outside on a sunny day. De Saussure's rudimentary panel reached temperatures of up to 190°F—a full 54°F hotter than the world record open-air temperature.

FIVE-MINUTE EGGS
Another way to collect solar energy is to build solar ponds. At their simplest, these are lakes of salty water that gradually collect the sun's heat in the deepest, most salty layers. This happens because of the pattern of circulation in saltwater ponds. In a freshwater pond, convection currents keep lifting the warm water, so that it mixes with cooler water and loses its heat. But in a saltwater pond the saltiest layers are the densest, so they sink to the bottom and stay there, counteracting the process of convection. Insulated in this way by the cooler upper layers, the bottom layers of the pond go on absorbing heat from the sun, and their temperature can keep rising until it reaches the boiling point.

To prove this, researchers in New Mexico have boiled eggs in 5 minutes by suspending them in a solar pond. Israel already generates some electricity from the heat that solar ponds accumulate. And by the year 2000 Israel plans to generate 20 percent of its electricity in this way.

THE FIRES BELOW
Some countries are trying to tap the heat of the earth—what scientists call geothermal energy. In most parts of the world the temperature of the earth's crust rises only about 70 degrees with each mile in depth, which means that only very deep holes can tap high temperatures. But in some volcanic areas, such as Iceland, temperatures as high as 680°F exist close to the earth's surface and can be tapped relatively easily.

In Denmark and Iceland, engineers use this heat by piping hot water from under the ground to warm nearby homes, offices, and factories. An outdoor swimming pool in Iceland's capital, Reykjavik, is heated so efficiently by this method that it remains open and in use all year round.

San Francisco already derives more than 600 megawatts of electricity, about half its energy needs, from natural steam created by geothermal energy. The city hopes to triple the output from its geothermal sources to 1,900 megawatts in the next few years.

SOAKING UP THE SUN *Scores of giant mirrors swivel to follow the sun each day at Adrano in Sicily, site of the world's first solar power station connected to a national grid. Opened in 1981, the plant, known as Eurelios, uses the mirrors to focus the sun's rays onto a boiler. Steam from the boiler drives a conventional turbine and generator. The plant can generate up to 1 million watts (1 megawatt).*

WHY THE WINDS BLOW

Weather phenomena are caused by differences in temperature on the surface of the earth. The moving force behind the weather is the sun. At the equator the sun is never far from being directly overhead, and its heat is concentrated. Near the poles, however, the sun's rays strike obliquely, and its heat is spread more thinly. It is these unequal air temperatures that cause the winds.

Near the equator, where the sun's rays are hottest, warmed air expands, rises, and billows out at high altitudes. As it cools, most of it subsides back to earth just beyond the tropics, about 30°N and 30°S. Its weight then creates regions of high pressure. Surface winds blow from there back into the low-pressure zone around the equator. The earth's rotation deflects these winds, so that they blow from the northeast in the Northern Hemisphere and the southeast in the Southern Hemisphere. These are the great trade winds, so named by the merchant sailors in the 17th century who made use of them to speed their ships.

In the polar regions, air chilled by the ground sinks, creating a high-pressure zone from which the winds at ground level blow outward to warmer latitudes.

Where cold air meets warm

Between the tropical and polar winds in each hemisphere are the winds of the temperate latitudes. There, cold polar air meets warm tropical air, creating low-pressure eddies, known as cyclones, that bring rain, winds, and gales.

The pattern of these major air currents is complicated by the presence of large areas of land. Because land surfaces heat up and cool down more quickly than water, the continents are hotter than the sea in summer, cooler in winter. In India and other parts of the tropics, air rising from the hot land creates low-pressure areas, which suck in the monsoon winds in summer. The same effect causes daily sea breezes in coastal areas during hot weather. In the afternoon, breezes blow shoreward as cooler air from the sea replaces hot air rising above the land. During the night and early morning, breezes blow seaward from the cooler land to the warmer sea.

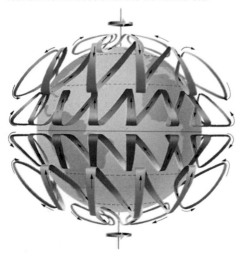

THE WINDS OF THE WORLD *Each hemisphere has three major wind systems: the trade winds, the westerlies, and the polar winds. In the Southern Hemisphere the westerlies blow most strongly at latitudes around 40°S, where there is little land to interrupt the airflow. This is the region sailors call the Roaring Forties. Along the equator, by contrast, sailing ships can be becalmed in the windless doldrums.*

HOT DOG DAYS The warmest days of summer, usually from about July 3 until August 15 in temperate latitudes of the Northern Hemisphere, were named the dog days by the Romans. The brightest star in the sky at that time was Sirius, the Dog Star, and the Romans associated weather patterns with the stars.

RED FOR ALL CLEAR "Red sky at night, sailor's delight; red sky in the morning, sailor take warning."

That old rhyme will prove more often right than wrong. When the sun is low in the sky, morning or evening, it tends to glow red, whatever the weather conditions. But we do not see the glow if there are clouds in the way. So if the redness is visible in the evening, in a relatively cloud-free sky, it means that the air to the west—the direction from which most of the weather comes in temperate latitudes—is fairly cloudless and dry. So the following day should be clear. If, on the other hand, the redness is visible in the morning, it means that the clear weather is to the east—and less favorable weather may be on the way from the west.

Sayings about red skies date back at least to the Greek Peripatetic philosopher and naturalist Theophrastus (372–287 B.C.), a student of Aristotle. In the 16th chapter of the Gospel according to St. Matthew the adage is expressed in these words:

When it is evening, ye say, it will be fair weather: for the sky is red. And in the morning, it will be foul weather today: for the sky is red and lowring.

Blue moons do occasionally occur—when there are dust particles in the air of a critical size that scatter more light at the red end of the rainbow spectrum than at the blue end. When this happens, the red light vanishes against the blackness of the night sky. The unscattered light shining through makes the moon itself look blue. One of the most recent examples was on September 26, 1950, when dust from extensive forest fires in Canada entered the earth's atmosphere. The moon also appeared blue after a huge volcanic explosion on the Indonesian island of Krakatoa in 1883.

ACID RAIN Rain is slightly acidic even in unpolluted air, because carbon dioxide in the atmosphere and other natural acid-forming gases dissolve in the water. But in parts of Europe and North America rainwater is sometimes more acidic than lemon juice. Damage to forest and freshwater ecosystems, as well as to buildings and monuments, has been extensive in Canada, Scandinavia, and the northeastern United States. Although other factors have been cited, the increasing acidity of rain has been largely caused by the burning of fossil fuels, such as oil and coal, at power plants, in industry, and in the home.

The main product of the burning is carbon dioxide—the same gas that all animals, including humans, exhale. But many fuels also contain small amounts of nitrogen oxides and sulfur dioxide (SO_2). When the sulfur compounds dissolve in rain in the atmosphere, they form a weak solution of sulfuric acid (H_2SO_4). Nitrogen oxides dissolve similarly, to form nitric acid (HNO_3).

Northern lakes and ponds get a particularly heavy dose of acid in the spring, from the runoff of melting acid snow.

CHILLING OUT Air temperature is not the only factor that makes the weather feel cold. The wind plays a powerful role too. Even in temperate latitudes, this wind-chill factor is capable of making the air feel much colder than the thermometer alone would indicate. As the temperature drops, the chilling effect of the wind becomes more pronounced. But as a rule of thumb, subtract 1 degree from the temperature for every 1 m.p.h. of wind speed. Thus a strong breeze of 30 m.p.h. in an air temperature of about 60°F will feel as cold as if there were no wind and the temperature were about 30°F.

WHIRLPOOL IN THE SKY *A spiral of clouds, hundreds of miles across, wheels across the earth over the northern Pacific Ocean. The counterclockwise spiral is typical of a Northern Hemisphere cyclone: a low-pressure system that brings rain and stormy winds to the surface below. A Southern Hemisphere cyclone would spin in the opposite direction.*

Weather patterns

SITTING OUT A STORM It is safer to be in a car during a thunderstorm than it is to be in a house. If lightning does strike, it flashes over the outside of the car—which is virtually a metal cage—and runs to ground through the tires. Although the tires are made of rubber, an insulator, they contain enough other materials to make them conductors of electricity.

HUMAN HAILSTONES Thermal updrafts in large clouds reach speeds of 60 m.p.h., and they can be killers. In 1930 five glider pilots bailed out into a thundercloud over the Rhön Mountains in Germany.

Only one survived the drop. The others, held aloft by thermals, became entombed in icelike giant hailstones before the cloud finally released them.

On September 26, 1982, an Australian parachutist, Rick Collins, was trapped for 28 minutes in a thundercloud over Brisbane. He jumped from 6,000 feet, opened his parachute—and was lifted by thermal air currents back up to 12,500 feet. Battered by hailstones and in danger of passing out from lack of oxygen, Collins escaped by jettisoning his main parachute, free-falling through the cloud to 1,500 feet, then opening his reserve parachute to make a safe landing.

People who say they can feel the weather in their bones may be telling the truth. Even so, what their bones tell them is not the future state of the weather but present conditions (which may indicate the future pattern). Why the ability exists is not entirely clear. But some people, for instance, find they get headaches when the air is damp or charged with static electricity, which is often the case before a thunderstorm. Others find that an aching bone or a corn throbs more when the barometer falls abruptly; and falling air pressure usually indicates approaching bad weather.

UNDERSTANDING A SATELLITE PHOTOGRAPH

Since the 1960s, satellites have helped to keep a weather eye on the climate and make meteorological prediction more precise.

Remote-controlled cameras on the satellites take sequences of photographs that are radioed back to receiving stations on earth at regular intervals. Placed together, the pictures show the pattern of weather across the globe. Patterns of cloud, photographed by the satellite, can be related to weather charts drawn up by meteorologists. The commonest symbols on those charts are isobars, contours that join places of equal atmospheric pressure.

At the center of a high-pressure region, the weather is usually dry; at the center of a low-pressure region, it is generally rainy. Wind direction is usually marked by arrows on the isobars. The closer the isobars are together, the stronger are the winds around centers of pressure. Boundaries between warm and cool air are called fronts. A warm front (marked on a weather chart by rounded humps) brings a period of fairly steady rain. It forms where warm air is replacing cold air at the earth's surface. A cold front (marked by spiky humps) usually brings showers with sunny intervals. It forms where cold air is replacing warm air.

OUTLOOK COOL *Satellite photography has revolutionized meteorology by revealing the global sweep of weather patterns—patterns that had been impossible to observe directly from the ground. Here, meteorological symbols have been superimposed on a satellite shot taken on a chilly October morning. The outline of Britain can be seen right of center. Numbers on the chart represent millibars of atmospheric pressure. Arrows show wind direction.*

KILLER WINDS The great storms of the tropics, with winds from 75 to 190 m.p.h., are called typhoons in the North Pacific, hurricanes in the Atlantic, and cyclones in the Indian Ocean and Australia. All are concentrated low-pressure zones spawned over the sea near the equator.

Most of these storms collapse within about 10 days, becoming ordinary rain-bearing depressions. But while they last their power is awesome. A hurricane releases as much energy as four hundred 20-megaton H-bombs every minute.

The first person to name hurricanes was a 19th-century Australian weatherman, Clement L. Wragge. He liked biblical names, such as Sacar, Talmon, and Uphaz.

BIG BREEZE LOUISE A whistling U.S. radio operator started the 20th-century system of naming hurricanes and typhoons. He was overheard whistling a line from a popular song, "Louise," just as news of a storm was being broadcast during World War II. The storm was instantly named Louise, and the custom caught on.

The U.S. Weather Bureau began to use female names in 1953. The Australian weather forecasting service began to allocate male and female names equally in 1975, and the World Meteorological Organization followed suit in 1978.

TERROR OF THE TORNADO Tornadoes are spinning funnels of cloud, usually only 80 to 160 feet across, which descend from the base of storm clouds. If the funnel touches ground, it causes considerable damage—both because of the raging winds it contains and because the winds suck air out of the funnel's core, leaving the air pressure inside drastically lower. The most destructive and most frequent tornadoes occur in the prairies of North America. The drastically lower air pressure inside a tornado has some bizarre effects. Several chickens were plucked alive by a tornado at Linslade, England, on May 21, 1950, and survived. As the tornado passed over the coop, the normal air pressure inside the birds' quills was suddenly much higher than the pressure outside, so that the feathers exploded from their skins. For the same reason, houses in the path of a tornado can explode. For people in a house in the path of a tornado, the best bet is to open all doors and windows on the side away from the approaching storm. This helps equalize the air pressure inside and out.

A tornado's whirling winds, which can reach speeds nearing 300 m.p.h., can twist the tops off trees as easily as a person can twist the stalk from an apple. On the storm's fringes, by contrast, the winds can be astonishingly gentle. On September 4, 1981, a tornado that struck the Italian port of Ancona lifted a baby in its carriage 50 feet into the air and set it down safely 300 feet away. The baby didn't even wake up.

HIGH-SPEED FLASH Lightning travels at speeds of between 100 and 1,000 miles per second on its downward track to ground. But it can reach a speed of 87,000 miles per second on the return stroke.

The enormous spark heats the surrounding air explosively, creating the sonic boom we hear as thunder. In rare cases, the spark can generate a temperature of 54,000°F—about six times hotter than the surface of the sun.

At any given moment there are about 1,800 thunderstorms raging around the world, generating between them about 6,000 flashes of lightning every minute.

THE BISHOP OF RAIN Meddling English monks are to blame for the old legend that if it rains on St. Swithin's Day, July 15, it will rain for the next 40 days. Swithin, bishop of Winchester, died in A.D. 862. He had asked to be buried "in a vile and unworthy place, under the drip of the eaves, where the sweet rain of heaven may fall upon my grave." When he was canonized in 971, the monks at Winchester decided to move

TERRIBLE TWINS *Rare twin hurricanes whirl together across the Atlantic Ocean. The storms get their name from Huracán, a West Indian god of storms. Winds immediately around a hurricane's "eye," which is usually about 20 miles across, reach more than 190 m.p.h. But in the eye itself—seen here as a dark spot at the center of each spiral—the weather is eerily clear and calm. A hurricane moves forward at a rate typically between 5 and 15 m.p.h.*

FACTS ABOUT THE EARTH

his body to a more fitting place in the cathedral choir. They moved his body on July 15, and it rained for the next 40 days—the saint's protest, so legend has it, against the move.

There is no scientific basis for the prediction, and at least one gaping hole in the story. It was based on the Julian calendar, which Britain scrapped in 1752 and replaced with the modern Gregorian calendar. The Julian July 15 would now fall in early August.

BURSTS OF BAD LUCK More than 30 airplane crashes and near-crashes since 1964 have been blamed on a single cause, a type of wind disturbance called a microburst. It occurs when there is a sudden change in wind speed or direction, a condition meteorologists call wind shear. The result can be a sharp loss of airflow over a plane's wings, followed by a stall. If the plane is high enough off the ground, the pilot can take steps to recover lift, but during take-off and landing the loss of lift can be disastrous.

PRESIDENTIAL WEATHER JINX So often have U.S. presidents been inaugurated in rain, snow, or bitter cold that miserable weather on Inauguration Day is something of an American tradition. The bad weather has been just as consistent since Inauguration Day was changed from March 4th to January 20th in 1937. It was at his 1841 inauguration that William Henry Harrison, the first president to die in office, caught a chill that led to his death from pneumonia a month later on April 4, 1841.

Toward the end of World War II, U.S. B-29s were making high-altitude bombing runs on Japan—and the pilots were bewildered by a strange phenomenon. As they flew eastward toward Japan, their planes were sometimes stopped almost dead, as if by an invisible hand. On the way back, westward, they sometimes traveled at almost twice their aircraft's top speed. Unknowingly, the pilots had discovered the jet stream, a meandering globe-circling current of westerly air that moves at speeds of up to 300 m.p.h. Since then, pilots have learned to use the jet stream to cut flying times, and meteorologists have discovered that changes in its path can affect weather around the world.

RISING DAMP *Like the blast from a nuclear explosion, a vast thundercloud mushrooms upward above the Amazon basin in South America, carrying with it thousands of tons of water, which it will shed as rain. Scientists have learned how to encourage clouds to unload their water by seeding them with chemicals, such as silver iodide crystals. But nobody yet knows how to make rain to order unless the right sorts of cloud are in the right place to start with.*

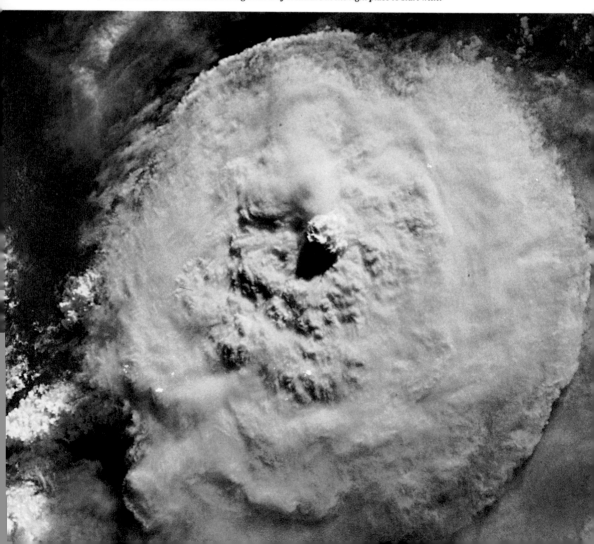

THE MESSAGE IN THE CLOUDS

Clouds are the handwriting of the weather. They are formed when cooling causes some of the water vapor in the air to condense into visible water droplets or ice crystals. In most cases, the cooling is the result of the air rising. Some weather systems are heralded by thick clouds; others by hardly any clouds at all.

If a cloud is deep enough and lasts long enough, some water droplets or ice crystals grow and produce raindrops and snowflakes that are large enough to overcome the rising air currents and fall out of the cloud as rain or snow. In temperate latitudes, much of the rain starts life as snow and melts during its fall to the ground. In very deep convective clouds, hail (frozen rain) may form instead.

Clouds and rain are generally associated with low-pressure systems. This is because low-pressure systems occur in areas where a lot of air is rising, cooling as it does so. In regions of high pressure, by contrast, the air is sinking toward the ground, warming as it falls. As a result, water droplets in the air evaporate into invisible water vapor, and the clouds formed from the droplets break up and disappear.

There are 10 main types of clouds. Each carries its own message about the weather to come.

CIRRUS *High-altitude ice-crystal cloud. It is often a sign of bad weather to come.* ▼

CIRROCUMULUS *High-altitude rippling cloud. It often forms on the edge of unsettled weather.* ▼

CIRROSTRATUS *High, milky cloud. It often brings showers or rain within 12 hours.* ▼

ALTOCUMULUS *Mid-altitude banded masses. They usually break up to give sunny periods.* ▼

ALTOSTRATUS *Mid-altitude, thin blue or gray sheet. It can develop into rain clouds.* ▼

NIMBOSTRATUS *A solid mass of low-lying cloud. A sign that rain is imminent.* ▼

STRATOCUMULUS *Low rolls of cloud. They are usually associated with dry but overcast weather.* ▼

STRATUS *Low, shapeless, foggy clouds that often blanket hills. They commonly bring drizzle.* ▼

CUMULUS *Fluffy, low, cauliflowerlike clouds. They are associated with sunny spells.* ▼

CUMULONIMBUS *Tall, often anvil-shaped clouds. They usually bring showers and thunder.* ▼

FACTS ABOUT THE EARTH

Natural disasters

DOUBLE DISASTER

Most of the 99,000 people who perished in a massive earthquake that struck the Japanese capital of Tokyo in 1923 died not in the quake itself but in firestorms that raged through the city immediately after the first shock, just before noon. The earthquake set off several fires as it brought down power cables and shattered gas mains. But hundreds of other fires started when family cooking stoves fell to the ground, igniting the wood and paper from which most of the houses were built. Almost half the city was destroyed in the quake, but about 95 percent of the damage was caused by fire. Almost half a million houses burned down in the conflagration that swept Tokyo.

LIFESAVING SENTENCE

A prisoner in the basement of a stone jail—a stevedore named August Cyparis, who had been jailed for brawling—was one of only three survivors of one of the world's worst volcanic eruptions. The jail was the only building in the city of St.-Pierre—on the Caribbean island of Martinique—that withstood the volcanic blast and the fire that followed.

St.-Pierre was wiped out in 3 minutes when Mont Pelée, which loomed over the city, erupted on May 8, 1902, releasing a cloud of red-hot gas and rock dust that raced down the volcano's flanks. The eruption killed the entire population of 28,000 except Cyparis, a priest, and a man driving a pony carriage on the city outskirts.

UNWELCOME DIVERSION

An attempt to divert a lava flow after an eruption on Mount Etna in Sicily in 1669 caused a local war. The citizens of nearby Catania tried to save their city from the lava by forcing it to flow in a different direction. However, they were attacked by the inhabitants of Paterno, a village threatened by the lava's new course. The Catanians were routed, and the lava quickly flowed back on its original course. It eventually destroyed the western half of Catania.

LASTING REMINDER

Fifteen years after being destroyed by the terrible earthquake of 1972, downtown Managua, Nicaragua, was still devastated. The center of the city was little more than an overgrown field dotted with ruins. Yet the inhabitants were still giving directions as if the old streets, buildings, and landmarks still existed.

MITIGATED DISASTER

In 1985 alone, forest and brushfires burned 1.5 million acres of land in the United States and Canada. Most of the fires were started by lightning and destroyed millions of dollars' worth of trees and other commercially valuable property. But foresters have become increasingly aware that fire is nature's way of cleaning out old, weak, or diseased trees and overgrown forests, opening the way for new and healthier generations of trees. The strongest trees tend to survive even a bad fire, and they repopulate the burned and cleared ground with strong new specimens.

BURIED ALIVE

An earthquake devastated China's densely populated Shenshi Province in 1556, killing an estimated 830,000 people in the worst quake disaster ever recorded. Many of the victims were buried alive when their cave homes collapsed, and others perished from the famine and disease that followed. Another severe earthquake struck Tientsin and Tangshan in 1976, killing some 655,000 people.

TERROR OF THE TSUNAMIS

Tsunamis are often called tidal waves, although they have nothing to do with tides. They start out as barely noticeable deep-water ripples caused by underwater

---

THE RICHTER SCALE

The Richter scale measures the total energy released during an earthquake. The scale is open-ended and is a logarithmic progression. An increase of one point on the scale indicates that the force of the earthquake is 10 times greater than the number below. So an earthquake of magnitude 5 is ten times more powerful than a quake of magnitude 4, a hundred times more powerful than one of magnitude 3, and 1,000 times more powerful than a quake of magnitude 2.

The largest earthquakes ever recorded, such as the Lisbon earthquake in 1755, have measured about 8.9 on the scale.

More than 300,000 shocks with magnitudes between 2 and 2.9 occur every year. Jolts of less than 1 can be detected only on a seismograph. Humans only begin to feel shocks with a magnitude of 2 or more, although animals can detect smaller tremors. Earthquakes over 5 cause minor damage, and those over 8 can produce almost total destruction.

The scale was devised in 1935 by Charles F. Richter (1900–85), an American seismologist.

THE MERCALLI SCALE

The severity of an earthquake is also measured by scientists using a scale first devised in 1902 by an Italian geologist, Giuseppe Mercalli.

The scale, known as the Modified Mercalli, is used to assess the effects of a quake on people at a particular place, rather than to measure the quake's overall power.

Intensity 0 Registered only by seismographs.
Intensity 1 Not felt, except in perfectly still conditions.
Intensity 2 Felt by a few at rest. Suspended objects swing.
Intensity 3 Felt noticeably indoors. Parked cars may rock.
Intensity 4 Usually felt indoors. People awakened. Windows rattle.
Intensity 5 Felt generally. Some falling plaster. Dishes, windows broken.
Intensity 6 Felt by all. Chimneys damaged. Furniture moved. Difficult to walk.
Intensity 7 Felt in moving cars. Moderate damage.
Intensity 8 Damage to weak structures. Monuments and walls fall down.
Intensity 9 Total destruction of weak structures. Ground fissured.
Intensity 10 Only strongest buildings survive. Ground badly cracked. Rails bent.
Intensity 11 Few buildings survive. Broad fissures. Underground pipes broken.
Intensity 12 Total destruction. Ground waves seen.

FUNNEL OF DEATH *A whirling tornado, hanging below the storm clouds that power it, sweeps across a prairie in Nebraska. Tornadoes generate the world's highest known wind speeds: the record is 280 m.p.h., measured in a tornado that roared over Wichita Falls, Texas, on April 2, 1958. The most destructive tornado on record smashed through Annapolis, Missouri, on March 18, 1925. It cut a 1,000-foot-wide swath through the town, tearing up massive oak trees, splitting open stone buildings, throwing cars over rooftops, and derailing passenger trains. In minutes it was gone—leaving 823 people dead and 2,990 injured.*

earthquakes or volcanic eruptions. But they build up in shallow water into crests that can be more than 200 feet high. At sea they race through the water at speeds of up to 490 miles per hour. As they approach the land they suck back the sea, beaching ships in harbors. The giant waves then crash onto the shore, causing enormous destruction.

The largest known tsunami, an estimated 280 feet high, roared past Ishigaki-shima, largest island in the Ryukyu chain in the western Pacific Ocean, in April 1971. But the wave is not known to have caused any damage; instead, it dissipated its power in the open sea.

Tsunamis occur most often in the Pacific Ocean, whose basin is ringed by volcanoes. The term comes from Japanese *tsu* ("port") and *nami* ("waves").

Astonishingly, the largest known wave was not a

tsunami. It was caused by a landslide that sent some 100 million tons of rock crashing into remote Lituya Bay in Alaska in 1958. The slide produced a single immense crest, which swamped the hills on the opposite side of the bay to a height of nearly 1,700 feet. Then the monster surge bounced back into the bay and, as a mere 200-foot-high wave, raced harmlessly out to sea.

THE ISLAND THAT BLEW UP
Some 36,000 people were killed by the tsunamis that followed a violent eruption on the volcanic island of Krakatoa (Krakatau) on August 27, 1883. But even though the entire northern part of the island collapsed into the sea, no one died in the eruption itself, which was heard as far as 3,000 miles away. Volcanic dust spread over the world, causing vivid sunrises and sunsets. The shock was felt in California, 9,000 miles distant from Krakatoa—which is in the Sunda Strait between the Indonesian islands of Java and Sumatra. The killer tsunamis raced along the coasts of Java and Sumatra, surging up to 10 miles inland and smashing trees and houses.

Since 1883, volcanic vents on and around Krakatoa have erupted more than 30 times, the last occasion being in October 1981. However, the eruptions were minor and caused no known deaths. One of the vents—known as Anak Krakatoa, meaning "Child of Krakatoa"—has grown into a separate island 500 feet above sea level.

LONG-DISTANCE DESTRUCTION
Homes and cars were swallowed up when the streets of Anchorage, Alaska, buckled and cracked during a violent earthquake whose epicenter was 100 miles away. The earthquake took place on Good Friday, 1964, and registered 8.5 on the Richter scale. Its seismic waves made the land rise and fall visibly over an area estimated at 80,000 square miles.

The earthquake was followed by a 25-foot-high tsunami that destroyed the waterfront at Valdez in southern Alaska. A few hours later another and slightly smaller tsunami caused by the earthquake struck the shore about 1,800 miles away, at Crescent City, California, and killed 12 people.

DUST OVER EUROPE
In 1783 the Laki volcano in Iceland erupted, killing one in five of the island's inhabitants and covering Europe with a pall of dust that took months to disperse. One of the world's largest volcanic eruptions, the blast opened up a fissure 18 miles long, from which lava spread over an area of 221 square miles.

Laki belched out dust and poisonous gas in vast quantities, causing disease and famine that killed more than 10,500 people and three-quarters of Iceland's livestock.

EYEWITNESS TO POMPEII'S DESTRUCTION
The earliest recorded scientific account of a volcanic eruption was given in A.D. 79 by the Roman writer Pliny the Younger (c. A.D. 62–c. 113), who witnessed the eruption of Vesuvius and the resulting destruction of the cities of Pompeii and Herculaneum. The initial explosion came on August 24 and produced a thick ash cloud that, wrote Pliny, spread over "the earth like a flood."

He observed the disaster form a spot 20 miles away and described how the "black and dreadful cloud ...burst open in twisted and quivering gusts to reveal long flames resembling large flashes of lightning." Strong shocks caused buildings to sway "as if they had been torn from their foundations. The next day Pliny

went to the coast and found that earth tremors had caused the sea to "roll back on itself," revealing the seabed. Later in the day black ash enveloped Pliny's vantage point in a darkness so thick that he felt he was "in a sealed room without light." Several hours later the cloud dispersed, and a landscape "covered by a thick layer of ash that resembled snow" emerged.

About 20,000 people died in the disaster. Pompeii disappeared beneath ash, and Herculaneum was engulfed by a boiling mudflow. After some initial looting, the cities were abandoned. Pompeii was not rediscovered until 1748, by an engineer named Alcubierre, who was working for the king of Naples.

POMPEII OF THE NORTH
In 1973 a fishing port on the island of Heimaey off Iceland was partially buried by a volcanic eruption, the first time this had happened to a town since Pompeii and Herculaneum were buried by the eruption of Vesuvius in southern Italy in A.D. 79. But, thanks to an efficient evacuation operation, only one person died beneath the thick lava flow from the Icelandic volcano: a man looking for alcohol who was asphyxiated in a gas-filled cellar.

The town has since been completely rebuilt, and the population has returned. Curiously, the eruption did bring the town's fishermen one major benefit. Part of the lava stream flowed into the harbor and formed a perfect natural breakwater across the entrance.

VOLCANIC FLAK
Only some skillful flying by the pilot of an Australian airliner on January 21, 1951, prevented the plane from being shot down by flak—from a volcano. The aircraft, belonging to the Australian airline Qantas, was passing over Mount Lamington in Papua New Guinea. Unknown to scientists, the mountain was a dormant volcano. It suddenly erupted, spouting ash and pumice 36,000 feet into the air. Bits of pumice stone pounded against the airliner's wings and fuselage, but the pilot kept control and flew the aircraft out of the danger zone.

The people living near Mount Lamington were not so fortunate. Almost 3,000 died in incandescent ash clouds that gushed from the volcano in the wake of the blast.

CHRISTMAS EVE CATASTROPHE
In December 1953 a Coronation Tour of New Zealand by Queen Elizabeth coincided with one of the country's worst natural disasters. On Christmas Eve a huge mudflow composed of some 600 million gallons of hot acidic water and debris burst from the crater lake of Ruapehu, a volcano on the North Island.

The mudflow raced down the Whangaehu River, demolishing the Tangiwai Bridge, which carried the main Auckland-to-Wellington railway line. Five minutes after the bridge collapsed, a night express train plunged into the ravine and was swept away by the mudflow; 151 passengers lost their lives.

BOULDER BOMBS
Large boulders exploded like bombs during an earthquake that struck the mountains of northern Assam, India, in August 1950. According to an eyewitness, F. Kingdon-Ward, a British naturalist, the shock's vibrations blurred the surrounding trees and ridges, and long fissures appeared in the ground.

Despite the earthquake's violence, Kingdon-Ward escaped unharmed. A spilled glass of water in his tent was the only evidence of the shock. Elsewhere in the region between 1,500 and 2,000 people died as a result of the earthquake and subsequent floods.

THE WORLD'S WORST NATURAL DISASTERS

The death tolls given in the following list are based on commonly accepted data but are not definitive.

Deaths	Date	Cause	Place
75,000,000	Mid-14th century	Bubonic plague (Black Death)	Europe and Asia
22,000,000	1918	Influenza	Worldwide
20,000,000	1969–71	Famine	Northern China
10,000,000	1939	Floods/famine	Northern China
9,500,000	1877–78	Famine	China
3,700,000	1931	Flood	Yellow River, China
3,000,000	1669–70	Famine	Bombay/Madras, India
1,500,000	1943–44	Famine	Bengal, India
1,000,000	1201	Earthquake	Syria/Egypt
1,000,000	1846–47	Famine	Ireland
900,000	1887	Flood	Honan Province, China
830,000	1556	Earthquake	Shensi, China
800,000	1838	Famine	Northwestern India
655,000	1976	Earthquake	Tientsin/Tangshan, China
500,000	1970	Typhoon/flood	Bangladesh
300,000	1737	Earthquake	Calcutta, India
300,000	1881	Typhoon	Haiphong, Indochina
300,000	1642	Flood	Yellow River, China
250,000	526 B.C.	Earthquake	Antioch, Syria
215,000	1876	Tsunami	Bay of Bengal, India
200,000	1703	Earthquake	Tokyo, Japan
200,000	856	Earthquake	Persia
180,000	1920	Earthquake	Kansu Province, China
?	1983–	Famine (continuing)	Africa, eastern and southern

SON OF KRAKATOA *A jet of ash bursts from Anak Krakatoa (left), a volcano that appeared off the Indonesian coast in 1952. It thunders on the site of Krakatoa, which exploded cataclysmically in 1883, and its name means "Child of Krakatoa." Now about 500 feet high, it is still active.*

EARTHQUAKE ISLAND *Sicilians, many of whom live near Mount Etna, have coexisted for centuries with quakes as well as the volcano. A quake shattered this town in 1968.*

STORM WARNING *Ominous clouds darken the waterfront of Hong Kong as a typhoon sweeps in from the South China Sea. Winds in a typhoon—a Pacific hurricane—can reach almost 200 m.p.h.*

Time and the calendar

WHY MINUTES HAVE 60 SECONDS

Hours and degrees of longitude are divided into 60 minutes, and minutes into 60 seconds, because 60 was the number base used by the Sumerians, the first people known to have written down a workable counting system, 5,000 years ago in Mesopotamia.

DAYS OF THE GODS

English and the related Germanic languages, such as German, Dutch, Danish, and Swedish, derive most of their names for the days of the week from Germanic and Norse mythology. French and other Romance languages, such as Italian and Spanish, derive theirs from Latin and classical mythology.

ENGLISH	FRENCH
Sunday (Sun day)	Dimanche (*Dies Dominica,* "Lord's Day")
Monday (Moon day)	Lundi (*Lunae dies,* "Moon day")
Tuesday (Tiw's day. Germanic god identified with Mars)	Mardi (*Martis dies,* "Mars's day")
Wednesday (Woden's, or Odin's, day)	Mercredi (*Mercurii dies,* "Mercury's day")
Thursday (Thor's day)	Jeudi (*Jovis dies,* "Jove's day")
Friday (Frigg's, or Freya's, day)	Vendredi (*Veneris dies,* "Venus's day")
Saturday (Saturn's day)	Samedi (*Sabbati dies,* "Sabbath day")

HOW THE MONTHS WERE NAMED

All the English names for the months of the year have Roman origins. The last four get their names from the Latin numbers 7 to 10, because the early Romans began their year in March. January was named after Janus, the god of gateways, because the god's festival happened to fall at that time of year. When in about 150 B.C. the Romans moved back the date for taking up official office (and hence the start of a new year) from March to January, the choice made years before to name the month for Janus must have seemed especially appropriate.

MONTH	ORIGIN
January	Janus, god of gateways
February	Februa, festival of purification
March	Mars, god of war
April	*aperio,* the Latin "to open," because of the unfolding of buds and blossoms in spring
May	Maia, goddess of fertility
June	Juno, goddess of women
July	Julius Caesar
August	Augustus, the first Roman emperor
September	*septem,* the Latin "seven"
October	*octo,* the Latin "eight"
November	*novem,* the Latin "nine"
December	*decem,* the Latin "ten"

WHY DAYS HAVE 24 HOURS

The custom of dividing each day into 24 parts seems to have originated with the ancient Egyptians in about 3500 B.C. They divided daylight and darkness into periods of 12 hours each. But this meant that the length of each hour changed during the year as the nights lengthened and shortened. It was Babylonian astronomers who, in about 300 B.C., adopted the now universal practice of making all 24 hours equal in length, regardless of when the sun rose or set.

In Europe, however, equal hours did not become standard until about A.D. 1350, some 70 years after the introduction of mechanical clocks.

THE LONGEST YEAR

By 46 B.C. the Roman republican calendar then in use had become hopelessly out of step with the seasons. The spring equinox, which should have coincided with the end of March, was arriving in the middle of May. The calendar, devised some time between the 5th and 1st centuries B.C., was based on lunar months of $29\frac{1}{2}$ days. It consisted of 12 months and originally began on March 1, the start of the farmer's year and the time when Roman officials took office. There were 355 days, $10\frac{1}{4}$ days short of the solar year. In an attempt to prevent a slip in the seasons—so that midsummer would always fall in June, for example—an extra, short month was added every other year. But this resulted in an average year of $366\frac{1}{4}$ days, one day more than the solar year.

In 46 B.C., Julius Caesar commissioned Sosigenes, a Greek astronomer, to devise a new calendar. Sosigenes recommended that it be based on the solar year, with 365 days and an extra day every fourth year—the first leap year. But before this new, Julian, system could be put into effect, the discrepancy between seasons and date had to be corrected.

An extra 23 days were due anyway in February of 46 B.C. Caesar added another 67 days in the form of 2 extra months between November and December, so that 46 B.C. lasted a total of 445 days. It became known as the Year of Confusion. But by its end, January fell where March had been, and the spring equinox was back at the end of March.

IMPERIAL JEALOUSY

The month of August lasts 31 days because of an emperor's jealousy, according to a popular historical anecdote. In 8 B.C. August was named after Augustus, the first Roman emperor. Before that it had been called Sextilis (then the sixth month), from the time when the Roman year began on March 1. Sextilis, however, had only 30 days—one fewer than July, named after Julius Caesar—and Augustus could not bear to be outdone. So he had August extended to 31 days to match July, and he reduced February to 28 days, making it the year's shortest month.

THE DAYS DON'T DWINDLE DOWN

Each day is longer than the one it follows—by 0.00000002 second—because the earth's spin is gradually slowing down. Too small to notice, the delay adds up over time. One century ago the day was shorter by 0.00073 second. The slowing is caused by tidal friction brought about by the moon's gravitational pull on shallow seas.

THE INACCURATE EARTH

Until atomic clocks were invented in the 1940s and 1950s, all clocks were inaccurate because they were based on the earth's rotation, which is itself irregular. In addition to being slowed fractionally each day by the dragging effect of the tides, the earth spins at slightly different speeds from day to day because of the complex gravitational forces acting on it.

In 1967 an international agreement finally broke the link between the measurement of time and the earth's spin. Previously, the second had been defined as 1/86,400 of a day. The agreement replaced that definition with another: the time taken for an atom of the metal cesium to vibrate 9,192,631,770 times.

NO MONEY, NO TIME

Britain's Royal Greenwich Observatory, which has been keeper of Greenwich mean time, the world standard, since 1884, announced in March 1986 that it could no longer afford to keep its six atomic clocks running.

JUST A SECOND

Clocks around the world were put back by 1 second at midnight Greenwich Mean Time on July 1, 1983. It was the 11th such "leap second" to be introduced to the calendar since 1972. The purpose of the adjustments is to keep clock time in line with astronomical time.

COUNTDOWN TO DISASTER

Although navigators have known for centuries how to measure latitude—how far north or south they are—by taking sightings of the stars, they had no reliable way of working out longitude, how far east or west they were, until the 18th century. To reckon longitude, the exact time must be known. As the earth spins, the sun reaches its highest point in the sky at different times—an hour later for every 1/24th of the earth's circumference. By comparing midday locally with the time at a known point, therefore, navigators can work out how far east or west of that point they are.

Until the 18th century most navigators made do with dead reckoning, which meant working out their position by calculating how fast their ships had been sailing for how long and in what direction. But this method was extremely inaccurate, since there was no way of allowing for the effects of ocean currents, and in 1707 it contributed to a British naval disaster. On October 22, 1707, three ships, including the admiral's flagship, were wrecked off the Scilly Isles. More than 2,000 men died. The tragedy helped to spur the British Admiralty to set up a board of longitude, which offered a reward of £20,000 to anyone who could devise a means of measuring longitude at sea to within half a degree, or about 30 miles. The solution—an accurate clock—was devised by a Yorkshire carpenter, John Harrison. The chronometer he made, after

FIRST DATE *A total eclipse of the sun—like this one photographed from India on February 16, 1980—once blacked out the sky over Mesopotamia during a savage battle between Lydians, from present-day Turkey, and Medes, from what is now Iran. Terrified by what they took to be an omen, the armies downed weapons and made peace on the spot. Because eclipses are now known to fall at predictable intervals, modern astronomers have pinpointed the day as May 28, 585 B.C.—and the battle is now the earliest historical event for which a precise date is known.*

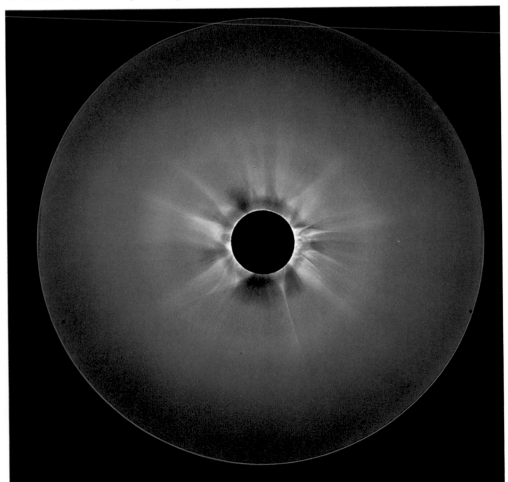

40 years of work, was tested by the navy in 1762 and found to be only 5 seconds off after 81 days at sea—an accuracy precise enough to enable a ship to work out its longitude to within about 2 miles.

But Harrison did not get the full reward because the navy claimed that the achievement was a fluke. After another trial in 1763 the board grudgingly handed over

part of the reward: £5,000. But it refused to hand over the rest on the grounds that the clock was too complicated and difficult to manufacture. After years of lobbying both Parliament and George III, Harrison finally settled in 1773 for what many believe to have been the full amount, but may not have been. He died 3 years later at the age of 82.

DIVIDING UP THE YEAR WITH THE SUN OR THE MOON

Most Western nations now use the Gregorian calendar, named for Pope Gregory XIII (1502–85) and revised by him from the Julian calendar devised by the Greek astronomer Sosigenes for Julius Caesar in 46 B.C. The Gregorian calendar is based on the 365.242 days the earth takes to revolve around the sun. The Hebrew and Muslim calendars are based on the moon. The ancient Chinese calendar, also based on the moon, is out of favor in modern China but is still the preferred calendar in some other Asian countries. The Hebrew calendar

periodically includes an extra month, known as First Adar, and the Chinese calendar does so occasionally. In the Muslim calendar an extra day is added to the last month in some years to ensure that the first day of the new year coincides with the new moon.

The Hebrew calendar is dated from 3761 B.C., the supposed year of the creation of the world. The Muslim calendar is dated from A.D. 622, the year in which Muhammad moved from Mecca to Medina, the city where he eventually died in 632.

GREGORIAN
A widely used calendar matching the seasons, with a 365.242-day year.

Month	days
January	31
February (in leap year 29)	28
March	31
April	30
May	31
June	30
July	31
August	31
September	30
October	31
November	30
December	31

HEBREW
The year 5748 coincides with September 24, 1987 – September 11, 1988.

Month	days
Tishri (Sept – Oct)	30
Heshvan (Oct – Nov) (in some years 30)	29
Kislev (Nov – Dec) (in some years 30)	29
Tevet (Dec – Jan)	29
Shevat (January – February)	30
Adar (February – March) (in leap year 30)	29
Nisan (March – April)	30
Iyar (April – May)	29
Sivan (May – June)	30
Tammuz (June – July)	29
Av (July – August)	30
Elul (August – Sept)	29

MUSLIM
The year 1408 coincides with August 26, 1987 – August 13, 1988.

Month	days
Muharram	30
Safar	29
Rabī I	30
Rabī II	29
Jumādā I	30
Jumādā II	29
Rajab	30
Sha'ban	29
Ramadān	30
Shawwāl	29
Dhū al-Qa'dah	30
Dhū al-Hijjah	29 or 30

CHINESE
The ancient Chinese agricultural calendar has 24 seasonal segments, each of about a fortnight. The Gregorian dates given are approximate.

Fortnight	Gregorian dates
Li Chun (Spring Begins)	February 5 – 19
Yu Shui (Rain Water)	February 19 – March 5
Jing Zhe (Excited Insects)	March 5 – 20
Chun Fen (Vernal Equinox)	March 20 – April 4/5
Qing Ming (Clear and Bright)	April 4/5 – 20
Gu Yu (Grain Rains)	April 20 – May 5
Li Xia (Summer Begins)	May 5 – 21
Xiao Man (Grain Fills)	May 21 – June 5
Mang Zhong (Grain in Ear)	June 5 – 21
Xia Zhi (Summer Solstice)	June 21 – July 7
Xiao Shu (Slight Heat)	July 7 – 23
Da Shu (Great Heat)	July 23 – August 7
Li Qiu (Autumn Begins)	August 7 – 23
Chu Shu (Limit of Heat)	August 23 – September 7
Bai Lu (White Dew)	September 7 – 23
Qui Fen (Autumn Equinox)	September 23 – October 8
Han Lu (Cold Dew)	October 8 – 23
Shuang Jiang (Frost Descends)	October 23 – November 7
Li Dong (Winter Begins)	November 7 – 22
Xiao Xue (Little Snow)	November 22 – December 7
Da Xue (Heavy Snow)	December 7 – 22
Dong Zhi (Winter Solstice)	December 22 – January 6
Xiao Han (Little Cold)	January 6 – 21
Da Han (Severe Cold)	January 21 – February 5

THE UNIVERSE

Early astronomers

HOW TO MEASURE THE WORLD

The distance around the earth was first accurately measured by the Greek astronomer Eratosthenes (c. 276–195 B.C.). His calculations were based on the fact that at midday on midsummer day the sun was directly above Aswan in Egypt, where it shone down a well without casting a shadow. On the same day in another year, he measured the angle of the sun at midday in Alexandria—where he was the director of the library—and compared it with that at Aswan, about 500 miles due south.

Eratosthenes found that there was a difference in angle of one-fiftieth of a circle—about 7 degrees—between the two cities. So he deduced that the distance between Alexandria and Aswan was about one-fiftieth of the earth's total circumference. His figure of about 25,000 miles for the earth's circumference through the poles almost matches the accepted modern measurement of 24,859 miles.

PTOLEMY ACCUSED

Many of the findings of the Greco-Egyptian astronomer Ptolemy (c. A.D. 120–80) were based upon lies—or so says a 20th-century American astronomer, Robert Russell Newton. He accuses Ptolemy of inventing bogus observations to support his theories and of altering, for the same reason, genuine observations made by earlier astronomers. Ptolemy, who lived and worked in Alexandria, Egypt, recorded his views in a 13-volume treatise, now known by its Arabic title as the *Almagest*, meaning "The Greatest." Newton bases his attack on close analysis of the treatise's contents.

In his book *The Crime of Claudius Ptolemy*, published in 1978, Newton asserts that Ptolemy reported an observation that would have been impossible. He gave the time of a lunar eclipse that took place in 200 B.C. on September 22 as the equivalent of 6.30 P.M.

But the moon did not rise until half an hour later on that date. To give the bogus observation credibility, Ptolemy attributed it to an earlier and widely respected Greek astronomer, Hipparchus, whose own records have long since vanished. And since Hipparchus was thought by his contemporaries to be a man above suspicion, Newton is in no doubt about who did the faking. Far from being a genius, he insists, Ptolemy was a fraud.

THE MAN WITH THE GOLDEN NOSE

The wealthy Danish astronomer Tycho Brahe (1546–1601) had a large part of his nose sliced off during a sword fight. He had a replacement made from gold, silver, copper, and wax, then painted this nosepiece the color of flesh, glued it in place, and wore it until his death more than 30 years later at the age of 54. The duel in which he had lost most of his real nose was with a young nobleman over who was the better mathematician. Six years before the duel, at the age of 14, Tycho had witnessed a partial eclipse of the sun and determined to become an astronomer against his family's wish that he become a lawyer.

His career took off in November 1572 when he observed a brilliant supernova—an exploding star—which was subsequently named Tycho's Star. It was the brightest supernova to have been seen for 1,000 years, and Tycho's description of it disproved the belief, which dated back to the Greeks, that the heavens were unchanging.

HERESY THROUGH A TELESCOPE

Although the Italian astronomer Galileo Galilei (1564–1642) was the first person to use a telescope for systematic observations of the skies, he did not invent the device. It is thought to have been invented by accident in 1608 by the children of a Dutch lens grinder, Hans Lipperhey.

While the children were playing one day in their father's workshop in the town of Middleburg, they are said to have put together a concave spectacle lens and a short-focus convex lens. Lipperhey used the telescope, as he called it, to observe a distant weather vane, which appeared larger and nearer.

The following year Galileo heard of the telescope and made a more powerful model for himself in his studio in Padua. His observations, which led him to support Copernicus's revolutionary theories, at first caused little stir among the establishment, but in 1614 were denounced as heresy by the Roman Catholic Church, and Galileo was later put on trial for his life. He was found guilty, but was spared after he recanted his heretical views.

Galileo spent the last 8 years of his life under house arrest near Florence. But although, to save his life, Galileo may have denied his findings in public, he never recanted in private. He continued to believe that the earth moved and the sun stood still.

THREE VIEWS OF THE SOLAR SYSTEM

In the history of astronomy there have been three major theories about the workings of the solar system: those of the Greek astronomer Claudius Ptolemy, the Polish astronomer Nicholas Copernicus, and the Danish astronomer Tycho Brahe. With modifications, Copernicus's theory is the one now accepted by scientists.

Ptolemy In the Ptolemaic theory, the sun and planets were thought to orbit the stationary earth in epicycles—that is, small circles whose centers moved around the circumference of larger circles. Ptolemy evolved a complex and clumsy system to explain the irregular orbits of the planets.

Copernicus The Ptolemaic system was challenged by Copernicus in the 16th century. He believed, correctly, that the earth orbited the sun. But he also believed—mistakenly—that the sun was the center of the entire universe, that the planets were all of the same size, and that they moved in perfect circles. The German astronomer Johannes Kepler (1571–1630), a student of Tycho Brahe, established in the early 17th century that the planets in fact move in ellipses (ovals).

Brahe Tycho Brahe attempted to reconcile the theory of Ptolemy with that of Copernicus. He felt that Ptolemy's theory did not explain the movements of the planets, and he believed Copernicus's theory to be heretical. So he suggested that the planets revolved around the sun, and that the sun and moon, in turn, revolved around the earth.

THE EARTH GOES AROUND AND AROUND

The first person to assert that the earth spins on its axis and revolves around the sun was not Copernicus but the Greek astronomer Aristarchus of Samos (c. 310–c. 250 B.C.). He anticipated later astronomers by declaring that the earth's rotation causes daylight and darkness, that the inclination of its axis causes the seasonal changes each year, and that the sun is larger than the earth.

Aristarchus also tried to measure the sizes and relative distances of the sun and the moon by using observation and calculation. But although his method was theoretically sound, he lacked the instruments that could obtain accurate measurements. He calculated that the sun was 18 to 20 times more distant than the moon, whereas the correct figure is about 390 times.

His heliocentric, or sun-centered, theory was reviled in his lifetime—and Aristarchus was threatened with prosecution for his alleged impiety. But his views were vindicated by Copernicus 1,800 years later.

THE STARS DO NOT FORETELL

Astrology, the age-old practice of predicting people's futures by casting their horoscopes based on the positions of the stars, the planets, and the moon, is a lot of moonshine. That is the opinion of most scientists, and one held by two 20th-century French researchers, Michel and Francoise Gauquelin, who have spent 20 years investigating the subject. They examined the birth data of more than 40,000 people throughout Europe to try to find correlations between birth signs, jobs, and personalities.

The Gauquelins' computerized findings were published in 1983. There was not one piece of evidence, they concluded, to show that astrology was anything but a sham. One of their experiments was to offer free "personalized" horoscopes to 150 people. But to each of the 150 they sent the same horoscope, that of a mass murderer named Dr. Marcel Petiot. Asked if they were pleased with their "personalized" horoscope, 141 respondents answered yes!

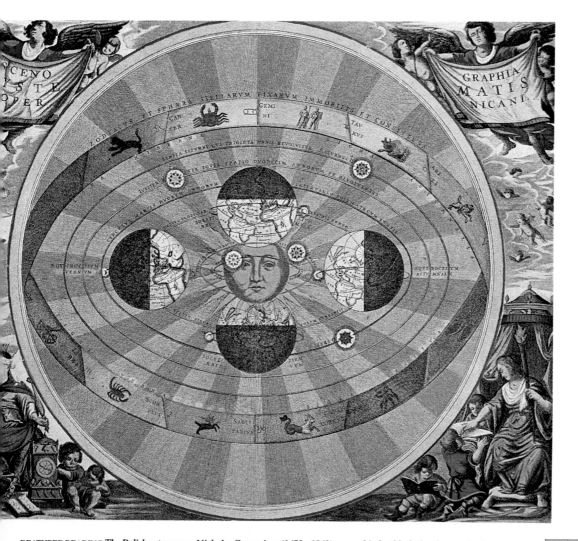

DEATHBED READING *The Polish astronomer Nicholas Copernicus (1473–1543) was on his deathbed when he saw the first printed copy of his book,* On the Revolutions of the Celestial Spheres. *It put forward his belief, illustrated here in a 17th-century diagram, that the earth was not the fixed center of the universe but merely a planet spinning around the sun. Copernicus had been convinced of this since about 1510 but in an era of religious controversy hesitated to publish his findings. Martin Luther opposed publication; the Vatican later condemned the book and did not remove it from the Index of Prohibited Books until 1758. By then the Copernican theory, which forms the basis of modern astronomy, was generally accepted, at least among enlightened scientists. Ironically, Copernicus had dedicated his great work to Pope Paul III.*

Modern astronomers

AN APPLE, APOCRYPHAL OR ACTUAL

The story that the English physicist Sir Isaac Newton (1642–1727) worked out his law of gravity after watching the fall of an apple is probably true, although nobody can ever know for sure. What makes some scholars doubt the story is that most of Newton's early biographers made no mention of it—an extraordinary omission, considering the importance of the discovery.

There are only two sources for the tale, and neither was an eyewitness. One is a clergyman, the Reverend William Stukely, who reported in his biography of Newton—written in the 18th century but not published until the 20th century—that the scientist told him of the incident while they were having tea together in the apple orchard at Newton's home.

The other source is Newton's niece, Catherine Barton Conduitt, who looked after Newton in his later years. Mrs. Conduitt's report, the first published account of the incident, appeared in *Elements of Newtonian Philosophy* by the French philosopher Voltaire. Voltaire's book was published in 1738, eleven years after Newton's death and more than 70 years after the apple was said to have fallen.

KARL'S SPARKS

The science of radio astronomy was born in 1931 when the U.S. engineer Karl Jansky (1905–50) intercepted radio waves from the Milky Way by accident. He made his discovery while investigating static on long-distance radio communications for the Bell Laboratories in New Jersey, using an improvised aerial built partly from a dismantled Ford car. Jansky never followed up his discovery, because his published findings aroused little interest.

After Jansky's discovery, the advance of radio astronomy in the United States owed much to Grote Reber (1911–), whose experiments inspired new studies of cosmic radio waves after World War II.

TOMB WITH A VIEW

The telescope at Lick Observatory on Mount Hamilton, in California, also serves as a tomb. The 36-inch refracting telescope is mounted on a pillar that contains the remains of James Lick (1796–1876), a wealthy financier and philanthropist who financed the observatory's construction and after whom it is named.

ACCIDENTAL OVERLOAD

The Van Allen belts (radiation-charged zones that girdle the earth) were discovered by accident. In 1958 the United States launched its first satellite, *Explorer 1*. It carried instruments to measure the intensity of cosmic radiation from space. But as the satellite soared out beyond the atmosphere, the radiation count on the meters suddenly dropped to zero—or seemed to.

Scientists on the ground were baffled until the U.S. astrophysicist James Van Allen (1914–) deduced that the satellite's meters had simply been overloaded, and so had broken down. The radiation belts now named after Van Allen lie between 400 and 40,000 miles above the earth.

FOUNDATIONS OF MODERN COSMOLOGY

Issac Newton's *Principia*, published in 1687, introduced the concept of universal gravitation and inspired a new generation of astronomers and cosmologists. The universe that Newton defined was a static and unchanging one. In it, space and time were unrelated.

In 1915 Albert Einstein's general theory of relativity showed the interrelation of matter, energy, gravity, space, and time. But despite evidence that contradicted Newton's model for a static universe, Einstein was unable to provide a new model.

The four basic forces

Edwin Hubble (1889–1953) was the first to suggest that the entire universe is expending, not static, with the more distant galaxies receding from the earth faster than the closer ones. This discovery led to the Big Bang theory, which states that the universe was created by an explosion 15 billion years ago. The discovery in 1965 of cosmic background radiation, which was assumed to be radiation left over from the early moments of the birth of the universe, supported the Big Bang theory.

Armed with a theory for the origin of the universe, cosmologists began theorizing about its evolution and ultimate fate. They became convinced that four basic forces—gravity, electromagnetism, strong nuclear forces, and weak nuclear forces—explain all the interactions in the universe.

GUTs

Next came grand unified theories (GUTs), which are an attempt to explain two or more of the basic forces by a single set of physical laws, and super GUTs, which seek to explain all four forces. GUTs suggest that all four forces were equivalent just after the Big Bang. Gravity was the first to emerge separately, followed by the strong nuclear force, electromagnetism, and finally the weak nuclear force. From that moment on, the universe behaved according to physical laws with which we are familiar, and the evolution of the universe as we know it began.

Most scientists believe that the universe will continue to expand, but that at a certain point, matter will collapse into huge black holes. Hydrogen and helium, which today constitute most of the universe, will be used up in thermonuclear fire of stars, about 10^{12} years from now. No new stars will be born, and the universe will consist of dead stars, meteoroids, rocks, and other cosmic debris.

Beyond the ultimate black holes

Eventually, after trillions of years have passed, two stars within a galaxy will collide with enough energy to kick one of the stars out of the galaxy. The other stars remaining in the galaxy will fall into a lower energy orbit closer to the center of the galaxy. Then, owing to the emission of gravitational radiation, these stars will fall into the galaxy's center, coalescing into one huge black hole.

When the universe is 10^{27} years old, it will consist of huge black holes surrounded by dead stars. After more time, entire galxies will spiral toward each other and collapse into supergalactic black holes. Eventually, after about 10^{106} years, these black holes will evaporate in a burst of particles and radiation equal to the explosion of a billion 1-megaton H-bombs.

WINDOWS ON THE UNIVERSE

Modern astronomers use three different types of telescope to probe the depths of space.

REFRACTING First developed early in the 17th century, refracting telescopes collect and magnify light through glass lenses. Their chief drawback is that the lenses can be supported only around their edges. As a result, very large lenses tend to sag, producing distortions, and this limits their useful size. The world's largest refracting telescope, built in 1897, is at Yerkes Observatory, in Wisconsin. Its largest lens is 40 inches across.

REFLECTING First built by the English physicist and mathematician Sir Isaac Newton in about 1668, a reflecting telescope uses a concave mirror to collect the light from stars. It can be larger than a refracting telescope, because the mirror can be supported across its entire width. The largest reflecting telescope is a Soviet instrument built in the 1970s near

Zelenchukskaya, in the Caucasus Mountains. Its largest mirror, which weighs about 75 tons, is 236 inches across. The telescope is powerful enough to spot the light from a single candle 15,000 miles away.

RADIO The first true radio telescope was built by the U.S. astronomer Grote Reber in 1937. Radio telescopes collect radio waves from space on a dish-shaped reflector in much the same way that a reflecting telescope collects light waves on a dish-shaped mirror. The world's largest single-dish radio telescope is slung like a hammock between the hills at the Arecibo Observatory in Puerto Rico. Completed in 1963, it has a dish 1,000 feet across. Near Socorro, New Mexico, astronomers have used computers to link together twenty-seven 85-foot-diameter parabolic dishes arranged in the shape of a huge Y. Completed in 1980, the array gives a radio view of the sky equivalent to that of a single dish 17 miles across.

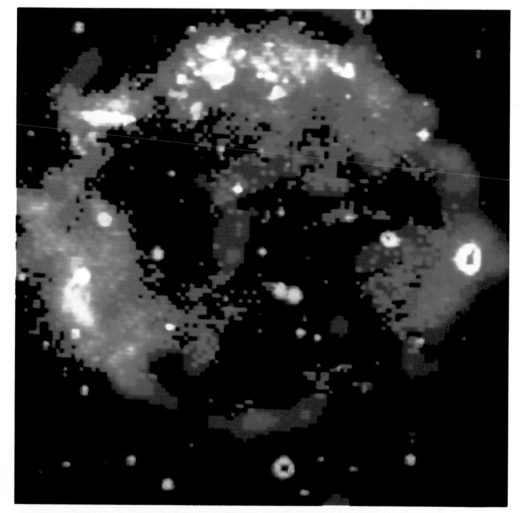

THREE IN ONE *Tycho's Star, named after the Danish astronomer Tycho Brahe, exploded in 1572 and grew so bright for a few weeks that it was visible to the naked eye even in broad daylight. Then it faded again. It was rediscovered in 1948 in the Northern Hemisphere constellation of Cassiopeia. Through an ordinary telescope little evidence of the blast can be seen. Its awesome scale becomes apparent only when other views are superimposed, as in this triple composite put together by U.S. researcher John Dickel. The yellow and red patches are visible through an optical telescope; the blue areas show up on a radio telescope; and the green regions emerge on film sensitive to X-rays.*

Origins of the universe

FAR HORIZONS

Space is so vast that astronomers have had to devise special units to keep their figures manageable. Their basic unit of distance is the light-year—the distance light travels in 1 year, or about 6 trillion miles (6 followed by 12 zeros). But astronomers also use an even larger unit known as the parsec, which is equivalent to 3.26 light-years.

BIG BANG EVIDENCE

In the 1940s George Gamow proposed that, right after the Big Bang, the universe was so hot that thermonuclear reactions could occur throughout space. This would mean that the early universe was filled with high-energy, shortwave photons (particles of light). In the 1960s, though unfamiliar with Gamow's ideas, Robert Dicke and J. E. Peebles of Princeton University in New Jersey theorized that the original radiation

left over from the Big Bang reactions would consist of low-energy photons that had been considerably stretched by the expansion of the universe. Dicke and Peebles decided to build an antenna to look for such radiation.

At about the same time, in another part of New Jersey, Arno Penzias and Robert Wilson, radio astronomers at Bell Laboratories, decided to use the Labs' new microwave horn antenna (designed to relay telephone calls to a communications satellite) for a purely scientific experiment: looking for radio waves emitted from our galaxy. They suspected that the noise they were trying to detect would be very faint—if they heard any noise at all.

To their surprise, they almost immediately heard a lot of static at the very short wavelength, or microwave, end of the spectrum. This noise came from all directions and did not vary with the time of day or, as the year progressed, with the seasons. For a brief time

COSMIC BLAST-OFF *The fan-shaped Orion Nebula, which glows in Orion's sword (inset), 1,600 light-years away from the earth, consists of a cloud of hot gases and dust spread out over at least 30 light-years of space. Yet the material it contains is so rarefied that a core sample taken from it, 1 inch across and 30 light-years long, would weigh less than a dime. Nebulas are the parents of stars, which form—frequently in clusters—as the result of the tug of gravity within the clouds. In the photograph below, the nebula is illuminated by the hot newborn stars in its center.*

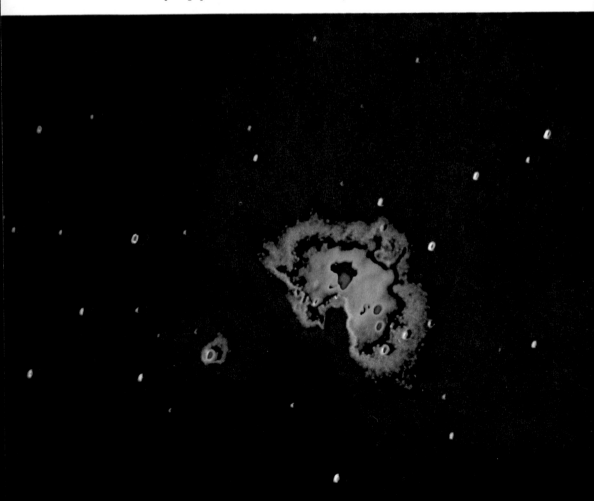

after their discovery, the scientists thought the noise might be caused by the droppings of pigeons roosting on the antenna. They removed the birds, cleaned the equipment—and still heard the noise.

By chance, talking to a colleague about another matter, Penzias learned of Peebles's and Dicke's efforts to find cosmic background radiation as evidence for the Big Bang theory. What the Princeton pair sought, the Bell Labs duo had found. Penzias and Wilson received the 1978 Nobel Prize in physics.

FIRST MOMENTS

Scientists have been able to construct a history of the universe back to a tiny fraction of a second after the Big Bang took place. At that moment, it is reckoned, there occurred the first comprehensible event in the origin of the universe: gravity emerged as a separate force from the single unifying force that had hitherto existed.

What happened before this is still a mystery. But scientists estimate that gravity broke free 10^{-43} seconds after the Big Bang—or a decimal point followed by 42 zeros and a 1.

CREATION'S CRUCIBLE

The figures involved in the concept of the universe's origin are, in every sense, astronomical. A fraction of a second after the universe was born, its temperature is calculated to have been more than 100 billion °Celsius (180 billion °F). Only 60 seconds later it had fallen to 10 billion °C (18 billion °F).

Today the universe's average temperature is −454°F (−270°C), just 5°F (3°C) above absolute zero, the lowest possible temperature.

ARE WE ALIENS?

Life may have originated in space and been brought to earth aboard a comet, according to a theory published in 1978 by the English astronomer Sir Fred Hoyle and the Sri Lankan astronomer Chandra Wickramasinghe. The creation of living material involved too many coincidences for it to have occurred on earth, they say; it required all the resources of space.

The astronomers argue that life probably formed elsewhere, then was deposited here by accident and thrived in earth's favorable conditions.

RIDDLE OF THE NEUTRINO

Among the most mysterious components of the universe are neutrinos. They are unimaginably tiny subatomic particles. Yet some scientists suspect that neutrinos may form 90 percent of the mass of the universe, and provide enough gravitational pull to slow and eventually reverse the headlong flight of the galaxies.

Despite their possibly central role as the universe's glue, neutrinos carry no electrical charge and are so difficult to study that their nature remains elusive. The particles travel at the speed of light and can pass right through the earth without even slowing down. Millions will pass through this page, and through you, while you are reading it.

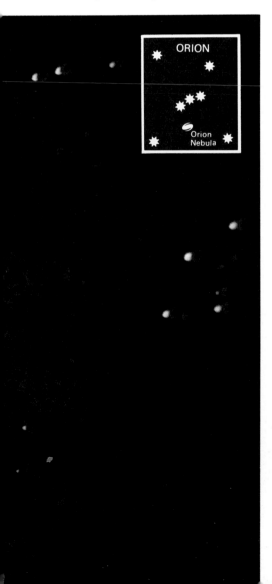

ORION

Orion
Nebula

BEGINNING WITH A BANG

Most astronomers now believe that the universe started with a gigantic explosion—the Big Bang—about 15 billion years ago (in any case, between 13 and 20 billion years ago). According to the theory, a "minute cosmic egg" of immeasurable energy exploded. Matter, gravity, and electromagnetism were created in the unimaginable blast, galaxies formed, and the universe began to expand at enormous speed, as it is still doing today.

Two other concepts have been proposed to explain the birth of the universe: the Oscillating Universe and the Steady State.

Oscillating Universe

The Big Bang idea is taken a step further by the Oscillating Universe theory. The present expansion, it says, will be followed by a contraction, brought on by the force of gravity. The outward-speeding galaxies will slow and stop, like balls tossed straight up in the air, then fall back toward the center. Finally, they will collide, triggering a new Big Bang; the cycle is repeated about once every 80 billion years.

Steady State

In the 1940s the idea of the Big Bang was challenged by the Steady State theory, which was put forward by a series of scientists, among them Britain's Sir Fred Hoyle. The scientists propounded a universe with no explosive start and an eternal life. Galaxies passing out of observable space, the theory holds, are replaced by new matter created from nothing and below the level of detectability.

But the theory was progressively discarded, notably after the discovery of cosmic background radiation by Arno Penzias and Robert Wilson in the United States. Present knowledge tends to support the Big Bang theory. But nothing is yet definitely known about why the Big Bang happened, only that it was a moment of infinite density, before which space and time were indistinguishable.

Voyaging beyond the earth

BLOWTORCH BLAST-OFF

In March 1926 the American physicist Robert Goddard (1882–1945) conducted the first tests with liquid-fuel rockets—in a field on his Aunt Effie's farm in Auburn, Massachusetts. His first rocket was fired from the back of a truck and ignited by means of a blowtorch. His early rockets were only about 4 feet tall. But in 1929 Goddard fired a far bigger rocket, which carried a small camera, a barometer, and a thermometer. The rocket made so much noise that the neighbors complained to the police.

Goddard's work received no official backing, and he and his colleagues frequently ran out of money. They got into further trouble with the police for illegally launching rockets from out-of-the-way spots. Their test models were often seized by the authorities or by angry farmers in whose fields the rockets had landed. However, with the aid of a $50,000 grant from the philanthropist David Guggenheim, Goddard set up an experimental rocket station in the New Mexico desert. There, he built rockets that reached heights of up to 8,000 feet and speeds of 700 m.p.h.

In 1935 Goddard became the first person to fire a liquid-fuel rocket that traveled faster than the speed of sound—at sea level, this is about 740 m.p.h. Altogether, he took out more than 200 rocketry patents, including one for a multistage rocket, the forerunner of modern three-stage booster rockets.

BLEEP . . . BLEEP . . . BLEEP

The first space vehicle to go into orbit around the earth was launched on October 4, 1957, the 40th anniversary of the Communist seizure of power in the Russian Revolution. It was the Soviet *Sputnik I*, which weighed only 185 pounds and was launched by means of a multistage rocket. *Sputnik I* traveled at 17,500 m.p.h.—then the highest speed ever achieved by a man-made object—and transmitted a radio bleep that could be picked up by listeners around the world.

The first U.S. artificial satellite, *Explorer 1*, was launched 4 months later, on January 31, 1958. It remained in orbit for 12 years and 2 months.

HOPE FOR AMERICAN COLONIES

A U.S. presidential panel has proposed a $700 billion space effort that would put human settlements on the moon in 30 years and permanent colonies on Mars by 2027. The program calls for the development of new space vehicles, one for cargo and one for passengers, that could be put into a low earth orbit. From these vehicles a transfer ship would carry passengers and cargo to the moon and beyond. The settlements would be sustained by permanent interplanetary space stations that would function as factories and supply depots.

The panel envisoned a time when a million passengers a day would be transported to new colonies in space.

BIG BOOST

The total power developed by all three stages of the United States' *Saturn V* booster rocket—used for all the Apollo moon shots—is almost 9 million pounds of thrust. It would take the engines of 50 Boeing 747 jumbo jets, a combined total of 200 engines, to match this amount of power.

LARGEST, SLOWEST, SAFEST

The Crawler, the huge transporter that takes the space shuttle to its launch pad, is the world's largest and slowest vehicle. It weighs 3,300 tons, and its top speed is 2 m.p.h. Nevertheless, in the interests of safety, the driver is ordered to wear a seat belt.

PRECIOUS STONES

The 12 Apollo astronauts who landed on the moon from 1969 through 1972, when the U.S. lunar landing program ended, brought back to earth a total of 842 pounds of lunar rocks and dust. Divided into the total cost of the Apollo program, estimated at $40 billion by the end of the project, the moon samples cost roughly $3 million per ounce. At that price, they are worth thousands of times their own weight in gold.

The astronauts left behind them the remains of six lunar landers, three lunar rover vehicles, and more than 50 tons of litter—scientific equipment, empty containers, and other rubbish—probably the most expensive waste materials in history.

MISSING THE MOON

The Apollo landings proved a great stimulus to computer engineers, mainly because of the guidance computers needed by the spacecraft. These navigational computers had to be hundreds of times more accurate than pevious models. An error of only 1 m.p.h. in the spacecraft's top speed would have resulted in its missing the moon by about 1,000 miles.

A YEAR IN SPACE

The world's most traveled man is the Soviet cosmonaut Valery Ryumin. In October 1980 he returned to earth from his second long-duration stay aboard the space station *Salyut 6*. His total time in space was 362 days—almost a full year.

During his space trips Ryumin circled the world 5,750 times, covering 150 million miles—a distance greater than a trip to Mars and back.

CALLING EARTH . . . QUIETLY

The radio transmitters that beam information back to earth from space shots are usually less powerful than the ones used in walkie-talkies or CB radios. The unmanned U.S. Voyager probers launched in 1977, for example, sent back spectacular pictures of Saturn and reams of scientific data across 800 million miles of space with transmitters that consumed only 28 watts. This is about half the power used by an ordinary light bulb. Weight is so important on a space mission that it is cheaper to have very sensitive receivers on the ground than to carry more powerful—but also heavier—transmitters into space.

SIGNAL SENSITIVITY

The radio antennae at U.S. tracking stations that monitor the transmissions from space shots are so sensitive that they can detect incoming signals with a strength of only one hundredth of a million million millionth (10^{-20}) of a watt.

This is so weak that if a signal of such strength were collected for the entire 4.6-billion-year history of the solar system, the total accumulated energy would be enough to light a 7.5-watt Christmas tree bulb for a mere 1/5000 of a second.

DREAM COME TRUE *To visit worlds beyond our own was a journey made only in the human imagination until the United States undertook the Apollo program. On May 25, 1961, President John F. Kennedy urged the nation to "commit itself to achieving the goal, before this decade is out, of landing a man on the moon and returning him safely." Eight years later, on July 20, 1969, the* Apollo 11 *mission put Neil Armstrong and Edwin Aldrin on the moon. A total of six moon landings was achieved, 1969–72. Shown above is the fourth landing, by the* Apollo 15 *mission (July–August 1971), on which astronauts James Irwin (saluting flag) and David Scott drove 17 miles over the lunar surface in the "dune buggy" at the right of the picture.*

HIGHER FLIERS

Astronauts can be 2 inches taller temporarily at the end of a space flight. The reason is that, without the pressure of gravity, cartilage discs in the spine expand, increasing the body's total length. For the same reason, people are fractionally taller in the morning, because the discs have expanded during the night.

The National Aeronautics and Space Administration has a collective name for all the physiological changes that affect astronauts in space: space adaptation syndrome. It includes the common malady of space sickness, whose symptoms resemble motion sickness on the earth, and a wide variety of other conditions. Among them are bone decalcification, changes in posture, general cardiovascular and muscle deterioration, decreased production of red blood cells, and increased fluid retention in the head, eyes, and chest cavities.

Fortunately, the human body seems to adapt to the very low gravity of space travel. In the U.S. Skylab missions, the astronauts who stayed up the longest returned in the best physical shape. This may have been due in part to the accumulating benefits of the exercise program followed by the Skylab crews.

BEWARE: ORBITING GARBAGE

There are about 1,000 artificial satellites in orbit around the earth, but they represent only about 5 percent of the man-made objects up there. The rest is junk and refuse, everything from dead satellites and discarded rocket stages to about 40,000 chunks of trash smaller than 8 inches in diameter, plus an estimated hundred billion very tiny objects, such as paint chips.

All this junk, orbiting mainly between 300 and 1,200 miles above the earth, has officials of the National Aeronautics and Space Administration worried, so worried that NASA has set up an office of orbital debris. Its director, Donald Kessler, warns, "If we don't have a coherent policy for managing space debris, an artificial asteroid belt will begin to circle the earth within 10 years. It will become common for satellites to collide with space debris."

SIX-MILLION-DOLLAR CLEANING BILL

Although most space debris is burned up by friction when it enters the atmosphere, there are costly and potentially dangerous exceptions. On January 24, 1978, for instance, a Soviet nuclear-powered satellite, *Cosmos 954,* crashed over northwestern Canada, spilling radioactive debris. The Canadian government presented the Soviet Union with a $6 million bill for the cleanup operation—of which, after protracted wrangling, the Soviets paid half.

Later that year two French farmers were narrowly missed by a 45-pound chunk of a reentering Soviet rocket that landed in a potato field. And in July 1979 the 80-ton U.S. space station *Skylab* fell in red-hot fragments across parts of Western Australia. This had its compensation for one young Australian, who flew to California with charred pieces of *Skylab* to collect a $10,000 reward offered by the San Francisco *Examiner.*

DOG THAT DIED IN SPACE

The first animal to travel into outer space was a dog called Laika, which was launched in a spacecraft by the Soviet Union in November 1957. The capsule was not designed to return to earth, and about a week later Laika died of asphyxiation when the oxygen ran out—provoking a worldwide outcry from animal lovers. Three years later, in August 1960, the Soviet Union sent two more dogs—Strelka and Belka—on a 24-hour spaceflight. This time the capsule was parachuted safely back to earth, and the animals were said to be none the worse for their experience.

DEATH OF AN ASTRONAUT

On April 12, 1961, the Soviet astronaut Yuri Gagarin (1934–68) became the first man to be rocketed into orbit around the earth. His 5-ton vehicle, the *Vostok* (meaning "east"), circled the earth once in just over 89 minutes, and the entire flight lasted 1 hour and 48 minutes from beginning to end. The *Vostok* returned safely after reaching a maximum altitude of 195 miles. Ironically, having survived this pioneering flight, the astronaut was killed 7 years later when a jet he was flying crashed during a training flight.

REQUIEM FOR A COW

In November 1960 an American rocket launched from Cape Canaveral, Florida, went off course and crashed in Cuba, killing a cow. The Cuban government gave the cow an official funeral as the victim of "imperialist aggression."

LIVING AND WORKING IN SPACE

The first space station, *Salyut*—meaning "Salute"—was launched by the Soviet Union in April 1971. It was designed to test the long-term capabilities of man to live and work in space, and to allow experimental work to be done in the fields of solar power, industrial processes, and medicine.

The United States launched its first space station, *Skylab,* in May 1973. It was larger than *Salyut*—about 20 feet long and 21 feet wide—and had two main compartments: a workshop and living quarters. There was a lavatory, a shower, solar-powered electric ovens, and hot plates. Sleeping bags were attached vertically to the walls. There was even an exercise bicycle for the astronauts. Three teams of astronauts manned *Skylab* for a total of 172 days. Then the last astronauts returned to earth, and the empty space station was left in orbit. In July 1979 it reentered the atmosphere and broke up as it fell to earth. Some 500 pieces of debris struck the earth, but hit nobody.

By then the Soviets had launched a series of Salyut stations. The last of these, *Salyut 7,* was launched in April 1982 and was still usable in 1986, when a bigger Soviet space station, *Mir* ("Peace"), was orbited.

CRADLE OF THE MIND

Although space travel is a 20th-century achievement, the idea of exploring space has fascinated mankind for centuries. The French dramatist and novelist Cyrano de Bergerac (1619–55)—model for Edmond de Rostand's 1897 play of the same name—predicted one day people would travel to the moon by rocket. The possibility of putting an artificial satellite in orbit was proposed in 1687 by the English mathematician and physicist Sir Isaac Newton. And in the 1890s a Russian scientist, Konstantin Tsiolkovsky (1857–1935), advocated rockets as the ideal way of traveling into outer space. "The earth is the cradle of the mind," he stated, "and man will not stay in the cradle forever!" He concluded that a multistage rocket could lift a space vehicle free of the earth's gravitational force, and proposed a "passenger rocket train" consisting of 20 single rockets.

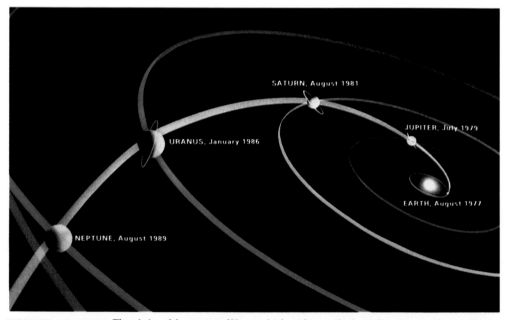

SATURN, August 1981

URANUS, January 1986

JUPITER, July 1979

EARTH, August 1977

NEPTUNE, August 1989

UNMANNED AND MANNED *The mission of the unmanned* Voyager 2 *(above) has sent back startling pictures of Jupiter, Saturn, and Uranus; and in 1989 it is expected to reveal much about Neptune as well. The spacecraft's launch in August 1977 was timed to catch the four planets in the so-called grand tour alignment—which occurs once every 176 years—and allow* Voyager *to investigate all four in just 12 years. By contrast, putting human beings into space, as in the space shuttle program (right), is far more costly and risky. Yet even after the* Challenger *tragedy in January 1986, the commitment to manned space programs remains strong in both the U.S.A., where shuttle launches are expected to resume in 1988, and in the Soviet Union, whose plans include a manned mission to Mars.*

MEN AND WOMEN IN SPACE

Manned spaceflight programs have so far been confined to the U.S.A. and the U.S.S.R. The current U.S. effort is concentrated on the development of reusable spacecraft and orbiting space stations, while the Soviets focus on long-duration flights, with Mars as a target. The key voyages into space, along with the names of the astronauts involved, are listed here.

April 12, 1961 (U.S.S.R.) First manned spaceflight. Yuri Gagarin, *Vostok 1*.

May 5, 1961 (U.S.A.) First U.S. manned spaceflight (suborbital). Alan Shepard, *Freedom 7*.

February 20, 1962 (U.S.A.) First U.S. orbital spaceflight. John Glenn, *Friendship 7*.

August 11 – 15, 1962 (U.S.S.R.) First simultaneous spaceflights. Andrian Nikolayev, *Vostok 3*, and Pavel Popovich, *Vostok 4*.

June 16, 1963 (U.S.S.R.) First woman in space. Valentina Tereshkova, *Vostok 6*.

March 18, 1965 (U.S.S.R.) First space walk. Alexei Leonov, *Voskhod 2*.

June 3, 1965 (U.S.A.) First U.S. space walk. Edward White, *Gemini 4*.

January 27, 1967 (U.S.A.) Virgil Grissom, Edward White, and Roger Chaffee died during a practice countdown for *Apollo 1* when the cockpit caught fire. Apollo program delayed for 18 months.

December 21 – 27, 1968 (U.S.A.) First manned flight around the moon. Frank Borman, James Lovell, William Anders, *Apollo 8*.

January 16, 1969 (U.S.S.R.) First transfer of crew members from one spacecraft to another. Yevgeny Khrunov and Aleksei Yeliseyev space walked from *Soyuz 5* to *Soyuz 4*.

July 20, 1969 (U.S.A.) First men walk on the moon. Neil Armstrong followed by Buzz Aldrin, *Apollo 11*. (Michael Collins stayed behind in the command module orbiting the moon.)

April 19, 1971 (U.S.S.R.) First space station launched, *Salyut 1*. It was manned for 23 days (June 6 – 30) by Georgi Dobrovolsky, Viktor Patseyev, and Vladislav Volkov, but all three men were killed on the return flight in *Soyuz 11*.

December 11, 1972 (U.S.A.) Last Apollo moon mission touches down on moon. Eugene Cernan, Harrison Schmitt, *Apollo 17*.

May 15, 1973 (U.S.A.) First U.S. space station, *Skylab*, launched. Last crew splashed down February 8, 1974.

July 16 – 18, 1975 (U.S.S.R./U.S.A.) First international space docking. *Soyuz 19* (Alexei Leonov and Valeri Kubasov) and *Apollo 18* (Thomas Stafford, Donald Slayton, and Vance Brand).

April 12 – 14, 1981 (U.S.A.) First flight of reusable space vehicle. John Young, Robert Crippen, space shuttle *Columbia*.

June 18, 1983 (U.S.A.) First U.S. woman in space, Sally Ride. Space shuttle *Challenger*.

January 28, 1986 (U.S.A) Space shuttle *Challenger* explodes barely a minute after lift-off, killing the crew of two women and five men: Christa McAuliffe, Judith Resnik, Gregory Jarvis, Ronald McNair, Ellison Onizuka, Francis Scobee, and Michael Smith.

387

COLLISION THEORY OF MOON BIRTH The origin of our moon has long been a mystery, but a new theory suggests that it may have been formed by a collision between earth and a smaller planet. Using the world's most powerful computers to create simulations of long-ago conditions in our solar system, proponents of the theory say that the collision occurred 4.5 billion years ago, when a crust was just forming around the mainly molten earth. In the infant solar system, planetesimals ("little planets") pulled together to form the present inner planets (Mercury, Venus, Earth, Mars). At this point, another planet entered earth's orbit, and the two planets collided. The surfaces of both planets vaporized, and a jet of superhot material shot upward, free of their gravitational pull. Then this material cooled, coalesced, and fell into orbit around the earth. Eventually this orbiting material evolved into our moon.

This so-called impact theory of moon formation, while still very controversial, helps explain why the earth's outer mantle is rich in some of the heavy metals, such as gold and platinum. According to widely accepted geological models, these metals should be more deeply buried, but the impact theory says the metals are nearer the surface because they come from the planet that collided with earth.

IS ANYONE OUT THERE? Two space probes launched by the United States, *Pioneer 10* and *Pioneer 11,* provided the first close-ups of Jupiter and Saturn. The spacecraft then continued on trajectories that will never return them to our solar system. On June 13, 1983, *Pioneer 10* became the first probe to move beyond the orbit of any known planet.

Both spacecraft carry metal plaques intended for any alien beings that might intercept the probes as they drift among the stars in the future. Each plaque shows a map of the solar system, the location of our sun, and sketches of a human female and male.

Voyager 1 and *Voyager 2,* launched to examine the outer planets (Jupiter and beyond), are following *Pioneer 10* into the depths of space. They each carry long-playing records that contain electronically encoded pictures of Earth, as well as spoken greetings,

sound effects, and a selection of music from around the world.

The Pioneer and Voyager spacecraft are hurtling along at about 30,000 m.p.h., faster than any man-made object has ever traveled. But even if they were aimed (which they are not) at the nearest star, Alpha Centauri, they would take 100,000 years to get there.

LOST DISCOVERERS OF NEPTUNE After Uranus was discovered in 1781, astronomers noticed that the planet was not keeping to its predicted path in the sky. One possible explanation was that it was being tugged off course by another planet, as yet unknown, which would be the eighth in the solar system. In 1846 the French astronomer Urbain Leverrier calculated where this eighth planet might lie and wrote to the Berlin Observatory to ask astronomers there to look for it. The letter arrived on September 23, the birthday of the observatory's director, Johann Encke. Since Encke was taking the evening off to attend his birthday party, he passed the information on to his assistant, Johann Galle, who, together with the 24-year-old student Heinrich d'Arrest (later to win fame for his studies of the nebulas), sighted the new planet that evening. So, simply because it was his birthday, Encke lost the distinction of discovering the planet now called Neptune.

Leverrier was not the only person to predict the position of Neptune. In England, John Couch Adams had made a similar prediction the year before, in 1845. He sent his results to the astronomer royal, Sir George Airy. However, Airy for some reason did not follow up on Adams's data until he heard about Leverrier's calculations. Only then did Airy direct James Challis, a professor at Cambridge University, to undertake a search for the predicted planet.

One night in 1846 Challis saw an object that he thought might be the planet but decided to wait until the following night to check it further. The next evening he lingered over tea after dinner with a colleague, and when the two men reached the observatory, the sky had clouded over. By the time the weather cleared and Challis could resume his observations, it was too late. Galle in Berlin had already discovered Neptune. Challis was denied credit for the discovery of a planet—by a cup of tea.

Although earth's atmosphere extends more than 2,000 miles outward, about 80 percent of the atmosphere's mass is concentrated within 10 miles of the earth's surface. This portion, called the troposphere, is the natural home of all known living things. Above it are the atmospheric layers called the stratosphere, the mesosphere, the thermosphere, and the exosphere, from which molecules occasionally escape into outer space.

THE LONGEST DAY The combination of spin and orbit can create unearthly calendars on some bodies in the solar system. Jupiter, for instance, makes a complete rotation on its axis, the common definition of a day, in about 10 hours and takes almost 12 Earth years to make one complete revolution around the sun, the common definition of a year. Thus a Jupiter year is almost 10,400 Jupiter days long.

Our own moon rotates on its axis in exactly the same time, just under 28 days, that it takes to revolve once around Earth. This is why we always see only one side of the moon. If the moon were a planet and the Earth its sun, a moon year would be only about 28 Earth days. On the day side of the moon, the sun would never set; and on the night side, the sun would never rise.

The slow rotation and fast solar orbit of Mercury, the planet nearest the sun, add up to a Mercury year of 88 Earth days and a Mercury day of about 2 Earth months.

GAS GIANT *Whirling bands of gas perpetually shroud the surface of Jupiter, the solar system's largest planet. In this photograph, taken by the U.S. space probe* Voyager 1 *in 1979, two of Jupiter's 16 known moons are visible: Europa, the ice-white ball at the extreme right; and Io, the orange ball near the planet's right-hand edge. The planet is huge. Io is bigger than the Earth's moon; and the planet's Great Red Spot (visible at the lower left) is large enough to swallow the entire Earth.*

THE SOLAR SYSTEM

The earth is one of nine planets orbiting the sun that together make up the solar system. The planets, in order of their distance from the sun, are:

Mercury 3,100 miles in diameter and 36 million miles from the sun. No moons. Rotates once in 59 Earth days; orbits sun once in 88 Earth days.

Venus 7,500 miles in diameter and 67 million miles from the sun. No moons. Rotates once in 243 Earth days; orbits sun once in 225 Earth days.

Earth 7,926 miles in diameter at the equator and 93 million miles from the sun. One moon. Rotates once in 24 hours; orbits sun once in 365 days.

Mars 4,218 miles in diameter at its equator and 142 million miles from the sun. Two moons. Rotates once in 24.4 Earth hours; orbits sun once in 687 Earth days.

Jupiter 89,400 miles in diameter at its equator and 483 million miles from the sun. Sixteen known moons. Rotates once in 10 Earth hours; orbits sun once in 11.86 Earth years.

Saturn 75,000 miles in diameter at its equator and 886 million miles from the sun. Twenty known moons. Rotates once in 10.4 Earth hours; orbits sun once in 29.46 Earth years.

Uranus 32,300 miles in diameter at its equator and 1.8 billion miles from the sun. Fifteen known moons. Rotates once in about 17 Earth hours; orbits sun once in 84 Earth years.

Neptune 30,000 miles in diameter at its equator and 2.8 billion miles from the sun. Three known moons. Rotates once in about 18–22 Earth hours; orbits sun once in 165 Earth years.

Pluto Approximately 1,900 miles in diameter and averages 3.7 billion miles from the sun. One moon. Rotates once in 6.4 Earth days; orbits sun once in 248 Earth years.

VERY DEADLY PLANET An astronaut unlucky enough to crash-land on Venus would be simultaneously suffocated, crushed, and roasted. Asphyxiation would quickly result from breathing the carbon dioxide atmosphere. The gas bears down with a crushing pressure nearly 100 times that of Earth's atmosphere, and it traps heat like a very efficient greenhouse, so that the surface temperature of Venus is estimated to be about 900°F.

What little was left of the astronaut would be eaten away by acid in the air. Thick clouds of sulfuric acid surround Venus, and the acid is far more corrosive than that in a car battery.

AT THE EDGE OF THE SOLAR SYSTEM In 1929 a major photographic search for new planets began at Lowell Observatory, Flagstaff, Arizona. As a result of the search, the ninth planet, Pluto, was discovered by U.S. astronomer Clyde Tombaugh on February 18, 1930.

Pluto turned out to be much smaller than expected, and to have a wayward orbit—so wayward that Pluto is sometimes closer to the sun than the eighth planet, Neptune. This happens, for instance, between January 1979 and March 1999. During this period, therefore, Neptune is the outermost planet in the solar system.

Pluto was found only 6 degrees from the position calculated for it by the U.S. astronomer Percival Lowell in 1915. Curiously, Lowell's calculations were based on perturbations in the motion of Neptune, but it turned out that Pluto was far too small to have produced them. There are still irregularities in the motions of the outer planets that are not fully accounted for, but which cannot be the result of Pluto's gravitational pull. The irregularities may be due to a combination of slight inaccuracies in computing the orbits of the outer planets, plus the gravitational effect of a belt of comets that some astronomers believe may exist at the edge of the solar system.

The planets

THE SUN ▶
THE STARS ▶
COMETS ▶

MOST WEIRD Miranda, the fifth largest moon of Uranus, is less than 200 miles in diameter—and one of the most puzzling bodies in the solar system. "If you can imagine taking all the bizarre forms in the solar system and putting them on one object, you'll find them on Miranda," said U.S. Geological Survey scientist Lawrence Soderblom after viewing photographs taken by *Voyager 2* in 1986. Because of its relatively small size, Miranda was expected to have had a fairly dull geological history, according to Soderblom. But the *Voyager 2* photos show the moon's surface to be heavily grooved and cratered in some places, and almost completely smooth elsewhere.

PLANET THAT SPINS BACKWARD Unlike the other planets in the solar system, Venus spins not from west to east but from east to west. And the planet takes longer to spin on its axis than it does to orbit the sun, so that a Venusian day is longer than a Venusian year. The reason for the reverse rotation is unknown. Until 1980 many scientists believed that the planet was set off on its backward spin when it collided with another embryonic planet or moon during the formation of the solar system about 4.6 billion years ago. But a mathematical analysis of Venus's movement has shown that theory to be incorrect and, so far, no fully accepted new theory has been put forward.

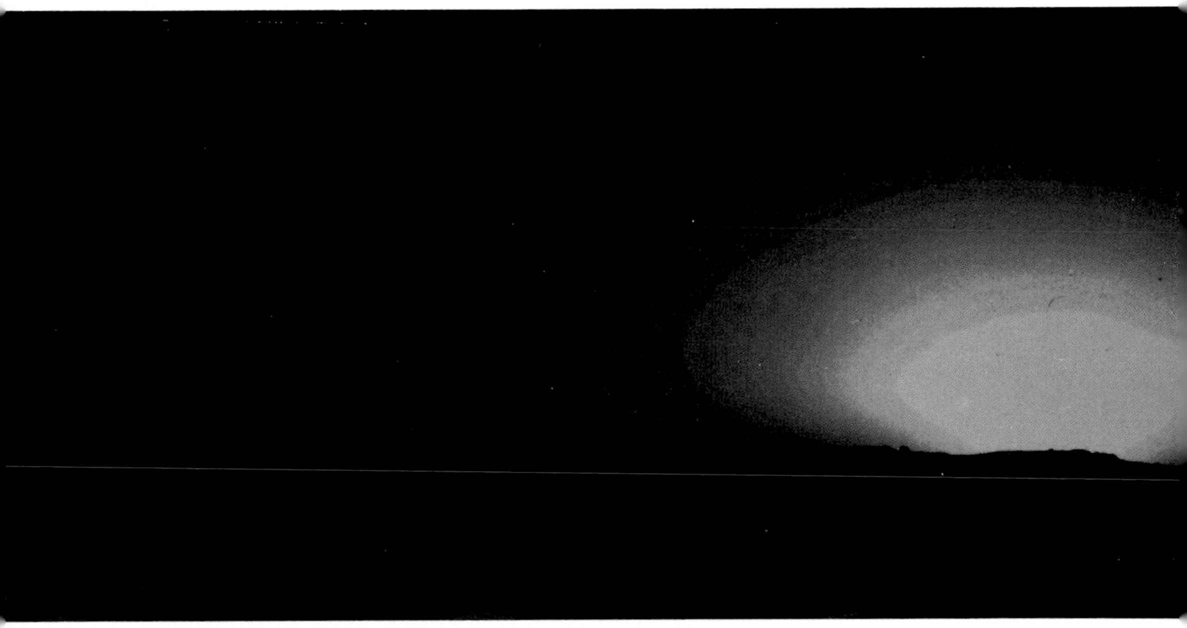

THE RED PLANET *The sinking sun reveals the inhospitable landscape of Mars, captured by the Viking space probes between July and September 1976. The probes confirmed that Mars consists mainly of dusty plains, craters, mountains, valleys, and canyons. Although dried-up streambeds in some valleys suggest that there was once water on the planet, organic soil tests showed that life was extremely unlikely to exist. The intelligent, warlike Martians of British novelist H. G. Wells's* The War of the Worlds *remain fiction, not fact.*

VOLCANO AND THE VALLEY The largest volcano known is on Mars. Olympus Mons, 370 miles wide and 79,000 feet high, is nearly three times higher than Mount Everest, and the 40-mile-wide crater at its summit is large enough to swallow the state of Rhode Island. Mars also has a massive rift valley called Valles Marineris, which is approximately 2,500 miles long, 50 to 300 miles wide, and up to 4 miles deep. The valley would stretch across the entire United States, from Los Angeles to New York City.

RINGS AROUND THE PLANETS Saturn is not the only planet in the solar system to have rings. Smaller but similar belts of debris, invisible from the surface of the earth, have been discovered around both Uranus and Jupiter. Nine Uranus rings were detected in 1977 with the help of a telescope aboard a U.S. airplane, and two more were photographed by *Voyager 2* in 1986.

The single ring around Jupiter was discovered by the *Voyager 1* space probe in 1979.

THE FASTEST MOONS Two tiny satellites of Jupiter whip around the giant planet in just about 7 hours. Andrastea, discovered by *Voyager 1* in 1979 and known also as J XIV, makes the circuit in about 0.299 Earth day. Metis, or J XVI, discovered in 1981, takes 0.295 Earth day. The speed of these moons, which are only about 25 miles in diameter, is estimated at over 70,400 m.p.h.—fast enough to circle Earth in little more than 20 minutes.

THE ROLLING PLANET Uranus is tilted on its axis more than any other planet. While Earth, for instance, is tilted at only 23 degrees, Uranus is tilted at about 98 degrees—more or less on its side. Since at times one or the other of its poles is pointing at the sun, Uranus actually rolls along its path through space. The tilt also creates the solar system's longest seasons: winters and summers that are 21 Earth years long. In winter, temperatures are estimated to drop to −362°F, less than 100 degrees above absolute zero.

FACTS ABOUT THE UNIVERSE

Space

INSPIRATION EXPRESS The modern theory of why the stars, including the sun, shine was worked out by a scientist doodling on a piece of paper during a railway journey. In 1938 the German-born U.S. physicist Hans Bethe (1906–) was returning to Cornell University by train after attending a conference in Washington, D.C. Musing on the nature of the heat source at the heart of any star, Bethe started scribbling on a sheet of paper—and before the end of the journey he had worked out the nuclear reaction that makes a star shine. Hydrogen deep in the core, he realized, was converted to helium, with carbon and nitrogen acting as catalysts. Bethe's doodles on the train helped to win him the Nobel Prize in physics in 1967.

SPOTTING THE SUNSPOTS The 11-year cycle of sunspots—giant magnetic disturbances that affect the weather and radio transmissions on earth—was discovered accidentally by a German pharmacist and amateur astronomer. Heinrich Schwabe (1789–1875) began studying the sun because he was searching for a planet that was thought to lie within the orbit of Mercury. Schwabe hoped to spot the planet as it passed across the sun. But while watching in vain for the planet (now known to be nonexistent), he became interested in the dark spots that appear and disappear periodically on the sun's brilliant surface. Schwabe began sketching the spots and kept on observing them every sunny day for 17 years.

By 1843 he had worked out their pattern. The number of spots reached a maximum about every 11 years, coinciding exactly with the periods when the aurora borealis and the aurora australis (the northern lights and the southern lights) were most often visible. The last sunspot peak was in 1980, and the next is due in 1991.

BRIGHTER THAN WHITE The solar storms known as sunspots, one of which can be several times larger than the entire earth, appear darker than the rest of the sun's surface only because their temperatures (about 7,200°F) are more than 1,800 degrees lower than the temperature of the solar surface.

LINES OF GENIUS Joseph von Fraunhofer (1787–1826), the German optician who made it possible for scientists to discover the chemical composition of the stars, owed his success to a disaster: the collapse of the building where he lived. The son of a poor but talented glazier, Fraunhofer was orphaned as a child and apprenticed to a glass cutter and mirror maker in Munich, the capital of Bavaria. His employer made his life a misery of constant hunger and overwork.

Fraunhofer was only 14 when the rickety tenement he lived in collapsed. During the rescue operation, the future Maximilian I of Bavaria, Maximilian Joseph (1756–1825), came to watch. Fraunhofer was the only survivor and, moved by the boy's plight, Maximilian gave him 18 ducats, which Fraunhofer used to buy glass-working equipment, books on optics, and his release from apprenticeship. In 1806 Fraunhofer began working in the optical shop of a Munich company that made scientific instruments.

It was while testing a prism in 1814 that Fraunhofer became fascinated by the spectral lines now known as Fraunhofer lines. When sunlight is broken up into the familiar colors of the rainbow, the spectrum also contains a number of dark lines. These lines had been spotted in 1802 by an English scientist, William Wollaston. But Wollaston had thought they were merely boundaries between the bands of color and ignored them. Fraunhofer realized that the lines were permanent—and significant—though he did not know why. He went on to plot more than 574 of them. There are now known to be about 25,000 lines in the sun's spectrum, and similar ones appear in the spectra of other stars.

The significance of the lines was worked out after Fraunhofer's death by two other German scientists: Gustav Kirchhoff (1824–87) and Robert Bunsen (1811–99), inventor of the Bunsen burner. They solved the problem in 1859 when they found that the position of the lines in the spectrum corresponded exactly to the position of lines in the spectra created when certain elements are heated to incandescence in the laboratory. The lines thus gave a direct indication of which elements were present, and so enabled Kirchhoff, Bunsen, and later scientists to analyze the chemical composition of the sun and the stars.

The temperature at the center of the sun is about 27 million °F. The U.S. physicist George Gamow (1904–68) once calculated that if a pinhead could be brought to the same temperature as the material at the core of the sun, heat from the pinhead would set fire to everything for 60 miles around.

ECLIPSE ESCAPE The 19th-century French astronomer Jules Janssen (1824–1907) risked his life to see a solar eclipse. From the earth, the sun's outer atmosphere, called the corona, can be seen clearly only during a total eclipse. Janssen knew that such an eclipse was due to pass across Oran in Algeria on December 22, 1870; but he was trapped in Paris by the besieging German Army at the height of the Franco-Prussian War. Determined to get to Oran, he made a daring escape from Paris by balloon, floating across the German lines, and then hurried south by ground transportation.

But Janssen missed the eclipse. It happened on schedule, and he was in the perfect location to see it. Unfortunately, the sky was solidly overcast, and he saw nothing at all. Other balloon journeys served Janssen better. He was one of the first scientific champions of aviation, and while floating aloft one day he conceived the idea of an aeronautic compass that gave instant readings of speed and direction.

RADIO SUNSHINE The sun, like most other stars, broadcasts radio waves as well as light. The sun's transmissions were discovered in 1942 during World War II by a team of British scientists under John Hey. When the scientists first picked up the crackling noise on their receivers, they did not realize that the interference came from the sun. They thought the Germans were jamming British radio communications.

A RIGHT-SIZE SUN If our sun were much larger or smaller than it is, life on earth could not exist. Because larger stars burn their fuel more quickly, the sun would have burned out already had it been, say, just twice its size. Were it much smaller, it would give out so little heat that the earth would be locked in a permanent freeze, and would be far too cold for any form of life to survive.

PLANET SWALLOWER Toward the end of its life, some 5 billion years from now, the sun will swell up into a red giant that will engulf the planets, including Earth, as far out as Mars. Most of the sun's bulk will then be a glowing ball of gas containing about half of its total mass. The remaining half will be a much denser and much smaller core. If that red-giant sun were the size of an ordinary living room, its energy-generating core would, on the same scale, be no larger than the period at the end of this sentence.

INSIDE THE SUN *By isolating light given off at different wavelengths, scientists can study the sun's ordinarily invisible atmosphere in detail. This color-coded picture—taken from Skylab at ultraviolet wavelengths—reveals how gas clouds (shown as red) clump together in the atmosphere's lower layers. The solar flare at the top juts some 300,000 miles; the earth (shown as boxed dot, right, at the same scale) would fit into its length nearly 40 times.*

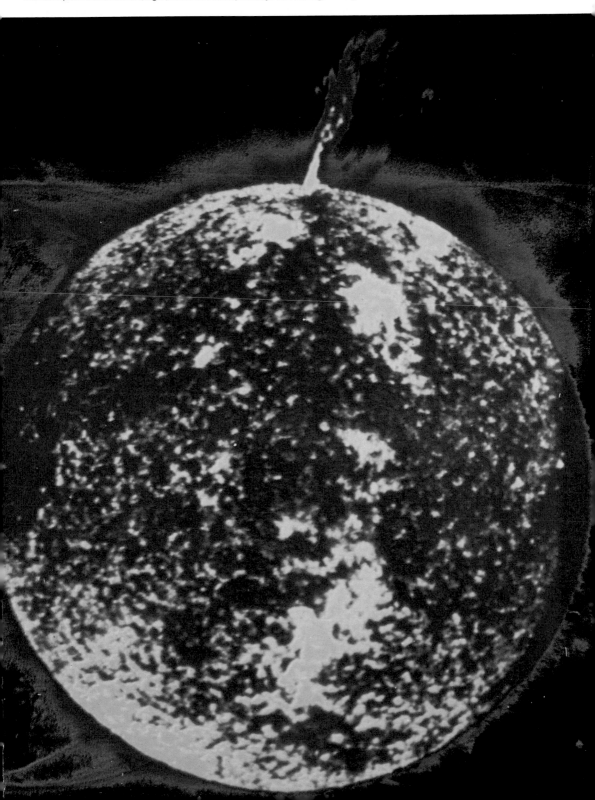

Space

LIGHT OF THE PARTY The first supernova (exploding star) to be discovered outside our own galaxy was spotted in August 1885—during a party in Hungary. The party was given by the Baroness de Podmaniczky, who also happened to be an avid amateur astronomer. On her lawn she had set up a telescope and turned it toward a celestial object then known as the Andromeda Nebula (now known to be a galaxy beyond our own).

Gazing through her telescope, the baroness noticed what seemed to be a "little star" in the nebula, and this was confirmed by one of her guests, a professional astronomer for whom only a last name, de Kövesligethy, is known. The baroness was one of several independent observers to discover the supernova within a few days of one another.

Some 2 million light-years from the earth, S. Andromedae (the official name of the supernova) was, at its peak, no less than 15 million times more luminous than the sun. Then it faded again. However, in apparent magnitude (its brilliance as it appeared in the sky), S. Andromedae remains the brightest supernova ever to have been seen in an outer galaxy.

BY THE LIGHT OF A SUPERNOVA An amateur Australian astronomer, Robert Evans, discovered a new supernova in the galaxy Centaurus A in May 1986. Not only was Evans extraordinarily lucky, since a supernova explodes in an average galaxy only once every 100 years or so, but his discovery may shed light on the strange dust clouds that shroud Centaurus A. The light from the exploding star is so brilliant that it shines through the dust. By measuring the spectrum of light that is absorbed by the dust, scientists can then make inferences about the dust's chemical composition. Early results indicate that the dust contains both sodium and calcium.

Centaurus A is approximately 13 million light-years away from our planet, which means that the newly discovered supernova exploded before human beings began to walk the earth.

LIGHTHOUSES IN THE SKY The smallest stars known are neutron stars, so called because their electrons and protons have been crushed together to form the subatomic particles called neutrons. A typical neutron star is only about 20 miles across, yet it may have as much mass as a star the size of the sun. A pinhead of material from a neutron star might weigh about a million tons, as much as two of the world's largest supertankers together.

Neutron stars are believed to be the remnants of large stars that have erupted at the end of their lives into supernovas. The intense gravity of neutron stars has the effect of concentrating the powerful radiation they give off into beams of particles. Since many neutron stars also spin, the radiation sweeps across space like the beams from a lighthouse. As the beams flash past the earth, the star seems to be pulsing with energy, which is why rotating neutron stars are known as pulsars.

The first pulsar was discovered by radio astronomers at Cambridge, England, in 1967. Hundreds of others have been mapped since then. The first pulsar to be identified optically as well as from its radio waves was the small, faint star at the core of the Crab Nebula. Spotted in 1968, the star spins 30 times per second. Since then, other pulsars have been spotted that spin thousands of times per second.

STAR BILLING

Astronomers classify stars in two main ways: by their surface temperature and by their brightness.

Temperature
The system for classifying stars by their surface temperature was devised by the U.S. astronomer Edward Pickering (1846–1919) with the aid of several investigators, including Annie Cannon, Williamina Fleming, and Antonia Maury. They listed the types alphabetically, starting with A for the hottest. Later discoveries made the list alphabetically chaotic.

In a modern form the list contains seven categories: O, B, A, F, G, K, and M. O-type stars are the hottest. Generally, stars of types O, A, and B are white or bluish; F-type stars are slightly yellow; G-type stars are yellow; K are orange; and M are orange-red. The sun is a G-type star.

Brightness
The brightness of a celestial object is measured in terms of its magnitude: either its *apparent* magnitude (as it appears in the sky) or its *absolute* magnitude (as it would appear at a fixed distance).

The first scale of magnitudes was drawn up by the Greek astronomer Hipparchus (c. 190–125 B.C.), who divided the stars into six groups, ranging from the faintest he could see (sixth magnitude) to the brightest (first magnitude). Modern astronomers have adjusted the scale so that a first-magnitude star is exactly 100 times as bright as a sixth-magnitude star. Objects fainter than magnitude 6, which are visible only through telescopes, are given larger magnitude values. The faintest objects detectable are about magnitude +25. Objects brighter than magnitude 0 are given negative values. The sun has an apparent magnitude of −26.8.

The scale of absolute magnitude is used to compare the actual light output of stars, allowing for their different distances from earth. An object's absolute magnitude, which can be estimated from its spectrum, is the brightness it would have if it were 32.6 light-years from earth. At this distance, the sun would be very faint, with a magnitude of only +4.79. By contrast, Eta Carinae, in the Southern Hemisphere constellation of Carina, has an absolute magnitude of −9, some 6 million times brighter than the sun.

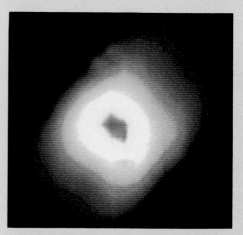

STAR BRIGHT *Eta Carinae, seen here in an infrared photograph with the hottest parts shown as blue, is one of the brightest known stars. Aging fast because of its ferocious energy output, it will explode as a supernova in a few thousand years.*

HELLO . . . HELLO One of the largest stars known is Betelgeuse, a red supergiant that marks the right shoulder of Orion. If Betelgeuse were positioned where the sun is now, it would engulf the orbits of Mercury, Venus, Earth, and Mars.

If it were possible to make a telephone call from one side to the other, your voice, traveling at the speed of light, would take half an hour to reach the other side of Betelgeuse—even if the call were routed straight through the star's center. If the call were routed around the surface of the star, your voice would take an hour and a half to get through.

Some astronomers believe that a mysterious and invisible object in the stellar group known as Epsilon Aurigae may be still larger. The object has not been observed directly, but every so often it seems to cause a partial eclipse of its visible neighbor—for a staggering 2 years at a time.

By observing these effects, some astronomers calculate that if the object is a star, it may be more than 2 billion miles across—large enough, if it were in our solar system, to engulf all the planets out to Saturn.

THE GREATER BEAR The group of stars known as the Big Dipper (part of the constellation called the Great Bear) has eight stars, not seven. One of the seven stars visible to the naked eye, Mizar—the second star from the handle end—is actually two stars. They are known as Mizar A, the brighter of the pair, and Mizar B. To the naked eye they appear as one star. Mizar B becomes separately visible only with a small telescope.

Many stars are, like Mizar, grouped in stellar families. One of the largest families is known collectively as Castor, in the constellation Gemini. A bright single star to the naked eye, Castor actually consists of a total of six stars orbiting each other in three pairs.

CALLING EARTH The U.S. astronomer Carl E. Sagan (1934–) has estimated that there may be as many as a million advanced alien civilizations in existence on planets orbiting the stars in our galaxy alone. In 1960 another American, radio astronomer Frank D. Drake (1930–), made the first deliberate attempt to pick up possible incoming messages from beings beyond the earth. He turned the 85-foot-diameter radio telescope of the National Radio Astronomy Observatory, Green Bank, West Virginia, toward two nearby stars, Tau Ceti and Epsilon Eridani. Listening for 2 months, Drake heard nothing.

Since then, other astronomers have searched for alien radio messages from approximately 1,000 stars without success. But as there are more than 100 billion stars in our own galaxy, and—if Sagan is right—only a million with advanced life, the odds are that we will need to listen to at least 100,000 stars before we can expect to pick up a signal.

Nevertheless, astronomers around the world are continuing the search, which may take until the end of the century to complete.

BAD OMEN, GOOD OMEN Halley's Comet, which orbits the sun about once every 76 years and passed through earth's neighborhood in 1985 and 1986, was an object of dread for centuries. Its appearance in 1066, for instance, is recorded on the Bayeux tapestry, which shows it blazing above terrified Saxons before the Battle of Hastings. For the Norman invader, William the Conqueror, on the other hand, it was an

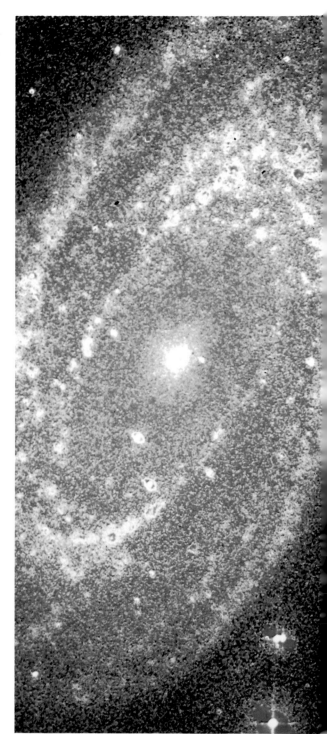

HEAVENLY TWIN *The galaxy known as M81—in the Northern Hemisphere constellation of Ursa Major (the Great Bear)—is a twin of our own. Like the Milky Way, it is a spiral galaxy about 100,000 light-years across. Older stars, concentrated mostly toward the galaxy's center, show up as yellow or red. Younger stars, which show up as blue, lie mostly along the slender arms.*

Space

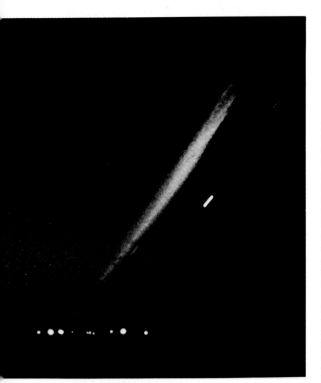

PASSING STRANGER *Comet Ikeya-Seki soars above Table Mountain, South Africa, in a photograph taken in November 1965. Astronomers do not expect it to return, if at all, for 880 years. Comet tails—streams of gas and dust boiled off from the nucleus by the sun's heat and pushed by a solar wind of charged particles—always point away from the sun, so that a comet travels tailfirst as it heads back out to the edge of the solar system.*

omen of good fortune. His battle cry at Hastings was: "A new star, a new king." During a later appearance in 1456, when Christians and Turks were at war, Pope Calixtus III officially condemned the comet as an agent of the devil. Despite his verdict, the comet seemed to be on the side of the Christians. At the Battle of Belgrade in the same year, its tail, shaped like a drawn sword, was seen pointing toward the Turks. The Christian armies, apparently encouraged by the omen, won the battle.

The comet is named after Edmund Halley (1656–1742), the English astronomer who first calculated its orbit in 1705. On March 13, 1986, the European Space Agency's *Giotto* spacecraft passed within 375 miles of the comet and took 2,000 pictures, the most spectacular of which were of the comet's nucleus. The pictures revealed that the nucleus measured about 5 miles by 10 miles, more than twice as large as previously thought, and was "black, absolutely black, blacker than coal, almost like velvet," in the words of an awed West German observer.

CONSTANT BOMBARDMENT Each day about three or four fist-size meteoroids, each weighing a few pounds, fall into the earth's atmosphere, where more often than not they burn up. The very few that do reach the earth's surface, at which point they become known as meteorites, are usually large ones. On average, a large meteorite—in the 50,000-ton range, or about the gross tonnage of the *Titanic*—hits the earth once every 100,000 years.

> *The earth increases in weight by about 25 tons each day. The extra material is mainly composed of space dust, micrometeors that are too small to see.*

DINOSAUR ZAPPER An asteroid caused the extinction of the dinosaurs, according to a theory developed by a group of researchers from the University of California, Berkeley, led by Luis Alvarez, a physicist, and his son Walter, a geologist. The Alvarezes say the asteroid, about 6 or 7 miles in diameter, hit the earth at the end of the Cretaceous period about 65 million years ago. The impact sent quadrillions of tons of rock into the earth's stratosphere, 10 miles above the earth's surface. This created a dust layer that for several years blocked out so much sunlight that huge quantities of land and sea plants died off, denying food to many species, including dinosaurs, and leading to their extinction.

The chemical evidence for this theory is an iridium-rich layer in marine clay deposited at the end of the Cretaceous. The proportion of iridium, rare in ordinary rocks but abundant in asteroids and meteorites, is 30 times greater than normal in the marine-clay layer. Some paleontologists and geologists think that a comet should be substituted for the asteroid favored by the Alvarezes.

BLOW FROM THE BLUE The only person known to have been hit by a meteorite is Mrs. Hewlett Hodges, of Sylacauga, Alabama. On November 30, 1954, a 9-pound meteorite crashed through the roof of her house, bounced off a radio, and struck Mrs. Hodges on the hip, causing massive bruises but no permanent injury.

Comets, meteorites, and asteroids

DIMINISHING RETURNS Comets get smaller every time they go around the sun. They normally resemble enormous dirty snowballs—bits of rocky debris held together by frozen gases and water in outer space. But each time they approach the sun, some of the ice is evaporated and some of the gases are boiled away by the sun's heat, leaving the comets smaller. Some of the comets that were seen regularly in the 19th century have now vanished, disintegrated by the sun. Others have died more spectacularly by plunging straight into the sun.

In 1846 one comet, Biela's Comet, which used to appear at intervals of 6.75 years, surprised astronomers by breaking in half. The two halves were observed from earth for the last time in 1852. The comet's legacy was a shower of hundreds of thousands of meteors formed from its remaining fragments. But by the 1980s this meteor shower, a November occurrence, had dwindled to almost nothing.

IRON FROM SPACE Eskimos in Greenland used iron tools for centuries—even though they had no idea how to smelt iron. They mined the metal in almost pure form from three large meteorites that had fallen on Greenland in ancient times. U.S. explorer Robert Peary shipped the largest of the three, which weighed more than 35 tons, to New York City in 1897. It is now in the Museum of Natural History.

SHOWERS FROM SPACE

Meteor showers happen when the earth passes through a swarm of space debris, which is made up of rock particles or chunks called meteors or meteoroids. As the swarm enters our atmosphere, its particles burn and produce a spectacular array of shooting stars. Although the shooting stars seem to radiate from a single point in space, this is an illusion of perspective, because the meteors actually travel in parallel paths. This list gives the names of the major showers, with the dates on which they appear each year and the constellations from which they seem to radiate.

Name	Date	Apparent origin
Quadrantids	Jan 1–6	Boötes
Lyrids	Apr 19–24	Lyra
Eta Aquarids	May 1–8	Aquarius
Perseids	July 25–Aug 18	Perseus
Orionids	Oct 16–26	Orion
Taurids	Oct 20–Nov 30	Taurus
Leonids	mid Nov	Leo
Phoenicids	Dec 4–5	Phoenix
Geminids	Dec 7–15	Gemini
Ursids	Dec 17–24	Ursa Minor

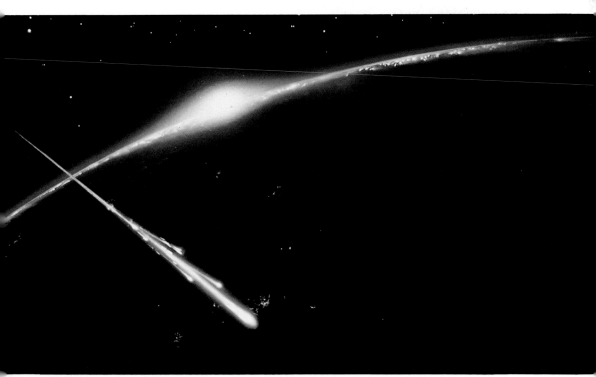

ROCKS FROM THE SKY *Rocks of all sizes whirl through space. Depending on whether or not they reach the earth's surface, they are called meteoroids, meteors, or meteorites. The terms* meteor *and* meteoroid *refer to rock particles in space whose origin is not definitely known, though some are fragments of comets. When a meteoroid hits our atmosphere, it heats up and may completely vaporize, so that only dust is left. The heat generates light, visible as a streak of light in the night sky. This streak is also known as a meteor, or a falling star or shooting star. If a meteoroid gets through our atmosphere and falls to the earth's surface as a rock large enough to see, it is called a meteorite. About 100 million meteoroids hurtle into the atmosphere each day, and most vaporize before they reach the earth's surface. The largest surviving meteorite, weighing some 65 tons, was found in South Africa in 1920.*

The limits of space

DISTANT NEIGHBORS

The stars nearest to us, after the sun, are those of the Alpha Centauri system, which are more than 4 light-years away. If it were possible to drive through space at a steady, law-abiding 55 m.p.h., you could reach the sun in 193 years. But at the same speed it would take 52 million years to reach Alpha Centauri.

ASTRONOMICAL ERRORS

Concepts of the universe were vastly inaccurate until the 20th century. The size of the sun, for instance, was wildly underestimated. In the 6th century B.C. the Greek philosopher Heraclitus estimated the diameter of the sun to be about 1 foot. In fact, it is nearly 870,000 miles across.

In about A.D. 150 the Greco-Egyptian astronomer Ptolemy calculated the distance from the earth to the sun at 5 million miles. The first reasonably close estimate was not made until 1672, by the Italian-born French astronomer Giovanni Domenico Cassini (1625–1712). The distance is now known to be 92,959,000 miles—nearly 20 times greater than Ptolemy thought.

In 1917 the U.S. astronomer Harlow Shapley (1885–1972) calculated that the Milky Way Galaxy was about 100,000 light-years across, a figure very close to the current estimate. The size of the universe as a whole did not become clear until the 1920s. Before then, astronomers had thought that the Milky Way encompassed the entire universe. But in the early 1920s another American, Edwin Hubble (1889–1953), confirmed the existence of galaxies beyond our own.

HIGH-SPEED WORLD

Like everything else in the universe, our earth is rushing headlong through space. Every point on the equator is moving at about 1,000 m.p.h. as the earth spins on its own axis. Nearer the poles the speed is less. On its annual journey around the sun, the earth as a whole moves at about 67,000 m.p.h. As our galaxy—the Milky Way—spins around its own center,

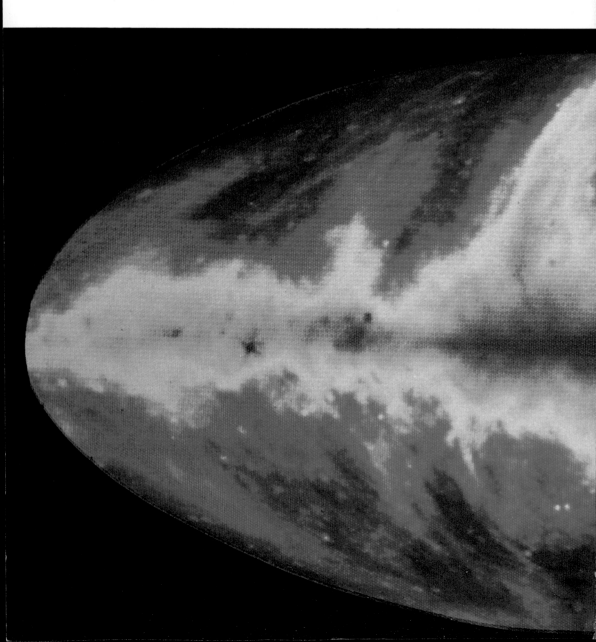

completing one revolution every 230 million years, the whole solar system moves with it, traveling at about 492,000 m.p.h.

Finally, the most distant galaxies are rushing away from our own at speeds close to that of light—which means in turn that, from their point of view, the Milky Way is rushing in the opposite direction at nearly 186,000 miles per second.

EARTH CALLING ANYONE
Since 1974 a radio message has been racing outward from earth at the speed of light. It was broadcast from the Arecibo radio telescope in Puerto Rico, the world's largest single radio astronomy dish. The dish, which is 1,000 feet across, is set in a natural hollow between hills and scans the sky overhead as the earth spins. It is so powerful that it could communicate with an identical twin of itself anywhere in our galaxy. The message, transmitted on November 16, 1974, was beamed toward a cluster of 300,000 stars called M13 in the constellation of Hercules. It consisted of 1,679 on-off pulses, which can be arranged to form a picture that shows the biochemistry of life on earth, a figure of a human being, and a map of the solar system. The number was chosen to avoid ambiguity: 1,679 pulses can be formed into a rectangular pattern only as a grid of 23 pulses by 73.

The message was the strongest radio transmission ever to leave the earth. But even if there are any aliens at home in M13 to answer the interstellar call, the cluster is so far away that no reply will arrive until about the year 50,000.

WEIGHED DOWN
Black holes—the collapsed remnants of giant stars— are so dense that not even light can escape their awesome gravitational pull. If a telephone directory weighing no more than 2 pounds were brought to within 20 feet of a black hole, it would weigh more than a trillion tons.

THE SKIES AT NIGHT *Three telescopes—in Britain, West Germany, and Australia—worked together for 12 years to produce this radio map of the entire sky, both the northern and southern hemispheres. The map is color-coded so that the brightest areas show up red, and others fade through yellow, green, and blue to black. The sky is dominated by the Milky Way (horizontal axis), seen edge on from earth. An ordinary observer sees the Milky Way as an evenly powdered band, because cosmic dust clouds block much of the light where the stars are thickest. But radio wavelengths cut through the dust, so that our galaxy's heart (center) gleams here with its true brilliance.*

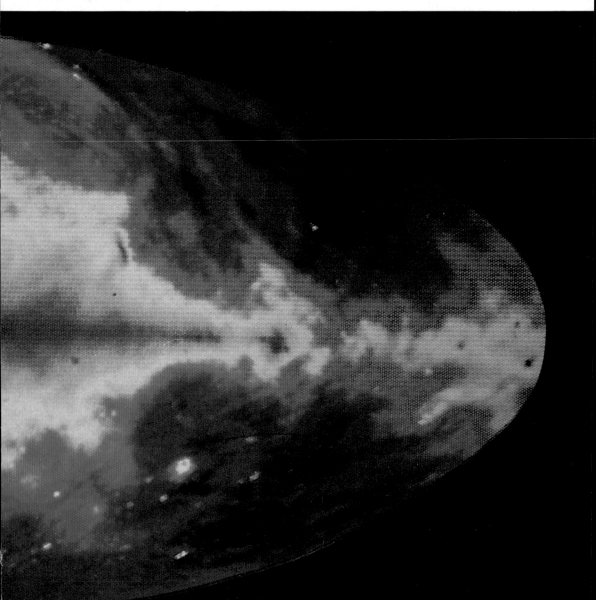

DISTANT HEART *Our Milky Way galaxy and the Local Group of galaxies to which it belongs are just part of what astronomers call the Local Supercluster of galaxies. At the center of the supercluster and some 50 million light-years from earth is the Virgo Cluster, which has about 1,000 galaxies. The galaxy known as M87 (above) is the brightest in the Virgo Cluster. It glitters at the heart of the spinning cluster, as the core of the whole supercluster. A mysterious jet of radiation streams out from M87's center some 5,000 light-years into space. The brightest point on the jet's length (visible to the right of the galaxy's center) shines with the strength of 40 million suns.*

EDUCATING ALBERT

For years many parents of underachieving schoolchildren have taken comfort in the belief that even Albert Einstein (1879–1955) got poor grades in school. But the school records of the German-born physicist who devised the theory of relativity show that in fact Einstein's marks were exceptional. He excelled particularly in physics, mathematics, and music.

The misunderstanding may have arisen because during Einstein's last year at school in Aarau, Switzerland, in 1896, the school's system of marking was reversed. Grade 6, which had been the lowest mark, became the highest, and Grade 1, which had been the highest, became the lowest. To anyone who did not know of the change, it could have appeared that Einstein's marks had plummeted.

Einstein did fail entrance exams for the Federal Technical Academy in Zurich, but this may have been because of his one area of weakness: French. It may also have been because he took the exams at the age of 16—2 years younger than normal. After spending 2 years at Aarau, Einstein reapplied to the Zurich institute and was admitted.

DEPTH OF VISION

The farthest object clearly visible to the naked eye is a spiral galaxy named M31 in the constellation of Andromeda. On a clear night it appears as a small, hazy patch. The Andromeda Galaxy is 2.2 million light-years away, which means that the light we now see from it began its journey when our apelike ancestors were still roaming the plains of Africa.

CHEMICAL TWINS

Carbon atoms often link with others in such a way that two molecules can have the same number of atoms and the same structure—and yet be different because the twins are mirror images of each other. Like a pair of gloves, the twins are not interchangeable, and in living organisms only one of them is likely to be useful.

Amino acids, the building blocks for proteins, occur mostly as one type of these pairs, while their mirror-image molecules cannot be used to make protein. No convincing explanation (other than pure chance) has been found for why life on earth has developed on one side of this twin relationship and not on the other.

Scientists have speculated that life elsewhere might be based on similar molecules but with the opposite sets to those on earth. A visitor from such a planet would starve to death on earth because he would be unable to digest the proteins in earthly food.

THE EDGES OF SPACE

Most modern astronomers believe that man may already be able to see nearly as much of the universe as will ever be possible. The belief rests on a discovery made by the U.S. astronomer Edwin Hubble. In 1929 he found that the more distant a galaxy was from our own, the faster it was moving away. Hubble made his discovery by analyzing the light from distant galaxies.

His discovery owed much to the earlier work of Vesto Slipher (1875–1969) at the Lowell Observatory at Flagstaff, Arizona. In 1912 Slipher had found that the light from distant galaxies was shifted toward the red end of the spectrum. Hubble worked out why. If an object is moving toward us, its wavelength is shortened; if it is moving away, its wavelength is lengthened—shifted toward the long-wave, or red, end of the spectrum. Thus, Hubble concluded, the galaxies are moving away from the earth, and the farther galaxies, with more pronounced red shifts, are moving away faster than the nearer ones. The amount of the shift gave a clue to the speed of a galaxy. The relationship between this speed and the galaxy's distance is known as Hubble's constant. In its modern form, the constant suggests that for every billion light-years between any two galaxies, their relative speed of separation increases by somewhat less than 10 percent of the speed of light.

If Hubble's constant holds good to the most extreme distances, there will finally come a point where galaxies are receding from us at the full speed of light. As a result, their light—along with any other radiation they emit—will never reach us, and no human observer will ever be able to detect them.

This critical distance for the boundary of the observable universe—though not necessarily the boundary of the universe itself—is believed to be about 15 billion light-years from earth.

THE FARTHEST GALAXY

The most distant objects known are quasars—named from the phrase "*quasi*-stella*r* radio source." They are enormously powerful starlike objects, some of which are as bright as 100 galaxies combined. A quasar known as PKS 2000-330 was discovered in 1982 by a team of international astronomers working in Australia. It is racing away from our galaxy at about 170,000 miles per second, or 91 percent of the speed of light.

Its distance is estimated to be at least 13 billion light-years, putting it close to the boundary of the observable universe.

In addition, because the quasar's light has taken 13 billion years to reach earth, astronomers are seeing the quasar as it was then. And since the universe itself is thought to be about 15 billion years old, observations of such distant galaxies enable astronomers to see the universe as it was quite early in its existence.

REMARKABLE RELATIVITY

The theory of relativity—published in two parts in 1905 and 1915 by Albert Einstein—rests on a remarkable realization: that when objects move at very high speeds, commonsense assumptions break down.

Common sense dictates, for example, that two cars traveling toward each other at 55 m.p.h will pass at a relative speed of 110 m.p.h. And they do. But if one of the cars is replaced by a beam of light, the ordinary assumption does not work. No matter how fast the remaining car travels toward or away from the beam, the light will always hit it at exactly the same speed: approximately 186,000 miles per second.

Einstein's starting point
Experiments in the 1880s had shown that the speed of light was unaffected by the earth's motion, and from this starting point Einstein went on to conclude that the speed of light was the universe's only constant, and that size, mass, and even time were all relative; measurements of any of them depend on the position and relative speed of the observer.

Einstein also deduced that mass and energy are interchangeable, and related by the equation $E = mc^2$, where E is the energy and m the mass of a particle, and c is the speed of light.

Modern experiments have confirmed the existence of many of the effects predicted by Einstein's theory. In 1972, for instance, sensitive atomic clocks carried on spacecraft and then compared with identical clocks on the ground after the flight were found to have slowed down—meaning that time itself had passed more slowly aboard the spacecraft.

Particle accelerators, used in the study of subatomic particles, have to be specially designed to take account of the increased mass of particles boosted to significant proportions of light speed. And $E = mc^2$, which shows that a small amount of mass can be converted into a huge amount of energy, has been utilized in nuclear reactors and atomic bombs.

How time slows down
As the speed of any object increases, its properties, relative to an observer at rest, change. Its mass increases, its length in the direction of travel decreases, and time slows down. At ordinary earthbound speeds—even those of a jet plane—the changes are infinitesimal.

At very high speeds, however, the changes become extremely important. An astronaut traveling at 90 percent of the speed of light, for instance, would not feel any different from his hypothetical twin on earth. But the mass of his spacecraft would be more than double, its length would be less than half, and a clock on board would take an hour to record 26 minutes, because time would have slowed—and he would therefore be aging at less than half the rate of his earthbound brother.

At the speed of light, the mass of the spacecraft would theoretically become infinite, its length would shrink to nothing, and time aboard it would slow to a complete stop.

INDEX

Page numbers in **bold** type indicate a major treatment of a subject. Page numbers in *italics* indicate that the subject is illustrated.

O

P

PICTURE CREDITS

Photographs appearing in this book came from the sources listed below. Positions on the page are indicated by the abbreviations *l* left, *r* right, *t* top, *c* center, and *b* bottom. Work commissioned by Reader's Digest is shown in italics.

Unless the artist is mentioned, all the artwork comes from the following books first published by Reader's Digest: *Great Illustrated Dictionary; Great World Atlas; Library of Modern Knowledge; Living World of Animals;* and *Inventions That Changed the World.*

COVER
tl NASA/Colorfic! *tr* British Aircraft Corporation. *c* Lee Boltin, USA *bl* artwork, Reader's Digest *br* Bob Clemenz Photography.

FACTS ABOUT PEOPLE
9 *l* Peter Jones © National Geographic Society; *r* National Museums of Kenya. 11 *c* Hans Hinz, Switzerland; *b* Jean Vertut. 12 by courtesy of the Trustees of the British Museum. 13 Eric Lessing/Magnum/John Hillelson Agency. 14 Michael Holford. 15 The Metropolitan Museum of Art, Rogers Fund, 1912. 17 *l* Michael Holford; *r* Lee Boltin/Anthony Blake Picture Library. 18 both courtesy of the Cultural Relics Bureau, Beijing, and The Metropolitan Museum of Art. 19 Robert Harding Picture Library. 20 Michael Holford. 20–21 by courtesy of the Trustees of the British Museum. 22 by permission of the Museum of Folk Culture, Chiba. 23 Rainbird/Robert Harding Picture Library. 24 Ronald Sheridan Photo Library. 25 The Metropolitan Museum of Art, Rogers Fund, 1912. 26 Leonard von Matt. 27 *l* courtesy, Museum of Fine Arts, Boston; *b* reproduced by courtesy of the Trustees of the British Museum; *cr* Ray Skibinski. 28 *t* Michael Holford; *b* The Metropolitan Museum of Art, Gift and Bequest of Alice K. Bache, 1974 and 1977. 29 from the Collection of Senor Mujica Gallo, Lima/Photo Michael Holford. 30 *t* Museum of the American Indian, Heye Foundation, New York; *b* © Justin Kerr, 1978; 31 all Kodansha, Japan. 32 Leonard von Matt. 33 *c* Mansell Collection; *b* Leonard von Matt. 34 *t* by courtesy of the Trustees of the British Museum; *b* Ashmolean Museum of Art and Archaeology, Oxford. 35 E.T. Archive Ltd. 36 Brown Brothers. 37 E.T. Archive Ltd. 38 *t* National Army Museum; *c* Mansell Collection; *b* National Park Service. 39 *t* Mary Evans Picture Library; *b* Imperial War Museum. 40 Cartoon by Zec © *Daily Mirror.* 41 Reuters/Bettmann Newsphotos. 42 *l* Michael Holford; *r* Mansell Collection; *b* William MacQuitty International Collection. 43 *t* by courtesy of the Trustees of the Pierpont Morgan Library, New York; *b* courtesy of the Trustees of the British Museum. 44 *t* Ann Ronan Picture Library; *b* Bibliothèque publique et universitaire, Genève. 45 *t* Bancroft Library, University of California; *b* FPG International/Photoworld. 46 Eric Lessing/Magnum/John Hillelson Agency. 47 Library of Congress. 48 *t* Mansell Collection; *b* Mary Evans Picture Library. 49 Reader's Digest. 50 *l* Wellcome Institute Library, London; others Ann Ronan Picture Library. 51 NASA. 52 Konrad Helbig/ZEFA. 53 *t* British Tourist Authority; *b* Copyright reserved. Reproduced by gracious permission of Her Majesty the Queen. 54 Michael Holford. 55 Mary Evans Picture Library. 56 Ronald Woolf/Camera Press/Photo Trends. 57 L. Lautenberger and E.

Romano/CBS Photography/reproduced by permission of Sullivan Productions, Inc. 59 Museum of London. 60 *l* by courtesy of the Trustees of the Victoria and Albert Museum; *r* Copyright reserved. Reproduced by gracious permission of Her Majesty the Queen. 61 *l* Musées de la Ville, Strasbourg Chateau des Rohan; *r* Popperfoto; *b* E.T. Archive Ltd. 62 *t* Popperfoto; *b* Michael Holford. 63 *t* Mansell Collection; *b* Mary Evans Picture Library. 64 courtesy, the Henry Francis du Pont Winterthur Museum. 65 Eisenhower Library/Johns Hopkins University, Baltimore. 66 BBC Hulton Picture Library. 67–68 Mansell Collection. 69 both Western Americana Picture Library. 70 Mary Evans Picture Library. 71 *t* to *b* Abilene Reflector Chronicle, New York *Herald Tribune, Daily News* (New York), all from John Frost Historical Collection. 73 *l* and *tr* Mary Evans Picture Library; *c* David Jones. 74 *t* cartoon by Vicki, Associated Newspaper Group PLC. 75 *t* © Photographers International/Outline; *b* National Portrait Gallery, London. 76 *l* to *r* Popperfoto. BBC Hulton Picture Library. Brown Brothers. 77 *l* The Granger Collection, New York; *r* Library of Congress. 78 *l* to *r* Eddie Adams/Gamma-Liaison. AP/Wide World Photos. Photo by Wu Jiquo/Eastfoto. 79 The Granger Collection, New York. 81 Reader's Digest. 82 The Bettmann Archive. 83 Illustrated London News Picture Library. 84–85 Illustrated London News Picture Library. 85 Mansell Collection. 88 *l* by courtesy of the Trustees of the British Museum; *r* AP/Wide World Photos. 89 Mansell Collection. 90–91 Michael Holford. 94–95 artist *Andrew Aloof.* 97 Mansell Collection. 98 *bl* UPI/Bettmann Newsphotos; others from "Of Graves and Epitaphs," Kenneth Lindley, Hutchinson, 1965. 100 Michael Holford. 101 The Warburg Institute, University of London. 102 Michael Holford. 103 Photographie Giraudon. 104 Michael Holford. 105–07 Mansell Collection. 108 Michael Holford. 109–12 Mansell Collection. 113 Mary Evans Picture Library. 114 *bl* Mansell Collection; *tr* Mary Evans Picture Library. 115 all Mary Evans Picture Library. 116 E.T. Archive Ltd. 119 BBC Hulton Picture Library. 120 Det Kongelige Bibliotek, Copenhagen. 121 Michael Holford. 122 Courtesy of The American Museum of Natural History. 123 Mary Evans Picture Library. 124 William MacQuitty International Collection. 124–25 Michael Holford. 127 by courtesy of the Trustees of the British Museum. 128 Mary Evans Picture Library.

FACTS ABOUT PLACES
130–31 artist *Hayward and Martin.* 132 S. Sassoon/Robert Harding Picture Library. 133 Popperfoto. 134 Media Productions Ltd, Gaborone. 135 *l* L. Nelson/Hutchison Camera Pix; *r* B. Norman/Ronald Sheridan Picture Library. 137 The Bridgeman Art Library/Joseph and Earle Vanderkar, London. 139 *l* The Bridgeman Art Library/Victoria and Albert Museum; *r* by courtesy of the Trustees of the British Museum. 141 by courtesy of the Trustees of the British Museum. 142 J. Pate/Hutchison Camera Pix. 143 Hutchison Camera Pix. 145 Michael Holford. 146 Ronald Sheridan Picture Library. 147 by courtesy of the Trustees of the Victoria and Albert Museum. 148 *l* Walters Art Gallery, Baltimore; *r* Ashmolean Museum of Art and Archaeology, Oxford. 149 Werner Forman Archive. 152–53 © 1984 Peter B. Kaplan. 154 Mary Evans Picture Library. 155–56 BBC Hulton Picture Library. 157 Vivien Fifield. 159 BBC Hulton Picture Library. 161 Vivien Fifield. 166 Mary Evans Picture Library. 167 Bob Clemenz Photography. 168–69 D. Goulston/Bruce Coleman Ltd. 169–70 Mary Evans Picture Library. 171 *t* George Rodger/Magnum/John Hillelson Agency; *b* Tony and Marion Morrison, South American Pictures. 172 Bruno Barbey/Magnum/John Hillelson Agency. 173 Mary Evans Picture Library. 174–75 Georg Gerster/John Hillelson Agency. 175–76 Mary Evans Picture Library 177 *t* Mary Evans Picture Library; *b* Georg Gerster/ John Hillelson Agency. 178 artist *Bob Larkin, Artright Artists.* 178–79 M. Macintyre/Hutchison Camera Pix. 181

Sonia Halliday and Laura Lushington. 183 Eliot Elisofon/Life © Time Inc., 1968. 184–85 *b* Loren McIntyre. 185 *t* and 186 *b* artist *Hayward and Martin.* 186–87 John Cleare, Mountain Camera. 188–89 A. Howarth/Susan Griggs Agency. 189 *t* and 191 *t* artist *Hayward and Martin.* 191 Franz Lazi, Stuttgart.

FACTS ABOUT SCIENCE & TECHNOLOGY
195 Copyright reserved. Reproduced by gracious permission of Her Majesty the Queen. 196–97 all Biophoto Associates. 199 Neils A. Lassen, M.D., Bispebierg Hospital, Denmark. 200 both Bibliothèque Nationale, Paris. 201 Mary Evans Picture Library/Sigmund Freud Copyrights. 202 *l* by permission of the Trustees of the Science Museum. Copyright reserved; *r* Wellcome Institute Library, London. 203 Hirmer Fotoarchiv, Munich. 204 *r* to *r* Wellcome Institute Library, London. Federico Arborio Mella, Milan. Reader's Digest. 205 Mansell Collection. 206 UPI/Bettmann Newsphotos. 207 *l* to *r* Wellcome Institute Library, London. Photo Deutsches Museum, Munich. Bayer AG. 209 Public Record Office, London. 211 Leonard von Matt. 212 by permission of the Trustees of the Science Museum. 213 *cr* The Metropolitan Museum of Art, Purchase, Mr. and Mrs. Charles Wrightsman Gift, 1977; *bl* Eileen Tweedy, object Science Museum; *br* by permission of the Trustees of the Science Museum. 217 by permission of the Trustees of the Science Museum 218 by permission U.S. Army Signal Corps. 219 *t* by permission of the Trustees of the Science Museum: *b* Imperial War Museum. 221 Public Record Office, London. 223 Jose Lopez/NYT Pictures. 225 *tl* Bodleian Library, Oxford; *tr* George A. Plimpton Collection, Rare Book and Manuscript Library, Columbia University; *cl* The British Library; *cr* and *bl* New York Public Library, Rare Book Division; *br* David Eugene Smith Collection, Rare Book and Manuscript Library, Columbia University. 229 by permission of the Trustees of the Science Museum. 230 Scientific American. 231 *l* Intel Corp., Inc.; *r* Paul Brierly. 233 Culver Pictures. 234 *l* Comsat; *r* Patrick Thurston. 236 Mansell Collection. 238–40 artist *Hayward and Martin.* 239 The Photo Source. 241 Nigel Press Ass. Ltd. 243 artists *Gross Thurston.* 244–45 artist *Robert Micklewright.* 247 artists *Edward Williams Arts.* 249 New York Public Library. 250–51 artist *Malcolm McGregor.* 252–53 all by permission of the Trustees of the Science Museum. 254–55 artist *Lancelot Jones.* 256 P. Marlow/Sygma/John Hillelson Agency.

FACTS ABOUT ANIMALS & PLANTS
259 Science Photo Library. 263 *r*, 265, 267 *r*, 269 and 271 *r* Reader's Digest, from the Linnean Society. 292–93 artist *Eric Robson.* 295 W. Williams/Planet Earth Pictures. 297 *tl* E. Lindgren/Ardea, London; *bl* Heather Angel; *r* M. Fogden/OSFPL. 298 both Heather Angel. 299 A. Bannister/NHPA. 301 S. Trevor/Bruce Coleman Ltd. 302–03 J. Foot/Bruce Coleman Ltd.

FACTS ABOUT THE ARTS & ENTERTAINMENT
307 A. Woolfitt/Susan Griggs Agency. 308–09 *Hayward and Martin.* 310 The Bridgeman Art Library/Mauritshuis. 311 *l* The Bridgeman Art Library/Mauritshuis. *r* The Bridgeman Art Library/Kenwood House. 312 both The Bridgeman Art Library/Private Collection. 313 Tate Gallery, London. 314–15 all Leon Bakst © SPADEM, 1984. 317 Historisches Museum der Stadt Wien (Vienna). 320 Mary Evans Picture Library. 321 *c* Tate Gallery, London; *tl* The Granger Collection, New York; *cl* National Portrait Gallery, London. 322 *t* to *b* National Portrait Gallery, London. National Portrait Gallery, London. Mary Evans Picture Library. Mary Evans Picture Library. Mary Evans Picture Library. Culver Pictures. Mary Evans Picture Library. 323 *l* all BBC Hulton Picture Library; *r, t* to *b* National Portrait Gallery, London. Mary Evans Picture Library. Mary Evans Picture Library. 324 *b*

Mary Evans Picture Library; others National Portrait Gallery, London. 325 *t* to *b* Mary Evans Picture Library. Mary Evans Picture Library. The Bettmann Archive. 326 *l* Niedersächsische Landesbibliothek, Hanover; *c* BBC Hulton Picture Library; *r The News*, Adelaide/John Frost Historical Collection. 327 *t* A. and F. Pears Ltd; *b* Alfred Dunhill Ltd. 328 *tl* National Film Institute Archive; others Kobal Collection. 329 *t* National Film Institute Archive: *b* RKO Radio U.S.A. 330 both Popperfoto. 331 artist *Andrew Aloof.* 332 artist *Andrew Aloof* based on a photo courtesy of AP/ Wide World Photos. 334 artist *Andrew Aloof* based on a photo courtesy of Neil Leifer. 336 artist *Andrew Aloof* based on a photo courtesy of AP/Wide World Photos. 338 artist *Andrew Aloof* based on a photo courtesy of Bruce Bennett. 340 artist *Andrew Aloof* based on a photo courtesy of AP/Wide World Photos. 341 artist *Andrew Aloof* based on a photo © Caryn Levy, 1986. 342 artist *Andrew Aloof.* 343 artist

Andrew Aloof. 344 artist *Andrew Aloof* based on a photo courtesy of AP/Wide World Photos. 345 artist *Andrew Aloof* based on a photo courtesy of Neil Leifer. 346–47 *l* to *r* Michael Holford. The Bridgeman Art Library/Cecil Higgins Art Gallery. The Bridgeman Art Library/Private Collection. Michael Holford. 348 *t* Courtesy of The National Baseball Hall of Fame and Museum; *b* The Encyclopedia of Collectibles: Advertising Giveaways to Baskets, Photograph by David Arky © 1978 Time-Life Books Inc. 350–51 *l* to *r* Michael Holford. BBC Hulton Picture Library. BBC Hulton Picture Library. Mary Evans Picture Library. Mary Evans Picture Library. The Bridgeman Art Library, British Museum.

FACTS ABOUT THE EARTH
354 NASA/Colorfic! 371 Geopic Earth Satellite Corporation. 358–61 Reader's Digest. 363 A. Vergani/Image Bank. 364–65 Science Photo Library. 368 NASA/

Science Photo Library. 369 all Professor R. Scorer. 371 J. Allan Cash Photo Library. 373 *l* A. Compost/Bruce Coleman Ltd; *tr* B. Moser/Hutchison Camera Pix; *br* G. Morrison/Hutchison Camera Pix. 375 Dr. J. Durst/Science Photo Library.

FACTS ABOUT THE UNIVERSE
379 Mary Evans Picture Library. 381 Dr. J. Dickel/Science Photo Library. 382–83 Dr. F. Espanak/Science Photo Library. 385 NASA. 386 Rob Wood/Stansbury, Ronsaville, Wood Inc. 387 Spinelli/Susan Griggs Agency. 388–89 NASA/Woodmansterne. 390 artist *Hayward and Martin.* 390–93 NASA/ Science Photo Library. 394 R.Gehrz/Science Photo Library. 395 Dr. J. Lorre/Science Photo Library. 396 Daily Telegraph Colour Library/SF. 397 artist M. Paternostro/ Science Photo Library. 398–99 Max Planck Institute for Radio Astronomy/Science Photo Library. 400 S. Gull/Science Photo Library.

ACKNOWLEDGMENTS

A number of organizations and individuals gave assistance during the preparation of this book, and the publishers would like to thank them. They include:

The Advertising Association, London; Agricultural Research Council; BP Solar Systems, Aylesbury; British Information Service, New York, N.Y.; British Red Cross; The Buddhist Centre, London; Catholic Information Office; Central Electricity Generating Board; Department of Energy, London; Executive Compensation Service, Brussels; Federal Reserve Bank, Washington, D.C.; Prudence Grice; Institut der Deutschen Wirtschaft, Cologne; Institute of Criminology, University of Cape Town, South Africa; Institute of Jewish Affairs; International Advertising Association; London Zoo; Muslim Educational Trust; National Electronics Council; Norwegian Oil Industry Information Bureau; Panama Canal Commission; The Paul Press; Sikh Cultural Society; Starch INRA Hooper, Mamaroneck, N.Y; Uniform Crime Report Statistics, Federal Bureau of Investigation, Washington, D.C.; Union des Industries Metallurgiques et Minières, Paris; United Nations Information Centre, London; World Health Organization; World Wildlife Fund.

Numerous embassies, legations, consulates, and high commissions also provided help, and the publishers are grateful to them all.

The publishers also acknowledge their indebtedness to the following books and journals, which were consulted for reference:

Abraham Lincoln: The Prairie Years and the War Years, Carl Sandburg, Harcourt Brace; *An Actor Guide to the Talkies*, Richard B. Dimmitt and Andrew A. Aros, Scarecrow Press; *Acupuncture*, Marc Duke, Constable; *African Occasions*, Leslie Blackwell, Hutchinson; *The Airship: A History*, Basil

Collier, Hart-Davis; *Airshipwreck*, Len Deighton and Arnold Schwartzman, Cape; *Alexander the Great*, Frank Lipsius, Weidenfeld & Nicolson; *All the Best People . . . The Pick of Peterborough*, George Allen & Unwin; *Almost in Confidence*, Arthur Barlow, Juta, Capetown; *The Amazing Brain*, Robert Ornstein and Richard F. Thompson, Houghton Mifflin; *America in Legend*, Richard Dorson, Pantheon; *American Folklore*, Richard Dorson, University of Chicago; *The Americans: A Social History of the United States 1587/1914*, J. C. Furnas, Longman; *American Weather Stories*, U.S. Dept. of Commerce; *The Armchair Quarterback*, ed. John Thorn, Scribner's;

Bach, Eva and Sydney Grew, Dent; *Background to the "Long Search,"* Smart, BBC; *The Baseball Encyclopedia*, Macmillan; *Beethoven*, Marion M. Scott, Dent; *Before Civilisation*, Colan Renfrew, Jonathan Cape; *The Bible as History: Archaeology Confirms the Book of Books*, Werner Keller, Hodder & Stoughton; *The Big Umbrella: History of the Parachute*, John Lucas, Elm Tree Books; *A Biographical Dictionary of Scientists*, T. I. Williams, Black; *Biology*, Helena Curtis, Worth; *The body Almanac*, Neil McAleer, Doubleday; *The Brain*, R. Thompson, W. H. Freeman; *Bumblebees*, D.V. Alford, Davis-Poynter; *Burke's Royal Families of the World*, Hugh Montgomery-Massingberd, Burke's Peerage; *Butterflies and Moths in Britain and Europe*, D. Carter, Pan; *But Who On Earth Was . . .?*, Eileen Hellicar, David & Charles;

Chemistry, L. & P. Pauling, W. H. Freeman & Co.; *The Chemistry of Life*, Steven Rose, Penguin; *China*, Sarah Allan & Cherry Barnett, Cassell; *A Chinese View of China*, John Gittings, BBC; *Christopher Columbus*, Ernle Bradford, Michael Joseph; *The Churches of Rome*, Roloff Beny and Peter Gunn, Weidenfeld & Nicolson; *The City in History*, Lewis Mumford, Secker; *Classic Descriptions of Disease with Biographical Sketches of the Authors*, Ralph H. Major, Charles C. Thomas; *Complete Handbook of Poultry Keeping*, S. Banks, Ward Lock; *The Complete Poems of Emily Dickinson*, ed. Thomas H. Johnson, Little, Brown; *Computer Appreciation*, T. F. Fry, Butterworths; *The Computer Book*, Peter Laurie, BBC; *Computer Dictionary and Handbook*, ed. Sippl & Sippl, Howard Sams; *Computer Software*, Scientific American editors, W. H. Freeman; *Concise Encyclopaedia of Archaeology*, ed. Leonard Cottrell, Hutchinson; *Concise Encyclopaedia of Living Faiths*, ed. R. C. Zaehner, Hutchinson; *Concise Encyclopaedia of the Arts*, T. Rowland-Entwistle and Cooke, Purnell; *Current Biography*, H. W. Wilson;

David Livingstone: His Triumph, Decline and Fall, C. Northcott, Lutterworth Press; *Death on the Road: A Study in Social Violence*, F. Whitlock, Tavistock Publications; *The Decline and Fall of the Roman Empire*, Edward Gibbon, Dent; *Dermatology in Internal Medicine*, S. Shuster, OUP; *The Desert*, J. L. Cloudsley-Thompson, Orbis; *Design of Cities*, Edmund N. Bacon, Thames & Hudson; *Dictionary of American Biography*, Scribner's; *Dictionary of Antiques*, George Savage, Barrie & Jenkins; *Dictionary of Art and Artists*, P. and L. Murray, Penguin; *A Dictionary of Biographical Quotation*, Justin Wintle and Richard Kenin, Routledge & Kegan Paul; *A Dictionary of Comparative Religions*, ed. S. G. F. Brandon, Weidenfeld & Nicolson; *Dictionary of Scientific Biography*, Scribner's;

Earth, Frank Press and Raymond Siever, W. H. Freeman; *Edith Wharton and Henry James, The Story of Their Friendship*, Millicent Bell, George Braziller; *Encyclopaedia of Espionage*, Ronald Seth, N.E.L.; *Encyclopaedia of Military History*, Dupuy, Macdonald; *Encyclopaedia of Mountaineering*, Walter Unsworth, Robert Hale; *Encyclopaedia of Myths and Legends of All Nations*, H. S. Robinson and K. Wilson, Kaye & Ward Ltd; *Encyclopaedia of Philosophy*, ed. Paul Edwards, Collier-Macmillan; *Encyclopaedia of the Plant Kingdom*, A. Huxley, Salamander Books; *Encyclopedia of Religion and Ethics*, ed. J. Hastings, Scribner's; *Encyclopaedia of Southern Africa*, Eric Rosenthal, Warne; *Encyclopaedia of Superstitions*, E. and M. Radford, Arrow; *Encyclopaedia of Witchcraft and Magic*, Venetia Newall, Hamlyn; *The Encyclopedia of Space Travel and Astronomy*, ed. John Man, Octopus; *Encyclopedia of World Art*, McGraw-Hill; *Everyman's Scientific Facts and Feats*, Magnus Pike and Patrick Moore, Dent;

Field Guide to the Butterflies of Britain and Europe, L. G. Higgins and N. D. Riley, Collins; *A Field Guide to the Insects of Britain and Europe*, Michael Chinery, Collins; *Field Guide to the Reptiles and Amphibians of Britain and Europe*, E. N. Arnold and J. A. Burton, Collins; *A Field Guide to the Sea Birds of Southern Africa and the World*, J. Tuck and H. Heinzel, Collins; *First Across!*, Richard K. Smith, U.S. Naval Inst. Press; *The First Cities*, Ruth Whitehouse, Phaidon; *The First Emperor of China*, Arthur Cotterell, Macmillan; *First Flight: The Untold Story of the Wright Brothers*, J. E. Walsh, Allen & Unwin; *The First Great Civilisations*, Jacquetta Hawkes, Hutchinson; *The First Three Minutes*, Steven Weinberg, Basic; *Fishes of the World*, Alan Cooper, Hamlyn; *Five Hundred Years of Printing*, A. H.

Steinberg, Penguin; *Flags and Arms Across the World,* Whitney Smith, Cassell; *Flags of the World,* ed. E. M. C. Barraclough, Warne; *Football: Facts and Figures,* Dr. L. H. Baker, Farrar & Rinehart;

The Garden of Japan, Masao Hayakawa, Weatherhill; *The General Armoury of England, Scotland, Ireland and Wales,* Sir Bernard Burke, Burke's Peerage; *General Chemistry,* Donald A. McQuarrie and Peter A. Rock, W. H. Freeman; *The Genius of China,* William Watson, Barron's Education Series; *The Geology of New York City and Environs,* Christopher J. Schuberth, Natural History Press; *George Stephenson,* Hunter Davies, Weidenfeld & Nicolson; *Georg Philipp Telemann,* Richard Petzoldt, Benn; *Giants in the Sky,* M. J. H. Taylor and David Mondey, Jane's; *Giving Up the Gun: Japan's Reversion to the Sword, 1543–1879,* Noel Perrin, Shambhala; *The Glory That Was Greece,* J. C. Stobart, Sidgwick & Jackson; *The Golden Bough,* Sir James Frazer, Macmillan; *Gossamer Odyssey,* M. Grosser, Michael Joseph; *The Grandeur That Was Rome,* J. C. Stobart, Sidgwick & Jackson; *Grzimek's Animal Life Encyclopedia,* Bernhard Grzimek, Van Nostrand and Reinhold;

Habits: Why You Do What You Do, John Nicholson, Pan; *Haiti: Black Peasants and Their Religion,* Alfred Métraux, Harrap; *Halliwell's Filmgoer's Companion,* Granada; *Hall of Fame,* A. P. Cartwright, CNA; *Haydn,* Rosemary Hughes, Dent; *Hear That Lonesome Whistle Blow,* Dee Brown, Chatto & Windus; *Heaven, Hell and Hara Kiri: The Rise and Fall of the Japanese Superstate,* James Kirkup, Angus & Robertson; *The Helicopter,* H. F. Gregory, Yoseloff; *Helicopters and Autogyros of the World,* Paul Lambermont and Anthony Pirie, Cassell; *Helicopters and Other Rotorcraft Since 1907,* Kenneth Munson, Blandford; *Henry VIII,* J. C. Scarisbrick, Eyre Methuen; *Heritage of Persia,* Richard N. Frye, Weidenfeld; *A History of Medicine,* Arturo Castiglioni, Aronson; *A History of Medicine,* Fielding H. Garrison, W. B. Saunders; *A History of Playing Cards,* Catherine Hargrave, Dover; *A History of Polar Exploration,* David Mountfield, Hamlyn; *A History of Railways in Britain,* Frank Ferneyhough, Osprey; *A History of Scotland,* Plantagenet and Fiona Somerset Fry, Routledge & Kegan Paul; *History of Technology,* ed. Charles Singer, OUP; *History of the Ancient Olympic Games,* Lynn and Gray Poole, Obolensky;

Ice, Fred Hoyle, Hutchinson; *I. K. Brunel, A Biography,* L. T. C. Rolt, Penguin; *Illustrated Atlas of the Bible Lands,* T. Rowland-Entwistle, Longman; *Illustrated Atlas of the World's Great Buildings,* ed. P. Bagenal and J. Meades, Salamander Books; *An Illustrated Encyclopaedia of Traditional Symbols,* J. C. Cooper, Thames & Hudson; *The Illustrated History of Seaplanes and Flying Boats,* Louis S. Casey and John Batchelor, Hamlyn; *Illustrating Computers,* Colin Day and Donald Alcock, Pan; *IMM's General Textbook of Entomology,* ed. O. W. Richards and R. G. Davies, Chapman & Hall; *Incendiary Weapons,* S.I.P.R.I., Stockholm; *Indian Asia,* Philip Rawson, Elsevier-Phaidon; *Industrial Biography: Ironworkers and Tool Makers,* Samuel Smiles and John Murray, Kelley; *Infantry Weapons of the World,* Foss & Gander, I. Allan; *In Flanders Fields,* Wolff, Penguin; *Insect Life,* Tweedie, Collins; *Insect Life: The World You Never See,* T. Rowland-Entwistle, Hamlyn;

Jamaican Song and Story, Walter Jekyll, Dover; *Jane's World Railways 1982–3,* ed. G. F. Allen, Jane's Pub. Co.; *Japan,* Pat Barr, Batsford; *Japan Behind the Fan,* James Kirkup, Dent; *Japanese Culture: A Short History,* H. Paul Varley, Faber; *Jerusalem,* Colin Thubron, Time-Life;

K.G.B.: Secret Work of Soviet Secret Agents, John Barron, Hodder; *K.G.B.: The Eyes of Russia,* Harry Rositzke, Sidgwick; *King George V,* Harold Nicolson, Constable; *Kings Over the Water: The Saga of the Stuart Pretenders,* Theo Aronson, Cassell; *Kino: History of the Russian and Soviet Film,* Jay Leyda, Allen & Unwin;

Learning, Sarnoff A. Mednick, Prentice-Hall; *Left Brain, Right Brain,* Sally P. Springer and Georg Deutsch, W. H. Freeman; *The Legacy of China,* Raymond Dawson, Clarendon Press; *Legends of the World,* ed. Richard Cavendish, Orbis; *Lempriere's Classical Dictionary,* Routledge & Kegan Paul; *Lenten Fare and Food for Fridays,* Constance Cruikshank, Faber; *Lewis and Clark and the Crossing of North America,* David Holloway, Weidenfeld; *Lexicon of Musical Invective: Critical Assaults on Composers since Beethoven's Time,* Nicholas Slonimsky, University of Washington Press; *The Life and Times of George I,* Joyce Marlow, Weidenfeld & Nicolson; *The Life and Times of Henry VIII,* Robert Lacey, Weidenfeld & Nicolson; *The Life and Times of Tycho Brahe,* John Allyne Gode, Greenwood Press; *Life of Marsupials,* H. Tyndale-Briscoe, E. Arnold; *The Life of Reptiles,* Angus Bellairs, Weidenfeld & Nicolson; *Life on Earth,* David Attenborough, Collins;

Man, Myth and Magic, IPC; *Man the Tool-maker,* Kenneth P. Oakley, British Museum; *Marine Mammals,* R. J. Harrison and J. E. King, Hutchinson; *Mathematics and Mathematicians,* P. Dedron and J. Itard, Open UP; *Mathematics in Western Culture,* Morris Kline, Penguin; *The Mating Game,* Robert Burton, Elsevier; *A Matter of Trust: MI5 1945–72,* Nigel West, Weidenfeld; *Maya: The Riddle and Rediscovery of a Lost Civilisation,* Charles Gallenkamp, Penguin; *McGraw-Hill Encyclopedia of Science and Technology; The Medieval Machine: Industrial Revolution of the Middle Ages,* Jean Gimpel, Futura; *Men of Ideas,* ed. Bryan Magee, BBC; *Mermaids and Mastodons,* Richard Carrington, Chatto; *Meteorites and Their Origins,* G. J. McCall, David & Charles; *MI5: British Security Service Operations 1909–45,* Nigel West, Bodley Head; *MI6: British Secret Intelligence Service Operations 1909–45,* Nigel West, Weidenfeld; *Milestones in Medicine,* George Bankoff, Museum; *A Million and One Nights: A History of the Motion Picture,* Terry Ramsaye, Cass; *Mimicry in Plants and Animals,* Wolfgang Wickler, Weidenfeld; *Miracle of Flight,* S. Dalton, S. Low; *Model Girl,* Charles Castle, David & Charles; *Model Soldiers,* Henry Harris, Weidenfeld & Nicolson; *The Monkey Puzzle: A Family Tree,* John Gribbin and Jeremy Cherfas, Bodley Head;

National Geographic *World* Magazine; *Naturalised Animals of the British Isles,* Christopher Lever, Paladin; *Nature, Mother of Invention: Engineering of Plant Life,* F. R. Paturi, Penguin; *The Netherlands in Brief,* Ministry of Foreign Affairs, The Hague; *The New Columbia Encyclopedia,* Columbia University Press; *The New Dog Encyclopedia,* Galahad Books; *The New English Bible,* CUP; *New Shell Guide to England,* Michael Joseph; *The New Solar System,* Beatty, O'Leary, and Chaikin, CUP; *New York,* Carole Chester, Batsford; *Non-verbal Communication,* ed. R. A. Hinde, CUP; *Norway,* Ronald Popperwell, Benn; *No. 10 Downing Street: A House in History,* R. J. Minney, Cassell;

The Origin and Diversification of Language, M. Swadesh, Routledge; *Origin of Japanese Architecture,* Kenze Tange; *The Origin of Species,* Charles Darwin; *Origins,* Richard E. Leakey and Roger Lewin, Macdonald & Jane's; *The Oscar Movies From A to Z,* Roy Pickard, Muller; *Out of the Darkness: Planet Pluto,* Clyde Tombaugh, Lutterworth Press; *Owls: Their Natural and Unnatural History,* Sparks and Soper, David & Charles; *Oxford Book of Invertebrates,* David Nichols and John A. L. Cooke, OUP; *Oxford Book of Literary Anecdotes,* ed. Sutherland, OUP; *Oxford Book of Vertebrates,* Nixon and Whiteley, OUP; *Oxford Classical Dictionary,* ed. Hammond and Scullard, OUP; *Oxford Companion to American Literature,* James D. Hart, OUP;

The Plants, F. W. Went, Life Nature Library, Time-Life International; *Pompeii, Naples and Southern Italy,* Anthony Pereira, Batsford; *The Popes,* Friedrich Gontard, Barrie; *Popular Encyclopaedia of Plants,* V. H. Heywood and S. R. Chant, CUP; *Porcelain Through the Ages,* George Savage, Penguin; *Portugal, A Book of Folk Ways,* Rodney Gallop, Cambridge; *Pregnancy,* Gordon Bourne, Cassell; *Prehistoric Animals,* Barry Cox, Hamlyn; *Prehistoric England,* Grahame Clark, Batsford; *The Prime Ministers,* ed. Herbert Van Thal, Allen & Unwin; *Prime Ministers of Britain From Walpole to Callaghan,* Eileen Hellicar, David & Charles; *Principles of Insect Physiology,* V. B. Wigglesworth, Methuen; *Prodigal Genius—The Life of Nikola Tesla,* John O'Neill, Panther; *Prolegomena to the Study of Greek Religion,* Jane Ellen Harrison, Merlin Press; *Purnell's Pictorial Encyclopaedia of Nature,* ed. T. Entwistle and P. Cooke;

The Queens of England, Barbara Softly, David & Charles; *Queen Victoria,* Lytton Strachey, Chatto; *Queen Victoria: Her Life and Times,* Cecil Woodham-Smith, Hamish Hamilton;

Recent Advances in Endocrinology and Metabolism, ed. J. L. H. O'Riordan, Churchill Livingstone; *Renaissance Florence,* Gene Brucker, John Wiley; *Reptiles and Amphibians,* John Stidworthy, Macdonald; *Respiratory Physiology—The Essentials,* J. B. West, Blackwell; *Restless Earth,* Nigel Calder, BBC; *Rise and Fall of the Third Reich,* Shirer, Secker & Warburg; *The Rise of Big Business,* C. Northcote Parkinson, Weidenfeld & Nicolson; *The Rise of Man,* Sampson Low; *The Road to Sarajevo,* Vladimir Dedijer, MacGibbon & Kee; *Rodents: Their Lives and Habits,* P. W. Hanney, David & Charles; *Roman Art and Architecture,* Sir Mortimer Wheeler, Thames & Hudson;

Secrets of the Great Pyramid, Peter Tompkins, Harper; *Semantics: A New Outline,* F. R. Palmer, CUP; *The Shadows Lengthen,* P. Van Der Byl, Timmins; *Shell Book of Firsts,* Patrick Robertson, Michael Joseph, 2nd ed. 1983; *The Shogun Inheritance,* Michael MacIntyre, Collins; *A Short History of Buddhism,* Dr. Edward Conze, Allen & Unwin; *A Short History of China,* Hilda Hookham, Longman; *A Short History of Technology from the Earliest Times to A.D. 1900,* T. K. Derry and Trevor I. Williams, OUP; *A Short Textbook of Clinical Physiology,* P. F. Binnion, Lloyd-Luke; *A Short Textbook of Medical Microbiology,* D. C. Turk and I. A. Porter, Hodder; *Sketches of Great Pianists and Great Violinists,* George T. Ferris, Wm. Reeves; *The Sky Is Falling,* Arthur Weingarten, Hodder; *The Skyscraper,* Paul Goldberger, Knopf; *Smuts,* S. G. Millin, Faber; *Snakes of the World,* John Stidworthy, Hamlyn; *Subatomic Particles,* Steven Weinberg, Scientific American Library;

Tacitus, Annals; La Terra in Piazza: An Interpretation of the Palio of Siena, Alessandro Falassi and Alan Dundes, University of California Press; *Texas, a Bicentennial History,* Joe B. Frantz, Norton; *A Textbook of Clinical Pharmacology,* H. J. Rogers, Hodder & Stoughton; *Textbook of Endocrinology,* ed. R. H. Williams, W. B. Saunders; *Textbook of Medical Physiology,* A. C. Guyton, W. B. Saunders; *Textbook of Surgery,* Frederick Christopher, W. B. Saunders; *This Is Japan,* Colin Simpson, Angus; *Thoracic Medicine,* ed. P. Emerson, Butterworths;

Underwater Medicine, S. Miles & D. E. MacKay, Adlard Coles Ltd; *Unfinished History of the World,* Hugh Thomas, Hamish Hamilton; *The United Nations,* Victoria Schofield, Wayland; *The United Nations: First Twenty-Five Years,* Edwin Tetlow, Peter Owen; *United States,* ed. S. Birnbaum, Penguin; *Universe,* William J. Kaufmann, W. H. Freeman;

The Vanishing Hitchhiker: American Urban Legends and Their Meanings, Jan H. Brunvand, Norton; *Verdi,* Dynely Hussey, Dent; *Vertebrate Paleontology,* Alfred Romer, University of Chicago Press; *Victoria R.I.,* Elizabeth Longford, Weidenfeld; *Voodoo in Haiti,* Alfred Métraux, Deutsch;

Webster's New Geographical Dictionary, Merriam; *Wedgwood Ware,* W. B. Honey, Faber; *West Indian Folk Tales,* Philip Sherlock, OUP; *What World Religions Teach,* E. G. Parrinder, Harrap; *Who Played Who in the Movies,* Roy Pickard, Muller; *Who Was Who in America 1974–76,* Marquis Who's Who Inc; *Who's Who in the Ancient World,* ed. Betty Radice, Penguin; *Wicked Uncles In Love,* Morris Marples, Michael Joseph;

The Yachtsman's Pocket Almanac, ed. N. Dent, Mitchell Beazley; *Your Guide to Lebanon,* Nina Nelson, Redman;

The Zulu War 1879, Alan Lloyd, Hart-Davis.